Trusts and Trustees:
Cases and Materials

AF831973

Trusts and Trustees: Cases and Materials

by R. H. Maudsley
LL.D., B.C.L., M.A., Hon. LL.D. (U.S.D.), S.J.D.
of Lincoln's Inn, Barrister; Professor of Law at New York Law School and University of San Diego Law School; formerly Professor of Law in the University of London

and E. H. Burn
B.C.L., M.A.
of Lincoln's Inn, Barrister, Student of Christ Church, Oxford, Lecturer in Law of Land in the Inns of Court

London
Butterworths
1978

England London	Butterworth & Co (Publishers) Ltd 88 Kingsway WC2B 6AB
Australia Sydney	Butterworths Pty Ltd 586 Pacific Highway, Chatswood, NSW 2067 Also at Melbourne, Brisbane, Adelaide and Perth
Canada Toronto	Butterworth & Co (Canada) Ltd 2265 Midland Avenue, Scarborough M1P 4S1
New Zealand Wellington	Butterworths of New Zealand Ltd 77–85 Customhouse Quay
South Africa Durban	Butterworth & Co (South Africa) (Pty) Ltd 152/154 Gale Street
USA Boston	Butterworth (Publishers) Inc 19 Cummings Park, Woburn, Mass 01801

© Butterworth & Co (Publishers) Ltd 1978

All rights reserved. No part of this publication may be reproduced or transmitted in any form or by any means, including photocopying and recording, without the written permission of the copyright holder, application for which should be addressed to the publisher. Such written permission must also be obtained before any part of this publication is stored in a retrieval system of any nature.

This book is sold subject to the Standard Conditions of Sale of Net Books and may not be re-sold in the UK below the net price fixed by Butterworths for the book in our current catalogue.

ISBN—Casebound 0 406 62322 8
Limp 0 406 62323 6

Photoset, printed and bound in Great Britain by
R. J. Acford Limited, Industrial Estate, Chichester, Sussex

Trusts and Trustees: Cases and Materials

by R. H. Maudsley
LL.D., B.C.L., M.A., Hon. LL.D. (U.S.D.), S.J.D.
of Lincoln's Inn, Barrister; Professor of Law at New York Law School and University of San Diego Law School; formerly Professor of Law in the University of London

and E. H. Burn
B.C.L., M.A.
of Lincoln's Inn, Barrister, Student of Christ Church, Oxford, Lecturer in Law of Land in the Inns of Court

London
Butterworths
1978

England London	Butterworth & Co (Publishers) Ltd 88 Kingsway WC2B 6AB
Australia Sydney	Butterworths Pty Ltd 586 Pacific Highway, Chatswood, NSW 2067 Also at Melbourne, Brisbane, Adelaide and Perth
Canada Toronto	Butterworth & Co (Canada) Ltd 2265 Midland Avenue, Scarborough M1P 4S1
New Zealand Wellington	Butterworths of New Zealand Ltd 77–85 Customhouse Quay
South Africa Durban	Butterworth & Co (South Africa) (Pty) Ltd 152/154 Gale Street
USA Boston	Butterworth (Publishers) Inc 19 Cummings Park, Woburn, Mass 01801

© Butterworth & Co (Publishers) Ltd 1978

All rights reserved. No part of this publication may be reproduced or transmitted in any form or by any means, including photocopying and recording, without the written permission of the copyright holder, application for which should be addressed to the publisher. Such written permission must also be obtained before any part of this publication is stored in a retrieval system of any nature.

This book is sold subject to the Standard Conditions of Sale of Net Books and may not be re-sold in the UK below the net price fixed by Butterworths for the book in our current catalogue.

ISBN—Casebound 0 406 62322 8
Limp 0 406 62323 6

Photoset, printed and bound in Great Britain by
R. J. Acford Limited, Industrial Estate, Chichester, Sussex

conscious of the host of practical problems which remain unsettled in this area.

There are smaller changes. The order of Chapters has been altered. It seemed more logical to treat Express Trusts first, along with the Chapter 6 on Trusts and Taxes; then treat Resulting Trusts and Constructive Trusts; and place Chapter 9, Non-Charitable Purpose Trusts, at the end of Part I, and immediately before Charitable Trusts. Chapter 9 has been re-cast, and largely re-written. Chapter 7, Resulting Trusts, has been changed to conform with the end of the Vandervell litigation, and contains an excellent treatment of the problem of the Member's Club cases in *Re Sick and Funeral Society of St. John's Sunday School, Golcar*. Chapter 8, on Constructive Trusts, contains fuller treatment of Mutual Wills and of the problem of the claimant who has killed the testator, and it also reflects a number of new and adventurous developments in the search for justice in this uncharted sea. Chapter 2 deals with some of the problems still left by the litigation over Mr. Baden's Trust Deed, and Chapter 1 contains a new short section on the Crown as a Trustee.

We have as usual attempted to follow the ipsissima verba of the cases and statutes. This, of course, produces many inconsistencies of style and spelling; but these are inconsistencies of different centuries, and, as the material is produced as authoritative, we feel that it is not for us to change or attempt to improve it. The questions which appear at the end of most of the Chapters and in other places in the book, are intended to raise questions of principle. Many great teachers have said that the best way to understand is to ask, or to be required to answer, penetrating questions. We have attempted to do this, rather than to provide questions of the type which may be expected to be found in the examination paper.

Finally, we wish to thank a number of friends, colleagues and pupils, who have given advice and encouragement at various times, including Mr. David Niddrie, research assistant and second year student at the University of San Diego, who did yeoman work with the proofs which had to be read in California against a strict time schedule; and also our Publishers for undertaking the compilation of the Tables of Statutes and Cases and for their ready and expert help at all times.

R.H.M.
New York Law School
University of San Diego Law School

E.H.B.
Christ Church, Oxford

April 5, 1978

Preface

This second edition incorporates the many changes which have taken place in the law relating to Trusts and Trustees since 1972, when the first edition appeared. The purpose of the book remains the same; namely, to provide for students a collection of the most significant readings in this subject which do not appear in the text books. The principles of law are best indicated from the expositions of the judges; and the many relevant statutory provisions can only be understood by a detailed study of the statutes themselves. Many other sources are included in order to introduce new and different viewpoints, and the leading text books are referred to at every stage. We take this opportunity to express our thanks to those persons and institutions who have given us permission to reproduce copyright material.

One great problem, of course, is the decision on what to omit. We have attempted to give adequate treatment to the subject-matter covered in courses in Law Faculties and Law Departments, and to provide the authorities which are needed to understand the academic principles of the subject, and also the questions and problems met in professional practice. Indeed, the more we work in this field, the less significant we find the commonly-made distinction between the two.

An understanding of the relevant tax law is crucial to the understanding of the modern law of Trusts and Trustees, because present practice is dominated by fiscal considerations. The previous edition contained a Chapter on Tax Saving Trusts. In those happy days, trust lawyers knew how to avoid liability to estate duty. Trusts practice has been wholly changed by the introduction of Capital Transfer Tax in the Finance Act 1975. An outline explanation, together with the most important statutory provisions, is contained in Chapter 6. We commend a detailed study of these provisions to any student who intends to practice in this area. Tax statutes are no easier to understand if read after graduation, and the best plan is to tackle them at the time when the principles of Trust Law are being studied. But we are conscious of the fact that many teachers do not share this view, and we must repeat what we said in the Preface to the First Edition, that the chapter is one which "those who do not enjoy the technicalities of estate duty may well decide to omit." Of course, the statutes need further supplementation. We have done our best in the space available.

The Law of Charities is an area where development is rapid, and largely independent of case law or statute. The Charity Commissioners produce excellent and informative Annual Reports, and the source material has been enriched by the Report of Lord Goodman's Committee, and by the Tenth Report from the Expenditure Committee of the House of Commons. Any reader conscious of the sheer volume of available material will sympathise with the authors who have to select from it. We have retained the leading cases, the provisions of the Charities Act 1960, and have brought the materials up to date with extracts from the various Reports. We remain

Acknowledgements

We gratefully acknowledge the permissions which were granted to reproduce extracts from the following publications:

Law Reports and Statutes:

The Incorporated Council of Law Reporting for England and Wales
The Commonwealth Law Reports

Textbooks and Treatises:

Cretney: Principles of Family Law (2nd Edn. 1976, Sweet & Maxwell)
Goff & Jones: Law of Restitution (1966, Sweet & Maxwell)
Hallett's Conveyancing Precedents (1965, Sweet & Maxwell)
Hanbury and Maudsley: Modern Equity (10th Edn. 1976, Sweet & Maxwell)
Harris: Variation of Trusts (1975, Sweet & Maxwell)
Jarman on Wills (8th Edn. 1951, Sweet & Maxwell)
Josling: Apportionments for Executors and Trustees (4th Edn. 1976, Oyez)
Key & Elphinstone: Conveyancing Precedents (15th Edn. 1953, Sweet & Maxwell)
Lewin on Trusts (16th Edn. 1964, Sweet & Maxwell)
Maitland: Lectures on Equity (1969, Cambridge University Press)
Miller: Machinery of Succession (1977, Professional Books)
Morris and Leach: Rule Against Perpetuities (2nd Edn. 1962, Sweet & Maxwell)
Parker & Mellows: Modern Law of Trusts (3rd Edn. 1975, Sweet & Maxwell)
Perspectives of Law: Essays for Austin Wakeman Scott (1964, Little, Brown and Co.)
Pettit: Equity and the Law of Trusts (3rd Edn. 1974, Butterworths)
Scott: Trusts (3rd Edn. 1967, Little, Brown and Co.)
Tudor on Charities (6th Edn. 1967, Sweet & Maxwell)
Underhill: Law of Trusts and Trustees (12th Edn. 1970, Butterworths)
Wheatcroft & Hewson: Capital Transfer Tax (1975, Sweet & Maxwell)

Restatement of Law:

Restitution (1936, American Law Institute)
Trusts (2nd Edn. 1959, American Law Institute)

Journals:

Conveyancer and Property Lawyer
Current Legal Problems
Law Quarterly Review
Modern Law Review
Solicitors' Journal

Reports:

Charity Commissioners for England and Wales: Annual Reports
Goodman Committee Report on Charity Law and Voluntary Organisations
House of Commons Expenditure Committee: Tenth Report

Cross-References

The following books have been cross-referenced, and abbreviated as follows:

H & M	Hanbury and Maudsley: Modern Equity (10th Edn. 1976)
K & S	Keeton and Sheridan: Law of Trusts (10th Edn. 1974)
P & M	Parker and Mellows: The Modern Law of Trusts (3rd Edn. 1975)
Pettit	Equity and the Law of Trusts (3rd Edn. 1974)
Snell	Principles of Equity (27th Edn. 1973)

Contents

Table of Statutes

References in this Table to *"Statutes"* are to Halsbury's Statutes of England (Third Edition) showing the volume and page at which the annotated text of the Act will be found.
Page references printed in bold type indicate where the section of an Act is set out in part or in full.

Table of Cases

In the following Table references are given to the English and Empire Digest showing where the cases appear in that work. Cases which are set out in this work are indicated by page numbers in bold type.

PAGE

PAGE

PAGE

I

J

PAGE

M

PAGE

R

Part One. Trusts

1. The Nature of a Trust

I. Introduction

For many reasons, it may be better to avoid having the whole of the capital of a family owned by one person. In some circumstances it will be preferable to provide for successive enjoyment; in others for the enjoyment to be shared; or to provide protection against creditors; or to provide for interests to arise in the future. These situations, and others, can be effected by means of a trust. When property is held in a way other than in the absolute ownership of one person, it is usually held under some form of trust. Courses on Land Law show clearly how this has been done, in the case of land, by the use of a strict settlement or a trust for sale.

The beneficiaries under a trust are the owners in equity of the beneficial interests given to them. The trustees are the legal owners. Trustees' ownership is wholly burdensome. The trusteeship obligates them to manage the property in the exclusive interest of the beneficiaries, and imposes onerous duties and liabilities upon them. All the advantage is with the beneficiaries.

Trusts may be created *inter vivos* or by will. On death, the owner of property has to do something with it. He cannot take it with him. He may give it to a devisee or legatee absolutely, or may create successive interests. It is common for a man to leave the bulk of his estate to his wife for her life and after her death to the children. Within limits, a testator can do as he wishes with his property. He will usually discuss with his family, his friends and his solicitor what will be the best thing to do. Any property owner, including owners of policies of insurance, should make his will early in life and at the latest on his marriage.

Inter vivos trusts are usually created for tax-saving purposes. There is no point in keeping more property than one reasonably can need. A large investment income is highly taxed[1]. Capital transfer tax is imposed on

[1] The maximum rate is 98%, which is payable on a taxable income in excess of £21,000, of which £2,000 is investment income. See p. 147, post. Under the Budget Proposals of April 11, 1978, this rate is payable on taxable income in excess of £23,000, of which £2,250 is investment income.

transfers of capital[2], but, up to £310,000, the rates are lower on *inter vivos* transfers than on transfers on death. Tax advantages can thus be obtained by the creation of family trusts which spread the beneficial interest in the family capital among various members. Men of property should consult their legal advisers to ascertain how the best use can be made of that part of their property which they cannot foreseeably need. Similarly, consideration should be given to the tax aspects of the dispositions contained in a will. Efficient and far-sighted tax planning becomes more important, and more complex, as each year goes by.

Such trusts are intentionally created by the settlor or the testator. Their existence depends upon a manifestation of his intention to create a trust. A trust can also arise however without any such intention being manifested. In some circumstances, discussed in Chapter 7, a trust results in favour of the settlor and this is usually, but not necessarily, consistent with the settlor's intention. Constructive trusts are imposed by equity independently of any indication of intention. They arise in a wide variety of circumstances, as explained in Chapter 8, the most significant of which is the prevention of fraud.

Trusts may be created for public (i.e. charitable) purposes as well as for private individuals. Charitable trusts form a large and important area of the law of trusts. They are specially favoured by the law, being in effect free from liability to tax, and being permitted to continue in perpetuity. Many English charities are ancient; and, until the Charities Act 1960 provided that charities (with exceptions) should be registered, no-one had any idea how many existed. The total number of charities registered with the Charity Commissioners at the end of 1976 was 122,715[3].

II. Definition[4]

Maitland: *Selected Essays*, p. 129

"If we were asked what is the greatest and most distinctive achievement performed by Englishmen in the field of jurisprudence I cannot think that we should have any better answer to give than this, namely, the development from century to century of the trust idea."

Underhill's Law of Trusts and Trustees (12th Edn) p. 3

"A trust is an equitable obligation, binding a person (who is called a trustee) to deal with property over which he has control (which is called the trust property), for the benefit of persons (who are called beneficiaries or *cestuis que trust*), of whom he may himself be one, and any one of whom may enforce the obligation. Any act or neglect on the part of a trustee which is not authorised or excused by the terms of the trust instrument, or by law, is called a breach of trust."[5]

[2] The rate on inter vivos transfers over £210,000 is 50%. This rate is reached on transfers on death at £110,000. See Chap. 6, post.

[3] See the Report of the Charity Commissioners for England and Wales 1976, para. 37.

[4] H & M, p. 117; K & S, pp. 2–6; P & M, pp. 4–6; Pettit, pp. 16–17; Snell pp. 87–89.

[5] Approved by COHEN J in *Re Marshall's Will Trusts* [1945] Ch 217 at 219, [1945] 1 All ER 550 at 551; and by ROMER LJ in *Green v Russell* [1959] 2 QB 226 at 241, [1959] 2 All ER 525 at 531. *Cestuis que trust* is the correct plural: (1910) 26 LQR 196 (C. Sweet).

Maitland: *Lectures on Equity* (2nd Edn) p. 44

"Where judges and text-writers fear to tread professors of law have to rush in. I should define a trust in some such way as the following—When a person has rights which he is bound to exercise upon behalf of another or for the accomplishment of some particular purpose he is said to have those rights in trust for that other or for that purpose and he is called a trustee.

It is a wide vague definition, but the best that I can make. I shall comment on it by distinguishing cases of trust from some other cases."

Scott: *Trusts* (3rd Edn) § 2.3

"Even if it were possible to frame an exact definition of a legal concept, the definition would not be of great practical value. A definition cannot properly be used as though it were a major premise so that rules governing conduct can be deduced from it. Our law, at least, has not grown in that way. When the rules have been arrived at from other sources, it may be possible to attempt to frame a definition. But the definition results from the rules, and not the rules from the definition.

All that one can properly attempt to do is to give such a description of a legal concept that others will know in a general way what one is talking about. It is possible to state the principal distinguishing characteristics of the concept so that others will have a general idea of what the writer means. With this in mind, those responsible for the Restatement of Trusts proposed the following definition or description of an express trust. It is 'a fiduciary relationship with respect to property, subjecting the person by whom the title to property is held to equitable duties to deal with the property for the benefit of another person, which arises as a result of a manifestation of an intention to create it.' In this definition or description the following characteristics are to be noticed: (1) a trust is a relationship; (2) it is a relationship of a fiduciary character; (3) it is a relationship with respect to property, not one involving merely personal duties; (4) it involves the existence of equitable duties imposed upon the holder of the title to the property to deal with it for the benefit of another; and (5) it arises as a result of a manifestation of an intention to create the relationship. The combination of these things characterizes the notion of the trust as that notion has been developed in the Anglo-American law." (Footnotes omitted.)

Hanbury & Maudsley: *Modern Equity* (10th Edn) p. 117

"Many attempts have been made to define a trust[6], but none of them has been wholly successful. It is not thought that a dissection and criticism of earlier definitions are very rewarding; rather it is better to describe than to define a trust, and then to distinguish it from related but distinguishable concepts."

[6] Co Litt 272b; *Underhill's Law of Trusts and Trustees* (12th Edn), p. 2; used by COHEN J in *Re Marshall's Will Trusts* [1945] Ch 217 at 219, [1945] 1 All ER 550 at 551, and by ROMER LJ in *Green v Russell* [1959] 2 QB 226 at 241, [1959] 2 All ER 525 at 531; Lewin, *Practical Treatise on Law of Trusts* (16th Edn), p. 1; K & S, pp. 2–6; Snell, p. 87; *Halsbury's Laws of England* (3rd Edn), vol. 38, pp. 809–810; *Restatement of Trusts* (U.S.A.), § 2; Scott, *Law of Trusts*, § 2; (1955) 71 LQR 39 (A. W. Scott).

III. Distinctions[7]

A. Bailment[8]

Maitland: *Lectures on Equity* (2nd Edn) p. 45

"3. We must distinguish the trust from the bailment. This is not very easy to do, for in some of our classical text-books perplexing language is used about this matter. For example, Blackstone defines a bailment thus: 'Bailment, from the French *bailler*, is a delivery of goods in trust, upon a contract expressed or implied, that the trust shall be faithfully executed on the part of the bailee' (*Comm.* II, 451).

Here a bailment seems to be made a kind of trust. Now of course in one way it is easy enough to distinguish a bailment from those trusts enforced by equity, and only by equity, of which we are speaking. We say that the rights of a bailor against his bailee are legal, are common law rights, while those of a *cestui que trust* against his trustee are never common law rights. But then this seems to be a putting of the cart before the horse; we do not explain why certain rights are enforced at law while other rights are left to equity.

Let us look at the matter a little more closely. On the one hand we will have a bailment—A lends B a quantity of books—A lets to B a quantity of books in return for a periodical payment—A deposits a lot of books with B for safe custody. In each of these cases B receives rights from A, and in each of these cases B is under an obligation to A; he is bound with more or less rigour to keep the books safely and to return them to A. Still we do not I think conceive that B is bound to use on A's behalf the rights that he, B, has in the books. Such rights as B has in them he has on his own behalf, and those rights he may enjoy as seems best to him. On the other hand, S is making a marriage settlement and the property that he is settling includes a library of books; he vests the whole ownership of these books in T and T′ who are to permit S to enjoy them during his life and then to permit his firstborn son to enjoy them and so forth. Not unfrequently valuable chattels are thus settled so that whoever dwells in a certain mansion during the continuance of the settlement shall have the use of the pictures, books, plate, and so forth. Now here T and T′ are full owners of the chattels. S and the other *cestui que trusts* have no rights in the chattels, but T and T′ are bound to use their rights according to the words of the settlement, words which compel them to allow S and the other *cestui que trusts* to enjoy those things.

You may say the distinction is a fine one, almost a metaphysical one—and very likely I am not stating it well—but there are two tests which will bring out the distinction. The one is afforded by the law of sale, . . .

(*a*) A is the bailor, B is the bailee of goods; B sells the goods to X, the sale not being authorised by the terms of the bailment and not being made in market overt or within the Factors' Acts. X, though he purchases in good faith, and though he has no notice of A's rights, does

[7] H & M, pp. 118–132; K & S, pp. 6–16; P & M, pp. 7–14; Pettit, pp. 17–32; Snell, pp. 89–98.

[8] H & M, p. 118; K & S, pp. 12–13; Pettit, p. 17; Snell, p. 89; Crossley Vaines, *Personal Property* (5th Edn 1973), Ch 6.

not get a good title to the goods. A can recover them from him; if he converts them to his use he wrongs A. Why? Because he bought them from one who was not owner of them. Turn to the other case. T is holding goods as trustee of S's marriage settlement. In breach of trust he sells them to X; X buys in good faith and has no notice of the trust. X gets a good title to the goods. T was the owner of the goods; he passed his rights to X; X became the owner of the goods and S has no right against X—for it is an elementary rule, to which I must often refer hereafter, that trust rights can not be enforced against one who has acquired legal (*i.e.* common law) ownership *bona fide*, for value, and without notice of the existence of those trust rights. Here you see one difference between the bailee and the trustee . . .

Cases can be conceived where it would be difficult to say whether there was a bailment by deposit or a trust. For instance, I go abroad in a hurry and do not know whether I shall return. I send a piano to a friend, and I say to him, 'Take care of my piano and if I don't return give it to my daughter.' This may be construed both ways, as a bailment or as a trust. Perhaps the age of my daughter—a thing strictly irrelevant—would decide which way it would go."

B. Agency[9]

The relationship between trustee and beneficiary, and that between principal and agent, is *fiduciary*. For that reason there are many similarities between them. The crucial distinction is that the agency relationship is *personal*; the trust relationship *proprietary*.

LISTER & CO v STUBBS
(1890) 45 ChD 1 (CA, COTTON, LINDLEY and BOWEN LJJ)

The defendant, Stubbs, was authorised by the plaintiff company to purchase materials for use in their business as silk-spinners, dyers and manufacturers. In the course of his duties, Stubbs secretly and improperly received from Varley & Co., who were trade customers, large sums by way of commission, which he was liable to pay over to the plaintiffs.

In order to ensure the repayment of the money, the plaintiffs sought to follow the money into certain investments which Stubbs had purchased with it; and to obtain an interlocutory injunction to restrain Stubbs from dealing with an investment in land and for an order to bring the other investments and cash into court.

Held. The plaintiffs failed. They were not owners of the money wrongly taken, nor of the investments purchased. Stubbs merely owed the money to them as their debtor.

LINDLEY LJ: The relation between Messrs. *Varley* and *Stubbs* is that of debtor and creditor—they pay him. Then comes the question, as between *Lister & Co.* and *Stubbs*, whether *Stubbs* can keep the money he has received

9 H & M, pp. 118–119; K & S, p. 16; P & M, p. 13; Pettit, p. 18; Snell, pp. 89–90; (1892) 8 LQR 220 (C. Sweet); Hanbury, *Principles of Agency* (2nd Edn), pp. 3–10; *Bowstead on Agency* (14th Edn, 1976), p. 10.

without accounting for it? Obviously not. I apprehend that he is liable to account for it the moment that he gets it. It is an obligation to pay and account to Messrs. *Lister & Co.*, with or without interest, as the case may be. I say nothing at all about that. But the relation between them is that of debtor and creditor; it is not that of trustee and *cestui que trust*. We are asked to hold that it is—which would involve consequences which, I confess, startle me. One consequence, of course, would be that, if *Stubbs* were to become bankrupt, this property acquired by him with the money paid to him by Messrs. *Varley* would be withdrawn from the mass of his creditors and be handed over bodily to *Lister & Co.* Can that be right? Another consequence would be that, if the Appellants are right, *Lister & Co.* could compel *Stubbs* to account to them, not only for the money with interest, but for all the profits which he might have made by embarking in trade with it. Can that be right? It appears to me that those consequences shew that there is some flaw in the argument. If by logical reasoning from the premises conclusions are arrived at which are opposed to good sense, it is necessary to go back and look again at the premises and see if they are sound. I am satisfied that they are not sound—the unsoundness consisting in confounding ownership with obligation. It appears to me that the view taken of this case by Mr. Justice *Stirling* was correct, and that we should be doing what I conceive to be very great mischief if we were to stretch a sound principle to the extent to which the Appellants ask us to stretch it, tempting as it is to do so as between the Plaintiffs and *Stubbs*. I think that the appeal ought to be dismissed[10].

C. Contract[11]

Trust and contract are very different concepts. Contract is a common law concept based upon agreement, requiring either a deed or consideration, and creates a personal right against the other party. Trust is equitable, dependent essentially upon the intention of the settlor, and creating a proprietary interest in the beneficiary. Nevertheless, there are situations in which the dividing line is not clear. Difficulties most commonly arise in distinguishing trust from debt, and this situation will be considered here. The other situations will merely be mentioned now, and discussed in other sections of the book.

i. DEBT[12]

A debt is a personal obligation. A trust is proprietary.

MORLEY v MORLEY
(1678) 2 Cas in Ch 2 (Lord NOTTINGHAM LC)

The Defendant was Trustee for the Plaintiff an Infant, and received for

[10] See also *Mareva Compania Naviera SA of Panama v International Bulkcarriers SA* (1975) 119 Sol Jo 660, [1975] 2 Lloyd's Reports 509; *Aluminium Industrie Vassen BV v Romalpa Aluminium Ltd* [1976] 1 WLR 676, [1976] 2 All ER 552; (1976) 92 LQR 360, 528 (R. M. Goode), demonstrating a modern extension, in the commercial field, of the tracing remedy denied in the principal case; p. 634, post.

[11] H & M, pp. 119–121; K & S, pp. 6–12; P & M, pp. 7–10; Pettit, pp. 17–18; Snell, pp. 90–94.

[12] H & M, pp. 120–121.

him 40l. in Gold; a Servant of the Defendant living in the House with him robbed his Master of 200l. and the 40l. out of his House. The Robbery, *viz.* That the Defendant was robbed of Money, was proved; the Sum of 40l. was proved by only the Defendant's Oath.

LORD CHANCELLOR: He was to keep it but as his own, and allowed it on Account; so in Case of a Factor; so in Case of a Person robbed, for he cannot possibly have other Proof.

BARCLAYS BANK LTD v QUISTCLOSE INVESTMENTS LTD

[1970] AC 567, [1968] 3 All ER 651 (HL, Lords REID, MORRIS OF BORTH-Y-GEST, GUEST, PEARCE and WILBERFORCE)

Rolls Razor Ltd. had declared a dividend upon their ordinary shares. They were in serious financial difficulties and were unable to pay the dividend without a loan of £209,719 8s. 6d., which the respondents Quistclose Investments Ltd. agreed to make on the condition "that it is used to pay the forthcoming dividend due on July 24 next."

The cheque for £209,719 8s. 6d. was paid into a separate account at Barclays Bank Ltd. with whom it was agreed that the account would "only be used to meet the dividend due on July 24, 1964".

Before the dividend was paid, Rolls Razor Ltd. went into liquidation. The question was whether Barclays Bank Ltd. could set that sum against Rolls Razor's overdraft; or whether they held it on trust for Quistclose.

Held. Barclays Bank held the money on trust for Quistclose. The fact that the transaction was a loan did not prevent there being also a trust.

LORD WILBERFORCE: Two questions arise, both of which must be answered favourably to the respondents if they are to recover the money from the bank. The first is whether as between the respondents and Rolls Razor Ltd. the terms upon which the loan was made were such as to impress upon the sum of £209,719 8s. 6d. a trust in their favour in the event of the dividend not being paid. The second is whether, in that event, the bank had such notice of the trust or of the circumstances giving rise to it as to make the trust binding upon them.

It is not difficult to establish precisely upon what terms the money was advanced by the respondents to Rolls Razor Ltd. There is no doubt that the loan was made specifically in order to enable Rolls Razor Ltd. to pay the dividend. There is equally, in my opinion, no doubt that the loan was made only so as to enable Rolls Razor Ltd. to pay the dividend and for no other purpose. This follows quite clearly from the terms of the letter of Rolls Razor Ltd. to the bank of July 15, 1964, which letter, before transmission to the bank, was sent to the respondents under open cover in order that the cheque might be (as it was) enclosed in it. The mutual intention of the respondents and of Rolls Razor Ltd., and the essence of the bargain, was that the sum advanced should not become part of the assets of Rolls Razor Ltd., but should be used exclusively for payment of a particular class of its creditors, namely, those entitled to the dividend. A necessary consequence from this, by process simply of interpretation, must be that if, for any reason, the dividend could not be paid, the money was to be returned to the respondents: the word "only" or "exclusively" can have no other meaning or effect.

That arrangements of this character for the payment of a person's creditors by a third person, give rise to a relationship of a fiduciary character or trust, in favour, as a primary trust, of the creditors, and secondarily, if the primary trust fails, of the third person, has been recognised in a series of cases over some 150 years.

In *Toovey v Milne* (1819) 2 B & A 683 part of the money advanced was, on the failure of the purpose for which it was lent (viz., to pay certain debts), repaid by the bankrupt to the person who had advanced it. On action being brought by the assignee of the bankrupt to recover it, the plaintiff was nonsuited and the nonsuit was upheld on a motion for a retrial. In his judgment Abbot CJ said, at p. 684:

> "I thought at the trial, and still think, that the fair inference from the facts proved was that this money was advanced for a special purpose, and that being so clothed with a specific trust, no property in it passed to the assignee of the bankrupt. Then the purpose having failed, there is an implied stipulation that the money shall be repaid. That has been done in the present case; and I am of opinion that that repayment was lawful, and that the nonsuit was right."

The basis for the decision was thus clearly stated, viz., that the money advanced for the specific purpose did not become part of the bankrupt's estate. This case has been repeatedly followed and applied: see *Edwards v Glynn* (1859) 2 E & E 29; *Re Rogers, ex parte Holland and Hannen* (1891) 8 Morr 243; *Re Drucker (No. 1)* [1902] 2 KB 237; *Re Hooley, ex parte Trustee* [1915] HBR 181. *Re Rogers* (1891) 8 Morr 243 was a decision of a strong Court of Appeal. In that case, the money provided by the third party had been paid to the creditors before the bankruptcy. Afterwards the trustee in bankruptcy sought to recover it. It was held that the money was advanced to the bankrupt for the special purpose of enabling his creditors to be paid, was impressed with a trust for the purpose and never became the property of the bankrupt. Lindley LJ decided the case on principle but said (at p. 248) that if authority was needed it would be found in *Toovey v Milne* (1819) 2 B & A 683 and other cases. Bowen LJ said (8 Morr 243 at 248) that the money came to the bankrupt's hands impressed with a trust and did not become the property of the bankrupt divisible amongst his creditors, and the judgment of Kay LJ, at p. 249, was to a similar effect.

These cases have the support of longevity, authority, consistency and, I would add, good sense. But they are not binding on your Lordships and it is necessary to consider such arguments as have been put why they should be departed from or distinguished . . .

The second, and main, argument for the appellant was of a more sophisticated character. The transaction, it was said, between the respondents and Rolls Razor Ltd., was one of loan, giving rise to a legal action of debt. This necessarily excluded the implication of any trust, enforceable in equity, in the respondents' favour: a transaction may attract one action or the other, it could not admit of both.

My Lords, I must say that I find this argument unattractive. Let us see what it involves. It means that the law does not permit an arrangement to be made by which one person agrees to advance money to another, on terms that the money is to be used exclusively to pay debts of the latter, and if, and so far as not so used, rather than becoming a general asset of the latter available to his creditors at large, is to be returned to the lender. The lender is obliged, in such a case, because he is a lender, to accept, whatever the mutual wishes of lender and borrower may be, that the money he was willing to make available for one purpose only shall be freely available for others of the borrower's creditors for whom he has not the slightest desire to provide.

I should be surprised if an argument of this kind—so conceptualist in character—had ever been accepted. In truth it has plainly been rejected by the eminent judges who from 1819 onwards have permitted arrangements of this type to be enforced, and have approved them as being for the benefit of creditors and all concerned. There is surely no difficulty in recognising the co-existence in one transaction of legal and equitable rights and remedies: when the money is advanced, the lender acquires an equitable right to see that it is applied for the primary designated purpose (see *Re Rogers* (1891) 8 Morr 243 where both Lindley LJ and Kay LJ recognised this): when the purpose has been carried out (i.e., the debt paid) the lender has his remedy against the borrower in debt: if the primary purpose cannot be carried out, the question arises if a secondary purpose (i.e., repayment to the lender) has been agreed, expressly or by implication: if it has, the remedies of equity may be invoked to give effect to it, if it has not (and the money is intended to fall within the general fund of the debtor's assets) then there is the appropriate remedy for recovery of a loan. I can appreciate no reason why the flexible interplay of law and equity cannot let in these practical arrangements, and other variations if desired: it would be to the discredit of both systems if they could not. In the present case the intention to create a secondary trust for the benefit of the lender, to arise if the primary trust, to pay the dividend, could not be carried out, is clear and I can find no reason why the law should not give effect to it.

I pass to the second question, that of notice. I can deal with this briefly because I am in agreement with the manner in which it has been disposed of by all three members of the Court of Appeal. I am prepared, for this purpose, to accept, by way of assumption, the position most favourable to the bank, i.e., that it is necessary to show that the bank had notice of the trust or of the circumstances giving rise to the trust, at the time when they received the money, viz., on July 15, 1964, and that notice on a later date, even though they had not in any real sense given value when they received the money or thereafter changed their position, will not do. It is common ground, and I think right, that a mere request to put the money into a separate account is not sufficient to constitute notice. But on July 15, 1964, the bank, when it received the cheque, also received the covering letter of that date which I have set out above: previously there had been the telephone conversation between Mr. Goldbart and Mr. Parker, to which I have also referred. From these there is no doubt that the bank was told that the money had been provided on loan by a third person and was to be used only for the purpose of paying the dividend. This was sufficient to give them notice that it was trust money and not assets of Rolls Razor Ltd.: the fact, if it be so, that they were unaware of the lender's identity (though the respondent's name as drawer was on the cheque) is of no significance. I may add to this, as having some bearing on the merits of the case, that it is quite apparent from earlier documents that the bank were aware that Rolls Razor Ltd. could not provide the money for the dividend and that this would have to come from an outside source and that they never contemplated that the money so provided could be used to reduce the existing overdraft. They were in fact insisting that other or additional arrangements should be made for that purpose. As was appropriately said by Russell LJ ([1968] Ch 540 at 563F) it would be giving a complete windfall to the bank if they had established a right to retain the money.

In my opinion, the decision of the Court of Appeal was correct on all points and the appeal should be dismissed[13].

ii. CONTRACTS FOR THE BENEFIT OF A THIRD PARTY[14]

The English rule of privity of contract requires that only the parties to a contract may sue or be sued upon it. There are of course many exceptions. And there have been many attempts to circumvent the rule, and to change it. One such attempt is based upon the theory that a third party may sue upon a contract if one of the parties contracted as trustee for the third party; the third party then becomes a beneficiary of a trust of the promise, a chose in action; he can require his trustee to sue upon it[15], and a successful action by the trustee will recover damages for the injury suffered by the third party[16]. This theory has met with success in some cases, but is now discredited as a method of enabling a third party to sue upon a contract[17]. The main reason for its failure was the difficulty of deciding whether there was or was not a trust of the promise. There is no difficulty, as will be seen[18], in creating a trust of a promise, or of a chose in action. A trust of a debt, or of a bank account are simple examples. The difficulty arose in the "third party contract" situation because of the attempts by the common law courts to find that a trust existed in some situations in which the basic requirement for the creation of a trust was not met. That requirement, as will be seen[19], is that there should be a manifestation of an intention to create a trust.

The problem of the enforcement of a contract by a person who is not a party to it is not therefore a situation in which there is a difficulty of determining whether there is a contract or a trust. So far as the third

[13] *Selangor United Rubber Estates Ltd v Cradock (No. 3)* [1968] 1 WLR 1555, [1968] 2 All ER 1073; p. 217, post; *Re Kayford Ltd (in liquidation)* [1975] 1 WLR 279, [1975] 1 All ER 604 (purchase money retained in separate account by mail order company held in trust for customers); cf. *Potters v Loppert* [1973] Ch 399, [1973] 1 All ER 658 (estate agent held entitled to retain interest earned by deposit held as stakeholder).

[14] Cheshire & Fifoot, *Law of Contract* (9th Edn), p. 434 et seq.; Treitel, *Law of Contract* (4th Edn), p. 437 et seq.; H & M, pp. 602–611; (1930) 46 LQR 12 (A. L. Corbin).

[15] *Tomlinson v Gill* (1756) Amb 330; *Les Affréteurs Réunis Société Anonyme v Leopold Walford (London) Ltd* [1919] AC 801.

[16] *Lloyd's v Harper* (1880) 16 ChD 290.

[17] *Beswick v Beswick* [1968] AC 58, [1967] 2 All ER 1197.

[18] See p. 96, post.

[19] See p. 32, post.

party is concerned, there is no contract, because of the privity rule. The question is whether or not there was an intention to create a trust of a promise. This is more relevant to Chapter 2.

iii. UNINCORPORATED ASSOCIATIONS

An unincorporated association is not a "legal person", and questions arise as to the means by which the property of such an association is held. Is it owned by the members jointly? Or held by the committee members or club officials on trust for the members? Or for the purposes of the association? Or held by them subject to contractual rights in favour of the members?

The answers to these questions can determine the validity of a gift to an unincorporated association, and are also relevant to the solution of problems concerning the disposal of assets on a dissolution. They are discussed in Chapters 2 and 7.

iv. SETTLEMENTS AND COVENANTS TO SETTLE

It is important also to distinguish between the creation of a trust or settlement and a covenant or contract to create one. Once a settlement is created, the beneficiaries become owners in equity of their share of the settled property. But if the settlor has covenanted to create a settlement or to add property to an existing settlement, the rights of the intended beneficiaries depend on whether or not they can compel the settlor to complete the settlement. Generally, they cannot do so if they are volunteers; for equity does not assist a volunteer. The matter is discussed in detail in Chapter 3.

D. Conditions and Charges[20]

In *Attorney-General v The Cordwainers' Co* ((1833) 3 My & K 534)[1] the testator, by his will dated March 31, 1547, devised the Falcon Inn and adjoining premises in Fleet St. to the Cordwainers' Company "for the only interest, use and performation of this my last will and testament . . ." The will required the Cordwainers' Company to pay £6 a year to the testator's brother David and after David's death to his widow; to make certain payments to charity and to the officers of the company for attending certain masses; a gift over to David in fee, on failure by the Company to carry out the terms of the will, the Company then "to be clearly expelled, discharged, and put out of the premises".

The rents of the premises were £12 6s. 8d. in 1547. They had risen to £358 in 1833. The question was whether the Company, having carried out the terms of the will, was entitled to the surplus, or whether they held the premises as trustees, and were obligated to hold the surplus on charitable trusts. The Master of the Rolls (Sir John LEACH) held that they held the premises subject to a condition, and, upon due performance of

[20] H & M, pp. 121, 122; P & M, p. 13–14.

[1] See also *Re Oliver* (1890) 62 LT 533 (devise of real estate to nephew, "he also paying thereout" certain legacies. Held to create a charge and not a trust. The nephew not obligated to account for surplus).

the condition, were entitled to keep the surplus beneficially. He said (at p. 542): "The first question is whether this testator intended the corporation to take as mere trustees, or whether he intended to give them any beneficial interest. The next consideration is whether, if the corporation were to take as trustees, they were to be trustees for mere charitable purposes.

It does not appear to me that the words of this devise do constitute this corporation mere trustees. The estate is absolutely given to them; not upon trust, but for the use, interest, and performance of the testator's will. It is rather a gift upon condition, than a gift upon trust. They are to take the estate so devised to them, upon condition that they perform the duties which by the terms of the will are imposed upon them. Those duties are not for mere charitable purposes. Half the property that this testator disposes of is disposed of to his brother; an annuity of £6 is given to his brother for his life; and after his brother's death there is no disposition of this annuity, except that £2 a year are given to his widow if she survived him. These are not charitable purposes. It is plain that a beneficial estate was intended to be given to the Cordwainers' Company, because the testator expressly declares that, if the condition upon which this estate is devised to the corporation be not performed, the brother shall enter and defeat the estate given to the Cordwainers' Company. Defeat what estate? An estate given to them in mere trust, from which they were to derive no benefit? Is it to be supposed that this was considered by the testator in the nature of a penalty? The imposition of a penalty for non-performance of the condition implies a benefit, if the condition be performed, and is inconsistent with any other intention, than that the testator meant to give a beneficial interest to the company upon the terms of complying with the directions contained in his will. There is, therefore, no trust, either express or implied, for charitable purposes further than to the extent of the special charge imposed; and, upon all the principles applied in this Court to such a case, this information must be dismissed."

In *Re Frame* ([1939] Ch 700, [1939] 2 All ER 865) a testator bequeathed property to Mrs. Ada Taylor, his housekeeper "on condition that she adopt my daughter Alma Edwards and also gives to my daughters Jessie Edwards and May Alice Edwards the sum of 5*l* each, and a like sum of 5*l* to my son Alexander Edwards." SIMONDS J construed this gift as a trust for the maintenance of Alma, and held that Mrs. Taylor was bound to provide maintenance for her even if, as happened, she was unsuccessful in an application to adopt her. He said, in considering the effect of the words quoted above (at p. 703): "The question is what those words mean. I have listened to an able and interesting argument on these questions: Whether the condition is a condition subsequent or a condition precedent; whether, if it be a condition precedent, the condition has become impossible of performance, and whether, if so, the gift fails; whether, if it be a condition subsequent, the donee has failed, through no fault of her own, to comply with the condition, and whether, in that event, the gift has failed. As I listened to that argument it impressed itself more and more on me that, after all, this was not a condition at all, for, in my view, on the true construction of this clause, the word 'condition' is not used in its strict legal sense. It is a gift to Mrs. Taylor on condition, in the sense of on the terms or on the trust that she does certain things, and that, I think, becomes clearer when it is realized that the condition relates not only to the adoption of one daughter, but to the payment of certain sums to other daughters. A devise, or bequest, on condition that the devisee or legatee makes certain payments does not import a condition in the strict sense of the word, but a trust, so that, though the devisee or legatee dies before the testator and the gift does not take effect, yet the payments must be made; for it is a trust, and no trust fails for want of trustees. When I come to look at the condition, it seems clear that what the testator intended was that Mrs. Taylor should receive certain moneys on the term that she performed certain acts. Much argument has been directed to what is involved in the condition that 'she adopts my daughter'. It seems clear that whether or not an adoption under the authority of an order made under the Adoption of Children Act, 1926, is necessary, what is intended is not any single formal act, but a series of acts to establish as between Mrs. Taylor and the testator's daughter the relationship of parent and child—in a word, Mrs. Taylor was to treat the child as if she were her daughter, because that is what adoption means. Is that a trust which the Court can enforce? It includes not only the parental duties of care, advice, and affection, but also the duty of maintenance. This Court cannot compel, so far as adoption involves the giving of care, advice and affection, that such things be given. But, seeing that it involves the duty of maintenance, that is a trust which the Court can enforce, directing, if necessary, an inquiry in that regard. It will not allow the whole trust to fail because in part it cannot be enforced.

Therefore, I come to the conclusion that the gift to Mrs. Taylor of all the money and insurance policies—what that means will have to be considered—on condition 'that she adopts my daughter' involves that she receives those things, whatever they may be, on trust to make proper provision for the maintenance of the child as her adopted daughter. That is a trust which can be enforced, and, if necessary, an inquiry can be directed in regard to it."

E. Interests Under a Will or Intestacy[2]

i. THE DISTINCTION BETWEEN A PERSONAL REPRESENTATIVE AND A TRUSTEE

ATTENBOROUGH v SOLOMON

[1913] AC 76 (HL, Viscount HALDANE, Lords ATKINSON and SHAW OF DUNFERMLINE)

The testator, who died on March 20, 1878, devised and bequeathed his residuary estate to his two sons, A. A. Solomon ("A.A.") and J. D. Solomon upon trust to sell, and to divide the proceeds of sale among his children equally. Within a year, the debts and legacies had been paid, and the residuary account passed, but the estate had not been finally distributed.

In 1892, A.A. pledged some silver plate, part of the residuary estate,

[2] H & M, pp. 122–127; K & S, p. 13; P & M, pp. 10–13; Pettit, pp. 30–32; Snell, pp. 96–98; (1955) 19 Conv (NS) 199 (B. S. Ker).

with George Attenborough and Sons, pawnbrokers, the appellants, to secure a personal loan. The appellants had no reason to believe that A.A. was not the absolute owner. The matter came to light when A.A. died in 1907.

The question was whether the appellants obtained any rights over the plate, as pawnbrokers. They would do so if A.A. had acted as an executor, since the power of disposal of personalty by executors is *several*; but not if A.A. were a trustee, because the trustee's power of disposal is *joint*.

Held. The appellants obtained no title because A.A. was a trustee.

VISCOUNT HALDANE LC: The general principles of law which govern this case are not doubtful. The position of an executor is a peculiar one. He is appointed by the will, but then, by virtue of his office, by the operation of law and not under the bequest in the will, he takes a title to the personal property of the testator, which vests him with the plenum dominium over the testator's chattels. He takes that, I say, by virtue of his office. The will becomes operative so far as its dispositions of personalty are concerned only if and when the executor assents to those dispositions. It is true that by virtue of his office he has a general power to sell or pledge for the purpose of paying debts and getting in the money value of the estate. He is executor and he remains executor for an indefinite time. Authorities were cited to us by [counsel for the appellants] to the effect that an executor can sell at a period long after the death of the testator, and that where it is a question of conveyancing, as for instance in the case of the sale of leaseholds by the executor, the purchaser is not entitled to make requisitions as to whether debts remain unpaid, because the executor's office remains intact and he may exercise his functions at any time. That is true as a general principle, and I have no comment to make upon it except that it is qualified by another principle, which is this: The office of executor remains, with its powers attached, but the property which he had originally in the chattels that devolved upon him, and over which these powers extended, does not necessarily remain. So soon as he has assented, and this he may do informally and the assent may be inferred from his conduct, the dispositions of the will become operative, and then the beneficiaries have vested in them the property in those chattels. The transfer is made not by the mere force of the assent of the executor, but by virtue of the dispositions of the will which have become operative because of this assent.

Now, my Lords, in view of the residuary account passed as it was and in the form it was, in view of the evidence of Mr. J. D. Solomon, and in view of the fourteen years which had passed since the testator died before the time when Mr. A. A. Solomon made the pledge to the appellants in 1892, I am of opinion that the true inference to be drawn from the facts is that the executors considered that they had done all that was due from them as executors by 1879, and were content when the residuary account was passed that the dispositions of the will should take effect. That is the inference I draw from the form of the residuary account; and the inference is strengthened when I consider the lapse of time since then, and that in the interval nothing was done by them purporting to be an exercise of power as executors. My Lords, if this be so, this appeal must be disposed of on the footing that in point of fact the executors assented at a very early date to the dispositions of the will taking effect. It follows that under these dispositions the residuary estate, including the chattels in question, became vested in the trustees as trustees. That they were the same persons as the executors does not affect the point, or in my opinion present the least obstacle to the inference. But if that was so, then the title to the silver plate of A.A. Solomon as executor had ceased to exist before he made the pledge of 1892. What then was the position of the appellants? By the law of England the property in a chattel must always be in one person or body of persons. When the person who owns the chattel makes a pledge of it to a pawnbroker he is not purporting to part with the full property or giving any thing which is in the nature of a title to that property to the pawnee, excepting to a limited extent. The expression has been used that the pawnee in such a case has got a special property in the chattel. My Lords, that is true in this sense, that the pawnbroker is entitled to hold the chattel upon the terms that when the possession has been lawfully given to him it is not to be taken away from him, and that if default is made in the redemption of the pledge, or it may be in the payment of interest, he may go further and by virtue of his contract, assuming it to be valid, sell the chattel. But the contract of pawn is simply an illustration of that contract of bailment of which Holt CJ gave the famous exposition in the great case of *Coggs v Bernard* ((1703) 2 Ld Raym 909); and it rests upon this foundation, that the property remains in the bailor, and that the bailee, whether it be a bailment by way of pawn or in any other form, simply takes at the outside a right to the possession dependent on the validity of the title of the bailor with the other rights possibly superadded to which I have referred. If that be true, upon no hypothesis did the appellants get a legal title to the property in the plate. When A. A. Solomon handed over these articles of silver to Messrs. Attenborough he had no property to pass as executor; and they got no contractual rights which could prevail against the trustees. The latter were the true owners and they are now in a position to maintain an action, which under the old forms would have been an action of trover or detinue, to recover possession of the chattels free from the restrictions on the right to reclaim possession which were sought to be imposed by the contract between A. A. Solomon and the appellants. My Lords, the property, if I am right in the inference which I draw from the circumstances of the case, was vested not in A. A. Solomon, but in A. A. Solomon and his co-trustee jointly in 1892, when the attempted pledge was made; and I see no answer to the case made for the respondents that the present trustees, in whom that property is now vested, are entitled to recover it.

In *Re King's Will Trusts* ([1964] Ch 542, [1964] 1 All ER 833) Pennycuick J held that personal representatives could not exercise the statutory powers of appointing new trustees nor could they rely upon the provisions of Trustee Act 1925, s. 40[3], to vest realty in newly appointed trustees, unless they had assented in writing in accordance with Administration of Estates Act 1925, s. 36 (4), to the vesting of the realty in themselves as trustees.

[3] See p. 440, post.

The testatrix, by her will dated June 12, 1939, appointed X, Y and Z to be her executors, and X and Y her trustees. The estate contained land. As a result of various deaths and purported appointments of new trustees, Mr. Assheton, the plaintiff, claimed that he was the sole surviving trustee, and that the legal estate was vested in him. The defendant was the sole surviving personal representative (by representation). The question was whether the various appointments of trustees by X and Y and their successors were valid appointments; and whether, if they were valid, the legal estate was now vested, by virtue of Trustee Act 1925, s. 40, in the plaintiff.

PENNYCUICK J decided that the legal estate was in the defendant. Before personal representatives could become trustees of land, it was necessary that they should formally assent in writing in their own favour under s. 36 (4), just as they would in favour of other persons. The deed of appointment of new trustees did not operate as such assent.

With personalty, therefore, an assent can be implied. With realty, it must be in writing. *Re King's Will Trusts* is contrary to the earlier practice of many conveyancers, and may cast doubt upon some existing titles[4].

ii. THE NATURE OF THE INTEREST OF A LEGATEE OR DEVISEE

COMMISSIONER OF STAMP DUTIES (QUEENSLAND) v LIVINGSTON[5]

[1965] AC 694, [1964] 3 All ER 692 (PC, Viscount RADCLIFFE, Lords REID, EVERSHED, PEARCE and UPJOHN)

A testator, H. D. Livingston, died domiciled in New South Wales, leaving to his widow absolutely an estate which consisted of real and personal property in Queensland and in New South Wales.

While the estate was still in the course of administration, the widow (Mrs. Coulson) died intestate, also domiciled in New South Wales.

One question was whether succession duty was payable on the widow's death in respect of the Queensland property left to her in the will. Under the relevant Queensland statute succession duty was payable in respect of "every devolution by law of any beneficial interest in property . . . upon the death of any person . . .".

Held. No duty was payable in Queensland. The widow did not hold a beneficial interest in the property, but merely a chose in action which was situated in New South Wales.

VISCOUNT RADCLIFFE: When Mrs. Coulson died she had the interest of a residuary legatee in the testator's unadministered estate. The nature of that

[4] (1964) 28 Conv (NS) 298 (J. F. Garner); (1964) 108 Sol Jo 698 at 719; (1964) 80 LQR 328 (R. R. A. Walker); (1976) 29 CLP 60 (E. C. Ryder); see also *Williams on Title* (4th Edn), p. 360 et seq.; Barnsley, *Conveyancing Law and Practice*, p. 290; *Emmet on Title* (16th Edn), p. 418; Farrand, *Contract and Conveyance* (2nd Edn), p. 111 et seq. The requirement of an assent is however supported by Key and Elphinstone, *Conveyancing Precedents* (15th Edn), Vol. 1, p. 238 (§ 14) and p. 248 (note p); Prideaux, *Conveyancing Forms and Precedents* (25th Edn), Vol 3, p. 909; Wolstenholme and Cherry, *Conveyancing Statutes* (12th Edn), Vol. 2, p. 1470, but the support is qualified in 13th Edn, Vol. 5, p. 61 (ed. J. T. Farrand).

[5] (1965) CLJ 44 (S. J. Bailey).

interest has been conclusively defined by decisions of long-established authority, and its definition no doubt depends upon the peculiar status which the law accorded to an executor for the purposes of carrying out his duties of administration. There were special rules which long prevailed about the devolution of freehold land and its liability for the debts of a deceased, but subject to the working of these rules whatever property came to the executor virtute officii came to him in full ownership, without distinction between legal and equitable interests. The whole property was his. He held it for the purpose of carrying out the functions and duties of administration, not for his own benefit; and these duties would be enforced upon him by the Court of Chancery, if application had to be made for that purpose by a creditor or beneficiary interested in the estate. Certainly, therefore, he was in a fiduciary position with regard to the assets that came to him in the right of his office, and for certain purposes and in some aspects he was treated by the court as a trustee. "An executor," said Kay J in *Re Marsden* ((1884) 26 ChD 783 at 789), "is personally liable in equity for all breaches of the ordinary trusts which in Courts of Equity are considered to arise from his office." He is a trustee "in this sense".

It may not be possible to state exhaustively what those trusts are at any one moment. Essentially, they are trusts to preserve the assets, to deal properly with them, and to apply them in a due course of administration for the benefit of those interested according to that course, creditors, the death duty authorities, legatees of various sorts, and the residuary beneficiaries. They might just as well have been termed "duties in respect of the assets" as trusts. What equity did not do was to recognise or create for residuary legatees a beneficial interest in the assets in the executor's hands during the course of administration. Conceivably, this could have been done, in the sense that the assets, whatever they might be from time to time, could have been treated as a present, though fluctuating, trust fund held for the benefit of all those interested in the estate according to the measure of their respective interests. But it never was done. It would have been a clumsy and unsatisfactory device from a practical point of view; and, indeed, it would have been in plain conflict with the basic conception of equity that to impose the fetters of a trust upon property, with the resulting creation of equitable interests in that property, there had to be specific subjects identifiable as the trust fund. An unadministered estate was incapable of satisfying this requirement. The assets as a whole were in the hands of the executor, his property; and until administration was complete no one was in a position to say what items of property would need to be realised for the purposes of that administration or of what the residue, when ascertained, would consist or what its value would be. Even in modern economies, when the ready marketability of many forms of property can almost be assumed, valuation and realisation are very far from being interchangeable terms.

At the date of Mrs. Coulson's death, therefore, there was no trust fund consisting of Mr. Livingston's residuary estate in which she could be said to have any beneficial interest, because no trust had as yet come into existence to affect the assets of his estate. The relation of her estate to his was exactly the same as that of Mrs. Tollemache's estate to that of her deceased husband's, as analysed in the well-known decision of *Lord Sudeley v A-G* ([1897] AC 11). Just as Mr. Tollemache's rights in the mortgages of New Zealand land were the property of his executors for the purposes of the administration of his estate, and no one else had any property interest in them, so Mr. Livingston's property in Queensland, real or personal, was vested in his executors in full right, and no beneficial property interest in any item of it belonged to Mrs. Coulson at the date of her death. In their Lordships' opinion the decision of the *Sudeley* case is conclusive on this issue. It is sufficient to quote the words of Lord Herschell, which do no more than reflect the reasoning and views of all the members of the House who took part in the decision. "I do not think," he said (at p. 18), speaking of Mrs. Tollemache's executors, "that they have any estate, right, or interest, legal or equitable, in these New Zealand mortgages so as to make them an asset of her estate."

It is evident that there would not have been the divisions of opinion in the Australian courts that have arisen in this case, if the proposition laid down by the *Sudeley* decision had always been regarded as being as final and comprehensive as, in their Lordships' opinion, it was intended to be. There has been a reluctance to accept Lord Herschell's words at their face value and, it would seem, a feeling that they ought to be treated as subject to some limitation that does justice to the "interest" that a residuary legatee possesses in his testator's estate. The judgment of Jordan CJ in *McCaughey v Stamp Duties Comr.* ((1945) 46 SR (NSW) 192) contains a reasoned statement of some of these misgivings, which were again referred to in the High Court of Australia in *Smith v Layh* ((1953) 90 CLR 102 at 108–109); and cases in England such as *Cunliffe-Owen v IRC* ([1953] Ch 545, [1953] 2 All ER 196) indicate a certain unease at relating *Sudeley* to other English decisions. Basically, these criticisms appear to arise from an incomplete assessment of the legal position of assets which belong to an executor for the purposes of his administration and from a use of the word "interest" that is not sufficiently precise to meet the requirements of a taxing Act to which questions of locality and valuation are all important. But since these criticisms have been made, it is desirable that this opinion should notice and comment upon them . . .

. . . their Lordships regard it as clearly established that Mrs. Coulson was not entitled to any beneficial interest in any property in Queensland at the date of her death. What she was entitled to in respect of her rights under her deceased husband's will was a chose in action, capable of being invoked for any purpose connected with the proper administration of his estate; and the local situation of this asset, as much under Queensland law as any other law, was in New South Wales, where the testator had been domiciled and his executors resided and which constituted the proper forum of administration of his estate.

In *Lall v Lall* ([1965] 1 WLR 1249, [1965] 3 All ER 330) the question was whether the right of a widow under the Intestates' Estates Act 1952 to require the matrimonial home to be appropriated towards the satisfaction of her share of an intestate's estate gave the widow standing to defend an action for possession of the house. No grant of administration had been made. BUCKLEY J held, following *Commissioner of Stamp Duties (Queensland) v Livingston*, that it did not.

In *Eastbourne Mutual Building Society v Hastings Corporation* ([1965] 1 WLR 861, [1965] 1 All ER 779 PLOWMAN J quoted Viscount RADCLIFFE to summarise the principle of the *Livingston* case as follows: "Therefore, while it may well be said in a general way that a residuary legatee has an interest in the totality of the assets . . . it is in their Lordships' opinion inadmissible to proceed from that to the statement that such a person has an equitable interest in any particular one of those assets, for such a statement is in conflict with the authority of both *Sudeley* ([1897] AC 11) and *Barnardo* ([1921] 2 AC 1) and is excluded by the very premise on which those decisions were based."

(1970) 86 LQR 20 (P.V.B.)

"In *Re Leigh's Will Trusts* ([1970] Ch 277, [1969] 3 All ER 432), a testatrix specifically bequeathed 'all shares which I hold and any other interest or assets which I may have' in a named company. The testatrix never had any shares or interest of her own in the company, but both at the time she made her will and at her death she was the sole administratrix and beneficiary of her intestate husband's unadministered estate. That estate included some shares in and a debt due from the company. The question for Buckley J was whether those shares and debt passed under the bequest. The testatrix could not have bequeathed them in her capacity of administratrix, but what of her position as sole beneficiary?

The position of a person entitled to the residue or upon an intestacy while the administration is continuing was reviewed by Viscount Radcliffe in *Commissioner of Stamp Duties (Queensland) v Livingston* [1965] AC 694 and, as Buckley J observed, may be summarised in four propositions:

(1) The entire ownership of the assets of the estate remains during the course of administration in the personal representative;
(2) No person entitled to residue or upon an intestacy has any proprietary interest in any particular asset in the estate;
(3) Each such person has a right to require the deceased's estate to be duly administered;
(4) That right is a chose in action which is transmissible.

It follows that the only disposable interest which the testatrix had was the chose in action which could be transmitted to one or more beneficiaries. Buckley J held that the testatrix had 'an interest in the company both in respect of the shares and of the debt sufficient to answer the description in the specific bequest to the [specific legatee], which was accordingly effective to entitle [him] to receive such of the shares and so much of the debt as in the due administration of [the husband's] estate should eventually fall into the possession of the executors of the testatrix' (p. 654).

This decision is understandable on the facts of the case but may be difficult to apply in other circumstances. Suppose that the testatrix already had some shares in the company. Would the gift in the will have carried the additional shares comprised in the unadministered estate? Then again, suppose that the shares had been sold to pay the husband's debts. Could the specific legatee have recourse to the doctrine of marshalling and require to be compensated out of other assets of the husband's estate? And if they had not been sold, how far do the executors have to go to procure them? Buckley J said: 'What she could transmit was her own right to require the administrator of her husband's estate, whoever he might be, to administer his estate in any manner she or her personal representative might require consistent with the rights of any other persons having rights against the estate. This right she could transmit to her executor, coupled with a duty to exercise it in a particular manner. By her will she has, in my judgment, clearly indicated that her executor should so exercise this right as to procure the 51 shares, and the company's indebtedness should to the largest possible extent become available to satisfy the specific bequest' (p. 654). Is the executor bound, if necessary to save the shares, to use the testatrix's own estate to pay off the husband's debts? Alternatively, does the doctrine of ademption apply to any extent if the shares are sold (a) before the testatrix makes her will, or (b) before she dies, or (c) after her death? It may be some time before the implications of this decision are fully worked out."

iii. EXECUTOR'S DUTY IS TO THE ESTATE AS A WHOLE

In *Re Hayes Will Trusts* ([1971] 1 WLR 758, [1971] 2 All ER 341)[6] the testator appointed four persons to be executors and trustees of his will, of whom the testator's son was one. The will gave to the executors a power to sell certain land, expressly authorising sale to his son "despite his being a trustee".

The executors agreed to sell the land to the son at the agreed estate duty valuation. The other beneficiaries objected that the sale price was too low.

UNGOED-THOMAS J held that the executors were under no duty to agree an estate duty valuation which held an even balance between the beneficiaries, as trustees would have to do. Their duty was to the estate as a whole, and the estate duty valuation should be agreed in the ordinary way. He said at p. 764:

> "It is of course rightly common ground that 'my trustees' in agreeing the estate duty valuation were acting as executors under statutory powers conferred by section 15 (*f*) of the Trustee Act 1925. They were not acting under any powers conferred by the will, including in particular clause 5 (iii). I am completely satisfied that in fixing and agreeing the amount of the estate duty valuation Mr. Cooper, who was acting for the executors, was completely unaffected by the existence of the power to sell to the son. So this power to agree the estate duty valuation is to be considered as a purely personal representative administration power. It is well established that the estate being administered by a personal representative is the personal representative's property. Of course he has fiduciary duties with regard to it and their performance will be secured by the court; and he may be made liable for breaches of his fiduciary

[6] (1971) 36 Conv (NS) 136 (J. F. Mummery).

duties. But no legatee, devisee or next-of-kin has any beneficial interests in the assets being administered. His position is quite different from that of a trustee, who holds property for beneficiaries and has a duty to hold the balance evenly between the beneficiaries to whom the property belongs and for whom the trustee holds it. It does not necessarily follow that the duty of an executor in the course of administering the estate is subject to the trustee's duty of holding the balance evenly between the beneficiaries. Whether he has such a duty has to be independently considered in the light of his own different fiduciary functions and obligations: see *Stamp Duties Comr, Queensland v Livingston* [1965] AC 694 at 707, 708. Those functions are to get in the testator's estate, preserve its properties, discharge its liabilities and distribute the resulting net assets. The legal personal representatives would in due course be concerned to obtain a proper discharge for the net assets and thus to ascertain who were entitled to them and to ensure that the assets were distributed to those entitled. But even then they would not be concerned in the course of acting as legal personal representatives with any conflicting interests of beneficiaries under testamentary trusts but only with the trustees of that trust; and not the less so even if they themselves happen to be such trustees. In our case there is not even the possibility of argument that the farms were in the personal representatives' hands freed of administration and merely held for distribution; and therefore held by the legal personal representative on trust for the beneficiaries. Such an argument would be plainly contrary to the established facts. So the legal personal representative functions, so far at any rate as they arise in our case, are functions which relate to the process of ascertaining the net assets available for distribution and not at all functions in the distribution itself.

Much the most important authority on this part of this case is *Re Charteris* [1917] 2 Ch 379. It appears from the recital of facts in the report supplemented by Swinfen Eady LJ's references in the course of his judgment, that a testatrix gave her residue to her executors and trustees upon trust for sale and to raise a legacy to be held by them on trust for A for life and over. She gave them power to appropriate in satisfaction of the legacy and to postpone sale: and she provided that interest on the amount of the legacy in so far as there was no appropriation should be at 3½ per cent. and in so far as there was appropriation the interest would be the income of the appropriated investments. The balance of residue she gave to residuary legatees. It seems that the powers of the executors and trustees to postpone the sale of residue out of whose proceeds the legacy was to be paid and to appropriate it to the legacy were powers given to them in their capacity as executors: but even if they were given to them as trustees then a fortiori the observations made in the judgment would be applicable to them as executors, because, as already indicated, the fiduciary nexus between trustees and beneficiaries fastens directly on the trust property and is in that respect stronger than the fiduciary nexus between executor and beneficiary.

The executors decided to postpone sale and thus not to appropriate investments to the legacy. As the life tenant's interest on appropriated investments would be higher than the 3½ per cent. interest on the amount of the legacy, the life tenant objected to this course. The postponement in itself operated, as was fully realised by the executors when they made their decision, wholly in the interests of the residuary legatee and contrary to the interests of the pecuniary legatee. The bona fides of the executors was not questioned. The objection failed . . .

The most likely price, in the absence of consultation between the valuers representing conflicting interests, would presumably be the mean price. The habitual well-recognised process of arriving at that price is for executors to put in the lowest price within the range and then to confer with the district valuer who acts to safeguard the revenue. Such has been the accepted process of arriving at the price which the 'property would fetch if sold in the open market' and it seems to me to be as likely as any to arrive at that price within the margin which is the price most likely to be the market price. That was what was done in our case; and Mr. Cooper's evidence, which I accept, is that the price agreed was the fair and proper price and was in fact in this case the mean price within the marginal limits ranging from 10 per cent. above to 10 per cent. below it."

F. Powers[7]

A trust is imperative; a power discretionary. A trustee must perform the duties connected with his trust. A power, whether held in a fiduciary capacity or otherwise, may be exercised or not at the discretion of the donee of the power. Whether a particular disposition creates a power or a trust is a question of the intention of the settlor as ascertained from a construction of the language of the instrument.

Under a trust, the beneficiaries are the owners of the property. Under a power, the objects own nothing; they merely have a hope that the power will be exercised in their favour. Until it is exercised, equitable ownership is in those who will take in default of the exercise of the power; their interest is subject to defeasance on such exercise.

The distinction between trust and power becomes blurred in the case of discretionary trusts[8], especially in the case of "non-exhaustive" discretionary trusts—those in which the trustees may decide not to distribute any income at all, but rather to accumulate it. With an "exhaustive" discretionary trust, it is the duty of the trustees to exercise their discretion in favour of one or more members of the class of beneficiaries. If they fail to do so, the court will make an order for equal division among the beneficiaries, or in such proportions as is appropriate in the circumstances[9].

[7] H & M, pp. 127–132; K & S, pp. 14–16; P & M, pp. 62–72; Pettit, pp. 19–29; Snell, pp. 94–96; *Farwell on Powers* (3rd Edn); (1957) 35 Can BR 1060 (O. R. Marshall); (1953) 69 LQR 334 (D. M. Gordon); (1949) 13 Conv (NS) 20 (J. G. Fleming); (1954) 18 Conv (NS) 565 (F. R. Crane); [1971] CLJ 68 (J. A. Hopkins); (1971) 87 LQR 31 (J. W. Harris); (1976) 54 Can BR 229 (M. C. Cullity).

[8] See also (1970) ASCL 187 (J. D. Davies); (1974) 37 MLR 643 (Y. Grbich).

[9] *McPhail v Doulton* [1971] AC 424, [1970] 2 All ER 228.

Further, the class of beneficiaries, if they are of full age and under no disability, and if between them they are entitled to the whole of the beneficial interest, may terminate the trust[10].

The analysis is all the more difficult with non-exhaustive discretionary trusts. As Pettit says[11]: "It is submitted that the term 'non-exhaustive discretionary trust' in fact conceals the two alternatives referred to by Lord Wilberforce in *McPhail v Doulton*[12] viz. a power of distribution coupled with a trust to dispose of the undistributed surplus, by accumulation or otherwise, and a trust for distribution coupled with a power to withhold a portion and accumulate or otherwise dispose of it. The distinction between these alternatives does not appear to have been raised in *Gartside v IRC*[13] and it is submitted that it is only if the provision there in question was construed in the latter sense that it should properly have been called a discretionary trust. It was in fact consistently so called by their Lordships, though the language of the will is similar to that given as a typical example of a mere power by RUSSELL LJ in *Re Baden's Deed Trusts.*[14]"

Finally, it may be added that most of the recent cases upon the distinction between trusts and powers have arisen in connection with the question whether a disposition is void for uncertainty. These cases are now mentioned only in a footnote[15], because it was decided in *McPhail v Doulton*[16] that the test of certainty of objects in the case of discretionary trusts should be the same as that established for powers in *Re Gulbenkian's Settlements*[17].

i. DISCRETIONARY TRUSTS AND POWERS

In *Burrough v Philcox* ((1840) 5 My & Cr 72) John Walton, the testator, gave life interests in a trust fund to his two children with remainders to their issue, but if each of the children should die without leaving lawful issue (as happened), then the survivor of the children should have power to dispose, by will, "amongst my nephews and nieces, or their children, either all to one of them or to as many of them as my surviving child shall think proper". There was no gift in default.

The question was whether this language created a trust in favour of the nephews and nieces, or whether it was a power.

Lord COTTENHAM held that it was a trust. The living nephews and nieces took in equal shares. He said (at p. 89): "The question is, whether these nephews and nieces and their children, take any interest in the property, independently of the power; that is, whether the power given to the survivor of the son and daughter is a mere power, and the interests of the

[10] *Re Smith* [1928] 1 Ch 915, see p. 27, post.

[11] At p. 85.

[12] [1971] AC 424 at 448, [1970] 2 All ER 228 at 240.

[13] [1968] AC 553; [1968] 1 All ER 121.

[14] [1969] 2 Ch 388 at 401, [1969] 1 All ER 1016 at 1022. In *Re Weir's Settlement Trusts* [1971] Ch 145 at 164, [1970] 1 All ER 297 at 300, RUSSELL LJ referred to *Gartside v IRC* as "a case of a non-exhaustive discretionary power or trust.".

[15] *IRC v Broadway Cottages Trust* [1955] Ch 20, [1954] 3 All ER 120; *Re Hooper's 1949 Settlement* (1955) 34 ATC 3; *Re Sayer* [1957] Ch 423, [1956] 3 All ER 600; *Re Eden* [1957] 1 WLR 788, [1957] 2 All ER 430; *Re Saxone Shoe Co Ltd's Trust Deed* [1962] 1 WLR 943, [1962] 2 All ER 904; *Re Leek* [1969] 1 Ch 563, [1968] 1 All ER 793.

[16] [1971] AC 424, [1970] 2 All ER 228, p. 48, post.

[17] [1970] AC 508, [1968] 3 All ER 785, see p. 28, post.

nephews and nieces and their children were, therefore, to depend upon the exercise of it, or whether there was a gift to them, subject only to the power of selection given to the survivor of the son and daughter.

[His Lordship referred to *Duke of Marlborough v Lord Godolphin* (1750) 2 Ves Sen 61, *Brown v Higgs* (1800) 5 Ves 495 at 506, *Harding v Glyn* (1739) 1 Atk 469, and *Witts v Boddington* (1790) 3 Bro CC 95, and continued:] These and other cases shew that when there appears a general intention in favour of a class, and a particular intention in favour of individuals of a class to be selected by another person, and the particular intention fails, from that selection not being made, the Court will carry into effect the general intention in favour of the class. When such an intention appears, the case arises, as stated by Lord *Eldon* in *Brown v Higgs* ((1803) 8 Ves 561 at 574), of the power being so given as to make it the duty of the donee to execute it; and, in such case, the Court will not permit the objects of the power to suffer by the negligence or conduct of the donee, but fastens upon the property a trust for their benefit."

In *Re Week's Settlement* ([1897] 1 Ch 289) Mrs. Slade, by her will, gave a life interest in certain property to her husband "and I give to him power to dispose of all such property by will amongst our children . . ." The will contained no gift in default of appointment.

The husband failed to make any appointment. The question was whether the children were entitled in equal shares or whether the property passed to the heir at law of Mrs. Slade. ROMER J held that the heir at law was entitled. He said (at p. 292): "Now, apart from the authorities, I should gather from the terms of the will that it was a mere power that was conferred on the husband, and not one coupled with a trust that he was bound to exercise. I see no words in the will to justify me in holding that the testatrix intended that the children should take if her husband did not execute the power.

This is not a case of a gift to the children with power to the husband to select, or to such of the children as the husband should select by exercising the power.

If in this case the testatrix really intended to give a life interest to her husband and a mere power to appoint if he chose, and intended if he did not think fit to appoint that the property should go as in default of appointment according to the settlement, why should she be bound to say more than she has said in this will?

I come to the conclusion on the words of this will that the testatrix only intended to give a life interest and a power to her husband—certainly she has not said more than that.

Am I then bound by the authorities to hold otherwise? I think I am not. The authorities do not shew, in my opinion, that there is a hard and fast rule that a gift to A for life with power to A to appoint among a class and nothing more must, if there is no gift over in the will, be held a gift by implication to the class in default of the power being exercised. In my opinion the cases shew (though there may be found here and there certain remarks of a few learned judges which, if not interpreted by the facts of the particular case before them, might seem to have a more extended operation) that you must find in the will an indication that the testatrix did intend the class or some of the class to take—intended in fact that the power should be regarded in the nature of a trust—only a power of selection being given, as, for example, a gift to A for life with a gift over to such of a class as A shall appoint."

ii. TERMINATION OF A DISCRETIONARY TRUST BY ALL MEMBERS OF THE CLASS OF BENEFICIARIES

In *Re Smith* ([1928] Ch 915) a fund was held by trustees upon trust "to pay or apply the whole or any part of the annual income . . . . thereof or if they shall think fit from time to time any part of the capital thereof unto and for the maintenance and personal support and benefit of. . . Lilian Aspinall". There was provision for accumulation of the surplus, the accumulations and the remainder after her death to be held in trust for such of her sons who should attain the age of twenty-one years and such of her daughters who should attain that age or marry.

Mrs. Aspinall had three children, all of whom attained the age of twenty-one years, and one of whom had died. Mrs. Aspinall was past the age of child-bearing.

Mrs. Aspinall, her two surviving children and the legal representatives of her deceased child, mortgaged to the Legal and General Assurance Co. their interests under the trust. The question was whether the trustees should pay the income of the trust to the mortgagees, or whether they retained the discretion to pay to Mrs. Aspinall.

ROMER J held that the mortgage to the Legal and General Assurance Co. was valid. He said (at p. 917): "The question I have to determine is whether the Legal and General Assurance Company are now entitled to call upon the trustees to pay the whole of the income to them. It will be observed from what I have said that the whole of this share is now held by the trustees upon trusts under which they are bound to apply the whole income and eventually pay over or apply the whole capital to Mrs. Aspinall and the three children or some or one of them. So far as the income is concerned they are obliged to pay it or apply it for her benefit or to pay it or apply it for the benefit of the children. So far as regards the capital they have a discretion to pay it and to apply it for her benefit and, subject to that, they must hold it upon trust for the children. Mrs. Aspinall, the two surviving children and the representatives of the deceased child are between them entitled to the whole fund. In those circumstances it appears to me, notwithstanding the discretion which is reposed in the trustees, under which discretion they could select one or more of the people I have mentioned as recipients of the income, and might apply part of the capital for the benefit of Mrs. Aspinall and so take it away from the children, that the four of them, if they were all living, could come to the Court and say to the trustees: 'Hand over the fund to us.' It appears to me that that is in accordance with the decision of the Court of Appeal in a case of *Re Nelson* ([1928] Ch 920n), of which a transcript of the judgments has been handed to me, and is in accordance with principle. What is the principle? As I understand it it is this. Where there is a trust under which trustees have a discretion as to applying the whole or part of a fund to or for the benefit of a particular person, that particular person cannot come to the trustees and demand the fund; for the whole fund has not been given to him but only so much as the trustees think fit to let him have. But when the trustees have no discretion as to the amount of the fund to be applied, the fact that the trustees have a discretion as to the method in which the whole of the fund shall be applied for the benefit of the particular person does not prevent that particular person from coming and saying: 'Hand over the fund to me.' That appears to be the result of the two cases which were cited to me: *Green v Spicer* ((1830) 1 Russ & My 395) and *Younghusband v Gisborne* ((1844) 1 Coll 400).

Now this third case arises. What is to happen where the trustees have a discretion whether they will apply the whole or only a portion of the fund for the benefit of one person, but are obliged to apply the rest of the fund, so far as not applied for the benefit of the first named person, to or for the benefit of a second named person? There, two people together are the sole objects of the discretionary trust and, between them, are entitled to have the whole fund applied to them or for their benefit. It has been laid down by the Court of Appeal in the case to which I have referred that, in such a case as that you treat all the people put together just as though they formed one person, for whose benefit the trustees were directed to apply the whole of a particular fund. The case before the Court of Appeal was this: A testator had directed his trustees to stand possessed of one-third of his residuary estate upon trust during the lifetime of the testator's son Arthur Hector Nelson: 'to apply the income thereof for the benefit of himself and his wife and child or children or of any such persons to the exclusion of the others or other of them as my trustees shall think fit.' What happened was something very similar to what happened in the case before me. Hector Nelson, his wife and the only existing child of the marriage joined together in asking the trustees to hand over the income to them, and it was held by the Court of Appeal that the trustees were obliged to comply with the request, in other words, to treat all those persons who were the only members of the class for whose benefit the income could be applied as forming together an individual for whose benefit a fund has to be applied by the trustees without any discretion as to the amount so to be applied."

iii. CERTAINTY

In the past ten years, important changes have been made in the rules relating to the certainty of identification of objects of a power and beneficiaries of a trust. Certainty in relation to beneficiaries of a trust is dealt with below[18]; and it will there be seen that the rule laid down in *Re Gulbenkian's Settlements*[19] in relation to powers, has been adopted in the case of discretionary trusts; but not for fixed trusts. Here we are concerned only with the development of the rule relating to powers.

In *Re Gulbenkian's Settlements* ([1970] AC 508, [1968] 3 All ER 785) a settle-

[18] See p. 47, post.

[19] [1970] AC 508, [1968] 3 All ER 785.

ment contained a power to appoint in favour of Nubar Gulbenkian "and any wife and his children or remoter issue . . . and any person . . . in whose house or apartments or in whose company or under whose care or control or by or with whom [he] may from time to time be employed or residing." The question was whether the power was void for uncertainty. It was unanimously upheld by the House of Lords. A power is valid if it could be said with certainty whether any given individual was or was not a member of the class. Lord UPJOHN said at p. 523: "In my opinion, this clause is not void for uncertainty, and the Court of Appeal were quite right to overrule the decision of Harman J in *Re Gresham* [1956] 1 WLR 573 where he held a similar clause was void on that ground.

My Lords, that is sufficient to dispose of the appeal, but, as I have mentioned earlier, the reasons of two members of the Court of Appeal went further and have been supported by counsel for the respondents with much force and so must be examined.

The Master of the Rolls ([1968] Ch 126 at 134E) propounded a test in the case of powers collateral, namely, that if you can say of one particular person meaning thereby, apparently, any one person only that he is clearly within the category the whole power is good though it may be difficult to say in other cases whether a person is or is not within the category, and he supported that view by reference to authority. Winn L.J. (at p. 138E) said that where there was not a complete failure by reason of ambiguity and uncertainty the court would give effect to the power as valid rather than hold it defeated since it will have wholly failed, which put—though more broadly—the view expressed by the Master of the Rolls. Counsel for the respondents in his second line of argument relied upon these observations as a matter of principle but he candidly admitted that he could not rely upon any authority. Moreover, the Master of the Rolls (at p. 133B) expressed the view that the different doctrine with regard to trust powers should be brought into line with the rule with regard to conditions precedent and powers collateral . . .

But with respect to mere powers, while the court cannot compel the trustees to exercise their powers, yet those entitled to the fund in default must clearly be entitled to restrain the trustees from exercising it save among those within the power. So the trustees or the court must be able to say with certainty who is within and who is without the power. It is for this reason that I find myself unable to accept the broader proposition advanced by Lord Denning M.R. and Winn L.J. mentioned earlier, and agree with the proposition as enunciated in *Re Gestetner's Settlement* [1953] Ch 672 and the later cases."

In *Re Manisty's Settlement* ([1974] Ch 17, [1973] 1 All ER 1203)[20] a clause in a settlement executed in 1970 gave to the trustees power to declare that any person corporation or charity (other than members of an "Excepted Class") should be included in the class of beneficiaries under the settlement.

The trustees purported to add the mother of the settlor and any widow he may leave. The question was whether such a power was valid. TEMPLEMAN J

[20] (1973) 37 Conv (NS) 355 (F. R. Crane); [1974] CLJ 66 (J. A. Hopkins).

upheld it. He said at p. 22: "Invalidity, based on uncertainty, was the subject of *Re Gulbenkian's Settlements* [1970] AC 508 relating to special powers in favour of a class, and *Re Baden's Deed Trusts* [1971] AC 424, known as *Baden* (*No. 1*), relating to discretionary trusts in favour of a class. Those authorities establish that such a power or trust is valid if it can be said with certainty that any given individual is or is not a member of the class. The principle of the rule thus established does not strike down an intermediate power provided that, having regard to the definition of excepted persons, it can be said with certainty that any given individual is or is not an object of the power. The principle for which Mr. Horne contends may be adopted from the summary of the effect of *Re Gulbenkian's Settlements* to be found in the dissenting speech of Lord Guest in *Baden (No. 1)* [1971] AC 424 where he said, at p. 445: 'In the case of a power it is only necessary for the trustees to know whether a particular individual does or does not come within the ambit of the power.' Mr. Horne says, applying that principle to the present case, the definition of excepted class being certain, it follows that there is no uncertainty about the power.

The cases of *Gulbenkian* and *Baden* (*No. 1*) also establish, or rather reiterate, the rule that trustees of a power must consider from time to time whether and how to exercise the power, for in the words of Lord Reid in *Gulbenkian* [1970] AC 508 at 518:

> 'A settlor or testator who entrusts a power to his trustees must be relying on them in their fiduciary capacity so they cannot simply push aside the power and refuse to consider whether it ought in their judgment to be exercised. And they cannot give money to a person who is not within the classes of persons designated by the settlor: the construction of the power is for the court.'

In *Baden* (*No. 1*) [1971] AC 424 at 449, Lord Wilberforce, referring to special powers, suggested that

> 'Any trustee would surely make it his duty to know what is the permissible area of selection and then consider responsibly, in individual cases, whether a contemplated beneficiary was within the power and whether, in relation to other possible claimants, a particular grant was appropriate.'

He added, at p. 457, referring to special powers and to discretionary trusts in favour of a class that 'in each case the trustees ought to make such a survey of the range of objects or possible beneficiaries as will enable them to carry out their fiduciary duty.'

It is said that if a power is too wide the trustees cannot perform the duty reiterated in *Gulbenkian* and *Baden* (*No. 1*) of considering from time to time whether and how to exercise the power and the court cannot determine whether or not the trustees are in breach of their duty. In my judgment, however, the mere width of a power cannot make it impossible for trustees to perform their duty nor prevent the court from determining whether the trustees are in breach . . ."

G. Where the Crown is Trustee

In considering the use of the term "trust" in relation to the Crown, Lord

Selborne LC said in *Kinloch v Secretary of State for India* ((1882) 7 App Cas 619 at 625): "Now the words 'in trust for' are quite consistent with, and indeed are the proper manner of expressing, every species of trust—a trust not only as regards those matters which are the proper subjects for an equitable jurisdiction to administer, but as respects higher matters, such as might take place between the Crown and public officers discharging, under the directions of the Crown, duties or functions belonging to the prerogative and to the authority of the Crown. In the lower sense they are matters within the jurisdiction of, and to be administered by, the ordinary courts of equity; in the higher sense they are not. What their sense is here, is the question to be determined, looking at the whole instrument and at its nature and effect."

And Lord Diplock in *Town Investments Ltd v Department of the Environment* ([1977] 2 WLR 450 at 457): "My Lords, I would not exclude the possibility that an officer of state, even though acting in his official capacity, may in some circumstances hold property subject to a trust in private law for the benefit of a subject; but clear words would be required to do this and, even where the person to be benefited is a subject, the use of the expression 'in trust' to describe the capacity in which the property is granted to an officer of state is not conclusive that a trust in private law was intended; for 'trust' is not a term of art in public law and when used in relation to matters which lie within the field of public law the words 'in trust' may do no more than indicate the existence of a duty owed to the Crown by the officer of state, as servant of the Crown, to deal with the property for the benefit of the subject for whom it is expressed to be held in trust, such duty being enforceable administratively by disciplinary sanctions and not otherwise: *Kinlock v Secretary of State for India* (1882) 7 App Cas 619, per Lord Selborne LC, at pp. 615–626. But even if the legal relationship of trustee and cestui qui trust under a trust in private law is capable of existing between an officer of state in his official capacity and a subject, the concept of such relationship being capable of existing between him as trustee and the Crown as cestui qui trust is in my view wholly irreconcilable with the legal nature in public law of the relationship between the Crown and its servants or, in more modern parlance, the government and the ministers who form part of it."[1]

[1] See also *Tito v Waddell (No. 2)* [1977] 2 WLR 496 at 596, per Megarry V-C.

2. The Requirements of a Trust

The essential factor in the creation of a trust is a manifestation of an intention by the settlor to create a trust.

There are however other factors.

I. Formalities[1]

A. Inter Vivos

i. DECLARATION AND DISPOSITION

LAW OF PROPERTY ACT 1925

53. Instruments required to be in writing.—(1) Subject to the provisions hereinafter contained with respect to the creation of interests in land by parol—

(*b*) a declaration of trust respecting any land or any interest therein must be manifested and proved by some writing signed by some person who is able to declare such trust or by his will;

(*c*) a disposition of an equitable interest or trust subsisting at the time of the disposition, must be in writing[2] signed by the person disposing of the same[3], or by his agent thereunto lawfully authorised in writing or by will.

(2) This section does not affect the creation or operation of resulting, implied or constructive trusts[4].

[1] H & M, pp. 156–164; K & S, pp. 62–64 ; P & M, pp. 20–25; Pettit, pp. 51–60; Snell, pp. 104–106.

[2] The writing need not contain details of the trust where the assignee is to hold in a fiduciary capacity. *Re Tyler* [1967] 1 WLR 1269, [1967] 3 All ER 389; see p. 39, post.

[3] This may be satisfied by joinder of documents. *Re Danish Bacon Co Ltd Staff Pension Fund Trusts* [1971] 1 WLR 248, [1971] 1 All ER 486; see p. 33, post; cf. L.P.A. 1925, s. 40 (1); *Timmins v Moreland Street Property Co Ltd* [1958] Ch 110, [1957] 3 All ER 265.

[4] *Bannister v Bannister* [1948] 2 All ER 133; *Oughtred v IRC* [1960] AC 206, [1959] 3 All ER 623, see p. 37, post; *Hodgson v Marks* [1971] Ch 892, [1971] 2 All ER 684; (1971) 35 Conv (NS) 255, at 260–266 (I. Leeming); *Ottaway v Norman* [1972] Ch 698, [1971] 3 All ER 1325, p. 115, post.

ii. METHODS OF DISPOSITION

It will be seen that the application of section 53 (1) (*c*) in diffierent types of situation has been inconsistent.

(a) Assignment of Equitable Interest

In *Re Danish Bacon Co Ltd Staff Pension Fund Trusts* ([1971] 1 WLR 248, [1971] 1 All ER 486) an employee had the right to nominate a person to receive benefits due under the company's pension fund in the case of death before qualifying for a pension. An employee had, in the approved form, duly signed and witnessed, nominated his wife. He then, by letter to the company, changed the nomination. The question was whether, on the assumption that s. 53 (1)(*c*) applied, the documents together could supply the necessary writing. MEGARRY J said at p. 254: "I have been referred to no authority on the point relating to the words in section 53 (1) (*c*) which run 'a disposition . . . must be in writing . . .'; indeed, despite the riches of authority on this point under section 40, section 53 (1) (*c*) appears to be wholly barren. However, if a statutory requirement that a 'memorandum' shall be 'in writing' may be satisfied by two or more documents, I do not see why two or more documents should not satisfy the requirement that a 'disposition' shall be 'in writing'. True, section 40 (1) is merely directed to providing written evidence of a transaction, whereas under section 53 (1) (*c*) (unlike section 53 (1) (*b*)) the matter is one not merely of evidence but of the disposition itself. Yet two documents are used in constituting a strict settlement of land or establishing a trust for sale of land, and there are well-established rules for the incorporation of documents in a will; and if two or more documents, when read together, dispose of an equitable interest, I do not see why the court should insist on separating them and subjecting each separately to the test of section 53 (1) (*c*)."

(b) Direction to Trustees to Hold on Trust for Another

In *Grey v Inland Revenue Commissioners* ([1960] AC 1, [1959] 3 All ER 603)[5] the question was whether an instruction by a beneficiary to the trustees to hold upon different trusts was a "disposition" within Law of Property Act 1925, s. 53 (1) (*c*). As it was put in argument by Pennycuick QC (at p. 4): "If X holds property in trust for A as absolute equitable owner and A then directs X to hold the property on the settlement trusts for the benefit of B, C and D, and X accepts the trust, is that direction a 'disposition' of a subsisting equitable interest within the meaning of section 53?"

The settlor, Mr. Hunter, had made six settlements of nominal sums in favour of grandchildren. Subsequently he transferred substantial blocks of shares to the trustees, which they held on trust for him. Then he orally instructed the trustees to hold the shares upon the trusts of the six settlements. Finally, documents were executed in confirmation of the oral declaration, and these were executed by Mr. Hunter. The question was whether the trusts of the shares were created by the oral declaration or by the later documents.

Upon this depended the liability to stamp duty. Stamp duty is payable *ad valorem* upon a "conveyance on sale", which includes "every instrument

[5] [1960] CLJ 31 (J. W. A. Thornely).

. . . whereby any property, or any estate or interest in any property, upon the sale thereof is transferred to or vested in a purchaser, or any other person on his behalf or by his direction"[6]. Thus "the thing which is made liable to the duty is an 'instrument'. If a contract of purchase and sale, or conveyance by way of purchase and sale, can be, or is carried out without an instrument, the case is not within the section, and no tax is imposed. It is not the transaction of purchase and sale which is struck at; it is the instrument whereby the purchase and sale are effected which is struck at."[7]

Whether the trusts of the shares in *Grey v Inland Revenue Commissioners* were created by the oral direction or by the later documents depended on whether the oral declaration was valid. It would be valid as an oral *declaration* of a trust of personalty; but not if it was a *disposition* of an equitable interest.

The House of Lords decided that it was a disposition. The equitable interest was to pass from Mr. Hunter to the beneficiaries. That "amounted in any ordinary sense of the words to a 'disposition of an equitable interest or trust subsisting at the time of the disposition'". (per Lord RADCLIFFE at 15). There was no necessity to construe the word "disposition" in the light of the language of the earlier Statute of Frauds, which dealt with "grants and assignments". The passing of the interest could only be effected by an instrument in writing. It was thus effected by the later document, and that document was liable to *ad valorem* stamp duty.

(c) Conveyance of Legal Estate by Nominee

In *Vandervell v Inland Revenue Commissioners* ([1967] 2 AC 291, [1967] 1 All ER 1)[8] Vandervell decided to give to the Royal college of Surgeons sufficient money to endow a Chair of Pharmacology. This was to be done by transferring a holding of shares in Vandervell Products Ltd., which were vested in the National Provincial Bank Ltd. on trust for Vandervell, to the Royal College of Surgeons, and then declaring dividends on the shares, for which the Royal College would be free of liability to tax because it is a charity. An option to re-purchase the shares for £5,000 was given to Vandervell Trustees Ltd., a company which acted as trustee for the Vandervell family trusts. The Bank transferred the shares, and the dividends were declared.

The Revenue assessed Vandervell to surtax on the dividends on the ground that he had not absolutely divested himself of all interest in the shares[9]. This was upheld. Vandervell Trustees Ltd. held the option on a resulting trust for Vandervell. One argument for the Revenue was that the Bank had conveyed only the legal estate in the shares to the Royal College of Surgeons; the equitable interest remained in Vandervell because he had failed to effect its disposition in writing as required by s. 53 (1) (*c*). In rejecting this argument, Lord UPJOHN said (at p. 311): "[Section 53 (1) (*c*) was] applied in *Grey*[10] and *Oughtred*[11] to cases where the legal estate

[6] Stamp Act 1891, s. 54.

[7] Per Lord ESHER in *IRC v Angus* (1889) 23 QBD 579 at 589.

[8] (1966) 24 CLJ 19 (G. H. Jones); (1967) 31 Conv (NS) 175 (S. M. Spencer); *IRC v Hood-Barrs (No. 2)* (1963) 41 TC 339; p. 173, post.

[9] See I.C.T.A. 1970, s. 457.

[10] [1960] AC 1, [1959] 3 All ER 603, p. 33, ante.

[11] [1960] AC 206, [1959] 3 All ER 623, p. 37, post.

remained outstanding in a trustee and the beneficial owner was dealing and dealing only with the equitable estate. That is understandable; the object of the section, as was the object of the old Statute of Frauds, is to prevent hidden oral transactions in equitable interests in fraud of those truly entitled, and making it difficult, if not impossible, for the trustees to ascertain who are in truth his beneficiaries. But when the beneficial owner owns the whole beneficial estate and is in a position to give directions to his bare trustee with regard to the legal as well as the equitable estate there can be no possible ground for invoking the section where the beneficial owner wants to deal with the legal estate as well as the equitable estate. . . .

Counsel for the Crown admitted that where the legal and beneficial estate was vested in the legal owner and he desired to transfer the whole legal and beneficial estate to another he did not have to do more than transfer the legal estate and he did not have to comply with section 53 (1) (*c*); and I can see no relevant difference between that case and this."

(d) Declaration of Trust with Consent of Beneficial Owner

In 1961 Vandervell Trustees Ltd. exercised the option, taking £5,000 from the Vandervell children's settlement for the purpose. The Royal College of Surgeons transferred the shares to Vandervell Trustees Ltd. The Revenue made a further claim on the ground that Vandervell Trustees Ltd. had held the shares on trust for Vandervell. In 1965 Vandervell executed a deed, formally transferring to the children's settlement any right or interest which he might still have in the shares.

Vandervell having died, his estate sued Vandervell Trustees Ltd. for the return of the dividends paid on the shares since 1961. They succeeded before MEGARRY J, but failed in the Court of Appeal (*Re Vandervell's Trusts (No.2)* [1974] Ch 269). On the question of the way in which the equitable interest, previously enjoyed in the option, had left Vandervell, Lord DENNING said at p. 320: "Mr. Balcombe for the executors admitted that the intention of Mr. Vandervell and the trustee company was that the shares should be held on trust for the children's settlement. But he said that this intention was of no avail. He said that during the first period, Mr. Vandervell had an equitable interest in the property, namely, a resulting trust; that he never disposed of this equitable interest (because he never knew he had it): and that in any case it was the disposition of an equitable interest which, under section 53 of the Law of Property Act 1925, had to be in writing, signed by him or his agent, lawfully authorised by him in writing (and there was no such writing produced). He cited *Grey v IRC* [1960] AC 1 and *Oughtred v IRC* [1960] AC 206.

There is a complete fallacy in that argument. A resulting trust for the settlor is born and dies without any writing at all. It comes into existence whenever there is a gap in the beneficial ownership. It ceases to exist whenever that gap is filled by someone becoming beneficially entitled. As soon as the gap is filled by the creation or declaration of a valid trust, the resulting trust comes to an end. In this case, before the option was exercised, there was a gap in the beneficial ownership. So there was a resulting trust for Mr. Vandervell. But, as soon as the option was exercised and the shares registered in the trustees' name, there was created a valid trust of the shares in favour of the children's settlement. Not being a trust of land, it could be created without any writing. A trust of personalty can be created without writing. Both Mr. Vandervell and the trustee company had done everything which needed to be done to make the settlement of these shares binding on them. So there was a valid trust: see *Milroy v Lord* (1862) 4 De GF & J 264 at 274, *per* Turner LJ."

But STEPHENSON LJ had doubts. He said at p. 322: "To expound my doubts would serve no useful purpose; to state them shortly may do no harm. The cause of all the trouble is what the judge called [[1974] Ch 269 at 298] 'this ill-fated option' and its incorporation in a deed which was 'too short and simple' to rid Mr. Vandervell of the beneficial interest in the disputed shares, as a bare majority of the House of Lords held, not without fluctuation of mind on the part of one of them (Lord Upjohn), in *Vandervell v IRC* [1967] 2 AC 291 at 314–317. The operation of law or equity kept for Mr. Vandervell or gave him back an equitable interest which he did not want and would have thought he had disposed of if he had ever known it existed. It is therefore difficult to infer that he intended to dispose or ever did dispose of something he did not know he had until the judgment of Plowman J. in *Vandervell v IRC* [1966] Ch 261 at 273, which led to the deed of 1965, enlightened him, or to find a disposition of it in the exercise by the trustee company in 1961 of its option to purchase the shares. And even if he had disposed of his interest, he did not dispose of it by any writing sufficient to comply with section 53 (1) (*c*) of the Law of Property Act 1925."

(e) Declaration by Equitable Owner of Himself as Trustee

(1958) 74 LQR 180 at p. 182 (P.V.B.)

"Does a declaration of trust [by an equitable owner] operate to transfer the equitable interest from donor to donee? It is suggested that when the donor declares himself a trustee of his equitable interest, he retains his equitable interest but a subsidiary equitable interest becomes vested in the donee. He might well have active duties, if, for example, he had declared a discretionary trust. Trusts of equitable interests do not seem to have received much attention in this country but are well recognised on the other side of the Atlantic and referred to in Scott on *Trusts* (2nd ed., 1956), p. 645 as subtrusts. Thus the *Restatement of the Law of Trusts,* Vol. 1, s. 83 declares that "an equitable interest, if transferable, can be held in trust" and gives the following illustration: "A, the owner of a bond, declares himself a trustee of it for B. B declares himself a trustee for C of his interest in the bond. B is trustee for C of his equitable interest in the bond." On the other hand, when the donor directs the trustees to hold property on trust for the donee, the donor does indeed disappear from the picture. Whether he says to the trustees, "I assign my equitable interest to you to hold upon the trusts of the settlements," so that it merges in the legal interest, or says more simply, "I direct you to hold the property" upon such trusts, he has, it would seem, purported to assign or dispose of his equitable interest in the property, which he cannot do orally."

(f) Oral Contract for the Sale of Shares

OUGHTRED v INLAND REVENUE COMMISSIONERS

[1960] AC 206, [1959] 3 All ER 623 (HL, Viscount RADCLIFFE, Lords COHEN, KEITH OF AVONHOLM, DENNING and JENKINS)

100,000 preference shares and 100,000 ordinary shares in William Jackson and Son Ltd. were held upon trust for Mrs. Oughtred for life and after her death on trust for her son Peter absolutely. Mrs. Oughtred also held 72,700 shares absolutely.

On Mrs. Oughtred's death, estate duty would be payable at the rate applicable to the aggregated value of the settled property and her own free estate. In order to reduce the liability to estate duty[12], Mrs. Oughtred and Peter orally agreed that she would transfer to him her 72,700 shares, and Peter would release to his mother his remainder interest in the 200,000 preference and ordinary shares. Subsequently, documents covering these transfers were executed. The Revenue claimed stamp duty upon the transfer of Peter's interest in the 200,000 shares.

Held (Viscount RADCLIFFE and Lord COHEN dissenting). Stamp duty was payable.

LORD JENKINS: It is said further that in the present case the disputed transfer transferred nothing beyond a bare legal estate, because, in accordance with the well-settled principle applicable to contracts of sale, between contract and completion the appellant became under the oral agreement beneficially entitled in equity to the settled shares, subject to the due satisfaction by her of the purchase consideration, and accordingly the entire beneficial interest in the settled shares had already passed to her at the time of the execution of the disputed transfer, and there was nothing left upon which the disputed transfer could operate except the bare legal estate.

The Commissioners of Inland Revenue seek to meet this argument by reference to section 53 (1) (*c*) of the Law of Property Act, 1925. They contend that as the agreement of June 18, 1956, was an oral agreement it could not, in view of section 53 (1) (*c*), effect a disposition of a subsisting equitable interest or trust, and accordingly that Peter's subsisting equitable interest under the trusts of the settlement, in the shape of his reversionary interest, remained vested in him until the execution of the disputed transfer, which in these circumstances operated as a transfer on sale to the appellant of Peter's reversionary interest and additionally as a transfer not on sale to the appellant of the legal interest in the settled shares. It was by this process of reasoning that the Commissioners arrived at the opinion expressed in the case stated that the disputed transfer attracted both the ad valorem duty exigible on a transfer on sale of the reversionary interest and also the fixed duty of 10s.

This argument is attacked on the appellant's side by reference to subsection (2) of section 53 of the Act of 1925, which excludes the creation or operation of resulting, implied or constructive trusts from the provisions of subsection (1). It is said that inasmuch as the oral agreement was an

[12] Estate duty has now been abolished. Capital transfer tax is payable on gratuitous transfers *inter vivos* and on death. See Chap. 6, post.

agreement of sale and purchase it gave rise, on the principle to which I have already adverted, to a constructive trust of the reversionary interest in favour of the appellant subject to performance by her of her obligation to transfer to Peter the free shares forming the consideration for the sale. It is said that this trust, being constructive, was untouched by section 53 (1) (*c*) in view of the exemption afforded by section 53 (2), and that the appellant's primary argument still holds good.

I find it unnecessary to decide whether section 53 (2) has the effect of excluding the present transaction from the operation of section 53 (1) (*c*), for, assuming in the appellant's favour that the oral contract did have the effect in equity of raising a constructive trust of the settled shares for her untouched by section 53 (1) (*c*), I am unable to accept the conclusion that the disputed transfer was prevented from being a transfer of the shares to the appellant on sale because the entire beneficial interest in the settled shares was already vested in the appellant under the constructive trust, and there was accordingly nothing left for the disputed transfer to pass to the appellant except the bare legal estate. The constructive trust in favour of a purchaser which arises on the conclusion of a contract for sale is founded upon the purchaser's right to enforce the contract in proceedings for specific performance. In other words, he is treated in equity as entitled by virtue of the contract to the property which the vendor is bound under the contract to convey to him. This interest under the contract is no doubt a proprietary interest of a sort, which arises, so to speak, in anticipation of the execution of the transfer for which the purchaser is entitled to call. But its existence has never (so far as I know) been held to prevent a subsequent transfer, in performance of the contract, of the property contracted to be sold from constituting for stamp duty purposes a transfer on sale of the property in question. Take the simple case of a contract for the sale of land. In such a case a constructive trust in favour of the purchaser arises on the conclusion of the contract for sale, but (so far as I know) it has never been held on this account that a conveyance subsequently executed in performance of the contract is not stampable ad valorem as a transfer on sale. Similarly, in a case like the present one, but uncomplicated by the existence of successive interests, a transfer to a purchaser of the investments comprised in a trust fund could not, in my judgment, be prevented from constituting a transfer on sale for the purposes of stamp duty by reason of the fact that the actual transfer had been preceded by an oral agreement for sale.

In truth, the title secured by a purchaser by means of an actual transfer is different in kind from, and may well be far superior to, the special form of proprietary interest which equity confers on a purchaser in anticipation of such transfer.

This difference is of particular importance in the case of property such as shares in a limited company. Under the contract the purchaser is no doubt entitled in equity as between himself and the vendor to the beneficial interest in the shares, and (subject to due payment of the purchase consideration) to call for a transfer of them from the vendor as trustee for him. But it is only on the execution of the actual transfer that he becomes entitled to be registered as a member, to attend and vote at meetings, to effect transfers on the register, or to receive dividends otherwise than through the vendor as his trustee.

VISCOUNT RADCLIFFE (dissenting): The reasoning of the whole matter, as I see it, is as follows: On June 18, 1956, the son owned an equitable reversionary interest in the settled shares: by his oral agreement of that date he created in his mother an equitable interest in his reversion, since the subject-matter of the agreement was property of which specific performance would normally be decreed by the court. He thus became a trustee for her of that interest sub modo: having regard to subsection (2) of section 53 of the Law of Property Act, 1925, subsection (1) of that section did not operate to prevent that trusteeship arising by operation of law. On June 26 Mrs. Oughtred transferred to her son the shares which were the consideration for her acquisition of his equitable interest: upon this transfer he became in a full sense and without more the trustee of his interest for her. She was the effective owner of all outstanding equitable interests. It was thus correct to recite in the deed of release to the trustees of the settlement, which was to wind up their trust, that the trust fund was by then held upon trust for her absolutely. There was, in fact, no equity to the shares that could be asserted against her, and it was open to her, if she so wished, to let the matter rest without calling for a written assignment from her son. Given that the trustees were apprised of the making of the oral agreement and of Mrs. Oughtred's satisfaction of the consideration to be given by her, the trustees had no more to do than to transfer their legal title to her or as she might direct. This and no more is what they did.

It follows that, in my view, this transfer cannot be treated as a conveyance of the son's equitable reversion at all. The trustees had not got it: he never transferred or released it to them: how then could they convey it? With all respect to those who think otherwise, it is incorrect to say that the trustees' transfer was made either with his authority or at his direction. If the recital as to Mrs. Oughtred's rights was correct, as I think that it was, he had no remaining authority to give or direction to issue. A release is, after all, the normal instrument for winding up a trust when all the equitable rights are vested and the legal estate is called for from the trustees who hold it. What the release gave the trustees from him was acquittance for the trust administration and accounts to date, and the fact that he gave it in consideration of the legal interest in the shares being vested in his mother adds nothing on this point. Nor does it, with respect, advance the matter to say, correctly, that at the end of the day Mrs. Oughtred was the absolute owner of the shares, legal and equitable. I think that she was: but that is description, not analysis. The question that is relevant for the purpose of this appeal is how she came to occupy that position; a position which, under English law, could be reached by more than one road.

(g) Disposition to Fiduciary

In *Re Tyler* ([1967] 1 WLR 1269, [1967] 3 All ER 389) Miss Tyler, by her will, appointed Mr. King and Mrs. Green her executors. Shortly after its execution, she placed £1,500 in the hands of Mr. King, and on May 9, 1951 she wrote a letter instructing him to use as much of the money, income or capital, as was needed to provide reasonable care and comfort for Mrs.

Green; and to dispose of the surplus at Mrs. Green's death as the testatrix had previously indicated to Mr. King. The testatrix died, then Mr. King and then Mrs. Green.

The instructions for disposal of the surplus on Mrs. Green's death were that £500 should be paid to Mr. King's executors if (as happened) he should die before Mrs. Green, and the rest divided among a number of charitable institutions.

This summons was brought to determine on what trusts the fund was held on Mrs. Green's death.

PENNYCUICK J held that the evidence to support the executors' claim to £500 was insufficient, and that that sum was held, on a resulting trust for Miss Tyler's estate. The balance of the fund went to charity. On the question of the observance of the necessary formalities, he said at p. 1274: "We do not know whether there was an interval of time between the payment by Miss Tyler to Mr. King of the £1,500 and the statement by her to him of her wishes with regard to it. On that footing there would have been an interval of time during which Mr. King held the £1,500 on a resulting trust for Miss Tyler. The first question which has been argued is whether a trust was validly constituted as regards formalities, having regard, in particular, to section 53 of the Law of Property Act, 1925, which contains the following provision: . . .

It is now well established that that requirement applies to equitable interest in personalty as well as in land. It seems to me that, even on the view of the facts most unfavourable to the creation of a valid trust for this purpose, that is that there was a payment to Mr. King before any trusts were declared, there has been in this case sufficient compliance with the requirements of section 53. The letter of May 9 constitutes, it seems to me, a valid assignment in writing of an equitable interest by Miss Tyler to Mr. King, assuming that such an equitable interest existed. There is nothing in section 53 which requires that, where the assignee is to hold in a fiduciary capacity, the writing shall comprise the particulars of the trust. I conclude, then, that in May, 1951, a trust was validly created so far as formality is concerned."

(h) Under Variation of Trusts Act 1958

The question of the operation of section 53 (1) (*c*) in relation to the equitable interests of consenting adults when a variation of a trust is effected under the Variation of Trusts Act 1958 was discussed in *Re Holt's Settlement* ([1969] 1 Ch 100, [1968] 1 All ER 470). This is dealt with in Chapter 16, below.

(i) Right of Nomination of Benefits under Staff Pension Fund

In *Re Danish Bacon Co Ltd Staff Pension Fund Trusts* ([1971] 1 WLR 248, [1971] 1 All ER 486; (p. 33, ante)), it was not necessary to decide whether the interest was one to which section 53 (1) (*c*) applied. MEGARRY J said at p. 255: "Whether section 53 (1) (*c*) does apply is a matter upon which I am by no means clear; and in view of what I have already decided on the section, I do not have to resolve that point. However, it has been extensively argued, and I think I should give some indication of my views. What I am concerned with is a transaction whereby the deceased dealt with something which ex hypothesi could never be his. He was not disposing of his pension, nor of his right to the contributions and interest if he left the company's service. He was dealing merely with a state of affairs that would arise if he died while in the company's pensionable service, or after he had left it without becoming entitled to a pension. If he did this, then the contributions and interest would, by force of the rules, go either to his nominee, if he had made a valid nomination, or to his personal representatives, if he had not. If he made a nomination, it was revocable at any time before his death.

The question is thus whether an instrument with this selective, contingent and defeasible quality, which takes effect only on the death of the person signing it, can fairly be said to be 'a disposition of an equitable interest or trust subsisting at the time of the disposition'. Mr. Ferris put much emphasis on the word 'subsisting': however wide the word 'disposition' might be in its meaning, there was no disposition of a subsisting equity, he said. I should hesitate to describe an instrument which has a mere possibility of becoming a 'disposition' as being in itself a disposition ab initio; and I agree that the word 'subsisting' also seems to point against the nomination falling within section 53 (1) (*c*) . . . I very much doubt whether the nomination falls within section 53 (1) (*c*); but as I have indicated, I do not have to decide that point, and I do not do so."

(j) Disclaimer of Beneficial Interest

In *Re Paradise Motor Co Ltd* ([1968] 1 WLR 1125, [1968] 2 All ER 625) the question arose whether the disclaimer of a beneficial interest in shares was required to be evidenced in writing under section 53 (1) (*c*). In holding that it did not, Danckwerts LJ said at p. 1143: "The . . . argument was that there could here be no disclaimer of the beneficial interest in the shares because a disclaimer would, by re-transfer, be a disposition of an equitable interest in property, and neither of the suggested disclaimers was in writing signed by [the disclaimant]: see the Law of Property Act, 1925, section 53 (2). We think that the short answer to this is that a disclaimer operates by way of avoidance and not by way of disposition. For the general aspects of disclaimer we refer briefly to the discussion in *Re Stratton's Disclaimer, Stratton v IRC* [1958] Ch 42, [1957] 2 All ER 594."[13]

B. By Will[14]

WILLS ACT 1837

9. Every will to be in writing, and signed or acknowledged by the testator in the presence of two witnesses.—No will shall be valid unless it shall be in writing, and executed in manner herein-after mentioned; (that is to say,) it shall be signed at the foot or end thereof[15] by the testator, or by some

[13] A disclaimer of an interest under a deceased person's estate, if made within two years of the death, or of an interest in settled property, is free of liability to capital transfer tax: F.A. 1975, s. 47 (2), (4).

[14] H & M, pp. 163–164; K & S, p. 64; P & M, pp. 24–25; Pettit, p. 60; Snell, p. 105. For detailed commentary on this section, see Bailey, *Law of Wills* (7th Edn) pp. 46 et seq.; *Jarman on Wills* (8th Edn) pp. 117 et seq.; *Theobald on Wills* (13th Edn) paras. 113–122. And for its relation to secret trusts see pp. 114–129, post. For testamentary formalities in the Conflict of Laws, see Wills Act 1963.

[15] Wills Act Amendment Act 1852.

other person in his presence and by his direction; and such signature shall be made or acknowledged by the testator in the presence of two or more witnesses present at the same time, and such witnesses shall attest and shall subscribe the will in the presence of the testator, but no form of attestation shall be necessary.

II. Certainty[16]

There can be no trust unless there is certainty in respect of the intention to create a trust, and in respect of the property which is the subject matter of the trust, and (charitable trusts apart) in respect of the beneficiaries. These are the "three certainties".[17] The principles to be applied in solving problems which arise in this context can be extracted from the cases; but each question can only be answered by careful construction of the language of the instrument under consideration.

The three aspects of the "certainty" problem are here treated separately. In many cases, however, they overlap. Thus, "uncertainty in the subject of the gift has a reflex action upon the previous words, and throws doubt upon the intention of the testator, and seems to shew that he could not possibly have intended his words of confidence, hope, or whatever they may be—his appeal to the conscience of the first taker—to be imperative words."[18] Similarly, a division of property among various claimants may create uncertainty both as to the property and the claimants[19].

There is sometimes confusion between these rules of certainty and some related rules. First, the certainty rules apply quite differently to charitable trusts[20]. There, the requirement is that the trust must be exclusively charitable; there must be no doubt about that. But there is no need to specify which particular charity is to benefit. Second, the rule that the objects of a trust (the beneficiaries) must be certain leaves open the question, discussed below[21], whether there can be a non-charitable purpose trust, without human beneficiaries. In so far as this is possible, the purposes must be sufficiently certain[1]. Third, it is important to appreciate the relationship between these rules and discretionary trusts[2]. It is possible to leave uncertain which members of a group of beneficiaries will benefit and which share any one will receive; provided that the property available for distribution is certain, the class of beneficiaries is sufficiently certain, and the discretionary power of selection is vested in some person or persons. If no provision is made for the exercise of the discretion, the disposition is void for uncertainty[3]. Fourth, problems of uncertainty also arise where the gift is to

16 H & M, pp. 164–172; K & S, pp. 90–104; P & M, pp. 51–56; Pettit, pp. 25–28, 34–43; Snell, pp. 111–115.

17 *Knight v Knight* (1840) 3 Beav 148 at 173, per Lord LANGDALE MR.

18 *Mussoorie Bank v Raynor* (1882) 7 App Cas 321 at 331, per Sir Arthur HOBHOUSE; *Re Adams and The Kensington Vestry* (1884) 27 ChD 394. See p. 43 et seq., post.

19 *Boyce v Boyce* (1849) 16 Sim 476.

20 See pp. 274, 365, post.

21 See pp. 242 et seq., post.

1 *Re Astor's Settlement Trusts* [1952] Ch 534, [1952] 1 All ER 1067, see p. 248, post.

2 See p. 47, post.

3 *Sprange v Barnard* (1789) 2 Bro CC 585.

ascertainable beneficiaries, but their qualification is subjected to a condition[4].

A. Certainty of Intention

The requirement that a settlor must manifest an intention to create a trust is strictly applied. A testator may say that he "hopes" or "expects" or "has full confidence" that a legatee will apply property for the benefit of others. Somehow a line has to be drawn between requests and obligations. The approach of the courts has varied on this question. In the early 19th century, an intention to create a trust would readily be found[5]. Later a stricter construction was applied, the turning point being usually said to be the Court of Appeal decision in *Lambe v Eames* in 1871[6].

RE ADAMS AND THE KENSINGTON VESTRY
(1884) 27 ChD 394 (CA, BAGGALLAY, COTTON and LINDLEY, LJJ)

George Smith, the testator, provided in his will as follows: "I give, devise, and bequeath all my real and personal estate and effects whatsoever and wheresoever unto and to the absolute use of my wife, Harriet Smith, her executors, administrators and assigns, in full confidence that she will do what is right as to the disposal thereof between my children, either in her lifetime or by will after her decease."

The question was whether this was an absolute gift, or whether the property was subject to a trust in favour of the children.

Held. The widow took absolutely.

COTTON, LJ: The question before us is whether, upon the true construction of the will of *George Smith*, he imposed upon his wife *Harriet* a trust. Now just let us look at it, in the first instance, alone, and see what we can spell out of it, and see what was expressed by the will. Reading that will, and I will not repeat it, because it has been already read, it seems to me perfectly clear what the testator intended. He leaves his wife his property absolutely, but what was in his mind was this: "I am the head of the family, and it is

[4] *Re Tuck's Settlement Trusts* [1978] 2 WLR 411, [1978] 1 All ER 1047, p. 469, post.

[5] H & M, pp. 164–166.

[6] (1871) 6 Ch App 597; for other cases where it was held that no trust was created, see *Mussoorie Bank Ltd v Raynor* (1882) 7 App Cas 321 ("feeling confident that she will act justly to our children in dividing the same when no longer required by her"); *Re Diggles* (1888) 39 ChD 253 ("it is my desire that she allows A.G. an annuity of £25 during her life"); *Re Hamilton* [1895] 2 Ch 370 ("I wish them to bequeath the same equally between the families of O and P"); *Re Williams* [1897] 2 Ch 12 ("in the fullest trust and confidence that she will carry out my wishes in the following particulars"); *Re Johnson* [1939] 2 All ER 458 ("I request that C on her death leave her property to my four sisters"). Contrast *Comiskey v Bowring-Hanbury* [1905] AC 84 (testator gave to his wife "the whole of my real and personal estate . . . in full confidence that she will make such use of it as I should have made myself and that at her death she will devise it to such one or more of my nieces as she may think fit and in default of any disposition by her thereof by her will . . . I hereby direct that all my estate and property acquired by her under this my will shall at her death be equally divided among the surviving said nieces"). H.L. held by a majority that there was an intention to make a gift to the wife, with an executory gift over of the whole property at her death to such of her nieces as should survive her, shared according to the wife's will, and otherwise equally. Lord LINDLEY (dissenting) construed the limitation as showing an intention to give an absolute gift to the wife.

laid upon me to provide properly for the members of my family—my children: my widow will succeed me when I die, and I wish to put her in the position I occupied as the person who is to provide for my children." Not that he entails upon her any trust so as to bind her, but he simply says, in giving her this, I express to her, and call to her attention, the moral obligation which I myself had and which I feel that she is going to discharge. The motive of the gift is, in my opinion, not a trust imposed upon her by the gift in the will. He leaves the property to her; he knows that she will do what is right, and carry out the moral obligation which he thought lay on him, and on her if she survived him, to provide for the children. But it is said that the testator would be very much astonished if he found that he had given his wife power to leave the property away. That is a proposition which I should express in a different way. He would be much surprised if the wife to whom he had left his property absolutely should so act as not to provide for the children, that is to say, not to do what is right. That is a very different thing. He would have said: "I expected that she would do what was right, and therefore I left it to her absolutely. I find she has not done what I think is right, but I cannot help it, I am very sorry that she has done so." That would be the surprise, I think, that he would express, and feel, if he could do either, if the wife did what was unreasonable as regards the children.

But, then, it is said there is authority against that, and I am in no way disposed, if there be any definite canon or rule of construction established, to depart from that, because that must introduce great uncertainty. But undoubtedly, to my mind, in the later cases, especially *Lambe v Eames* ((1871) 6 Ch App 597) and *Re Hutchinson and Tenant* ((1878) 8 ChD 540), both the Court of Appeal and the late Master of the Rolls shewed a desire really to find out what, upon the true construction, was the meaning of the testator, rather than to lay hold of certain words which in other wills had been held to create a trust, although on the will before them they were satisfied that that was not the intention. I have no hesitation in saying myself, that I think some of the older authorities went a great deal too far in holding that some particular words appearing in a will were sufficient to create a trust. Undoubtedly confidence, if the rest of the context shews that a trust is intended, may make a trust, but what we have to look at is the whole of the will which we have to construe, and if the confidence is that she will do what is right as regards the disposal of the property, I cannot say that that is, on the true construction of the will, a trust imposed upon her. Having regard to the later decisions, we must not extend the old cases in any way, or rely upon the mere use of any particular words, but, considering all the words which are used, we have to see what is their true effect, and what was the intention of the testator as expressed in his will. In my opinion, here he has expressed his will in such a way as not to shew an intention of imposing a trust on the wife, but on the contrary, in my opinion, he has shewn an intention to leave the property, as he says he does, to her absolutely.

In *Re Steele's Will Trusts*[7] ([1948] Ch 603, [1948] 2 All ER 193) the testatrix,

[7] (1968) 32 Conv (NS) 361 (P. St. J. Langan); Pettit, p. 36

who died in 1929, provided by clause 2 of her will as follows: "I give my diamond necklace to my son to go and be held as an heirloom by him and by his eldest son on his decease and to go and descend to the eldest son of such eldest son and so on to the eldest son of his descendants as far as the rules of law and equity will permit (and I request my said son to do all in his power by his will or otherwise to give effect to this my wish)." This provision was basically the same as that which had been held in *Shelley v Shelley* (1868) LR 6 Eq 540 to create a trust.

Wynn-Parry J, while noting the extent to which the construction placed upon precatory expressions had changed since 1868, upheld it. He said (at p. 609): "The case of *Shelley v Shelley* has stood for eighty years and I have before me a will which, as I have already observed, is, as regards the relevant passage, couched in exactly the same language mutatis mutandis as that which was considered by Wood V-C in *Shelley v Shelley*. That appears to me to afford the strongest indication that the testatrix in this case, by her will, which appears clearly upon the face of it to have been a will prepared with professional aid, indicated that the diamond necklace in question should devolve in the same manner as the jewellery was directed to devolve by the order in *Shelley v Shelley*. Having regard to that strong indication of intention, and having regard to the fact that I cannot see any good reason why, notwithstanding the admitted trend of modern decisions, I should treat *Shelley v Shelley* as wrongly decided and therefore a case which I ought not to follow, I come to the conclusion that I must declare that upon the true construction of the will of the testatrix the diamond necklace should have been held upon trust for Charles Steele for his life and after his death for the second plaintiff Charles Ronald Steele for his life and after his death for David Steele, the third plaintiff, for his life and after the death of the survivor of them upon trust for the eldest son or grandson of the third plaintiff David Steele and otherwise in the manner decided in *Shelley v Shelley* including the ultimate trust in default of any male issue of David Steele (who takes an absolutely vested interest) in favour of Charles Steele absolutely and that the order in this case will follow mutatis mutandis the minutes which appear in the case of *Shelley v Shelley*."

B. Certainty of Subject Matter

In *Palmer v Simmonds* ((1854) 2 Drew 221) the testatrix, by her will, gave her residuary estate to Thomas Harrison "for his own use and benefit, as I have full confidence in him, that if he should die without lawful issue he will . . . leave the bulk of my said residuary estate unto" certain named persons.

The expression of confidence was sufficient, according to the practice at that time, to manifest an intention to create a trust. The question was whether the subject matter of the trust was sufficiently certain. Kindersley VC held that it was not. He said (at p. 227): "What is the meaning then of bulk? The appropriate meaning, according to its derivation, is something which bulges out, &c. [His Honor referred to *Todd's Johnson and Richardson's* Dictionary for the different meanings and etymology of the word.] Its popular meaning we all know. When a person is said to have given the bulk of his property, what is meant is not the whole but the greater part, and that is in fact consistent with its classical meaning. When, therefore, the testatrix uses that term, can I say she has used a term expressing a definite, clear, certain part of her estate, or the whole of her estate? I am bound to say she has not designated the subject as to which she expressses her confidence; and I am therefore of opinion that there is no trust created; that *Harrison* took absolutely, and those claiming under him now take."

RE GOLAY'S WILL TRUSTS[8]

[1965] 1 WLR 969, [1965] 2 All ER 600 (ChD, UNGOED-THOMAS J)

By his will, the testator directed his executors "to let Tossy—[whom he named]—to enjoy one of my flats during her lifetime and to receive a reasonable income from my other properties. . . ."

The question was whether the gift of the income was void for uncertainty.

Held. The gift was valid.

UNGOED-THOMAS J: Another question that arises is whether this gift of reasonable income fails for uncertainty.

There are two classes of case with which I am concerned in interpreting this particular provision in the will: the first is where a discretion is given to specified persons to quantify the amount; the other class of case is where no such discretion is expressly conferred upon any specified person.

The question therefore comes to this: Whether the testator by the words "reasonable income" has given a sufficient indication of his intention to provide an effective determinant of what he intends so that the court in applying that determinant can give effect to the testator's intention.

Whether the yardstick of "reasonable income" were applied by trustees under a discretion given to them by a testator or applied by a court in course of interpreting and applying the words "reasonable income" in a will, the yardstick sought to be applied by the trustees in the one case and the court in the other case would be identical. The trustees might be other than the original trustees named by the testator and the trustees could even surrender their discretion to the court. It would seem to me to be drawing too fine a distinction to conclude that an objective yardstick which different persons sought to apply would be too uncertain, not because of uncertainty in the yardstick but as between those who seek to apply it.

In this case, however, the yardstick indicated by the testator is not what he or some other specified person subjectively considers to be reasonable but what he identifies objectively as "reasonable income". The court is constantly involved in making such objective assessments of what is reasonable and it is not to be deterred from doing so because subjective influences can never be wholly excluded. In my view the testator intended by "reasonable income" the yardstick which the court could and would

[8] (1965) 81 LQR 481 (R.E.M.). See also *Sprange v Barnard* (1789) 2 Bro CC 585 ("the remaining part of what is left"); *Boyce v Boyce* (1849) 16 Sim 476 ("all my other houses"); *Re Jones* [1898] 1 Ch 438 ("said parts of my . . . estate as she shall not have sold"); *In the Estate of Last* [1958] P 137, [1958] 1 All ER 316 ("anything that is left"); *Re London Wine Co (Shippers) Ltd* (1976) 126 NL Jo 978 ("your wines").

apply in quantifying the amount so that the direction in the will is not in my view defeated by uncertainty.

C. Certainty of Objects

Prior to *McPhail v Doulton*[9] the requirement of certainty was expressed by one rule for powers and another rule for trusts. As explained above[10], powers and trusts are different concepts. It is not inevitable that the test for validity on the grounds of certainty should be the same for each. The rule for powers was settled in *Re Gulbenkian's Settlements*[11] which laid down that the requirement of certainty was met if it was possible to determine with certainty whether any given individual was or was not a member of the class[12].

The rule for trusts, before *McPhail v Doulton,* was stricter. It had been laid down in *Inland Revenue Commissioners v Broadway Cottages Trust*[13] that a trust was void unless it was possible to make, at the time when the trust came into operation, a list of all the beneficiaries. This rule was thought to be necessary in order to make a distribution possible if the trustees, in breach of their duty, failed to make a selection. The method of distribution, it was said, would be by equal division among the members of the class of beneficiaries on the principle that Equality is Equity; and equal division was only possible if it was known how many shares there would be[14]. As will be seen, *McPhail v Doulton* applied, as the test for certainty of beneficiaries under a *discretionary* trust, the test which had been applied to powers in *Re Gulbenkian's Settlements*. The problem of determining the division if the trustees failed to select was not insuperable: the court would find a way. The problem was artificial, in that it had never arisen in the form of trustees refusing to select; rather in their asking whether a selection would be valid. Reluctant trustees could in any case be replaced. And, in modern trusts with the employees of a business tycoon as beneficiaries, and not merely members of the family, as was usually the case with older trusts, equal division would be absurd.

The older, stricter, rule, however, still applies to fixed trusts.

A fixed trust is a trust where the interest or share of a beneficiary is laid down in the trust instrument: for example, "on trust for my children in equal shares". A discretionary trust is a trust in which the share of each member of the class of beneficiaries is determined by the discretion of the trustees; but there is still an obligation upon the trustees to make the division; for example: "on trust for such of my children as my trustees shall select." A power enables the donee of the power to make a gift by exercising the power if he thinks fit: for example, "with power to appoint in favour of such of my children and in such proportions as he shall

9 [1971] AC 424, [1970] 2 All ER 228, p. 48, post.
10 See p. 24, ante.
11 [1970] AC 508, [1968] 3 All ER 785; p. 28, ante.
12 Following the formulation of the rule in *Re Gestetner Settlement* [1953] Ch 672 at 688, per Harman J: "whether any given postulant is a member of the specified class"; see p. 29, ante.
13 [1955] Ch 20, [1954] 3 All ER 120.
14 *Burrough v Philcox* (1840) 5 My & Cr 72; p. 25, ante.

think fit"; or, to give a more sophisticated example: "to my children, grandchildren and their spouses and the employees and ex-employees and their dependants of X Company and in such proportions . . . etc.". In the case both of a power to appoint among such a group and also in the case of a discretionary trust in favour of such a group, the test of certainty is that laid down in *Re Gulbenkian's Settlements* and in *McPhail v Doulton*. If the trust was a *fixed* trust, and the trust property were to be divided among such a group in equal shares, it could, as a practical matter, only be shared equally among the members of the group of beneficiaries if it was possible to make an exact and precise list of the members. In the case of a fixed trust, therefore, the rule of *Broadway Cottages* must apply. This point should be borne in mind when reading *McPhail v Doulton*.

Finally, a word of warning on terminology. The language of the cases dealing with the requirement of certainty in trusts and powers must be read with some care. The dividing line between trusts and powers is not always made clear; the very use of phrases such as "trust powers" and "powers in the nature of a trust" shows this. Such phrases refer to trusts in which the trustees have a power of selection; as in a discretionary trust.

McPHAIL v DOULTON[15]
[1971] AC 424, [1970] 2 All ER 228 (HL, Lords REID, HODSON, Viscount DILHORNE, Lords GUEST and WILBERFORCE)

A deed, executed on July 17, 1941, by the settlor, Mr. Bertram Baden, provided that a fund was to be held upon certain trusts in favour of the staff of Matthew Hall and Co. Ltd. and their relatives and dependants.

The deed provided (clause 9 (*a*)) that the trustees should apply the net income in making grants at their absolute discretion "to or for the benefit of any of the officers and employees or ex-officers or ex-employees of the company or to any relatives or dependants of any such persons in such amounts at such times and on such conditions (if any) as they think fit. . . ."

The trustees were under no obligation to exhaust the income in any one year. They could realise capital for the purpose of making such grants if the income was insufficient. It was also provided (clause 10) that "no person shall have any right title or interest in the fund otherwise than pursuant to the exercise of such discretion."

Two main questions arose: whether the deed created a power or a trust; and whether it was void for uncertainty. At first instance[16], GOFF J held that it was a power and not a trust and that it was valid: applying as the test of certainty that applied by the Court of Appeal in *Re Gulbenkian's Settlements*[17]: namely, that a power was valid if it was sufficiently certain to enable any one claimant to show that he comes within the description.

15 (1970) 34 Conv (NS) 287 (F. R. Crane); (1971) CLJ 68 (J. Hopkins); (1971) CLP 133 (H. Cohen); (1971) 87 LQR 31 (J. W. Harris); (1973) 5 NZ ULR 348; (1974) 37 MLR 643 (Y. F. R. Grbich); (1973) 7 VUWLR 258 (L. Mckay); (1975) 4 Anglo-American LR 442 (S. Fradley); Law Com No. 58, para. 68.

16 [1967] 1 WLR 1457, [1967] 3 All ER 159.

17 [1968] Ch 126, [1967] 3 All ER 15, following *Re Allen* [1953] Ch 810, [1953] 2 All ER 898; *Re Leek* [1967] Ch 1061, [1967] 2 All ER 1660; affd. [1969] 1 Ch 563, [1968] 1 All ER 793; *Re Gibbard's Will Trusts* [1967] 1 WLR 42, [1966] 1 All ER 273.

The Court of Appeal[18] agreed (HARMAN and KARMINSKI LJJ; RUSSELL LJ dissenting) that it was a power and not a trust; but remitted the case to the Chancery Division to determine the validity upon the application of the test for certainty of powers which had been laid down by the House of Lords in *Re Gulbenkian's Settlements*[19].

Held. (i) The deed created a trust and not a power; (ii) (Lords HODSON and GUEST dissenting). The test for certainty was the same as that for powers: i.e. whether it could be said with certainty that any given individual was or was not a member of the class.

The case was remitted to the Chancery Division for a determination of validity upon this basis. In *Re Baden's Deed Trusts (No. 2)*[20] the Court of Appeal, affirming BRIGHTMAN J, upheld it.

LORD WILBERFORCE: In this House, the appellants contend, and this is the first question for consideration, that the provisions of clause 9 (a) constitute a trust and not a power. If that is held to be the correct result, both sides agree that the case must return to the Chancery Division for consideration, on this footing, whether this trust is valid. But here comes a complication. In the present state of authority, the decision as to validity would turn on the question whether a complete list (or on another view a list complete for practical purposes) can be drawn up of all possible beneficiaries. This follows from the Court of Appeal's decision in *IRC v Broadway Cottages Trust* [1955] Ch 20 as applied in later cases by which, unless this House decides otherwise, the Court of Chancery would be bound. The respondents invite your Lordships to review this decision and challenge its correctness. So the second issue which arises, if clause 9 (a) amounts to a trust, is whether the existing test for its validity is right in law and, if not, what the test ought to be.

Before dealing with these two questions some general observations, or reflections, may be permissible. It is striking how narrow and in a sense artificial is the distinction, in cases such as the present, between trusts or as the particular type of trust is called, trust powers, and powers. It is only necessary to read the learned judgments in the Court of Appeal to see that what to one mind may appear as a power of distribution coupled with a trust to dispose of the undistributed surplus, by accumulation or otherwise, may to another appear as a trust for distribution coupled with a power to withhold a portion and accumulate or otherwise dispose of it. A layman and, I suspect, also a logician would find it hard to understand what difference there is.

It does not seem satisfactory that the entire validity of a disposition should depend on such delicate shading. And if one considers how in practice reasonable and competent trustees would act, and ought to act, in the two cases, surely a matter very relevant to the question of validity, the distinction appears even less significant. To say that there is no obligation to exercise a mere power and that no court will intervene to compel it, whereas a trust is mandatory and its execution may be compelled, may be legally correct enough but the proposition does not contain an exhaustive

[18] [1969] 2 Ch 388, [1969] 1 All ER 1016.
[19] [1970] AC 508, [1968] 3 All ER 785; p. 28, ante.
[20] [1973] Ch 9, [1971] 3 All ER 985; p. 56, post.

comparison of the duties of persons who are trustees in the two cases. A trustee of an employees' benefit fund, whether given a power or a trust power, is still a trustee and he would surely consider in either case that he has a fiduciary duty: he is most likely to have been selected as a suitable person to administer it from his knowledge and experience, and would consider he has a responsibility to do so according to its purpose. It would be a complete misdescription of his position to say that, if what he has is a power unaccompanied by an imperative trust to distribute, he cannot be controlled by the court unless he exercised it capriciously, or outside the field permitted by the trust (cf. *Farwell on Powers,* 3rd ed., p. 524). Any trustee would surely make it his duty to know what is the permissible area of selection and then consider responsibly, in individual cases, whether a contemplated beneficiary was within the power and whether, in relation to other possible claimants, a particular grant was appropriate.

Correspondingly a trustee with a duty to distribute, particularly among a potentially very large class, would surely never require the preparation of a complete list of names, which anyhow would tell him little that he needs to know. He would examine the field, by class and category; might indeed make diligent and careful inquiries, depending on how much money he had to give away and the means at his disposal, as to the composition and needs of particular categories and of individuals within them; decide upon certain priorities or proportions, and then select individuals according to their needs or qualifications. If he acts in this manner, can it really be said that he is not carrying out the trust?

Differences there certainly are between trust (trust powers) and powers, but as regards validity, should they be so great as that in one case complete, or practically complete, ascertainment is needed, but not in the other? Such distinction as there is would seem to lie in the extent of the survey which the trustee is required to carry out: if he has to distribute the whole of a fund's income, he must necessarily make a wider and more systematic survey than if his duty is expressed in terms of a power to make grants. But just as, in the case of a power, it is possible to underestimate the fiduciary obligation of the trustee to whom it is given, so, in the case of a trust (trust power), the danger lies in overstating what the trustee requires to know or to inquire into before he can properly execute his trust. The difference may be one of degree rather than of principle: in the well-known words of Sir George Farwell, *Farwell on Powers,* 3rd ed. (1916), p. 10, trusts and powers are often blended, and the mixture may vary in its ingredients.

With this background I now consider whether the provisions of clause 9 (a) constitute a trust or a power. I do so briefly because this is not a matter on which I or, I understand, any of your Lordships have any doubt. Indeed, a reading of the judgments of Goff, J. and of the majority in the Court of Appeal leave the strong impression that, if it had not been for their leaning in favour of possible validity and the state of the authorities, these learned judges would have found in favour of a trust. Naturally read, the intention of the deed seems to me clear: clause 9 (a), whose language is mandatory ("shall"), creates, together with a power of selection, a trust for distribution of the income, the strictness of which is qualified by clause 9 (b), which allows the income of any one year to be held up and (under clause 6 (a)) either placed, for the time, with a bank, or, if thought fit, invested. Whether there is, in any technical sense, an accumulation seems to me in the present context a jejune inquiry: what is relevant is that clause 9 (c) marks the difference between "accumulations" of income and the capital of the fund: the former can be distributed by a majority of the trustees, the latter cannot. As to clause 10, I do not find in it any decisive indication. If anything, it seems to point in favour of a trust, but both this and other points of detail are insignificant in the face of the clearly expressed scheme of clause 9. I therefore agree with Russell LJ and would to that extent allow the appeal, declare that the provisions of clause 9 (a) constitute a trust and remit the case to the Chancery Division for determination whether on this basis clause 9 is (subject to the effects of section 164 of the Law of Property Act, 1925) valid or void for uncertainty.

This makes it necessary to consider whether, in so doing, the court should proceed on the basis that the relevant test is that laid down in *IRC v Broadway Cottages Trust* [1955] Ch 20 or some other test.

That decision gave the authority of the Court of Appeal to the distinction between cases where trustees are given a *power* of selection and those where they are bound by a *trust* for selection. In the former case the position, as decided by this House, is that the power is valid if it can be said with certainty whether any given individual is or is not a member of the class and does not fail simply because it is impossible to ascertain every member of the class (*Re Gulbenkian's Settlements* [1970] AC 508). But in the latter case it is said to be necessary, for the trust to be valid, that the whole range of objects (I use the language of the Court of Appeal) should be ascertained or capable of ascertainment.

The respondents invited your Lordships to assimilate the validity test for trusts to that which applies to powers. Alternatively they contended that in any event the test laid down in the *Broadway Cottages* case [1955] Ch 20 was too rigid, and that a trust should be upheld if there is sufficient practical certainty in its definition for it to be carried out, if necessary with the administrative assistance of the court, according to the expressed intention of the settlor. I would agree with this, but this does not dispense from examination of the wider argument. The basis for the *Broadway Cottages* principle is stated to be that a trust cannot be valid unless, if need be, it can be executed by the court, and (though it is not quite clear from the judgment where argument ends and decision begins) that the court can only execute it by ordering an equal distribution in which every beneficiary shares. So it is necessary to examine the authority and reason for this supposed rule as to the execution of trusts by the court.

Assuming, as I am prepared to do for present purposes, that the test of validity is whether the trust can be executed by the court, it does not follow that execution is impossible unless there can be equal division.

As a matter of reason, to hold that a principle of equal division applies to trusts such as the present is certainly paradoxical. Equal division is surely the last thing the settlor ever intended: equal division among all may, probably would, produce a result beneficial to none. Why suppose that the court would lend itself to a whimsical execution? And as regards authority, I do not find that the nature of the trust, and of the court's powers over trusts, calls for any such rigid rule. Equal division may be sensible and has been decreed, in cases of family trusts, for a limited class; here there is life in the maxim "equality is equity", but the cases provide numerous examples where this has not been so, and a different type of execution has been ordered, appropriate to the circumstances.

Mosely v Moseley (1673) Fin 53 is an early example, from the time of equity's architect, where the court assumed power (if the executors did not act) to nominate from the sons of a named person as it should think fit and most worthy and hopeful, the testator's intention being that the estate should not be divided. In *Clarke v Turner* (1694) Free Ch 198, on a discretionary trust for relations, the court decreed conveyance to the heir-at-law judging it "most reputable for the family that the heir-at-law should have it." In *Warburton v Warburton* (1702) 4 Bro PC 1, on a discretionary trust to distribute between a number of the testator's children, the House of Lords affirmed a decree of Lord Keeper Wright that the eldest son and heir, regarded as necessitous, should have a double share, the court exercising its own discretionary judgment against equal division.

These are examples of family trusts but in *Richardson v Chapman* (1760), 7 Bro PC 318 the same principle is shown working in a different field. There was a discretionary trust of the testator's "options" (namely, rights of presentation to benefices or dignities in the Church) between a number of named or specified persons, including present and former chaplains and other domestics; also "my worthy friends and acquaintance, particularly the Reverend Dr. Richardson of Cambridge." The House of Lords (reversing Lord Keeper Henley) set aside a "corrupt" presentation and ordered the trustees to present Dr. Richardson as the most suitable person. The grounds of decision in this House, in accordance with the prevailing practice, were not reported, but it may be supposed that the reported argument was accepted that where the court sets aside the act of the trustee, it can at the same time decree the proper act to be done, not by referring the matter to the trustee's discretion, but by directing him to perform as a mere instrument the thing decreed (ibid., 326, 327). This shows that the court can in a suitable case execute a discretionary trust according to the perceived intention of the trustee. It is interesting also to see that it does not seem to have been contended that the trust was void because of the uncertainty of the words "my worthy friends and acquaintance". There was no doubt that Dr. Richardson came within the designation.

In the time of Lord Eldon, the Court of Chancery adopted a less flexible practice: in *Kemp v Kemp*, (1801) 5 Ves Junr 849 Sir Richard Arden MR, commenting on *Warburton v Warburton,* (1702) 4 Bro PC 1 ("a very extraordinary" case), said that the court now disclaims the right to execute a power (i.e., a trust power) and gives the fund equally. But I do not think that this change of attitude, or practice, affects the principle that a discretionary trust *can,* in a suitable case, be executed according to its merits and otherwise than by equal division. I prefer not to suppose that the great masters of equity, if faced with the modern trust for employees, would have failed to adapt their creation to its practical and commercial character. Lord

Eldon himself, in *Morice v Bishop of Durham,* (1805) 10 Ves Junr 522, laid down clearly enough that a trust fails if the object is insufficiently described or if it cannot be carried out, but these principles may be fully applied to trust powers without requiring a complete ascertainment of all possible objects. His earlier judgment in the leading, and much litigated, case of *Brown v Higgs* (1803), 8 Ves Junr 561 shows that he was far from fastening any rigid test of validity upon trust powers. After stating the distinction, which has ever since been followed, between powers, which the court will not require the donee to execute, and powers in the nature of a trust, or trust powers, he says of the latter that if the trustee does not discharge it, the court will, *to a certain extent,* discharge the duty in his room and place. To support this, he cites *Harding v Glyn* (1739), 1 Atk 469, an early case where the court executed a discretionary trust for "relations" by distributing to the next-of-kin.

I dwell for a moment upon this point because, not only was *Harding v Glyn* described by Lord Eldon (8 Ves Junr 561 at 570) as having been treated as a clear authority in his experience for a long period, but the principle of it was adopted in several nineteenth-century authorities. When the *Broadway Cottages Trust* case came to be decided in 1955, these cases were put aside as anomalous (see [1955] Ch at 33, 35), but I think they illustrate the flexible manner in which the court, if called on, executes trust powers for a class. At least they seem to prove that the supposed rule as to equal division does not rest on any principle inherent in the nature of a trust. They prompt me to ask why a practice, or rule, which has been long followed and found useful in "relations" cases should not also serve in regard to "employees", or "employees and their relatives", and whether a decision which says the contrary is acceptable.

I now consider the modern English authorities, particularly those relied on to show that complete ascertainment of the class must be possible before it can be said that a discretionary trust is valid.

Re H.J. Ogden [1933] Ch 678 is not a case which I find of great assistance. The argument seems to have turned mainly on the question whether the trust was a purpose trust or a trust for ascertained objects. The latter was held to be the case and the court then held that all the objects of the discretionary gift could be ascertained. It is weak authority for the requirement of complete ascertainment.

The modern shape of the rule derives from *Re Gestetner Settlement* [1953] Ch 672, where the judgment of Harman J, to his later regret, established the distinction between discretionary powers and discretionary trusts. The focus of this case was upon powers. The judgment first establishes a distinction between, on the one hand, a power collateral, or appurtenant, or other powers "which do not impose a trust on the conscience of the donee" (at p. 684), and on the other hand a trust imposing a duty to distribute. As to the first, the learned judge said (ibid.): "I do not think it can be the law that it is necessary to know of all the objects in order to appoint to one of them." As to the latter he uses these words (at p. 685): "It seems to me there is much to be said for the view that he must be able to review the whole field in order to exercise his judgment properly." He then considers authority on the validity of powers, the main stumbling-block in the way of his own view being some words used by Fry J in *Blight v Hartnoll* (1881) 19 ChD 294 at 301, which had been adversely commented on in *Farwell on Powers* (3rd Ed, at pp. 168, 169), and I think it worth while quoting the words of his conclusion. He says ([1953] Ch 672 at 688, 689):

> "The settlor had good reason, I have no doubt, to trust the persons whom he appointed trustees; but I cannot see here that there is such a duty as makes it essential for these trustees, before parting with any income or capital, to survey the whole field, and to consider whether A is more deserving of bounty than B. That is a task which was and which must have been known to the settlor to be impossible, having regard to the ramifications of the persons who might become members of this class.
>
> "If, therefore, there be no duty to distribute, but only a duty to consider, it does not seem to me that there is any authority binding on me to say that this whole trust is bad. In fact, there is no difficulty, as has been admitted, in ascertaining whether any given postulant is a member of the specified class. Of course, if that could not be ascertained the matter would be quite different, but of John Doe or Richard Roe it can be postulated easily enough whether he is or is not eligible to receive the settlor's bounty. There being no uncertainty in that sense, I am reluctant to introduce a notion of uncertainty in the other sense, by saying that the trustees must worry their heads to survey the world from China to Peru, when there are perfectly good objects of the class in England."

Subject to one point which was cleared up in this House in *Re Gulbenkian's Settlements* [1970] AC 508, all of this, if I may say so, seems impeccably good sense, and I do not understand the learned judge to have later repented of it. If the judgment was in any way the cause of future difficulties, it was in the indication given—not by way of decision, for the point did not arise—that there was a distinction between the kind of certainty required for powers and that required for trusts. There is a difference perhaps but the difference is a narrow one, and if one is looking to reality one could hardly find better words than those I have just quoted to describe what trustees, in either case, ought to know. A second look at this case, while fully justifying the decision, suggests to me that it does not discourage the application of a similar test for the validity of trusts.

So I come to *IRC v Broadway Cottages Trust* [1955] Ch 20. This was certainly a case of trust, and it proceeded on the basis of an admission, in the words of the judgment, "that the class of 'beneficiaries' is incapable of ascertainment". In addition to the discretionary trust of income, there was a trust of capital for all the beneficiaries living or existing at the terminal date. This necessarily involved equal division and it seems to have been accepted that it was void for uncertainty since there cannot be equal division among a class unless all the members of the class are known. The Court of Appeal applied this proposition to the discretionary trust of income, on the basis that execution by the court was only possible on the same basis of equal division. They rejected the argument that the trust could be executed by changing the trusteeship, and found the relations cases of no assistance as being in a class by themselves. The court could not create an arbitrarily restricted trust to take effect in default of distribution by the trustees. Finally they rejected the submission that the trust could take effect as a power: a valid power could not be spelt out of an invalid trust.

My Lords, it will have become apparent that there is much in this which I find out of line with principle and authority but before I come to a conclusion on it, I must examine the decision of this House in *Re Gulbenkian's Settlements* [1970] AC 508 on which the appellants placed much reliance as amounting to an endorsement of the *Broadway Cottages* case [1955] Ch 20. But is this really so?

[His Lordship examined the case and continued:] What this does say, and I respectfully agree, is that, in the case of a trust, the trustees must select from the class. What it does not say, as I read it, or imply, is that in order to carry out their duty of selection they must have before them, or be able to get, a complete list of all possible objects.

So I think that we are free to review the *Broadway Cottages* case [1955] Ch 20. The conclusion which I would reach, implicit in the previous discussion, is that the wide distinction between the validity test for powers and that for trust powers is unfortunate and wrong, that the rule recently fastened upon the courts by *IRC v Broadway Cottages Trust* ought to be discarded, and that the test for the validity of trust powers ought to be similar to that accepted by this House in *Re Gulbenkian's Settlements* [1970] AC 508 for powers, namely, that the trust is valid if it can be said with certainty that any given individual is or is not a member of the class.

I am interested, and encouraged, to find that the conclusion I had reached by the end of the argument is supported by distinguished American authority. Professor Scott in his well-known book on trusts (*Scott on Trusts* (1939)) discusses the suggested distinction as regards validity between trusts and powers and expresses the opinion that this would be "highly technical" (s. 122, p. 613). Later in the second *Restatement of Trusts* (1959), s. 122 (which *Restatement* aims at stating the better modern view and which annotates the *Broadway Cottages* case), a common test of invalidity is taken, whether trustees are "authorised" or "directed": this is that the class must not be so indefinite that it cannot be ascertained whether any person falls within it. The reporter is Professor Austin Scott. In his abridgment, published in 1960 (*Scott's Abridgment of The Law of Trusts*, s. 122, p. 239), Professor Scott maintains the same position:

> "It would seem that if a power of appointment among the members of an indefinite class is valid, the mere fact that the testator intended not merely to confer a power but to impose a duty to make such an appointment should not preclude the making of such an appointment. It would seem to be the height of technicality that if a testator *authorises* a legatee to divide the property among such of the testator's friends as he might select, he can properly do so, but that if he *directs* him to make such a selection, he will not be permitted to do so."

Assimilation of the validity test does not involve the complete assimilation of trust powers with powers. As to powers, I agree with my noble and learned friend Lord Upjohn in *Re Gulbenkian's Settlements* that although the trustees may, and normally will, be under a fiduciary duty to consider whether or in what way they should exercise their power, the court will not normally compel its exercise. It will intervene if the trustees exceed their powers, and possibly if they are proved to have exercised it capriciously. But in the case of a trust power, if the trustees do not exercise it, the court will: I respectfully adopt as to this the statement in Lord Upjohn's opinion (p. 525). I would venture to amplify this by saying that the court, if called upon to execute the trust power, will do so in the manner best calculated to give effect to the settlor's or testator's intentions. It may do so by appointing new trustees, or by authorising or directing representative persons of the classes of beneficiaries to prepare a scheme of distribution, or even, should the proper basis for distribution appear by itself directing the trustees so to distribute[21]. The books give many instances where this has been done, and I see no reason in principle why they should not do so in the modern field of discretionary trusts (see *Brunsden v Woolredge* (1765) Amb 507, *Supple v Lowson* (1773) Amb 729, *Liley v Hey* (1842) 1 Hare 580 and *Lewin on Trusts*, 16th Edn (1964), p. 630). Then, as to the trustees' duty of inquiry or ascertainment, in each case the trustees ought to make such a survey of the range of objects or possible beneficiaries as will enable them to carry out their fiduciary duty (cf. *Liley v Hey*). A wider and more comprehensive range of inquiry is called for in the case of trust powers than in the case of powers.

Two final points: first, as to the question of certainty. I desire to emphasise the distinction clearly made and explained by Lord Upjohn ([1970] AC 508 at 524) between linguistic or semantic uncertainty which, if unresolved by the court, renders the gift void, and the difficulty of ascertaining the existence or whereabouts of members of the class, a matter with which the court can appropriately deal on an application for directions. There may be a third case where the meaning of the words used is clear but the definition of beneficiaries is so hopelessly wide as not to form "anything like a class" so that the trust is administratively unworkable or in Lord Eldon's words one that cannot be executed (*Morice v Bishop of Durham* (1805) 10 Ves Junr 522 at 527). I hesitate to give examples for they may prejudice future cases, but perhaps "all the residents of Greater London" will serve. I do not think that a discretionary trust for "relatives" even of a living person falls within this category[22].

I would allow the appeal. . . .

On remittance to the Chancery Division, BRIGHTMAN J and the Court of Appeal (SACHS, MEGAW and STAMP LJJ) (in *Re Baden's Deed Trusts (No. 2)* [1973] Ch 9, [1972] 2 All ER 1304)[1] found that the test of certainty was satisfied. The wide differences in their application of the test demonstrates how difficult it may prove to be in practice.

SACHS LJ: The next point as regards approach that requires consideration is the contention, strongly pressed by Mr. Vinelott, that the court must

[21] *Re Locker's Settlement Meachen v Sachs*, [1977] 1 WLR 1323, [1978] 1 All ER 216.

[22] See *Blausten v IRC* [1972] Ch 256 at 271–273; [1972] 1 All ER 41 at 49–51, where some of these points are further discussed; *Re Manisty's Settlement* [1974] Ch 17 at 27–29, [1973] 2 All ER 1203; where TEMPLEMAN J, discussing this point in the context of intermediate powers, said, at p. 27; "A power to benefit 'residents of Greater London' is capricious because the terms of the power negative any sensible intention on the part of the settlor." (1974) 38 Conv (NS) 269 (L. Mackay).

[1] (1973) 36 Conv (NS) 351 (D. J. Hayton); (1973) CLJ 36 (J. A. Hopkins): *Re Bethel* (1971) 17 DLR (3d) 652: (1971) ASCL 377.

always be able to say whether any given postulant is *not* within the relevant class as well as being able to say whether he is within it. In construing the words already cited from the speech of Lord Wilberforce in the *Baden* case (as well as those of Lord Reid and Lord Upjohn in the *Gulbenkian* case), it is essential to bear in mind the difference between conceptual uncertainty and evidential difficulties . . .

As Mr. Vinelott himself rightly observed, "the court is never defeated by evidential uncertainty," and it is in my judgment clear that it is conceptual certainty to which reference was made when the "is or is not a member of the class" test was enunciated. (Conceptual uncertainty was in the course of argument conveniently exemplified, rightly or wrongly matters not, by the phrase " someone under a moral obligation" and contrasted with the certainty of the words "first cousins.") Once the class of person to be benefited is conceptually certain it then becomes a question of fact to be determined on evidence whether any postulant has on inquiry been proved to be within it: if he is not so proved, then he is not in it. That position remains the same whether the class to be benefited happens to be small (such as "first cousins") or large (such as "members of the X Trade Union" or "those who have served in the Royal Navy"). The suggestion that such trusts could be invalid because it might be impossible to prove of a given individual that he was *not* in the relevant class is wholly fallacious—and only Mr. Vinelott's persuasiveness has prevented me from saying that the contention is almost unarguable . . .

In agreement with the practical approach of Brightman J [1972] Ch. 607 at 625, I consider that the trustees, or if necessary the court, are quite capable of coming to a conclusion in any given case as to whether or not a particular candidate could properly be described as a dependant—a word that, as the judge said, "conjures up a sufficiently distinct picture". I agree, too, that any one wholly or partly dependent on the means of another is a "dependant". There is thus no conceptual uncertainty inherent in that word and the executors' contentions as to the effect of its use fail.

As regards "relatives" Brightman J, after stating, at p. 625, "It is not in dispute that a person is a relative of an . . . employee . . . , if both trace legal descent from a common ancestor:" a little later said: "In practice, the use of the expression 'relatives' cannot cause the slightest difficulty." With that view I agree for the reasons he gave when he correctly set out the evidential position.

Megaw LJ: The main argument of Mr. Vinelott was founded upon a strict and literal interpretation of the words in which the decision of the House of Lords in *Re Gulbenkian's Settlements* [1970] AC 508 was expressed. That decision laid down the test for the validity of powers of selection. It is relevant for the present case, because in the previous excursion of this case to the House of Lords [1971] AC 424 it was held that there is no relevant difference in the test of validity, whether the trustees are given a power of selection or, as was held by their Lordships to be the case in this trust deed, a trust for selection. The test in either case is what may be called the *Gulbenkian* test. The *Gulbenkian* test, as expressed by Lord Wilberforce at p. 450, and again in almost identical words at p. 454 is this:

". . . the power is valid if it can be said with certainty whether any given individual is or is not a member of the class and does not fail simply because it is impossible to ascertain every member of the class."

The executors' argument concentrates on the words "or is not" in the first of the two limbs of the sentence quoted above: "if it can be said with certainty whether any given individual is *or is not* a member of the class". It is said that those words have been used deliberately, and have only one possible meaning; and that, however startling or drastic or unsatisfactory the result may be—and Mr. Vinelott does not shrink from saying that the consequence is drastic—this court is bound to give effect to the words used in the House of Lords' definition of the test. It would be quite impracticable for the trustees to ascertain in many cases whether a particular person was *not* a relative of an employee. The most that could be said is: "There is no proof that he is a relative." But there would still be no "certainty" that such a person was not a relative. Hence, so it is said, the test laid down by the House of Lords is not satisfied, and the trust is void. For it cannot be said with certainty, in relation to any individual, that he is not a relative.

I do not think it was contemplated that the words "or is not" would produce that result. It would, as I see it, involve an inconsistency with the latter part of the same sentence: "does not fail simply because it is impossible to ascertain every member of the class". The executors' contention, in substance and reality, is that it *does* fail "simply because it is impossible to ascertain every member of the class".

The same verbal difficulty, as I see it, emerges also when one considers the words of the suggested test which the House of Lords expressly rejected. That is set out by Lord Wilberforce in a passage immediately following the sentence which I have already quoted. The rejected test was in these terms [1971] AC 424 at 450: ". . . it is said to be necessary . . . that the whole range of objects . . . should be ascertained or capable of ascertainment". Since that test was rejected, the resulting affirmative proposition, which by implication must have been accepted by their Lordships, is this: a trust for selection will not fail simply because the whole range of objects cannot be ascertained. In the present case, the trustees could ascertain, by investigation and evidence, many of the objects: as to many other theoretically possible claimants, they could not be certain. Is it to be said that the trust fails because it cannot be said with certainty that such persons are not members of the class? If so, is that not the application of the rejected test: the trust failing because "the whole range of objects cannot be ascertained"?

In my judgment, much too great emphasis is placed in the executors' argument on the words "or is not". To my mind, the test is satisfied if, as regards at least a substantial number of objects, it can be said with certainty that they fall within the trust; even though, as regards a substantial number of other persons, if they ever for some fanciful reason fell to be considered, the answer would have to be, not "they are outside the trust", but "it is not proven whether they are in or out". What is a "substantial number" may well be a question of common sense and of degree in relation to the particular trust: particularly where, as here, it would be fantasy, to use a mild word, to suggest that any practical difficulty would arise in the fair, proper and sensible administration of this trust in respect of relatives and dependants.

I do not think that this involves, as Mr. Vinelott suggested, a return by this court to its former view which was rejected by the House of Lords in the *Gulbenkian* case. If I did so think, I should, however reluctantly, accept Mr. Vinelott's argument and its consequences. But as I read it, the criticism in the House of Lords of the decision of this court in that case related to this court's acceptance of the view that it would be sufficient if it could be shown that *one single person* fell within the scope of the power or trust. The essence of the decision of the House of Lords in the *Gulbenkian* case, as I see it, is *not* that it must be possible to show with certainty that any given person is *or is not* within the trust; but that it is not, or may not be, sufficient to be able to show that one individual person is within it. If it does not mean that, I do not know where the line is supposed to be drawn, having regard to the clarity and emphasis with which the House of Lords has laid down that the trust does not fail because the whole range of objects cannot be ascertained.

I would dismiss the appeal.

Stamp LJ: Mr. Vinelott, fastening on those words, "if it can be said with certainty that any given individual is or is not a member of the class", submitted in this court that a trust for distribution among officers and employees or ex-officers or ex-employees or any of their relatives or dependants does not satisfy the test. You may say with certainty that any given individual is or is not an officer, employee, ex-officer or ex-employee. You may say with certainty that a very large number of given individuals are relatives of one of them; but, so the argument runs, you will never be able to say with certainty of many given individuals that they are not. I am bound to say that I had thought at one stage of Mr. Vinelott's able argument that this was no more than an exercise in semantics and that the phrase on which he relies indicated no more than that the trust was valid if there was such certainty in the definition of membership of the class that you could say with certainty that some individuals were members of it: that it was sufficient that you should be satisfied that a given individual presenting himself has or has not passed the test and that it matters not that having failed to establish his membership—here his relationship—you may, perhaps wrongly, reject him. There are, however, in my judgment serious difficulties in the way of a rejection of Mr. Vinelott's submission.

The first difficulty, as I see it, is that the rejection of Mr. Vinelott's submission involves holding that the trust is good if there are individuals —or even one—of whom you can say with certainty that he is a member of the class. That was the test adopted by and the decision of the Court of Appeal in the *Gulbenkian* case where what was under consideration was a power of distribution among a class conferred upon trustees as distinct from a trust for distribution: but when the *Gulbenkian* case came before the House of Lords that test was decisively rejected and the more stringent test upon which Mr. Vinelott insists was adopted. Clearly Lord Wilberforce in expressing the view that the test of validity of a discretionary trust ought to be similar to that accepted by the House of Lords in the *Gulbenkian* case did not take the view that it was sufficient that you could find individuals who were clearly members of the class; for he himself remarked, towards the end of his speech as to the trustees' duty of inquiring or ascertaining, that in each case the trustees ought to make such a survey of the range of objects or possible beneficiaries as will enable them to carry out their fiduciary duty. It is not enough that trustees should do nothing but distribute the fund among those objects of the trust who happen to be at hand or present themselves. Lord Wilberforce, after citing that passage which I have already quoted from the speech of Lord Upjohn in the *Gulbenkian* case, put it more succinctly by remarking that what this did say (and he agreed) was that the trustees must select from the class, but that passage did not mean (as had been contended) that they must be able to get a complete list of all possible objects. I have already called attention to Lord Wilberforce's opinion that the trustees ought to make such a survey of the range of objects or possible beneficiaries as will enable them to carry out their fiduciary duty, and I ought perhaps to add that he indicated that a wider and more comprehensive range of inquiry is called for in the case of what I have called discretionary trusts than in the case of fiduciary powers. But, as I understand it, having made the appropriate survey, it matters not that it is not complete or fails to yield a result enabling you to lay out a list or particulars of every single beneficiary. Having done the best they can, the trustees may proceed upon the basis similar to that adopted by the court where all the beneficiaries cannot be ascertained and distribute upon the footing that they have been: see, for example, *Re Benjamin* [1902] 1 Ch 723. What was referred to as "the complete ascertainment test" laid down by this court in the *Broadway Cottages* case is rejected. So also is the test laid down by this court in the *Gulbenkian* case. Validity or invalidity is to depend upon whether you can say of any individual—and the accent must be upon that word "any", for it is not simply the individual whose claim you are considering who is spoken of—"is or is not a member of the class", for only thus can you make a survey of the range of objects or possible beneficiaries.

If the matter rested there, it would in my judgment follow that, treating the word "relatives" as meaning descendants from a common ancestor, a trust for distribution such as is here in question would not be valid. Any "survey of the range of the objects or possible beneficiaries" would certainly be incomplete, and I am able to discern no principle upon which such a survey could be conducted or where it should start or finish. The most you could do, so far as regards relatives, would be to find individuals who are clearly members of the class—the test which was accepted in the Court of Appeal, but rejected in the House of Lords, in the *Gulbenkian* case.

The matter does not, however, rest there . . . *Harding v Glyn* (1739) 1 Atk 469 . . . was an early case where the court executed a discretionary trust for "relations"—and it is a discretionary trust for relations that I am considering—by distributing to the next of kin in equal shares . . .

Harding v Glyn accordingly cannot be regarded simply as a case where in default of appointment a gift to the next of kin is to be implied as a matter of construction, but as authority endorsed by the decision of the House of Lords [1971] AC 424 that a discretionary trust for "relations" was a valid trust to be executed by the court by distribution to the next of kin. The class of beneficiaries thus becomes a clearly defined class and there is no difficulty in determining whether a given individual is within it or without it.

Does it then make any difference that here the discretionary trust for relations was a reference not to the relations of a deceased person but of one who was living? I think not. The next of kin of a living person are as readily ascertainable at any given time as the next of kin of one who is dead.

Hanbury and Maudsley: *Modern Equity* (10th Edn) p. 171

(b) *Many Certain Categories: One Uncertain.* Further difficulties could arise with a definition of a class of beneficiaries which contained a long series of categories which complied with the *McPhail v Doulton* test, but to which there was added one category which did not. What, for example, would the court say to a trust in the same language as that in *McPhail v Doulton* but to which there was added "any person to whom I may be under a moral obligation and any of my old friends?" . . . which is, let it be assumed, conceptually uncertain. The same problem as we have seen could arise in a case of power.

In this situation, the class as the whole does not satisfy the test. It would however be unfortunate to declare the whole trust void because of the final addition. After all, the trust is eminently workable as it is. Such a trust, however, may be held void. Alternatively, it could be valid by applying Megaw LJ's construction of the *McPhail v Doulton* test. Or even by excising the offending phrase by the operation of a species of severance; a suggestion which is made on more than one occasion[2]. It would of course be valid if a return was made to the *Gibbard* test[3].

III. A Special Problem Relating to Unincorporated Associations[4]

A corporation, like a human being, is a legal person, and can own property. An unincorporated association is not a legal person; but many unincorporated associations exist and operate, and have done so for many years. The question which must be investigated now is this: what is the proper legal analysis of the way in which they hold property?

The variety of unincorporated associations is limitless. In order to determine into which category any particular association fits, it is necessary for the court to construe the language of its constitution or rules or of the instrument which created it. Certain types may be categorised in order to show some of the possibilities.

[2] Per SACHS LJ in *Re Leek* [1969] 1 Ch at 586; and in the case of a power by WINN LJ in *Re Gulbenkian's Settlements* [1968] Ch 126 at 138.

[3] [1967] 1 WLR 42, [1966] 1 All ER 273.

[4] See Morris and Leach, *Rule Against Perpetuities* (2nd Edn), pp. 313–318; Ford, *Unincorporated Non-Profit Associations*, pp. 1–49; H & M, pp. 172–175.

(i) An unincorporated association or group of trustees holding property on charitable trusts; as, for example, on trust for the relief of poverty. This is valid. It is exempt from most forms of taxation, and may continue for ever. Charitable trusts are discussed in Chapter 10.

(ii) An unincorporated association whose funds are required by its rules to be applied for non-charitable purposes. For example: a trust for the preservation of the independence and integrity of newspapers. Generally speaking, a trust for non-charitable purposes is void. The matter is discussed in Chapter 9.

(iii) An unincorporated association whose committee or officers hold property on trust for the members of the association; for example, to the Treasurer for the time being of a school old boys' society[5]. This may be construed as an ordinary trust for beneficiaries. But difficulties can arise in connection with the following questions: whether beneficiaries are sufficiently ascertainable; whether such a beneficial interest under a trust can be obtained or released by joining or leaving an association; and whether the rule against perpetuities applies so as to render void the beneficial interest of any member who joins outside the period.

(iv) An unincorporated association in which the members have a right based upon contract to claim a share of the property. For example, a members' club, such as a golf club. This situation is outside the law of trusts, but it is mentioned here in order to complete the categories by including an explanation of the most common type of unincorporated association. Legal difficulties can of course arise in this analysis. In many cases the members of the association will be unaware of the existence or the terms of the contract. And other difficulties arise if members are minors.

The subject of unincorporated associations is included here, because in some of the categories, especially category (iii), questions arise relating to the requirements of a trust. This aspect of the problem is quite recent. Prior to the decision of the Privy Council in *Leahy v A-G for New South Wales*[6], the courts did not analyse the theoretical basis of property holding by unincorporated associations in terms of category (iii), and did not in consequence put such an unincorporated association "at risk" of invalidity by reason of failure to comply with the requirements of a trust for beneficiaries. Before 1959, the courts seemed satisfied so long as the society could, by its rules, alienate its property and did not create a perpetuity[7]. The matter, and the earlier cases[8] are discussed in *Leahy*, below.

But the analysis of an unincorporated association on the basis of a trust was sometimes made in the context of a resulting trust arising upon the *dissolution* of the society, and the disposal of the surplus funds. This question is related to the one under discussion here, but its detailed consideration is postponed to the chapter on Resulting Trusts, Chapter 7. It will there

[5] See *Re Drummond* [1914] 2 Ch 90, as discussed in *Leahy v A-G for New South Wales* [1959] AC 457 at 479, p. 63, post.

[6] [1959] AC 457, [1959] 2 All ER 300.

[7] *Carne v Long* (1860) 2 De GF & J 75.

[8] *Re Drummond* [1914] 2 Ch 90; *Re Patten* [1929] 2 Ch 276; *Re Prevost* [1930] 2 Ch 383, (1937) 53 LQR 24 at p. 46 (W. O. Hart); *Re Price* [1943] Ch 422, [1943] 2 All ER 505; *Re Macaulay's Estate* (HL July 10, 1933) [1943] Ch 435n.

be seen that the disposal of the surplus can depend on the question whether the situation is analysed as being one where the property is held on trust, or whether it is held subject to the contractual rights of the members. Where a friendly society, a mutual insurance society, a golf club, or whatever, is wound up, and there is a surplus, should the surplus be paid out to the existing members? Or to past and present members? Or to those who contributed the funds, whether they are members or not? And whether they can be identified or not? Or, should the surplus be treated as one without a claimant, and paid to the Crown as *bona vacantia?* It will be seen in Chapter 7 that each of these solutions has at times been applied. Again, much depends on whether the situation is analysed as one of contract or trust.

LEAHY v ATTORNEY-GENERAL FOR NEW SOUTH WALES

[1959] AC 457, [1959] 2 All ER 300 (PC, Viscount SIMONDS, Lords MORTON OF HENRYTON, COHEN, SOMERVELL OF HARROW and DENNING)

An Australian testator provided by clause 3 of his will, *inter alia,* that his property, known as "Elmslea" should be held upon trust for "such order of nuns of the Catholic Church or the Christian Brothers as my executors and trustees shall select". Such orders included some purely contemplative orders, which were not legally "charitable".

The New South Wales Conveyancing Act 1919–54, s. 37 (D) provided that a trust should not be invalid on the ground that the property might be applicable to objects some of which were charitable and some of which were not.

The question was whether the property could be applied, as being a valid private trust, in favour of the individual members of contemplative orders. Or whether it should be treated as an endowment of the orders selected; and valid only, as a charitable trust, under the New South Wales Conveyancing Act 1919–54, s. 37 (D)[9]; and, as such, applicable only in favour of such orders as were charitable.

Held. The trust was intended as an endowment of the orders selected. It could not take effect as a private trust, but was validated by the New South Wales Conveyancing Act.

VISCOUNT SIMONDS: The disposition made by clause 3 must now be considered. As has already been pointed out, it will in any case be saved by the section so far as Orders other than Contemplative Orders are concerned, but the trustees are anxious to preserve their right to select such Orders. They can only do so if the gift is what is called an absolute gift to the selected Order, an expression which may require examination.

Upon this question there has been a sharp division of opinion in the High Court. Williams and Webb JJ agreed with Myers J that the disposition by clause 3 was valid. They held that it provided for an immediate gift to the particular religious community selected by the trustees and that it was immaterial whether the Order was charitable or not because the gift was not a gift in perpetuity. "It is given" they said (and these are the significant words) "to the individuals comprising the community

[9] See p. 370, post.

selected by the trustees at the date of the death of the testator. It is given to them for the benefit of the community". Kitto J reached the same conclusion. He thought that the selected Order would take the gift immediately and absolutely and could expend immediately the whole of what it received. "There is," he said, "no attempt to create a perpetual endowment". A different view was taken by the Chief Justice and McTiernan J. After an exhaustive examination of the problem and of the relevant authorities they concluded that the provision made by clause 3 was intended as a trust operating for the furtherance of the purpose of the Order as a body of religious women or, in the case of the Christian Brothers, as a teaching Order. "The membership of any Order chosen," they said, "would be indeterminate and the trust was intended to apply to those who should become members at any time. There was no intention to restrain the operation of the trust to these presently members or to make the alienation of the property a question for the Governing Body of the Order chosen or any section or part of that Order." They therefore held that unless the trust could be supported as a charity it must fail.

The brief passages that have been cited from the judgments in the High Court sufficiently indicate the question that must be answered and the difficulty of solving it. It arises out of the artificial and anomalous conception of an unincorporated society which, though it is not a separate entity in law, is yet for many purposes regarded as a continuing entity and, however inaccurately, as something other than an aggregate of its members. In law a gift to such a society simpliciter (i.e., where, to use the words of Lord Parker in *Bowman v Secular Society Ltd* ([1917] AC 406 at 437), neither the circumstances of the gift nor the directions given nor the objects expressed impose on the donee the character of a trustee) is nothing else than a gift to its members at the date of the gift as joint tenants or tenants in common. It is for this reason that the prudent conveyancer provides that a receipt by the treasurer or other proper officer of the recipient society for a legacy to the society shall be a sufficient discharge to executors. If it were not so, the executors could only get a valid discharge by obtaining a receipt from every member. This must be qualified by saying that by their rules the members might have authorised one of themselves to receive a gift on behalf of them all.

It is in the light of this fundamental proposition that the statements, to which reference has been made, must be examined. What is meant when it is said that a gift is made to the individuals comprising the community and the words are added "it is given to them for the benefit of the community"? If it is a gift to individuals, each of them is entitled to his distributive share (unless he has previously bound himself by the rules of the society that it shall be devoted to some other purpose). It is difficult to see what is added by the words "for the benefit of the community." If they are intended to import a trust, who are the beneficiaries? If the present members are the beneficiaries, the words add nothing and are meaningless. If some other persons or purposes are intended, the conclusion cannot be avoided that the gift is void. For it is uncertain, and beyond doubt tends to a perpetuity.

The question then appears to be whether, even if the gift to a selected

Order of Nuns is prima facie a gift to the individual members of that Order, there are other considerations arising out of the terms of the will, or the nature of the society, its organisation and rules, or the subject-matter of the gift which should lead the court to conclude that, though prima facie the gift is an absolute one (absolute both in quality of estate and in freedom from restriction) to individual nuns, yet it is invalid because it is in the nature of an endowment and tends to a perpetuity or for any other reason. This raises a problem which is not easy to solve, as the divergent opinions in the High Court indicate.

The prima facie validity of such a gift (by which term their Lordships intend a bequest or devise[10]) is a convenient starting point for the examination of the relevant law. For as Lord Tomlin (sitting at first instance in the Chancery Division) said in *Re Ogden* ([1933] Ch 678), a gift to a voluntary association of persons for the general purposes of the association is an absolute gift and prima facie a good gift. He was echoing the words of Lord Parker in *Bowman's* case ([1917] AC 406 at 442), that a gift to an unincorporated association for the attainment of its purposes "may . . . be upheld as an absolute gift to its members". These words must receive careful consideration, for it is to be noted that it is because the gift can be upheld as a gift to the individual members that it is valid, even though it is given for the general purposes of the association. If the words "for the general purposes of the association" were held to import a trust, the question would have to be asked, what is the trust and who are the beneficiaries? A gift can be made to persons (including a corporation) but it cannot be made to a purpose or to an object: so also, a trust may be created for the benefit of persons as cestuis que trust but not for a purpose or object unless the purpose or object be charitable. [His Lordship referred to *Cocks v Manners* (1871) LR 12 Eq 574 (a share of residue to the "Dominican Convent at Carisbrooke payable to the Superior for the time being); *Re Smith* [1914] 1 Ch 937 (bequest to "the society or institution known as the Franciscan Friars of Clevedon County of Somerset"); *Re Clarke* [1901] 2 Ch 110 (bequest to "the committee for the time being of the Corps of Commissionaires in London"); *Re Drummond* [1914] 2 Ch 90 (residuary testamentary gift upon trust for "the Old Bradfordians Club, London"); *Re Taylor* [1940] Ch 481, [1940] 2 All ER 637(residuary testamentary gift upon trust for "the Midland Bank Staff Association, Liverpool and District Centre"); *Re Price* [1943] Ch 422, [1943] 2 All ER 505 (residuary testamentary gift to "the Anthroposophical Society in Great Britain"); *Re Prevost* [1930] 2 Ch 383 (residuary testamentary gift to "the trustees of the London Library"); *Re Ray's Will Trusts* [1936] Ch 520, [1936] 2 All ER 93 (bequest to "the person who, at the time of my death, shall be or shall act as the abbess of the Franciscan Convent, Woodchester, Gloucestershire") and continued:]

The cases that have been referred to (and many others might have been referred to in the courts of Australia, England and Ireland) are all cases in which gifts have been upheld as valid either on the ground that, where a society has been named as legatee, its members could demand that the gift should be dealt with as they should together think fit; or on the

[10] The report says demise; but presumably devise is intended.

ground that a trust had been established (as in *Re Drummond* ([1914] 2 Ch 90)) which did not create a perpetuity. It will be sufficient to mention one only of the cases in which a different conclusion has been reached, before coming to a recent decision of the House of Lords which must be regarded as of paramount authority. In *Carne v Long* ((1860) 2 De GF & J 75) the testator devised his mansion-house after the death of his wife to the trustees of the Penzance Public Library to hold to them and their successors for ever for the use, benefit, maintenance and support of the said library. It appeared that the library was established and kept on foot by the subscriptions of certain inhabitants of Penzance, that the subscribers were elected by ballot and the library managed by officers chosen from amongst themselves by the subscribers, that the property in the books and everything else belonging to the library was vested in trustees for the subscribers and that it was provided that the institution should not be broken up so long as 10 members remained. It was urged that the gift was to a number of private persons and there were in truth no other beneficiaries. But Campbell LC rejected the plea in words which, often though they have been cited, will bear repetition (ibid., at 79): "If the devise had been in favour of the existing members of the society, and they had been at liberty to dispose of the property as they might think fit, then it might, I think, have been a lawful disposition and not tending to a perpetuity. But looking to the language of the rules of this society, it is clear that the library was intended to be a perpetual institution, and the testator must be presumed to have known what the regulations were." This was perhaps a clear case where both from the terms of the gift and the nature of the society a perpetuity was indicated.

Their Lordships must now turn to the recent case of *Re Macaulay's Estate*, which appears to be reported only in a footnote to *Re Price* ([1943] Ch. 422 at 435, [1943] 2 All ER 505). There the gift was to the Folkestone Lodge of the Theosophical Society absolutely for the maintenance and improvement of the Theosophical Lodge at Folkestone. It was assumed that the donee, "the Lodge," was a body of persons. The decision of the House of Lords in July 1933, to which both Lord Buckmaster and Lord Tomlin were parties, was that the gift was invalid. A portion of Lord Buckmaster's speech may well be quoted. He had previously referred to *Re Drummond* ([1914] 2 Ch 90) and *Carne v Long* ((1860) 2 De GF & J 75), "A group of people," he said, "defined and bound together by rules and called by a distinctive name can be the subject of gift as well as any individual or incorporated body. The real question is what is the actual purpose for which the gift is made. There is no perpetuity if the gift is for the individual members for their own benefit, but that, I think, is clearly not the meaning of this gift. Nor again is there a perpetuity if the society is at liberty in accordance with the terms of the gift to spend both capital and income as they think fit . . . If the gift is to be for the endowment of the society to be held as an endowment and the society is according to its form perpetual, the gift is bad: but, if the gift is an immediate beneficial legacy, it is good." In the result he held the gift for the maintenance and improvement of the Theosophical Lodge at Folkestone to be invalid. Their Lordships respectfully doubt whether the passage in

Lord Buckmaster's speech in which he suggests the alternative ground of validity: viz., that the society is at liberty in accordance with the terms of the gift to spend both capital and income as they think fit, presents a true alternative. It is only because the society, i.e., the individuals constituting it, are beneficiaries, that they can dispose of the gift. Lord Tomlin came to the same conclusion. He found in the words of the will "for the maintenance and improvement" a sufficient indication that it was the permanence of the Lodge at Folkestone that the testatrix was seeking to secure and this, he thought, necessarily involved endowment. Therefore a perpetuity was created. A passage from the judgment of Lord Hanworth MR (which has been obtained from the records) may usefully be cited. He said: " The problem may be stated in this way. If the gift is in truth to the present members of the society described by their society name so that they have the beneficial use of the property and can, if they please, alienate and put the proceeds in their own pocket, then there is a present gift to individuals which is good: but if the gift is intended for the good not only of the present but of future members so that the present members are in the position of trustees and have no right to appropriate the property or its proceeds for their personal benefit then the gift is invalid. It may be invalid by reason of there being a trust created, or it may be by reason of the terms that the period allowed by the rule against perpetuities would be exceeded."

It is not very clear what is intended by the dichotomy suggested in the last sentence of the citation, but the penultimate sentence goes to the root of the matter. At the risk of repetition their Lordships would point out that, if a gift is made to individuals, whether under their own names or in the name of their society, and the conclusion is reached that they are not intended to take beneficially, then they take as trustees. If so, it must be ascertained who are the beneficiaries . . .[11].

It must now be asked, then, whether in the present case there are sufficient indications to displace the prima facie conclusion that the gift made by clause 3 of the will is to the individual members of the selected Order of Nuns at the date of the testator's death so that they can together dispose of it as they think fit. It appears to their Lordships that such indications are ample.

In the first place, it is not altogether irrelevant that the gift is in terms upon trust for a selected Order. It is true that this can in law be regarded as a trust in favour of each and every member of the Order. But at least the form of the gift is not to the members, and it may be questioned whether the testator understood the niceties of the law. In the second place, the members of the selected Order may be numerous, very numerous perhaps, and they may be spread over the world. If the gift is to the individuals it is to all the members who were living at the death of the testator, but only to them. It is not easy to believe that the testator intended an "immediate beneficial legacy" (to use the words of Lord Buckmaster) to such a body of beneficiaries. In the third place, the subject-matter of the gift cannot be ignored. It appears from the evidence filed in the suit that

[11] Which would now be decided according to the test laid down in *Mc Phail v Doulton*, [1971] AC 424, [1970] 2 All ER 288; p. 48, ante.

Elmslea is a grazing property of about 730 acres, with a furnished homestead containing 20 rooms and a number of outbuildings. With the greatest respect to those judges who have taken a different view, their Lordships do not find it possible to regard all the individual members of an Order as intended to become the beneficial owners of such a property. Little or no evidence has been given about the organisation and rules of the several Orders, but it is at least permissible to doubt whether it is a common feature of them, that all their members regard themselves or are to be regarded as having the capacity of (say) the Corps of Commissionaires (see *Re Clarke* ([1901] 2 Ch 110) to put an end to their association and distribute its assets. On the contrary, it seems reasonably clear that, however little the testator understood the effect in law of a gift to an unincorporated body of persons by their society name, his intention was to create a trust, not merely for the benefit of the existing members of the selected Order, but for its benefit as a continuing society and for the furtherance of its work.

Different views have been held upon the question whether the legal title remains in the will trustees after they have selected an Order. Kitto J (expressly) and Williams and Webb JJ (by implication) held that "when a body is selected by the trustees the property will be at home" and will vest presumably in some authorised person or persons. (The Roman Catholic Charities Land Act of 1942 was not invoked in the High Court and becomes irrelevant if the chosen Order is not a charity.) The Chief Justice and McTiernan J were of opinion that the trustees were intended, subject to the power of sale, to remain the repository of the whole legal title and to administer the trust by affording the enjoyment to the selected Order. The latter view is attractive if only because of the difficulty of transferring title when the above-mentioned Act does not apply. But their Lordships do not think it necessary for the purpose of this case to decide the question. No difficulty will arise if only a charitable body can be selected. If the choice is wider, the question will not arise. The dominant and sufficiently expressed intention of the testator is in their opinion (again in the words of Lord Buckmaster) that "the gift is to be an endowment of the society to be held as an endowment", and that "as the society is according to its form perpetual" the gift must, if it is to a non-charitable body, fail.

Their Lordships, therefore, humbly advise Her Majesty that the appeal should be dismissed, but that the gift made by clause 3 of the will is valid by reason only of the provisions of section 37(D) of the Conveyancing Act, 1919–54, and that the power of selection thereby given to the trustees does not extend to Contemplative Orders of Nuns. The costs of all parties will be paid out of the estate of the testator. The costs of all the respondents will be taxed as between solicitor and clients.

In *Neville Estates Ltd v Madden* ([1962] Ch 832, [1961] 3 All ER 769) the trustees of Catford Synagogue entered into a contract to sell some land. The question arose whether the consent of the Charity Commissioners was required. Consent would be required if the land was held upon charitable trusts and if the Charitable Trusts Act 1853, s. 62[12] did not apply. The members of the Synagogue claimed that they were entitled to the purchase money.

CROSS J decided that the land was held on charitable trusts and that consent was required. In considering the claim of the members, he discussed the question of the nature of gifts in favour of unincorporated associations. He said (at p. 849): "I turn now at last to the legal issues involved. The question of the construction and effect of gifts to or in trust for unincorporated associations was recently considered by the Privy Council in *Leahy v A-G for New South Wales* ([1959] AC 457, [1959] 2 All ER 300). The position, as I understand it, is as follows. Such a gift may take effect in one or other of three quite different ways. In the first place, it may, on its true construction, be a gift to the members of the association at the relevant date as joint tenants, so that any member can sever his share and claim it whether or not he continues to be a member of the association. Secondly, it may be a gift to the existing members not as joint tenants, but subject to their respective contractual rights and liabilities towards one another as members of the association. In such a case a member cannot sever his share. It will accrue to the other members on his death or resignation, even though such members include persons who became members after the gift took effect. If this is the effect of the gift, it will not be open to objection on the score of perpetuity or uncertainty unless there is something in its terms or circumstances or in the rules of the association which precludes the members at any given time from dividing the subject of the gift between them on the footing that they are solely entitled to it in equity.

Thirdly, the terms or circumstances of the gift or the rules of the association may show that the property in question is not to be at the disposal of the members for the time being, but is to be held in trust for or applied for the purposes of the association as a quasi-corporate entity. In this case the gift will fail unless the association is a charitable body. If the gift is of the second class, i.e., one which the members of the association for the time being are entitled to divide among themselves, then, even if the objects of the association are in themselves charitable, the gift would not, I think, be a charitable gift. If, for example, a number of persons formed themselves into an association with a charitable object—say the relief of poverty in some district—but it was part of the contract between them that, if a majority of the members so desired, the assocation should be dissolved and its property divided between the members at the date of dissolution, a gift to the association as part of its general funds would not, I conceive, be a charitable gift."

Compare the approach of the High Court of Australia in *Bacon v Pianta* ((1966) 114 CLR 634[13]), with that of BRIGHTMAN J in *Re Recher's Will Trusts* ([1972] Ch 526, [1971] 3 All ER 401).

[12] Which exempts charities which are wholly or partly maintained by voluntary subscription.
[13] (1971) 8 Melbourne Law Review 1 (P. W. Hogg).

In *Bacon v Pianta*, the question was whether a bequest was valid which gave the whole of the testator's estate "To the Communist Party of Australia for its sole use and benefit". This was held void. The High Court said at p. 638: "The question for our decision is whether a bequest in the terms stated is valid or whether the whole of the estate passes to the persons entitled thereto as upon an intestacy. In the Supreme Court Hart J was of opinion that the bequest was void and the appeal is brought from the order which, on that view, he made disposing of the suit.

The difficulty in the case arises from the fact that The Communist Party of Australia is an unincorporated voluntary association. Cases dealing with the problem which arises from such a circumstance with respect to testamentary dispositions are numerous and some of them are, to say the least, not readily reconcilable. However, in the recent case of *Leahy v A-G for New South Wales* ([1959] AC 457, [1959] 2 All ER 300) many of them were referred to and reviewed and the guiding principles were restated. It was accepted that, as had been held in cases such as *Bowman v Secular Society* ([1917] AC 406) and *Re Ogden* ([1933] Ch 678), a gift to an unincorporated association operates, prima facie, as a gift to the individual members at the time when the bequest becomes operative. However, circumstances may appear which preclude this conclusion; it may appear that the disposition amounts to a trust for the benefit of both present and future members, or, that it is not for the benefit of individuals at all but stands revealed as a trust for some purpose or purposes disclosed by the terms of the bequest. In the former of these two cases the gift may well fail as infringing the rule against perpetuities and, in the latter case, it will fail unless the purpose is, in the legal sense, charitable. Indications sufficient to rebut the prima facie presumption may be found to some extent in the form which the gift takes, in the number and disposition of the members of the association, in the subject matter of the gift and in the capacity of the members to put an end to their association and distribute its assets. As was said of the disposition in question in *Leahy's Case* ([1959] AC 457 at 485, 486, [1959] 2 All ER 300). [His Lordship quoted the paragraph p. 67, ante and continued:] We do not think that this passage was intended as an exhaustive catalogue of the matters which might induce a court to hold that the prima facie conclusion was displaced; they were matters which presented themselves for consideration in *Leahy's Case* and they were thought to lead to the conclusion which is stated in the last sentence of the passage which we have quoted.

In the instant case it is, we think, impossible for a number of reasons to regard the disposition as effectively making a gift collectively to the existing members of The Communist Party of Australia at the time of the testator's death. In form, the gift is to The Communist Party of Australia for *its* sole use and benefit and, there being nothing to show that the testator knew that that organization was not a legal entity, this provides some, albeit slight, indication that he did not intend to make such an immediate gift. Indeed, it is reasonable to suppose that the testator was unaware of the difficulties which would be occasioned by the fact that, in truth, the designated beneficiary was an unincorporated body. When there is added to the form in which the disposition is made the fact that The Communist Party had an extensive membership throughout Australia and that its membership seems to have been subject to very substantial fluctuation from time to time the additional difficulty arises of regarding the disposition as a gift to those individuals throughout Australia who should happen to be members of the organization at the time of his death. Some indication of the extent of the membership of the Party and the fluctuations in membership may be gathered from the evidence although it dealt primarily only with changes in the membership during a period of less than two years after the testator's death. To the best of the defendants' knowledge—exact records not having been kept at the office of the Central Committee—the number of members of the Party in Australia at the testator's death was some 5,274 of whom 2,515 were residents of New South Wales, 1,375 residents of Victoria, 826 residents of Queensland, 295 residents of South Australia, 194 residents of Western Australia, 51 residents of Tasmania and 18 residents of the Northern Territory. Of the total number specified 420 ceased to be members by the end of 1965 by reason of resignation, death or expulsion and, in the same period, 776 persons became members. Further, we think, upon consideration of the 1961 constitution of the Party—which, so far as we can see, is entirely silent concerning property of the Party or its transmission—it is impossible to say that at the time when the bequest, if effective, became operative the members of the Party had any, or any practical, capacity to put an end to their association and to distribute its assets. In our view, the observations made in *Re Macaulay's Estate* ([1943] Ch 435), which were cited and commented upon by Viscount Simonds in *Leahy's Case* ([1959] AC 457, [1959] 2 All ER 300), and the reasons for the decision in the last-mentioned case, lead to the conclusion that the cumulative effect of these considerations compel us to dismiss the appeal. In our view, it would be quite artificial to hold that the bequest operated as a bequest beneficially to the existing members of The Communist Party of Australia and we are satisfied that the correct conclusion is that it was a bequest to the members, both present and future, in trust for the purposes of the Party. That being so the bequest was void and, accordingly, the appeal should be dismissed."

In *Re Recher's Will Trusts* ([1972] Ch 526, [1971] 3 All ER 401)[14] one question was whether a gift to the London and Provincial Anti-Vivisection Society was valid. The Society was unincorporated[15]. Its main object was to secure the total abolition of vivisection[16]. It consisted of ordinary and life members, and the constitution was laid down in its Rules.

BRIGHTMAN J considered the various ways in which the property of the society could be held, and continued (at p. 538): "Having reached the conclusion that the gift in question is not a gift to the members of the London & Provincial society at the date of death, as joint tenants or tenants in common, so as to entitle a member as of right to a distributive share, nor an attempted gift to present and future members beneficially, and

[14] (1971) 35 Conv (NS) 381 (J. Mummery)

[15] It later merged with The National Anti-Vivisection Society and was incorporated in 1963 as The National Anti-Vivisection Society Ltd.

[16] Which is not charitable. *National Anti-Vivisection Society v IRC* [1948] AC 31, [1947] 2 All ER 217, p. 331, post.

is not a gift in trust for the purposes of the society, I must now consider how otherwise, if at all, it is capable of taking effect.

As I have already mentioned, the rules of the London & Provincial society do not purport to create any trusts except in so far as the honorary trustees are not beneficial owners of the assets of the society, but are trustees upon trust to deal with such assets according to the directions of the committee.

A trust for non-charitable purposes, as distinct from a trust for individuals, is clearly void because there is no beneficiary. It does not, however, follow that persons cannot band themselves together as an association or society, pay subscriptions and validly devote their funds in pursuit of some lawful non-charitable purpose. An obvious example is a members' social club. But it is not essential that the members should only intend to secure direct personal advantages to themselves. The association may be one in which personal advantages to the members are combined with the pursuit of some outside purpose. Or the association may be one which offers no personal benefit at all to the members, the funds of the association being applied exclusively to the pursuit of some outside purpose. Such an association of persons is bound, I would think, to have some sort of constitution; that is to say, the rights and liabilities of the members of the association will inevitably depend on some form of contract inter se, usually evidenced by a set of rules. In the present case it appears to me clear that the life members, the ordinary members and the associate members of the London & Provincial society were bound together by a contract inter se. Any such member was entitled to the rights and subject to the liabilities defined by the rules. If the committee acted contrary to the rules, an individual member would be entitled to take proceedings in the courts to compel observance of the rules or to recover damages for any loss he had suffered as a result of the breach of contract. As and when a member paid his subscription to the association, he would be subjecting his money to the disposition and expenditure thereof laid down by the rules. That is to say, the member would be bound to permit, and entitled to require, the honorary trustees and other members of the society to deal with that subscription in accordance with the lawful directions of the committee. Those directions would include the expenditure of that subscription, as part of the general funds of the association, in furthering the objects of the association. The resultant situation, on analysis, is that the London & Provincial society represented an organisation of individuals bound together by a contract under which their subscriptions became, as it were, mandated towards a certain type of expenditure as adumbrated in rule 1. Just as the two parties to a bi-partite bargain can vary or terminate their contract by mutual assent, so it must follow that the life members, ordinary members and associated members of the London & Provincial society could, at any moment of time, by unanimous agreement (or by majority vote, if the rules so prescribe), vary or terminate their multi-partite contract. There would be no limit to the type of variation or termination to which all might agree. There is no private trust or trust for charitable purposes or other trust to hinder the process. It follows that if all members agreed, they could decide to wind up the London & Provincial society and divide the net assets among themselves beneficially. No one would have any locus standi to stop them so doing. The contract is the same as any other contract and concerns only those who are parties to it, that is to say, the members of the society.

The funds of such an association may, of course, be derived not only from the subscriptions of the contracting parties but also from donations from non-contracting parties and legacies from persons who have died. In the case of a donation which is not accompanied by any words which purport to impose a trust, it seems to me that the gift takes effect in favour of the existing members of the association as an accretion to the funds which are the subject-matter of the contract which such members have made inter se, and falls to be dealt with in precisely the same way as the funds which the members themselves have subscribed. So, in the case of a legacy. In the absence of words which purport to impose a trust, the legacy is a gift to the members beneficially, not as joint tenants or as tenants in common so as to entitle each member to an immediate distributive share, but as an accretion to the funds which are the subject-matter of the contract which the members have made inter se.

In my judgment the legacy in the present case to the London & Provincial society ought to be construed as a legacy of that type, that is to say, a legacy to the members beneficially as an accretion to the funds subject to the contract which they had made inter se. Of course, the testatrix did not intend the members of the society to divide her bounty between themselves, and doubtless she was ignorant of that remote but theoretical possibility. Her knowledge or absence of knowledge of the true legal analysis of the gift is irrelevant. The legacy is accordingly in my view valid, subject only to the effect of the events of January 1, 1957.

A strong argument has been presented to me against this conclusion and I have been taken through most, if not all, of the cases which are referred to in *Leahy's* case, [1959] AC 457, as well as later authorities. It has been urged upon me that if the gift is not a purpose gift, there is no half-way house between, on the one hand, a legacy to the members of the London & Provincial society at the date of death, as joint tenants beneficially, or as tenants in common beneficially, and, on the other hand, a trust for members which is void for perpetuity because no individual member acting by himself can ever obtain his share of the legacy. I do not see why the choice should be confined to these two extremes. If the argument were correct it would be difficult, if not impossible, for a person to make a straightforward donation, whether inter vivos or by will, to a club or other non-charitable association which the donor desires to benefit. This conclusion seems to me contrary to common sense."

QUESTIONS

1. Do you think that the test for certainty laid down in *Re Gulbenkian's Settlements* and *McPhail v Doulton* is sound? How would you formulate the test after reading *Re Baden's Deed Trusts* (*No 2*) [1973] Ch 9, [1972] 2 All ER 1304. See H & M, pp 141, 171.
2. To what extent does a trustee of a discretionary trust run the risk of personal liability if he disposes of the fund without considering a

beneficiary of whom he was unaware? How should he protect himself? H & M, p. 172; (1970) 34 Conv (NS) 287 (F. R. Crane); T.A. 1925, s. 61; p. 622, post.

3. Take as an example any club that you know; or of which you are a member. Then consider who is the legal owner of the land or premises occupied by the club, of any investments held, and of its current bank account. Could each member claim a share now? On the ground that he is a beneficial owner? Or on the basis of a contract? Could each member claim a share of the assets on a dissolution? If so, on what basis? See p. 193, post.

3. The Constitution of Trusts; Volunteers[1]

An express trust only exists where the trust property is vested in the trustee and the terms of the trust have been properly declared. Questions relating to the rules concerning the declaration of trusts have been considered. We are now concerned with the further requirement that the trust property must be vested in the trustee.

I. Transfer of the Trust Property to Trustees[2]

The method of transfer varies with the property in question. A legal estate in land must be transferred by deed[3], stocks and shares by an appropriate form of transfer[4], equitable interests[5] and copyright by writing[6]; chattels by deed of gift or by an intention to give coupled with a delivery of possession[7]; a bill of exchange by indorsement[8]; and various other types of property by their own special procedure. The vesting of the trust property in the trustee *constitutes* the trust. In a completely constituted trust, there is no need for consideration.

MILROY v LORD
(1862) 4 De GF & J 264 (CA in Ch, KNIGHT BRUCE and TURNER LJJ)

The settlor executed a voluntary deed, purporting to transfer fifty shares in the Bank of Louisiana to Samuel Lord to be held on trust for the plaintiffs, and later handed to him the share certificates. At the time, Lord held a general power of attorney, which would have entitled him to transfer the settlor's shares. However the shares could only be transferred by registration of the transferee in the books of the bank, and this was

[1] H & M, pp. 176–198; K & S, pp. 82–89; P & M, pp. 38–51; Pettit, pp. 60–83; Snell, pp. 118–126.
[2] H & M, pp. 179–184; K & S, pp. 82–84; P & M, pp. 38–41; Pettit, pp. 60–64; Snell, pp. 120–122.
[3] L.P.A. 1925, s. 52 (1).
[4] See Companies Act 1948, s. 75, Sch. 1, Table A, paras. 22 and 23; Stock Transfer Act 1963, s. 1.
[5] L.P.A.1925, s. 53 (1), p. 32, ante.
[6] Copyright Act 1956, s. 36 (3).
[7] *Ryall v Rowles* (1750) 1 Ves Sen 348; *Irons v Smallpiece* (1819) 2 B & Ald 551; *Cochrane v Moore* (1890) 25 QBD 57; *Lock v Heath* (1892) 8 TLR 295; *Kilpin v Raltey* [1892] 1 QB 582; *Re Cole* [1964] Ch 175, [1963] 3 All ER 433; (1964) 27 MLR 357 (A. C. Diamond); see also [1953] CLJ 355 (J. W. A. Thornely).
[8] Bills of Exchange Act 1882, s. 31; *Whistler v Forster* (1863) 14 CBNS 248; see, however, Cheques Act 1957, ss. 1, 2.

never done. The question was whether a trust of the shares had been created in favour of the plaintiffs.

Held (reversing STUART V-C). No trust existed.

TURNER LJ: Under the circumstances of this case, it would be difficult not to feel a strong disposition to give effect to this settlement to the fullest extent, and certainly I spared no pains to find the means of doing so, consistently with what I apprehend to be the law of the Court; but, after full and anxious consideration, I find myself unable to do so. I take the law of this Court to be well settled, that, in order to render a voluntary settlement valid and effectual, the settlor must have done everything which, according to the nature of the property comprised in the settlement, was necessary to be done in order to transfer the property and render the settlement binding upon him. He may of course do this by actually transferring the property to the persons for whom he intends to provide, and the provision will then be effectual, and it will be equally effectual if he transfers the property to a trustee for the purposes of the settlement, or declares that he himself holds it in trust for those purposes; and if the property be personal, the trust may, as I apprehend, be declared either in writing or by parol; but, in order to render the settlement binding, one or other of these modes must, as I understand the law of this Court, be resorted to, for there is no equity in this Court to perfect an imperfect gift. The cases I think go further to this extent, that if the settlement is intended to be effectuated by one of the modes to which I have referred, the Court will not give effect to it by applying another of those modes. If it is intended to take effect by transfer, the Court will not hold the intended transfer to operate as a declaration of trust, for then every imperfect instrument would be made effectual by being converted into a perfect trust. These are the principles by which, as I conceive, this case must be tried.

Applying, then, these principles to the case, there is not here any transfer either of the one class of shares or of the other to the objects of the settlement, and the question therefore must be, whether a valid and effectual trust in favour of those objects was created in the defendant *Samuel Lord* or in the settlor himself as to all or any of these shares. Now it is plain that it was not the purpose of this settlement, or the intention of the settlor, to constitute himself a trustee of the bank shares. The intention was that the trust should be vested in the defendant *Samuel Lord*, and I think therefore that we should not be justified in holding that by the settlement, or by any parol declaration made by the settlor, he himself became a trustee of these shares for the purposes of the settlement. By doing so we should be converting the settlement or the parol declaration to a purpose wholly different from that which was intended to be effected by it, and, as I have said, creating a perfect trust out of an imperfect transaction . . . .

The more difficult question is, whether the Defendant *Samuel Lord* did not become a trustee of these shares? Upon this question I have felt considerable doubt; but in the result, I have come to the conclusion that no perfect trust was ever created in him. The shares, it is clear, were never legally vested in him; and the only ground on which he can be held to have become a trustee of them is, that he held a power of attorney under which he might have transferred them into his own name; but he held that power of attorney as the agent of the settlor; and if he had been sued by the Plaintiffs as trustee of the settlement for an account under the trust, and to compel him to transfer the shares into his own name as trustee, I think he might well have said—These shares are not vested in me; I have no power over them except as the agent of the settlor, and without his express directions I cannot be justified in making the proposed transfer, in converting an intended into an actual settlement. A Court of Equity could not, I think, decree the agent of the settlor to make the transfer, unless it could decree the settlor himself to do so, and it is plain that no such decree could have been made against the settlor. In my opinion, therefore, this decree cannot be maintained as to the fifty *Louisiana Bank* shares.

In *Paul v Paul* ((1882) 20 ChD 742) property was settled, in a marriage settlement, upon the spouses successively for life, with remainder to the children of the marriage. If there were no children of the marriage, the wife took absolutely on surviving the husband; and, if she died in his lifetime, she was given a power to appoint by will, and in default of appointment, the property passed to the wife's next of kin excluding the husband.

There were no children of the marriage. The spouses asked that the capital of the fund should be paid to them because the only persons who had any interest therein were the next of kin who were volunteers, and whose interest the wife could defeat by exercising her power of appointment, or by surviving her husband.

The Court of Appeal refused the application. The funds were settled. The trust in favour of the next of kin was constituted. It was immaterial that they were volunteers.

In *Re Bowden* ([1936] Ch 71)[9] a settlor, by a voluntary settlement executed in 1868, prior to becoming a nun, purported to convey to trustees all the property to which she might become entitled under her father's will. This could not create a trust, because there was no existing trust property[10]. However, the settlor's father died in 1869, and, during the next five years, the settlor's share of her father's estate was transferred to the trustees. In 1935, the settlor requested the trustees to return to her the funds then representing the property. BENNETT J. refused. The property had been effectively settled, and was held upon the trusts of the settlement.

RE RALLI'S WILL TRUSTS

[1964] Ch 288, [1963] 3 All ER 940 (ChD, BUCKLEY J)

A testator, who died in 1899, left his residuary estate on trust for his wife for life, and then for his daughters, Helen and Irene absolutely.

[9] See also *Re Adlard* [1954] Ch 29, [1953] 2 All ER 1437 (convenant to settle).

[10] See pp. 98–104, post. *Re Ellenborough* [1903] 1 Ch 697.

Helen, by her marriage settlement, covenanted to settle after-acquired property in favour, in the events which happened, of the children of Irene. On the death of Helen and of the testator's widow, the plaintiff, who was Irene's husband, was sole surviving trustee, both of the will trusts and of the marriage settlement; and Helen's share of the residuary estate was thus vested in him. The question was whether the plaintiff held it on trust for those interested under Helen's will, or on the trusts of Helen's marriage settlement.

Held. The plaintiff held Helen's share upon the trusts of the marriage settlement. The property was vested in the trustee of the marriage settlement, and it made no difference that it came to him in his capacity as trustee of the will trusts.

BUCKLEY J: The investments representing the share of residue in question, which I shall call "the fund", stand in the name of the plaintiff. This is because he is now the sole surviving trustee of the testator's will. Therefore, say the defendants, he holds the fund primarily on the trusts of the will, that is to say, in trust for them as part of Helen's estate. The plaintiff is, however, also the sole surviving covenantee under clause 7 of the settlement as well as the sole surviving trustee of that settlement. This, however, affords him no answer, say the defendants, to their claim under the will unless the plaintiff, having transferred the fund to them in pursuance of the trusts of the will, could compel them to return it in pursuance of their obligation under the covenant, and this, they say, he could not do. In support of this last contention they rely on *Re Plumptre's Marriage Settlement* ([1910] 1 Ch 609), *Re Pryce* ([1917] 1 Ch 234) and *Re Kay's Settlement* ([1939] Ch 329, [1939] 1 All ER 245).

The plaintiff, on the other hand, contends that, as he already holds the fund, no question of his having to enforce the covenant arises. The fund, having come without impropriety into his hands, is now, he says, impressed in his hands with the trusts upon which he ought to hold it under the settlement; and because of the covenant it does not lie in the mouth of the defendants to say that he should hold the fund in trust for Helen's estate. He relies on *Re Bowden* ([1936] Ch 71)[11] . . . The plaintiff also relies on *Re Adlard* ([1954] Ch 29, [1953] 2 All ER 1437), where Vaisey J followed *Re Bowden*, and on the observations of Upjohn J in *Re Burton's Settlements* ([1955] Ch 82 at 104, [1954] 3 All ER 193).

Mr. Goff for the defendants says that *Re Bowden* and *Re Adlard* are distinguishable from the present case because in each of those cases the fund had reached the hands of the trustees of the relevant settlement and was held by them in that capacity, whereas in the present case the fund is, as he maintains, in the hands of the plaintiff in the capacity of trustee of the will and not in the capacity of trustee of the settlement. He says that *Re Burton's Settlements*, the complicated facts of which I forbear to set out here, should be distinguished on the ground that, when the settlement there in question was made, the trustee of that settlement and the trustee of the settlement under which the settlor had expectations was the same, so that the settlor by her settlement gave directions to the trustee of the

[11] See p. 77, ante.

settlement under which she had expectations, who then already held the relevant fund.

Sir Milner Holland, for the plaintiff, says that the capacity in which the trustee has become possessed of the fund is irrelevant. Thus in *Strong v Bird* ((1874) LR 18 Eq 315) an imperfect gift was held to be completed by the donee obtaining probate of the donor's will of which he was executor, notwithstanding that the donor died intestate as to her residue and that the donee was not a person entitled as on her intestacy. Similarly in *Re James* ([1935] Ch 449) a grant of administration to two administrators was held to perfect an imperfect gift by the intestate to one of them, who had no beneficial interest in the intestate's estate.

In my judgment the circumstance that the plaintiff holds the fund because he was appointed a trustee of the will is irrelevant. He is at law the owner of the fund, and the means by which he became so have no effect upon the quality of his legal ownership. The question is: For whom, if anyone, does he hold the fund in equity? In other words, who can successfully assert an equity against him disentitling him to stand upon his legal right? It seems to me to be indisputable that Helen, if she were alive, could not do so, for she has solemnly covenanted under seal to assign the fund to the plaintiff, and the defendants can stand in no better position. It is, of course, true that the object of the covenant was not that the plaintiff should retain the property for his own benefit, but that he should hold it on the trusts of the settlement. It is also true that, if it were necessary to enforce performance of the covenant, equity would not assist the beneficiaries under the settlement, because they are mere volunteers; and that for the same reason the plaintiff, as trustee of the settlement, would not be bound to enforce the covenant and would not be constrained by the court to do so, and indeed, it seems, might be constrained by the court not to do so. As matters stand, however, there is no occasion to invoke the assistance of equity to enforce the performance of the covenant. It is for the defendants to invoke the assistance of equity to make good their claim to the fund. To do so successfully they must show that the plaintiff cannot conscientiously withhold it from them. When they seek to do this, he can point to the covenant which, in my judgment, relieves him from any fiduciary obligation he would otherwise owe to the defendants as Helen's representatives. In so doing the plaintiff is not seeking to enforce an equitable remedy against the defendants on behalf of persons who could not enforce such a remedy themselves: he is relying upon the combined effect of his legal ownership of the fund and his rights under the covenant. That an action on the covenant might be statute-barred is irrelevant, for there is no occasion for such an action.

Buckley J also held that a clause in the settlement providing that "all the property comprised within the terms of [the covenant] shall become subject in equity to the settlement hereby covenanted to be made thereof" had the effect of imposing a trust independently of the vesting of the property in the trustee. It is difficult, however, to see that the provision could be more than a future declaration of a trust of unascertained property, and therefore void. See *Re Anstis* (1886) 31 ChD 596.

RE ROSE[12]

[1952] Ch 499, [1952] 1 All ER 1217 (CA, EVERSHED MR, JENKINS and MORRIS LJJ)

On March 30, 1943 the settlor made two transfers of shares in an unlimited company in the form required by its Articles of Association. The directors of the company could, under the Articles, refuse, at their discretion, to register a transfer. The transfers were registered on June 30, 1943. The settlor died at a time at which estate duty would be payable on the shares if the effective date of the transfer was June 30, but not if it was March 30. The Crown claimed the duty.

Held (affirming ROXBURGH J). No duty payable. The settlor had done everything in his power to effect the transfer.

EVERSHED MR: The burden of the case presented by the Crown may be briefly put as it was formulated in reply by Mr. Pennycuick. This document, he said, on the face of it, was intended to operate and operated, if it operated at all, as a transfer. If for any reason it was at its date incapable of so operating, it is not legitimate, either by reference to the expressed intention in the document or on well-established principles of law, to extract from it a wholly different transaction—that is, to make it take effect not as a transfer but as a declaration of trust. Now I agree that on the face of the document it was obviously intended (if you take the words used) to operate and operate immediately as a transfer—"I do hereby transfer to the transferee" these shares "to hold unto the said transferee, subject to the several conditions on which I held the same at the time of the execution hereof". It plainly was intended to operate immediately as a transfer of rights. To some extent at least, it is said, it could not possibly do so. To revert to the illustration which has throughout been taken, if the company had declared a dividend during this interregnum, it is not open to question that the company must have paid that dividend to the deceased. So that vis-à-vis the company, this document did not, and could not, operate to transfer to Mrs. Rose the right against the company to claim and receive that dividend. Shares, Mr. Pennycuick says, are property of a peculiar character consisting, as it is sometimes put, of a bundle of rights—that is, rights against or in the company. It has followed from his argument that if such a dividend had been paid, the deceased could, consistently with the document to which he has set his hand and seal, have retained that dividend, and, if he had handed it over to his wife, it would have been an independent gift. I think myself that such a conclusion is startling. Indeed, I venture to doubt whether to anybody but a lawyer such a conclusion would even be comprehensible—at least without a considerable amount of explanation. That again is not conclusive; but I confess that I approach a matter of this kind with a pre-conceived notion that a conclusion that offends common sense, so much as this would prima facie do, ought not to be the right conclusion.

[His Lordship examined *Milroy v Lord* in detail, and referred to the dictum of TURNER LJ which is reprinted above at p. 76.]

Those last few sentences form the gist of the Crown's argument and

[12] (1976) 40 Conv (NS) 139 (L. McKay).

on it is founded the broad, general proposition that if a document is expressed as, and on the face of it intended to operate as, a transfer, it cannot in any respect take effect by way of trust—so far I understand the argument to go. In my judgment, that statement is too broad and involves too great a simplification of the problem; and is not warranted by authority. I agree that if a man purporting to transfer property executes documents which are not apt to effect that purpose, the court cannot then extract from those documents some quite different transaction and say that they were intended merely to operate as a declaration of trust, which ex facie they were not: but if a document is apt and proper to transfer the property—is in truth the appropriate way in which the property must be transferred—then it does not seem to me to follow from the statement of Turner LJ that, as a result, either during some limited period or otherwise, a trust may not arise, for the purpose of giving effect to the transfer. The simplest case will, perhaps, provide an illustration. If a man executes a document transferring all his equitable interest, say, in shares, that document, operating, and intended to operate, as a transfer, will give rise to and take effect as a trust; for the assignor will then be a trustee of the legal estate in the shares for the person in whose favour he has made an assignment of his beneficial interest. And, for my part, I do not think that the case of *Milroy v Lord* ((1862) 4 De GF & J 264) is an authority which compels this court to hold that in this case —where, in the terms of Turner LJ's judgment, the settlor did everything which, according to the nature of the property comprised in the settlement, was necessary to be done by him in order to transfer the property—the result necessarily negatives the conclusion that, pending registration, the settlor was a trustee of the legal interest for the transferee.

The view of the limitations of *Milroy v Lord*, which I have tried to express, was much better expressed by Jenkins J in the recent case which also bears the same name of *Re Rose* ([1949] Ch 78, [1948] 2 All ER 971) (though that is a coincidence). It is true that the main point, the essential question to be determined, was whether there had been a transfer eo nomine of certain shares within the meaning of a will. The testator in that case, Rose, by his will had given a number of shares to one Hook but the gift was subject to this qualification, "if such shares have not been transferred to him previously to my death". The question was, had the shares been transferred to him in these circumstances? He had executed (as had this Mr. Rose) a transfer in appropriate form and handed the transfer and the certificate to Hook; but, at the time of his death, the transfer had not been registered. It was said, therefore, that there had been no transfer; and (following Mr. Pennycuick's argument) there had been no passing to Hook of any interest, legal or beneficial, whatever, by the time the testator died. If that view were right then, of course, Hook would be entitled to the shares under the will. But my brother went a little more closely into the matter, because it was obvious that on one view of it, if it were held that there was a "transfer" within the terms of the will, though the transfer was inoperative in the eye of the law and not capable of being completed after the death, then Mr. Hook suffered the misfortune of getting the shares neither by gift inter vivos nor by testamentary benefaction.

Therefore, my brother considered the case of *Milroy v Lord*, and in regard to it he used this language ([1949] Ch 78 at 89); "I was referred on that to the well known case of *Milroy v Lord*, and also to the recent case of *Re Fry* ([1946] Ch 312, [1946] 2 All ER 106). Those cases, as I understand them, turn on the fact that the deceased donor had not done all in his power, according to the nature of the property given, to vest the legal interest in the property in the donee. In such circumstances it is, of course, well settled that there is no equity to complete the imperfect gift. If any act remained to be done by the donor to complete the gift at the date of the donor's death the court will not compel his personal representatives to do that act and the gift remains incomplete and fails. In *Milroy v Lord* the imperfection was due to the fact that the wrong form of transfer was used for the purpose of transferring certain bank shares. The document was not the appropriate document to pass any interest in the property at all." Then he refers to *Re Fry*, which is another illustration. "In this case, as I understand it, the testator had done everything in his power to divest himself of the shares in question to Mr. Hook. He had executed a transfer. It is not suggested that the transfer was not in accordance with the company's regulations. He had handed that transfer together with the certificate to Mr. Hook. There was nothing else the testator could do." I venture respectfully to adopt the whole of the passage I have read which, in my judgment, is a correct statement of the law. If that be so, then it seems to me that it cannot be asserted on the authority of *Milroy v Lord*, and I venture to think it also cannot be asserted as a matter of logic and good sense or principle, that because, by the regulations of the company, there had to be a gap before Mrs. Rose could, as between herself and the company, claim the rights which the shares gave her vis-à-vis the company, the deceased was not in the meantime a trustee for her of all his rights and benefits under the shares. That he intended to pass all those rights, as I have said, seems to me too plain for argument. I think the matter might be put perhaps in a somewhat different fashion, though it reaches the same end. Whatever might be the position during the period between the execution of this document and the registration of the shares, the transfers were on June 30, 1943, registered. After registration, the title of Mrs. Rose was beyond doubt complete in every respect; and if the deceased had received a dividend between execution and registration and Mrs. Rose had claimed to have that dividend handed to her, what would have been the deceased's answer? It could no longer be that the purported gift was imperfect; it had been made perfect. I am not suggesting that the perfection was retroactive. But what else could he say? How could he, in the face of his own statement under seal, deny the proposition that he had, on March 30, 1943, transferred the shares to his wife?—and by the phrase "transfer the shares" surely must be meant transfer to her "the shares and all my right title and interest thereunder." Nothing else could sensibly have been meant. Nor can he, I think, make much of the fact that this was a voluntary settlement on his part. Being a case of an unlimited company, as I have said, Mrs. Rose had herself to undertake by covenant to accept the shares subject to their burdens—in other words, to relieve the deceased of his liability as a corporator. I find it unnecessary to pursue the question of consideration, but it is, I think, another feature which would make exceedingly difficult and, sensibly impossible, the assertion on the deceased's part of any right to retain any such dividend. Nor is the Crown's argument made any easier by the circumstance that another emanation of the Crown has adjudicated that stamp duty ad valorem under section 74 of the Act of 1910 was payable upon this transfer as a disposition of the subject-matter transferred.

II. Declaration of Self as Trustee[13]

If the settlor declares himself trustee, there is no problem of constitution of the trust. The property is already vested in the settlor. The problem in this context relates to the *declaration* of the trust. "Men often mean to give things to their kinsfolk, they do not often mean to constitute themselves trustees."[14] It is necessary to show that the settlor manifested an intention to declare himself trustee. Nothing else will do. An intention to give will not be construed as an intention to declare himself trustee. "An imperfect gift is no declaration of trust."[14]

JONES v LOCK
(1865) LR 1 Ch App 25 (CA in Ch, Lord Cranworth LC)

On returning from a business visit to Birmingham, Robert Jones was reproved by his family for not bringing a present for his baby son. He produced a cheque for £900, and said: "Look you here, I give this to baby; it is for himself, and I am going to put it away for him, and will give him a great deal more along with it." He placed the cheque in the baby's hand. His wife feared that the baby might tear it, and Jones added: "Never mind if he does; it is his own, and he may do what he likes with it." He then took the cheque back and locked it in the safe. Six days later he died. The question was whether the baby was entitled to the cheque.

Held. There had been no gift to the baby, and no declaration of trust in his favour.

Lord Cranworth LC: This is a special case, in which I regret to say that I cannot bring myself to think that, either on principle or on authority, there has been any gift or any valid declaration of trust. No doubt a gift may be made by any person *sui juris* and *compos mentis*, by conveyance of a real estate or by delivery of a chattel; and there is no doubt also that, by some decisions, unfortunate I must think them, a parol declaration of trust of personalty may be perfectly valid even when voluntary. If I give any chattel that, of course, passes by delivery, and if I say, expressly or impliedly, that I constitute myself a trustee of personalty, that is a trust executed, and capable of being enforced without consideration. I do not think it necessary to go into any of the authorities cited before me; they all turn upon the question, whether what has been said was a declaration of trust or an imperfect gift. In the latter case the parties

13 H & M, pp. 183–184; K & S, pp. 85; P & M, pp. 41–42; Pettit, p. 63; Snell, p. 122.
14 Maitland, *Equity* (2nd Edn) p. 72.

would receive no aid from a Court of equity if they claimed as volunteers. But when there has been a declaration of trust, then it will be enforced, whether there has been consideration or not. Therefore the question in each case is one of fact; has there been a gift or not, or has there been a declaration of trust or not? I should have every inclination to sustain this gift, but unfortunately I am unable to do so; the case turns on the very short question whether *Jones* intended to make a declaration that he held the property in trust for the child; and I cannot come to any other conclusion than that he did not. I think it would be of very dangerous example if loose conversations of this sort, in important transactions of this kind, should have the effect of declarations of trust.

[His Lordship then commented on the evidence, and said that no doubt it was a fair representation of what actually took place, and that the father really had an intention of settling something on the child, and that his giving the note to the child was symbolical of what he meant to do; but it was not his meaning to enable the child, by his next friend, to bring an action of trover for the cheque or file a bill for the £900, but he merely meant to say that now he could make a provision for the boy; and what he said to the solicitor was quite consistent with it.]

It was all quite natural, but the testator would have been very much surprised if he had been told that he had parted with the £900, and could no longer dispose of it. It all turns upon the facts, which do not lead me to the conclusion that the testator meant to deprive himself of all property in the note, or to declare himself a trustee of the money for the child. I extremely regret this result, because it is obvious that, by the act of God, this unfortunate child has been deprived of a provision which his father meant to make for him.

RICHARDS v DELBRIDGE
(1874) LR 18 Eq 11 (Chancery, Sir George JESSEL MR)

John Delbridge was tenant of premises where he carried on business as a bone manure merchant. He was assisted by Edward Bennetto Richards, who was his infant grandson. Shortly before Delbridge's death, he indorsed on the lease, and signed the following memorandum: "This deed and all thereto belonging I give to *Edward Bennetto Richards* from this time forth, with all the stock-in-trade." He delivered the document to Richard's mother to hold for him. The question was whether, on Delbridge's death, the lease and business passed to Richards, or whether it passed under the will.

Held. It passed under the will. There was no conveyance to, or declaration of trust in favour of, Richards.

SIR GEORGE JESSEL MR: The principle is a very simple one. A man may transfer his property, without valuable consideration, in one of two ways: he may either do such acts as amount in law to a conveyance or assignment of the property, and thus completely divest himself of the legal ownership, in which case the person who by those acts acquires the property takes it beneficially, or on trust, as the case may be; or the legal owner of the property may, by one or other of the modes recognised as amounting to a valid declaration of trust, constitute himself a trustee, and, without an actual transfer of the legal title, may so deal with the property as to deprive himself of its beneficial ownership, and declare that he will hold it from that time forward on trust for the other person. It is true he need not use the words, "I declare myself a trustee," but he must do something which is equivalent to it, and use expressions which have that meaning; for, however anxious the Court may be to carry out a man's intention, it is not at liberty to construe words otherwise than according to their proper meaning. . . .

The true distinction appears to me to be plain, and beyond dispute: for a man to make himself a trustee there must be an expression of intention to become a trustee, whereas words of present gift shew an intention to give over property to another, and not retain it in the donor's own hands for any purpose, fiduciary or otherwise.

In *Milroy v Lord* ((1862) 4 De GF & J 264 at 274) Lord Justice *Turner*, after referring to the two modes of making a voluntary settlement valid and effectual, adds these words: "The cases, I think, go further, to this extent, that if the settlement is intended to be effectuated by one of the modes to which I have referred, the Court will not give effect to it by applying another of those modes. If it is intended to take effect by transfer, the Court will not hold the intended transfer to operate as a declaration of trust, for then every imperfect instrument would be made effectual by being converted into a perfect trust."

In *Middleton v Pollock* ((1876) 2 ChD 104)[15] Mr. Pollock, a solicitor, received money for investment from various clients. The money was so intermingled that it was impossible to trace that invested by each client. Pollock died heavily insolvent.

Before his death, he made declarations of trust in favour of selected clients, mostly relatives and friends. The one selected for trial as a representative case was that of a relative, Miss Elliott.

Miss Elliott's money had never been invested. Before he died, Pollock indorsed a bill of exchange in her favour, and signed a declaration that he held certain leaseholds on trust for her to secure the repayment to her of the money owed, plus interest. Miss Elliott knew nothing of this. The question was whether Miss Elliott (and the others similarly placed) was entitled to the property in preference to the general creditors. Sir George JESSEL MR held that she was; as there had been a valid declaration of trust in favour of Miss Elliott. The trust could not be avoided as a fraudulent preference under 13 Eliz. c. 5[16], as it was made bona fide and for valuable consideration.

In *Paul v Constance* ([1977] 1 WLR 527, [1977] 1 All ER 195) Mr. Constance was separated from his wife and lived with the plaintiff. He

[15] *Gee v Liddell* (1866) 35 Beav 621.
[16] See p. 137, post.

received £950 as damages resulting from an injury at work, and he and the plaintiff decided to put it into a deposit account at Lloyds Bank.

Because of the embarrassment which would be caused by having an account in two different names, the account was opened in Mr. Constance's name only. He indicated on various occasions that he wished it to be hers as much as his. On his death, Mrs. Constance claimed the deposit as part of her husband's estate. The plaintiff sought a declaration that the deposit was held on trust for her.

In finding for the plaintiff, SCARMAN LJ, after referring to *Jones v Lock*[17] and *Richards v Delbridge*[18], said at p. 531: "There is no suggestion of a gift by transfer in the present case. The facts of the two cases do not, therefore, very much help the submission of Mr. Blythe but he was able to extract from them this principle: that there must be a clear declaration of trust and that means there must be clear evidence from what is said or done of an intention to create a trust—or, as Mr. Blythe put it, 'an intention to dispose of a property or a fund so that somebody else to the exclusion of the disponent acquires the beneficial interest in it'. He submitted that there was no such evidence.

When one looks at the detailed evidence to see whether it goes as far as that—and I think that the evidence does have to go as far as that—one finds that from the time that the deceased received his damages right up to his death he was saying, on occasions, that the money was as much the plaintiff's as his. When they discussed the damages, how to invest them or what to do with them and when they discussed the bank account, he would say to her: 'The money is as much yours as mine'.

The judge, rightly treating the basic problem in the case as a question of fact, reached this conclusion. He said: 'I have read through my notes and I am quite satisfied that it was the intention of Mrs. Paul and Mr. Constance to create a trust in which both of them were interested.'

In this court the issue becomes: was there sufficient evidence to justify the judge in reaching that conclusion of fact? In submitting that there was, Mr. Wilson draws attention first and foremost to the words used. When one bears in mind the unsophisticated character of the deceased and his relationship with the plaintiff during the last few years of his life, Mr. Wilson submits that the words that he did use on more than one occasion, 'This money is as much yours as mine', convey clearly a present declaration that the existing fund was as much the plaintiff's as his own. The judge accepted that conclusion. I think that he was well justified in doing so and, indeed, I think that he was right to do so.

It might, however, be thought that this was a borderline case, since it is not easy to pin-point a specific moment of declaration, and one must exclude from one's mind any case built upon the existence of an implied or constructive trust, for this case was put forward at the trial and is now argued by the plaintiff as one of express declaration of trust. It was so pleaded and it is only as such that it may be considered in this court. The question, therefore, is whether, in all the circumstances, the use of those words on numerous occasions as between the deceased and the plaintiff

[17] (1865) 1 Ch App 25, p. 83, ante.
[18] (1874) LR 18 Eq 11, p. 84, ante.

constituted an express declaration of trust. The judge found that they did. For myself, I think that he was right so to find. I therefore would dismiss the appeal."

III. Covenants to Settle[19]

A. Unenforceable by Volunteers

Where there is no settlement, but only a covenant to settle, consideration becomes material. Persons who have given consideration (including those within the marriage consideration) may enforce a covenant. Volunteers may not.

The question commonly arises in connection with family settlements; either where the covenantor has failed to comply with a covenant to establish a settlement, or where a spouse, being a beneficiary under a marriage settlement, covenants to settle after-acquired property and fails to do so. Some writers are critical of the law which leaves covenants unenforceable by volunteers. Various suggestions have been made for overcoming it, and these will be considered.

PULLAN v KOE[20]
[1913] 1 Ch 9 (ChD, SWINFEN EADY J)

A marriage settlement dated May 1859 contained a provision that the wife should settle after-acquired property of the value of £100 or upwards.

In 1879, she received a present of £285 from her mother. The money was paid into her husband's bank account, on which she had power to draw. Part was then invested in Cape of Good Hope bearer bonds or debentures; and the interest paid to the account. The bonds remained at the bank.

In 1909, the husband died. The trustees of the settlement, acting on behalf of the wife and children claimed the bonds from the husband's executor. The defendants relied on the Statutes of Limitation.

Held. The trustees succeeded. The £285 was subject to a trust in favour of those within the marriage consideration, and was now represented by the bonds.

SWINFEN EADY J: It was contended that the bonds never in fact became trust property, as both the wife and husband were only liable in damages for breach of covenant, and that the case was different from cases where property which has once admittedly become subject to the trusts of an instrument has been improperly dealt with, and is sought to be recovered. In my opinion as soon as the 285*l*. was paid to the wife it became in equity

[19] H & M, pp. 185–193; K & S, pp. 84–89; P & M, pp. 42–47; Pettit, pp. 64–74; Snell, pp. 124–126. See also (1960) 76 LQR 100 (D. W. Elliott); (1962) 78 LQR 228 (J. A. Hornby); [1965] 23 CLJ 46 (G. H. Jones); (1966) 29 MLR 397 (D. Matheson); [1967] ASCL 387 (J. D. Davies); (1969) 85 LQR 213 (W. A. Lee); (1975) 91 L.Q.R. 236 (J. L. Barton); (1976) 92 LQR 427 (R. P. Meagher and J. R. F. Lehane); *Perspectives of Law*, p. 240 (R. H. Maudsley).

[20] *Re D'Angibau* (1880) 15 ChD 228; *Re Plumptre's Marriage Settlement* [1910] 1 Ch 609; *Re Cook's Settlement Trusts* [1965] Ch 902, [1964] 3 All ER 898, p. 91, post; cf. *Paul v Paul* (1882) 20 ChD 742.

bound by and subject to the trusts of the settlement. The trustees could have claimed that particular sum, could have obtained at once the appointment of a receiver of it, if they could have shewn a case of jeopardy, and, if it had been invested and the investment could be traced, could have followed the money and claimed the investment.

This point was dealt with by Jessel MR in *Smith v Lucas* ((1881) ChD 531 at 543), where he said: "What is the effect of such a covenant in equity? It has been said that the effect in equity of the covenant of the wife, as far as she is concerned, is that it does not affect her personally, but that it binds the property: that is to say, it binds the property under the doctrine of equity that that is to be considered as done which ought to be done. That is in the nature of specific performance of the contract no doubt. If, therefore, this is a covenant to settle the future-acquired property of the wife, and nothing more is done by her, the covenant will bind the property."

Again in *Collyer v Isaacs* ((1881) ChD 342 at 351) Jessel MR said: "A man can contract to assign property which is to come into existence in the future, and when it has come into existence, equity, treating as done that which ought to be done, fastens upon that property, and the contract to assign thus becomes a complete assignment. If a person contract for value, e.g., in his marriage settlement, to settle all such real estate as his father shall leave him by will, or purports actually to convey by the deed all such real estate, the effect is the same. It is a contract for value which will bind the property if the father leaves any property to his son."

The property being thus bound, these bonds became trust property, and can be followed by the trustees and claimed from a volunteer.

Again the trustees are entitled to come into a Court of Equity to enforce a contract to create a trust, contained in a marriage settlement, for the benefit of the wife and the issue of the marriage, all of whom are within the marriage consideration. The husband covenanted that he and his heirs, executors, and administrators should, as soon as circumstances would admit, convey, assign, and surrender to the trustees the real or personal property to which his wife should become beneficially entitled. The trustees are entitled to have that covenant specifically enforced by a Court of Equity. In *Re D'Angibau* ((1880) 15 ChD 228 at 242) and in *Re Plumptre's Marriage Settlement* ([1910] 1 Ch 609 at 616) it was held that the Court would not interfere in favour of volunteers, not within the marriage consideration, but here the plaintiffs are the contracting parties and the object of the proceeding is to benefit the wife and issue of the marriage.

RE KAY'S SETTLEMENT

[1939] Ch 329, [1939] 1 All ER 245 (ChD, Simonds J)

In 1907 Mary Winifred Kay, a spinster, executed a voluntary conveyance in favour of herself for life and after her death for her issue, containing a covenant to settle after-acquired property. She married and had three children and became entitled to other property. She refused a request by the trustees of the settlement to bring in the property on the ground that, as the settlement was purely voluntary, they ought not to take steps to enforce the covenant or to recover damages.

Held. Trustees directed not to take any such steps.

SIMONDS J: The trustees have issued this summons, making as parties to it, first, the settlor herself and, secondly, her infant children, who are beneficiaries under the settlement. But, be it observed, though beneficiaries, her children are, for the purpose of this settlement, to be regarded as volunteers, there being no marriage consideration, which would have entitled them to sue, though they are parties to this application. The trustees ask whether, in the event which has happened of the settlor having become entitled to certain property, they should take proceedings against her to compel performance of the covenant or to recover damages on her failure to implement it. . . . The settlor has appeared by Mr. Evershed and has contended, as she was entitled to contend, that the only question before the Court was whether the trustees ought to be directed to take such proceedings; that is to say, she contended that the only question before the Court was precisely that question which Eve J had to deal with in *Re Pryce* ([1917] 1 Ch 234). She has said that the question before me is not primarily whether, if she were sued, such an action would succeed (as to which she might have a defence, I know not what), but whether, in the circumstances as they are stated to the Court, the trustees ought to be directed to take proceedings against her.

As to that, the argument before me has been, on behalf of the children of the marriage, beneficiaries under the settlement, that, although it is conceded that the trustees could not successfully take proceedings for specific performance of the agreements contained in the settlement, yet they could successfully, and ought to be directed to, take proceedings at law to recover damages for the non-observance of the agreements contained in the settlement. . . . In the circumstances I must say that I felt considerable sympathy for the argument which was put before me by Mr. Winterbotham on behalf of the children, that there was, at any rate, on the evidence before the Court to-day, no reason why the trustees should not be directed to take proceedings to recover what damages might be recoverable at law for breach of the agreements entered into by the settlor in her settlement. But on a consideration of *Re Pryce* it seemed to me that so far as this Court was concerned the matter was concluded and that I ought not to give any directions to the trustees to take the suggested proceedings.

In *Re Pryce* the circumstances appear to me to have been in no wise different from those which obtain in the case which I have to consider. In that case there was a marriage settlement made in 1887. It contained a covenant to settle the wife's after-acquired property. . . .

[His Lordship set out the after-acquired property and continued:] The husband died in 1907, and there was no issue of the marriage. Subject to his widow's life interest in both funds, the ultimate residue of the wife's fund was held in trust for her statutory next of kin, and the husband's fund was held in trust for him absolutely. The widow was also tenant for life under her husband's will. The trustees of the marriage settlement in that case took out a summons "to have it determined whether these interests and funds were caught by the provisions of the settlement, and, if so, whether they should take proceedings to enforce them". . . .

Eve J, in a considered judgment, held that although the interests to which I have referred were caught by the covenant of the wife and the agreement by the husband respectively, yet the trustees ought not to take any steps to recover any of them. In the case of the wife's fund he said that her next of kin were volunteers, who could neither maintain an action to enforce the covenant nor for damages for breach of it, and that the Court would not give them by indirect means what they could not obtain by direct procedure; therefore he declined to direct the trustees to take proceedings either to have the covenant specifically enforced or to recover damages at law. The learned judge, as I have said, took time to consider his judgment. Many of the cases which have been cited to me, though not all of them apparently, were cited to him, and after deciding that no steps should be taken to enforce specific performance of the covenant he used these words ([1971] 1 Ch at 214): "The position of the wife's fund is somewhat different, in that her next of kin would be entitled to it on her death; but they are volunteers, and although the Court would probably compel fulfilment of the contract to settle at the instance of any persons within the marriage consideration—see per Cotton LJ in *Re D'Angibau* ((1880) 15 ChD 228 at 242)—and in their favour will treat the outstanding property as subjected to an enforceable trust—*Pullan v Koe* ([1913] 1 Ch 9)—'volunteers have no right whatever to obtain specific performance of a mere covenant which has remained as a covenant and has never been performed'; see per James LJ in *Re D'Angibau* (at p. 246). Nor could damages be awarded either in this Court, or, I apprehend, at law, where, since the Judicature Act, 1873, the same defences would be available to the defendant as would be raised in an action brought in this Court for specific performance or damages."

That is the exact point which has been urged on me with great insistence by Mr. Winterbotham. Whatever sympathy I might feel for his argument, I am not justified in departing in any way from this decision, which is now twenty-one years old. The learned judge went on: "In these circumstances, seeing that the next of kin could neither maintain an action to enforce the covenant nor for damages for breach of it, and that the settlement is not a declaration of trust constituting the relationship of trustee and cestui que trust between the defendant and the next of kin, in which case effect could be given to the trusts even in favour of volunteers, but is a mere voluntary contract to create a trust, ought the Court now for the sole benefit of these volunteers to direct the trustees to take proceedings to enforce the defendant's covenant? I think it ought not; to do so would be to give the next of kin by indirect means relief they cannot obtain by any direct procedure, and would in effect be enforcing the settlement as against the defendant's legal right to payment and transfer from the trustees of the parents' marriage settlement." It is true that in those last words the learned judge does not specifically refer to an action for damages, but it is clear that he has in his mind directions both with regard to an action for specific performance and an action to recover damages at law—or, now, in this Court.

In those circumstances it appears to me that I must follow the learned judge's decision and I must direct the trustees not to take any steps either to compel performance of the covenant or to recover damages through her failure to implement it.

RE COOK'S SETTLEMENT TRUSTS
[1965] Ch 902, [1964] 3 All ER 898 (ChD, BUCKLEY J)

In 1934, by an agreement and subsequent settlement of family property, made between Sir Herbert Cook Bart., Sir Francis Cook (his son) and the trustees of the settlement, certain pictures became the absolute property of Sir Francis Cook. In the settlement, Sir Francis covenanted (cl. 6) for valuable consideration that if any of those pictures should be sold during his lifetime, the net proceeds of sale should be paid to the trustees of the settlement to be held upon the trusts of the settlement.

In 1962, Sir Francis gave a Rembrandt (a picture of Titus) to his wife. She desired to sell it. The question was whether, on the sale of the Rembrandt, the trustees were obligated to take steps to enforce the performance of the covenant.

Held. As the beneficiaries had given no consideration for the covenant, they could not require the trustees to take steps to enforce it. Nor were they beneficiaries of a trust of the promise[1].

BUCKLEY J: Mr. Goff, appearing for Sir Francis, has submitted first that, as a matter of law, the covenant contained in clause 6 of the settlement is not enforceable against him by the trustees of the settlement . . . [He] submits that the covenant was a voluntary and executory contract to make a settlement in a future event and was not a settlement of a covenant to pay a sum of money to the trustees. He further submits that as regards the covenant all the beneficiaries under the settlement are volunteers, with the consequence that not only should the court not direct the trustees to take proceedings on the covenant but it should positively direct them not to take proceedings. He relies upon *Re Pryce* ([1917] 1 Ch 234) and *Re Kay's Settlement* ([1939] Ch 329, [1939] 1 All ER 245).

Counsel for the second and third defendants have contended that on the true view of the facts there was an immediate settlement of the obligation created by the covenant, and not merely a covenant to settle something in the future. It was said, as Mr. Monckton put it, that by the agreement Sir Herbert bought the rights arising under the covenant for the benefit of the cestuis que trustent under the settlement and that, the covenant being made in favour of the trustees, these rights became assets of the trust. He relied on *Fletcher v Fletcher* ((1844) 4 Hare 67); *Williamson v Codrington* ((1750) 1 Ves Sen 511) and *Re Cavendish Browne's Settlement Trusts* ([1916] WN 341). I am not able to accept this argument. The covenant with which I am concerned did not, in my opinion, create a debt enforceable at law, that is to say, a property right, which, although to bear fruit only in the future and upon a contingency, was capable of being made the subject of an immediate trust, as was held to be the case in *Fletcher v Fletcher*. Nor is this covenant associated with property which was the subject of an immediate trust as in *Williamson v Codrington*. Nor did the covenant relate to property

[1] Appeal compromised. The picture was later sold at Christies for 760,000 guineas. See Times Newspaper, November 7, 1964, p. 5 and March 20, 1965, p.10.

which then belonged to the covenantor, as in *Re Cavendish Browne's Settlement Trusts*. In contrast to all these cases, this covenant upon its true construction is, in my opinion, an executory contract to settle a particular fund or particular funds of money which at the date of the covenant did not exist and which might never come into existence. It is analogous to a covenant to settle an expectation or to settle after-acquired property. The case, in my judgment, involves the law of contract, not the law of trusts.

As an alternative argument, Mr. Brightman formulated this proposition, which he admitted not to be directly supported by any authority, but he claimed to conflict with none: that where a covenantor has for consideration moving from a third party covenanted with trustees to make a settlement of property, the court will assist an intended beneficiary who is a volunteer to enforce the covenant if he is specially an object of the intended trust or (which Mr. Brightman says is the same thing) is within the consideration of the deed. In formulating this proposition Mr. Brightman bases himself on language used by Cotton LJ in *Re d'Angibau* ((1880) 15 ChD 228 at 242) and by Romer J in *Cannon v Hartley* ([1949] Ch 213 at 223, [1949] 1 All ER 50). As an example of a case to which the proposition would apply, Mr. Brightman supposes a father having two sons who enters into an agreement with his elder son and with trustees whereby the father agrees to convey an estate to his elder son absolutely in consideration of the son covenanting with his father and the trustees, or with the trustees alone, to settle an expectation on trusts for the benefit of the younger son. The younger son is a stranger to the transaction, but he is also the primary (and special) beneficiary of the intended settlement. A court of equity should, and would, Mr. Brightman contends, assist the younger son to enforce his brother's covenant and should not permit the elder son to frustrate the purposes of the agreement by refusing to implement his covenant although he has secured the valuable consideration given for it. The submission is not without attraction, for it is not to be denied that, generally speaking, the conduct of a man who, having pledged his word for valuable consideration, takes the benefits he has so obtained and then fails to do his part, commands no admiration. I have, therefore, given careful consideration to this part of the argument to see whether the state of the law is such as might justify me (subject to the construction point) in dealing with the case on some such grounds.

There was no consideration for Sir Francis's covenant moving from the trustees; nor, of course, was there any consideration moving from Sir Francis's children. [His Lordship referred to *A-G v Jacobs-Smith* (1895) 2 QB 341 at 353; *Hill v Gomme* (1839) 5 My & Cr 250 at 254; *Harvey v Ashley* (1748) 3 Atk 607 at 610; *Re D'Angibau* (1880) 15 ChD 228; *Green v Paterson* (1886) 32 ChD 95, and continued:]

These authorities show that there is an equitable exception to the general rule of law which I have mentioned where the contract is made in consideration of marriage and the intended beneficiary who seeks to have the contract enforced is within the marriage consideration. They do not support the existence of any wider exception save perhaps in the case of a beneficiary who is not within the marriage consideration but whose interests under the intended trusts are closely interwoven with interests or others who are within that consideration. They do not support the view that any such exception exists in favour of a person who was not a party to the contract and is not to be treated as though he had been and who has given no consideration and is not to be treated as if he had given consideration. Where the obligation to settle property has been assumed voluntarily it is clear that no object of the intended trusts can enforce the obligation. Thus in *Re Kay's Settlement* ([1939] Ch 329, [1939] 1 All ER 245), a spinster made a voluntary settlement in favour of herself and her issue which contained a covenant to settle after-acquired property. She later married and had children who, as volunteers, were held to have no right to enforce the covenant. Mr. Brightman distinguishes that case from the present on the ground that in *Re Kay's Settlement* the settlement and covenant were entirely voluntary, whereas Sir Francis received consideration from Sir Herbert; but Sir Francis received no consideration from his own children. Why, it may be asked, should they be accorded an indulgence in a court of equity which they would not have been accorded had Sir Herbert given no consideration? As regards them the covenant must, in my judgment, be regarded as having been given voluntarily. A plaintiff is not entitled to claim equitable relief against another merely because the latter's conduct is unmeritorious. Conduct by A which is unconscientious in relation to B so as to entitle B to equitable relief may not be unconscientious in relation to C so that C will have no standing to claim relief notwithstanding that the conduct in question may affect C. The father in Mr. Brightman's fictitious illustration could after performing his part of the contract release his elder son from the latter's covenant with him to make a settlement on the younger son, and the younger son could, I think, not complain. Only the covenant with the trustees would then remain, but this covenant would be a voluntary one, the trustees having given no consideration. I can see no reason why in these circumstances the court should assist the younger son to enforce the covenant with the trustees. But the right of the younger son to require the trustees to enforce their covenant, could not, I think, depend on whether the father had or had not released his covenant. Therefore, as it seems to me, on principle the younger son would not in any event have an equitable right to require the trustees to enforce their covenant. In other words, the arrangement between the father and his elder son would not have conferred any equitable right or interest upon his younger son.

I reach the conclusion that Mr. Brightman's proposition is not well-founded. There is no authority to support it and *Green v Paterson* ((1886) 32 ChD 95) is, I think, authority the other way. Accordingly, the second and third defendants are not, in my judgment, entitled to require the trustees to take proceedings to enforce the covenant even if it is capable of being construed in a manner favourable to them.

[His Lordship then held that the words "in case any of such pictures shall be sold" in clause 6 of the settlement following the covenant that Sir Francis would not during his lifetime sell without previous notice in writing to the trustees, only referred to a sale by Sir Francis and did not contain any embargo on a disposition of the works of art in any other way, e.g., by gift.]

In *Cannon v Hartley* ([1949] Ch 213, [1949] 1 All ER 50) a deed of separation, dated 1941, executed by the husband (the defendant) the wife and the daughter, provided that the defendant would settle, in favour of the wife and daughter, half of what the husband should receive under the will of either of his parents, being worth more than £1,000.

In 1944, the defendant inherited property in excess of £1,000. In 1946, the wife died. The daughter sued, as a party to the deed of separation, for damages for breach of covenant, and succeeded. She would have been unable, as a volunteer, to insist on the property being settled.

B. Should Volunteers be Able to Enforce?

i. ACTION FOR DAMAGES BY TRUSTEES

Pettit: *Equity and the Law of Trusts* (3rd Edn), pp. 66–67

(ii) *Cestui que trust a volunteer*—The fact that the obligation is contained in a deed makes no difference in equity which has no special regard to the form of a seal[2]. It may well be asked, however, whether the trustees with whom the covenant is made can, or should, bring an action at law for damages since the common law regards consideration and a seal as alternative requirements. On this question it has been held that volunteers cannot compel trustees to take proceedings for damages, and further, that if the trustees ask the court for directions as to what they should do, they will be directed not to take any steps either to compel performance of the covenant or to recover damages through the failure to implement it. Thus in the leading case of *Re Pryce*[3] there was a marriage settlement under which the wife covenanted to settle after-acquired property. The beneficial limitations of funds brought into the settlement by the wife (including any after-acquired property) were successive life interests to the wife and the husband, remainder to the children of the marriage (of whom there were never in fact any), and an ultimate remainder to the wife's next-of-kin, who were of course volunteers. The husband was dead and the wife did not wish the covenant to be enforced. The court held that the trustees ought not to take any steps to compel the transfer or payment to them of the after-acquired property. The principle of *Re Pryce* has been strongly criticised[4], and it has been further contended[5] that the court should not in such cases have left it open whether the trustees could sue for damages for breach of covenant if they wished, but should have directed them to sue, on the ground that there was a completely constituted trust of the benefit of the covenant. Since these critical articles, however, *Re Pryce*[3] and *Re Kay's Settlement*[6] have been followed in *Re Cook's Settlement Trusts*[7] and have found academic support[8]. On the cases as they stand there is no clear authority as to the

[2] See e.g. *Jefferys v Jefferys* (1841 Cr & Ph 138; *Kekewich v Manning* (1851) 1 De GM & G 176.

[3] [1971] 1 Ch 234; *Re Kay's Settlement,* [1939] Ch 329, [1939] 1 All ER 245, see p. 88, ante.
See generally *Perspectives of Law*, p. 240 (R. H. Maudsley).

[4] (1960) 76 LQR 100 (D. W. Elliott).

[5] (1962) 78 LQR 228 (J. A. Hornby).

[6] [1939] Ch 329, [1939] 1 All ER 245.

[7] [1965] Ch 902, [1964] 3 All ER 898, see p. 91, ante. And see [1965] CLJ 46 (G. H. Jones).
Cf. *Re Ralli's Will Trusts* [1964] Ch 288, [1963] 3 All ER 940, see p. 77, ante.

[8] (1967) ASCL, pp. 387 et seq. (J. D. Davies); (1969) 85 LQR 213 (W. A. Lee).

position if the trustees do not ask the court for directions, but choose to bring an action. Professor Elliott[9] takes the view that if an action would lie any damages recovered would become trust property, and that such damages would be substantial[10]. The authorities for this view are not very weighty, and even if valid as regards a covenant to pay money or transfer specific property, do not establish the point in the case of a covenant to settle after-acquired property[11]. Lee[12] considers that any damages recovered would be held on a resulting trust for the settlor.

(iii) *Cestui que trust a covenantee*—Even where the *cestui que trust* is a volunteer, there is a clear decision at first instance[13], that if the covenant is made with him, there is no answer to an action by him at common law on the covenant, and substantial damages for breach thereof will be awarded.

(iv) *Performance of unenforceable covenant*—It is clear that if the settlor has in fact transferred property to trustees in compliance with an unenforceable covenant to settle the same in favour of volunteers, he thereby completely constitutes the trust, and cannot thereafter claim to recover the property, which must be held by the trustees on the declared trusts[14].

In *Re Cavendish Browne's Settlement Trusts* ([1916] WN 341) Catherine Penelope Cavendish Browne made a voluntary settlement containing a covenant "to convey and transfer to the trustees all the property, both real and personal, to which she was absolutely entitled by virtue of the joint operation of the wills of" J.H. and A.C.B. When Catherine died, she had not yet assured to the trustees a share of unconverted real estate in Canada, to which she had become entitled under the two wills. The question was whether the value of the share or any part of it ought to be paid to the trustees by way of damages for breach of covenant. YOUNGER J "without delivering a final judgment, held on the authority of *Williamson v Codrington* (1750) 1 Ves Sen 511; *Cox v Barnard* (1850) 8 Hare 310; *Fletcher v Fletcher* (1884) 4 Hare 67; *Re Parkin* [1892] 3 Ch 510; *Ward v Audland* (1847) 16 M & W 862; *Lloyd's v Harper* (1880) 16 ChD 290; *Davenport v Bishopp* (1843) 2 Y & C Ch Cas 451; *Clough v Lambert* (1839) 10 Sim 174; *Synge v Synge* [1894] 1 QB 466; *Spickernell v Hotham* (1854) Kay 669; *Re Plumptre's Marriage Settlement* [1910] 1 Ch 609 that the trustees were entitled to recover [from Catherine's administrators] substantial damages for breach of the covenant to assure, and that the measure of damages was the value of the property which would have come to the hands of the trustees if the covenant had been duly performed."

---

[9] Loc. cit.

[10] See (1960) 76 LQR 100 (D. W. Elliott), citing, inter alia *Re Cavendish Browne's Settlement Trusts* [1916] WN 341.

[11] See R. H. Maudsley, op cit, p. 244, and J. D. Davies, op cit, p. 392.

[12] Loc. cit.

[13] *Cannon v Hartley* [1949] Ch 213, [1949] 1 All ER 50, see p. 94, ante.

[14] *Paul v Paul* (1882) 20 ChD 742; *Re Adlard* [1954] Ch 29, [1953] 2 All ER 1437; *Re Ralli's Will Trusts* [1964] Ch 288, [1963] 3 All ER 940, see p. 77, ante.

ii. TRUST OF THE PROMISE

If there was a trust of the promise, there would be a constituted trust of a chose in action, and such a trust could be enforced by the trustee for the benefit of the beneficiary[15], or by the beneficiary for his own benefit, joining the trustee as co-plaintiff or as defendant[16].

FLETCHER v FLETCHER
(1844) 4 Hare 67 (Chancery, WIGRAM V-C)

By a voluntary deed, Ellis Fletcher covenanted with trustees, to pay to them £60,000, which the trustees were to hold upon trust for, in the events which happened, Ellis's illegitimate son, Jacob. The trustees were unaware of the deed, which was found among Ellis's papers after his death. The trustees did not wish to establish the trust except under an order of the court. The question was whether Jacob could enforce the covenant against the executor of Ellis.

Held. Jacob was entitled to enforce the covenant, although it was voluntary.

WIGRAM V-C: It is not denied that, if the Plaintiff in this case had brought an action in the name of the trustees, he might have recovered the money; and it is not suggested, that if the trustees had simply allowed their name to be used in the action, their conduct could have been impeached. There are two classes of cases, one of which is in favour of, and the other, if applicable, against, the Plaintiff's claim. The question is, to which of the two classes it belongs.

In trying the equitable question I shall assume the validity of the instrument at law. If there was any doubt of that it would be reasonable to allow the Plaintiff to try the right by suing in the name of the surviving trustee. The first proposition relied upon against the claim in equity was, that equity will not interfere in favour of a volunteer. That proposition, though true in many cases, has been too largely stated. A court of equity, for example, will not, in favour of a volunteer, enforce the performance of a contract in specie. That it will, however, sometimes act in favour of a volunteer is proved by the common case of a volunteer on a bond who may prove his bond against the assets. Again, where the relation of trustee and *cestui que trust* is constituted, as where property is transferred from the author of the trust into the name of a trustee, so that he has lost all power of disposition over it, and the transaction is complete as regards him, the trustee, having accepted the trust, cannot say he holds it, except for the purposes of the trust; and the Court will enforce the trust at the suit of a volunteer. According to the authorities, I cannot, I admit, do anything to perfect the liability of the author of the trust, if it is not already perfect. This covenant, however, is already perfect. The covenantor is liable at law, and the Court is not called upon to do any act to perfect it. One question made in argument has been, whether there can be a trust of a covenant the benefit of which shall belong to

[15] *Lloyd's v Harper* (1880) 16 ChD 290.
[16] *Les Affréteurs Réunis Société Anonyme v Leopold Walford (London) Ltd* [1919] AC 801.

a third party; but I cannot think there is any difficulty in that. Suppose, in the case of a personal covenant to pay a certain annual sum for the benefit of a third person, the trustee were to bring an action against the covenantor; would he be afterwards allowed to say he was not a trustee? If he cannot do so after once acknowledging the trust, then there is a case in which there is a trust of a covenant for another. In the case of *Clough v Lambert* ((1839) 10 Sim 174) the question arose; the point does not appear to have been taken during the argument, but the Vice-Chancellor of England was of opinion that the covenant bound the party; that the *cestui que trust* was entitled to the benefit of it; and that the mere intervention of a trustee made no difference. The proposition, therefore, that in no case can there be a trust of a covenant is clearly too large, and the real question is whether the relation of trustee and *cestui que trust* is established in the present case.

Perspectives of Law (ed. R. Pound), p. 248

"There was, then, a trust of the promise, and the plaintiff as beneficiary of this trust, could enforce it. But it seems to me that there are one or two difficulties in holding that a trust of a chose in action was created on the facts of this particular case. In the first place, positive evidence of intention is lacking. Ellis Fletcher, the covenantor, covenanted that he would pay the £60,000 to trustees 'to be held on the following trusts'. There is clearly a trust which will affect the money once it is received by the trustee, but no manifestation of an intention by either party to create a trust of a chose in action. Secondly . . . it seems to me that a trust of this nature should be created, if at all, by the obligee and not by the obligor; and there was evidence of the fact that the trustee did not enter into the arrangement intending to be a trustee of a promise, for he did not know about it, and wished to decline the trust as soon as he did hear about it. A trust of tangible property is declared by the owner of the property, whether he keeps the property himself or transfers it to another on trust; a trust of a debt is declared by the creditor. A covenantor should not claim, at one swoop, to burden himself with the promise of the payment of money to a promisee, and impose trusts upon the promisee behind his back. It is not as if he were assigning the benefit of a promise, or transferring the money; in such cases he could of course impose trusts on the promise or on the money. The logic of the matter seems to me to be that if A covenants to pay money to B which B is to hold on trust for C, the trusts on which money will be held, when paid over, can be declared by A; but a trust of A's promise should be declared by the person who has the benefit of the promise, namely B; and this will usually be proved by showing that B contracted as trustee for the persons nominated by the covenantor. Both these difficulties are overcome by the rules of the Restatement that the inference in these cases is that the promisee becomes trustee of his rights under the promise, and that, in the case of a voluntary covenant to settle, the settlor is the promisor.[17]"

[17] § 26, Comment (n).

IV. Trusts of Future Property[18]

In *Norman v Federal Commissioner of Taxation* ((1963) 109 CLR 9) WINDEYER J said, at p. 24: "As to attempted assignments of things not yet in existence:

As it is impossible for anyone to own something that does not exist, it is impossible for anyone to make a present gift of such a thing to another person, however sure he may be that it will come into existence and will then be his to give. He can, of course, promise that when the thing is his he will make it over to the intended donee. But in the meantime he may change his mind and when the time comes refuse to carry out his promise, even though it were by deed. A court of law could not compel him to perform it. A court of equity would not. Courts of equity never had the objections to all agreements about future interests that, until the seventeenth century, were deeply rooted in the common law. Equity did not share the view that such agreements were void on the ground of maintenance. But things not yet in existence could only be the subject of agreement, not of present disposition. And, in relation to promises and agreements, equity has been faithful to its maxim that it does not come to the aid of volunteers. For equity a deed does not make good a want of consideration.

If we turn from attempted gifts of future property to purported dispositions of it for value, the picture changes completely. The common law objection remains. But in equity a would-be present assignment of something to be acquired in the future is, when made for value, construed as an agreement to assign the thing when it is acquired. A court of equity will ensure that the would-be assignor performs this agreement, his conscience being bound by the consideration. The purported assignee thus gets an equitable interest in the property immediately the legal ownership of it is acquired by the assignor, assuming it to have been sufficiently described to be then identifiable. The prospective interest of the assignee is in the meantime protected by equity. These principles, which now govern assignments for value of property to be acquired in the future, have been developed and established by a line of well-known cases, of which *Holroyd v Marshall* ((1862) 10 HL Cas 191), *Collyer v Isaacs* ((1881) 19 ChD 342), *Tailby v Official Receiver* ((1888) 13 App Cas 523), and *Re Lind*, ([1915] 2 Ch 345) are the most important. 'And so', to use *Maitland's* words, 'lawyers easily slipped into the way of saying that in equity one could make an assignment of goods hereafter to be acquired though one could not do so at law. This was a compendious way of putting the matter and was not likely to deceive any equity lawyer': *Maitland, Equity,* 2nd ed. (1936) p. 150."

RE ELLENBOROUGH

[1903] 1 Ch 697 (ChD, BUCKLEY J)

By a voluntary settlement, Miss Emily Towry Law, a sister of Lord Ellenborough, purported to assign to the trustees the property to which she might become entitled under the wills of her brother and her sister.

[18] H & M, pp. 193–195; Pettit, p. 73; Snell, pp. 80–82; (1966) 30 Conv (NS) 286 (M. C. Cullity and H. A. J. Ford).

She received property under her sister's will and conveyed it to the trustees. On her brother's death in 1902, she received property under his will, and declined to transfer it to the trustees. The question was whether she was obligated to do so.

Held. She could not be compelled to hand over the property.

BUCKLEY J: The question is whether a volunteer can enforce a contract made by deed to dispose of an expectancy. It cannot be and is not disputed that if the deed had been for value the trustees could have enforced it. If value be given, it is immaterial what is the form of assurance by which the disposition is made, or whether the subject of the disposition is capable of being thereby disposed of or not. An assignment for value binds the conscience of the assignor. A Court of Equity as against him will compel him to do that which ex hypothesi he has not yet effectually done. Future property, possibilities, and expectancies are all assignable in equity for value: *Tailby v Official Receiver* ((1888) 13 App Cas 523 at 543). But when the assurance is not for value, a Court of Equity will not assist a volunteer. In *Meek v Kettlewell* ((1842) 1 Hare 464), affirmed by Lord Lyndhust ((1843) 1 Ph 342), the exact point arose which I have here to decide, and it was held that a voluntary assignment of an expectancy, even though under seal, would not be enforced by a Court of Equity. "The assignment of an expectancy", says Lord Lynhurst ((1843) 1 Ph at 347), "such as this is, cannot be supported unless made for a valuable consideration." It is however suggested that that decision was overruled or affected by the decision of the Court of Appeal in *Kekewich v Manning* ((1851) 1 DM & G 176 at 187), and a passage in White and Tudor's Leading Cases in Equity, 7th ed. vol. ii, p. 851, was referred to upon the point. In my opinion *Kekewich v Manning* has no bearing upon that which was decided in *Meek v Kettlewell*. The assignment in *Kekewich v Manning* was not of an expectancy, but of property. "It is on legal and equitable principles", said Knight Bruce LJ "we apprehend, clear that a person sui juris, acting freely, fairly, and with sufficient knowledge, ought to have and has it in his power to make, in a binding and effectual manner, a voluntary gift of any part of his property, whether capable or incapable of manual delivery, whether in possession or reversionary, and howsoever circumstanced." The important words there are "of his property". The point of *Meek v Kettlewell* and of the case before me is that the assignment was not of property, but of a mere expectancy. On December 22, 1893, that with which the grantor was dealing was not her property in any sense. She had nothing more than an expectancy. In *Re Tilt* ((1896) 74 LT 163) there was again a voluntary assignment of an expectancy, and the point was not regarded as arguable. "It was rightly admitted" said Chitty J, "that as, when this plaintiff executed the deed of 1880, she had no interest whatever in the fund in question, which was a mere expectancy, the deed was wholly inoperative both at law and in equity, being entirely voluntary." By "wholly inoperative" there the learned judge of course did not mean that if the voluntary settlor had handed over the funds the trustees would not have held them upon the trusts, but that the grantees under the deed could not enforce it as against the settlor in a Court of Equity or elsewhere. In my judgment the interest of the plaintiff as sole heiress-at-law and next of kin of the late Lord

Ellenborough was not effectually assigned to the trustees by the deed, and the trustees cannot call upon her to grant, assign, transfer, or pay over to them his residuary real and personal estate.

In *Re Brooks' Settlement Trusts* ([1939] Ch 993, [1939] 3 All ER 920) property was held under a marriage settlement on trust for X for life, and after her death on trust for such of her issue as she might by deed or will appoint, and in default of appointment on trust for her children in equal shares. One child, A, conveyed to trustees "all the part or share . . . and other interest whether vested or contingent to which the settlor is now or may at any time hereafter become entitled whether in default of appointment or under any appointment hereafter to be made". X appointed the sum of £3,517 to A. The question was whether the trustees of the marriage settlement, who were also the trustees of A's settlement, should pay the money to A. FARWELL J held that they should pay. A could not settle property to which he might become entitled under a future appointment; for in that property he had only an expectancy. He could settle property to which he would become entitled in default of appointment; for in that property he had a vested interest subject to divestment. This case does not appear to have been cited in *Re Ralli's Will Trusts* ([1964] Ch 288, [1964] 3 All ER 940; p. 77, ante.

In *Williams v Commissioner of Inland Revenue* ([1965] NZLR 395)[19] Williams, who had a life interest under a trust, executed a voluntary deed, in which "the assignor by way of gift hereby assigns to the assignee for the religious purposes of the Parish of the Holy Trinity Gisborne for the four years commencing on 30 June 1960 the first £500 of the net income which shall accrue to the assignor personally while he lives in each of the said four years from the Trust. . . . And the assignor hereby declares that he is trustee for the sole use and benefit of the assignee for the purpose aforesaid of so much (if any) of the said income as may not be capable of assignment (or may come to his hands)."

The question arose whether Williams had effectively divested himself of his interest in the £500 so as not to be liable for income tax on it. The New Zealand Court of Appeal held that he had not.

TURNER J (delivering the judgment of NORTH P and himself) said: "Mr. Thorp, for the appellant, submitted that what was assigned by this document was a defined share in the existing life estate of the assignor in the trust property, and hence that the deed of assignment took effect, as at its date, to divest the assignor of the annual sums of £500 so that he did not thereafter derive them for taxation purposes in the years under consideration. For the respondent Commissioner it was contended that the deed was ineffective to divest the assignor of the sums, and that its effect was no more than that of an order upon the trustees still revocable by the assignor until payment.

[19] (1965) ASCL 328 (J. D. Davies); see also *Shepherd v Taxation Comr* (1965) 113 CLR 385.

The life interest of the appellant in the trust was at the date of the execution of the deed an existing equitable interest. This cannot be doubted, and it was so conceded by the learned Solicitor-General. Being an existing interest, it was capable in equity of immediate effective assignment. Such an assignment could be made without consideration, if it immediately passed the equitable estate: *Kekewich v Manning* (1851) 1 De GM & G 176, 42 ER 519. There is no doubt that if the deed before us had purported to assign, not "the first £500", but the whole of the appellant's life interest under the trust, such an assignment would have been good in equity.

But while equity will recognise a voluntary assignment of an existing equitable interest, it will refuse to recognise in favour of a volunteer an assignment of an interest, either legal or equitable, not existing at the date of the assignment, but to arise in the future. Not yet existing, such property cannot be owned, and what may not be owned may not be effectively assigned: *Holroyd v Marshall* (1862) 10 HL Cas 191 at 210, 11 ER 999 at 1006, per Lord Westbury LC. If, not effectively assigned, it is made the subject of an agreement to assign it, such an agreement may be good in equity, and become effective upon the property coming into existence (ibid., 211; 1007) but if, and only if, the agreement is made for consideration (as in *Spratt v Commissioner of Inland Revenue* [1964] NZLR 272), for equity will not assist a volunteer: *Re Ellenborough* [1903] 1 Ch 697.

The deed on which this appeal is founded was not made for consideration. The simple question is therefore—was that which it purported to assign (*viz.* 'the first five hundred pounds of the net income which shall accrue') an existing property right, or was it a mere expectancy, a future right not yet in existence? If the former, counsel agree that the deed was effective as an immediate assignment: if the latter, it is conceded by Mr. Thorp that it could not in the circumstances of this case have effect.

What then was it that the assignor purported to assign? What he had was the life interest of a *cestui que trust* in a property or partnership adventure vested in or carried on by trustees for his benefit. Such a life interest exists in equity as soon as the deed of trust creating it is executed and delivered. Existing, it is capable of immediate assignment. We do not doubt that where it is possible to assign a right completely it is possible to assign an undivided interest in it. The learned Solicitor-General was therefore right, in our opinion, in conceding that if here, instead of purporting to assign 'the first £500 of the income', the assignor had purported to assign (say) an undivided one-fourth share in his life estate, then he would have assigned an existing right, and in the circumstances effectively.

But in our view, as soon as he quantified the sum in the way here attempted, the assignment became one not of a share or a part of his right, but of moneys which should arise from it. Whether the sums mentioned were ever to come into existence in whole or in part could not at the date of assignment be certain. In any or all of the years designated the net income might conceivably be less than five hundred pounds; in some or all of them the operations of the trust might indeed result in a loss. The first £500 of the net income, then, might or might not (judging the matter on the date of execution of the deed) in fact have any existence.

We accordingly reject Mr. Thorp's argument that what was here assigned was a part or share of the existing equitable right of the assignor. He did not assign part of his right to income; he assigned a right to a part of the income, a different thing. The £500 which was the subject of the purported assignment was five hundred pounds *out of the net income*. There could be no such income for any year until the operations of that year were complete, and it became apparent what debits were to be set off against the gross receipts. For these reasons we are of opinion that what was assigned here was money; and that was something which was not presently owned by the assignor. He had no more than an expectation of it, to arise, it is true, from an existing equitable interest—but that interest he did not purport to assign. . . .

It was argued in the alternative by Mr. Thorp, but somewhat faintly, that if the document were not effective as an assignment it was effective as a declaration of trust, and that this result was sufficient to divest the appellant of the enjoyment of the annual sums so that he did not derive them as income. It will be recalled in this regard that the text of the deed includes an express declaration of trust. Mr. Thorp's submission was that this express declaration is effective even if the assignment fails. We agree that there may be circumstances in which a purported assignment, ineffective for insufficiency of form or perhaps through lack of notice, may yet perhaps be given effect by equity by reason of the assignor having declared himself to be a trustee; but it is useless to seek to use this device in the circumstances of the present case. Property which is not presently owned cannot presently be impressed with a trust any more than it can be effectively assigned; property which is not yet in existence may be the subject of a present agreement to impress it with a trust when it comes into the hands of the donor; but equity will not enforce such an agrement at the instance of the *cestui que trust* in the absence of consideration: *Ellison v Ellison* (1802) 6 Ves Jun 656 at 662, 31 ER 1243 at 1246 per Lord Eldon LC; *Brennan v Morphett* (1908) 6 CLR 22 at 30 per Griffith CJ; cf. *Underhill's Law of Trusts and Trustees,* 11th ed. 43. For the same reasons therefore as apply in this case to the argument on assignment, Mr. Thorp's second alternative submission must also fail."

Perspectives of Law (ed. R. Pound), p. 250

"A contract for consideration to convey future property to trustees upon trust is valid[20] and, in most cases, specifically enforceable[1]. A gratuitous covenant under seal to convey property to trustees is actionable at the instance of the beneficiary, if the court finds, on a proper construction of the situation, that the promisee became trustee of the promise for the beneficiaries[2]. A purported assignment of an expectancy cannot be a conveyance because there is nothing to convey. If consideration is given for the purported conveyance, it will be construed as a contract to assign

[20] *Re Lind* [1915] 2 Ch 345; *Re Gillott's Settlement* [1934] Ch 97; *Re Haynes' Will Trusts* [1949] Ch 5, [1948] 2 All ER 423.

[1] *Pullan v Koe,* [1913] 1 Ch 9, p. 87, ante.

[2] *Fletcher v Fletcher* (1844) 4 Hare 67, p. 96, ante.

and enforceable as such[3]. But if it is made gratuitously it is a nullity[4]. In *Re Ellenborough*[5], the sister of Lord Ellenborough purported to convey by voluntary settlement the property which she would receive under her brother's will. On his death she declined to transfer the property to the trustees, and Buckley J held that the trustees could not compel her to do so.

The question is whether such a gratuitous covenant or assignment in respect of future property can ever be effective as a declaration of trust, so that the trust will become effective when the property vests in the trustee. The situation can arise if the property, on falling in, is transferred to trustees without a further declaration of the trusts, or where the property vests in the settlor after he has declared the trusts on which he is to hold it.

We have seen that, in England, a covenant in a marriage settlement to settle after-acquired property is not enforceable at the suit of the next of kin because they are volunteers[6]; and it is clear that a deed purporting to grant future property on trust is ineffective[7]. But if, in either of these cases, the property found its way into the hands of the trustees, it would presumably be held upon the trusts declared in the relevant documents[8]. If the settlor, in either case, conveyed the property to the trustees, that action could be construed as a further declaration of the trusts; but if the property reaches the trustees by another route, being conveyed perhaps by the executors of the testator from whom the property came, or coming into the hands of the trustee in a different capacity[9], the possibility of finding that there was a further declaration of trust is less strong. There appear to be three possible solutions to such a case: that the trustees take beneficially, that they hold on trust for the settlor, or that they hold on the trusts declared in the previous document. The first is obviously unsatisfactory; the second involves the proposition that the settlor could claim back in equity property which he had covenanted or purported to settle. The third avoids the necessity of making the ultimate destination of the property depend upon the route by which it reached the trustees; it is consistent with the expressed intention of the parties, and appears to be the most satisfactory solution[10].

Where the property comes to the settlor himself, it is possible for the court to hold that a previous declaration of trust, followed by the vesting of the property in himself as trustee, constitutes the trust. The question is whether he will be treated as making the declaration at the moment he receives the property[11]. It is clear that a previous declaration is not

3 Snell, *Equity* (26th Edn) p. 91.

4 *Meek v Kettlewell* (1842) 1 Hare 464; *Re Ellenborough* [1903] 1 Ch 697; *Re Brooks' Settlement Trusts* [1939] Ch 993, [1939] 3 All ER 920.

5 [1903] 1 Ch 697.

6 *Re D'Angibau* (1880) 15 ChD 228; *Re Plumptre's Marriage Settlement* [1910] 1 Ch 609.

7 *Re Ellenborough* [1903] 1 Ch 697; *Re Brooks' Settlement Trusts* [1939] Ch 993, [1939] 3 All ER 920.

8 *Re Ellenborough* [1903] 1 Ch 697; Miss Emily Towry Law had already handed over to the trustees the property which she received under her sister's will and no attempt was made to recover it; *Re Adlard* [1954] Ch 29, [1953] 2 All ER 1437; *Re Ralli's Will Trusts* [1964] Ch 288, [1963] 3 All ER 940, p. 77, ante.

9 *Re Ralli's Will Trusts* [1964] Ch 288, [1963] 3 All ER 940.

10 *Re Ralli's Will Trusts*, supra.

11 Restatement of Trusts 2d § 26, Comments *k* and *l*; § 86, Comment *c*.

of itself sufficient[12]; subsequent confirmation of a previous declaration is sufficient[13]. In less obvious cases it is no doubt a question of construction to determine whether or not the settlor is to be taken to have made a subsequent declaration or to have affirmed a previous one. If he made the declaration every day, the last declaration being made the moment before he received the property, this would no doubt be sufficient. But in the absence of authority, in England at least, it is unsafe to predict to what extent an argument on these lines might be acceptable. What is clear in these cases . . . is that the beneficiaries must show that the trust was properly declared and properly constituted. In connection with the declaration, there are again very difficult points of construction, the solution of which will largely depend on the view the court takes on the policy question whether or not trusts ought to be created in this way. There appears to be nothing intrinsically wrong in holding that the declaration of a trust may precede its constitution."

QUESTIONS

1. Consider whether the doctrine expounded by EVERSHED MR in *Re Rose* ([1952] Ch 499, [1952] 1 All ER 1217, p. 80, ante) is inconsistent with the principles laid down in other parts of this chapter? Would it apply if the transfer was never registered? Do you think that the transfer of shares is a special situation? (H & M, pp. 181–183).
2. What would be the result in *Re Ellenborough* ([1903] 1 Ch 697, p. 98, ante) if Miss Towry Law had, instead of purporting to assign what she would receive under her brother's will, declared herself a trustee of it? *Matter of Gurlitz* (1918) 105 Misc 30, 172 NY Supp 523; *Brennan v Morphett* (1908) 6 CLR 22; *Williams v Commissioner of Inland Revenue* [1965] NZLR 395, see p. 100, ante; *Re Northcliffe* ([1925] Ch 651; *Perspectives of Law*, pp. 257–258.)
3. It appears from cases in section III that equity will not assist a volunteer (nor direct his trustees) to enforce a covenant to settle after-acquired property. Consider the effect of the House of Lords decision in *Beswick v Beswick* [1968] AC 58, [1967] 2 All ER 1197, on this; and, in particular, where the settlor has given valuable consideration, and an attempt to enforce the covenant is made by
   a) the settlor, or his estate
   b) the trustees,
   c) a beneficiary who is a volunteer.
   (*Re Cook's Settlement Trusts* [1965] Ch 902, [1964] 3 All ER 898; *Coulls v Bagot's Executor and Trustee Co* (1967) 40 ALJR 471 at 477; H & M, pp. 190–193; Pettit, pp. 68–70; (1967) ASCL 387–396 (J. D. Davies). Treitel, *Law of Contract* (4th Edn 1975), pp. 416–427.)
4. After reading the articles quoted on p. 87, note 19, what do you think of *Re Pryce* and *Re Kay's Settlement*?
5. What exceptions exist to the rule that Equity will not assist a volunteer?

[12] *Matter of Gurlitz*, 105 Misc 30, 172 NY Supp 523 (1918); *Brennan v Morphett* (1908) 6 CLR 22.
[13] *Re Northcliffe* [1925] Ch 651.

H & M, pp. 195–198; K & S, pp. 88–89; P & M, pp. 46–51; Pettit, pp. 74–83; Snell, pp. 122–134.

What is the relationship between the rule in *Strong v Bird* (1874) LR 18 Eq 315 and *Re Ralli's Will Trusts* [1964] Ch 288, [1963] 3 All ER 940, p. 77, ante? See *Re Gonin* [1977] 3 WLR 379, [1977] 2 All ER 720.

4. Testamentary Dispositions which Fail to Comply with the Wills Act 1837[1]

I. Introduction

The Wills Act 1837, s. 9 (p. 41, ante) prescribes the formalities which are necessary for the validity of a testamentary disposition. It is important that strict formalities should attend a will. If a problem should arise, the testator is no longer with us and cannot be consulted. The imposition of certain formalities reduces the chance of mistake, or of ill-considered and hasty dispositions. There are many decisions on the question whether the formalities have been observed, but they do not concern us here[2]. It should, however, be said that wills of members of the armed forces made on active service are not required to observe the same formalities[3].

What should be done however if the testator's intention is obvious, but a formality is lacking? Perhaps there was only one witness; or perhaps two witnesses attested the will, but not in the presence of the testator or in that of each other. In this situation, the well-intentioned formalities become a burden, unnecessarily invalidating the will. Further, what should the court do if a beneficiary fraudulently obtains a benefit for himself?—as by promising orally that he would hold certain property, left to him in the will, on trust for another[4]? Equity strives, where possible, to prevent a statute being used as a cloak for fraud. The secret trust doctrines grew up in this context, and reasonably clear rules were laid down to meet the situation where, by the terms of the will, the gift was made to a legatee absolutely (a "fully secret" trust); for there was in that situation a possibility of fraud. The problem is more difficult where the gift is to a legatee "on such trusts as I have declared (or shall declare)" (a "half-secret" trust). The legatee here takes in a fiduciary capacity, and cannot

[1] H & M, pp. 199–216; K & S, pp. 64–78; P & M, pp. 26–35; Pettit, pp. 89–96; Snell, pp. 104–111; (1915) 28 HLR 237, 366 (P. Costigan); (1937) 53 LQR 501 (W. S. Holdsworth); (1947) 12 Conv (NS) 28 (J. G. Fleming); (1951) 67 LQR 314 (L. A. Sheridan); (1963) 27 Conv (NS) 92 (J. A. Andrews); (1972) 36 Conv (NS) 113 (R. Burgess); (1972) 23 NILQ 263 (R. Burgess).

[2] See Bailey, *Law of Wills* (6th Edn) pp. 45 et seq.; *Jarman on Wills* (8th Edn) pp. 117 et seq.; *Theobald on Wills* (13th Edn) paras. 113–122.

[3] Wills Act 1837, s. 11 (as amended).

[4] A similar problem arises where land is conveyed inter vivos to a donee on an oral trust for a third party; thus failing to comply with L.P.A. 1925, s. 53 (1) (b), (p. 32, ante). An oral trust will be enforced where this is necessary to prevent fraud. *Taylor v Salmon* (1838) 4 My & Cr 134; *Davies v Otty (No. 2)* (1865) 35 Beav 208; *Rochefoucauld v Boustead* [1897] 1 Ch 196; *Bannister v Bannister* [1948] 2 All ER 133; *Re Nichols* [1974] 1 WLR 296 at 301, [1973] 3 All ER 362.

fraudulently claim for himself. It would be strange if the mention of the trust *prevented* its being enforced as a secret trust; but, there being no possibility of fraud, its enforcement must be upon some doctrine other than that of fraud.

Secret trusts however are only one of various methods of effecting testamentary dispositions without spelling out the disposition in the will. They will be considered in order.

II. Incorporation by Reference

IN THE GOODS OF SMART[5]

[1902] P 238 (PD, GORELL BARNES J)

By a will made in 1895, the testatrix directed that, after a life interest, her trustees should give to such of her friends as she might designate certain articles to be specified in a book or memorandum to be found with her will.

Such a book or memorandum was prepared in 1898 or 1899. Subsequently (July 27, 1900) a codicil was executed which confirmed the will, but did not refer to the book.

Held. The "book or memorandum" was referred to as a future document and could not be admitted to probate.

GORELL BARNES J: The question is, therefore, whether the book, so far as it is referred to, if referred to at all, in that clause which I read from the will, is to be incorporated with the will and codicil. I have already practically intimated my view that it ought not to be incorporated, and I might have contented myself with saying that I come to that conclusion in consequence, principally, of a decision of the President in the case of *Durham v Northern* ([1895] P 66), but Mr. Deane argued that that case was inconsistent with other authorities, and that the authorities were in conflict amongst themselves; so I desired to look through them to see if that contention could be properly supported. Before referring very briefly to the cases, it seems to me desirable to state how the principle upon which this matter ought to be decided appears to my mind. It seems to me that it has been established that if a testator, in a testamentary paper duly executed, refers to an existing unattested testamentary paper, the instrument so referred to becomes part of his will; in other words, it is incorporated into it; but it is clear that, in order that the informal document should be incorporated in the validly executed document, the latter must refer to the former as a written instrument then existing—that is, at the time of execution—in such terms that it may be ascertained. A leading case upon this subject is *Allen v Maddock* ((1858) 11 Moo PCC 427), and it is desirable also to refer to *In the Goods of Mary Sunderland* ((1866) LR 1 P & D 198). It will be seen from a statement of the principle in the form I have just given, that the document which it is sought

[5] *Allen v Maddock* (1858) 11 Moo PCC 427; *Re Jones* [1942] Ch 328, [1942] 1 All ER 642; *Re Edwards' Will Trusts* [1948] Ch 440, [1948] 1 All ER 821, see p. 110, post; *Re Schintz's Will Trusts* [1951] Ch 870, [1951] 1 All ER 1095; *Re Tyler* [1967] 1 WLR 1269, [1967] 3 All ER 389; cp. *In the Goods of Lady Truro* (1866) LR 1 P & D 201; *Jarman on Wills* (8th Edn) p. 154.

to incorporate must be existing at the time of the execution of the document into which it is to be incorporated, and there must be a reference in the properly executed document to the informal document as an existing one, and not as a future document. If the document is not existing at the time of the will, but comes into existence afterwards, and then, after that again, there is a codicil confirming the will, the question arises, as it has done in a number of these cases, whether that document is incorporated. It appears to me that, following out the principle which I have already referred to, the will may be treated, by the confirmation given by the codicil, as executed again, and as speaking from the date of the codicil, and if the informal document is existing then, and is referred to in the will as existing, so as to identify it, there will be incorporation; but if the will, treated as being re-executed at the date of the codicil, still speaks in terms which shew that it is referring to a future document, then it appears to me there is no incorporation. I might put a clear concrete case. Suppose that the will said, "I wish certain articles to be disposed of by my executors in accordance with a list which I shall hereafter write", and the testator then wrote a list such as was contemplated, and then, after that, a codicil was made confirming the will, one of the conditions at the date of the codicil which is necessary for incorporation would be fulfilled, namely, the execution of a document; but the other condition would not be fulfilled, because the will, even speaking from the date of its so-called re-execution by that confirmation by the codicil, would still in terms refer to something which even then was future. I have, perhaps, stated a little more fully than is necessary what was very clearly and shortly said by the President (Sir F. H. Jeune) in the case to which I have referred. . . .[6]

Therefore, to my mind, it is clear that if the terms of the reference in this case indicate a document of a future character there is no incorporation. The words are: "I direct my trustees to give to such of my friends as I may designate in a book or memorandum that will be found with this will." That reference, made at the date of the will, was, I think, clearly made as to a future document. A document next comes into existence, and a codicil is afterwards made; but if you treat the will according to the cases, as speaking at the date of the codicil, the reference is still in terms to a document which, even then, is future, and therefore does not comply with one of the necessary conditions, namely, that it must refer to a document as existing at the date when the will is re-executed.

III. Facts of Independent Legal Significance

Jarman on Wills (8th Edn) p. 153

"In *Stubbs v Sargon*[7] it was contended that, on the same principle, a devise of realty to 'the persons who shall be in co-partnership with me at the time of my decease, or to whom I shall have disposed of my business' was void, as leaving it for the testator by some further act, not authorised by the Statute of Frauds, to select the devise. But Lord Langdale, and

[6] *Durham v Northern* [1895] P 66.

[7] (1837) 2 Keen 255; *on appeal* (1838) 3 My & Cr 507.

on appeal Lord Cottenham, held the devise good. Lord Cottenham compared the case to that of a father having two sons, and devising his property to such one of them as should not become entitled to an estate from a third person; here the act of a third person determines who shall take the father's estate. But the act is not testamentary; if it were, one man would be making another man's will. And if not testamentary when done by a third person, it cannot be so when done by the testator himself; otherwise a testator could not devise to such person as, at his death, should be his wife or servant. And Lord Langdale said, if the description was such as to distinguish the devisee from every other person, it was sufficient without entering into the question whether the description was acquired by the devisee after the date of the will, or by the testator's own act in the ordinary course of his affairs, or in the management of his property.

The question is, therefore: Is the supplementary act testamentary? If it is, the devise is void; if it is not, then, although it is the sole act of the testator, the devise is good.

The point frequently arises where a testator by his will directs part of his property to be disposed of in such way as he shall by letter, memorandum, etc., or the like, direct; it is clear that no such document can have any testamentary operation, unless executed as a will, or incorporated by a subsequent will or codicil[8]."

Scott; *Trusts* (3rd Edn) § 54.2.

"Where disposition is determined by facts of independent significance. There is another doctrine of the law of wills which is sometimes confused with the doctrine of incorporation by reference. Even though a disposition cannot be fully ascertained from the terms of the will, it is not invalid if it can be ascertained from facts which have significance apart from their effect upon the disposition in the will. Indeed it is frequently necessary to resort to extrinsic evidence to identify the persons who are to take or the subject matter of a disposition. Thus a bequest to the children or the heirs or next of kin of a named person requires a resort to extrinsic evidence to establish their identity, but it is of course valid. So also a disposition in favor of persons who are in the employ of the testator at the time of his death, or a disposition in favor of such person or institution as may care for the testator during his old age or last illness, is valid. So too the property given may be ascertained by extrinsic facts; thus a bequest of money in banks, securities in a safe-deposit box, or furniture in a designated room or house, is valid. On the other hand, the disposition is invalid where the facts from which it is to be ascertained have no independent significance; thus a disposition in favor of such persons as may be named in an unattested memorandum, or such property as may be designated in such a memorandum, is invalid unless it can be upheld on the doctrine of incorporation by reference, since the designation in the memorandum has no significance apart from the disposition of the property by the will . . . this doctrine, like that of incorporation by reference, is a general doctrine of the law of wills . . ."

[8] See *Re Jones* [1942] Ch 328, [1942] 1 All ER 642.

IV. Gifts to Trustees of an Existing Settlement

A testamentary gift may be made as an addition to an existing settlement by "incorporating" the settlement into the will by reference in accordance with the principles explained in Section II. But difficulties will obviously arise where the settlement is amended; for the amended settlement will be a new document. If the rules of the doctrine of incorporation by reference are strictly observed, it seems that the only alternative solutions are either to hold that the settlement is void, or to enforce it in its *un*amended form. Neither solution is satisfactory.

In *Re Edwards' Will Trusts* ([1948] Ch 440, [1948] 1 All ER 821)[9] a settlor, in 1936, made a 'pilot' settlement of £100, the fund to be held upon trust, as to income and capital, for such persons as the settlor should direct, and subject thereto, upon trust for his wife and children. By his will, made on the same date but afterwards, the settlor directed that his residuary estate should be held upon the trusts of the settlement "so far as such trusts and provisions are subsisting and capable of taking effect."

By a subsequent memorandum dated November 1937, he laid down certain trusts upon which part of the fund was to be held. Seven years later, he died. The question was whether the residuary estate was held upon the trusts of the settlement; and, if so, whether these were the original trusts, or those laid down in the memorandum of 1937. The Court of Appeal held that the will incorporated the settlement in its original unamended form. Lord GREENE MR said (at p. 446): "The settlement here is a document which can be perfectly well identified, and there is no rule of law to the contrary. It can accordingly be incorporated as a piece of writing into the testamentary disposition. Indeed, if the settlement, instead of being a thing having value and force in itself, had been merely a memorandum previously executed to which, in his will, he referred, it could perfectly well have been admitted to probate as a testamentary instrument. The question then would have arisen, what provisions in this instrument are valid and what are invalid? I start then with the proposition that the incorporation of this document into the will is a permissible and easy matter. When I say incorporation, I am referring to what I may perhaps call the mechanical act of incorporation by reading the language of it into the will itself. We have now got therefore to a stage where there is a will, part of the directions of which cannot operate any more than they could operate if they had been contained, as in the case of *Re Jones* ([1942] Ch 328, [1942] 1 All ER 642) in the will itself. The presence of that invalid provision in the case of *Re Jones* did not involve its being struck out of the probate and treated as not being part of the will, nor do I see any reason why the invalidity of a provision contained in this settlement should be any reason for excluding it from the testamentary directions of the deceased. The result of his having in that identifiable document included something which the law does not allow to have effect, is a matter to be considered after probate when the question of the validity of his testamentary dispositions arises. The result therefore

[9] *Re Jones* [1942] Ch 328, [1942] 1 All ER 642; *Re Schintz's Will Trusts* [1951] Ch 870, [1951] 1 All ER 1095; *Re Colin Cooper* [1939] Ch 811, [1939] 3 All ER 586.

is that there is here a composite will consisting of a combination of the actual will itself plus the provisions of the settlement. . . .

It seems to me that the directions for incorporation are directions to read into the will the entirety of a document which the testator no doubt thought would be effective. But if, on writing them into the will, it turns out that part of them is invalid from some rule of law, as in the present case, I cannot read the testator's directions as meaning that, therefore, the whole process of incorporation must be abandoned. I think that the effect of it is that so much of the settlement as can validly have operation as part of a testamentary disposition is left to take effect according to its true construction. I have formed that view quite apart from a point which appears to me to confirm it, namely, that in cl. 2 of the will, after the direction that the residuary estate is to be held upon the trusts of the settlement, appear the words 'so far as such trusts, powers and provisions are subsisting and capable of having effect'. I see no reason myself for reading those words as not extending to a case where some of the trusts are invalid through a rule of law. When the settlement is written into the will there are a string of trusts. Some of them are capable of taking effect; some are incapable of taking effect. It is perfectly true that this form of phrase generally operates in the common case where some trusts in the document referred to have expired through the effluxion of time or the extinction of a family or the birth of children, or something of that kind. But I do not read the words as limited to that class of case. I think a trust which is prevented from operating by a rule of law is a trust which can be fairly described as a trust which is not subsisting and capable of taking effect. I have come to the same conclusion without reference to those words, but I think their presence confirms the view that I have taken."

Miller: *The Machinery of Succession* (1977) pp. 217–219

"Facts of Independent Legal Significance

An alternative approach to testamentary gifts on the trusts of *inter vivos* settlements has been advocated and has achieved some acceptance in the United States[10]. The proponents of this approach point out that there are a number of situations where it is necessary and permissible to have regard to acts or events occurring either before or after the execution of a will in order to identify a legatee or the subject matter of a legacy. Thus, if a testator makes a gift to the persons who are in his employment at the time of his death, it is necessary to have regard to the facts existing at his death in order to ascertain the beneficiaries. Extrinsic evidence as to the identity of such persons is admissible for such facts have significance apart from their relevance to the testamentary gift. It is possible for the testator during his lifetime to discharge employees and to employ other persons and such acts will have the effect of modifying the testamentary disposition. However, such acts are not testamentary for they were not done for the purpose of supplementing the will. They are relevant to ascertaining

[10] See Scott, *Trusts and the Statute of Wills* (1930) 43 Harvard LR 521, at p. 544 et seq.; Evans, *Non-testamentary Acts and Incorporation by reference* (1949) 16 Univ of Chicago LR 635.

the persons who are to take under the testamentary gift, but they also have independent legal significance.

In the same way, it is argued that the terms of a testamentary gift can be regarded as determined by a fact of independent legal significance, namely, the *inter vivos* trust as it exists at the date of death, i.e., even though modified after the date of the will. Again, it can be argued that, although modifications after the date of the will have the effect of modifying the terms of the testamentary gift, such modifications should not be regarded as testamentary acts for they were not done for the purpose of supplementing the will, but for the purpose of modifying the terms of the *inter vivos* trust. In other words, they have a significance independent of their effect on the will.

Even in the United States not all courts have been prepared to accept this approach in relation to trusts liable to amendment after the date of the will[11]. However, a number of States have now adopted the Uniform Testamentary Additions to Trusts Act 1960 which permits a gift by will to the trustees of a settlement to be governed by the terms of the settlement as they stand at the date of the testator's death, i.e., even though amended after the date of the will. The Uniform Probate Code[12] also contains a provision authorising gifts by will to the trustees of a trust established, or to be established, by the testator or another, if the trust is identified in the will and its terms are set forth in a written instrument executed before or concurrently with the execution of the testator's will. The gift is not invalid because the trust is liable to amendment or revocation or because it was amended after the execution of the will or after the death of the testator. Unless the testator's will otherwise provides, the property so given is not deemed to be held under a testamentary trust of the testator, but becomes a part of the trust to which it is given[13].

Such an approach has not been accepted, at least openly, in England. Professor Scott stated that there were numerous English cases in which, after creating a trust *inter vivos*, the settlor had by will left property upon the same trust, merely making reference to the prior disposition. He argued that in many of these cases there was no reference to a particular instrument so that the doctrine of incorporation by reference was inapplicable[14]. It is true that in the cases cited by him the words used to refer to the existing trust may in some respects leave room for debate, but in each case the trust referred to had been created prior to the execution of the will and was irrevocable[15]. Some support for the approach may perhaps be found in *Re Playfair*[16] where the testator bequeathed £20,000 to trustees to be held on the trusts of a marriage settlement. The testator's son, who had

[11] See the survey and criticism by Lauritzen, *Can a Revocable Trust be Incorporated by Reference?* (1950) 45 North Western Univ LR 583.

[12] Section 2–512. There is a separate section dealing with Events of Independent Significance: s. 2–513.

[13] See also the Report of the Ontario Law Commission Relating to Testamentary Additions to Trusts; Appendix V to the Proceedings of the 49th Meeting of the Conference of Commissions of Uniformity of Legislation in Canada.

[14] (1930) 43 Harvard LR 521 at p. 547.

[15] *Berchtoldt v Hertford* (1844) 7 Beav 172; *Ford v Ruxton* (1844) 1 Coll 403; *Re Finch and Chew's Contract* [1903] 2 Ch 486; *Re Beaumont* [1913] 1 Ch 325; *Re Powell* [1918] 1 Ch 407; *Re Gooch* [1929] 1 Ch 740; *Re Shelton's Settled Estates* [1945] Ch 158, [1945] 1 All ER 283.

[16] [1951] Ch 4, [1950] 2 All ER 285.

a vested interest under the marriage settlement, predeceased the testator so that it was necessary to consider whether his estate could derive any benefit from the disposition in the will. If the marriage settlement had been incorporated into the will, then as a purely testamentary gift it would have lapsed. However, it was held that the gift was an addition to the funds of the marriage settlement so that the gift did not lapse and the son's estate was entitled. In this case too the settlement was not liable to amendment.

The adoption of such an approach is not without difficulty. Professor Scott acknowledged that if the *inter vivos* trust was of a nominal sum and was created simply for the purpose of avoiding the necessity of spelling out the trusts in the will it would not in substance be a fact of independent significance[17]. How substantial must the *inter vivos* trust be to have independent significance? Looked at in another way it could present the difficult question of deciding whether a particular amendment of the *inter vivos* trust was testamentary or not[18].

In considering the extent to which effect should be given to gifts by will on the trusts of an *inter vivos* settlement liable to amendment, the potential threat to the policy of the Wills Act must be borne in mind. This applies as much to any extension of the doctrine of incorporation by reference as to any development of the doctrine of facts of independent legal significance. How far should a testator be permitted to reserve for himself a power to make future dispositions which do not comply with the Wills Act? If the trustee of the *inter vivos* trust is a trust corporation, and if the signatures are all carefully witnessed, then it can be argued that the evils which the Wills Act seeks to prevent have been successfully guarded against. On the other hand if the trustee is the testator himself, and the *inter vivos* settlement is at all times subject to his unfettered control, there is a real danger of the underlying policy of the Wills Act being thwarted[19]."

American Uniform Testamentary Additions to Trusts Act 1960

Section 1. Testamentary Additions to Trusts.—A devise or bequest, the validity of which is determinable by the law of this state, may be made by a will to the trustee or trustees of a trust established or to be established by the testator or by the testator and some other person or persons or by some other person or persons (including a funded or unfunded life insurance trust, although the trustor has reserved any or all rights of ownership of the insurance contracts) if the trust is identified in the testator's will and its terms are set forth in a written instrument (other than a will) executed before or concurrently with the execution of the testator's will or in the valid last will of a person who has predeceased the testator (regardless of the existence, size, or character of the corpus of the trust). The devise or bequest shall not be invalid because the trust is amendable

[17] Loc cit., p. 549.
[18] See Lauritzen, loc. cit., pp. 609–610.
[19] See Lauritzen, loc. cit., pp. 612–613.

or revocable, or both, or because the trust was amended after the execution of the will or after the death of the testator. Unless the testator's will provides otherwise, the property so devised or bequeathed (a) shall not be deemed to be held under a testamentary trust of the testator but shall become a part of the trust to which it is given and (b) shall be administered and disposed of in accordance with the provisions of the instrument or will setting forth the terms of the trust, including any amendments thereto made before the death of the testator (regardless of whether made before or after the execution of the testator's will), and, if the testator's will so provides, including any amendments to the trust made after the death of the testator. A revocation or termination of the trust before the death of the testator shall cause the devise or bequest to lapse.

Section 2. Effect on Prior Wills.—This Act shall have no effect upon any devise or bequest made by a will executed prior to the effective date of this Act.

Section 3. Uniformity of Interpretation.—This Act shall be so construed as to effectuate its general purpose to make uniform the law of those states which enact it.

V. Secret Trusts[20]

A. Fully Secret Trusts

A testator sometimes makes a gift by will which is absolute on its face, but which is intended to be held by the legatee (or devisee) upon trust. This may be, as was commonly the situation in the older cases, a method of giving property to a mistress or to an illegitimate child, without the fact being made public by inclusion in the will. The testator could give the legacy to a trusted friend, absolutely, relying on the friend to hand over the legacy as required. The situation commonly arises also where an aged testatrix is unable to make up her mind as to her wishes, usually in relation to trinkets; she leaves the property to a solicitor, and he will see to its disposal according to later verbal instructions.

The difficulty is that such intended trusts do not comply with the necessary formalities of the Wills Act 1837. If they are not to be enforced in favour of the intended beneficiaries, what should happen? It is inequitable for the legatee to keep it for himself. Equity will not allow a statute to be used as an engine of fraud. Fraud would be prevented if the legatee was required to hold upon a resulting trust for the estate. But this of course is a denial of the testator's intention. Provided that the intended trusts are communicated to the legatee *prior to* the testator's death, such trusts are enforced in favour of the intended beneficiary[1].

[20] H & M, pp. 205–216; K & S, pp. 64–78; P & M, pp. 26–35; Pettit, pp. 89–96; Snell, pp. 106–111; see articles referred to at p. 106, note 1, ante.

[1] The same principle applies where an existing legacy is not revoked (*Chamberlaine v Chamberlaine* (1678) Freem Ch 34; *Moss v Cooper* (1861) 1 John & H 352); and where an ancestor, in reliance upon the undertaking of an heir, fails to make a will (*Stickland v Aldridge* (1804) 9 Ves 516), and where a legatee undertakes to dispose of property in a particular manner (*Ottaway v Norman*, [1972] Ch 698, [1971] 3 All ER 1325, p. 115, post).

THYNN v THYNN

(1684) 1 Vern 296 (Chancery. Earl of GUILDFORD. Lord Keeper)

The Case was. that Mr. *Thynn,* of *Eagham,* Deceased. having made a Will. and thereby made his Wife sole Executrix; the Defendant Mr. *Thynn* the Son. hearing of this Will. came to his Mother in the Life-time of his Father. and perswaded her. that there being many Debts. the Executorship would be troublesome to her; and desired that he might be nam'd Executor[2];—for that he by reason of his Privilege of Parliament could struggle the better with the Creditors. and perswaded his Mother to move his Father in it; declaring that he would be only an Executor in Trust for her: And the Mother accordingly prevails on the Father that it might be so: And thereupon Mr. *Thynn* the Son gets a new Will drawn. whereby a Legacy of 50*l.* only is given to his Mother. and therein he makes himself sole Executor; and cancels the former Will. tho' the Father opposed the doing thereof; and the last Will was read over so low. that the Testator could not hear it; and when he called to have it read louder. the Scrivenor cried. he was afraid of disturbing his Worship. The Defendant having thus made himself sole Executor. and procured this Will to be executed. where only a Legacy of 50*l.* was given to his Mother. set up for himself. and denied the Trust for his Mother: And in his two first Answers he denied the Will was drawn by his Directions. and that the 50*l.* therein given to his Mother was without the Testator's Privity; but in his third Answer he confessed it.

Upon the whole Matter. it appeared to be. as well as a Fraud. as also a Trust. the Lord *Keeper,* notwithstanding the Statute of *Frauds* and *Perjuries,* tho' no Trust was declar'd in Writing. decreed it for the Plaintiff. and Order'd that the Defendant should be examined on Interrogatories for discovery of the Estate.

OTTAWAY v NORMAN

[1972] Ch 698. [1971] 3 All ER 1325[3] (ChD. BRIGHTMAN J)

By his will, dated March 8, 1960, Harry Ottaway devised his freehold bungalow, called "Ashcroft" and its contents to Miss Hodges, his housekeeper; and one half of his residuary estate to her, and the other half to his son, William.

During his lifetime Harry orally communicated his intention to Miss Hodges that she should leave the bungalow and its contents. and it was alleged. so much of her residuary estate as should remain undisposed of at her death. to the plaintiffs. William and William's wife. Dorothy.

A few months after Harry's death in 1963. Miss Hodges made a will which accorded with this arrangement. But in 1967 she made a new will in which she devised the bungalow to the defendant and his wife. The plaintiff alleged that Miss Hodges had agreed to leave the bungalow. its contents and her residuary estate to them. and brought an action for a declaration that the defendant, who was Miss Hodges's executor, held the property on a constructive trust for them. In the evidence. the undertaking

2 Before the Executors Act 1830, an executor was permitted to retain beneficially property not otherwise disposed of by the will.

3 (1972) 36 conv (NS) 113 (R. Burgess), 129 (D. J. Hayton); (1973) 36 MLR 210 (S. M. Bandali), p.228, post.

in respect of the bungalow was established, but not that in respect of the residuary estate.

Held. The defendant held the bungalow on a constructive trust for the plaintiffs.

BRIGHTMAN J: It will be convenient to call the person upon whom such a trust is imposed the "primary donee" and the beneficiary under that trust the "secondary donee." The essential elements which must be proved to exist are: (i) the intention of the testator to subject the primary donee to an obligation in favour of the secondary donee; (ii) communication of that intention to the primary donee; and (iii) the acceptance of that obligation by the primary donee either expressly or by acquiescence. It is immaterial whether these elements precede or succeed the will of the donor. I am informed that there is no recent reported case where the obligation imposed on the primary donee is an obligation to make a will in favour of the secondary donee as distinct from some form of inter vivos transfer. But it does not seem to me that there can really be any distinction which can validly be taken on behalf of the defendant in the present case. The basis of the doctrine of a secret trust is the obligation imposed on the conscience of the primary donee and it does not seem to me that there is any materiality in the machinery by which the donor intends that that obligation shall be carried out.

Mr. Buckle, for Mr. Norman, relied strongly on *McCormick v Grogan* (1869) LR 4 HL 82. In that case a testator in 1851 had left all his property by a three line will to his friend Mr. Grogan. In 1854 the testator was struck down by cholera. With only a few hours to live he sent for Mr. Grogan. He told Mr. Grogan in effect that his will and a letter would be found in his desk. The letter named various intended beneficiaries and the intended gifts to them. The letter concluded with the words:

> "I do not wish you to act strictly on the foregoing instructions, but leave it entirely to your own good judgment to do as you think I would, if living, and as the parties are deserving;"

An intended beneficiary whom Mr. Grogan thought it right to exclude sued. I will read an extract from the speech of Lord Westbury, at p. 97, because Mr. Buckle relied much upon it.

> ". . . the jurisdiction which is invoked here by the appellant is founded altogether on personal fraud. It is a jurisdiction by which a Court of Equity, proceeding on the ground of fraud, converts the party who has committed it into a trustee for the party who is injured by that fraud. Now, being a jurisdiction founded on personal fraud, it is incumbent on the court to see that a fraud, a malus animus, is proved by the clearest and most indisputable evidence."

Lord Westbury continued, at p. 97:

> "You are obliged, therefore, to shew most clearly and distinctly that the person you wish to convert into a trustee acted malo animo. You must shew distinctly that he knew that the testator or the intestate was beguiled and deceived by his conduct. If you are not in a condition to affirm that without any misgiving, or possibility of mistake, you are not warranted in affixing on the individual the delictum of fraud, which

> you must do before you convert him into a trustee. Now are there any indicia of fraud in this case?"

Lord Westbury then examined the facts with which that case was concerned.

Founding himself on Lord Westbury Mr. Buckle sought at one stage to deploy an argument that a person could never succeed in establishing a secret trust unless he could show that the primary donee was guilty of deliberate and conscious wrongdoing of which he said there was no evidence in the case before me. That proposition, if correct, would lead to the surprising result that if the primary donee faithfully observed the obligation imposed on him there would not ever have been a trust at any time in existence. The argument was discarded, and I think rightly. Mr. Buckle then fastened on the words "clearest and most indisputable evidence" and he submitted that an exceptionally high standard of proof was needed to establish a secret trust. I do not think that Lord Westbury's words mean more than this: that if a will contains a gift which is in terms absolute, clear evidence is needed before the court will assume that the testator did not mean what he said. It is perhaps analogous to the standard of proof which this court requires before it will rectify a written instrument, for there again a party is saying that neither meant what they have written . . .

Having heard the evidence I have no doubt in my mind that I have received an accurate account of all essential facts from William and Mrs. Dorothy Ottaway (the plaintiffs). I find as a fact that Mr. Harry Ottaway intended that Miss Hodges should be obliged to dispose of the bungalow in favour of the plaintiffs at her death; that Mr. Harry Ottaway communicated that intention to Miss Hodges; and that Miss Hodges accepted the obligation. I find the same facts in relation to the furniture, fixtures and fittings which passed to Miss Hodges under clause 4 of Mr. Harry Ottaway's will. I am not satisfied that any similar obligation was imposed and accepted as regards any contents of the bungalow which had not devolved on Miss Hodges under clause 4 of Mr. Harry Ottaway's will.

I turn to the question of money. In cross-examination William said the trust extended to the house, furniture and money:

> "Everything my father left to Miss Hodges was to be in the trust. The trust comprised the lot. She could use the money as she liked. She had to leave my wife and me whatever money was left."

In cross-examination Mrs. Dorothy Ottaway said that her understanding was that Miss Hodges was bound to make a will giving her and her husband the bungalow, contents and any money she had left. "She could please herself about the money. She did not have to save it for us. She was free to spend it." It seems to me that two questions arise. First, as a matter of fact, what did the parties intend should be comprised in Miss Hodges's obligation? All money which Miss Hodges had at her death including both money which she had acquired before Mr. Harry Ottaway's death and money she acquired after his death from all sources? Or only money acquired under Mr. Harry Ottaway's will? Secondly, as a matter of law, if such an obligation existed would it create a valid trust? On the second question I am content to assume for present purposes but without so deciding that if property is given to the primary donee on the understanding that the primary donee will dispose by his will of such assets, if any, as he may have at his command at his death in favour of the secondary donee, a valid trust is created in favour of the secondary donee which is in suspense during the lifetime of the primary donee, but attaches to the estate of the primary donee at the moment of the latter's death. There would seem to be at least some support for this proposition in an Australian case to which I was referred: *Birmingham v Renfrew* (1937) 57 CLR 666. I accept that the parties mentioned money on at least some occasions when they talked about Mr. Harry Ottaway's intentions for the future disposition of Ashcroft. I do not, however, find sufficient evidence that it was the intention of Mr. Harry Ottaway that Miss Hodges should be compelled to leave all her money, from whatever source derived, to the plaintiffs. This would seem to preclude her giving even a small pecuniary legacy to any friend or relative. I do not think it is clear that Mr. Harry Ottaway intended to extract any such far-reaching undertaking from Miss Hodges or that she intended to accept such a wide obligation herself. Therefore the obligation, if any, is in my view, to be confined to money derived under Mr. Harry Ottaway's will. If the obligation is confined to money derived under Mr. Harry Ottaway's will, the obligation is meaningless and unworkable unless it includes the requirement that she shall keep such money separate and distinct from her own money. I am certain that no such requirement was ever discussed or intended. If she had the right to mingle her own money with that derived from Mr. Harry Ottaway, there would be no ascertainable property upon which the trust could bite at her death. This aspect distinguishes this case from *Re Gardner* [1920] 2 Ch 523.

There is another difficulty. Does money in this context include only cash or cash and investments, or all movable property of any description? The evidence is quite inconclusive. In my judgment the plaintiff's claim succeeds in relation to the bungalow and in relation to the furniture, fixtures and fittings which devolved under paragraph 4 of Mr. Harry Ottaway's will subject, of course, to normal wastage, fair wear and tear, but not to any other assets.

In *Re Boyes* (1884) 26 ChD 531) a legacy was given to the testator's solicitor, who was told that it was to be held upon trust, but he was not informed, until after the testator's death, what the trusts were. Among the testator's papers, a letter was found which said that the residuary estate was to be held on trust for a lady to whom the testator was not married. The solicitor desired to carry out the testator's wishes.

Kay J held that he took as trustee, holding on trust for the next of kin, and hoping that they "will consider the claim which this lady has upon their generosity."

The delivery of a sealed letter during the testator's lifetime is a sufficient communication provided that it is known to contain the terms of a trust and is accepted as such. For "a ship which sails under sealed orders, is sailing under orders though the exact terms are not ascertained by the captain till later."[4]

B. Half-Secret Trusts

The gift may be to a legatee, not absolutely, but in a fiduciary capacity. Different questions then arise. If the legacy is "to X upon such trusts as I have orally declared (or shall orally declare) to him", it is clear that X can never claim beneficially. The property is given to him as trustee. We saw that the reason which the judges gave for enforcing fully secret trusts was the prevention of fraud. If, in a half-secret trust, there is no possibility of fraud, how can the court justify the imposition of a trust on that ground?

One possible solution is to refuse to enforce half-secret trusts and to hold that the beneficial interest returns to the testator's estate by way of resulting trust.

It would however be a strange rule of law which says that a gift to X absolutely (on a fully secret trust) makes X hold upon trust for Y; yet a gift to X *upon trust* (on a half-secret trust) will be held on a resulting trust. That would mean that the mention of the intended trust in the will would prevent its taking effect.

It seems therefore that (a) half-secret trusts should be no less readily enforced than fully secret trusts; (b) fraud is not an adequate basis for the enforcement of half-secret trusts: (c) some other and better rationale is required. The cases will show that some courts have used the analogy of the doctrine of incorporation by reference to meet this problem; with the result that half-secret trusts communicated before or at the time of the will may be enforced; but not those communicated between the date of the will and the death of the testator. Clearly this is inadequate. An attempt is made at the end of this chapter to suggest a theory which is capable of providing a rational basis for the enforcement of secret trusts.

But the problem is wider than this. The question is not merely: on what basis can we enforce these trusts? The question should be: bearing in mind the sound policy in favour of formalities in wills, and the express terms of the Wills Act 1837, s. 9, are the reasons for the enforcement of informal dispositions so compelling that it is necessary to enforce them, or some of them? Having answered that question, the earlier one becomes relevant.

BLACKWELL v BLACKWELL
[1929] AC 318 (HL, Lord HAILSHAM LC, Viscount SUMNER, Lords BUCKMASTER CARSON and WARRINGTON)

The testator, John Duncan Blackwell, by a codicil to his will, gave to five persons the sum of £12,000, the income to be applied "for the purposes indicated by me to them," with power to apply £8,000 of the capital "to such person or persons indicated by me to them", as they thought fit.

The objects of the trust were communicated orally to the trustees, and accepted by them prior to the execution of the codicil. These were in favour

[4] *Re Keen* [1937] Ch 236 at 242, per Lord WRIGHT MR; *Re Boyes* (1884) 26 ChD 531 at 536.

of a lady and her illegitimate son. The widow challenged the validity of the trust and claimed the £12,000 as part of the residue.

Held. The trust was valid, and oral evidence was admissible to prove it.

VISCOUNT SUMNER: In itself the doctrine of equity, by which parol evidence is admissible to prove what is called "fraud" in connection with secret trusts, and effect is given to such trusts when established, would not seem to conflict with any of the Acts under which from time to time the Legislature has regulated the right of testamentary disposition. A Court of conscience finds a man in the position of an absolute legal owner of a sum of money, which has been bequeathed to him under a valid will, and it declares that, on proof of certain facts relating to the motives and actions of the testator, it will not allow the legal owner to exercise his legal right to do what he will with his own. This seems to be a perfectly normal exercise of general equitable jurisdiction. The facts commonly but not necessarily involve some immoral and selfish conduct on the part of the legal owner. The necessary elements, on which the question turns, are intention, communication, and acquiescence. The testator intends his absolute gift to be employed as he and not as the donee desires; he tells the proposed donee of this intention and, either by express promise or by the tacit promise, which is signified by acquiescence, the proposed donee encourages him to bequeath the money in the faith that his intentions will be carried out. The special circumstance, that the gift is by bequest only makes this rule a special case of the exercise of a general jurisdiction, but in its application to a bequest the doctrine must in principle rest on the assumption that the will has first operated according to its terms. It is because there is no one to whom the law can give relief in the premises, that relief, if any, must be sought in equity. So far, and in the bare case of a legacy absolute on the face of it, I do not see how the statute-law relating to the form of a valid will is concerned at all, and the expressions, in which the doctrine has been habitually described, seem to bear this out. For the prevention of fraud equity fastens on the conscience of the legatee a trust, a trust, that is, which otherwise would be inoperative; in other words it makes him do what the will in itself has nothing to do with; it lets him take what the will gives him and then makes him apply it, as the Court of conscience directs, and it does so in order to give effect to wishes of the testator, which would not otherwise be effectual.

To this two circumstances must be added to bring the present case to the test of the general doctrine, first, that the will states on its face that the legacy is given on trust but does not state what the trusts are, and further contains a residuary bequest, and, second, that the legatees are acting with perfect honesty, seek no advantage to themselves, and only desire, if the Court will permit them, to do what in other circumstances the Court would have fastened it on their conscience to perform.

Since the current of decisions down to *Re Fleetwood* ((1880) 15 ChD 594) and *Re Huxtable* ([1902] 2 Ch 793) has established that the principles of equity apply equally when these circumstances are present as in cases where they are not, the material question is whether and how the Wills Act affects this case. It seems to me that, apart from legislation, the application of the principle of equity, which was made in *Fleetwood's* and *Huxtable's* cases, was logical, and was justified by the same considerations as in the cases of fraud and absolute gifts. Why should equity forbid an honest trustee to give effect to his promise, made to a deceased testator, and compel him to pay another legatee, about whom it is quite certain that the testator did not mean to make him the object of this bounty? In both cases the testator's wishes are incompletely expressed in his will. Why should equity, over a mere matter of words, give effect to them in one case and frustrate them in the other? No doubt the words "in trust" prevent the legatee from taking beneficially, whether they have simply been declared in conversation or written in the will, but the fraud, when the trustee, so called in the will, is also the residuary legatee, is the same as when he is only declared a trustee by word of mouth accepted by him. I recoil from interfering with decisions of long standing, which reject this anomaly, unless constrained by statute.

The answer is put in the phrase, "this is making the testator's will for him", instead, that is, of limiting him to the will made in statutory form. What then of the legislation? Great authorities seem to have expressed an opinion, that this equitable principle, as a whole, conflicts with s. 9 of the Wills Act. Lord Cairns in 1868 says that when a devisee seeks to apply what has been devised to him otherwise than in accordance with the testator's intentions, communicated by him and accepted, "it is in effect a case of trust, and in such case the Court will not allow the devisee to set up the Statute of Frauds, or, rather, the Statute of Wills. . . . But in this the Court does not violate the spirit of the statutes; but for the . . . prevention of fraud, it engrafts the trusts on the devise by admitting evidence which the statute would in terms exclude, in order to prevent a devisee from applying property to a purpose foreign to that for which he undertook to hold it": *Jones v Badley* ((1868) 3 Ch App 362 at 364).

In the following year in *McCormick v Grogan* ((1869) LR 4 HL 82) . . . [His Lordship discussed the relationship between the equitable principle and the Wills Act 1837, s. 9, and continued:] Accordingly, I think the conclusion is confirmed, which the frame of s. 9 of the Wills Act seems to me to carry on its face, that the legislation did not purport to interfere with the exercise of a general equitable jurisdiction, even in connection with secret dispositions of a testator, except in so far as reinforcement of the formalities required for a valid will might indirectly limit it. The effect, therefore, of a bequest being made in terms on trust, without any statement in the will to show what the trust is, remains to be decided by the law as laid down by the Courts before and since the Act and does not depend on the Act itself.

The limits, beyond which the rules as to unspecified trusts must not be carried, have often been discussed. A testator cannot reserve to himself a power of making future unwitnessed dispositions by merely naming a trustee and leaving the purposes of the trust to be supplied afterwards, nor can a legatee give testamentary validity to an unexecuted codicil by accepting an indefinite trust, never communicated to him in the testator's lifetime: *Johnson v Ball* ((1851) 5 De G & Sm 85), *Re Boyes* ((1884) 26 ChD 531), *Riordan v Banon*((1876) 10 IR Eq 469), *Re Hetley* ([1902] 2 Ch

866). To hold otherwise would indeed be to enable the testator to "give the go-by" to the requirements of the Wills Act, because he did not choose to comply with them. It is communication of the purpose to the legatee, coupled with acquiescence or promise on his part, that removes the matter from the provision of the Wills Act and brings it within the law of trusts, as applied in this instance to trustees, who happen also to be legatees. If I am right in thinking that there is no contradiction of the Wills Act in applying the same rule, whether the trustee is or is not so described in the will, and the whole topic is detached from the enforcement of the Wills Act itself, then, whether the decisions in equity are or are not open to doubt in themselves, I think that, in view of the subject-matter of these decisions and the length of time during which they have been acquiesced in, your Lordships may well in accordance with precedent refuse to overrule them lest titles should be rendered insecure and settlements, entered into in reliance on their authority, should now be disturbed. It is to be remembered that the rule as to trusts not expressed in a will is not limited to relations such as the testator in this case was concerned to provide for, but may have been applied in many other connections. I pretend to no means of knowledge of my own, but it seems to me probable that effect has been given to these cases to a substantial extent and therefore that, to avoid possible injustice, your Lordships should refuse to interfere with them now. Accordingly in my opinion the appeal fails on all grounds.

RE KEEN

[1937] Ch 236, [1937] 1 All ER 452 (CA, Lords WRIGHT MR, GREENE and ROMER LJJ)

A testator, Harry Augustus Keen, by clause 5 of his will, gave £10,000 to trustees "to be held upon trust and disposed of by them among such person, persons or charities as may be notified by me to them . . . during my lifetime".

Prior to the execution of the will, he handed to one of the trustees a sealed envelope, containing the name of a lady who was to be the beneficiary. The trustee did not open the envelope until after the testator's death, but he was aware of the fact that it contained the beneficiary's name.

Held. The reservation of a power to make future unattested dispositions is contrary to the Wills Act 1837. Furthermore, the communication, being prior to the execution of the will, was inconsistent with the terms of the will. The legacy therefore fell into residue.

LORD WRIGHT MR: The summons came before Farwell J, who decided adversely to the claims of the lady on the short ground that she could not prove that she was a person notified to the trustees by the testator during his lifetime within the words of clause 5. His opinion seems to be that the clause required the name and identity of the lady to be expressly disclosed to the trustees during the testator's lifetime so that it was not sufficient to place these particulars in the physical possession of the trustees or one of them in the form of a memorandum which they were not to read till the testator's death.

I am unable to accept this conclusion, which appears to me to put too narrow a construction on the word "notified" as used in clause 5 in all the circumstances of the case. To take a parallel, a ship which sails under sealed orders, is sailing under orders though the exact terms are not ascertained by the captain till later. I note that the case of a trust put into writing which is placed in the trustees' hands in a sealed envelope, was hypothetically treated by Kay J. as possibly constituting a communication in a case of this nature: *Re Boyes* ((1884) 26 ChD 531 at 536). This, so far as it goes, seems to support my conclusion. The trustees had the means of knowledge available whenever it became necessary and proper to open the envelope. I think Mr. Evershed was right in understanding that the giving of the sealed envelope was a notification within clause 5.

This makes it necessary to examine the matter on a wider basis, and to consider the principles of law which were argued both before Farwell, J. and this Court, but which the judge found it merely necessary to mention. There are two main questions: first, how far parol evidence is admissible to define the trust under such a clause as this, and, secondly and in particular, how far such evidence if admissible at all would be excluded on the ground that it would be inconsistent with the true meaning of clause 5.

It is first necessary to state what, in my opinion, is the true construction of the words of the clause.

These words, in my opinion, can only be considered as referrring to a definition of trusts which have not yet at the date of the will been established and which between that date and the testator's death may or may not be established. Mr. Roxburgh has strenuously argued, basing himself in particular on the word "may", that the clause even though it covers future dispositions, also includes a disposition antecedent to or contemporaneous with the execution of the will. I do not think that even so wide a construction of the word "may" would enable Mr. Roxburgh's contention to succeed, but in any case I do not feel able to accept it. The words of the clause seem to me to refer only to something future and hypothetical, to something as to which the testator is reserving an option whether to do or not to do it. . . .

The principles of law or equity relevant in a question of this nature have now been authoritatively settled or discussed by the House of Lords in *Blackwell v Blackwell* ([1929] AC 318). In 1869 in *McCormick v Grogan* ((1869) LR 4 HL 82) the House of Lords had held that a secret trust, that is a trust created by an expression of the testator's wishes communicated to and accepted by the legatee, bound the conscience of the legatee, though in the terms of the will the bequest was absolute. Such a trust was held to be altogether outside the will; the will took effect according to its terms and the property passed absolutely to the legatee: but the Court, it was held, would compel the legatee to apply that property according to the undertaking he had assumed to carry out the wishes of the testator. It would be a fraud or breach of faith not to fulfil the undertaking which the legatee had given to carry out the purposes for which the bequest to him was made.

No complication was involved in such a case by reason of s. 9 of the Wills Act, 1837. The testamentary disposition, which had been duly attested, received full effect. But a different question had to be considered when in the will itself the property was left to the legatee in trust, but neither the nature of the trust nor its beneficiaries were defined in the will. That was the case decided in *Blackwell v Blackwell*. . . .

As in my judgment clause 5 should be considered as contemplating future dispositions and as reserving to the testator the power of making such dispositions without a duly attested codicil simply by notifying them during his lifetime, the principles laid down by Lord Sumner must be fatal to the appellant's claim. Indeed they would be equally fatal even on the construction for which Mr. Roxburgh contended, that the clause covered both anterior or contemporaneous notifications as well as future notifications. The clause would be equally invalid, but, as already explained, I cannot accept that construction. In *Blackwell v Blackwell; Re Fleetwood* ((1880) 15 ChD 594) and *Re Huxtable* ([1902] 2 Ch 793) the trusts had been specifically declared to some or all of the trustees at or before the execution of the will and the language of the will was consistent with that fact. There was in these cases no reservation of a future power to change the trusts, in whole or in part. Such a power would involve a power to change a testamentary disposition by an unexecuted codicil and would violate s. 9 of the Wills Act. This was so held in *Re Hetley* ([1902] 2 Ch 866). *Johnson v Ball* ((1851) 5 De G & Sm 85) is again a somewhat different example of the rule against dispositions made subsequently to the date of the will in cases where the will in terms leaves the property on trust, and shows that the position may be different from the position where the will in terms leaves the gift absolutely. The trusts referred to but undefined in the will must be described in the will as established prior to or at least contemporaneously with its execution.

But there is still a further objection which in the present case renders the appellant's claim unenforceable; the trusts which it is sought to establish by parol evidence would be inconsistent with the express terms of the will. That such an objection is fatal appears from the cases already cited, such as *Re Huxtable*. In that case an undefined trust of money for charitable purposes was declared in the will as in respect of the whole corpus, and accordingly evidence was held inadmissible that the charitable trust was limited to the legatee's life so that he was free to dispose of the corpus after his death. Similarly in *Johnson v Ball* the testator by the will left the property to trustees upon the uses contained in a letter signed "by them and myself": it was held that evidence was not admissible to show that though no such letter was in existence at the date of the will, the testator had made a subsequent declaration of trust; the Court held that these trusts could not be enforced. Lord Buckmaster in *Blackwell's* case ([1929] AC 318 at 331) described *Johnson v Ball* as an authority pointing to "a case where the actual trusts were left over after the date of the will to be subsequently determined by the testator". That in his opinion would be a contravention of the Wills Act. I know of no authority which would justify such a contravention. Lord Buckmaster also quotes (at p. 330) the grounds on which Parker V-C based his decision as being both "that the letter referred to in the will had no existence at the time when the will was made and that supposing it referred to a letter afterwards signed it is impossible to give effect to it as a declaration of the trusts, since it would admit the document as part of the will and it was unattested".

In the present case, while clause 5 refers solely to a future definition or to future definitions of the trust subsequent to the date of the will, the sealed letter relied on as notifying the trust was communicated (as I find the facts) before the date of the will. That it was communicated to one trustee only and not to both would not, I think, be an objection (see Lord Warrington's observation in the *Blackwell* case (at p. 341)). But the objection remains that the notification sought to be put in evidence was anterior to the will and hence not within the language of clause 5, and inadmissible simply on that ground as being inconsistent with what the will prescribes.

It is always with reluctance that a Court refuses to give effect to the proved intention of the testator. In the present case it may be said that the objection is merely a matter of drafting and that the decision in *Blackwell v Blackwell* would have been applicable if only clause 5 had been worded as applying to trusts previously indicated by the testator. The sealed letter would then have been admissible, subject to proof of the communication and acceptance of the trust. This may be true, but the Court must deal with the matter as in fact it is. It would be impossible to give effect to the appellant's contention without not merely extending the rule laid down in *Blackwell v Blackwell*, but actually contravening the limitations which have been placed on that rule as necessarily arising from the Wills Act and, in addition, from the fact that the conditions prescribed by the will cannot be contradicted.

The appeal must be dismissed and the decision of Farwell J affirmed.

In *Re Bateman's Will Trusts* ([1970] 1 WLR 1463, [1970] 3 All ER 817) a testator directed his trustees to set aside £24,000 and pay the income "to such persons and in such proportions as shall be stated by me in a sealed letter in my own handwriting addressed to my trustees." There was no evidence as to whether a sealed letter had been written and addressed to the trustees by the testator at the date of the will. PENNYCUICK V-C held that the direction was invalid, and said at p. 1468:

"These words clearly, I think, import that the testator may, in the future, after the date of the will, give a sealed letter to his trustees. It is impossible to confine the words to a sealed letter already so given. If that is the true construction of the wording, it is not in dispute that the direction is invalid.

I was referred to one or two cases on the point, in particular, *Re Keen's Estate* [1937] Ch 236, [1937] 1 All ER 452 in the Court of Appeal, and *Re Jones* [1942] Ch 328, [1942] 1 All ER 642, per Simonds J. I do not think it necessary to go further into those cases because it is really clear and not in dispute that once one must construe the direction as admitting of a future letter then the direction is invalid, as an attempt to dispose of the estate by a non-testamentary instrument."

C. Tenants in Common and Joint Tenants

In *Re Stead* ([1900] 1 Ch 237) FARWELL J had to consider a gift by will to two persons as joint tenants which had been made upon the faith of an antecedent promise by one of them to hold upon secret trusts. He said: "If A induces B either to make, or to leave unrevoked, a will leaving property to A and C as tenants in common, by expressly promising, or tacitly consenting, that he and C will carry out the testator's wishes, and C knows nothing of the matter until after A's death, A is bound, but C is not bound: *Tee v Ferris* ((1856) 2 K & J 357); the reason stated (at p. 368) being, that to hold otherwise would enable one beneficiary to deprive the rest of their benefits by setting up a secret trust. If, however, the gift were to A and C as joint tenants, the authorities have established a distinction between those cases in which the will is made on the faith of an antecedent promise by A and those in which the will is left unrevoked on the faith of a subsequent promise. In the former case, the trust binds both A and C: *Russell v Jackson* ((1852) 10 Hare 204), *Jones v Badley* ((1868) 3 Ch App 362), the reason stated being that no person can claim an interest under a fraud committed by another; in the latter case A and not C is bound: *Burney v Macdonald* ((1845) 15 Sim 6) and *Moss v Cooper* ((1861) 1 J & H 352), the reason stated (at p. 367) being that the gift is not tainted with any fraud in procuring the execution of the will. Personally I am unable to see any difference between a gift made on the faith of an antecedent promise and a gift left unrevoked on the faith of a subsequent promise to carry out the testator's wishes; but apparently a distinction has been made by the various judges who have had to consider the question. I am bound, therefore, to decide in accordance with these authorities . . ."

(1972) 88 LQR at p. 228 (B. Perrins)

"The 'reasons stated' by Farwell J in *Re Stead* are at first sight contradictory. One consideration is that a person must not be allowed, by falsely setting up a secret trust, to deprive another of his benefits under the will. Apparently this is decisive if the parties are tenants in common but not if they are joint tenants. On the other hand one person must not profit by the fraud of another. Apparently this is decisive only if the parties are joint tenants and not if they are tenants in common. Yet again it is apparently only fraud in procuring the execution of a will that is relevant, and not fraud in inducing a testator not to revoke a will already made. All very confusing, but add *Huguenin v Baseley* ((1807) 14 Ves 273) and the whole picture springs into focus and the confusion disappears. Returning to A and C, whether they are tenants in common or joint tenants, C is not bound *if his gift was not induced by the promise of A* because to hold otherwise would be to enable A to deprive C of his benefit by setting up a secret trust; but C is bound *if his gift was induced by the promise of A* because he cannot profit by the fraud of another; and if the trust was communicated to A after the will was made, then C takes free *if his gift was not induced by the promise of* A because if there is no inducement there is no fraud affecting C.

This, it is submitted, is what was decided by the cases cited in Farwell J's judgment."

D. Theoretical Basis of Secret Trusts[5]

In *Re Young* ([1951] Ch 344, [1950] 2 All ER 1245) a testator made a bequest to his wife, and imposed a condition that she should, *inter alia,* make certain bequests which he had communicated to her. One of them was a gift of £2,000 in favour of Thomas Cobb, the testator's chauffeur. Cobb attested the will. An attesting witness cannot receive a legacy under the will[6]. DANCKWERTS J held that Cobb was entitled to the £2,000. This was a gift to him under an oral trust declared by the testator and not a bequest under the will. He said (at p. 350): "There is one other point, which is rather interesting, concerning the validity of one of these legacies. The widow has testified that the testator's intention, as communicated to her, was that the man who had been employed by the testator for many years as chauffeur and general factotum should receive a legacy of £2,000. The chauffeur was one of the two attesting witnesses to the will, and if he takes the legacy under the terms of the will the result of s. 15 of the Wills Act, 1837, is to make his legacy ineffective. The question is whether he takes the legacy under the will. Mr. Christie, on behalf of the next-of-kin, referred to *Re Fleetwood* ((1880) 15 ChD 594), a case of a secret trust, decided by Hall V-C, where it was held that, as a woman intended to be a beneficiary was one of the attesting witnesses to the fourth codicil, the trust for her failed as to her beneficial interest, as it would have done, Hall V-C said, had it been declared in the codicil. It appears that the point was not argued in that particular case, which was concerned with a number of other points; and it seems to me that that particular decision is contrary to principle. The whole theory of the formation of a secret trust is that the Wills Act has nothing to do with the matter because the forms required by the Wills Act are entirely disregarded, since the persons do not take by virtue of the gift in the will, but by virtue of the secret trusts imposed upon the beneficiary, who does in fact take under the will.

In the Irish case of *O'Brien v Condon* ([1905] 1 IR 51) Sir Andrew Porter MR had to consider the matter with the decision of *Re Fleetwood* before him. He pointed out in a judgment which seems to me to be entirely in accordance with principle and common sense that *Re Fleetwood* was inconsistent with the principle of the matter, and inconsistent with certain other cases, one of which was a decision of the House of Lords on an Irish appeal, namely *Cullen v A-G for Ireland* ((1866) LR 1 HL,190). Sir Andrew Porter MR pointed out in *O'Brien v Condon* (at p. 59) that the point was not argued before Hall V-C in *Re Fleetwood*, and accordingly he decided to differ from the decision in *Re Fleetwood* and to apply what seems to me to be the proper statement of the principle. I agree with the decision in *O'Brien v Condon* and I think it right to follow it in the circumstances of this case, because the particular point was not argued before Hall V-C and I think that his judgment on it was given per incuriam.

It seems to me that according to *Cullen v A-G for Ireland*, and the later decision of *Re Gardner* ([1923] 2 Ch 230), every consideration connected

[5] See articles referred to at p. 106, note 1, ante.
[6] Wills Act 1837, s. 15; Wills Act 1968.

with this principle requires me to reach the conclusion that a beneficiary under a secret trust does not take under the will, and that he is not, therefore, affected by s. 15 of the Wills Act, 1837."

Hanbury & Maudsley: *Modern Equity* (10th Edn), pp. 213–214

"It is one thing to say that the trust operates outside the will, but it is another to say just how and when the trust takes effect. . . . the most natural way for this to occur is to treat the communication to the trustee as the declaration of trust, and the vesting of the property in the trustee by the will as the constitution of the trust. If this is so, the declaration is *inter vivos*, the Wills Act has no effect upon it, and the only statutory formalities that are relevant are Law of Property Act 1925, s. 53 (1) (*b*)[7], which requires that declarations of trusts of land should be evidenced in writing; but this would not affect the rule requiring a fraudulent trustee in a fully secret trust of land to hold on a constructive trust[8]. There would be no awkward distinction between declarations prior to and subsequent to the will in semi-secret trusts[9], the sole question would be whether or not a trust was declared of the property before the death, and whether that trust became properly constituted by the vesting of the property in the trustee.

We have seen that the usual rule in the case of property coming to a person who had previously declared himself trustee of it was that the trust did not become constituted without a further manifestation of intention[10]. It was submitted that where a third person accepted an instruction to hold the property on certain trusts and the settlor subsequently transferred the property to him without further declaration, the trust would be constituted. It should make no difference whether the property passed to the trustee by conveyance *inter vivos* or by a will[11]. It will probably fail however if the trustee predeceases the testator[12]. . . .

Until the property has so vested, the declaration can have no effect and cannot create property rights. It can be revoked or altered, and no doubt, if the settlor (or testator) acts as if he had forgotten the declaration or assumed it to be no longer existent, it will be treated as having expired. And no rational theory, it is suggested, can be found which will justify the remarkable decision in *Re Gardner (No. 2)*[13].

We have seen that a wife left her estate to her husband for life[14], and that after his death, it was to be held on secret trust for five named beneficiaries. One of the beneficiaries predeceased the wife. The representatives of the deceased beneficiary successfully claimed the share.

7 See p. 32, ante; *Re Baillie* (1886) 2 TLR at 661.

8 L.P.A. 1925, s. 53 (2).

9 *Re Keen* [1937] Ch 236, p. 122, ante; *Re Bateman's Will Trusts* [1970] 1 WLR 1463, [1970] 3 All ER 817, p. 125, ante.

10 See p. 103, ante; *Brennan v Morphett* (1908) 6 CLR 22; *Matter of Gurlitz,* 105 Misc 30, 172 NY Supp 523 (1918); *Re Northcliffe* [1925] Ch 651.

11 As with the property received by Miss Towry Law from her sister and conveyed to the trustees: *Re Ellenborough* [1903] 1 Ch 697, p. 98, ante; *Re Adlard* [1954] Ch 29, [1953] 2 All ER 1437; *Re Ralli's Will Trusts* [1964] Ch 288, [1963] 3 All ER 940, p. 77, ante.

12 Per Cozens-Hardy LJ in *Re Maddock* [1902] 2 Ch 220 at 251.

13 [1923] 2 Ch 230.

14 *Re Gardner (No. 1)* [1920] 2 Ch 523.

A gift by will normally fails if the donee predeceases the testator[15], and the estate of the donee can only claim if the donee acquired some interest in the property before he died. No such interest could exist in this case; and the theory which suggests that a secret trust can be treated as a declaration of trust *inter vivos* does not suggest that any interest is obtained by any beneficiary prior to the constitution of the trust by the vesting of the legal estate in the trustee."

QUESTIONS

1. Should secret trusts be classified as express, implied or constructive trusts? Why? Is this a matter of practical significance? H & M, pp. 215–216; (1951) 67 LQR 314 at 323 et seq. (L. A. Sheridan); *Ottaway v Norman* [1972] Ch 698, [1971] 3 All ER 1325.
2. Can you suggest any rational ground to support *Re Gardner* (*No, 2*) [1923] 2 Ch 230; H & M, pp. 214–215.
3. Is it advisable, as a matter of policy to enforce (a) fully secret trusts, (b) half-secret trusts? H & M, p. 216; (1951) 67 LQR 314 at 328; Scott, *Trusts* (3rd Edn) §55. 9.
4. To what extent does the doctrine of secret trusts apply to *inter vivos* dispositions? (1951) 67 LQR 314 at 323.

   V sells and conveys two cottages to P. By a separate oral agreement P allows V to occupy one of the cottages rent free for so long as he desires. Consider how V can be protected if P claims possession. By a constructive trust (*Bannister v Bannister* [1948] 2 All ER 133)? By an estoppel licence? If both methods are applicable, which is to be preferred? Maudsley and Burn, *Land Law*: *Cases and Materials* (3rd Edn, 1975) p. 460.
5. Would you recommend legislation in England on the lines of the American Uniform Testamentary Additions to Trusts Act (pp. 113, et seq. ante)?

[15] 39 *Halsbury's Laws*, paras. 1417 et seq.; *Jarman on Wills* (8th Edn) p. 438: a special exception is made in the case of children of the testator who predeceased him, leaving issue: Wills Act 1837, s. 33.

5. Trusts and Creditors

I. Introduction[1]

Property which a debtor owns beneficially is normally available to his creditors for the payment of his debts. A settlor, on setting up a trust, intends however to benefit the beneficiaries, and not to give the money to their creditors. We consider in Section II the extent to which a trust can be created so as to deprive the creditors of the beneficiary from recourse to the fund. But it may be that the settlor is worried about his own creditors. To what extent can he escape from them by creating trusts of his property in favour of members of his family? That is the subject of Section III.

II. Protective Trusts[2]

A. General

A protective trust is a useful way of protecting a beneficiary against the effects of misfortune or his own extravagance. It represents a compromise between two forces: the desire on the one hand to make a man's property available for his creditors; and on the other to enable family property to be available for the support of the family in the event of the insolvency of the head of the family. As here described, a protective trust shows the furthest extent to which English law will permit property to be denied to creditors. Most American jurisdictions allow beneficial interests under trusts to be inalienable, and this has allowed the development of what they call "spendthrift trusts"[3].

[1] H & M, pp. 217–225; 337–345; K & S, pp. 141–155; P & M, pp. 103–118; Pettit, pp. 83–89; 136–153; Snell, pp. 134–141.

[2] H & M, pp. 217–225; K & S, pp. 151–155; P & M, pp. 112–118; Pettit, pp. 87–89; Snell, pp. 134–138; (1957) 21 Conv (NS) 110, 323 (L. A. Sheridan); (1967) 31 Conv (NS) 117 (A. J. Hawkins).

[3] Scott, *Law of Trusts*, §152; Griswold, *Spendthrift Trusts* (2nd Edn, 1947). In England it was possible from the early 19th century to 1935 to create a trust for the separate use of a married woman and to impose a restraint upon anticipation or alienation. See Law Reform (Married Women and Tortfeasors) Act 1935 and Married Women (Restraint upon Anticipation) Act 1949.

The basis of a protective trust is a determinable life interest[4], determinable upon a stated event, which is usually any situation in which the income or any part of it becomes payable to anyone other than the beneficiary. A settlor cannot create in himself an interest which is determinable upon his own bankruptcy[5]. He may make it determinable upon any event *other than* bankruptcy[6]. And he may create an interest in *another* person which is determinable upon that other's bankruptcy.

When the determining event occurs, the life interest is forfeited. That is not necessarily a disaster; forfeiture means that the life tenant is no longer entitled; therefore, his creditors (or the trustee in bankruptcy) cannot claim. But on the forfeiture of the life interest, other trusts then arise; which, in the case of the protective trust provisions contained in Trustee Act 1925, s. 33, will be discretionary trusts, with the original life tenant a member of the class of beneficiaries.

As will be seen, a settlor may spell out the terms of a protective trust. But, since 1925, he may take advantage of Trustee Act 1925, s. 33, and declare that property is held "on protective trusts"[7].

B. Trustee Act 1925, s. 33

TRUSTEE ACT 1925

33. Protective Trusts.—(1) Where any income, including an annuity or other periodical income payment, is directed to be held on protective trusts for the benefit of any person (in this section called "the principal beneficiary") for the period of his life or for any less period, then, during that period (in this section called the "trust period") the said income shall, without prejudice to any prior interest, be held on the following trusts, namely:

(i) Upon trust for the principal beneficiary during the trust period or until he, whether before or after the termination of any prior interest, does or attempts to do or suffers any act or thing, or until any event happens, other than an advance under any statutory or express power, whereby, if the said income were payable during the trust period to the principal beneficiary absolutely during that period, he would be deprived of the right to receive the same or any part thereof, in any of which cases, as well as on the termination of the trust period, whichever first happens, this trust of the said income shall fail or determine;

(ii) If the trust aforesaid fails or determines during the subsistence of the trust period, then, during the residue of that period, the said income shall be held upon trust for the application thereof for the maintenance or support, or otherwise for the benefit, of all

[4] Which must be distinguished from a gift subject to a condition subsequent; *Brandon v Robinson* (1811) 18 Ves Jnr 429; *Rochford v Hackman* (1852) 9 Hare 475.

[5] *Re Burroughs-Fowler* [1916] 2 Ch 251; Trustee Act 1925, s. 33 (3), p. 132, post.

[6] *Re Detmold* (1889) 40 ChD 585, p. 132, post.

[7] Or words making clear that this was intended; *Re Wittke* [1944] Ch 166 ("upon protective trusts for the benefit of my sister"); *Re Platt* (1949) unreported, Current Law Cases 10917 ("for a protective life interest").

or any one or more exclusively of the other or others of the following persons (that is to say)—

(*a*) the principal beneficiary and his or her wife or husband, if any, and his or her children or more remote issue, if any; or

(*b*) if there is no wife or husband or issue of the principal beneficiary in existence, the principal beneficiary and the persons who would, if he were actually dead, be entitled to the trust property or the income thereof or to the annuity fund, if any, or arrears of the annuity, as the case may be;

as the trustees in their absolute discretion, without being liable to account for the exercise of such discretion, think fit.

(2) This section does not apply to trusts coming into operation before the commencement of this Act, and has effect subject to any variation of the implied trusts aforesaid contained in the instrument creating the trust.

(3) Nothing in this section operates to validate any trust which would, if contained in the instrument creating the trust, be liable to be set aside.

C. Forfeiture

The courts have often had to determine whether or not a particular event has effected a forfeiture. When the question arises upon an express trust, the result depends, of course, upon a construction of the language of the forfeiture provision, which may or may not differ materially from the Trustee Act 1925, s. 33. It will be seen that in some of the cases it is to the advantage of the life tenant to establish that there was a forfeiture; sometimes not. The termination of the principal beneficiary's life interest does not give rise to a charge to capital transfer tax[8].

In *Re Detmold* ((1889) 40 ChD 585) under a marriage settlement of the settlor's own property, the income was payable to himself "during his life, or till he shall become bankrupt, or shall . . . suffer something whereby [the income], or some part thereof, would . . . by operation or process of law, if belonging absolutely to him, become vested in or payable to some other person", and after the determination of the trust in favour of the settlor, upon trust to pay the income to his wife. In July 1888 an order was made appointing a judgment creditor of the settlor to be receiver of the income; and in September 1888 the settlor was adjudicated bankrupt.

NORTH J in holding that the wife was entitled to the income, said (at p. 588): "The limitation of the life interest to the settlor was validly determined by the fact that, in consequence of the order appointing the receiver, he ceased to be entitled to receive the income. This took place before the bankruptcy, and, therefore, the forfeiture is valid against the trustee in bankruptcy."

---

[8] F.A. 1975, Sch. 5, para. 18; F.A. 1976, Sch. 14, para. 19.

In *Re Balfour's Settlement* ([1938] Ch 928, [1938] 3 All ER 259) the income of a settled fund was payable to Nigel Balfour for life or until he should "do or suffer something whereby the same or some part thereof would through his act or default or by operation or process of law or otherwise if belonging absolutely to him become vested in or payable to some other person", with a discretionary trust over. During 1933 to 1936 the sole trustee advanced to him part of the capital at his request and in breach of trust. Balfour was then adjudicated bankrupt. FARWELL J held that his interest had determined, because the trustees had asserted their right to impound the income prior to the date of the bankruptcy; and therefore nothing passed to the trustee in bankruptcy[9].

In *Re Baring's Settlement Trusts* ([1940] Ch 737, [1940] 3 All ER 20) under a family settlement a wife had a protected life interest with the income payable to her "until some event should happen whereby the income . . . would become . . . payable to . . . some other person", with a discretionary trust over. Her husband obtained a sequestration order against her property on her failure to obey a court order to return her infant children to the jurisdiction of the court. When she eventually returned with the children, the question arose whether the life interest was forfeited. MORTON, J. held that it was, although the sequestration order was only temporary. The settlor "had intended that there should be a continuous benefit to the beneficiaries so that either the tenant for life should be in a position to have the income or the discretionary trust should arise"[10].

In *Re Dennis's Settlement Trusts* ([1942] Ch 283, [1942] 1 All ER 520)[11] under a family settlement of 1923 the settlor's son, then an infant, was given a protected life interest "until any act or event should happen whereby the income would . . . become vested in . . . some other person." On his attaining twenty-one in 1935, a supplemental deed was executed providing that for the next six years the trustees should pay to him only part of the income and accumulate the balance for him. FARWELL J held that this rearrangement caused a forfeiture.

In *Re Tancred's Settlement* ([1903] 1 Ch 715 at 723) Sir Seymer Tancred was entitled under a deed of 1891 to income for life or "until he should dispose or attempt to dispose of the . . . income . . . or do something whereby the income . . . would become payable to or vested in some other person". In 1896 he assigned his life interest to the trustees of his marriage settlement, of which he was tenant for life and solely entitled to the income, and appointed them his attorneys to receive the income; and authorised them to charge their expenses to the fund. BUCKLEY J held that there was no forfeiture.

---

[9] Cf. *Re Brewer's Settlement* [1896] 2 Ch 503, where the bankruptcy took place before the trustees exercised their right.

[10] At p. 753.

[11] (1942) 58 LQR 312 (R.E.M.).

In *Re Westby's Settlement* ([1950] Ch 296, [1950] 1 All ER 479) the Court of Appeal held that there was no forfeiture where the tenant for life under a protective trust was of unsound mind, and fees became payable out of the estate to the Supreme Court Funds under section 148 (3) of the Lunacy Act 1890[12].

In *Re Oppenheim's Will Trusts* ([1950] Ch 633, [1950] 2 All ER 86) HARMAN J, in holding that, where a tenant for life under a protective trust was certified as a person of unsound mind, the appointment of a receiver did not effect a forfeiture, said (at p. 636): "I think that a man who has a statutory agent, as this man has, can give by his agent a personal discharge no less than . . . if he were on the top of Mount Everest, his banker could give a personal discharge on his behalf. It seems to me also that the forfeiture was not intended to operate in a case of this kind where no one else will be entitled to the benefit of the income in the event which has happened. It was intended to prevent the income from getting into other hands. That does not occur in the present case."

In *Re Longman* ([1955] 1 WLR 197, [1955] 1 All ER 455) a son was entitled to the income from a trust fund subject to a forfeiture "if he should commit any act whereby any part of the income . . . became vested in or payable to any other person". In 1953 he authorised his trustees to pay money to his creditors "from the dividend due to me in July next from [a certain company]". The company, however, did not declare a dividend. DANCKWERTS J held that this prevented a forfeiture and said (at p. 199): "It seems to me that the authorities given by the son were completely nugatory, and that there was nothing on which they could operate and they never did operate on anything."

In *Re Mair* ([1935] Ch 562) FARWELL J held that an order made under section 57 of the Trustee Act 1925[13], authorising the trustees to raise money to enable a tenant for life under a protective trust to "pay certain pressing liabilities" did not effect a forfeiture. He said (at p. 565): "If and when the Court sanctions an arrangement or transaction under s. 57, it must be taken to have done it as though the power which is being put into operation had been inserted in the trust instrument as an overriding power . . . The forfeiture clause remains attached to the income which is payable to the tenant for life from time to time . . .

It must, however, be remembered that if a scheme sanctioned by the Court involves, as in *Re Salting* ([1932] 2 Ch 57), an agreement or covenant by the tenant for life to pay premiums on policies or other like payments with a proviso that if they are not duly paid the trustees are to pay them out of income, the failure to pay by the tenant for life will create a forfeiture, since it will be that act or omission of the tenant for life that

[12] See now Mental Health Act 1959, s. 112 (6).
[13] See p. 559, post.

creates the forfeiture and not the exercise by the Court of its overriding power."

Hanbury & Maudsley: *Modern Equity* (10th Edn, 1976), pp. 223–224

"It is not clear whether a forfeiture is effected when an order is made in the Family Division of the High Court which alters a protected life interest under a marriage settlement[14]. In *Re Richardson's Will Trusts*[15], the court ordered that the principal beneficiary should charge his interest with an annual payment of £50 in favour of his divorced wife. The charge was held to create a forfeiture. On the other hand, in *General Accident Fire and Life Assurance Corporation Ltd v IRC*[16] an order of the Divorce Court diverting part of the income from the life tenant in favour of a former wife was held not to effect a forfeiture.

These cases are distinguishable on a narrow ground of construction of s. 33[17]. But the broader ground of the decision, that this situation has no relevance to the real purpose of protective trusts, would seem to apply to the charge in *Re Richardson's Will Trusts*[18] as much as to the diversion of part of the income in the *General Accident* case. It is submitted that the principle of the *General Accident* case is sound. As Donovan LJ said[19], '. . . the section is intended as a protection to spendthrift or improvident or weak life tenants. But it can give . . . no protection against the effect of a court order such as was made here. Furthermore, if such an order involves a forfeiture much injustice could be done.' Perhaps the problem can be rationalised with the cases on s. 57 by saying with Russell LJ, who made clear, however, that he did not rest his decision on this approach: 'the settlement throughout was potentially subject in all its trusts to such an order as was made[1].' *Re Richardson's Will Trusts*[2] was not mentioned; but an earlier case on the Matrimonial Causes Act 1859 in favour of forfeiture, *Re Carew*[3], was overruled. It is tempting to say that *Re Richardson's Will Trusts* is wrong; but it should be noted that in that case, as in *Re Carew*, the decision in favour of forfeiture forwarded the broad policy of s. 33; for the forfeiture in those cases allowed the discretionary trusts to operate when otherwise the trustee in bankruptcy would have claimed the interest."

(1958) 74 LQR 184 (R.E.M.)

"This sequence of events points a moral for draftsmen. Hitherto the normal course of drafting has been to give a life interest simply 'on protective trusts', with or without variations. The result is that a single mistaken

[14] Which the court has power to do under Matrimonial Causes Act 1973, s. 24 (1), p. 563, post.
[15] [1958] Ch 504, [1958] 1 All ER 538; *Edmonds v Edmonds* [1965] 1 WLR 58, [1965] 1 All ER 379 . . . .
[16] [1963] 1 WLR 1207, [1963] 3 All ER 259.
[17] Ibid., see DONOVAN LJ at p. 1217 and RUSSELL LJ at p. 1221; (1963) 27 Conv (NS) 517 (F. R. Crane).
[18] [1958] Ch 504, [1958] 1 All ER 538.
[19] [1963] 1 WLR 1207, at p. 1218.
[1] [1963] 1 WLR 1207, at p. 1222.
[2] [1958] Ch 504, [1958] 1 All ER 538.
[3] (1910) 103 LT 658.

act by the beneficiary may deprive him of his determinable life interest and reduce him for the rest of his life to the status of merely one of the beneficiaries of a discretionary trust. *Re Richardson* suggests that there may be advantages in setting up a series of protective trusts, *e.g.*, one set until the beneficiary is twenty-five, another from twenty-five to thirty-five, a third from thirty-five to forty-five, and another for the rest of his life. The result would be that a youthful indiscretion at, say, twenty-two, would not irretrievably condemn the beneficiary to the mere hopes of a beneficiary under a discretionary trust, dependent upon the exercise of the trustees' discretion, but would give him a fresh start when he was twenty-five. Again, a bankruptcy at the age of thirty would not *per se* mean that when he was twice that age he would still have not an income as of right, but a mere hope of a well-exercised discretion. Indeed, instead of relating the stages to the age of the beneficiary, they might be related to a period of time (*e.g.*, five years) after the occurrence of any event which had made the initial trust pass from Stage 1 to Stage 2. England lacks the device of the spendthrift trust in the American sense, but it is far from clear that the fullest possible use is being made of the existing machinery of protective and discretionary trusts."

D. The Effect of Forfeiture

In *Re Gourju's Will Trusts* ([1943] Ch 24, [1942] 2 All ER 605) Mrs. Gourju was a protected life tenant under her husband's will. She resided at Nice. That part of France was occupied by the Germans in June, 1940. By the Trading with the Enemy Act 1939 and Orders made thereunder[4], she became disentitled to receive the income of the fund, and her protected life interest was forfeited. The Custodian of Enemy Property could not claim the income, for he had no better claim than Mrs. Gourju. The discretionary trusts came into effect. The trustees wished to accumulate the income and pay it at the end of the war to Mrs. Gourju. SIMONDS J held that they could not do so. Their duty was to pay to one or more of the members of the discretionary class.

Underhill's Law of Trusts and Trustees (12th Edn, 1970) p. 100

"Another point that not infrequently arises is whether, under a discretionary trust (such as the statutory trust above set forth) *where the settlor is a third party*, and the defeasible life interest has been forfeited either by bankruptcy or alienation (voluntary or involuntary), the trustees can, *under the discretion* vested in them, continue to pay the income to the person whose life interest has determined. Obviously the object of such trusts is to enable this to be done if it can be. The authorities are, however, against the right of the trustees to do this[5], on the ground apparently that the life tenant, being

[4] Trading With the Enemy (Custodian) Order 1939 (S.R. & O. 1939 No. 1198). Later Orders contained a proviso that vesting in the Custodian of Enemy Property should not take place if it would cause a forfeiture.

[5] *Re Coleman* (1888) 39 ChD 443; *Re Neil* (1890) 62 LT 649, explained by STIRLING LJ in *Re Fitzgerald* [1904] 1 Ch 573 at 593.

bound in conscience to hand over to his creditor or assignee whatever his interest in the income may be, is none the less bound with regard to such part of the income as may be paid to him by the trustees in the exercise of their discretion; and that they, having notice of this equity, are equally bound not to pay him. This may seem to be a *reductio ad absurdum,* since the trustees could not under any circumstances pay any part of the income to the creditor or assignee[6], so that it is difficult to see how the latter could suffer by the payment being made to the life tenant himself, or what claim he could have upon the trustees. Nevertheless, trustees under such circumstances have been made liable to the creditor or assignee[7], although, curiously enough, it is well settled that they are at liberty to *expend* the income for his benefit[8]. In one case it was held that the trustees might apply such part as they thought fit of the income for the benefit of the person whose life interest had determined without reference to any debt which such person might owe to the trust estate[9]. This case is distinct from that which has been more frequently before the courts where the contest is between the tenant of a protected life interest and his own assignee. The law is, therefore, in an anomalous and unsatisfactory state; and it is not considered that it has been in any way altered by the introduction by s. 33 of the Trustee Act 1925[10] of the statutory 'protective trusts'.

It need scarcely be said that, until they have notice of an act amounting to forfeiture, the trustees are justified in paying the income to the first beneficiary[11].

III. Attempts to Deprive Creditors of the Settlor[12]

We discussed in Section II the extent to which it was possible to give to a person an interest which would be kept from his creditors on his bankruptcy. We now consider the extent to which creditors can claim property which the debtor has given away in the form of a voluntary settlement.

A. Voluntary Settlements Independent of Bankruptcy

LAW OF PROPERTY ACT 1925

172. Voluntary conveyances to defraud creditors voidable[13].—(1) Save as

[6] *Re Bullock* (1891) 64 LT 736; *Train v Clapperton* [1908] AC 342; *Re Laye* [1913] 1 Ch 298; *Re Hamilton* (1921) 124 LT 737. But cf. *Lord v Bunn* (1843) 2 Y & C Ch Cas 98; which seems *contra* at first sight but really turned on a question of construction.

[7] *Re Coleman* (1888) 39 ChD 443; *Re Neil* (1890) 62 LT 649, explained by Stirling LJ in *Re Fitzgerald* [1904] 1 Ch 573 at 593.

[8] *Re Bullock*, supra; and cf. *Re Coleman*, supra; and *Re Neil*, supra. But see *Re Ashby* [1892] 1 QB 872, where Vaughan Williams J thought that the bankrupt might be liable to account for sums paid to him.

[9] *Re Eiser's Will Trusts* [1937] 1 All ER 244.

[10] See p. 131, ante.

[11] *Re Long* [1901] WN 166.

[12] H & M, pp. 337–345; K & S, pp. 141–151; P & M, pp. 103–111; Pettit, pp. 136–153; Snell, pp. 138–141.

[13] Replacing 13 Elizabeth I, c. 5.

provided in this section, every conveyance of property made, whether before or after the commencement of this Act, with intent to defraud creditors, shall be voidable, at the instance of any person thereby prejudiced.

(2) This section does not affect the operation of a disentailing assurance, or the law of bankruptcy for the time being in force.

(3) This section does not extend to any estate or interest in property conveyed for valuable consideration and in good faith or upon good consideration and in good faith to any person not having, at the time of the conveyance, notice of the intent to defraud creditors.

i. "INTENT TO DEFRAUD"

There has long been disagreement as to the meaning of "intent to defraud"; and whether the intent needs to be affirmatively proved, or may be ascertained from surrounding circumstances.

In *Freeman v Pope* ((1870) 5 Ch App 538 at 541) Lord HATHERLEY LC said: "If a person owing debts makes a settlement which subtracts from the property which is the proper fund for the payment of those debts, an amount without which the debts cannot be paid, then, since it is the necessary consequence of the settlement (supposing it effectual) that some creditors must remain unpaid, it would be the duty of the Judge to direct the jury that they must infer the intent of the settlor to defeat or delay his creditors, and that the case is within the statute."

In *Re Wise, ex parte Mercer* ((1886) 17 QBD 290) Wise, a master mariner, was engaged to Miss Vyse. He sailed to Hongkong and married someone else. In August 1881, Miss Vyse commenced an action for breach of promise[14]. In October, Wise inherited £500 from his mother, and nine days later he executed a voluntary settlement of that sum upon his wife and himself and his family. On obtaining judgment in her action, Miss Vyse attempted to have the settlement set aside. She failed; because there was insufficient evidence of an intent to defraud. Lord ESHER MR said at p. 298:

"The argument was first put in this way—it is necessary to prove that the bankrupt, at the date of the voluntary settlement, intended to defeat and delay a creditor or his creditors generally; the necessary consequence of what he did was to defeat and delay his creditors; and, therefore, as a proposition of law, the tribunal which had to consider whether he did intend to defeat and delay his creditors was bound fo find that he did. In support of that proposition dicta of great and eminent judges were cited. I will venture to say as strongly as I can that to my mind that proposition is monstrous."

[14] This action was abolished by L.R. (Miscellaneous Provisions) Act 1970.

LLOYDS BANK LTD v MARCAN[15]

[1973] 1 WLR 339, [1973] 2 All ER 359 (PENNYCUICK V-C); and [1973] 1 WLR 1387, [1973] 3 All ER 754 (CA, RUSSELL and CAIRNS LJJ and GOULDING J).

David Marcan had guaranteed the indebtedness of Marcan Industries Ltd. to Lloyds Bank. In order to cover his liabilities to the Bank, including that under the guarantee, he executed in 1966 a legal mortgage of the land on which his family lived and carried on a horticultural business. The Bank immediately called for payment of the guarantee; and on September 1, 1967 commenced proceedings for possession.

On March 11, 1968, David Marcan granted a lease of the premises to his wife, Betty, for a term of 20 years at a rent to be determined by a qualified surveyor. Betty was added as a defendant, as was David's trustee in bankruptcy[16] after his adjudication in August 1969.

The question was whether the lease was voidable under section 172.

Held. The lease had been granted with an intent to defraud.

CAIRNS LJ: My mind fluctuated much during the argument of this appeal and it is only by a narrow margin and with some reluctance that I agree that the appeal should be dismissed. Both under the Statute of Elizabeth I and under section 172 of the Law of Property Act 1925 it is clear from the words of the enactment that fraud has to be established before a transaction can be avoided. In my opinion, fraud involves dishonesty and I cannot go with Pennycuick V-C in his observation [1973] 1 WLR 339, 344 that the word "defraud" in section 172 "is not intended to be confined to cases of fraud in the ordinary modern sense of that word, i.e., as involving actual deceit or dishonesty". It is clear enough that deceit is not a necessary element, but in my view dishonest intention is, at any rate when the conveyance is for consideration. That is shown by *Copis v Middleton* (1818) 2 Madd 410, *Wood v Dixie* (1845) 7 QB 892, *Alton v Harrison* (1869) 4 Ch App 622, *Re Johnson* (1881) 20 ChD 389 and *Re David and Adlard* [1914] 2 KB 694.

Other cases make it clear that if the conveyance is voluntary it is easier to infer a dishonest intention than when it is made for consideration or even that no dishonest intention need then be established: see *Freeman v Pope* (1870) 5 Ch App 538, *Ideal Bedding Co Ltd v Holland* [1907] 2 Ch 157, *Re Eichholz*, [1959] Ch 708, [1959] 1 All ER 166. It does, however, appear that a conveyance for good consideration will be regarded as fraudulent if made with the deliberate intention of hindering creditors and for the benefit of the debtor himself rather than as a bona fide family arrangement or an arrangement which merely prefers one set of creditors to another set. To that effect was *Re Fasey* [1923] 2 Ch 1, decided by a very strong Court of Appeal (Lord Sterndale MR, Warrington and Atkin LJJ).

In the present case the debtor let the property at a rent which was honestly fixed; he was unaware (as Pennycuick V-C found) that the land would be worth more with vacant possession than when subject to the lease; he acted at least in part for the sake of his wife and family; and he took legal advice

[15] (1975) 91 LQR 86 (B. J. F. Longstaff), 317 (B. Elkan).

[16] The settlement would in any case have been void against the trustee in bankruptcy under the Bankruptcy Act 1914, s. 42, p. 142, post.

before granting the lease. These facts tend to support the view that he acted honestly.

The elements which in the end persuade me that he acted with intent to defraud his creditors are that he granted the lease at a time when he knew that the bank was seeking possession; that he must have known that it would have been more convenient for the bank to have vacant possession than merely to have possession of the rents and profits; and that while his wife was the grantee of the lease it was obviously for his own benefit that he wished her to be in possession rather than the bank. . . .

I accordingly agree that the appeal must be dismissed.

---

ii. "ANY PERSON THEREBY PREJUDICED"

In *Re Butterworth, ex parte Russell* (1882) 19 ChD 588) Charles Butterworth was a successful baker in Manchester. He decided to purchase a grocery business—a trade in which he had no experience. Before doing so, he made a voluntary settlement, dated August 8, 1878, of substantially the whole of his property, in favour of his family. The grocery business lost money, but he sold it six months later for the same price as he paid, and continued his bakery business only. In 1881 he became bankrupt, owing money to many creditors; but all the debts owing at the date of the settlement had been paid.

The Court of Appeal held that the settlement was void under the Bankruptcy Act 1869, and fraudulent under 13 Eliz. I, c. 5, because it was executed with a view to putting property out of the reach of creditors if the grocery business should fail. JESSEL MR said (at p. 598): "As regards the other point it is not absolutely necessary to decide it, but I think that the County Court Judge was right. The principle of *Mackay v Douglas* ((1872) LR 14 Eq 106), and that line of cases, is this, that a man is not entitled to go into a hazardous business, and immediately before doing so settle all his property voluntarily, the object being this: 'If I succeed in business, I make a fortune for myself. If I fail, I leave my creditors upaid. They will bear the loss.' That is the very thing which the statute of *Elizabeth* was meant to prevent. The object of the settlor was to put his property out of the reach of his future creditors. He contemplated engaging in this new trade and he wanted to preserve his property from his future creditors. That cannot be done by a voluntary settlement. That is, to my mind, a clear and satisfactory principle."

In *Cadogan v Cadogan* ([1977] 1 WLR 1041, [1977] 1 All ER 200) Mr. and Mrs. Cadogan purchased a house as their matrimonial home. The wife paid part of the purchase price but the house was conveyed into the husband's name alone. In 1949 they separated. In October 1973 the husband petitioned for divorce, and the wife, when acknowledging service of the petition, stated that she wished to apply for financial relief. The husband then executed a voluntary conveyance of the house to their son, the defendant. In December 1973 the husband was granted a decree nisi, but died intestate before the decree absolute. The effect of his death was that the wife's right to apply to the court for relief abated. The wife claimed inter alia that the conveyance was void under Law of Property Act 1925, s. 172 (1). At first instance, SLADE J struck out this claim under Ord. 18, r. 19, on the ground that it was unsustainable. The Court of Appeal reversed this decision. BUCKLEY LJ said at p. 1056:

"It does not seem to me to be wholly clear that before the commencement of the Act of 1925, the law of avoidance of fraudulent dispositions was one which could only be relied upon for the benefit of somebody who was, at the date of the application for relief, a creditor of the allegedly fraudulent disponent. If the judge was right in thinking that section 172 could only be invoked by creditors, he was right in thinking that the plaintiff could not succeed on a claim for relief based on that section. But it seems to me to be arguable, first, that the Statute of Elizabeth was not confined to protecting the interests of creditors only, as the judge thought, and, secondly, that the use of the word 'person' in section 172 was intended to make the protection of the section available to persons who were prejudiced, although they were not properly to be described as creditors and were not prejudiced in the capacity of creditors.

If there seems to be a respectable argument (by which I mean one which has a recognisable chance of success) in favour of the view that the plaintiff may be able to substantiate her claim under section 172, I do not think we ought now to decide the question whether she can or cannot. R.S.C. Ord. 18, r. 19 is not a rule which provides an opportunity to get points of law decided as preliminary issues: it is for the present purpose a rule which is directed to getting rid of embarrassing pleas—pleas which ought not to be on the face of the pleadings because they are clearly unsustainable. Only if any such argument would, as the judge thought, be clearly unsustainable, would it be right in my view to decide that question here and now and close the doors of the court to the plaintiff in relation to that question."

Hanbury & Maudsley: *Modern Equity* (10th Edn, 1976), p. 340

"The statute 13 Eliz. 1, c. 5, had given protection to persons taking in good faith 'upon good consideration'; but this had been held to include valuable consideration only (including marriage) and to exclude natural love and affection. The reason for this was that, as was said in *Twyne's Case*[17]: 'if consideration of nature and blood should be a good consideration within this proviso, the statute would serve for little or nothing, and no creditor would be sure of his debt." In other words, the most common way of defrauding creditors is to make settlements in favour of the family; to exclude such settlements from the operation of section 172 would render the section almost useless.

This aspect of section 172 has not been discussed by the courts. It was relevant in *Re Eichholz*[18], where Harman J, without referring to the point, treated the subsection as if it had made no alteration to the law. In that case:

[17] (1602) 3 Co Rep 80b at 81b.
[18] [1959] Ch 708, [1959] 1 All ER 166.

> Trustees administering the estate of Eichholz in bankruptcy claimed to recover from his widow a house and contents which he had purchased for her. He was hopelessly insolvent at that time, having, as a solicitor, misappropriated large amounts of clients' funds. His widow knew nothing of this, and was bona fide throughout. The trustees succeeded, no mention being made by Harman, J., nor apparently in argument, of the possibility of natural love and affection being a sufficient consideration to bring her within the protection of the section."

iii. PURCHASER FOR VALUE WITHOUT NOTICE

In *Halifax Joint Stock Banking Co v Gledhill* ([1891] 1 Ch 31) a settlement which was fraudulent and void against creditors under 13 Eliz. 1, c. 5, reserved a reversionary life interest to the settlor. The settlor subsequently charged this interest by way of equitable mortgage to a mortgagee who had no notice that the settlement was fraudulent. In an action by the creditor to have the settlement declared void, KAY J held that the equitable mortgagee was protected; but declared the settlement was otherwise void. He said (at p. 39): "I think that it is right to hold that sect. 5 does include a purchaser for value, without notice, of any interest under the deed impeached, whether that interest be legal or equitable, and prevents the deed being used against him."

B. Bankruptcy

BANKRUPTCY ACT 1914

42. Avoidance of certain settlements.—(1) Any settlement of property, not being a settlement made before and in consideration of marriage, or made in favour of a purchaser or incumbrancer in good faith and for valuable consideration, or a settlement made on or for the wife or children of the settlor of property which has accrued to the settlor after marriage in right of his wife, shall, if the settlor becomes bankrupt within two years after the date of the settlement, be void against the trustee in the bankruptcy, and shall, if the settlor becomes bankrupt at any subsequent time within ten years after the date of the settlement, be void against the trustee in the bankruptcy, unless the parties claiming under the settlement can prove that the settlor was, at the time of making the settlement, able to pay all his debts without the aid of the property comprised in the settlement, and that the interest of the settlor in such property passed to the trustee of such settlement on the execution thereof.

(2) Any covenant or contract made by any person (hereinafter called the settlor) in consideration of his or her marriage, either for the future payment of money for the benefit of the settlor's wife or husband, or children, or for the future settlement on or for the settlor's wife or husband or children, of property, wherein the settlor had not at the date of the marriage any estate or interest, whether vested or contingent, in possession or remainder, and not being money or property in right of the settlor's wife or husband, shall, if the settlor is adjudged bankrupt and the covenant or contract has not been executed at the date of the commencement of his

bankruptcy, be void against the trustee in the bankruptcy, except so far as it enables the persons entitled under the covenant or contract to claim for dividend in the settlor's bankruptcy under or in respect of the covenant or contract, but any such claim to dividend shall be postponed until all claims of the other creditors for valuable consideration in money or money's worth have been satisfied.

(3) Any payment of money (not being payment of premiums on a policy of life assurance) or any transfer of property made by the settlor in pursuance of such a covenant or contract as aforesaid shall be void against the trustee in the settlor's bankruptcy, unless the persons to whom the payment or transfer was made prove either—

(*a*) that the payment or transfer was made more than two years before the date of the commencement of the bankruptcy; or

(*b*) that at the date of the payment or transfer the settlor was able to pay all his debts without the aid of the money so paid or the property so transferred; or

(*c*) that the payment or transfer was made in pursuance of a covenant or contract to pay or transfer money or property expected to come to the settlor from or on the death of a particular person named in the covenant or contract and was made within three months after the money or property came into the possession or under the control of the settlor;

but, in the event of any such payment or transfer being declared void, the persons to whom it was made shall be entitled to claim for dividend under or in respect of the covenant or contract in like manner as if it had not been executed at the commencement of the bankruptcy.

(4) "Settlement" shall, for the purposes of this section, include any conveyance or transfer of property.

In *Re Carter and Kenderdine's Contract* ([1897] 1 Ch 776) a question was raised under a vendor and purchaser summons whether the vendors could make a good title. They derived their title under a voluntary settlement, which, said the purchasers, was liable to be set aside under section 47 of the Bankruptcy Act 1883[19]. The question therefore was whether the purchasers would obtain a good title if they purchased *bona fide* in reliance upon a voluntary settlement which had not been challenged but which might be challenged in the future.

The Court of Appeal, approving *Re Brall* ([1893] 2 QB 381) and *Re Holden* ((1887) 20 QBD 43), held that the vendors' title was good. LINDLEY LJ said: "Looking at that section, and looking at it with no more than ordinary care, we first find that it does not say that these settlements are to be void generally, or anything of the sort. It says that they will be void 'against the trustee in bankruptcy', which is a totally different thing. We must then ask ourselves, how can a settlement be void against the trustee in bankruptcy until there is a trustee in bankruptcy against whom it can be void? That remark leads to this question, 'Void', as from what time? That is the whole controversy. The section does not say a word about

[19] Replaced by the Bankruptcy Act 1914, s. 42, p. 142, ante.

it. You must look at it with reference to the language and the kind of transaction with which the section deals. Looking at the language only, it seems to me that when an enactment says a settlement 'shall be void against the trustee in bankruptcy', it does not mean that it shall be void before there is a trustee in bankruptcy."

QUESTION

The Restatement of Trusts §152 provides: "(1) Except as stated in §156 [where the settlor is a beneficiary] and 157 [particular classes of claimants], if by the terms of a trust the beneficiary is entitled to the income from the trust property for life or for a term of years and it is provided that his interest shall not be transferable by him and shall not be subject to the claims of his creditors, the restraint on the voluntary and involuntary transfer of his right to the income accruing during his life is valid. (2) A trust in which by the terms of the trust or by statute a valid restraint on the voluntary and involuntary transfer of the interest of the beneficiary is imposed is a spendthrift trust."

In some American jurisdictions, statutes provide that only that part of a beneficiary's interest which is required for his education and support shall be protected against his creditors.

Consider the differences between the American spendthrift trusts and the English protective trust developments. Would you favour the introduction of spendthrift trusts in England? (Scott: *Trusts*, §152; *Cases on Trusts*, p. 381).

6. Trusts and Taxes

I. Introduction

Any acquisition of, or any dealing with, money or property may involve liability to some form of taxation. Income is subject to income tax, at escalating rates; and unearned income is liable also to the investment income surcharge. Capital gains tax is payable in respect of a gain made on a disposal of property. And capital transfer tax, which replaced estate duty in respect of transfers made after March 26, 1974, is payable in respect of transfers of capital inter vivos or on death, and on capital distributions from a trust.

Tax legislation is directed towards the imposition of liability to tax upon existing or anticipated situations. People earn income; they dispose of capital to their children and relatives, and they die, owning capital. A tax lawyer and an accountant could tell them what tax is payable in any particular situation.

A tax or estate-planner will tackle the situation one stage further back. Rather than work out what tax has to be paid in a particular situation, it is better to reorganise the situation, and adjust it to one in which the tax charge is less, or is avoided altogether. A student of trusts thus needs to understand by what methods tax charges can be reduced or avoided. This is tax avoidance, not tax evasion. It involves the organisation of a client's affairs in such a way as to attract the minimum liability. As Potter and Monroe said: "By the expression 'tax planning' nothing more sinister is meant than that a man should make an intelligent appreciation of the incidence of tax and should take it into account as a relevant factor in planning what dispositions he will make of his property as between himself and the members of his family"[1].

In the modern capitalist world, fiscal considerations dominate the types of trust which are created. Until 1974, when capital transfer tax was introduced, the only charge upon capital transfers[2] was estate duty, which was payable when property passed on a death or within seven years before a death. Thus the transfer was tax-free if it was made more than seven years before the donor's death. The richer the donor, the more he could give away without noticing the difference; and it was common practice among rich families to make gifts, usually by setting up trusts before reaching an age at which death must soon be expected. Avoidance of estate duty was so easy that it was often described as a "voluntary tax".

Not only could the donor avoid estate duty by transferring property into a trust, but estate duty could also be avoided, until 1969, on the deaths of beneficiaries under a trust. Estate duty, as explained above, was payable when property "passed" on a death. It "passed" when a life tenant under a trust died[3]. But there was no "passing" on the death of a member of a class of beneficiaries under a discretionary trust[4]. It was possible, therefore, to avoid liability to estate duty on the death of the settlor and of all the beneficiaries if the settlor, more than seven years before his death, set up a discretionary trust. The discretionary trust could be designed to continue for the period of perpetuity[5]. The Finance Act 1969 imposed liability in the case of the death of a beneficiary under a discretionary trust who had (in general) received income from the trust during the seven years before his death. Duty was charged on the proportion of the capital which corresponded to the proportion of the income which he had received during that period[6].

That is all history; except for the fact that the seven year "claw-back" rule still applies in respect of gifts made prior to 1974[7]. But it is history which still leaves its mark. The creation of discretionary trusts was standard practice among rich families, and large numbers were in existence in 1974. The capital transfer tax legislation has borne hard on discretionary trusts, and they have moved from the top of the fiscal league to the bottom. Few are likely to be created in the future; the current problem is to know what to do with those which remain[8]. Many will be quickly terminated, and the assets distributed, and we shall see that tax reductions are available where distributions are made before April 1, 1980[9]. Many questions remain to be determined in relation to existing discretionary trusts, and that alone makes it important to understand the principles on which they were based.

While discretionary trusts were going out of favour for fiscal reasons,

1 Tax Planning: Preface to 1st Edn quoted 8th Edn p. *x*.
2 There may also be a charge to capital gains tax.
3 *Earl Cowley v IRC* [1899] AC 198.
4 *Gartside v IRC* [1968] AC 553, [1968] 1 All ER 121.
5 H & M, p. 230.
6 F.A. 1969, ss. 36, 37, introducing the "substituted 2 (1) (b)". See the previous edition of this book, pp. 221–224.
7 F.A. 1975, Sch. 11, Part I.
8 (1977) NLJ 31 (J. B. Morcom).
9 F.A. 1975, Sch. 5, para. 14.

accumulation and maintenance settlements are likely to come into greater prominence, for the same reasons. We will examine these two types of trust in this chapter. Reference should also be made, in connection with accumulation and maintenance settlements, to Chapter 15, sections VIII and IX, dealing with the trustees' powers of maintenance and advancement. To understand these trusts, it is necessary to have some background knowledge of the British fiscal system. The subject is too large for detailed treatment here. A few general statements will set the scene. Many qualifications and exceptions are omitted, and the reader is warned that the account is too condensed to be relied on in practice.

II. Taxation

A. Income Tax

"Income tax, if I may be pardoned for saying so," said Lord MACNAGHTEN nearly eighty years ago, "is a tax on income."[10] The basic rate is 34 per cent[11]. Certain reliefs may be deducted in calculating taxable income, the most important of which are: personal relief; marriage allowance; small income relief; children's relief; earned income relief and old age relief. Higher rates are payable on income in excess of £6,000, rising to 83% at £21,000. In addition, investment income in excess of £1,500 is subject to a surcharge of 10%, and that in excess of £2,000 to one of 15%. Thus a tax payer who earns £19,000 and has investment income of £2,001, will pay 98% on the last £ of his income[12a].

Ordinarily, liability to income tax only arises where the income is that of the taxpayer. But there is an exception in the case of income paid to or for the benefit of an unmarried minor child of the settlor. Such income is treated as the income of the settlor. Subject to complex provisions which need not be examined here, this liability does not, however, arise if the income is not paid out, but is accumulated. It will be seen that the aggregation provisions only apply where the income is paid to or for the benefit of a child of the *settlor*. Between April 1969 and the end of the tax year 1971–1972, there were further and much wider aggregation provisions. By Finance Act 1969, s. 15, all unearned income of a minor, who was unmarried and not regularly working[12], was to be treated as the income of the parent of the minor even though that parent was not the settlor. These provisions were repealed by Finance Act 1971, s. 16 (2) (b), the repeal taking effect from the beginning of the tax year 1972–1973. Their return has been promised since 1974.

B. Capital Gains Tax

Capital gains tax was introduced by the Finance Act 1965. The rate is 30

[10] *LCC v A-G* [1901] AC 26 at 35.

[11] I.C.T.A. (No. 2) 1970, s. 1; F.A. 1977, s. 17.

[12] Which included students.

[12a] Under the Budget proposals of April 11, 1978, higher rates are payable on income in excess of £7,000, rising to 83% at £23,000. Investment income in excess of £1,700 is subject to a surcharge of 10%, and that in excess of £2,250 to one of 15%. A taxpayer who earns £20,750 and has investment income of £2,251 will pay 98% on the last £.

per cent[13]. It is payable on a disposal of property and calculated upon the increase in value between the date of purchase and that of disposal; and also where a beneficiary under a trust becomes absolutely entitled to the property as against the trustee. There is no longer a deemed disposal on death[14]. If the property was owned on April 6, 1965 the value as at that date is (generally speaking) taken. Some property is exempt; the most important exemptions being the taxpayer's main or only residence and chattels worth less than £1,000. And no liability is incurred on the disposition of a beneficial interest under a trust[14a].

C. Capital Transfer Tax

i. CAPITAL TRANSFERS BY INDIVIDUALS

Tax is payable on voluntary transfers of value made by an individual after March 26, 1974[15], the date on which the tax was announced in the House of Commons. There is a transfer of value when a person makes a disposition as a result of which the value of his estate immediately after the disposition is less than it would have been but for the transfer; and the value transferred is the amount by which the estate is the less[16]. This covers inter vivos transfers and also transfers on death[17]. In the White Paper[18], the plan was to treat both in exactly the same way. But the Act provided two scales: Table 1, applying to transfers on death and within three years of death, and Table 2 applying to all other transfers. It will be seen that[19] the rates in Table 2 are half those in Table 1 up to £110,000, and that they are the same after £310,000.

There are various exceptions and reliefs, the most important of which are: transfers between spouses, inter vivos or on death; certain foreign property; and personal exemptions, which include £2,000 per annum per donor, and an additional £100 per annum per donee; gifts to charities, works of art, agricultural and business property and woodlands. There is no room to give details here[20].

Two important points need to be made to explain the nature of capital transfer tax. First, it is a single tax, affecting inter vivos transfers and transfers on death. The rate of tax increases as the amount of the transfer increases, and the rate will therefore be higher on subsequent gifts. And the transfer on death is necessarily the last of all. Thus, if A makes a first gift of £110,000, tax will be charged under Table 2 on the amount of the gift. A second gift of £100,000 would be taxed at the rate applicable under Table 2 on gifts between £110,000 and £210,000. If, more than three years later, he

[13] There is an alternative basis for individuals which is advantageous at lower income levels. It is not available to trustees: F.A. 1965, s. 21.

[14] F.A. 1965, s. 24 (1), as substituted by F.A. 1971, s. 59, Sch. 12, para. 1.

[14a] Under the Budget proposals of April 11, 1978, gains not exceeding £1,000 for the tax year are exempt. Gains in excess of £1,000 but under £5,000 are taxable at 15%. The exemption for chattels is increased to £2,000.

[15] F.A. 1975, s. 20 (5); other than exempt transfers: Sch. 6.

[16] Ibid., s. 20 (2), (3), (7). [17] Ibid., s. 22. [18] Cmnd. No. 5705 of 1974.

[19] See p. 154, post. The Tables show the rates applicable to transfers made after October 26, 1977, when the CTT threshhold was increased from £15,000 to £25,000, and the starting point of each taxable band in the rate scales similarly raised by £10,000; the size of each band and the rates are unchanged.

[20] F.A. 1975, Sch. 6.

dies, leaving £100,000, his estate will be taxed under Table 1 at the rates applicable to £210,000–£310,000.

Secondly, grossing up. Unless the donee pays the tax on a transfer, the donor is treated as making a gift of the amount transferred, plus the tax. That is the amount by which his estate is reduced by the transfer. To find out the tax due upon a gift of £110,000 from A to B, the tax is not that chargeable on £110,000; but rather the tax chargeable upon the sum which, after tax, leaves £110,000. In other words, it is necessary to gross up. This can be a complex calculation. Grossing up Tables are readily available[1]. From these it will be seen that a gift to B of £110,000 is treated as a transfer by A of £129,483, the tax on that figure being £19,483. If B paid the tax, he would pay only £14,125; but he would then only keep £95,875. Transfers on death are necessarily gross gifts, and there is no question of grossing up.

In order to calculate the tax on a transfer, it is necessary therefore to know what previous transfers have been made, and whether the transfers were gross or net. A record should be kept of capital transfers made. A method of doing so, showing a variety of gross and net gifts is given in Wheatcroft and Hewson, *Capital Transfer Tax* p. 10, reprinted below.

ii. CAPITAL TRANSFER TAX AND TRUSTS

Special provisions were necessary to make capital transfer tax applicable to trusts. It is necessary to determine both in what circumstances tax is payable, and also who should be treated as the donor for the purpose of bringing prior transfers into account.

(a) Trusts with An Interest in Possession

The answers were not difficult in the case of trusts in which a beneficiary had an interest in possession. Estate duty had always been payable on the death of a life tenant, and it was only to be expected that capital transfer tax would be charged on the termination of the life tenant's interest, by death or by other means, such as payment of the capital to remaindermen. The life tenant is treated as making the transfer; the rate of tax will depend on the amount of the transfer, and on his prior record of transfers (including those of his free estate).

(b) Trusts with No Interest in Possession

There was no such obvious solution in the case of trusts in which there was no interest in possession. Such trusts of course include discretionary trusts. And also many other types, of which the most important for our purposes is the accumulation and maintenance trust; where the property is held on trust for persons contingently on attaining a certain age.

There is no obvious answer to either of the two points referred to above. With discretionary trusts, there is no obvious occasion for the imposition of charge; and no obvious person to treat as the transferor. The matter is dealt with in Sched. 5 paras 6–13, of which paragraphs 7 and 8, which

[1] Wheatcroft & Hewson: *Capital Transfer Tax*, p. 9, p. 154, post; *Butterworth's Tax Tables.*

are some of the most complex parts of the Act, lay down the basis of calculation in relation to capital distributions from discretionary trusts. The general result of paragraphs 7 and 8, in the words of the Inland Revenue Circular dated April 8, 1975 is

> "*Paragraphs 7 to 9* establish the basis for calculating the rates chargeable on capital distributions. *Paragraph 7* applies to capital distributions where there has been a chargeable transfer in relation to the settlement (usually on its making) and therefore (normally) applies to settlements made after 26 March 1974 (sub-paragraph (1) in conjunction with paragraph 11 (2) and (3)). Sub-paragraph (2) establishes the rate to be applied when the gross amount of the capital distribution, taken with the total of previous distribution payments, does not exceed the initial value of the settled property. In this event the rate charged on a capital distribution is that which the settlor would have paid at the time of the settlement on a chargeable transfer equal to the value of the property in settlement (or, if more than one settlement was made on the same occasion, on a chargeable transfer equal to the aggregate values of the property in these "related" settlements). Under sub-paragraph (3) once the initial value is exceeded the rate charged on successive capital distributions is the rate which the settlor would have paid on successive chargeable transfers of the same amounts after making the settlement (or settlements).
>
> *Paragraph 8* applies where paragraph 7 does not apply—e.g. to capital distributions out of property settled before 27 March 1974. In that case, the tax chargeable on a capital distribution will be that which would have been due from an individual on a chargeable transfer equal to the capital distribution if he had already made chargeable transfers equal to the total of previous distribution payments (if any)."

There are separate provisions relating to Accumulation and Maintenance Settlements[2], Protective Trusts[3], Superannuation Schemes[4], Trusts for the Benefit of Employees[5], Trusts for Mentally Disabled Persons[6], and various compensation funds[7], such as those maintained by the Stock Exchange, Lloyd's and the Law Society, and since 1976, for Newspaper Trusts[8].

D. Wealth Tax

Side by side with the White Paper on Capital Transfer Tax[9] was a Green Paper on Wealth Tax[10]. The preface to the latter stated that "The Government is committed to use the taxation system to promote greater social and economic equality. This requires a redistribution of wealth as well as income". The two taxes should be regarded as inter-related methods

[2] F.A. 1975, Sch 5, para. 15, as amended, p. 169, post.
[3] Ibid., Sch. 5, para. 18, p. 171, post, p. 130, ante.
[4] Ibid., Sch. 5, para. 16.
[5] Ibid., Sch. 5, para. 17.
[6] Ibid., Sch. 5, para. 19.
[7] Ibid., Sch. 5, para. 21.
[8] F.A. 1976, s. 108.
[9] Cmnd. No. 5705 of 1974.
[10] Cmnd. No. 5704 of 1974.

of pursuing this policy. Capital Transfer Tax came first, because it makes no sense to announce a new tax on wealth, and allow rich people to dispose of it before the tax comes into force.

The Wealth Tax is an annual tax on capital. Legislation was promised for 1976; but it has so far proved impossible to reach agreement upon a number of important questions concerning the tax[11]. Even the rates are not settled. The Green Paper suggested two rates, each starting at 1% at £100,000. The lower scale increased to 2½%, and the higher to 5%, over £5,000,000. The matter remains in the realm, not of law, but of politics.

III. Statutes on Capital Transfer Tax

A. General

i. CAPITAL TRANSFERS

FINANCE ACT 1975

PART III

CAPITAL TRANSFER TAX

Main charging provisions

19. Capital transfer tax.—(1) A tax, to be known as capital transfer tax, shall be charged on the value transferred by a chargeable transfer.

(2) Schedule 4 to this Act shall have effect with respect to the administration and collection of the tax.

20. Transfers and chargeable transfers.—(1) The following provisions of this section shall have effect, subject to the other provisions of this Part of this Act, for determining for the purposes of capital transfer tax what is a chargeable transfer and what value is transferred by a chargeable transfer.

(2) Subject to subsections (3) and (4) below, a transfer of value is any disposition made by a person ("the transferor") as a result of which the value of his estate immediately after the disposition is less than it would be but for the disposition; and the amount by which it is less is the value transferred by the transfer.

(3) For the purposes of subsection (2) above no account shall be taken of the value of excluded property which ceases to form part of a persons's estate as a result of a disposition.

(4) A disposition is not a transfer of value if it is shown that it was not intended, and was not made in a transaction intended, to confer any gratuitous benefit on any person and either—

(*a*) that it was made in a transaction at arm's length between persons not connected with each other, or

(*b*) that it was such as might be expected to be made in a transaction at arm's length between persons not connected with each other:

[11] A Select Committee produced five minority reports (1975) H.C. 696.

but this subsection does not apply to a disposition by which a reversionary interest is acquired in the circumstances mentioned in section 23 (3) of this Act and does not apply to a sale of shares or debentures not quoted on a recognised stock exchange unless it is shown that the sale was at a price freely negotiated at the time of the sale or at a price such as might be expected to have been freely negotiated at the time of the sale.

In this subsection "transaction" includes a series of transactions and any associated operations.

(5) A chargeable transfer is any transfer of value made by an individual after 26th March 1974 other than an exempt transfer.

(6) A transfer of value made by an individual after that date and exempt only to a limited extent—

(*a*) is, if all the value transferred by it is within the limit, an exempt transfer; and

(*b*) is, if that value is partly within and partly outside the limit, a chargeable transfer of so much of that value as is outside the limit as well as an exempt transfer of so much of that value as is within the limit.

(7) For the purposes of this section, where the value of a person's estate is diminished and that of another person's estate is increased by the first-mentioned person's omission to exercise a right he shall be treated as having made a disposition at the time, or the latest time, when he could exercise the right, unless it is shown that the omission was not deliberate.

21. Settled property.—Schedule 5 to this Act shall have effect with respect to settled property.

22. Transfer on death.—(1) On the death of any person after the passing of this Act tax shall be charged as if, immediately before his death, he had made a transfer of value and the value transferred by it had been equal to the value of his estate immediately before his death, but subject to the following provisions of this section.

(2) Where the deceased was entitled to an interest in possession in settled property which on his death but during the life of the settlor reverted to the settlor, then, unless the settlor had acquired a reversionary interest in the property for a consideration in money or money's worth, the value of the settled property shall be left out of account in determining for the purposes of this Part of this Act the value of the deceased's estate immediately before his death.

(3) Where the deceased was entitled to an interest in possession in settled property and on his death the settlor's spouse became beneficially entitled to that property, then if—

(*a*) the settlor's spouse was at the time of the death domiciled in the United Kingdom . . .[12]; and

(*b*) neither the settlor nor the settlor's spouse had acquired a reversionary interest in the property for a consideration in money or money's worth;

[12] Words in sub-para. (*a*) repealed by F.A. 1976, Sch. 14, para. 13, and Sch. 15, Part V.

the value of the settled property shall be left out of account in determining for the purposes of this Part of this Act the value of the deceased's estate immediately before his death. [The references in this subsection to the settlor's spouse include, in a case where the settlor died less than two years before the deceased or the deceased died before 1st April 1977, references to the settlor's widow or widower.][13,14]

Meaning of estate and excluded property

23. Meaning of estate.—(1) For the purposes of this Part of this Act, a person's estate is the aggregate of all the property to which he is beneficially entitled, except that the estate of a person immediately before his death does not include excluded property.

(2) A person who has a general power which enables him, or would if he were sui juris enable him, to dispose of any property other than settled property, or to charge money on any property other than settled property, shall be treated as beneficially entitled to the property or money; and for this purpose "general power" means a power or authority enabling the person by whom it is exercisable to appoint or dispose of property as he thinks fit.

(3) Notwithstanding subsection (1) above, where a person entitled to an interest (whether in possession or not) in any settled property acquires a reversionary interest expectant (whether immediately or not) on the interest, the reversionary interest is not part of his estate for the purposes of this Part of this Act.

24. Excluded property.—(1) The following provisions of this section apply for determining what is excluded property for the purposes of this Part of this Act, in addition to property which is excluded property by virtue of any of the provisions of Schedule 7 to this Act, and subject to paragraph 2 of Schedule 5 to this Act.

(2) Property situated outside the United Kingdom is excluded property if the person beneficially entitled to it is an individual domiciled outside the United Kingdom.

(3) A reversionary interest is excluded property unless—

(*a*) it has at any time been acquired (whether by the person entitled to it or by a person previously entitled to it) for a consideration in money or money's worth; or

[(*aa*) it is one to which either the settlor or his spouse is beneficially entitled; or][15]

(*b*) it is the interest expectant on the determination of a lease treated as a settlement by virtue of paragraph 1 (3) of Schedule 5 to this Act.[16]

[13] Words in brackets were added by F.A. 1976, s. 110 (1).
[14] The omitted subsections deal with transitional provisions relating to estate duty.
[15] Para. (aa) in sub-s. (3) was inserted by F.A. 1976, s. 120 (1) with effect from April 16, 1976, except in relation to a reversionary interest under a settlement made before that date.
[16] See also F.A. 1977, s. 41 (2), (3), (4).

ii. CAPITAL TRANSFER TAX RATES[17]

Value of Transfer £	Table 1 Rate on Slice %	Table 1 Cumulative Tax £	Table 1 Effective Rate %	Table 2 Rate on Slice %	Table 2 Cumulative Tax £	Table 2 Effective Rate %
0–25,000	0	0	0	0	0	0
25–30,000	10	500	1.67	5	250	.83
30–35,000	15	1,250	3.57	7½	625	1.79
35–40,000	20	2,250	5.62	10	1,125	2.81
40–50,000	25	4,750	9.50	12½	2,375	4.75
50–60,000	30	7,750	12.92	15	3,875	6.46
60–70,000	35	11,250	16.07	17½	5,625	8.04
70–90,000	40	19,250	21.39	20	9,625	10.69
90–110,000	45	28,250	25.68	22½	14,125	12.84
110–130,000	50	38,250	29.42	27½	19,625	15.10
130–160,000	55	54,750	34.22	35	30,125	18.83
160–210,000	60	84,750	40.36	42½	51,375	24.46
210–260,000	60	114,750	44.13	50	76,375	29.37
260–310,000	60	144,750	46.69	55	103,875	33.51
310–510,000	60	264,750	51.91	60	223,875	43.90
510–1,010,000	65	589,750	58.39	65	548,875	54.34
1,010–2,010,000	70	1,289,750	64.17	70	1,248,875	62.13
Over 2,010,000	75	—	—	75	—	—

iii. GROSSING-UP

Wheatcroft and Hewson: *Capital Transfer Tax*, p. 9

"The value for tax of a net transfer must be ascertained by grossing up the net amount to calculate the tax and adding that tax to the net amount. To do this requires another Table, Table 3[18]. By using this Table the tax appropriate to a net gift of any amount can be found, and the value transferred by that gift is obtained by adding the tax to the net gift. It will be seen that when gifts are of substantial amounts the tax is high in relation to the net amount given.

Table 3

THE METHOD OF CALCULATING THE TAX ON THE VALUE TRANSFERRED BY A NET GIFT

Value of net gift £	*Tax*		
0– 25,000	0		
25,000– 29,750	5/95ths (5.26%)	of excess over	£25,000
29,750– 34,375	250 + 7.5/92.5ths (8.11%)	,, ,,	29,750
34,375– 38,875	625 + 10/90ths (11.11%)	,, ,,	34,375
38,875– 47,625	1,125 + 12.5/87.5ths (14.29%)	,, ,,	38,875
47,625– 56,125	2,375 + 15/85ths (17.65%)	,, ,,	47,625
56,125– 64,375	3,875 + 17.5/82.5ths (21.21%)	,, ,,	56,125
64,375– 80,375	5,625 + 20/80ths (25.00%)	,, ,,	64.375
80,375– 95,875	9,625 + 22.5/77.5ths (29.03%)	,, ,,	80,375
95,875–110,375	14.125 + 27.5/72.5ths (37.93%)	,, ,,	95,875
110,375–129,875	19,625 + 35/65ths (53.85%)	,, ,,	110,375

[17] The Tables show the rates applicable to transfers made after October 26, 1977. See p. 148, note 19, ante.

[18] This table is not in the Act and has been produced for the authors. This Table has also been amended: note 17, supra.

Value of net gift £	*Tax*			
129,875–158,625	30,125 + 42.5/57.5ths (73.91%)	,,	,,	129,875
158,625–183,625	51,375 + 50/50ths (100.00%	,,	,,	158,625
183,625–206,125	76,375 + 55/45ths (122.22%)	,,	,,	183,625
206,125–286,125	103,875 + 60/40ths (150.00%)	,,	,,	206,125
286,125–461,125	223,875 + 65/35ths (185.71%)	,,	,,	286,125
461,125–761,125	548,875 + 70/30ths (233.33%)	,,	,,	461,125
761,125–	1,248,875 + 75/25ths (300.00%)	,,	,,	761,125

The gross equivalent of a net gift is the net gift plus the tax."

iv. RECORD OF GIVING

Wheatcroft and Hewson: *Capital Transfer Tax*, pp. 9–10

To illustrate the tax on successive gifts let us start with a simple example (No. 1, see below) where an individual . . . makes three successive lifetime gifts in cash, in three successive years of £110,000 in the first year, followed by £100,000 in each of the later two years, and each time calculates the tax and deducts it from the amount handed over to the donee, so that each transfer is a gross transfer[19]. In year one the tax on the lower rate scale of Table 2 is £14,125 so the donee gets £95,875. In year two the tax on a further £100,000 is £37,250[20] so the donee gets £62,750 and in year three the tax on the third £100,000 is £52,500[21] so the donee gets £47,500. If there were three separate donees the last would benefit the least.

Let us now take another example (No. 2, see below) where all three gifts were net transfers as the donor paid the tax himself, with the aid of Table 3 we find that the tax on the first gift is £19,483[22] and the equivalent gross transfer is £129,483. To find the tax on the second net transfer of £100,000 it is necessary to calculate from Table 3 the tax on the total net transfers to date of £210,000 (which is £109,688)[1] and to deduct from that figure the tax on the previous transfer (£19,483) so that the tax on the second gift of £100,000 is £90,205 making total tax to date of £109,688 on the first two gifts of £210,000. Using the same method the total tax on the third transfer is £158,526[2]. When grossed up, the three gifts carry forward a cumulative total of value for tax of £578,214.

The calculations are more complicated when some of the gifts are gross and some are net. In Example 3 (below) we assume that the first and last transfers are net (the donor paying the tax) and the second transfer is gross (the donee paying the tax). Tax on the first net transfer is £19,483[3] but as the next transfer is gross we must now calculate the cumulative *gross* figure (£129,483) and calculate the tax from Table 1 on £229,483 which is £61,117; the tax on the second transfer therefore amounts to £41,634. It follows that the donee of the second gift only receives £58,366 and there is a carry

[19] This and the following examples assume (a) that no part of the gift is exempt (i.e. the donor has used up his annual £2,000 and £100 per donee and any "normal expenditure" exemption); but (b) that he has made no other chargeable transfers.

[20] This is calculated from the lower rate scale of Table 2 by deducting the tax on £110,000 (£14,125) from the tax on £220,000 (£51,375).

[21] Tax on £310,000 (£103,875) less tax on £210,000 (£51,375).

[22] £14,125 plus 27.5/72.5 of £14,125.

[1] £103,875 plus 60/40 of £3,875.

[2] £223,875 plus 65/35 of £23,875.

[3] See § 1–24.

forward of £229,483 gross and £168,366 net. As the third transfer is made net we must look at Table 3 to find the tax on net transfers totalling £268,366[4]. When the first and third gifts are grossed up the three gifts carry forward a cumulative total of value for tax of £465,603.

These three examples can be shown in tabular form which is how an individual's records can conveniently be kept[5].

	Net value of transfer	*Gross value of transfer*	*Tax on transfer*	*Cumulative net transfer*	*Cumulative gross transfer*	*Cumulative tax*
Example 1						
First gift	£95,875	£110,000	£14,125	£95,875	£110,000	£14,125
Second gift	£62,750	£100,000	£37,250	£158,625	£210,000	£51,375
Third gift	£47,500	£100,000	£52,500	£206,125	£310,000	£103,875
Example 2						
First gift	£110,000	£129,483	£19,483	£110,000	£129,483	£19,483
Second gift	£100,000	£190,205	£90,205	£210,000	£319,688	£109,688
Third gift	£100,000	£258,526	£158,526	£310,000	£578,214	£268,214
*Example*3						
First gift	£110,000	£129,483	£19,483	£110,000	£129,483	£19,483
Second gift	£58,366	£100,000	£41,634	£168,366	£229,483	£61,117
Third gift	£100,000	£236,120	£136,120	£268,366	£465,603	£197,237

B. Trusts

i. TRUSTS WITH AN INTEREST IN POSSESSION

FINANCE ACT 1975, Schedule 5

Interests in possession

3.—(1) A person beneficially entitled to an interest in possession in settled property shall be treated as beneficially entitled to the property in which the interest subsists.

(2) Where the person entitled to the interest is entitled to part only of the income (if any) of the property, the interest shall be taken to subsist in such part only of the property as bears to the whole thereof the same proportion as the part of the income to which he is entitled bears to the whole of the income.

(3) Where the part of the income of any property to which a person is entitled is a specified amount (or the whole less a specified amount) in any period, his interest in the property shall be taken, subject to sub-paragraph (4) below, to subsist in such part (or in the whole less such part) of the property as produces that amount in that period.

(4) The Treasury may from time to time by order made by statutory instrument[6] prescribe a higher and a lower rate for the purposes of this

[4] £197,237 less previous tax of £61,117 resulting in £136,120 tax on third gift.

[5] The examples have been amended to take account of the new rates applicable after October 26, 1977. See p. 148, note 19, ante.

[6] Capital Transfer Tax (Settled Property Income Yield) Order 1975, S.I. 1975 No. 610, prescribes from May 8, 1975 the 2½ per cent. Consols yield and the gross dividend yield of the All-Share Index from the F.T.-Actuaries Share Indices (published daily in the *Financial Times*).

paragraph; and where tax is chargeable in accordance with sub-paragraph (3) above by reference to the value of the part of a property which produces a specified amount or by reference to the value of the remainder (but not where chargeable transfers are made simultaneously and tax is chargeable by reference to the value of that part as well as by reference to the value of the remainder) the value of the part producing that specified amount—

(*a*) shall, if tax is chargeable by reference to the value of that part, be taken to be not less than it would be if the property produced income at the higher rate so prescribed; and

(*b*) shall, if tax is chargeable by reference to the value of the remainder, be taken to be not more than it would be if the property produced income at the lower rate so prescribed;

but the value to be taken by virtue of paragraph (*a*) above as the value of part of a property shall not exceed the value of the whole of the property.

(5) Where the person entitled to the interest is not entitled to any income of the property but is entitled, jointly or in common with one or more other persons, to the use and enjoyment of the property, his interest shall be taken to subsist in such part of the property as corresponds to the proportion which the annual value of his interest bears to the aggregate of the annual values of his interest and that or those of the other or others.

(6) Where, under paragraph 1 (3) of this Schedule, a lease of property is to be treated as a settlement, the lessee's interest in the property shall be taken to subsist in the whole of the property less such part of it as corresponds to the proportion which the value of the lessor's interest (as determined under Schedule 10 to this Act) bears to the value of the property.

(7) A statutory instrument made under this paragraph shall be subject to annulment in pursuance of a resolution of the House of Commons.

Termination of interest in possession treated as transfer of value

4.—(1) Where a person beneficially entitled to an interest in possession in any property comprised in a settlement disposes of his interest the disposal—

(*a*) is not a transfer of value; but

(*b*) shall be treated for the purposes of this Schedule as the coming to an end of his interest;

and tax shall be charged accordingly under the following provisions of this paragraph.

(2) Where at any time during the life of a person beneficially entitled to an interest in possession in any property comprised in a settlement his interest comes to an end, tax shall be charged, subject to the following provisions of this paragraph, as if at that time he had made a transfer of value and the value transferred had been equal to the value of the property in which his interest subsisted.

(3) If the person whose interest in the property comes to an end becomes

on the same occasion beneficially entitled to the property or to another interest in possession in the property tax shall not be chargeable under this paragraph, except in the case mentioned in sub-paragraph (10) (*b*) below.

(4) If the interest comes to an end by being disposed of by the person beneficially entitled thereto and the disposal is for a consideration in money or money's worth, tax shall be chargeable under this paragraph as if the value of the property in which the interest subsisted were reduced by the amount of the consideration; but in determining that amount the value of a reversionary interest in the property or of any interest in other property comprised in the same settlement shall be left out of account.

(5) If the interest comes to an end during the settlor's life and on the same occasion the property in which the interest subsisted reverts to the settlor, tax shall not be chargeable under this paragraph unless the settlor had acquired a reversionary interest in the property for a consideration in money or money's worth.

(6) If the interest comes to an end and on the same occasion the settlor's spouse becomes beneficially entitled to the settled property, then if—

(*a*) the settlor's spouse is then domiciled in the United Kingdom . . . ; and

(*b*) neither the settlor nor the settlor's spouse had acquired a reversionary interest in the property for a consideration in money or money's worth;

tax shall not be chargeable under this paragraph. [The references in this sub-paragraph to the settlor's spouse include, in a case where the settlor has died less than two years before the interest comes to an end or the interest comes to an end before 1st April 1977, references to the settlor's widow or widower][7].

(7) Where the person beneficially entitled to the interest is the surviving spouse of a person who has died before 13th November 1974, tax shall not be chargeable under this paragraph if the value of the property in which the interest subsists would, by virtue of section 22 (4) of this Act, have been left out of account in determining the value of his estate had he died immediately before the coming to an end of the interest.

(9) Where a transaction is made between the trustees of the settlement and a person who is, or is connected with—

(*a*) the person beneficially entitled to an interest in the property; or

(*b*) a person beneficially entitled to any other interest in that property or to any interest in any other property comprised in the settlement; or

(*c*) a person for whose benefit any of the settled property may be applied,

and, as a result of the transaction, the value of the first-mentioned property is less than it would be but for the transaction, a corresponding part

[7] The words in brackets were added by F.A. 1976, s. 110 (2) and are deemed always to have had effect.

of the interest shall be deemed for the purposes of this paragraph to come to an end, unless the transaction is such that, were the trustees beneficially entitled to the settled property, it would not be a transfer of value.

(10) References in this paragraph to any property and to an interest in any property include references to part of any property or interest; and—

(*a*) the tax chargeable under this paragraph on the coming to an end of part of an interest shall be charged as if the value of the property (or part) in which the interest subsisted were a corresponding part of the whole thereof; and

(*b*) if the value of the property (or part) to which or to an interest in which a person becomes entitled as mentioned in sub-paragraph (3) above is less than the value on which tax would be chargeable apart from that sub-paragraph, tax shall be chargeable on a value equal to the difference.

(11) Tax shall not be chargeable under this paragraph if the settled property is excluded property.

Relief for successive charges on interest in possession

5.—(1) Where the value transferred by a chargeable transfer falls to be determined by reference to the value of any settled property in which there subsists an interest in possession to which the transferor is entitled, and—

(*a*) the value transferred by an earlier chargeable transfer also fell to be determined by reference to the value of that property; and

(*b*) that earlier transfer either was or included the making of the settlement or was made after the making of the settlement;

then, if the period between those transfers is not more than four years, tax shall be charged as if the value of that property were reduced—

(i) by 80 per cent. if that period is one year or less;

(ii) by 60 per cent. if that period is more than one year but not more than two years;

(iii) by 40 per cent. if that period is more than two years but not more than three years; and

(iv) by 20 per cent. if that period is more than three years.

[(2) Where the transferor became entitled to the interest—

(*a*) on a death on which estate duty was payable in respect of the settled property; or

(*b*) in consequence of

(i) a gift inter vivos; or

(ii) a disposition or determination of a beneficial interest in possession in any property comprised in a settlement,

where, by reason of the gift or interest, estate duty or capital transfer tax under section 22 (5) of this Act was payable on a subsequent death in respect of the settled property, sub-paragraph (1) above shall apply as if the period referred to therein were the period between the death and the chargeable transfer.][8]

ii. TRUSTS WITH NO INTEREST IN POSSESSION. DISCRETIONARY TRUSTS

(a) Capital Distributions

FINANCE ACT 1975, Schedule 5

Charge on capital distributions of settled property

6.[9]—(1) Where a distribution payment is made out of property comprised in a settlement and at the time the payment is made no interest in possession subsists in the property or in the part of it out of which the payment is made, the payment is in this Schedule referred to as a capital distribution.

(2) Where a person becomes entitled to an interest in possession in the whole or any part of the property comprised in a settlement at a time when no such interest subsists in the property or that part, a capital distribution shall be treated as being made out of the property or that part of the property; and the amount of the distribution shall be taken to be equal to the value at that time of the property or, if the interest is in part only of that property, of that part.

(3) Where, at a time when no interest in possession subsists in property comprised in a settlement or in a part of that property, a transaction is made between the trustees of the settlement and a person who is, or is connected with—

(*a*) a person beneficially entitled to an interest in any of the settled property; or

(*b*) a person for whose benefit any of the settled property may be applied;

and, as a result of the transaction, the value of the property or part is less than it would be but for the transaction, a capital distribution shall be treated as being made out of the property or part of an amount equal to that by which that value is less, unless the transaction is such that, were the trustees beneficially entitled to the settled property, it would not be a transfer of value.

(4) Tax shall be charged on any capital distribution as on the value transferred by a chargeable transfer where—

(*a*) the value transferred less the tax payable on it is equal to the amount of the capital distribution; and

(*b*) the rate applicable is that specified in paragraphs 7 to 9 below;

and in those paragraphs "the assumed transferor" means the person who would be the transferor in relation to the chargeable transfer assumed by this sub-paragraph and the appropriate Table for the purposes of those paragraphs (including the calculation of any tax that would have been

[8] Sub-para. (2) was substituted by F.A. 1976, s. 97 (2), and deemed always to have had effect.
[9] See also F.A. 1975, s. 39, F.A. 1976, s. 98, dealing with close companies.

chargeable as mentioned in paragraph 7 (2) (*a*) below) is the Second Table set out in section 37 (3) of this Act.

(5) The reference in sub-paragraph (4) (*a*) above to the tax payable on a capital distribution does not include any tax which is payable by a person to whom a distribution payment is made [or, in the case of a capital distribution treated as made under sub-paragraph (2) above or paragraph 15 (3) below, any tax which is payable out of the property whose value is taken as the amount of the capital distribution; and in relation to a capital distribution treated as made under sub-paragraph (3) above or paragraph 12 or 24 (2) below, sub-paragraph (4) (*a*) above shall have effect as if the words "less the tax payable on it" were omitted][10].

(6) Notwithstanding sub-paragraph (1) above, a distribution payment which is made to the settlor or the settlor's spouse shall not be a capital distribution if the settlor or, as the case may be, the settlor's spouse is domiciled in the United Kingdom at the time the payment is made . . . [The references in this sub-paragraph to the settlor's spouse include, in the case of a distribution payment made less than two years after the settlor's death or made before 1st April 1977, references to the settlor's widow or widower.][11]

[(6A) Where the person referred to in sub-paragraph (2) above is the settlor, the settlor's spouse or, if the settlor has died less than two years before the time there referred to, the settlor's widow or widower, and is domiciled in the United Kingdom at that time, that sub-paragraph shall have effect as if the reference in it to a capital distribution were a reference to a distribution payment to the settlor or, as the case may be, the settlor's spouse, widow or widower.][12]

(7) . . .[13]

(8) Where a person entitled to an interest in possession in part of the property comprised in a settlement became so entitled as a member of a class, sub-paragraph (2) above shall not apply on his becoming entitled, as such a member, to an interest in possession in another part of that property, if he becomes so entitled on the death under full age of another member of that class.

---

105. Survivorship clauses.[14]—(1) Schedule 5 to the Finance Act 1975 shall have effect, and subject to subsections (2) and (3) below shall be deemed always to have had effect, as if paragraph 6 (7) were omitted and the following paragraph inserted after paragraph 22—

> "22A—(1) Where under the terms of a will or otherwise property is held for any person on condition that he survives another for a specified period of not more than six months, this Part of this Act shall

[10] The words in brackets were substituted by F.A. 1976, Sch. 14, para. 11.

[11] The words in brackets were substituted by F.A. 1976, s. 110 (3), and deemed always to have had effect.

[12] Sub-para. (6A) was inserted by F.A. 1976, Sch. 14, para. 12, and deemed always to have had effect.

[13] Sub-para. (7) was replaced by sub-para. 22A: F.A. 1976, s. 105 (1), infra.

[14] See note 13, supra.

apply as if the dispositions taking effect at the end of the period or, if he does not survive until then, on his death (including any such disposition which has effect by operation of law or is a separate disposition of the income from the property) had had effect from the beginning of the period.

(2) Sub-paragraph (1) above does not affect the application of this Part of this Act in relation to any distribution or application of property occurring before the dispositions there mentioned take effect.

(3) Where the death with which the period mentioned in sub-paragraph (1) above begins occurred before 13th March 1975, that sub-paragraph shall not apply in relation to any property, if or to the extent that, by virtue of section 121 (1) (*c*) of the Finance Act 1972 (relief for property given to a surviving spouse), the value attributable to it was disregarded for the purposes of estate duty charge-on that death."

(2) Subsection (1) above shall not have effect in a case where the period there mentioned ended before 7th April 1976 if the application at the end of the period of sub-paragraph (2) of paragraph 6 of the said Schedule 5 was excluded by sub-paragraph (7) of that paragraph.

(3) Where the person for whom property was held as mentioned in subsection (1) above—

(*a*) was the spouse of the other person there mentioned, and

(*b*) died before the end of 1976 and during the period there mentioned,

that subsection shall not have effect if the persons mentioned in subsection (4) below so elect by written notice given to the Board within twelve months of the second death or such longer time as the Board may allow.

(4) The persons referred to in subsection (3) above are the personal representatives of each spouse and the trustees of every settlement in which either of the spouses had an interest in possession immediately before his death.

(b) Rates of Charge

FINANCE ACT 1975, Schedule 5

Rates of charge on capital distributions following chargeable transfers

7.—(1) This paragraph applies where, at or after the relevant time and before the capital distribution, there has been a transfer of value which satisfies the conditions stated in paragraph 11 (2) below.

(2) So far as the amount on which tax is chargeable, when added to the amount of all previous distribution payments made out of property comprised in the settlement, does not exceed the initial value, the rate chargeable shall be equal to the fraction of which—

(*a*) the numerator is the amount of the tax which would have been charged on the value transferred by the relevant transfer, or such part of that amount as is attributable to the initial value, if the value so transferred had been equal to the aggregate of the initial values of the settlement and any related settlement; and

(*b*) the denominator is the initial value.

(3) So far as the amount on which tax is chargeable, when so added, exceeds the initial value, the rate or rates chargeable shall be the rate or rates that would be applicable if the assumed transferor had made previous chargeable transfers and the aggregate of the values transferred by them were equal to the aggregate of—

(*a*) the values transferred by any chargeable transfers which the person who made the relevant transfer had made before the relevant transfer;

(*b*) the aggregate of the initial values of the settlement and any related settlement; and

(*c*) the amounts of any previous distribution payments out of property comprised in the settlement, so far as the tax (if any) chargeable thereon is chargeable in accordance with this sub-paragraph.

Rate of charge on other capital distributions

8.—(1) This paragraph applies where paragraph 7 above does not apply.

(2) The rate or rates chargeable shall be the rate or rates that would be applicable if the assumed transferor—

(*a*) had made previous chargeable transfers in any case where there had been previous distribution payments made on or after 27th March 1974 out of the settled property; but

(*b*) had made no previous chargeable transfers in any other case;

and, where paragraph (*a*) above applies, the aggregate of the values transferred by the previous chargeable transfers were equal to the aggregate amounts of the previous distribution payments mentioned therein.

(c) Additions to Trust

FINANCE ACT 1975, Schedule 5

Further property added by settlor

9.—(1) The following provisions of this paragraph apply where, by a transfer of value made by the settlor at any time after the making of the settlement and after 26th March 1974 (in this paragraph referred to as "the subsequent transfer") further property is added to the property comprised in the settlement immediately before the subsequent transfer (in this paragraph referred to as "the previous property").

(2) The subsequent transfer shall be treated for the purposes of paragraphs 6 to 8 above as the making of a separate settlement and the further property as property comprised in that separate settlement, and the following provisions of this paragraph shall apply for determining the property out of which any capital distributions made after the subsequent transfer are to be treated as made.

(3) If paragraph 7 above would have applied to a capital distribution

made immediately before the subsequent transfer, any capital distribution made after the subsequent transfer shall be treated as made—

(*a*) out of the previous property, if or to the extent that the amount of the distribution, when added to the amount of all previous distribution payments made out of the settled property, does not exceed the previous value defined in sub-paragraph (4) below; and

(*b*) out of the further property in any other case.

(4) For the purposes of sub-paragraph (3) above the previous value is the initial value, increased, if there was an earlier transfer which is a "subsequent transfer" as defined above, by the value, immediately after the earlier transfer, of any property added by it to the settled property.

(5) If paragraph 7 above would not have applied to a capital distribution made immediately before the subsequent transfer, any capital distribution made after the subsequent transfer shall be treated as made—

(*a*) out of the previous property, if or to the extent that the amount of the distribution, when added to the amount of any previous distribution payment made since the subsequent transfer, does not exceed the value of the settled property immediately before the subsequent transfer; and

(*b*) out of the further property in any other case;

and accordingly, where paragraph (*b*) above applies, the rate or rates chargeable shall be determined in accordance with paragraph 7 above (and, where there is a further subsequent transfer, in accordance with sub-paragraphs (3) and (4) above).

(d) Termination of Interest of Settlor or Spouse

FINANCE ACT 1975, Schedule 5

Capital distributions after termination of interest of settlor or settlor's spouse

10. Where, after the termination of an interest in possession in a part (in this paragraph referred to as the chargeable part) of any property comprised in a settlement made after 26th March 1974, a capital distribution is made out of the chargeable part, and—

(*a*) the settlor or the settlor's spouse was the person entitled to the interest before its termination, and either the settlor or the settlor's spouse was entitled to an interest in possession in the chargeable part immediately after the making of the settlement; and

(*b*) the making of the settlement either was not a transfer of value or was an exempt transfer or a transfer exempt to the extent of the value of the chargeable part;

paragraphs 6 to 9 above shall apply as if the chargeable part were comprised in a separate settlement made by the person entitled to the first-mentioned interest on its termination and the termination of the interest were the relevant transfer; and as if the subsequent termination of any interest of his in any other part of the settled property were an addition made by him to the property comprised in that separate settlement.

[**10A.** Where a capital distribution is made on the same day and out of property comprised in the same settlement as a distribution payment that is not a capital distribution, the capital distribution shall for the purpose of paragraphs 7 to 9 above be treated as made before the distribution payment.][15]

(e) Interpretation

FINANCE ACT 1975, Schedule 5

Interpretation of paragraphs 6 *to* 10

11.—(1) The following provisions apply for the interpretation of paragraphs 6 to 10 above.

(2) The relevant transfer, in relation to any settlement, is the first transfer of value made at or after the relevant time which satisfies the conditions—[16].

(*a*) that the value of the property comprised in the settlement or of that part of it out of which the capital distributions are made was taken into account in determining the value transferred; and

(*b*) that the transfer was, or would but for paragraph 19 (2) below or paragraphs 2 to 7 of Schedule 6 to this Act [or section 76 of the Finance Act 1976][17] have been, a chargeable transfer; and

(*c*) that, if the settlement was made before 27th March 1974, the transfer was made neither under paragraph 4 above nor on death;

and where it was not a chargeable transfer [(or was a chargeable transfer of some only of the value transferred by it)][18] the reference in paragraph 7(2) (*a*) above to the tax which would have been charged is a reference to the tax which would have been charged but for paragraph 19 (2) below or paragraphs 2 to 7 of Schedule 6 to this Act [or section 76 of the Finance Act 1976][17]

(3) The relevant time, in relation to any settlement, is, if the settled property became comprised in the settlement on the death of any person, the time immediately before his death, and, in any other case, the time when the settlement was made.

(4) Where, by the same disposition, property ceases to be comprised in one settlement and becomes comprised in another settlement, the property shall be treated as remaining comprised in the first settlement.

(5) The amount of any distribution payment which is a capital distribution shall be taken (except for the purposes of paragraph 6 (4) (*a*)) to be the amount on which tax is chargeable in respect of it.

(6) A settlement is related to another if the same transfer of value is the relevant transfer in relation to both; and for this purpose transfers of value made by the same person on the same day shall be treated as one.

[15] Para. 10A was inserted by F.A. 1976, Sch. 14, para. 14, in relation to distribution payments made after April 15, 1976.

[16] See also F.A. 1976, Sch. 14, para. 15.

[17] The words in brackets were added by F.A. 1976, Sch. 11, para.4.

[18] The words in brackets were added by F.A. 1976, Sch. 14, para. 16.

(7) "Distribution payment" means, subject to sub-paragraph (8) below, any payment which—

(*a*) is not income of any person for any of the purposes of income tax and would not for any of those purposes be income of a person not resident in the United Kingdom if he were so resident; and

(*b*) is not a payment in respect of costs or expenses;

and "payment" includes the transfer of assets other than money.

(8) The amount of any capital distribution treated as made under paragraph 6 (2) or (3) above or paragraph 15 (3) or 24 (2) below shall also be deemed to be a distribution payment; but where, after an amount has been taken into account by virtue of this sub-paragraph [or paragraph 6 (6A) above][19] as a distribution payment made out of the whole or part of any property, one or more distribution payments are made (otherwise than under this sub-paragraph [or paragraph 6 (6A) above][19]) out of that property or part, the amount so taken into account shall be treated as reducing the amount of those payments.

(9) "Initial value", in relation to any settlement, means the value, immediately after the relevant transfer, of the property then comprised in the settlement.

(10) "Interest in possession" means an interest in possession to which an individual is beneficially entitled or, if the following conditions are satisfied, an interest in possession to which a company is beneficially entitled, the conditions being—

(*a*) that the business of the company consists wholly or mainly in the acquisition of interests in settled property; and

(*b*) that the company has acquired the interest for full consideration in money or money's worth from an individual who was beneficially entitled to the interest[20].

(11) References to settled property shall be construed as referring only to property which is not excluded property.

(f) Periodic Charge

FINANCE ACT 1975, Schedule 5

Periodic charge to tax

12.—(1) Where, at a relevant anniversary, no interest in possession subsists in the property comprised in a settlement or in a part of that property, a capital distribution of an amount equal to the value immediately before that anniversary of that property or part shall be treated as made out of that property or part, and tax shall be charged on a capital distribution so treated as made at 30 per cent. of the rate at which it would be chargeable under paragraphs 6 to 10 above on a capital distribution of the same amount made at the same date, but subject to any reduction under sub-paragraph (4) below.

[19] The words in brackets were added by F.A. 1976, Sch. 14, para. 12 (2), and deemed always to have had effect.

[20] See F.A. 1977, s. 50.

(2) Where the trustees of the settlement are not resident in the United Kingdom a capital distribution of a corresponding amount shall also be treated as made if no interest in possession subsists in the property or in a part thereof at the end of any year in the period of ten years ending with a relevant anniversary, except the last and except any year ending before 1st January 1976; and tax shall be charged on a capital distribution so treated as made at 3 per cent. of the rate at which it would be chargeable under paragraphs 6 to 10 above on a capital distribution of the same amount made at the same date

(3) Any tax charged by virtue of sub-paragraph (2) above shall be allowed as credit against the tax chargeable on the [next capital distribution made out of the property or, as the case may be, out of the part concerned, not being a capital distribution treated as made under that sub-paragraph.][1]

(4) Where the whole or part of the value mentioned in sub-paragraph (1) above is attributable to property—

(*a*) which was added by the settlor after the end of the first of the ten years ending with the relevant anniversary; or

(*b*) in which an interest in possession subsisted throughout at least one of those ten years;

the rate at which, under sub-paragraph (1) above, tax is chargeable on that value or that part of it shall be reduced by one-tenth for each of those ten years throughout which either the settled property did not include that property, or an interest in possession subsisted in that property.

(5) For the purposes of this paragraph trustees of a settlement shall be regarded as not resident in the United Kingdom unless the general administration of the settlement is ordinarily carried on in the United Kingdom and the trustees or a majority of them (and, where there is more than one class of trustees, a majority of each class) are for the time being resident in the United Kingdom.

(6) For the purposes of this paragraph a relevant anniversary, in relation to a settlement, is the end of the ten years beginning with the date of the transfer of value which is the relevant transfer in relation to the settlement (or would be the relevant transfer in relation to it if dispositions made or events happening at that date could be chargeable transfers and paragraph (*c*) of paragraph 11 (2) above were omitted) and the end of every subsequent ten years; but no date falling before 1st April 1980 is a relevant anniversary.

[(7) Paragraph 11 above shall apply for the interpretation of this paragraph as it applies for the interpretation of paragraphs 6 to 10, except that paragraph 11 (4) shall be disregarded in determining in relation to any settled property whether the trustees are resident in the United Kingdom.][2]

Tax credit for periodic charge

13.—(1) Subject to sub-paragraph (2) below, where tax is charged at

[1] The words in brackets were substituted by F.A. 1976, Sch. 14, para. 8 (1).

[2] Sub-para. (7) was substituted by F.A. 1976, Sch. 14, para. 17.

a relevant anniversary on any capital distribution treated by virtue of paragraph 12 (1) above as made out of any property, the effective rate at which that tax is charged (taking into account any reduction under paragraph 12 (4) above) shall reduce the rate at which, apart from this paragraph, tax would be chargeable on any capital distribution made out of that property on or not later than twenty years after that relevant anniversary [not being a capital distribution treated as made under paragraph 12 above.][3]

(2) The amounts by which tax on any capital distribution is reduced under sub-paragraph (1) above by reason of any tax charged under paragraph 12 (1) above shall not together exceed the amount of the tax so charged.

(3) In this paragraph "relevant anniversary" has the same meaning as in paragraph 12 above.

(g) Transitional Relief

FINANCE ACT 1975, Schedule 5

Transitional relief for settlements made before 27th March 1974

14.—(1) In relation to a settlement made before 27th March 1974 paragraphs 6 to 12 above shall apply with the following modifications.

(2) Subject to sub-paragraphs (3) to (5) below, the rate at which tax is chargeable on any capital distribution made before 1st April 1980 out of property comprised in the settlement (but not on any capital distribution which, under paragraph 9 above, is treated as made out of property comprised in a separate settlement made after 26th March 1974) shall be the following percentage of the rate at which it would be chargeable apart from this paragraph, that is to say—

(*a*) 10 per cent. if the capital distribution is made before 1st April 1976;

(*b*) 12½ per cent. if it is made after 31st March 1976 but before 1st April 1977;

(*c*) 15 per cent. if it is made after 31st March 1977 but before 1st April 1978; and

(*d*) 17½ per cent. if it is made after 31st March 1978 but before 1st April 1979; and

(*e*) 20 per cent. if it is made after 31st March 1979.

(3) Where any capital distribution made after 31st March 1976 but before 1st April 1977 could not have been made except as the result of some proceedings before a court, this paragraph shall have effect in relation to it as if it had been made before 1st April 1976.

(4) Sub-paragraph (2) above does not apply in relation to a capital distribution treated as made under paragraph 12 (2) above.

[3] The words in brackets were added by F.A. 1976, Sch. 14, para. 8 (2).

(5) Sub-paragraph (2) above does not apply—

(*a*) in relation to a capital distribution treated as made under paragraph 6 (2) above, unless the person becoming entitled as mentioned therein; or

(*b*) in relation to a capital distribution treated as made under paragraph 15 (3) below, unless each of the beneficiaries referred to therein [living at the time of the capital distribution][4]; or

(*c*) in relation to a distribution payment made for the benefit of any person, unless that person;

is an individual who is domiciled in the United Kingdom at the time the capital distribution is made . . .[5]

(6) In this paragraph expressions defined for the purposes of paragraphs 6 to 10 above have the same meanings as in those paragraphs.

iii. ACCUMULATION AND MAINTENANCE SETTLEMENTS

It has long been common to establish trusts in favour of children contingently upon attaining a specified age. During the minority of the children, the income can be applied by the trustees for the education and maintenance of the children under the statutory power of maintenance provided by Trustee Act 1925, s. 31[6], and income not so applied will be accumulated. On majority, the beneficiary becomes entitled to the income, even if his interest in the capital remains contingent. The statutory power of advancement, provided by Trustee Act 1925, s. 32[7], is also available. The problem of aggregation of the income of the children with that of the settlor has been mentioned.

Such trusts have not been actively discouraged in the recent legislation. During the minority of the beneficiaries, there is no interest in possession, but qualifying accumulation and maintenance trusts are not subjected to the burdens imposed on discretionary trusts. Nor is capital transfer tax charged upon a beneficiary obtaining a vested interest, nor on the payment of capital to a beneficiary; nor on the death of a beneficiary before obtaining a vested interest in the capital; nor is there a periodic charge. These advantages are closely controlled by the definition of "accumulation and maintenance settlement" in Sch. 5, para. 15, and Finance Act 1976, s. 106. They are sufficient to suggest that accumulation and maintenance settlements will be one of the most popular forms of trust in the future.

FINANCE ACT 1975, Schedule 5

Accumulation and maintenance settlements

15.—(1) This paragraph applies to any settlement where—

(*a*) one or more persons (in this paragraph referred to as beneficiaries) will, on or before attaining a specified age not exceeding twenty-five,

[4] The words in brackets were added by F.A. 1976, s. 106 (3).

[5] The deletion was made by F.A. 1976, Sch. 14, para. 13, and Sch. 15, Part V.

[6] See p. 541, post.

[7] See p. 548, post.

become entitled to, or to an interest in possession in, the settled property or part of it[8]; and

(*b*) no interest in possession subsists in the settled property or part and the income from it is to be accumulated so far as not applied for the maintenance, education or benefit of a beneficiary, and

(*c*) either—

[(i) not more than twenty-five years have elapsed since the day on which the settlement was made or, if it was later, since the time (or latest time) when the conditions stated in paragraphs (*a*) and (*b*) above became satisfied with respect to the property or part; or

(ii) all the persons who are or have been beneficiaries are or were either grandchildren of a common grandparent or children, widows or widowers of such grandchildren who were themselves beneficiaries but died before the time when, had they survived, they would have become entitled as mentioned in paragraph (*a*) above.][9]

(2) Where this paragraph applies to a settlement—

(*a*) a payment made to a beneficiary out of the settled property or part concerned shall not be a capital distribution and a capital distribution shall not be treated as made under paragraph 6 (2) above on a beneficiary's becoming entitled to an interest in the property or part; and

(*b*) no capital distribution shall be treated as made out of the property or part by virtue of paragraph 12 above at any time during the period for which the income is to be accumulated as mentioned in sub-paragraph (1) (*b*) above.

(3) Where no interest in possession subsists in the property comprised in a settlement or some part of that property but the conditions stated in paragraphs (*a*) and (*b*) of sub-paragraph (1) above are not satisfied with respect to the property or part, then, if those conditions become satisfied with respect to the property or any part thereof a capital distribution shall be treated as being made out of the property or part and the amount of the distribution shall be taken to be equal to the value of the property with respect to which those conditions become satisfied.

[(4) Where the conditions stated in paragraphs (*a*) and (*b*) of sub-paragraph (1) above were satisfied on 15th April 1976 with respect to any property comprised in a settlement made before that day, paragraph (*c*) (i) of that sub-paragraph shall have effect with the substitution of a reference to that day for the reference to the day on which the settlement was made, and the condition stated in paragraph (*c*) (ii) shall be treated as satisfied if—

(*a*) it is satisfied in respect of the period beginning with 15th April 1976; or

(*b*) it is satisfied in respect of the period beginning with 1st April 1977 and either there was no beneficiary living on 15th April 1976 or the beneficiaries on 1st April 1977 include a living beneficiary; or

[8] The Inland Revenue will, by concession, regard this as being satisfied even if no age is specified, provided it is clear that a beneficiary will in fact become entitled by the age of 25. See (1977) 127 NLJ 883.

[9] The words in brackets were added by F.A. 1976, s. 106 (1).

(*c*) there is no power under the terms of the settlement whereby it could have become satisfied in respect of the period beginning with 1st April 1977, and the trusts of the settlement have not been varied at any time after 15th April 1976.

(5) In sub-paragraph (1) above "persons" includes unborn persons; but the conditions stated in paragraphs (*a*) and (*b*) of that sub-paragraph shall be treated as not satisfied unless there is or has been a living beneficiary.

(6) Paragraph 11 above shall apply for the interpretation of this paragraph as it applies for the interpretation of paragraphs 6 to 10; and for the purposes of this paragraph a person's children shall be taken to include his illegitimate children, his adopted children and his step-children.][10]

iv. PROTECTIVE TRUSTS[11]

FINANCE ACT 1975, Schedule 5

Protective trusts

18.—(1) This paragraph applies to settled property held on trusts to the like effect as those specified in section 33 (1) of the Trustee Act 1925; and in this paragraph "the principal beneficiary" and "the trust period" have the same meanings as in that section.

(2) Where this paragraph applies to any settled property—

[(*a*) tax shall not be charged under paragraph 4 (2) above on the coming to an end of the principal beneficiary's interest in the property if the property is then held on discretionary trusts to the like effect as those specified in paragraph (ii) of the said section 33 (1).][12]

(*b*) a distribution payment made out of the settled property for the benefit of the principal beneficiary shall not be a capital distribution.

(3) Sub-paragraphs (5) to (9) of paragraph 17[13] above shall apply where this paragraph applies to any settled property as if the references to that paragraph were references to this paragraph and references to that paragraph ceasing to apply to the settled property included references to the coming to an end of the trust period.

[10] Sub-paras. (4) and (5) were substituted, and sub-para. (6) added by F.A. 1976, s. 106 (2).
[11] See p. 130, ante.
[12] Sub-para. 2(*a*) was substituted by F.A. 1976, Sch. 14, para. 19, with effect from 16th April 1976.
[13] Which provides for a postponement of the periodic charge in the case of trusts for the benefit of employees.

7. Resulting Trusts[1]

I. General

This chapter will deal with a miscellaneous group of situations in which the settlor has transferred property to other persons, but the beneficial interest returns, or "results" to the settlor. It was at one time common to say that such trusts arose as a result of the presumed or implied intention of the settlor. But that explanation is clearly inadequate in cases, such as *Vandervell v IRC*[2] where the existence of a resulting trust imposed a serious fiscal burden on the grantor. That was the last thing he intended.

The modern classification divides resulting trusts into "automatic" and "presumed" resulting trusts[3]. The first category is that in which property has been conveyed to trustees, and the beneficial interest has not been wholly disposed of. The trustees cannot enjoy it, and inevitably a resulting trust arises in favour of the settlor. The second category is that in which the conveyance is not made expressly upon trust; but, by reason of certain presumptions established by the law, the legal owner is required to hold the property upon trust for the settlor.

The presumptions are always rebuttable by evidence, and they may indeed give way to contrary, stronger presumptions, such as the presumption of advancement in favour of a person to whom the donor stood *in loco parentis*. The presumptions were developed in earlier centuries; they are not always consistent with modern ideas of property ownership, and are easily displaced. As Lord UPJOHN said in *Vandervell v IRC*[4]: "In reality the so-called presumption of a resulting trust is no more than a long-stop to provide the answer where the relevant facts and circumstances fail to reach a solution". There is no difference between an "automatic" and a "presumed" resulting trust once the trust has been established. The merit of the classification is that it provides an explanation for the existence of a resulting trust where there is no presumption, or evidence of intention to support it.

[1] H & M, pp. 253–275; K & S, pp. 173–190; P & M, pp. 119–150; Pettit, pp. 100–120; Snell, pp. 172–182.
[2] [1967] 2 AC 291, [1967] 1 All ER 1; p. 173, post.
[3] See *Re Vandervell's Trusts (No. 2)* [1974] Ch 269 at 294; p. 175, post.
[4] [1967] 2 AC 291 at 312, 313, [1967] 1 All ER 1 at 8.

Finally, it should be noted that resulting trusts overlap with constructive trusts. Thus, if a person obtains legal title to property by fraud, he will be compelled to hold it on trust for the transferor[5]; this may be regarded as a constructive trust or a resulting trust. As Lord DENNING MR said in *Hussey v Palmer*[6]: "Although the plaintiff alleged that there was a resulting trust, I should have thought that the trust in this case, if there was one, was more in the nature of a constructive trust; but this is more a matter of words than anything else. The two run together."

II. Conveyance to Trustees

A. No Declaration of Trust

VANDERVELL v INLAND REVENUE COMMISSIONERS
[1967] 2 AC 291, [1967] 1 All ER 1 (HL, Lords REID, PEARCE, UPJOHN, DONOVAN and WILBERFORCE)

RE VANDERVELL'S TRUSTS (No. 2)
[1974] Ch 269, [1974] 3 All ER 205 (CA, Lord DENNING MR, STEPHENSON and LAWTON LJJ)

Guy Anthony Vandervell decided to make a gift of money to the Royal College of Surgeons for the purpose of founding a Chair of Pharmacology. His plan was to arrange the transfer to the College of a block of shares in Vandervell Products Ltd., which were held by the National Provincial Bank as his nominee; to provide the bulk of the endowment by declaring dividends on those shares; and to enable Vandervell Trustees Ltd. (a private trustee company which acted as trustee for the Vandervell children's trust, among other private trusts) to re-purchase the shares for £5,000. In this way the dividends would not be taxable in the hands of the charity; and the shares would return after the payment of the dividends to the family's control.

The shares were transferred in 1958, and the dividends amounting to £266,000 gross were declared on the shares. But no express provision was made to declare the trusts on which Vandervell Trustees Ltd. held the option. If the option was held on trust for Vandervell, the settlor, he would be liable to pay surtax upon the whole of the dividends paid to the College, because he had failed to divest himself absolutely of all interest in the property within the Income Tax Act 1952, s. 415 (2)[7].

On receiving an assessment to surtax, Vandervell arranged, in October 1961, for Vandervell Trustees Ltd. to exercise the option. They did so, using £5,000 from the children's settlement for the purchase. The shares were transferred. Vandervell Trustees Ltd. treated them as being held on trust for the children's settlement, and paid to that settlement all dividends received during 1961–1965.

Vandervell was then assessed to surtax on these dividends, on the ground that the shares were, like the option, held on resulting trust for him.

[5] See p. 234, note 14, post.
[6] [1972] 1 WLR 1286 at 1289, [1972] 3 All ER 744 at 747. See pp. 234 et seq., post.
[7] Now I.C.T.A. 1970, s. 458 (2).

At last, on January 19, 1965, he executed a deed transferring to the trusts of the children's settlement any interest which he might have in the shares. He died in March 1967.

Before the assessment for 1961–1965 was settled, Vandervell's executors started an action against the trustee company, claiming that the dividends belonged to Vandervell. The Revenue asked to be joined as parties, but, on objection by the trustee company, were excluded: *Re Vandervell's Trusts* ([1971] AC 912, [1970] 3 All ER 16). The executors succeeded before MEGARRY J, but failed in the Court of Appeal.

In the first of the cases, *Vandervell v IRC* ([1967] 2 AC 291, [1967] 1 All ER 1) the House of Lords examined three alternative solutions: that the option was held on trust for the children's settlement; that Vandervell Trustees Ltd. held it beneficially; and that it was held on resulting trust for Vandervell. The third alternative was chosen.

LORD WILBERFORCE: On these findings it was, in my opinion, at once clear that the appellant's contention that the option became subject to the trusts of the children's settlement of 1949 must fail, for the reason that it was not the intention of the settlor, or of his plenipotentiary, Mr. Robins, at the time the option was exercised that this should be so. I need not elaborate this point since I understand that there is no disagreement about it. This was the appellant's main (if not the sole) contention before the special commissioners and Plowman J and it remained his first contention on this appeal. The alternative which . . . is expressed in the printed case as being that the option was held by the trustee company in equity as well as in law as the absolute owner thereof for the purposes of its business, is, of course, one which the appellant is entitled to put forward, as a contention of law, at any stage, provided that it is consistent with the facts as found by the special commissioners. It is on that contention that the appellant ultimately fell back. For my part, I cannot find that it is so consistent. . . .

Correspondingly, the evidence points clearly away from any conclusion that the trustee company held beneficially, or for the purpose of its business. It had no business, no function, except as a trustee; no assets, except as a trustee. The £5,000 to be paid if the option was to be exercised was, as a term of the arrangement between Mr. Vandervell and the college, part of the £150,000 benefaction; how could that come from the company's own resources? To extract from the findings a conclusion that the trustee company was to hold free from any trust but possibly subject to some understanding or gentleman's agreement seems to me, rather than even a benevolent interpretation of the evidence, a reconstruction of it. I may add that had this contention been put forward at the hearing before the special commissioners the Revenue might well have been tempted to explore, by cross-examination, the real control of the trustee company and to argue that the case came within section 415 (2) of the Income Tax Act 1952.

If, then, as I think, both the first two alternatives fail, there remains only the third, which, to my mind, corresponds exactly with Mr. Robins' intentions, namely, that the option was held by the trustee company on trusts which were undefined, or in the air.

As to the consequences, there has been some difference and possibly lack of clarity below. The special commissioners held that the initially undefined trusts could be defined later in a way which might benefit the appellant, and they found the benefit to the appellant in this circumstance. The Court of Appeal, starting from the fact that the trustee company took the option as a volunteer, thought that this was a case where the presumption of a resulting trust arose and was not displaced. For my part, I prefer a slightly different and simpler approach. The transaction has been investigated on the evidence of the settlor and his agent and the facts have been found. There is no need, or room, as I see it, to invoke a presumption. The conclusion, on the facts found, is simply that the option was vested in the trustee company as a trustee on trusts, not defined at the time, possibly to be defined later. But the equitable, or beneficial interest, cannot remain in the air: the consequence in law must be that it remains in the settlor. There is no need to consider some of the more refined intellectualities of the doctrine of resulting trust, nor to speculate whether, in possible circumstances, the shares might be applicable for Mr. Vandervell's benefit: he had, as the direct result of the option and of the failure to place the beneficial interest in it securely away from him, not divested himself absolutely of the shares which it controlled.

In the later case, *Re Vandervell's Trusts (No. 2),* the width of the difference of the analysis of MEGARRY J and that of the Court of Appeal makes it necessary to include extracts from the judgments in both courts. On the executors' failure to recover the money representing the dividends for 1961–1965, the Revenue accepted the situation, and the assessment was withdrawn.

MEGARRY J: It seems to me that the relevant points on resulting trusts may be put in a series of propositions which, so far as not directly supported, appear at least to be consistent with Lord Wilberforce's speech, and reconcilable with the true intent of Lord Upjohn's speech, though it may not be with all his words on a literal reading. The propositions are the broadest of generalisations, and do not purport to cover the exceptions and qualifications that doubtless exist. Nevertheless, these generalisations at least provide a starting point for the classification of a corner of equity which might benefit from some attempt at classification. The propositions are as follows.

(1) If a transaction fails to make any effective disposition of any interest it does nothing. This is so at law and in equity, and has nothing to do with resulting trusts. (2) Normally the mere existence of some unexpressed intention in the breast of the owner of the property does nothing: there must at least be some expression of that intention before it can effect any result. To yearn is not to transfer. (3) Before any doctrine of resulting trust can come into play, there must at least be some effective transaction which transfers or creates some interest in property. (4) Where A effectually transfers to B (or creates in his favour) any interest in any property, whether legal or equitable, a resulting trust for A may arise in two distinct classes of case. For simplicity, I shall confine my statement to cases in which the transfer or creation is made without B providing any valuable consideration, and where no presumption of advancement can arise; and I shall state the position for transfers without specific mention of the creation of new interests.

(a) The first class of case is where the transfer to B is not made on any trust. If, of course, it appears from the transfer that B is intended to hold on certain trusts, that will be decisive, and the case is not within this category; and similarly if it appears that B is intended to take beneficially. But in other cases there is a rebuttable presumption that B holds on a resulting trust for A. The question is not one of the automatic consequences of a dispositive failure by A, but one of presumption: the property has been carried to B, and from the absence of consideration and any presumption of advancement B is presumed not only to hold the entire interest on trust, but also to hold the beneficial interest for A absolutely. The presumption thus establishes both that B is to take on trust and also what that trust is. Such resulting trusts may be called "presumed resulting trusts".

(b) The second class of case is where the transfer to B is made on trusts which leave some or all of the beneficial interest undisposed of. Here B automatically holds on a resulting trust for A to the extent that the beneficial interest has not been carried to him or others. The resulting trust here does not depend on any intentions or presumptions, but is the automatic consequence of A's failure to dispose of what is vested in him. Since ex hypothesi the transfer is on trust, the resulting trust does not establish the trust but merely carries back to A the beneficial interest that has not been disposed of. Such resulting trusts may be called "automatic resulting trusts".

(5) Where trustees hold property in trust for A, and it is they who, at A's direction, make the transfer to B, similar principles apply, even though on the face of the transaction the transferor appears to be the trustees and not A. If the transfer to B is on trust, B will hold any beneficial interest that has not been effectually disposed of on an automatic resulting trust for the true transferor, A. If the transfer to B is not on trust, there will be a rebuttable presumption that B holds on a resulting trust for A.

I turn to the speech of Lord Wilberforce. At the outset (p. 324) he stated his concurrence with the view taken below, based on Mr. Vandervell's failure to divest himself of all interest in the option, and said that but for the division of opinion in the House he would have thought it sufficient to express his concurrence. He then turned to the facts, and after discussing them at some length, he rejected the contention that the option had become subject to the trusts of the children's settlement. He did this because it was not the intention of Mr. Vandervell or Mr. Robins "at the time the option was exercised that this should be so" (p. 327). I think that the word "exercised" probably should be read as "granted," for there does not seem to have been any evidence before the House as to the intentions which Mr. Vandervell or Mr. Robins had when the option was exercised in 1961; and, I may add, the reference on p. 327 to the alternative "numbered 3 above" is plainly not to the Arabic (3) on p. 326 but to the Roman (iii) on p. 325. Lord Wilberforce held that on the evidence the defendant company held the option not beneficially, subject to some understanding or gentleman's agreement, but on "trusts which were undefined, or in the air" (p. 328). He then referred to the decision of the Court of Appeal as being one where, starting from the fact that the defendant company took the option as a volunteer, the court thought that the presumption of a resulting trust arose and was not displaced. Lord Wilberforce then said, at p. 329: [quoted p. 175, ante].

Now as it seems to me this passage shows Lord Wilberforce as rejecting the application of what I have called the "presumption" class of resulting trust and accepting that the case falls into what I have called the "automatic" class. The grant of the option to the defendant company was, as he had held, on trust. There was thus no need, nor, indeed, any reason to consider whether the option was granted to the defendant company beneficially, or whether there was any presumption of a resulting trust, for that question had been foreclosed by the decision that the defendant company did not take beneficially but held on trust. The only question was whether Mr. Vandervell had ever effectually disposed of the beneficial interest that the defendant company, holding on trust, must hold on a resulting trust for him unless and until an effective trust for some other beneficiary was constituted. This had not been done, and so the defendant company continued to hold on a resulting trust for Mr. Vandervell.

If one bears in mind Lord Wilberforce's speech and the principles that I have tried to state it seems to me that when one looks again at Lord Upjohn's speech it is at least possible to read it as supporting what seems to me to be the right analysis of the case, namely, that the true grantor of the option was Mr. Vandervell, that the option was granted to the defendant company on trust, that no effective trusts were ever declared, and so the defendant company held the option on an automatic resulting trust for Mr. Vandervell. Indeed, that is what I think he was laying down. The question is whether, on the evidence before me, I ought to reach any other conclusion.

. . . My conclusion is that there is nothing in the evidence before me that warrants any conclusion different from that reached in *Vandervell No. 1*, namely, that the option was granted to the defendant company on trust, but that no effective trusts were ever established and so the defendant company held the option on a resulting trust for Mr. Vandervell.

(3) *Effect of children's £5,000.* The third issue is that of the effect of exercising the option with £5,000 of the moneys held by the defendant company on the trusts of the children's settlement. I shall deal with this main issue before I turn to estoppel and acquiescence. That issue is, in essence, whether trustees who hold an option on trust for X will hold the shares obtained by exercising that option on trust for Y merely because they used Y's money in exercising the option. Authority apart, my answer would be an unhesitating No. The option belongs to X beneficially, and the money merely exercises rights which belong to X. Let the shares be worth £50,000, so that an option to purchase those shares for £5,000 is worth £45,000, and it will at once be seen what a monstrous result would be produced by allowing trustees to divert from their beneficiary X the benefits of what they hold in trust for him merely because they used Y's money instead of X's . . .

I need only say that the consequences of recognising any rule to the effect that trustees of more than one trust can in effect transfer the assets of one trust to another trust simply by expending the money of that other trust on improving the assets seems to me to be incalculable . . . . I merely add that, as I have already mentioned, Mr. Balcombe has throughout accepted what he has pleaded, namely, that the plaintiffs' right to the shares is subject to a lien in favour of the children's settlement for the £5,000 paid for exercising the option with interest. This in effect will restore the status quo ante as regards this payment.

MEGARRY J then considered the effect of acquiescence and estoppel and concluded that the plaintiffs' claim was not affected on either of these grounds.

In the Court of Appeal:

LORD DENNING MR:

Summary of the claims

The root cause of all the litigation is the claim of the revenue authorities.

The first period—1958–1961: The revenue authorities claimed that Mr. Vandervell was the beneficial owner of the *option* and was liable for surtax on the dividends declared from 1958 to 1961. This came to £250,000. The claim of the revenue was upheld by the House of Lords: see *Vandervell v IRC* [1967] 2 AC 291, [1967] 1 All ER 1.

The second period—1961–1965: The revenue authorities claimed that Mr. Vandervell was the beneficial owner of the shares. They assessed him for surtax in respect of the dividends from October 11, 1961, to January 19, 1965, amounting to £628,229. The executors dispute the claim of the revenue. They appealed against the assessments. But the appeal was, by agreement, stood over pending the case now before us. The executors have brought this action against the trustee company. They seek a declaration that, during the second period, the dividends belonged to Mr. Vandervell himself, and they ask for an account of them. The revenue asked to be joined as parties to the action. This court did join them (see *Re Vandervell's Trusts* [1970] Ch 44, [1969] 3 All ER 496); but the House of Lords reversed the decision (see [1971] AC 912). So this action has continued—without the presence of the revenue, whose claim to £628,229 has caused all the trouble.

The third period—1965–1967: The revenue agree that they have no claim against the estate for this period.

The law for the first period

The first period was considered by the House of Lords in *Vandervell v IRC* [1967] 2 AC 291, [1967] 1 All ER 1. They held, by a majority of three to two, that, during this period, the trustee company held the option as a trustee. The terms of the trust were stated in two ways. Lord Upjohn (with the agreement of Lord Pearce) said that the proper inference was that "the trustee company should hold as trustee upon such trusts as he [Mr. Vandervell] or the trust company should from time to time declare" (see pp. 309, 315, 317). Lord Wilberforce said "that the option was held by the trustee company on trusts" "not at the time determined, but to be decided on at a later date"(see pp. 328, 325).

The trouble about the trust so stated was that it was too uncertain. The trusts were not declared or defined with sufficient precision for the trustees to ascertain who the beneficiaries were. It is clear law that a trust (other than a charitable trust) must be for ascertainable beneficiaries: see *Re Gulbenkian's Settlements* [1970] AC 508 at 523–524, *per* Lord Upjohn. Seeing that there were no ascertainable beneficiaries, there was a resulting trust for Mr. Vandervell. But if and when Mr. Vandervell should declare any defined trusts, the resulting trust would come to an end. As Lord Upjohn said [1967] 2 AC 291 at 317: "... until these trusts should be declared, there was a resulting trust for [Mr. Vandervell]."

During the first period, however, Mr. Vandervell did not declare any defined trusts. The option was, therefore, held on a resulting trust for him. He had not divested himself absolutely of the shares. He was, therefore, liable to pay surtax on the dividends.

The law for the second period

In October and November 1961, the trustee company exercised the option. They paid £5,000 out of the children's settlement. The Royal College of Surgeons transferred the legal estate in the 100,000 "A" shares to the trustee company. Thereupon the trustee company became the legal owner of the shares. This was a different kind of property altogether. Whereas previously the trustee company had only a chose in action of one kind—an option—it now had a chose in action of a different kind—the actual shares. This trust property was not held by the trustee company beneficially. It was held by them on trust. On this occasion a valid trust was created at the time of the transfer. It was manifested in clear and unmistakable fashion. It was precisely defined. The shares were to be held on the trusts of the children's settlement. The evidence of intention is indisputable: (i) The trustee company used the children's money—£5,000– with which to acquire the shares. This would be a breach of trust unless they intended the shares to be an addition to the children's settlement. (ii) The trustee company wrote to the revenue authorities the letter of November 2, 1961, declaring expressly that the shares "will henceforth be held by them upon the trusts of the [children's] settlement." (iii) Thenceforward all the dividends received by the trustees were paid by them to the children's settlement and treated as part of the funds of the settlement. This was all done with the full assent of Mr. Vandervell. Such being the intention, clear and manifest, at the time when the shares were conveyed to the trustee company, it is sufficient to create a trust.

Mr. Balcombe for the executors admitted that the intention of Mr. Vandervell and the trustee company was that the shares should be held on trust for the children's settlement. But he said that this intention was of no avail. He said that during the first period, Mr. Vandervell had an equitable interest in the property, namely, a resulting trust; that he never disposed of this equitable interest (because he never knew he had it): and that in any case it was the disposition of an equitable interest which, under section 53 of the Law of Property Act 1925, had to be in writing, signed by him or his agent, lawfully authorised by him in writing (and there was no such writing produced). He cited *Grey v IRC* [1960] AC 1; [1959] 3 All E.R. 603 and *Oughtred v IRC* [1960] AC 206.

There is a complete fallacy in that argument. A resulting trust for the settlor is born and dies without any writing at all. It comes into existence whenever there is a gap in the beneficial ownership. It ceases to exist whenever that gap is filled by someone becoming beneficially entitled. As soon as the gap is filled by the creation or declaration of a valid trust, the resulting trust comes to an end. In this case, before the option was exercised, there was a gap in the beneficial ownership. So there was a resulting trust for Mr. Vandervell. But, as soon as the option was exercised and the shares registered in the trustees' name, there was created a valid trust of the shares in favour of the children's settlement. Not being a trust of land, it could be created without any writing. A trust of personalty can be created without any writing. Both Mr. Vandervell and the trustee company had done everything which needed to be done to make the settlement of these shares binding on them. So there was a valid trust: see *Milroy v Lord* (1862) 4 De GF & J 264 at 274, *per* Turner LJ.

The law as to the third period

The executors admit that from January 19, 1965, Mr. Vandervell had no interest whatsoever in the shares. The deed of that date operated so as to transfer all his interest thenceforward to the trustee company to be held by them on trust for the children. I asked Mr. Balcombe: What is the difference between the events of October and November 1961, and the event of January 19, 1965? He said that it lay in the writing. In 1965, Mr. Vandervell disposed of his equitable interest in writing: whereas in 1961 there was no writing. There was only conduct or word of mouth. That was insufficient. And, therefore, his executors were not bound by it.

The answer to this argument is what I have said. Mr. Vandervell did not dispose in 1961 of any equitable interest. All that happened was that his resulting trust came to an end—because there was created a new valid trust of the shares for the children's settlement.

Estoppel

Even if Mr. Balcombe were right in saying that Mr. Vandervell retained an equitable interest in the shares, after the exercise of the option, the question arises whether Mr. Vandervell can in the circumstances be heard to assert that claim against his children. Just see what happened. He himself arranged for the option to be exercised. He himself agreed to the shares being transferred to the trustee company. He himself procured his products company to declare dividends on the shares and to pay them to the trustee company for the benefit of the children. Thenceforward the trustee company invested the money and treated it as part of the children's settlement. If he himself had lived, and not died, he could not have claimed it back. He could not be heard to say that he did not intend the children's trust to have it. Even a court of equity would not allow him to do anything so inequitable and unjust. Now that he has died, his executors are in no better position. If authority were needed, it is to be found in *Milroy v Lord* (1862) 4 De GF & J 264. In that case Thomas Medley assigned to Samuel Lord 50 shares in the Bank of Louisiana on trust for his niece: but the shares were not formally transferred into the name of Samuel Lord. The bank, however, paid the dividends to Samuel Lord. He paid them to the niece, and then, at Thomas Medley's suggestion, the niece used those dividends to buy shares in a fire insurance company—taking them in the name of Thomas Medley. After Thomas Medley's death, his executors claimed that the bank shares belonged to them as representing him, and also the fire insurance shares. The lords justices held that the executors were entitled to the bank shares, because "there is no equity in this court to perfect an imperfect gift": see p. 274. But the executors were not entitled to the fire insurance shares. Turner LJ said at p. 277:

> "the settlor [Mr. Medley] made a perfect gift to [his niece] of the dividends upon these shares, so far as they were handed over or treated by him as belonging to her, and these insurance shares were purchased with dividends which were so handed over or treated."

So here Mr. Vandervell made a perfect gift to the trustee company of the dividends on the shares, so far as they were handed over or treated by him as belonging to the trustee company for the benefit of the children. Alternatively, there was an equitable estoppel. His conduct was such that it would be quite inequitable for him to be allowed to enforce his strict rights (under a resulting trust) having regard to the dealings which had taken place between the parties: see *Hughes v Metropolitan Rly Co* (1877) 2 App Cas 439 at 448. . . . Every unjust decision is a reproach to the law or to the judge who administers it. If the law should be in danger of doing injustice, then equity should be called in to remedy it. Equity was introduced to mitigate the rigour of the law. But in the present case it has been prayed in aid to do injustice on a large scale—to defeat the intentions of a dead man—to deprive his children of the benefits he provided for them—and to expose his estate to the payment of tax of over £600,000. I am glad to find that we can overcome this most unjust result. The dividends for the second period were properly paid to the trustee company for the benefit of the children's settlement. There is no equity in Mr. Vandervell or his executors seeking to recover them. I would allow the appeal and dismiss the claim of the executors.

STEPHENSON LJ: I have had more doubt than Lord Denning MR and Lawton LJ whether we can overturn the judgment of Megarry J (ante, p. 273) in what I have not found an easy case. Indeed, treading a (to me) dark and unfamiliar path, I had parted from both my fellow-travellers and following the windings of Mr. Balcombe's argument had nearly reached a different terminus before the light which they threw upon the journey enabled me to join them at the same conclusion.

To expound my doubts would serve no useful purpose; to state them shortly may do no harm. The cause of all the trouble is what the judge called [[1974] Ch 269 at 298] "this ill-fated option" and its incorporation in a deed which was "too short and simple" to rid Mr. Vandervell of the beneficial interest in the disputed shares, as a bare majority of the House of Lords held, not without fluctuation of mind on the part of one of them (Lord Upjohn), in *Vandervell v Inland Revenue Commissioners* [1967] 2 AC 291 at 314–317. The operation of law or equity kept for Mr. Vandervell or gave him back an equitable interest which he did not want and would have thought he had disposed of if he had ever known it existed. It is therefore difficult to infer that he intended to dispose or ever did dispose of something he did not know he had until the judgment of Plowman J in *Vandervell v Inland Revenue Commissioners* [1966] Ch 261 at 273, which led to the deed of

1965, enlightened him, or to find a disposition of it in the exercise by the trustee company in 1961 of its option to purchase the shares. And even if he had disposed of his interest, he did not dispose of it by any writing sufficient to comply with section 53 (1) (*c*) of the Law of Property Act 1925.

But Lord Denning MR and Lawton LJ are able to hold that no such disposition is needed because (1) the option was held on such trusts as might thereafter be declared by the trustee company or Mr. Vandervell himself, and (2) the trustee company has declared that it holds the shares in the children's settlement. I do not doubt the first, because it was apparently the view of the majority of the House of Lords in *Vandervell v Inland Revenue Commissioners* [1967] 2 AC 291. I should be more confident of the second if it had been pleaded or argued either here or below and we had had the benefit of Megarry J's views upon it. If counsel for the trustee company in the court below had thought that the evidence supported it, he would not, I think, have sought and obtained the amendment of the defence which he did to allege what the judge rejected as an unusual and improbable form of trust which was not supported by the evidence. If counsel for the trustee company in this court had accepted it, I do not think that he would have opened this appeal as he did with references to perfecting or completing the trust but none to declaring it. I see, as perhaps did counsel, difficulties in the way of a limited company declaring a trust by parole or conduct and without resolution of the board of directors, and difficulties also in the way of finding any declaration of trust by Mr. Vandervell himself in October or November 1961, or any conduct then or later which would in law or equity estop him from denying that he made one.

However, Lord Denning MR and Lawton LJ are of opinion that these difficulties, if not imaginary, are not insuperable and that these shares went into the children's settlement in 1961 in accordance with the intention of Mr. Vandervell and the trustee company—a result with which I am happy to agree as it seems to me to be in accordance with the justice and the reality of the case.

B. Where an Express Trust Fails

In Essery v Cowlard ((1884) 26 ChD 191) a marriage settlement of 1877 declared that certain property of the intended wife had been transferred to trustees to be held by them in trust for herself, her intended husband and the issue of the marriage. The marriage never took place. The parties cohabited, and children were born. PEARSON J held that the contract for marriage had been rescinded. The trusts failed. Illegitimate children would not in those days have been able to take, nor could they be legitimated by the subsequent marriage of their parents. So, "If the father and mother were now to marry, and this deed were to be taken as their marriage settlement, their intention to provide for all their issue would be defeated." The trustees held on a resulting trust for the settlor (the wife), who could claim the return of the property.

RE AMES' SETTLEMENT

[1946] Ch 217, [1946] 1 All ER 694 (ChD, VAISEY J)

John Ames and Miss Hamilton married in 1908. Ames' father transferred £10,000 to trustees to be held on the usual trusts of a marriage settlement. The parties lived together for a number of years in England and Kenya. In 1926, the Supreme Court of Kenya declared the marriage null and void. The wife surrendered all her interests under the settlement. There was no issue. On the death of John Ames in 1945, the question was whether the £10,000 should be paid to those entitled under the settlement in default of issue, or to the representatives of the settlor.

Held. The marriage being void *ab initio*[8], the fund was held on resulting trust for the settlor.

VAISEY J: I regard the contest as merely this: The plaintiffs hold certain funds in their hands, and they ask to which of the alternative claimants they ought to make those funds over. I think it would not be incorrect to say that the problem is really which of those parties has the better equity. The persons who constitute the hypothetical next-of-kin say "Look at the deed of settlement. We are the persons there designated to take the fund, and there is no reason why we should not do so," and therefore claim to have the better equity. On the other hand it is said "But that trust, with the other trusts, were all based on the consideration and contemplation of a valid marriage, and now that it has been judicially decided that there never was a marriage that trust cannot possibly form the foundation of a good equitable right." The settlor's representatives say that theirs is the better equity because the money was only parted with by their testator on a consideration which was expressed but which in fact completely failed. It seems to me that the claim of the executors of the settlor in this case must succeed. I think that the case is, having regard to the wording of the settlement, a simple case of money paid on a consideration which failed. I do not think that that hypothetical class of next-of-kin (who were only brought in, so to speak, and given an interest in the fund on the basis and footing that there was going to be a valid marriage between John Ames and Miss Hamilton) have really any merits in equity, and I do not see how they can claim under the express terms of a document which, so far as regards the persons with whom the marriage consideration was concerned, has utterly and completely failed. If their claim be good, it is difficult to see at what precise period of time their interest became an interest in possession. But I hold that their claim is not good, and that they have not been able to establish it[9].

C. Incomplete Disposal of Beneficial Interest

RE THE TRUSTS OF THE ABBOTT FUND
[1900] 2 Ch 326 (ChD, STIRLING J)

Dr. Abbott, of Cambridge, died in 1844, leaving ample funds for the support of his family, including two daughters, Frederica and Katherine,

[8] A decree of nullity in England granted after July 31, 1971 in respect of a voidable marriage now has prospective and not retrospective effect: Matrimonial Causes Act 1973, s. 16; see also s. 24, under which the court has power to make property adjustment orders.

[9] See also *Morice v Bishop of Durham* (1804) 9 Ves 399; on appeal (1805) 10 Ves J 522, and *Chichester Diocesan Fund and Board of Finance (Incorporated) v Simpson* [1944] AC 341, [1944] 2 All ER 60, being examples of resulting trusts arising where an intended charitable trust failed.

who were deaf and dumb. But on the death of Dr. Abbott's surviving trustee in 1889, it was learned that all the money had disappeared.

Dr. Fawcett, and subsequently Mr. Smith, issued appeals to friends who subscribed money to a fund for the support of the two ladies. No provision was made for the disposal of the fund on the death of the survivor. This occurred in 1899, and there was then a surplus of £366 13s 9d.

Held. The fund was held upon a resulting trust for the subscribers.

STIRLING J: It seems to me . . . that I may treat the fund which was collected by Dr. Fawcett as really applicable to the same purposes, for that is the effect of it, as that which was subscribed in response to the circular issued by Mr. Smith. The ladies are both dead, and the question is whether, so far as this fund has not been applied for their benefit, there is a resulting trust of it for the subscribers. I cannot believe that it was ever intended to become the absolute property of the ladies so that they should be in a position to demand a transfer of it to themselves, or so that if they became bankrupt the trustee in the bankruptcy should be able to claim it. I believe it was intended that it should be administered by Mr. Smith, or the trustees who had been nominated in pursuance of the circular. I do not think the ladies ever became absolute owners of this fund. I think that the trustee or trustees were intended to have a wide discretion as to whether any, and if any what, part of the fund should be applied for the benefit of the ladies and how the application should be made. That view would not deprive them of all right in the fund, because if the trustees had not done their duty—if they either failed to exercise their discretion or exercised it improperly—the ladies might successfully have applied to the Court to have the fund administered according to the terms of the circular. In the result, therefore, there must be a declaration that there is a resulting trust of the moneys remaining unapplied for the benefit of the subscribers to the Abbott Fund[10].

In *Re Cochrane* ([1955] Ch 309, [1955] 1 All ER 222) a marriage settlement provided for funds to be held on trust for the wife "during her life so long as she shall continue to reside with the said W. J. B. Cochrane . . . and after [her] decease or the prior determination of the trust in her favour . . . upon trust to pay the said income to the said W. J. B. Cochrane (if then living) during his life and after the decease of the survivor of them . . . in trust for" such of their issue as they should jointly or as the survivor of them should appoint, and in default of appointment equally at the age of 21, or in the case of daughters, earlier marriage.

The wife ceased to reside with the husband. Her interest thus terminated and the income was paid to the husband. In 1953 the husband died. No appointment in favour of the children had been made. The question was whether the claim of the children was accelerated, or whether the fund

[10] Cp. *Re Andrew's Trust* [1905] 2 Ch 48 (surplus from fund for education of children of a deceased clergyman held payable to the children. The gift was construed as a gift to them, applicable primarily for their education). See also *Re Foord* [1922] 2 Ch 519; *Re Denley's Trust Deed* [1969] 1 Ch 373, [1968] 3 All ER 65; *Re Lipinski's Will Trusts* [1976] Ch 235, [1976] 1 All ER 33, p. 256, post.

was held on a resulting trust during the gap in the beneficial limitations following the husband's death.

HARMAN J, holding that a resulting trust arose, said (at p. 315): "Is it clear not only that something has been left out, but what it is that ought to be put in ?—the second, of course, being much the more difficult part. One can see that the limitations over do not marry with the prior trusts. It should have been obvious to the draftsman that the event might happen which in fact has happened. But is it clear that the gift over ought, so to speak, to be accelerated? I do not think so on this particular deed, and I base that decision on this: that I cannot see clearly what it is which should have been put in. There is a power for the spouses to appoint to issue; there is a power for the survivor to appoint. Now, it is clear and conceded that the wife, notwithstanding that she forfeited her interest in her husband's lifetime, still has for the rest of her life—or had, at any rate, after her husband's death—power to dispose of the fund as the survivor of the two, either by deed or by will. That power clearly did not stop with the cesser of her interest, so that she could alter the beneficial trust by appointing away from the children in favour of the grandchildren or by making an unequal division between her daughters; and it seems to me in the face of that that it is impossible to say that the gift over took effect at the date of the ceasing of the husband's interest.

It was admitted in fact before me that the fund could not be distributed so long as the power of appointment was outstanding in the survivor of the two spouses, and that alone seems to me to show that it could not be true to say that the gift over could operate until the event had happened which is stated to be the event in the deed; namely, the death of the survivor of the husband and wife.

The result of that is that the draftsman has failed to provide for the event which has happened. A resulting trust is the last resort to which the law has recourse when the draftsman has made a blunder or failed to dispose of that which he has set out to dispose of, but that seems to have happened here, and until the death of the survivor I think that there is a resulting trust of the income of the fund in favour of the settlors in proportion to their several interests."

RE GILLINGHAM BUS DISASTER FUND

[1958] Ch 300, [1958] 1 All ER 37 (ChD, HARMAN J)

In 1951, a squad of Royal Marine cadets was marching through a street in Gillingham, when a bus, out of control, struck them in the rear, killing 24, and injuring several others. A memorial fund was established by the Mayors of Gillingham, Rochester and Chatham, which was stated to be devoted "among other things, to defraying the funeral expenses, caring for the boys who may be disabled, and then to such worthy cause or causes . . . as the Mayors may determine."

The public contributed about £9,000, partly in identifiable sums from individual subscribers, but mainly from street collections and other untraceable sources. Various payments were made from the fund towards expenditure not covered by the common law liability accepted by the driver of the bus and his employees. There was a surplus, and the question arose as to its disposal.

Held. The surplus was held on a resulting trust for the donors.

HARMAN J: I have already decided that the surplus of this fund now in the hands of the plaintiffs as trustees ought not to be devoted to charitable purposes under a cy-près scheme. There arises now a further question, namely, whether, as the Treasury Solicitor claims, this surplus should be paid to the Crown as bona vacantia, or whether there is a resulting trust in favour of the subscribers, who are here represented by the Official Solicitor. The general principle must be that where money is held upon trust and the trusts declared do not exhaust the fund it will revert to the donor or settlor under what is called a resulting trust. The reasoning behind this is that the settlor or donor did not part with his money absolutely out and out but only sub modo to the intent that his wishes as declared by the declaration of trust should be carried into effect. When, therefore, this has been done any surplus still belongs to him. This doctrine does not, in my judgment, rest on any evidence of the state of mind of the settlor, for in the vast majority of cases no doubt he does not expect to see his money back: he has created a trust which so far as he can see will absorb the whole of it. The resulting trust arises where that expectation is for some unforeseen reason cheated of fruition, and is an inference of law based on after-knowledge of the event.

Counsel for the Crown admitted that it was for him to show that this principle did not apply to the present case. Counsel for the subscribers cited to me *Re Abbott* ([1900] 2 Ch 326). . . . Stirling J had no difficulty in coming to the conclusion that the ladies were not intended to become the absolute owners of the fund and therefore their personal representatives had no claim. It was never suggested in this case that any claim by the Crown to bona vacantia might arise. A similar result was reached in *Re Hobourn Aero Components Air Raid Distress Fund* ([1946] Ch 86, [1945] 2 All ER 711) where the judge found that though the objects of the fund were charitable no general charitable intent was shown in the absence of any element of public benefit and decided that the money belonged to the subscribers upon a resulting trust. Here again no claim was made on behalf of the Crown that the surplus constituted bona vacantia.

I was referred to two cases where a claim was made to bona vacantia and succeeded. The first of these was *Cunnack v Edwards* ([1896] 2 Ch 679). This was a case of a society formed to raise a fund by subscriptions and so forth from the members to provide for widows of deceased members. Upon the death of the last widow of a member it was found that there was a surplus. It was held by the Court of Appeal that no question of charity arose, that there was no resulting trust in favour of the subscribers, but that the surplus passed to the Crown as bona vacantia. . . .

The ratio decidendi seems to have been that having regard to the constitution of the fund no interest could possibly be held to remain in the contributor who had parted with his money once and for all under a contract for the benefit of his widow. When this contract had been carried into effect the contributor had received all that he contracted to get for his money and could not ask for any more.

A similar result was reached in the case of *Smith v Cooke* ([1891] AC 297), cited by A. L. Smith LJ ([1896] 2 Ch 679 at 683), though it does not appear from the report what the result was. Another case cited to me was *Braithwaite v A-G* ([1909] 1 Ch 510). Here again it was held that there was no room for a resulting trust and the claim to bona vacantia succeeded. The opponents there, it appears, were the last two surviving annuitants. Their claim was rejected on the ground that they had had or were having everything for which the contract provided. The claim of the Attorney-General on behalf of charity was rejected, it being held that there was no charity. A different result was reached by Kekewich J in *Re Buck* ([1896] 2 Ch 727), but it was on the ground that the society was a charity and the money was therefore directed to be applied cy-près. . . .

[His Lordship referred to "the three hospital cases": *Re Welsh Hospital (Netley) Fund* ([1921] 1 Ch 655)[11], *Re Hillier's Trusts* ([1954] 1 WLR 9, [1953] 2 All ER 1547)[12], and *Re Ulverston and District New Hospital Building Trusts* ([1956] Ch 622, [1956] 3 All ER 164)[13] and continued:]

It was argued for the Crown that the subscribers to this fund must be taken to have parted with their money out and out, and that there was here, as in *Cunnack v Edwards* ([1896] 2 Ch 679) and *Braithwaite v A-G,* no room for a resulting trust. But there is a difference between those cases and this in that they were cases of contract and this is not. Further, it seems to me that the hospital cases are not of great help because the argument centred round general charitable intent, a point which cannot arise unless the immediate object be a charity. I have already held there is no such question here. In my judgment the nearest case is the *Hobourn* case ([1946] Ch 86, [1945] 2 All ER 711), which, however, is no authority for the present because no claim for bona vacantia was made.

In my judgment the Crown has failed to show that this case should not follow the ordinary rule merely because there was a number of donors who, I will assume, are unascertainable. I see no reason myself to suppose that the small giver who is anonymous has any wider intention than the large giver who can be named. They all give for the one object. If they can be found by inquiry the resulting trust can be executed in their favour. If they cannot I do not see how the money could then, with all respect to Jenkins LJ, change its destination and become bona vacantia. It will be merely money held upon a trust for which no beneficiary can be found. Such cases are common and where it is known that there are beneficiaries the fact that they cannot be ascertained does not entitle the Crown to come in and claim. The trustees must pay the money into court like any other trustee who cannot find his beneficiary. I conclude, therefore, that there must be an inquiry for the subscribers to this fund[14].

D. Absolute Disposal of Donor's Interest

Where a donor intends to part absolutely with his interest, there is no room for a resulting trust. This statement seems obvious enough; but,

[11] See p. 191, post.
[12] On appeal [1954] 1 WLR 700, [1954] 2 All ER 59, p. 192, post.
[13] P. 192, post.
[14] The fund was wound up in 1965, when the remainder of the money was paid into court.

as the judgment of Harman J in the previous case shows, the distinction has not always been kept clear, although the inconvenience of a resulting trust in the case of street collections etc., has been recognised. As will be seen, provision is made in the Charities Act 1960[15] for the application *cy-près* of money given to charity, and obtained from gifts by unknown donors, even where it was given for a specific purpose only.

In *Cunnack v Edwards* ([1896] 2 Ch 679) a society was formed to raise funds, by the subscription, fines and forfeitures of its members to provide annuities for the widows of those members who died. By 1879, all the members had died, and by 1892, the last widow died. There was then a surplus of £1,250.

The Court of Appeal, reversing Chitty J, held that the Crown took the fund as *bona vacantia*. There was no room for a resulting trust because each member had paid his contributions without reserving any beneficial interest to himself. A. L. Smith LJ said (at p. 683): "As the member paid his money to the society, so he divested himself of all interest in this money for ever, with this one reservation, that if the member left a widow she was to be provided for during her widowhood. Except as to this he abandoned and gave up the money for ever". The benefits were for the widows and not for the members.

RE WEST SUSSEX CONSTABULARY'S WIDOWS, CHILDREN AND BENEVOLENT (1930) FUND TRUSTS[16]

[1971] Ch 1, [1970] 1 All ER 544 (ChD, Goff J)

A fund was established for the purpose of providing payments to widows and certain dependants of deceased members of the West Sussex Constabulary. Clause 10 of the Rules provided that, with exceptions, a member who resigned should forfeit all claims to the fund. Receipts to the fund came from members' subscriptions, the proceeds of entertainments, sweepstakes, raffles and collecting boxes and various donations and legacies. On the amalgamation of the constabulary with other police forces as from January 1, 1968 the operation of the fund came to an end. The question arose as to the distribution of the fund.

Held. (i) Where a donation or legacy was made for the specific purpose of the fund, the donor was entitled under a resulting trust. (ii) Money received from all other sources passed to the Crown as *bona vacantia*.

Goff J: I have already decided . . . that there were not at any time after December 31, 1967 any members of the fund capable of holding a meeting, amending the rules, or winding up the fund. I now have to determine what is its destination in those circumstances.

First, it was submitted that the fund belongs exclusively and in equal shares to all those persons now living who were members on December 31, 1967, and the personal representatives of all the then members since deceased, to all of whom I will refer collectively as "the surviving

[15] S. 14, p. 391, post.
[16] (1971) 87 LQR 464 (M. J. Albery).

members." That argument is based on the analogy of the members' club cases, and the decisions in *Re Printers and Transferrers Amalgamated Trades Protection Society* [1899] 2 Ch 184, *Re Lead Company's Workmen's Fund Society* [1904] 2 Ch 196 and the Irish case of *Tierney v Tough* [1914] 1 IR 142. The ratio decidendi of the first two of those cases was that there was a resulting trust, but that would not give the whole fund to the surviving members, unless rule 10 of the fund's rules could somehow be made to carry to them the contributions of the former members despite the failure of the purposes of the fund (as was pointed out by O'Connor MR in *Tierney v Tough,* at p. 155), and unless indeed the moneys raised from outside sources also could somehow be made to accrue to the surviving members. I agree with Ungoed-Thomas J that the ratio decidendi of *Tierney v Tough* is to be preferred: see *Re St Andrew's Allotment Association* [1969] 1 WLR 229 at 238.

This brings one back to the principle of the members' clubs, and I cannot accept that as applicable for three reasons; First, it simply does not look like it; this was nothing but a pensions or dependent relatives fund not at all akin to a club; secondly, in all the cases where the surviving members have taken, with the sole exception of *Tierney v Tough*, the club society or organisation existed for the benefit of the members for the time being exclusively, whereas in the present case, as in *Cunnack v Edwards* [1896] 2 Ch 679, only third parties could benefit. Moreover, in *Tierney v Tough* the exception was minimal and discretionary and can, I think, fairly be disregarded. Finally, this very argument was advanced and rejected by Chitty J in *Cunnack v Edwards* at first instance [1895] 1 Ch 489 at 496, and was abandoned on the hearing of the appeal. That judgment also disposes of the further argument that the surviving members of the fund had power to amend the rules under rule 14 and could therefore have reduced the fund into possession, and so ought to be treated as the owners of it or the persons for whose benefit it existed at the crucial moment. They had the power but they did not exercise it, and it is now too late.

Then it was argued that there is a resulting trust, with several possible consequences. If this be the right view there must be a primary division of the fund into three parts, one representing contributions from former members, another contributions from the surviving members, and the third moneys raised from outside sources. The surviving members then take the second, and possibly by virtue of rule 10, the first also. That rule is as follows:

> "Any member who voluntarily terminates his membership shall forfeit all claim against the fund, except in the case of a member transferring to a similar fund of another force, in which instance the contributions paid by the member to the West Sussex Constabulary's Widows, Children and Benevolent (1930) Fund may be paid into the fund of the force to which the member transfers."

Alternatively, the first part may belong to the past members on the footing that rule 10 is operative so long only as the fund is a going concern, or may be bona vacantia. The third is distributable in whole or in part between those who provided the money, or again is bona vacantia.

In my judgment the doctrine of resulting trust is clearly inapplicable to the contributions of both classes. Those persons who remained members until their deaths are in any event excluded because they have had all they contracted for, either because their widows and dependants have received or are in receipt of the prescribed benefits, or because they did not have a widow or dependants. In my view that is inherent in all the speeches in the Court of Appeal in *Cunnack v Edwards* [1896] 2 Ch 679. Further, whatever the effect of the fund's rule 10 may be upon the contributions of those members who left prematurely, they and the surviving members alike are also in my judgment unable to claim under a resulting trust because they put up their money on a contractual basis and not one of trust: see per Harman J in *Re Gillingham Bus Disaster Fund* [1958] Ch 300 at 314. The only case which has given me difficulty on this aspect of the matter is *Re Hobourn Aero Components Ltd's Air Raid Distress Fund* [1946] Ch 86, where in somewhat similar circumstances it was held there was a resulting trust. The argument postulated, I think, the distinction between contract and trust but in another connection, namely, whether the fund was charitable: see pp. 89 and 90. There was in that case a resolution to wind up but that was not, at all events as expressed, the ratio decidendi: see per Cohen J at p. 97, but, as Cohen J observed, there was no argument for bona vacantia. Moreover, no rules or regulations were ever made and although in fact £1 per month was paid or saved for each member serving with the forces, there were no prescribed contractual benefits. In my judgment that case is therefore distinguishable.

Accordingly, in my judgment all the contributions of both classes are bona vacantia, but I must make a reservation with respect to possible contractual rights. In *Cunnack v Edwards* [1895] 1 Ch 489 and *Braithwaite v A-G* [1909] 1 Ch 510 all the members had received, or provision had been made for, all the contractual benefits. Here the matter has been cut short. Those persons who died whilst still in membership cannot, I conceive, have any rights because in their case the contract has been fully worked out, and on a contractual basis I would think that members who retired would be precluded from making any claim by rule 10, although that is perhaps more arguable. The surviving members, on the other hand, may well have a right in contract on the ground of frustration or total failure of consideration, and that right may embrace contributions made by past members, though I do not see how it could apply to moneys raised from outside sources. I have not, however, heard any argument based on contract and therefore the declarations I propose to make will be subject to the reservation which I will later formulate. This will not prevent those parts of the fund which are bona vacantia from being paid over to the Crown as it has offered to give a full indemnity to the trustees.

I must now turn to the moneys raised from outside sources. Counsel for the Treasury Solicitor made an overriding general submission that there cannot be a resulting trust of any of the outside moneys because in the circumstances it is impossible to identify the trust property; no doubt something could be achieved by complicated accounting, but this, he submitted, would not be identification but notional reconstruction. I cannot accept that argument. In my judgment, in a case like the present, equity will cut the Gordian knot by simply dividing the ultimate surplus in proportion to the sources from which it has arisen. Chitty J in *Cunnack v Edwards* at first instance [1895] 1 Ch 489, particularly at pp. 497 and 498, was prepared to order an inquiry, notwithstanding the difficulty that it involved, going back over many years, and despite the fact that the early records were not available; but that was a difficulty of ascertaining the original contributions, not of working out surpluses or interest calculations year by year. Similarly it was not suggested that any such operation ought to be carried out, or that the necessity for it prevented the doctrine of resulting trust being applied in the *Re Printers and Transferrers* case [1899] 2 Ch 184. Yet in both those cases, although the matter was not further complicated by outside contributions, the problem of interest on invested funds, and of contributions and expenditure made at different times, must have presented itself. Again, in the *Printers* case, fines and forfeitures were ignored: see pp. 189 and 190. There may be cases of tolerable simplicity where the court will be more refined, but in general, where a fund has been raised from mixed sources, interest has been earned over the years and income—and possibly capital—expenditure has been made indiscriminately out of the fund as an entirety, and then the venture comes to an end prematurely or otherwise, the court will not find itself baffled but will cut the Gordian knot as I have said.

Then counsel divided the outside moneys into three categories, first, the proceeds of entertainments, raffles and sweepstakes; secondly, the proceeds of collecting-boxes; and, thirdly, donations, including legacies if any, and he took particular objections to each.

I agree that there cannot be any resulting trust with respect to the first category. I am not certain whether Harman J in *Re Gillingham Bus Disaster Fund* [1958] Ch 300 meant to decide otherwise. In stating the facts at p. 304 he referred to "street collections and so forth". In the further argument at p. 309 there is mention of whist drives and concerts but the judge himself did not speak of anything other than gifts. If, however, he did, I must respectfully decline to follow his judgment in that regard, for whatever may be the true position with regard to collecting-boxes, it appears to me to be impossible to apply the doctrine of resulting trust to the proceeds of entertainments and sweepstakes and such-like money-raising operations for two reasons: first, the relationship is one of contract and not of trust; the purchaser of a ticket may have the motive of aiding the cause or he may not; he may purchase a ticket merely because he wishes to attend the particular entertainment or to try for the prize, but whichever it be, he pays his money as the price of what is offered and what he receives; secondly, there is in such cases no direct contribution to the fund at all; it is only the profit, if any, which is ultimately received and there may even be none.

In any event, the first category cannot be any more susceptible to the doctrine than the second to which I now turn. Here one starts with the well-known dictum of P.O. Lawrence J in *Re Welsh Hospital (Netley) Fund* [1921] 1 Ch 655 at 660 where he said:

> "So far as regards the contributors to entertainments, street collections etc., I have no hesitation in holding that they must be taken to have parted with their money out-and-out. It is inconceivable that any

person paying for a concert ticket or placing a coin in a collecting-box presented to him in the street should have intended that any part of the money so contributed should be returned to him when the immediate object for which the concert was given or the collection made had come to an end. To draw such an inference would be absurd on the face of it."

This was adopted by Upjohn J in *Re Hillier's Trusts* [1954] 1 WLR 9, [1954] 2 All ER 59, where the point was actually decided. . . .

[The analysis of Upjohn J] was approved by Denning LJ in the Court of Appeal [1954] 1 WLR 700 although it is true he went on to say that the law makes a presumption of charity. I quote from p. 714:

"Let me first state the law as I understand it in regard to money collected for a specific charity by means of a church collection, a flag day, a whist drive, a dance, or some such activity. When a man gives money on such an occasion, he gives it, I think, beyond recall. He parts with his money out-and-out. . . ."

In *Re Ulverston and District New Hospital Building Trusts* [1956] Ch 622 at 633 Jenkins LJ threw out a suggestion that there might be a distinction in the case of a person who could prove that he put a specified sum in a collecting-box, and, in the *Gillingham* case [1958] Ch 300 Harman J after noting this, decided that there was a resulting trust with respect to the proceeds of collections. He said at p. 314: [quoting the last paragraph extracted, p. 187, ante:]

It will be observed that Harman J considered that *Re Welsh Hospital (Netley) Fund* [1921] 1 Ch 655; *Re Hillier's Trusts* [1954] 1 WLR 9, [1954] 2 All ER 9 and *Re Ulverston and District New Hospital Building Trusts* [1956] Ch 622, [1956] 3 All ER 164 did not help him greatly because they were charity cases. It is true that they were, and, as will presently appear, that is in my view very significant in relation to the third category, but I do not think it was a valid objection with respect to the second, and for my part I cannot reconcile the decision of Upjohn J in *Re Hillier's Trusts* with that of Harman J in the *Gillingham* case [1958] Ch 300, [1958] 1 All ER 37. As I see it, therefore, I have to choose between them. On the one hand it may be said that Harman J had the advantage, which Upjohn J had not, of considering the suggestion made by Jenkins LJ. On the other hand that suggestion with all respect, seems to me somewhat fanciful and unreal. I agree that all who put their money into collecting-boxes should be taken to have the same intention, but why should they not all be regarded as intending to part with their money out and out absolutely in all circumstances? I observe that P.O. Lawrence J in *Re Welsh Hospital* [1921] 1 Ch 655 at 661 used very strong words. He said any other view was inconceivable and absurd on the face of it. That commends itself to my humble judgment, and I therefore prefer and follow the judgment of Upjohn J in *Re Hillier's Trusts*. . . . [His Lordship referred to *Re Hillier's Trusts* [1954] 1 WLR 700, [1953] 2 All ER 1547, and continued:] Therefore, where, as in the present case, the object was neither equivocal nor charitable, I can see no justification for infecting the third category with the weaknesses of the first and second, and I cannot distinguish this part of the case from *Re Abbott Fund Trusts* [1900] 2 Ch 326.

I will hear counsel on the form of order and in any case will direct a minute to be signed and circulated, but in general I direct two inquiries: (1) What donations of specific amounts other than through collecting-boxes but including legacies were at any time given to the fund and by whom, and whether any living donors have since died and, if so, who are their personal representatives, and who are the personal representatives of any testators by whom such legacies were bequeathed; (2) What is the total amount of (a) the contributions made by the members since the inception of the fund, (b) the proceeds of entertainments, sweepstakes, collections and any similar money-raising activities, and (c) such donations including legacies. I then direct the total net assets after payment of costs to be divided between these three portions pro rata.

And I make the following declarations: First, that the portion attributable to donations and legacies is held on a resulting trust for the donors or their estates and the estates of the respective testators; secondly, that the remainder of the fund is bona vacantia.

These declarations are, however, without prejudice to (1) Any claim which may be made in contract by any person or the personal representatives of any person who was at any time a member, and (2) Any right or claim of the trustees to be indemnified against any such claim out of the whole fund including the portion attributable to donations and legacies.

Finally there will, of course, be general liberty to apply.

E. The Members' Club Cases

Where members contribute to the funds or property of a club or society which is established for their own benefit, the members will usually be held to be the owners of the property of the club or society. As has been seen[17], their entitlement may be based upon beneficial ownership under a resulting trust; or, as is shown by the modern cases to be much more likely, upon the basis of contractual rights. Such questions often arise where a club or association is dissolved[18], and the problem concerns the distribution of the surplus assets. If the members have no claim on either ground, the Crown may become entitled to the property as bona vacantia[19].

RE SICK AND FUNERAL SOCIETY OF ST. JOHN'S SUNDAY SCHOOL, GOLCAR[20]

[1973] Ch 51, [1972] 2 All ER 439 (ChD, MEGARRY J)

In 1866 a society was formed at a Sunday school near Huddersfield to provide for sickness and death benefits for its members. Teachers and children could join, and subscriptions were based on a sliding scale according to age; those under 13 paying ½d. per week (Rule 9) and those

[17] See pp. 62, 187 et seq., ante.

[18] As to when there is a dissolution so as to render the unspent assets distributable, see *Re William Denby & Sons Ltd Sick and Benevolent Fund* [1971] 1 WLR 973, [1971] 3 All ER 1196.

[19] Ing, *Bona Vacantia* (1971) pp. 180 et seq.

[20] See (1973) 92 Law Notes 297, 330 (A. Cooklin).

over 12 paying 1d. The benefits for those paying the full subscription were twice those of the smaller subscribers (Rules 12, 14).

On December 12, 1966, a meeting unanimously decided to wind up the Society as from December 31. No further subscriptions were paid. There was some £4,000 of surplus assets.

Before the assets were distributed among the current members, four ex-members, who had been excluded from membership for failure to pay subscriptions since 1963 (Rules 9, 17), claimed to pay up their arrears and to participate. A further meeting was held in September 1968 in which it was again resolved to wind up the Society and to distribute the assets among the persons who were members on December 31, 1966, and the personal representatives of such members who had subsequently died.

Held. Distribution accordingly; with full shares for full members and half shares for the children. The ex-members were excluded.

MEGARRY J (having held that the resolution of December 1966 was a valid resolution to wind up the Society): In my judgment the substantive rights of all concerned crystallised on December 31, 1966, when, in accordance with the resolution of December 12, 1966, the society ceased all its activities. . . . Accordingly, in my judgment the personal representatives of each deceased member are entitled to the share to which that member would have been entitled had he lived. . . .

I turn to question 2. This relates to the basis of distribution. Is each member entitled to an equal share, or is there to be a division into full shares and half-shares, with those paying ½d. week entitled only to a half-share, and those paying 1d. a week a full share? Or is the basis of distribution to be proportionate to the amounts respectively contributed by each member? The first step, in my view, is to decide between the first two contentions on the one hand and the third on the other: is the proper basis that of division per capita, whether in full or half-shares, or that of division in proportion to the amounts contributed? In discussing this, I speak, of course, in general terms, and subject to any other basis for division that is to be discerned in the rules or any other source.

The authorities are in a curious state. In *Re Printers and Transferrers Amalgamated Trades Protection Society* [1899] 2 Ch 184, Byrne J applied the amounts-contributed basis to a trade union, putting matters on the footing of a resulting trust, and directing division on that basis among the members existing at the time of the resolution for dissolution. In *Re Lead Company's Workmen's Fund Society* [1904] 2 Ch 196, Warrington J followed this decision in the case of an unregistered friendly society. In these cases payments for forfeitures, fines, sick benefits and so on, were disregarded. In *Tierney v Tough* [1914] 1 IR 142, another case of an unregistered friendly society, O'Connor MR was critical of the application of the law relating to resulting trusts to such cases. Despite his criticism, however, he directed division on the basis of the amounts contributed. On the other hand, in the case of clubs, *Brown v Dale* (1878) 9 ChD 78 supports the per capita basis, though it is so shortly reported as to provoke more questions than it answers. *Feeney and Shannon v MacManus* [1937] IR 23, another club case, also supports the same basis. The case is a little remarkable in that the headnote proclaims that *Tierney v Tough* [1914] 1 IR 142 was "applied"; and it appears from page 33 that the basis of the decision was not so much that equal division was right, but that equality was necessary because ascertaining the proportionate contributions was an impossibility. Finally, in *Re St Andrew's Allotment Association* [1969] 1 WLR 229, concerning an allotment association, Ungoed-Thomas J considered these cases, together with *Re Blue Albion Cattle Society* [1966] CLY 1274, The Guardian, May 28, 1966, where Cross J had applied the per capita basis to a cattle-breeding society. In the *St Andrew's* case Ungoed-Thomas J said, at p. 238:

> "If the true principle is that laid down in *Tierney v Tough* [1914] 1 IR 142 and that principle certainly seems to me preferable to the principle of the resulting trust adopted in *Re Printers and Transferrers Amalgamated Trades Protection Society* [1899] 2 Ch 184, then it would seem to me that prima facie the assets are distributable between members at the relevant date per capita. It is conceivable that a basis for distinguishing the friendly and mutual benefit society cases may be that, whereas in the club cases enjoyment ab initio and equality are contemplated, yet in the friendly and mutual benefit society cases what are contemplated are advantages related to contributions."

The reference to the principle laid down in *Tierney v Tough* must, I think, be to the comments of O'Connor MR which rejected the concept of resulting trust, rather than to the actual decision, which was on the basis of the proportionate contributions that flow from the concept of resulting trust.

It seems to me, with all respect, that much of the difficulty arises from confusing property with contract. A resulting trust is essentially a property concept: any property that a man does not effectually dispose of remains his own. If, then, there is a true resulting trust in respect of an unexpended balance of payments made to some club or association, there will be a resulting trust in respect of that unexpended balance, and the beneficiaries under that trust will be those who made the payments. If any are dead, the trust will be for their estates; death does not deprive a man of his beneficial interest. Yet in what I may call "the resulting trust cases," the beneficiaries who were held to be entitled were the members living at the time of the dissolution, to the exclusion of those who had died or otherwise ceased to be members. If, then, there was any resulting trust, it must be a trust modified in some way, perhaps by some unexplained implied term, that distinguishes between the quick and the dead. It cannot be merely an ordinary resulting trust.

On the other hand, membership of a club or association is primarily a matter of contract. The members make their payments, and in return they become entitled to the benefits of membership in accordance with the rules. The sums they pay cease to be their individual property, and so cease to be subject to any concept of resulting trust. Instead, they become the property, through the trustees of the club or association, of all the members for the time being, including themselves. A member who, by death or otherwise, ceases to be a member thereby ceases to be the part owner of any of the club's property: those who remain continue owners. If, then, dissolution ensues, there must be a division of the property of the club or association among those alone who are owners of that property, to the exclusion of former members. In that division, I cannot see what relevance there can be in the respective amounts of the contributions. The newest member, who has made a single payment when he joined only a year ago, is as much a part owner of the property of the club or association as a member who has been making payments for 50 years. Each has had what he has paid for: the newest member has had the benefits of membership for a year or so and the oldest member for 50 years. Why should the latter, who for his money has had the benefits of membership for 50 times as long as the former, get the further benefit of receiving 50 times as much in the winding up?

I have, of course, been speaking in the broadest of outlines; but I must say that the view taken on principle by O'Connor MR in *Tierney v Tough* [1914] 1 IR 142 and by Ungoed-Thomas J in *Re Andrew's Allotment Association* [1969] 1 WLR 229 seem to me to be preferable to the other view, despite certain difficulties in the basis of distinction between the club cases and the others tentatively suggested by Ungoed-Thomas J in the passage that I have read: [1969] 1 WLR 229 at 238. Accordingly, I reject the basis of proportionate division in favour of equality, or division per capita. But then the second question arises, namely, whether the principle of equality prevails not only when there is no more than one class of members but when there are two or more classes. Is the proposed division into shares and half-shares sound, or ought it to be rejected in favour of equality throughout?

On the footing that the rules of a club or association form the basis of the contract between all the members, I must look at the rules of the society to see whether they indicate any basis other than that of equality. It seems to me that they do. Those aged from five to 12 years old pay contributions at half the rate (rule 9), and correspondingly their allowances (rule 12) and death benefit (rule 14) are also paid at half the rate. Where the rules have written into them the basis of inequality among different classes of members in relation to the principal contractual burdens and benefits of membership, it seems to me to follow that this inequality ought also to be applied to the surplus property of the society. A distinction between classes of members is quite different from a distinction between individual members of the same class based on the amounts contributed by each member. At any given moment one can say that the rights and liabilities of all the members of one class differ in the same way from the rights and liabilities of all the members of the other class, irrespective of the length of membership or anything else. It was indeed suggested that the words "two classes of subscribers" in rule 9 did not mean that there were two classes of members, the word "subscribers" being in contrast with the word "member" used in the next sentence. But the rules are too ill-drafted for any such inferences to be drawn; and rule 5, providing for special meetings of the committee when requested by three "subscribers," and a general meeting if required by 20 of the "members," strongly suggests that the terms are used interchangeably. At any rate, I have heard no sensible explanations of the distinction . . .

I turn to question 3, the case of the four members who ceased to make any payments at some unspecified date in 1963 and then sought to tender all arrears at some unspecified date in 1967. Theirs is not a particularly attractive claim; for after having failed to discharge their obligations as members for over three years, they came forward to claim as members after the 1966 resolution to wind up the society had been passed and had come into such force as it had. Their claim is almost of necessity technical. They say that they were members, and that the machinery of the rules whereby a defaulting member ceases to be a member never took effect. They rely on rules 9 and 17, which I have already read, and in particular upon the fact that no "summons" under rule 9 had ever been served upon them.

I have already observed that the rules are not well drafted, and I do not intend to explore all the difficulties discussed in argument. The four respondents contend that for various reasons, and in particular the reference in rule 17 to "notice charges," the machinery of rule 9 for a summons and a discretionary power in the committee are imported into rule 17. Rule 17 accordingly does not, it is said, result in an automatic cessation of membership after two months' failure to make a quarterly payment. It is not admitted that the four were "out members" within rule 17, although it is accepted that they probably were and that the case can be dealt with on that footing, subject to the right to reopen the point if on investigation it proves that they were not "out members."

I should be very slow to accept that a member of a society may disregard all his obligations as a member for several years, and then, when it appears that there is some advantage in resuming his membership, assert that he is still a member because the correct procedure under the rules to terminate his membership has not been followed. The question, of course, is not one of expulsion, or of the society snatching at some trivial or short-lived breach of rules by a member to deny him membership: it is a question of a voluntary disregard of the obligations of membership over a continuous period of years. There must be many instances in clubs up and down the country in which this sort of thing happens. Yet if the contentions on behalf of the four members are right, either the society or the members concerned may, if it suits them, claim that the membership is still in being. Such members might find that the society is claiming many years' arrears of a substantial subscription, or the members might, as here, suddenly reassert their membership when some advantage turns up.

I do not think that this can be right. . . .

QUESTIONS

1. How would you have decided *Re Vandervell's Trusts (No. 2)* if it had gone on appeal to the House of Lords, and you had been sitting?
2. Re-examine the situations in which the court has found a solution based upon (i) a resulting trust, (ii) a contractual right, (iii) bona vacantia. Do you think that the choice was based upon logical analysis, or upon convenience of result, or upon chance?

III. The Presumptions[1]

A. Voluntary Conveyances

i. LAND

LAW OF PROPERTY ACT 1925

60. Abolition of technicalities in regard to conveyancing and deeds.— (3) In a voluntary conveyance a resulting trust for the grantor shall not be implied merely by reason that the property is not expressed to be conveyed for the use or benefit of the grantee.

In *Hodgson v Marks* ([1971] Ch 892, [1971] 2 All ER 684) Mrs. Hodgson, a widow and 83 years of age, was the owner of a house. Mr. Evans was her lodger. He gained her trust and affection, and supervised the investment of her money. A nephew of Mrs. Hodgson was suspicious of Mr. Evans and tried to persuade her to turn him out. In order to protect Mr. Evans, she transferred the house to him, under an oral agreement that she would continue to be the beneficial owner. Mr. Evans was registered as the absolute owner. He later sold it to Mr. Marks. The question was whether Mrs. Hodgson was entitled to protection against Mr. Marks as the owner of an overriding interest on the ground that she was a person in actual occupation of the land. The Court of Appeal held that Mr. Evans held the house upon a resulting trust for her and that she was, therefore, equitable owner of the house. Her right to the house constituted an overriding interest under Land Registration Act 1925, s. 70 (1) (*g*).

ii. PERSONALTY

In *Re Vinogradoff* ([1935] WN 68) Mrs. Vinogradoff, in 1926, gratuitously transferred a sum of £800 War Loan into the joint names of herself and of her infant granddaughter, Laura Jackson. The question was whether the stock was owned, on Mrs. Vinogradoff's death, by her estate or by Laura Jackson.

FARWELL J decided that it was held upon a resulting trust for the estate of Mrs. Vinogradoff. Section 20 of the Law of Property Act 1925, under which the appointment of an infant as trustee is void, did not affect the presumption of a resulting trust. "The stock was not the property of the infant, but formed part of the estate of the testatrix."

B. Presumption in Favour of a Purchaser

Purchase in the Name of Another, and Joint Purchase in the Name of One

In *Dyer v Dyer* (1788) 2 Cox Eq 92 at 93, EYRE CB explained the principle as follows: "The clear result of all the cases, without a single exception, is, that the trust of a legal estate, whether freehold, copyhold, or leasehold; whether taken in the names of the purchasers and others jointly, or in

[1] H & M, pp. 262–270; K & S, pp. 137–181; P & M, pp. 119–128; Pettit, pp. 100–115; Snell, pp. 175–182.

the name of others without that of the purchaser; whether in one name or several; whether jointly or *successive,* results to the man who advances the purchase-money. This is a general proposition supported by all the cases, and there is nothing to contradict it; and it goes on a strict analogy to the rule of the common law, that where a feoffment is made without consideration, the use results to the feoffor''.

FOWKES v PASCOE[2]
(1875) 10 Ch App 343 (CA in Ch, JAMES AND MELLISH LJJ)

Mrs. Baker made various purchases of $3\frac{1}{4}$ per cent. Annuities, amounting in all to £7,000 in the joint names of herself and John Pascoe, who was the son of Mrs. Baker's daughter-in-law.

By her will, Mrs. Baker gave her residuary estate to the daughter-in-law for life and after her death to John Pascoe and his sister in equal shares.

John Pascoe claimed to be entitled both to the capital sum and to the dividends due at Mrs. Baker's death, and afterwards received by him.

Held. Pascoe was entitled to the capital, but not to the dividends.

MELLISH LJ: Now, the presumption must, beyond all question, be of very different weight in different cases. In some cases it would be very strong indeed. If, for instance, a man invested a sum of stock in the name of himself and his solicitor, the inference would be very strong indeed that it was intended solely for the purpose of a trust, and the Court would require very strong evidence on the part of the solicitor to prove that it was intended as a gift; and certainly his own evidence would not be sufficient. On the other hand a man may make an investment of stock in the name of himself and some person, although not a child or wife, yet in such a position to him as to make it extremely probable that the investment was intended as a gift. In such a case, although the rule of law, if there was no evidence at all, would compel the Court to say that the presumption of trust must prevail, even if the Court might not believe that the fact was in accordance with the presumption, yet, if there is evidence to rebut the presumption, then, in my opinion, the Court must go into the actual facts. And if we are to go into the actual facts, and look at the circumstances of this investment, it appears to me utterly impossible, as the Lord Justice has said, to come to any other conclusion than that the first investment was made for the purpose of gift and not for the purpose of trust. It was either for the purpose of trust or else for the purpose of gift; and therefore any evidence which shews it was not for the purpose of trust is evidence to shew that it was for the purpose of gift. We find a lady of considerable fortune, having no nearer connections than Mr. *Pascoe,* who was then a young man living in her house, and for whom she was providing. We find her, manifestly out of her savings, buying a sum of £250 stock in the joint names of herself and him, and at the same time buying another sum of £250 stock, on the very same day, in the joint names of herself and a lady who was living with her

[2] *Young v Sealey* [1949] Ch 278, [1949] 1 All ER 92; (1969) 85 LQR 530 (M. C. Cullity).

as a companion. Then, applying one's common sense to that transaction, what inference is it possible to draw, except that the purchases were intended for the purpose of gifts? If they were intended for the purpose of trusts, what possible reason was there why the two sums were not invested in the same names? Besides, at the very same time the lady had a large sum of stock in her own name, and could anything be more absurd than to suppose that a lady with £4,000 or £5,000 in her own name at that time in the same stock, and having a sum of £500 to invest out of her savings, should go and invest £250 in the name of herself and a young gentleman who was living in her house, and another £250 in the name of herself and her companion, and yet intend the whole to be for herself? I cannot come to any other conclusion than that it must have been intended by way of a present after her death.

Then, when we have once arrived at the conclusion that the first investment was intended as a gift (and the second was exactly similar), and when we find that the account was opened for the purpose of gift, those facts appear to me to rebut the presumption altogether, because when an account is once found to be opened for the purpose of gift there is very strong reason to suppose that everything added to that account was intended for the purpose of gift also. Assuming the testatrix to know that she had made a gift, and had invested a sum of money in stock in the joint names of herself and *Pascoe* for the purpose of making a present to him, it would certainly be a very extraordinary thing that she should go and add other large sums to that account, not for the purpose of making a present to him, but for the purpose of his being a trustee. I cannot help coming to the conclusion that, as a matter of fact, these investments were intended for the purpose of gift.

There were one or two facts relied on against this conclusion. It was said that Mr. *Pascoe* kept the matter secret for a great number of years, and never revealed it. I do not greatly rely on that. Every one who has experience knows that some persons are very reticent about their affairs, and some persons are always talking about them. You cannot form any inference as to that. If he really and *bona fide* believed, and had no doubt that it was intended for a gift, and for his use, I do not see that there was anything extraordinary in his not mentioning it to the persons who now say it was not mentioned to them. The only fact that in the least degree, in my opinion, went against him was his not accounting for the dividend which was due at the death of the testatrix. I think it is not at all impossible that he might have honestly believed that that was his, although I entirely agree that in point of law it was not so; therefore on the whole I come to the same conclusion as the Lord Justice.

C. Presumption of Advancement

Where a voluntary conveyance is made to the wife or child of the donor, or to a person to whom he stands in *loco parentis,* the presumption is that a gift was intended. This is the Presumption of Advancement. It is a stronger presumption than the so-called presumption of a resulting trust, as is made clear in *Shephard v Cartwright*.[3] But it can be rebutted by evidence of a contrary intention.

In *Bennet v Bennet* ((1879) 10 ChD 474) JESSEL MR said at p. 476[4]: "The doctrine of equity as regards presumption of gifts is this, that where one person stands in such a relation to another that there is an obligation on that person to make a provision for the other, and we find either a purchase or investment in the name of the other, or in the joint names of the person and the other, of an amount which would constitute a provision for the other, the presumption arises of an intention on the part of the person to discharge the obligation to the other; and therefore, in the absence of evidence to the contrary, that purchase or investment is held to be in itself evidence of a gift.

In other words, the presumption of gift arises from the moral obligation to give.

That reconciles all the cases upon the subject but one, because nothing is better established than this, that as regards a child, a person not the father of the child may put himself in the position of one *in loco parentis* to the child, and so incur the obligation to make a provision for the child. . . .

A person *in loco parentis* means a person taking upon himself the duty of a father of a child to make a provision for that child. It is clear that in that case the presumption can only arise from the obligation, and therefore in that case the doctrine can only have reference to the obligation of a father to provide for his child, and nothing else.

But the father is under that obligation from the mere fact of his being the father, and therefore no evidence is necessary to shew the obligation to provide for his child, because that is part of his duty. In the case of a father, you have only to prove the fact that he is the father, and when you have done that the obligation at once arises; but in the case of a person *in loco parentis* you must prove that he took upon himself the obligation."

SHEPHARD v CARTWRIGHT

[1955] AC 431, [1954] 3 All ER 649 (HL, Viscount SIMONDS, Lords MORTON OF HENRYTON, REID, TUCKER and SOMERVELL OF HARROW)

In 1929 Philip Edward Shephard established certain private companies which prospered. The shares in these companies were divided among his three children, the appellants, one of whom was an infant. One reason for so dividing the shares was to obtain certain tax advantages which at that time were obtainable.

In 1934 he formed a public company which took over the private companies, paying £300,000 in cash and £400,000 in shares. The Shephard children signed the necessary documents at the request of their father.

Shephard in effect controlled the cash and the shares and obtained the

[3] [1955] AC 431, [1954] 3 All ER 649, infra.
[4] *Re Paradise Motor Co Ltd* [1968] 1 WLR 1125, [1968] 2 All ER 625.

children's signatures to all necessary documents, without their knowing what they were signing. By 1936 all the money properly due to the children was exhausted. On Shephard's death in 1949, the children sued the executors for an account. The defendants argued that the intention of the father since 1929 indicated clearly that he intended to treat the money and shares as his own.

Held. The estate was liable. The shares and money were owned beneficially by the children. Evidence of the activities of the father subsequent to the transfer of the shares to the children was not admissible in his favour[5].

VISCOUNT SIMONDS: I think it well to pause in this year 1929 and to ask what was the result in law or equity of the registration, in the names of his children of shares for which he supplied the cash, and I pause in order to examine the law, because it appears to me that the only two facts which are at this stage relied on to rebut the presumption of advancement, viz., that the children were ignorant and that certificates were not given to them, are of negligible value.

My Lords, I do not distinguish between the purchase of shares and the acquisition of shares upon allotment, and I think that the law is clear that on the one hand where a man purchases shares and they are registered in the name of a stranger there is a resulting trust in favour of the purchaser; on the other hand, if they are registered in the name of a child or one to whom the purchaser then stood in loco parentis, there is no such resulting trust but a presumption of advancement. Equally it is clear that the presumption may be rebutted but should not, as Lord Eldon said, give way to slight circumstances: *Finch v Finch* ((1808) 15 Ves 43).

It must then be asked by what evidence can the presumption be rebutted, and it would, I think, be very unfortunate if any doubt were cast (as I think it has been by certain passages in the judgments under review) upon the well-settled law on this subject. It is, I think, correctly stated in substantially the same terms in every textbook that I have consulted and supported by authority extending over a long period of time. I will take, as an example, a passage from Snell's Equity, 24th Edn., p. 153, which is as follows:

> "The acts and declarations of the parties before or at the time of the purchase, or so immediately after it as to constitute a part of the transaction, are admissible in evidence either for or against the party who did the act or made the declaration . . . But subsequent declarations are admissible as evidence only against the party who made them, and not in his favour."

I do not think it necessary to review the numerous cases of high authority upon which this statement is founded. It is possible to find in some earlier judgments reference to "subsequent" events without the qualifications contained in the textbook statement: it may even be possible to wonder in some cases how in the narration of facts certain events were admitted to consideration. But the burden of authority in favour of the broad propo-

[5] See Civil Evidence Act 1968, s. 2; Cross, *Evidence* (4th Edn, 1974) p. 22.

sition as stated in the passage I have cited is overwhelming and should not be disturbed.

But although the applicable law is not in doubt, the application of it is not always easy. There must often be room for argument whether a subsequent act is part of the same transaction as the original purchase or transfer, and equally whether subsequent acts which it is sought to adduce in evidence ought to be regarded as admissions by the party so acting, and if they are so admitted, further facts should be admitted by way of qualification of those admissions. . . .

The first question, then, is whether any subsequent events are admissible as part of the original transaction to prove that the deceased had not in 1929 the intention of advancement which the law presumes. My Lords, for nearly five years nothing happened which could by any means be regarded as throwing light upon his original intention, but an event did happen which would amply explain a change in that intention. For within a short time of their promotion the businesses of the six companies were prosperous beyond all expectation. In the year 1931 their combined profits were £57,780, in 1932 £128,525 and in 1933 £344,671. It is not surprising that in the light of this great success the deceased and his co-adventurer, Meyer, should form a public company to acquire all the shares of all the six companies. This they did.

[His Lordship reviewed the events subsequent to 1929, and continued:]

I have omitted to state one fact subsequent to the original transaction which, whether or not it is to be regarded as part of it and admissible in evidence under that head, is clearly admissible as an admission by the deceased against interest. Shortly before the completion of the agreement with the new company and no doubt as part of the arrangement, one of the old companies, New Ideal Homesteads Ld., declared and paid a dividend of £25 12s. per share. The deceased, acting presumably under the power of attorney to which I have referred, received the dividend attributable to the appellants' shares and, though retaining it for his own use, instructed the respondent Dunk, an accountant who acted for the deceased in the preparation of his income tax returns, that the dividend was the income of the appellants. It was so treated by Dunk, whose integrity has not been challenged. Similar information and instructions were given by the deceased to Dunk in regard to the sums placed to the deposit account of the appellants with Barclays Bank Ld., and to the untaxed interest payable in respect of those sums, and were acted on by him.

I turn, then, again to ask how these facts which I have briefly narrated can be adduced in evidence by the deceased or his estate. And I think it convenient at this stage to refer to a matter in which, with great respect, I think the Master of the Rolls fell into an error and, moreover, into an error which largely influenced him in the conclusion to which he came. For he treated the appellants' claim merely as a claim against a dead man's estate, and therefore (as he says and reiterates) as a claim in which a heavy onus lay on the claimants. But that is not, in my opinion, the way in which the claim should be regarded. It starts with the fact that in 1929 certain shares were placed by their father in the names of the appellants, and, that fact being admitted or proved, a presumption at once arises which it is for the respondents to rebut. They as executors are in no stronger position than their testator would be in if he were alive.

My Lords, at the outset of this opinion I said that there must often be room for argument whether subsequent events can be regarded as forming part of the original transaction so as to be admissible evidence of intention and in this case it has certainly been vigorously argued that they can. But, though I know of no universal criterion by which a link can for this purpose be established between one event and another, here I see insuperable difficulty in finding any link at all. The time factor alone of nearly five years is almost decisive, but, apart from that, the events of 1934 and 1935, whether taken singly or in their sum, appear to me to be wholly independent of the original transaction. It is in fact fair to say that, so far from flowing naturally and inevitably from it, they probably never would have happened but for the phenomenal success of the enterprise. Nor can I give any weight to the argument much pressed upon us that the deceased was an honourable man and therefore could not have acted as he did, if he had in 1929 intended to give the shares outright to his children. I assume that he was an honourable man as well in the directions in regard to income tax that he gave to Mr. Dunk as otherwise, but I think that he may well have deemed it consistent with honourable conduct and with paternal benevolence to take back part of what he had given when the magnitude of the gift so far surpassed his expectation.

If, then, these events cannot be admitted in evidence as part of the original transaction, can they be admitted to rebut the presumption on the ground that they are admissions by the appellants against interest? I conceive it possible, and this view is supported by authority, that there might be such a course of conduct by a child after a presumed advancement as to constitute an admission by him of his parent's original intention, though such evidence should be regarded jealously. But it appears to me to be an indispensable condition of such conduct being admissible that it should be performed with knowledge of the material facts. In the present case the undisputed fact that the appellants under their father's guidance did what they were told without inquiry or knowledge precludes the admission in evidence of their conduct and, if it were admitted, would deprive it of all probative value. It is otherwise, however, with the conduct of the deceased. I have already made it clear that the respondents have failed to discharge the burden which rests on them of rebutting the presumption of advancement. The appellants, therefore, in my opinion, need no reinforcement from subsequent events. But, since inevitably in a complex case like this, either upon the footing of being examined de bene esse or because they have been admitted for some other purpose than the proof of intention, all the facts relevant or irrelevant have been reviewed, I do not hesitate to say that the only conclusion which I can form about the deceased's original intention is that he meant the provision he then made for his children to be for their permanent advancement. He may well have changed his mind at a later date, but it was too late. He may have thought that, having made an absolute gift, he could yet revoke it. This is something that no one will ever know. The presumption which the law makes is not to be thus rebutted. If it were my duty to speculate upon these matters, my final question would be why the deceased should have put these several parcels of shares in six different companies into the names of his wife and three children unless he meant to make provision for them, and since counsel have not been able to suggest any, much less any plausible, reason why he should have done so, I shall conclude that the intention which the law imputes to him was in fact his intention. The reasoning which made so strong an appeal to Mellish LJ in *Fowkes v Pascoe* ((1875) 10 Ch App 343) has in this case also particular weight.

In my opinion, then, this appeal succeeds on the main question that has been argued before us[6].

WARREN v GURNEY

[1944] 2 All ER 472 (CA, Lord GREENE MR, FINLAY and MORTON LJJ)

In 1929, Elijah Gurney purchased a house, "Fairview", for £300. It was conveyed to his daughter, who was about to be married to Denis Warren. Elijah retained the title deeds.

In 1943 Elijah signed a document headed "my wish", in which he stated that the house was to be divided between his three daughters. No provision was made in his will. He died in 1944, and Catherine Warren, claiming to be absolute owner of "Fairview", sued Elijah's executors to recover possession of the deeds.

Held. Catherine held "Fairview" on trust for her father. The presumption of advancement was rebutted by the contemporaneous declarations of Elijah. The document headed "my wish" was inadmissible.

MORTON LJ: It is well established that when a parent buys a property and has it conveyed into the name of his child, there arises a presumption that the parent intended to make a gift or advancement to the child of that property. Of course, that is a presumption which can be rebutted by evidence that that was not the father's intention. The father retained the title deeds of the property and he still had them in his possession when he died in the year 1944. . . .

Three points were taken by counsel for the appellant. First of all, he contended that the judge was wrong in admitting as evidence a document headed "my wish", which he held was signed by Elijah Gurney, which was dated September 6, 1943. In my view counsel's contention under that heading was quite correct. The document headed "my wish" was not admissible in evidence. It was in the nature of a subsequent declaration by the alleged donor, which was not against his own interest, and it is clearly established that subsequent declarations by the alleged donor

[6] For the operation of the principle of advancement in the case of a joint banking account, see *Marshal v Crutwell* (1875) LR 20 Eq 328; *Re Roberts* [1946] Ch 1; *Hoddinott v Hoddinott* [1949] 2 KB 406; *Jones v Maynard* [1951] Ch 572, [1951] 1 All ER 802; *Re Bishop* [1965] Ch 450, [1965] 1 All ER 249; *Re Figgis* [1969] 1 Ch 123, [1968] 1 All ER 999; *Thompson v Thompson* (1970) 114 Sol Jo 455; *Heseltine v Heseltine* [1971] 1 WLR 342, [1971] 1 All ER 952 (money provided by wife); (1969) 85 LQR 530 (M. C. Cullity); H & M, pp. 265–269; Cretney, *Principles of Family Law* (2nd Edn) pp. 274–275. The problem of housekeeping money was dealt with by Married Women's Property Act 1964, under which equality of ownership is presumed in the absence of other evidence.

are only admissible if they are against his interest. The reason for that is quite obvious. If the rule were otherwise it would be extremely easy for persons to manufacture evidence, even although at the time when they made the purchase they in fact intended the child to have the gift of the property.

The second contention put forward by counsel for the appellants was that, on the admissible evidence, the judge was not justified in coming to the conclusion that the defendants had rebutted the presumption of advancement. In my view, there was ample evidence to justify that conclusion of the judge. In the first place, there is the fact that the father retained the title deeds from the time of purchase to the time of his death. I think that is a very significant fact, because title deeds, as it was said in COKE ON LITTLETON, are "sinews of the land". One would have expected the father to have handed them over, either to the plaintiff or her husband, if he had intended the gift. It is to be noted that the judge accepted the evidence given by the plaintiff's mother, Mary Ann Gurney, and by her brother, Meyrick George Gurney, and rejected the evidence of Denis Warren, the plaintiff's husband, where it conflicted with that given by those two witnesses.

I do not intend to travel all through the evidence given before the county court judge, but I wish to read one portion of it only, which, it seems to me, is of the utmost importance. Meyrick George Gurney gave evidence as follows:

> "I am the son of Elijah Gurney and his executor. In 1929 father said he had thought of buying one of the properties for plaintiff: asked me which I thought best."

Pausing there, the words "for plaintiff" might, if they had stood alone, seem to indicate that a gift was intended, but that possible meaning is displaced by what follows:

> "I said 'Fairview'. Father said he had been talking to Warren. Father said Warren had said if father bought the house he would pay for the house as he could. I went with father to Wadeson, the solicitor. Father required property made in my sister's name, so that there could be no trouble at a later date, as Warren had to pay for it at a later date. Father said he should keep the deeds as security."

There are other passages of importance in the evidence. There are passages in the evidence of Mary Ann Gurney, containing statements as to contemporaneous declarations by the testator. There are certain statements made by the plaintiff herself against her own interest: for instance, the statement that she had not enough money to pay any rent. But I need not go further into the evidence. It seems to me, on the passages which I have referred to alone, the county court judge was fully justified in coming to his conclusion. The passage I have read from the evidence of Meyrick Gurney is a passage of the evidence of a witness whom the judge believed, and it seems to me that those contemporaneous declarations are quite sufficient to rebut the presumption even if they stood alone.

It is quite clear that contemporaneous declarations by the alleged donor are admissible in evidence. I am satisfied that there was ample evidence upon which the judge could found his conclusion, and, indeed, it is difficult to see how, on the evidence which he believed, he could have reached any other conclusion.

The last point raised by counsel for the appellant was this. He said that, on the evidence, and on the findings of the judge, his client was entitled to become the absolute owner of this property on the payment of a sum of £250 into the estate. I express no view as to whether that contention is or is not correct, because, even if it were correct, it would clearly not justify the plaintiff's claim to be handed the title deeds now. If that contention were correct she could only have them on payment of £250, which has never in fact been paid.

For these reasons, I think that this appeal should be dismissed with costs.

In *Gascoigne v Gascoigne* ([1918] 1 KB 223) a husband took a lease of land in his wife's name, and built a bungalow on it with his own money. He used his wife's name, with her knowledge, because he was in debt and wanted to protect the property from his creditors. He claimed that she held the property on a resulting trust for him and sought to rebut the presumption of advancement by putting in evidence the scheme to defraud his creditors.

In rejecting the claim, LUSH J said at p. 226: "[The county court judge's] findings of fact must be taken to mean that the plaintiff, with his wife's knowledge and connivance, concocted the scheme of putting his property in her name, while retaining the beneficial interest, for the purpose of misleading, defeating, and delaying present or future creditors. This was the whole basis of the plaintiff's case, and it could not be put in any other way consistently with his claim to be owner of the property. It was the reason he himself gave for his conduct. Now, assuming that there was evidence to support the finding that the defendant was a party to the scheme which the plaintiff admitted, but without deciding it, what the learned judge has done is this: He has permitted the plaintiff to rebut the presumption which the law raises by setting up his own illegality and fraud, and to obtain relief in equity because he has succeeded in proving it. The plaintiff cannot do this; and, whether the point was taken or not in the county court this Court cannot allow a judgment to stand which has given relief under such circumstances as that."[7]

IV. Matrimonial Property[8]

Practical problems of resulting trusts have commonly arisen in recent years in the context of the ownership of the matrimonial home; or of the home occupied by a man and woman who have formed a reasonably "permanent" union. The problem now arises less often in this form; at

[7] See also *Re Great Berlin Steamboat Co* (1884) 26 ChD 616; *Re Emery's Investment Trust* [1959] Ch 410, [1959] 1 All ER 577; *Chettiar v Chettiar* [1962] AC 294, [1962] 1 All ER 494; *Tinker v Tinker* [1970] P 136, [1970] 1 All ER 540; *Cox v Hush* [1976] 239 Estates Gazette 123.

[8] See generally Bromley, *Family Law* (5th Edn, 1976) Chap. 14; Cretney, *Principles of Family Law* (2nd Edn, 1976) Chap. 7; Miller, *Family Property and Financial Provision* (1974), Chap. 2.

least among married couples. For spouses dispute over the matrimonial home when the marriage is collapsing; and these problems are commonly, and much better, determined under the wide jurisdiction now given to the court under Matrimonial Causes Act 1973.

Where the problem arises outside the context of a divorce jurisdiction, the doctrines of resulting trusts and the presumptions play their part. Where each of the spouses has contributed to the purchase price, a purchase money resulting trust may arise. Contribution to mortgage payments will count; as will a contribution by making substantial improvements. The question whether other general contributions to the marriage partnership may give a right to a share of the house has been the subject of conflicting views. The detail of these cases is more relevant to a study of Family Law; and a summary must suffice.

Pettit: *Equity and the Law of Trusts* (3rd Edn), pp. 112–114

"(*c*) *Contributions*[9] *by both spouses*[10] *to purchase price of property.* In this situation the role of the presumption of advancement is now negligible. Even if the property is conveyed into the name of the wife alone the strength of the presumption has diminished virtually to vanishing point[11]. The relevant law was discussed by the House of Lords in the recent cases of *Pettitt v Pettitt*[12] and *Gissing v Gissing*[13], from which it appears that in this sort of case by virtue of the contributions that a party has made towards the purchase price there will be a resulting trust in his favour to a proportionate extent no matter in whose name the legal title may be put. It was further pointed out in *Gissing v Gissing*[14] that the courts should make a serious attempt to evaluate the contribution made by each party, and should only fall back on the maxim "Equality is equity" where each has clearly made a substantial contribution but it is virtually impossible to quantify the contributions precisely.

A number of cases have come before the courts since *Gissing v Gissing*[13] and a difference of opinion has emerged as to the meaning of the House of Lords' decisions. In a series of cases[15] dealing mainly with the matrimonial home the Court of Appeal has stated the effect of these decisions in very broad terms, namely that if both husband and wife make substantial[16] contributions, whether directly or indirectly, in money or

[9] Including contributions before marriage with a view to setting up the matrimonial home: *Ulrich v Ulrich* [1968] 1 WLR 180, [1968] 1 All ER 67.

[10] Similar principles apply to a man and his mistress. *Richards v Dove* [1974] 1 All ER 888—though the result may be different because of the absence of the legal duty owed by a husband to his wife.

[11] Even Lord Upjohn in *Pettitt v Pettitt* [1970] AC 777, [1969] 2 All ER 385, thought that a wife would not be able to rely on the presumption of advancement unless the husband's contribution was very small. And see *Falconer v Falconer* [1970] 1 WLR 1333, [1970] 3 All ER 449.

[12] Supra.

[13] [1971] AC 886, [1970] 2 All ER 780.

[14] Supra, per Lord Reid at 897 and per Lord Pearson at 903.

[15] Including *Falconer v Falconer* [1970] 1 WLR 1333, [1970] 3 All ER 449; *Davis v Vale* [1971] 1 WLR 1022, [1971] 2 All ER 1021; *Hargrave v Newton* [1971] 1 WLR 1611, [1971] 3 All ER 866; *Hazell v Hazell* [1972] 1 WLR 301, [1972] 1 All ER 923; *Kowalczuk v Kowalczuk* [1973] 1 WLR 930, [1973] 2 All ER 1042.

[16] See *Falconer v Falconer* and *Hargrave v Newton*.

money's worth to the initial deposit or to the mortgage instalments, the court will impute, impose or infer a trust whereby the legal owner holds the house on trust for them both, giving to each a beneficial interest of such an extent as may in all the circumstances seem just. In relation to indirect contributions, in the case of a claim by a wife, for instance, if her efforts or her contributions relieved the husband of other expenses which he would otherwise have had to bear—so that he would not have been able to meet the mortgage instalments without her help—then she is regarded as having made an indirect contribution. Indeed, even if the husband does not strictly need the wife's help—because, for instance, he has enough money of his own, or could find it by cutting down his smoking or drinking, or selling his car—if in fact he accepts it, she becomes entitled to a share. The Court of Appeal has indeed expressly rejected[17] the argument that indirect contributions can only be taken into account if they are referable to the purchase of the property in question, though, as has been pointed out[18], it is doubtful whether the court is entitled to do this in the light of the speeches in *Gissing v Gissing*[19]. The Court of Appeal has relied mainly on the opinion of Lord Reid which, as pointed out by Bagnall J in *Cowcher v Cowcher*[20], in such significant respects did not accord with the other four opinions. Viscount Dilhorne, for instance, said[21] in so many words that proof of expenditure for the benefit of the family by one spouse will not of itself show any common intention as to the ownership of the matrimonial home.

Cowcher v Cowcher[1] is difficult to reconcile with the line of Court of Appeal decisions referred to above. Although Bagnall J made a gallant attempt to do so in respect of the decisions then available to him, the truth of the matter seems to be that his interpretation of the House of Lords decisions in *Pettitt v Pettitt*[2] and *Gissing v Gissing*[3] is inconsistent with that put upon them by the Court of Appeal. Bagnall J's view is that one must first determine the actual sources of the purchase money, that is from whose bank account or savings account or other resources it was provided. Prima facie the property will be held on a resulting trust for the spouses in corresponding proportions. Secondly, it may in some cases be possible to establish an express agreement ('interest consensus') showing an intention that the property shall be held on different trusts. These would be express trusts. If effective there will be no difficulty. If ineffective for any reason—it may, for instance, be oral but come within statutory provisions requiring writing—it will nevertheless preclude the possibility of any implied agreement and the *prima facie* resulting trust will operate. Thirdly, in the absence of an express agreement, the court must determine whether, from the whole of the evidence including acts of the parties before, at the time of and after the purchase, there can be

17 *Hargrave v Newton; Hazell v Hazell.*
18 (1972) 88 LQR 333 (J. M. Eekelaar) where the difficulties flowing from the absence of a requirement of referability are pointed out.
19 [1971] AC 886, [1970] 2 All ER 780.
20 [1972] 1 WLR 425, [1972] 1 All ER 943.
21 *Gissing v Gissing* at p. 901.
1 Supra, noted (1972) 88 LQR 333 (J. M. Eekelaar); (1972) 35 MLR 547 (J. Levin).
2 [1970] AC 777, [1969] 2 All ER 385.
3 [1971] AC 886, [1970] 2 All ER 780.

inferred an agreement as to the proportions in which they were to be treated as providing the purchase money. If so, there will be a resulting trust for the parties in corresponding proportions. It should be observed that the agreement last referred to, called by the judge 'money consensus', is to be distinguished from 'interest consensus'. By 'money consensus' he means an agreement that, irrespective of who makes the actual payments, as between themselves the parties are to be treated as contributing to the purchase price in certain agreed shares. Whoever held the legal title would then hold it on a corresponding resulting trust. By 'interest consensus' he means an agreement that, irrespective of their contributions to the purchase price, the property is to be held in an *express* trust for the parties in certain agreed shares. In Bagnall J's view it would be very difficult to infer interest consensus from conduct, and in any case he considers that the House of Lords contemplated money consensus.

It should be added that where there has been a divorce it is now seldom necessary to decide the exact property rights of husband and wife by reason of the wide powers given to the court under the Matrimonial Causes Act 1973, which enable the court to do what is just having regard to all the circumstances[4]. In other circumstances it may still be essential[5].

(d) *Improvements*. So far as improvements to matrimonial property are concerned the disputes in the cases have been silenced by the enactment of s. 37 of the Matrimonial Proceedings and Property Act 1970, which provides[6]:

> 'It is hereby declared that where a husband or wife contributes in money or money's worth to the improvement of real or personal property in which or in the proceeds of sale of which either or both of them has or have a beneficial interest, the husband or wife so contributing shall, if the contribution is of a substantial nature and subject to any agreement between them to the contrary express or implied, be treated as having then acquired by virtue of his or her contribution a share or an enlarged share, as the case may be, in that beneficial interest of such an extent as may have been then agreed or, in default of such agreement, as may seem in all the circumstances just to any court before which the question of the existence or extent of the beneficial interest of the husband or wife arises (whether in proceedings between them or in any other proceedings).'

The section has been held[7] to have retrospective effect and according to Lord Denning MR[8] is a declaration not only of what the law is now and is to be in the future, but also as to what it was before the Act. Even Lord Denning MR seems to agree, however, that under s. 37 only

[4] See *Wachtel v Wachtel* [1973] Fam at 81, [1973] 1 All ER 829, per Lord Denning MR at p. 92; *Kowalczuk v Kowalczuk* [1973] 1 WLR 930, [1973] 2 All ER 1042, per Lord Denning MR at p. 934; *Gordon v Gordon* (1973) 123 NJL 969; *Griffiths v Griffiths* [1974] 1 WLR 1350, [1974] 1 All ER 932.

[5] See e.g. *Re Cummins* [1972] Ch 62, [1971] 3 All ER 782.

[6] See (1970) 120 NLJ 1008 (R. T. Oerton) and the correspondence at p. 1082.

[7] *Davis v Vale* [1971] 1 WLR 1022, [1971] 2 All ER 1021.

[8] *Davis v Vale* at p. 1025; *Kowalczuk v Kowalczuk* [1973] 1 WLR 930, [1973] 2 All ER 1042. It is submitted, however, that there is much to be said for the view that before the Act improvements gave rise to no claim in the absence of agreement.

contributions referable to the improvement to the property can be taken into account[9]"

Cretney: *Principles of Family Law* (2nd Edn) pp. 268–269

"IMPOSING THE JUST SOLUTION. It is often difficult in matrimonial cases to reconcile the demands of doing justice on the facts with the rigid demands of orthodox property law. Two techniques were used in an attempt to do what is just, rather than simply what is the law:

(i) *Section 17 of the Married Women's Property Act 1882.* This gave power to a judge to 'make such order . . . as he thinks fit' where any question arose between husband and wife as to the title to or possession of property. It was claimed that this gave the court 'a free hand to do what is just' in all the circumstances, ignoring the strict legal rules governing the title to property[10]. The House of Lords denounced this view as heretical[11]: 'no Parliament of that era could have intended to put a husband's property at the hazard of the unfettered discretion of a judge (including a county court judge).'[12] This provision simply gives the parties the advantage of a summary procedure[13], and gives the court a discretion as to the *enforcement* of the parties' proprietary or possessory rights. The court may[14], for instance, while recognising that a husband is sole beneficial owner, yet prevent him from dealing with the property unless and until he provides the wife with suitable alternative accommodation.

(ii) *Lord Denning's view of the Trust.* In a number[15] of cases Lord Denning has suggested that the court may impose a trust wherever it would be 'inequitable' for the estate owner to keep the property for himself alone[16]. 'Inequitable' is not used in any technical sense: according to this view a trust may be imposed wherever justice and good conscience require it[17]. This may be because of the wife's contributions to the family budget[18], because of the husband's conduct[19], or because the

[9] *Kowalczuk v Kowalczuk*, supra, at p. 1045. See also *Griffiths v Griffiths* at first instance [1973] 1 WLR 1454, [1973] 3 All ER 1155.

[10] *Hine v Hine* [1962] 1 WLR 1124, [1962] 3 All ER 345, *Appleton v Appleton* [1965] 1 WLR 25 [1965] 1 All ER 44.

[11] *Pettitt v Pettitt* [1970] AC 777 at 793, per Lord REID.

[12] But note that 23 years previously Parliament had by s. 5 of the Matrimonial Causes Act 1859 given the courts (although not county courts) an entirely unfettered discretion to vary that most sacrosanct of Victorian institutions, the marriage settlement.

[13] The Act (as amended by the Matrimonial Causes (Property and Maintenance) Act 1958, s. 7) also gives the court power to order a sale, which it does not have under the discretionary powers of breakdown; see *Glenn v Glenn* [1973] 1 WLR 1016, [1973] 2 All ER 1187.

[14] See *National Provincial Bank Ltd v Ainsworth* [1965] AC 1175 at 1235, 1246; *Lee v Lee* [1952] 2 QB 489, [1952] 1 All ER 1299.

[15] See *Heseltine v Heseltine* [1971] 1 WLR 342, [1971] 1 All ER 952; *Davis v Vale* [1971] 1 WLR 1022, [1971] 2 All ER 1021; *Farquharson v Farquharson* (1971) 115 Sol Jo 444; *Hazell v Hazell* [1972] 1 WLR 301, [1972] 1 All ER 923; and see *Hussey v Palmer* [1972] 1 WLR 1286, [1972] 3 All ER 744; *Binions v Evans* [1972] Ch 359.

[16] *Heseltine v Heseltine* (supra) at 346F; *Binions v Evans* [1972] Ch 359 at 368; *Hussey v Palmer* [1972] 1 WLR 1286 at 1290.

[17] *Hussey v Palmer* (supra).

[18] As in *Hazell v Hazell* (supra) but not (apparently) to contributions not in money's worth: *Wachtel v Wachtel* (supra) at 92.

[19] As in *Heseltine v Heseltine* (supra).

property was acquired by joint efforts for joint *use*[20]. Lord Denning has in terms stated that it is not necessary to establish even an implied agreement or common intention[1]. It is also implicit in his judgments that the court may look at the circumstances as they exist at the time of the marriage breakdown, and do what seems just in the circumstances as they exist[2] (including the wife's right to maintenance[3]).

It is difficult to reconcile these views with the House of Lords' insistence on the application of orthodox property law concepts[4]. It is true that this insistence leads to artificiality and injustice[5]. But in the absence of legislation inferior courts are obliged to follow decisions of the House of Lords[6]. It is submitted that this doctrine does not do so. It is not in any case necessary to have recourse to doctrines of this kind to do justice between the parties when a marriage breaks down: the court has ample *discretionary* powers to deal with this situation on the basis of an adjustment of the parties' *personal* rights".

QUESTIONS

1. What part do presumptions play in this field today?
2. Do you think that resulting trust doctrines satisfactorily meet the problems of the husband and wife cases? Or are these problems better treated as situations of constructive trust? Or, is this a matter requiring the creation of new doctrines relating to the family situation, outside the law of trusts? (1975) 53 Can BR 366 (D. W. M. Waters); (1978) 94 LQR 26 (A. A. S. Zuckerman.

[20] As in *Cooke v Head* [1972] 1 WLR 518 at 520. This trust "applies to husband and wife, to engaged couples, to man and mistress, and maybe to other relationships too" (per Lord DENNING MR).

[1] See *Hazell v Hazell* (supra) at 303G; *Cooke v Head* (supra) at 520; *Hussey v Palmer* [1972] 1 WLR 1286 at 1290.

[2] *Heseltine v Heseltine*; *Davis v Vale*; *Farquharson v Farquharson* (supra).

[3] But this may be intended only to apply to *quantum*: see *Farquharson v Farquharson* (supra).

[4] See *Pettitt v Pettitt* [1970] AC 777, [1969] 2 All ER 385; *Gissing v Gissing* [1971] AC 886, [1970] 2 All ER 780.

[5] Cf. per BAGNALL J, *Cowcher v Cowcher* [1972] 1 WLR 425 at 430B.

[6] See *Broome v Cassell & Co Ltd* [1972] AC 1027.

8. Constructive Trusts[1]

I. General

A constructive trust is one which arises by operation of law. It can arise in a wide variety of circumstances. There is little agreement among writers as to the proper categories. There is much inconsistency in the use of terminology, and there are many situations involving overlap between the categories into which trusts are usually classified. Many of the issues which arise in this area appear also in other contexts. It is important for these reasons, among others, to clarify a few general points upon which the present account is based.

It is often assumed that a constructive trust, like any other trust, is a situation in which specific property is vested in a trustee on trust for ascertained beneficiaries. This is not always so; there are many differences between constructive trusts and others. A constructive trustee may not know that he is a trustee. Where the trust arises because a fiduciary has received a benefit in breach of a fiduciary obligation, it may be impossible to say what the trust property is. In many cases, the duty of a constructive trustee is less onerous than that of an express trustee; he is under no obligation to invest in authorised securities, nor to observe the usual duty of *exacta diligentia*. It would be unreasonable to impose such obligations in cases in which he did not know he was a trustee.

It is sometimes difficult to see the distinction between a constructive trust and a duty to account. Where an agent has obtained illegal profits, or taken bribes, should we say that he is a constructive trustee, or that he is under a duty to account? The former involves a proprietary claim by the plaintiff, the latter a personal claim. The difference may be considerable, but the terminology is indiscriminate[2].

This means that there is much confusion between cases of constructive trust and cases of the liability of fiduciaries[3]. So long as the defendant can pay, it makes little difference whether the claim is proprietary or

[1] H & M, pp. 135–136, 307–329; K & S, pp. 181–184, 191–218; P & M, pp. 151–160; Pettit, pp. 97–100, 120–125, 314–316; Snell, pp. 185–188; See generally (1913–14) 27 Harv LR 125; (1955) 71 LQR 39 (A. W. Scott); Waters, *The Constructive Trust* (1964); (1973) CLP 17 (A. J. Oakley).
[2] *Boardman v Phipps* [1967] 2 AC 46, [1966] 3 All ER 721.
[3] See pp. 217, 613 post.

personal. But if the defendant is insolvent, and the plaintiff can only be satisfied by a claim in priority to the general creditors, the distinction is crucial; just as it is in cases which are usually discussed in the context of the beneficiaries' right to "trace", or to "follow the trust property," or to make a "claim *in rem.*" By making a proprietary claim, the plaintiff can take any property which he can show to be his in equity; and he can make a claim in priority to the general creditors upon a mixed fund of money or investments. Further, if the investments have appreciated, he may wish to claim a share of the fund at this higher value.

We cannot explore these matters in detail now[4]; our present point is to indicate the connection between them. A claim involving only the defendant's personal liability to account has nothing to do with a constructive trust. A proprietary claim against a fiduciary may be a claim in respect of a specific item, but is more commonly against a fund, usually a mixed fund. The plaintiff may wish to have a charge on the fund to give him priority over the general creditors or he may, because of the increase in the value of the fund, wish to claim a share. Here we have a mixture of "constructive trust", "liability of fiduciaries" and "tracing". They are all inter-connected.

Finally, it may be asked whether we cannot somehow suggest a general principle which will determine the circumstances in which a constructive trust will exist. This would be a great improvement over the present miscellany. Some find this in the principle of unjust enrichment, arguing that where the defendant is unjustly enriched at the expense of the plaintiff, he should disgorge; and that, as the defendant should never have had the property, his creditors should not be entitled to share it. The first edition said that this was a heady doctrine for English equity; but recent formulations have gone further, treating a constructive trust as a doctrine which permits a desired result to be reached on a principle of justice and good conscience, regardless of the effect upon the rights of third parties of using a proprietary remedy to reach the solution[5]. This question will be taken up infra, p. 234. We must first examine the situations in which it has long been established that a constructive trust arises.

II. Categories of Constructive Trusts

A. Unauthorised Profit by a Trustee or Fiduciary

i. RENEWAL OF A LEASE[6]

KEECH v SANDFORD

(1726) Sel Cas temp King 61, 2 Eq Cas Abr 741, pl. 7 (KING LC)

The lessee of the profits of a market devised his estate to a trustee on trust for an infant. Prior to the expiration of the lease, the trustee applied

[4] See pp. 634 et seq., post.

[5] [1973] CLP 17 (A. J. Oakley); (1977) 28 NILQ 123 (R. H. Maudsley).

[6] White and Tudor's *Leading Cases in Equity* (9th Edn, 1928), pp. 648 et seq. *Re Knowles' Will Trusts* [1948] 1 All ER 866; *Re Jarvis* [1958] 1 WLR 815, [1958] 2 All ER 336. See too (1969) 33 Conv (NS) 161 (S. M. Cretney) on the historical reasons for the rule.

to the lessor for a renewal of the lease for the benefit of the infant. The lessor refused, on the ground that, because the lease was of the profits only and not of the land, his remedy for recovery of rent was not by distress, but upon the covenant only, by which an infant would not be bound. The trustee then took a lease for himself.

The infant sought to have the lease assigned to him.

Held. The lease should be assigned to the infant, with an account of the profits received by the trustee.

KING LC: I must consider this as a trust for the infant; for I very well see, if a trustee, on the refusal to renew, might have a lease to himself, few trust estates would be renewed to *cestui que use*; though I do not say there is a fraud in this case, yet he should rather have let it run out, than to have had the lease to himself. This may seem hard, that the trustee is the only person of all mankind who might not have the lease; but it is very proper that rule should be strictly pursued, and not in the least relaxed; for it is very obvious what would be the consequences of letting trustees have the lease, on refusal to renew to *cestui que use*.

In *Re Biss* ([1903] 2 Ch 40) John Biss had carried on a profitable business of a common lodging-house keeper on premises leased to him under a seven-year lease. On its expiration he continued as a yearly tenant. He died, leaving a widow and three children, one of whom was an infant. The widow, who was his administratrix, and an adult son continued the business, and they applied for a renewal of the lease. This was refused, but a new lease was then granted to the adult son. The question was whether he should be compelled, under the rule in *Keech v Sandford,* to hold the lease upon trust. The Court of Appeal decided that he could hold it beneficially. The son, in obtaining the lease, was not in breach of any fiduciary duty. COLLINS MR said (at p. 57):

"In the present case the appellant is simply one of the next of kin of the former tenant, and had, as such, a possible interest in the term. He was not, as such, a trustee for the others interested, nor was he in possession. The administratrix represented the estate and alone had the right to renew incident thereto, and she unquestionably could renew only for the benefit of the estate. But is the appellant in the same category? Or is he entitled to go into the facts to shew that he has not, in point of fact, abused his position, or in any sense intercepted an advantage coming by way of accretion to the estate? He did not take under a will or a settlement with interests coming after his own, but simply got a possible share upon an intestacy in case there was a surplus of assets over debts. It seems to me that his obligation cannot be put higher than that of any other tenant in common against whom it would have to be established, not as a presumption of law but as an inference of fact, that he had abused his position. If he is not under a personal incapacity to take a benefit, he is entitled to shew that the renewal was not in fact an accretion to the original term, and that it was not until there had been an absolute refusal on the part of the lessor, and after full opportunity to the administratrix to procure it for the estate if she could, that he accepted a proposal of renewal made to him by the lessor. These questions cannot be considered or discussed when the party is by his position debarred from keeping a personal advantage derived directly or indirectly out of his fiduciary or quasi-fiduciary position; but when he is not so debarred I think it becomes a question of fact whether that which he has received was in his hands an accretion to the interest of the deceased, or whether the connection between the estate and the renewal had not been wholly severed by the action of the lessor before the appellant accepted a new lease. This consideration seems to get rid of any difficulty that one of the next of kin was an infant. The right or hope of renewal incident to the estate was determined before the plaintiff intervened."[7]

ii. PURCHASE OF THE REVERSION

In *Thompson's Trustee in Bankruptcy* ([1974] 1 WLR 605, [1974] 1 All ER 1239)[8] PENNYCUICK V-C said at p. 606: "The action is concerned with a property known as Lissington Manor Farm in Lincolnshire, to which I shall refer as 'Lissington'. Summarily Mr. Thompson and Mr. Heaton acquired a leasehold interest in Lissington as partners in 1948. The partnership was dissolved in 1952 under some arrangement between them. Mr. Heaton and, subsequently the company [William T. Heaton Ltd., a private company whose shares were owned by Mr. and Mrs. Heaton] remained in sole occupation of Lissington. Mr. Heaton died in 1966. Then in 1967 his executors acquired the freehold reversion in Lissington on behalf of the company. Since the commencement of the action the company has sold Lissington at a very substantial profit. [Mr. Thompson having become bankrupt] the plaintiff trustee in bankruptcy now contends that he is entitled in effect to half of that profit [on the ground that the farm was an undistributed asset of the partnership].

It remains to consider whether the defendants are accountable to the plaintiff in respect of the freehold reversion and the proceeds of sale of the freehold. It is well established that where someone holding a leasehold interest in a fiduciary capacity acquires a renewal of the leasehold interest he must hold the renewed interest as part of the trust estate. This principle is known as the rule in *Keech v Sandford* (1726) Sel Cas Ch 61: *Snell's Principles of Equity,* 27th Edn (1973), p. 236. It is also, I think, well established that where someone holding a leasehold interest in a fiduciary capacity acquires the freehold reversion, he must hold that reversion as part of the trust estate: see *Protheroe v Protheroe* [1968] 1 WLR 519, where Lord Denning MR says, at p. 521:

> 'The short answer to the husband's contention is this: although the house was in the husband's name, he was a trustee of it for both. It was a family asset which the husband and wife owned in equal shares. Being a trustee, he had an especial advantage in getting the freehold. There is a long established rule of equity from *Keech v Sandford* (1726) Sel. Cas. Ch. 61 downwards that if a trustee, who owns the leasehold, gets in the freehold, that freehold belongs to the trust and he cannot take the property for himself.'

[7] *Brenner v Rose* [1973] 1 WLR 443, [1973] 2 All ER 535.
[8] (1974) 38 Conv (NS) 288 (F. R. Crane).

That decision is cited, with some implied criticism, in *Snell's Principles of Equity,* p. 238. It seems to me, however, that, apart from the fact that it binds me, this decision, like the rule in *Keech v Sandford* is really in modern terms an application of the broad principle that a trustee must not make a profit out of the trust estate. This principle applies to all kinds of collateral advantages, for instance directors' remuneration received by a trustee acting as a director for a company controlled through the shares of the trust. In *Phillips v Phillips* (1885) 29 ChD 673 the Court of Appeal applied the principle to the purchase of a reversion by a tenant for life. I ought to make one observation in this connection. Obviously the beneficiary under the trust in such circumstances cannot be compelled to accept and pay for the reversion. If he refuses to do so, either before or after the acquisition by the trustee, no doubt the latter is entitled to acquire and retain the reversion for his own use, but if the beneficiary does require that the reversion be brought into the trust estate, then the trustee must deal with it accordingly, subject of course to recoupment out of the trust estate.

There can, I think, be no doubt that so long as a partnership subsists each partner is under a corresponding obligation to his co-partners. See as to this point section 29 of the Partnership Act 1890 and *Lindley on Partnership* 13th Edn (1971), p. 337. . . .

The fiduciary relation here arises not from a trust of property but from the duty of good faith which each partner owes to the other. It is immaterial for this purpose in which partner the legal estate in the leasehold interest concerned is vested."

B. Strangers to the Trust. Trustees De Son Tort[9]

It was submitted above that a distinction should be made between (a) the personal liability of a fiduciary and (b) a constructive trust. The distinction becomes clear when the remedies of the beneficiaries are considered; the distinction between a proceeding against the plaintiff personally and one against property in his hands then becomes obvious. In many factual situations, these two basic kinds of liability will overlap.

It must be said however that recent judicial formulations, and most writers, treat both types of situation as cases of constructive trusts. The different views are made clear by the extract from KEKEWICH J in *Re Barney* ([1892] 2 Ch 265), and of BRIGHTMAN J in *Karak Rubber Co Ltd v Burden (No. 2)* ([1972] 1 WLR 602, [1972] 1 All ER 1210).

There is also difficulty in determining the proper test of liability of agents who participate in transactions which they do not know, but ought reasonably to have known that the transaction was improper. In *Selangor United Rubber Estates Ltd v Cradock (No. 3)* ([1968] 1 WLR 1555, [1968] 2 All ER 1073) and in *Karak Rubber Co Ltd v Burden (No. 2)* ([1972] 1 WLR 602, [1972] 1 All ER 1210), banks participated in a series of transactions and transfers which effectively enabled a company to use its own money to purchase its own shares[10]. The banks were in each case held liable

[9] H & M, pp. 314–318; K & S, pp. 212–213; P & M, pp. 156–159; Pettit, pp. 122–125; Snell, pp. 186–188.

[10] Which is forbidden under the Companies Act 1948, s. 54.

on the ground that they ought to have known. Their liability would have been obvious if trust property had been vested in themselves. A defendant in whom trust property has vested would be liable unless he could show that he was a bona fide purchaser of the legal estate for value without notice[11].

In *Re Barney* ([1892] 2 Ch 265) KEKEWICH J, refusing to hold liable persons who had, with the best possible intent, been involved in an unauthorised continuation of a testator's business, said (at p. 271):

"Undoubtedly there are persons who can be made responsible as trustees to the full extent of a trustee's responsibility, notwithstanding that they have never been properly appointed trustees, either by the parties or by the Court. That is established by a long series of authorities, and is succinctly expressed by Lord *Selborne* in the case of *Barnes v Addy* ((1874) 9 Ch App 244 at 251). He says: 'Those who create a trust clothe the trustee with a legal power and control'—mark the word—'over the trust property, imposing on him a corresponding responsibility. That responsibility may no doubt be extended in equity to others who are not properly trustees, if they are found either making themselves trustees *de son tort*, or actually participating in any fraudulent conduct of the trustee to the injury of the *cestui que trust.*' Fraud apart, they must, according to the language of Lord *Selborne*, and according to the language of all the cases to which I have been referred, make themselves what Lord *Selborne* calls, borrowing an expression from the law of executors, trustees '*de son tort*.' When once you have participation in a fraudulent act, then it is immaterial whether the person participating fills the position of trustee *de son tort* or not. The very participation in fraud is conclusive against him, and that is the explanation of more than one of the cases to be found in the books, and of more than one of those cases to which I have been referred. There is no suggestion in the case now before me of the existence of fraud; it has not been mentioned in the argument; it is not suggested by the evidence. Therefore I dismiss fraud from the case, and I have to inquire whether the Defendants, Messrs. *Mitchell* and *Appleford*, have made themselves trustees *de son tort*, and in order to answer that question I must consider what is meant by Lord *Selborne* by that phrase, and what is meant by other Judges by equivalent phrases in other cases.

A trustee, properly so called, must, according to my view, have property committed to his charge. I have had occasion to say before now, and I now say again, that in order to constitute a man a trustee there must be a person or persons for whom he is a trustee—called *cestui* or *cestuis que trust*—and there must be property vested in him of which he is trustee for such person or persons. I do not mean to say that he must have the legal estate. I do not mean to say that the Consols, if Consols be the subject-matter of the trust, must be standing in his name. He may only have the right to call for a transfer—the right to possess the property, as often happens where there is an interval between the appointment of a trustee and the conveyance of the trust property to him. But there must be that which is either vested in him in law, or for which he is entitled

[11] *Lee v Sankey* (1873) LR 15 Eq 204 at 211; *Nelson v Larholt* [1948] 1 KB 339, [1947] 2 All ER 751.

to call, about which there is no question; so that his duty plainly is to require that it should be vested in him. And if that is true of a trustee properly appointed, why is it not also true of a trustee *de son tort?* Why should I extend the phrase when I find a person irregularly acting in a certain way, and make him a trustee irregularly, although he would not be a trustee if he had been regularly appointed to act in the same way? I hold that it is essential to the character of a trustee that he should have trust property either actually vested in him, or so far under his control that he has nothing to do but require that, perhaps by one process, perhaps by another, it should be vested in him. That view seems entirely consistent with all the cases, and especially with those on which reliance is placed on behalf of the Plaintiffs."

In *Karak Rubber Co Ltd v Burden (No. 2)* ([1972] 1 WLR 602, [1972] 1 All ER 1210)[12] Barclays Bank Ltd. was held liable for breach of the contractual duty of care owed to its customer, Karak Rubber Co Ltd, in that the Bank had failed to make proper enquiries before allowing the directors of Karak (Mr. Burden and Mr. Cross) to pay over £99,504 of Karak's money to meet the Bank's draft.

The question was argued also on the basis of the Bank's liability as constructive trustee; BRIGHTMAN J held them liable on this ground also, and said (at p. 632): "My decision on the claim in contract is sufficient to dispose of the case so far as this court is concerned. I have, however, heard a full argument on the question of constructive trusteeship, and I must deal with that topic as well.

I must first touch on the plaintiff's [Karak's] claim against the trustee in bankruptcy of Mr. Burden and Mr. Cross. These claims have not been actively fought. I deal with them at this stage because the quality of the conduct of Mr. Burden and Mr. Cross is decisive of the question whether the claim against Barclays Bank in constructive trusteeship is capable of succeeding; that claim is based on the existence of their fraud and dishonesty. The plaintiff pleads that Mr. Burden and Mr. Cross procured that the amount of the Karak cheque should be misapplied in bad faith in providing out of Karak's money the purchase price of 40,804 shares and the expenses incidental to that purchase. In my judgment, on the evidence I have heard, and quite apart from admissions by Mr. Burden and Mr. Cross to which I will refer later, it is plain beyond the possibility of argument to the contrary that Mr. Burden, in deliberate and conscious fraud, procured that £99,504 10s. 6d. of Karak's money, that is to say, the amount of the Karak cheque, should be misapplied in financing the purchase of the Karak shares so as to be lost to Karak, and that Mr. Cross, either knowingly or recklessly, was implicated in that fraudulent and dishonest design. I did not understand Mr. Caplan, on behalf of Barclays Bank, to seek to argue otherwise.

It is convenient to make an initial distinction between (i) a person who is a constructive trustee because (though not nominated as a trustee)

[12] (1972) 36 Conv (NS) 213 (D. J. Hayton); *Competitive Insurance Co Ltd v Davies Investments Ltd* [1975] 1 WLR 1240, [1975] 3 All ER 254; *Rowlandson v National Westminster Bank Ltd* (1977) Times, 12th December.

he has received trust property with actual or constructive notice that it is trust property transferred in breach of trust, or because (not being a bona fide purchaser for value without notice) he acquires notice subsequent to such receipt and then deals with the property in a manner inconsistent with the trust, and (ii) a person who has not received and become chargeable with trust property in that manner but whom equity nevertheless fixes with liability as a constructive trustee on account of assistance which he has rendered to a breach of trust. This is not intended to be an exhaustive definition of constructive trusteeship, but to distinguish two categories thereof. There is included in the second category of constructive trusteeship the duly appointed agent of the trustees who is in receipt of trust property solely by virtue of the existence of such agency but who, by assisting in a breach of trust at the direction of trustees, is fixed with liability as a constructive trustee. The two categories are conveniently labelled in *Snell's Principles of Equity*, 26th Edn. (1966), pp. 202 and 203, with the catch-phrases 'knowing receipt or dealing' and 'knowing assistance', which seem to me an admirable shorthand description of their different natures.

The question of law which arises is, in what circumstances will a Court of Equity treat the second category of person as a trustee in order to provide an equitable remedy against that person on account of conduct which a Court of Equity considers unconscionable?

It is common ground that directors of a company, though not trustees in the strictest sense of that expression, are to be considered and treated as trustees of money which comes to their hands or is under their control. The fact that they are to be considered and treated as trustees bears upon the question whether the imposition of the equitable remedy of constructive trusteeship is available against those who have dealings with them. It is also common ground that a bank is not a trustee for its customer of the amount to his credit in his account. In the result, Mr. Burden and Mr. Cross are to be considered and treated as trustees in relation to the sum of money comprised in the Chartered cheque and paid into Karak's account with Barclays Bank, and Barclays Bank is to be considered and treated as the agent of such trustees.

The conclusion of law reached by Ungoed-Thomas J in the *Selangor* case [1968] 1 WLR 1555, in relation to the second category of constructive trustees, was as follows: (1) Strangers who act as the agents of trustees are liable as constructive trustees if they 'assist with knowledge in a dishonest and fraudulent design on the part of the trustees': see p. 1580 referring to *Barnes v Addy* (1874) 9 Ch App 244 at 252.

(2) 'The knowledge required to hold a stranger liable as constructive trustee in a dishonest and fraudulent design, is knowledge of circumstances which would indicate to an honest, reasonable man that such a design was being committed or would put him on inquiry, which the stranger failed to make, whether it was being committed': [1968] 1 WLR 1555 at 1590.

(3) What is 'a dishonest and fraudulent design' is to be judged 'according to the plain principles of a Court of Equity': see p. 1582.

'The governing consideration is to give effect to equitable rights, where it is not inequitable to do so, and when knowledge of the existence of those rights is material to granting equitable relief. In general, at any rate, it is equitable that a person with actual notice or constructive notice of those rights should be fixed with knowledge of them. This is in a context of producing equitable results in a civil action and not in the context of criminal liability': see pp. 1582 and 1583.

These conclusions were reached after consideration of a large number of authorities, ranging in time from the decision of Leach V-C in *Keane v Robarts* (1819) 4 Madd 332 down to the decision of the Privy Council in *Bank of New South Wales v Goulburn Valley Butter Co Proprietary Ltd* [1902] AC 543.

The formulation in the *Selangor* case of the law applicable to the second category of constructive trusteeship is based on the judgment of Lord Selborne LC in *Barnes v Addy* (1874) 9 Ch App 244, with which James and Mellish LJJ concurred. This was a case in which beneficiaries unsuccessfully sued solicitors who had been associated with the fraud of the trustee; it was found that the solicitors had no knowledge or suspicion of the fraud and that there was nothing to lead them to suppose that a fraud was intended. The test of liability—which it may be convenient to call the *Barnes v Addy* formula—in the words of Lord Selborne LC, was: 'they assist with knowledge in a dishonest and fraudulent design on the part of the trustees' at p. 252. This was paraphrased with approval by Lord Esher MR in *Soar v Ashwell* [1893] 2 QB 390 at 395 (a first category case) as 'he has knowingly assisted a nominated trustee in a fraudulent and dishonest disposition of the trust property'. The point on which the authorities were obscure, until the *Selangor* case, was what degree of 'knowledge' was required to satisfy that test. A person may have knowledge of an existing fact because in a subjective sense he is actually aware of that fact. In an appropriate context a court of law may attribute knowledge of an existing fact to that person because in a subjective sense he has knowledge of circumstances which would lead a postulated man to the conclusion that the fact exists or which would put a postulated man upon inquiry as to whether the fact exists. The claim against the District Bank was that it knew, or as a reasonable banker ought to have known, that Selangor's money was being applied for the purpose of giving financial assistance in connection with the purchase by Cradock of Selangor stock. It was not pleaded that the District Bank ought to have made inquiries. The decision, which went against the District Bank on constructive trusteeship as it did in negligence, was based on proof of facts which would have brought home the knowledge of such misapplication to the mind of a reasonable banker.

Mr. Caplan attacked the statement of law in the *Selangor* case [1968] 1 WLR 1555, principally on two grounds, (1) that it was inconsistent with the ratio decidendi of, and was impliedly overruled by the decision of, the Court of Appeal in *Carl Zeiss Stiftung v Herbert Smith & Co (No. 2)* [1969] 2 Ch 276, [1969] 2 All ER 367 and (2) because important and decisive cases were not brought to the attention of Ungoed-Thomas J. It will be observed that, according to the *Selangor* case, an objective test is to be applied both in assessing the defendant's 'knowledge' and in assessing the character of the 'design'. Mr. Caplan, in an argument of great penetration, accepted the objective test in relation to the 'design' but not in relation to 'knowledge' . . . In other words, the defendant is not liable as a constructive trustee if he had no actual or imputed knowledge of the design and did not intend to participate in it; on the other hand, he cannot successfully defend a claim by saying that he knew of the design but did not regard it as dishonest. Unless, it is submitted, a subjective test is applied to the acts, knowledge and intention of the defendant, it is not possible to charge him with the lack of probity which is the foundation of a stranger's liability as a constructive trustee. It is important to an understanding of this argument to appreciate the special sense given to the expression 'imputed knowledge', which in Mr. Caplan's formulation is brought about by the deliberate shutting of eyes so as to avoid actual knowledge.

The *Carl Zeiss* case [1969] 2 Ch 276, [1969] 2 All ER 367 was a dispute between the Carl Zeiss company of Jena ('the East German foundation') and the Carl Zeiss company of Würtemberg ('the West German foundation'). In the main action the East German foundation claimed (inter alia) that the assets of the West German foundation, including its property in England, were held by that foundation in trust for the East German foundation. The East German foundation later issued a writ against the current and former solicitors of the West German foundation claiming that when they were put in funds by their client, they had notice, via the East German foundation's pleadings in the main action and from other material, that such money belonged to the East German foundation, and it was said that the solicitors were accountable accordingly. The matter came on for trial as a preliminary issue.

The East German foundation based its claim on a submission that a man who receives trust property which he knows or ought to know is trust property and applies that property in a manner which he knows or ought to know is inconsistent with the terms of the trust, is accountable at the suit of the beneficiaries under that trust. The submission failed, on the ground that the solicitors only had knowledge of a disputed claim that the assets of the West German foundation were trust property; they did not have knowledge that such assets were *in fact* trust property. . . .

The *Selangor* case was certainly not expressly overruled by the *Carl Zeiss* case [1969] 2 Ch 276, [1969] 2 All ER 367. It was not even referred to in the judgments of Danckwerts and Edmund Davies LJJ. Nor do I think that it was overruled by necessary implication. . . . Accordingly I reject the submission that the *Selangor* judgment [1968] 1 WLR 1555 on constructive trusteeship is inconsistent with the ratio decidendi of the *Carl Zeiss* case.

In support of his proposition that lack of probity is an essential ingredient of the second category of constructive trusteeship, Mr. Caplan also referred me to five pre-*Keane v Robarts* (1819) 4 Madd 332 cases. These were *Nugent v Gifford* (1738) 1 Atk 463, *Mead v Lord Orrery* (1745) 3 Atk 235, *Scott v Tyler* (1788) 2 Dick 712, *Hill v Simpson* (1802) 7 Ves 152 and *M'Leod v Drummond* (1805) 14 Ves 353, (1810) 17 Ves 152. It may well be that these cases are consistent with the proposition that fraud or what is tantamount to fraud must be found before an agent who has not intermeddled is rendered accountable as a constructive trustee. They are not, in my view, decisive against the relevance of an objective test, that is to say, whether the circumstances would have indicated a dishonest and fraudulent design to a reasonable man or have put him upon inquiry. It must, I think, be remembered that equitable doctrines have developed over the passage of time and it would not be right to assume that principles expressed two centuries ago were being fully and exhaustively enunciated for all ages to come. . . .

I respectfully agree with the explanation of the *Barnes v Addy* (1874) 9 Ch App 244 formula which I find in the *Selangor* [1968] 1 WLR 1555 judgment. If, as seems to be established by the cases, an objective test of 'knowledge' is rightly applied in the context of the first category of constructive trusteeship (see, for example, *Reckitt v Barnett, Pembroke and Slater Ltd* [1929] AC 176 and *Nelson v Larholt* [1948] 1 KB 339, [1947] 2 All ER 751) I do not myself see any particular logic in denying it a similar role in the context of the second category of constructive trusteeship. To borrow the words of Lord Cranworth LC, spoken admittedly in a different context, 'Constructive notice is as good as any notice, if it does amount to notice' (*Cookson v Lee* (1853) 23 LJ Ch 473 at 478).

Applying the *Barnes v Addy* formula, as explained in the *Selangor* case, I reach the conclusion, for reasons already indicated in dealing with the claim in negligence, that a reasonable banker would have been put upon inquiry as to the propriety of the Karak cheque and that such inquiry would in all probability have revealed the impropriety. So I find the claim against Barclays Bank made good in equity as in contract."

(1969) 85 LQR 169 (P.V.B.)

"Neither loss to the plaintiff nor gain to the defendant are essential elements in this formulation. Moreover, the knowledge required is not necessarily knowledge of the dishonest design, but knowledge of the circumstances indicating such a design. No doubt banks will have to consider their procedures in the light of this case. One matter not explicitly dealt with is the manner in which knowledge is acquired. When banks are large corporations, and many of their processes are mechanised, it may be unrealistic and unjust to speak of 'the mind of a reasonable banker' unless one means the mind of a responsible officer of the bank. In the present case it was proved that responsible officers did know the relevant facts, but what if the cheques had been paid in across the counter?"

Other cases have suggested that an agent (usually a solicitor) in control of trust money will not be liable if he acts honestly and in accordance with the instructions of his principal[13]. In *Williams-Ashman v Price and Williams* ([1942] Ch 219, [1942] 1 All ER 310) solicitors had received trust money into the firm's account and, on the trustees' instructions, in some cases those of a sole trustee, made unauthorised investments. BENNETT J said at p. 228: "*Mara v Browne* ([1896] 1 Ch 199) seems to me to be a decision that

[13] *Morgan v Stephens* (1861) 3 Giff 226; *Barnes v Addy* (1874) 9 Ch App 244; *Mara v Browne* [1896] 1 Ch 199; *Competitive Insurance Co Ltd v Davies Investments Ltd* [1975] 1 WLR 1240, [1975] 3 All ER 254 (a liquidator unaware of the trust).

an agent in possession of money which he knows to be trust money, so long as he acts honestly, is not accountable to the beneficiaries interested in the trust money unless he intermeddles in the trust by doing acts characteristic of a trustee and outside the duties of an agent. After all, the beneficiaries have their remedy against the persons who are the real trustees. I have stated that, in my opinion, Mr. Alfred Williams acted throughout the transactions honestly. Indeed, the contrary is not suggested. He acted throughout on the instructions of his principals. He never intermeddled in the trust. He has, I think, acted incautiously. Many people might take the view that he ought to have ascertained by reference to the declaration of trust what the trusts were before he did what he was asked to do first by Dr. MacGowan and Mr. Streather [the trustees] and afterwards, when Mr. Streather had died, by Dr. MacGowan alone. But considerations of this kind do not assist the plaintiff unless he can establish that when the money came into the possession of the firm, Mr. Alfred Williams or the firm came under a duty to him as a beneficiary interested in the trust fund. It is only if the plaintiff can establish the existence of such a duty that he can establish a liability on the firm arising out of the breaches of trust committed by the express trustees.

The plaintiff is, I think, trying to use the passage from Stirling J's judgment and the statement from Underhill's Law of Trusts and Trustees to support a proposition which neither Stirling J nor the late Sir Arthur Underhill could have had in mind when they used the words relied on[14].

Blyth v Fladgate ([1891] 1 Ch 337) was plainly a case where the defendants, a firm of solicitors, were saddled with the liability of trustees because they had dealt with trust moneys in breach of trust and without instructions from their principals. The facts were that at a time when there was but one trustee of a marriage settlement, trust moneys had been invested in exchequer bills which had been deposited with the bankers of the solicitors and were so deposited when the sole trustee died. Afterwards, while there was no trustee, the bills were sold and the proceeds of sale were placed to the credit of the solicitors with their bankers and afterwards paid by the solicitors to a mortgagor who, as security for their repayment, executed a mortgage in favour of three persons who were subsequently appointed to be trustees of the settlement. The advance on this mortgage was held improper and a breach of trust, and for this breach the solicitors were held to be responsible as constructive trustees because, having in their possession money which they knew was trust money, they had made an improper investment of it without instructions from or the authority of any principal. Stirling J's observations must be read in relation to the facts with which he was dealing. In *Mara v Browne* ([1896] 1 Ch 199) the Court of Appeal laid down clearly the principles which govern the rights of the plaintiff and defendant firm in respect of the two sums of 200l. and 700l. received by the firm from Miss Pullen. On the facts, as I find them to be, the firm is not responsible to the plaintiff for the breaches

[14] "Where the trust funds come into the custody and under the control of a solicitor, or indeed of any one else, with notice of the trusts, he can only discharge himself of liability by showing that the property was duly applied in accordance with the trusts." Underhill, cited at p. 548, and relied on by STIRLING J in *Blyth v Fladgate* [1891] 1 Ch 337.

of trust committed by the express trustees of the declaration of trust in respect of these two sums. The result is that the action fails and must be dismissed with costs."

C. Mutual Wills[15]

Where two persons by agreement make wills which give the property of the first to die to the survivor, and after the survivor's death to agreed legatees, they are said to make mutual wills. The parties are commonly husband and wife, but not necessarily so; spinster sisters living together sometimes make mutual wills. The survivor may be given a life interest with remainders over to the agreed legatees; or perhaps an absolute interest with a substitutionary gift to the agreed legatees[16].

Assume that the first to die, the husband, dies with a will which takes effect in the agreed form. The widow then re-marries and decides to leave all her estate to her new husband. This would be a breach of the agreement. But the agreed legatees cannot sue (even if they knew about the agreement) because they were not parties to the agreement. Nor can the widow be prevented from making a new will, for an existing will is always revocable[17]. It is not right that the widow should be able to take advantage of her husband's will, and to ignore the obligations of the contract. It is established that a trust is imposed in favour of the agreed legatees. But that simple solution leaves a number of questions unanswered.

1. Is this an express trust, or a constructive trust? If an express trust, who declared it, and when, and in respect of which identifiable property?

If a constructive trust, upon what ground? The failure to carry out the contract is not a sufficient justification. But the receipt of benefits under the first will would be; but it has been said that such receipt is not necessary[18].

2. To what property does the trust attach?[19] To that received by the survivor from the first to die? To that owned by the survivor at the date of the first death? To all property owned by the survivor at the date of his death?

3. When does that trust come into effect? On the first death (which would prevent a lapse of the interest of one of the agreed beneficiaries)? Or when the survivor obtains a benefit under the will of the first to die (supra)? Or on the second death, at which time the property which is the subject of the trust would be identifiable?

4. Could the estate of the first to die take proceedings to enforce the agreement on the principle of *Beswick v Beswick?* ([1968] AC 58, [1967] 2 All ER 1197; H & M, p. 323.)

---

15 H & M, pp. 318–323; K & S, pp. 181–184; P & M, pp. 146–150; Pettit, pp. 97–100; Snell, pp. 182–184; (1951) 14 MLR 136 (J. D. B. Mitchell); (1951) 15 Conv (NS) 28 (G. B. Graham); (1970) 34 Conv (NS) 230 (R. Burgess).

16 *Re Green* [1951] Ch 148, [1950] 2 All ER 913.

17 *In the Estate of Hays* [1914] P 192.

18 *Stone v Hoskins* [1905] P 194 at 197; *Re Hagger* [1930] 2 Ch 190 at 195; (1951) 14 MLR at 138 (J. D. B. Mitchell).

19 [1951] 14 MLR at 139, 140 (J. D. B. Mitchell).

(1951) 14 MLR at p. 139 (J. D. B. Mitchell).

"*Scope of the Trust*

The date of creation has important consequences on the scope of the trust. It is obvious that where the first testator's will only gives a life interest to the survivor, no question arises in relation to that estate. It must be held upon trust to give effect to the whole will including the ultimate dispositions. Similarly even if it apparently gives an absolute interest, yet the survivor holds all that he receives thereunder on trust for himself for life and then for the ultimate beneficiaries[1]. The trust, however, where the doctrine applies, affects not only the estate of the first testator but also that of the survivor. The question is as to the extent to which it does so. Is the entirety comprised in it and if so is it the entirety as at the first death or does the trust also comprise after-acquired property?

The short answer would simply be that the extent of the trust is defined by the agreement. Thus in *Re Green* the trust was to operate on property received from the other party and on property which was derived from another trust[2]. This definition might be express, as in that case, or implied, by reason, for example, of the fact that the ultimate gifts are set out in specific sums and not as residuary dispositions. This short answer is not, judging from the few reported cases, satisfactory since the agreement is often silent or ambiguous on the point. In one case[3] the trust apparently only affected property held by the survivor at the first death. That restriction was perhaps dictated by the fact that the mutual wills were only intended to deal with the assets of the two testators which resulted from a business they had carried on together. It was therefore reasonable to allow the survivor a free hand with the fruits of his unaided labour. In *Re Oldham*[4] Astbury J seemed disposed to hold that the trust only binds the property held by the survivor at the time of his death, thus leaving unimpaired the power of disposition *inter vivos*. This seems to conflict with the decision as to lapse in *Re Hagger,* which implies that the interest of the beneficiaries is vested during the lifetime of the survivor. Moreover a devise to A with a direction to settle 'so much as he shall die seised of' has, by reason of uncertainty, been held incapable of creating a trust[5]. Yet, in effect, that is what the view of Astbury J amounts to. The significance of this question lies of course in the powers of the survivor over his own property during his life. It would seem absurd if the court is prepared to prevent his breaking faith with the first testator only to the extent of preventing inconsistent testamentary dispositions thus allowing him to make the arrangement nugatory by dispositions *inter vivos*. It seems, therefore, that the two arguments of certainty and good faith lead to the conclusion that, in the absence of any definition, the trust of the survivor's property must

[1] *Re Green* [1951] Ch 148, [1950] 2 All ER 913.

[2] In this respect *Re Green* does nothing more than make clear the effect of the agreement, which was implicit in earlier decisions such as *Re Hagger* [1930] 2 Ch 190 at p. 195, or *Re Oldham* [1925] Ch 75 where, had the trust been regarded as effective, there would nevertheless have been some free property. The arrangement in *Dufour v Pereira* (1769) 1 Dick 419 seems only to have covered residue. See 2 Hargr Jurid Arg, p. 305.

[3] *Re Hagger*, [1930] 2 Ch 190.

[4] [1925] Ch at 88.

[5] *Bland v Bland* (1745) 2 Cox Eq Cas 349. See also *Re Jones* [1898] 1 Ch 438.

be treated as embracing that which he holds at the death of the first testator together with subsequently acquired property; though clearly he will be entitled to deal freely with the income of the fund and accumulations of the income. Such indeed seems to be the implication to be drawn from Lord Camden's direction for accounts to be taken in *Dufour v Pereira,* and to have been the opinion of Lord Loughborough. It was one of his objections to finding an agreement in *Lord Walpole v Lord Orford*[6] that it would have resulted in an inability of the survivor to raise portions for his daughters by mortgage. This breadth of the scope of the trust, or at least the possibility of it, affords another reason for delimiting it in the agreement."

In *Re Hagger* ([1930] 2 Ch 190) a husband and wife made a joint will (to which the same principles apply) by which, inter alia, the survivor was given a life interest in the whole of their estate, and after the survivor's death, their property at Wandsworth was to be held on trust for sale, with Eleanor Palmer as one of nine beneficiaries. The wife died in 1904, Eleanor Palmer in 1923, and the husband in 1928. By his will the husband left all his property on different trusts.

The questions were whether the beneficiaries under the joint will could take on the husband's death; and, if so, whether Eleanor Palmer's interest lapsed by reason of her death before the husband. CLAUSON J held that all the beneficiaries, including Eleanor, could claim. He said, at p. 195:

"To my mind *Dufour v Pereira* (1 Dick 419, 2 Hargr Jurid Arg 304) decides that where there is a joint will such as this, on the death of the first testator the position as regards that part of the property which belongs to the survivor is that the survivor will be treated in this Court as holding the property on trust to apply it so as to carry out the effect of the joint will. As I read Lord Camden's judgment in *Dufour v Pereira* that would be so, even though the survivor did not signify his election to give effect to the will by taking benefits under it. But in any case it is clear that Lord Camden has decided that if the survivor takes a benefit conferred on him by the joint will he will be treated as a trustee in this Court, and he will not be allowed to do anything inconsistent with the provisions of the joint will. It is not necessary for me to consider the reasons on which Lord Camden based his judgment. The case must be accepted in this Court as binding. Therefore I am bound to hold that from the death of the wife the husband held the property, according to the tenor of the will, subject to the trusts thereby imposed upon it, at all events if he took advantage of the provisions of the will. In my view he did take advantage of those provisions.

The effect of the will was that the husband and wife agreed that the property should on the death of the first of them to die pass to trustees to hold on trusts inconsistent with the right of survivorship, and therefore the will effected a severance of the joint interest of the husband and wife. By the will they made a provision which was inconsistent with the survivor taking by survivorship. Therefore the property at the moment when, on

[6] (1797) 3 Ves 402 at 417. For the opposed view see however DIXON J in *Birmingham v Renfrew* (1937) 57 CLR 666 at 689.

the wife's death, it came within the ambit of the will ceased to be held by the two jointly, and the husband had no title to the wife's interest on her dying in his lifetime, save in so far as he took a life interest under the joint will. From the moment of the wife's death the Wandsworth property was held on trust for the husband for life with a vested interest in remainder as to one-sixth in E. Palmer. So far as the husband's interest in the property is concerned the will operated as a trust from the date of the wife's death. There is, accordingly, no lapse by reason of Eleanor Palmer's death in the husband's lifetime, but after the wife's death."

Similar questions arise, where, as in *Ottaway v Norman* ([1972] Ch 698, [1971] 3 All ER 1325) property is left to a legatee upon a secret trust to leave it by will to another. BRIGHTMAN J, as has been seen[7], upheld the trust.

(1973) 36 MLR at pp. 212–214 (S. M. Bandali)

"On the evidence [in *Ottaway v Norman*] BRIGHTMAN J found that the residue was not intended to be subject to trust. However, he went on to state a new principle, while making clear that this was *obiter*. 'I am content to assume for present purposes but without so deciding that if property is given to the primary donee on the understanding that the primary donee will dispose by will of such assets, if any, as he may have at his command at his death in favour of the secondary donee, a valid trust is created in favour of the secondary donee which is in suspense during the lifetime of the primary donee, but attaches to the estate of the primary donee at the moment of the latter's death.'[8] In the present case on the evidence there had been no such 'far-reaching undertaking' and, therefore, no trust arose as regards Eva's [the house-keeper's] residuary estate. Moreover, no obligation had been undertaken by Eva as regards the money she had received under H's will. Such an obligation could be binding provided the donor and donee had discussed and intended that the donee should keep the money distinct from her own money, but there was no such evidence here[9]. However, the above doctrine of a 'trust in suspense' calls for analysis, for apart from being a salutary, if bad, attempt at indicating the potential dynamism of equitable principles, the opinion ignores some difficulties.

There is no clear English authority on this concept. The court referred to *Birmingham v Renfrew*[10], an Australian decision, as giving some support to the proposition. This was a case of mutual wills where the survivor-husband revoked his will in breach of the undertaking he had given to his wife, and the High Court held that the agreement between them had created a constructive trust not of any specific property but of any residue of property, of whatever character, at the time of the survivor's death. The

[7] See p. 115, ante.

[8] *Ottaway v Norman* [1972] Ch 698 at 713, [1971] 3 All ER 1325 at 1334.

[9] The absence of this intention to keep the money distinct was, according to BRIGHTMAN J, the distinguishing factor from *Re Gardner* [1920] 2 Ch 523, where the half-secret trust clearly showed that the donee only had a life interest in the personal estate of the donor.

[10] (1937) 57 CLR 666.

obligation was a 'floating obligation, suspended, so to speak, during the lifetime of the survivor [and] can descend upon the assets at his death and crystallise into a trust.'[11] Let us consider theoretical difficulties.

First, there is the problem of determining the ownership of property in the interval. Is the property (i.e. which 'he may have at his command at his death') during the intervening period vested in the primary donee or the secondary donee? If the former, then the legal owner should logically be able to dispose of it subject to any possible remedy for a breach of contract which, again, would be subject to the rules of privity and consideration. If the ownership is vested in the secondary donee, then there is an immediate trust. But, according to Brightman J, the trust 'attaches . . . at the moment of the [primary donee's] death.' It is submitted that the difficulty cannot be avoided by holding that, in such circumstances, the primary donee has a life interest in such assets, for the fact is that the donor has been given a promise that property would be given ' if any' is left at the donee's death; this suggests that the donee is free to do what he likes with the property[12]. Moreover, if the trust attaches when the primary donee dies, what property could be subject to a life interest before that event?

Secondly, such an undertaking would in all probability fail to satisfy the requirement of certainty of the subject-matter of a trust. This requirement has to be satisfied at the time the trust comes into operation. Brightman J's words that the trust is, during the intervening period, in suspense suggests that the trust has its existence at the time the donor dies, though it does not 'bite' until the primary donee dies. If so, such a trust would fail to meet the test of certainty. The primary donee should then take the property absolutely. Moreover, the trust is open to the charge of inconsistency of directions if the primary donee is entitled to do what he likes with the property during his lifetime (an absolute ownership) but is bound by a promise to leave any residue of that property in a particular way at his death[13]. It is therefore submitted that the trust concept cannot legitimately be extended to deal with the situation envisaged by Brightman J. It would be theoretically better if the situation is left to be dealt with by the law of contract, i.e. the estate of the promisor should be subject to contractual obligation undertaken by the promisor.

Lastly, an important point was not raised by counsel nor averred to by the court. Equity holds that where a testator by his will gives his property absolutely to A but by the same will he gives away some of the property belonging to A to X, then A cannot take the former without observing the testator's intention as to the latter; he must take the burden with the benefit, though he is free to elect either against or under the instrument. It seems that *Ottaway v Norman* satisfied all the requirements of this doctrine, for Eva had given one-half of her residuary estate to the plaintiffs but had also taken the house and its contents from them and given these to N and his wife. . . .

[11] Ibid., per DIXON J at 689.

[12] Presumably, if the trust arises at death of the donee, and if the ultimate beneficiary predeceases the donee then, unlike in *Re Gardner* [1923] 2 Ch 230, the trust fails. Who would then be entitled to the property?

[13] Cf. *Re Golay's Will Trusts* [1965] 1 WLR 969, [1965] 2 All ER 660 and *Re Jones* [1898] 1 Ch 438.

In short *Ottaway v Norman* raises more problems than it solves. The machinery by which the primary donee is to carry out the terms of the secret trust is not as unimportant as Brightman J appears to suggest."

D. The Vendor under a Contract for the Sale of Land[14]

In *Rayner v Preston*[15] ((1881) 18 ChD 1) Preston agreed in 1878 to sell to Rayner for £3,100 a house in Suffolk Street, Liverpool, which had been insured by Preston against fire. The contract did not refer to the insurance. After the date of the contract but before the time fixed for completion, the house was damaged by fire to the amount of £330, and this sum was paid by the insurers to Preston. Rayner brought an action to establish his right to the sum, or to have it applied in repairing the house. The Court of Appeal held that Rayner was not entitled to the benefit of the insurance as against Preston.

The law on this point was changed by Law of Property Act 1925, s. 47, under which a purchaser may, on completion, recover from the vendor any money due under an insurance policy "in respect of any damage or destruction of property included in the contract". Cotton LJ[16] said at p. 6: "It was said that the vendor is, between the time of the contract being made and being completed by conveyance, a trustee of the property for the purchaser, and that as, but for the fact of the legal ownership of the building insured being vested in him, he could not have recovered on the policy, he must be considered a trustee of the money recovered. In my opinion, this cannot be maintained. An unpaid vendor is a trustee in a qualified sense only, and is so only because he has made a contract which a Court of Equity will give effect to by transferring the property sold to the purchaser, and so far as he is a trustee he is so only in respect of the property contracted to be sold. Of this the policy is not a part. A vendor is in no way a trustee for the purchaser of rents accruing before the time fixed for completion, and here the fire occurred and the right to recover the money accrued before the day fixed for completion. The argument that the money is received in respect of property which is trust property is, in my opinion, fallacious. The money is received by virtue or in respect of the contract of insurance, and though the fact that the insured had parted with all interest in the property insured would be an answer to the claim, on the principle that the contract is one of indemnity only, this is very different from the proposition that the money is received by reason of his legal interest in the property"

In *Shaw v Foster* ((1872) LR 5 HL 321) Lord Cairns said (at p. 338): "The vendor was a trustee of the property for the purchaser; the purchaser was the real beneficial owner in the eye of a Court of Equity of the property

[14] H & M, pp. 323–324; K & S, pp. 194–202; P & M, pp. 159–160; Pettit, pp. 120–121; Snell, p. 188; Farrand, *Contract and Conveyance* (2nd Edn, 1973) pp. 225–231; (1959) 23 Conv (NS) 173 (V. G. Wellings).

[15] *Lake v Bayliss* [1974] 1 WLR 1073, [1974] 2 All ER 1114; (1974) 38 Conv (NS) 357 (F. R. Crane).

[16] Brett LJ and James LJ (who dissented) expressed different views on the situation.

subject only to this observation, that the vendor, whom I have called the trustee, was not a mere dormant trustee, he was a trustee having a personal and substantial interest in the property, a right to protect that interest, and an active right to assert that interest if anything should be done in derogation of it. The relation, therefore, of trustee and *cestui que trust* subsisted, but subsisted subject to the paramount right of the vendor and trustee to protect his own interest as vendor of the property."[17]

E. The Mortgagee on Exercising the Power of Sale[18]

There is no doubt that a mortgagee, in possession of mortgage money after exercising the statutory power of sale, is trustee of the money. The Law of Property Act 1925, s. 105, says so. And this was the rule of equity before it became statutory.

On the other hand, he is not a trustee of the power of sale. In *Cuckmere Brick Co Ltd v Mutual Finance Ltd* ([1971] Ch 949, [1971] 2 All ER 633) Cross LJ said (at p. 969): "I shall first deal with the law applicable to this case. A mortgagee exercising a power of sale is in an ambiguous position. He is not a trustee of the power for the mortgagor for it was given him for his own benefit to enable him to obtain repayment of his loan. On the other hand, he is not in the position of an absolute owner selling his own property but must undoubtedly pay some regard to the interests of the mortgagor when he comes to exercise the power.

Some points are clear. On the one hand, the mortgagee, when the power has arisen, can sell when he likes, even though the market is likely to improve if he holds his hand and the result of an immediate sale may be that instead of yielding a surplus for the mortgagor the purchase price is only sufficient to discharge the mortgage debt and the interest owing on it. On the other hand, the sale must be a genuine sale by the mortgagee to an independent purchaser at a price honestly arrived at.

Suppose, however, that the mortgagee acts in good faith but that through the negligence either of the mortgagee himself or of an agent employed by him a smaller purchase price is obtained than would otherwise have been the case? . . .

There is no doubt that a mortgagee who takes possession of the security with a view to selling it has to account to the mortgagor for any loss occurring through his negligence or the negligence of his agent in dealing with the property between the date of his taking possession of it and the date of the sale, including, as in the *McHugh* case [1913] AC 299, steps

[17] See also *Lysaght v Edwards* (1876) 2 ChD 499 at 506, per Jessel MR ("The position of the vendor is something between what is called a naked or bare trustee, or a mere trustee (that is, a person without beneficial interest), and a mortgagee who is not, in equity (any more than a vendor), the owner of the estate, but is, in certain events, entitled to what the unpaid vendor is, viz. possession of the estate and a charge upon the estate for his purchase-money."); *Royal Bristol Permanent Building Society v Bomash* (1887) 35 ChD 390 at 397, per Kekewich J ("Of course we all know that he is only a trustee in a modified sense"); *Cumberland Consolidated Holdings Ltd v Ireland* [1946] KB 264 at 269, per Lord Greene MR ("His position is that of a quasi-trustee for the purchaser").

[18] Cheshire, *Modern Law of Real Property* (12th Edn, 1976), pp. 672–673; Megarry and Wade, *Law of Real Property* (4th Edn, 1975) pp. 911–912; see also *Palmer v Barclays Bank Ltd* (1972) 23 P & CR 30.

taken to bring the property to the place of sale. It seems quite illogical that the mortgagee's duty should suddenly change when one comes to the sale itself and that at that stage if only he acts in good faith he is under no liability, however negligent he or his agent may be. . . .

In my judgment, therefore, if either the [mortgagees or the auctioneers] were guilty of negligence in connection with the sale, the [mortgagees] are liable to compensate the [mortgagors] for any damage which they have suffered by reason of that negligence."

F. Acquisition of Property by Killing

(1973) 89 LQR 235 (T. G. Yardan)

" INTRODUCTION

It is a well-established general principle that a person who kills another is not entitled to enjoy any property which he would otherwise have acquired as a result of that death. However, the limits of the principle are ill-defined and the English courts have worked out no rational theory for their actions in depriving killers—actions that might seem to conflict with other well-established principles and, in many cases, might seem to contravene the language of the legislature[19].

It is the purpose of this article to examine the practical effect and theoretical basis of the principle. This examination will involve consideration of certain problems of causation; the types of killing that invoke the principle; and the different ways that acquisitions may be brought about by killing. Once the practical application of the principle has thus been clarified it will be shown that the principle is simply an example of the use of the constructive trust to prevent unjust enrichment. It will then be convenient to deal with the difficult question of who should benefit from the court's deprivation of the killer, i.e. who is the beneficiary of the constructive trust. . . .

A THEORETICAL BASIS

Ames, in his famous article 'Can a Murderer acquire Title by his Crime and keep it,'[20] said that three results were possible where a person acquires property by killing: (i) the legal title does not pass to the killer; (ii) the legal title passes to the killer, and he may retain it in spite of his crime; or (iii) the legal title passes to the killer, but equity will treat him as a constructive trustee of the title because of the unconscionable mode of its acquisition[1].

It has been shown that English courts have rejected the second possibility and generally they have considered that the killer does not gain legal title. However, there has been little discussion of the theoretical basis for a deprivation that in most cases might appear to contravene legislative provisions. There are two methods that have been used to justify this result.

[19] For an early review of this topic, see Chadwick *A Testator's Bounty to his Slayer* (1914) 30 LQR 211. See also Toohey, "Killing the Goose that lays the Golden Eggs" (1958) 23 Australian Law Journal 14.

[20] *Lectures on Legal History*, at p. 310.

[1] Ibid., at p. 311.

Both methods are sometimes employed in the same judgment and the difference between them is more superficial than real. The first approach is to say that all laws—whether made by statute or judicial precedent—must conform to a 'higher law.' The second approach is to interpret the law so as to make it conform to the judge's conception of what it should be. A case which is a good example of the former approach is *Riggs v Palmer*[2] where the New York Court of Appeals held that a legatee did not gain title to property which he would have received as the result of murdering his testator. Earl J said that there are certain principles that 'have their foundation in universal law administered in all civilised countries' and that 'all laws, as well as all contracts, may be controlled in their operation and effect by general, fundamental maxims of the common law.'[3] This approach is, however, generally recognised as being too open an example of judicial law-making and the courts that consider the killer does not acquire legal title usually arrive at such a result by liberal statutory interpretation.[4]. . .

The constructive trust approach to this situation has received considerable recognition in the United States[5] and, moreover, in the joint tenancy context courts in Canada[6], Australia[7], and New Zealand[8], finding it impossible to hold that the right of survivorship does not operate at common law, have accepted the constructive trust as the appropriate way to prevent the unjust enrichment of the killer. . . .

The Effect of the Killer's Deprivation

As the English courts have worked out no suitable justification for depriving the wrongdoer of property acquired as the result of the killing so no rational theory has been devised for working out who becomes entitled to the property[9]. However, if it is accepted that it is the constructive trust which is used to prevent the unjust enrichment of the wrongdoer the confusion is reduced and the person who is entitled to the property—the beneficiary of the constructive trust—is the person who, in the eyes of equity, has the best right to it[10]. Now, it might be argued that this simply begs the question which is, who has the best right to the property? The reply is that though the process for determining the answer to that question is equitable and therefore flexible nevertheless guide-lines are to be found from the other situations where the constructive trust is similarly

[2] (1889) 115 NY 506, 22 NE 188.
[3] Ibid., at p. 190.
[4] See Woerner, "Self-made Heirship through Murder" (1925) 10 St Louis Law Rev 34; a note "Succession by Murder—Applicability of the Constructive Trust" (1931) 29 Mich L Rev 745 at 746.
[5] Scott, *Trusts* (3rd Edn), s. 492; Restatement: Restitution, s. 187. See also *Ellerson v Westcott* (1896) 148 NY 149, 42 NE 540, where Andrews CJ rationalised *Riggs v Palmer* (1889) 115 NY 506, 22 NE 188 on the constructive trust theory.
[6] *Schobelt v Barber* (1967) 59 DLR (2d) 519 (Ont.).
[7] *Rasmanis v Jurewitsch* [1970] 1 NSWR 650. But cf. *Re Barrowcliff* [1927] SASR 147; *Kemp v The Public Curator of Queensland* [1969] Qd R 145.
[8] *Re Pechar* [1969] NZLR 574.
[9] See *Re Callaway* [1956] Ch 559, [1956] 2 All ER 451; *Re Peacock* [1957] Ch 310, [1957] 2 All ER 98.
[10] See Costigan (1915) 9 Ill L Rev 505.

employed[11], and from the decisions in this situation which, though generally unsupported by any or by inadequate reasoning, have achieved equitable results.

The principle is, it is suggested, that where there are circumstances showing that a particular person has a better equity than anybody else the property should be given to that person but otherwise it should be given to the estate of the victim[12] for lack of 'any other suitable recipient,'[13] and in all cases the wrongdoer or anyone (except a bona fide purchaser) claiming through him should be excluded. It will be convenient now to examine this principle in the context of each of the methods of acquisition discussed in this article. . . ."

G. Justice and Good Conscience

Recently, and especially in the context of parties' rights in a family home, or of the rights of a licensee to occupy land, there has been much emphasis on finding a constructive trust where in justice and good conscience such a trust should exist.

In *Eves v Eves* ([1975] 1 WLR 1338, [1975] 3 All ER 768)[14] Lord DENNING MR said at p. 1340: "I will call her Janet because she has had four surnames already. She was married for the first time at the age of 18; but that marriage only lasted about a year. Next at the age of 19 she met a man, Stuart Eves. He was a married man. They could not marry. So they started living together. She took his name and had two children by him. After 4½ years that relationship broke down. Now both have got divorces from their former spouses and have remarried. The question arises now as to the house where they lived. . .

The problem in this case is a familiar one. It often happens that a man and a woman set up house together and have children. They cannot marry because one or other or both are already married. But they intend to marry as soon as they are free to do so. She takes his name. They live as husband and wife. They are known to their neighbours as husband

[11] It is arguable that the constructive trust is similarly employed in other situations where a person would be unjustly enriched by the acquisition or retention of property, e.g. where he acquires it as the result of a secret trust arrangement; a mutual will arrangement; an informal *inter vivos* arrangement which does not comply with the required formalities; or acquiescence.

[12] In the unusual situation where a remainderman kills the *cestui que vie* of a prior life interest the beneficiary would not be the victim but the tenant *pur autre vie*.

[13] *Rasmanis v Jurewitsch* [1968] 2 NSWR 166 at 169, per STREET J (affd [1970] 1 NSWR 650).

[14] Cf. *Tanner v Tanner* [1975] 1 WLR 1346, [1975] 3 All ER 776. See also *Falconer v Falconer* [1970] 1 WLR 1333, [1970] 3 All ER 449; *Heseltine v Heseltine* [1971] 1 WLR 342, [1971] 1 All ER 953; *Davis v Vale* [1971] 1 WLR 1022, [1971] 2 All ER 1021; *Hargrave v Newton* [1971] 1 WLR 1611, [1971] 3 All ER 866; *Re Cummins* [1972] Ch 62, [1971] 3 All ER 782; *Binions v Evans* [1972] Ch 359, [1972] 2 All ER 70, [1973] CLJ 123 (R. J. Smith); cf. *Dodsworth v Dodsworth* (1973) 228 Estates Gazette 115; *Hazell v Hazell* [1972] 1 WLR 301, [1972] 1 All ER 923; *Cooke v Head* [1972] 1 WLR 518, [1972] 2 All ER 38; *Re Densham* [1975] 1 WLR 1519, [1975] 3 All ER 726; (1976) 92 LQR 489 (F. Webb); (1976) 40 Conv (NS) 351 (M. Richards); *D H N Food Distributors Ltd v Tower Hamlets London Borough Council* [1976] 1 WLR 852, [1976] 3 All ER 462; (1977) 93 LQR 170 (D. Sugarman and F. Webb); and in the context of a purchaser of registered land with knowledge of the existence of an unregistered equitable interest, see *Peffer v Rigg* [1977] 1 WLR 285; (1977) 41 Conv (NS) 207 (F. R. Crane); 93 LQR 341 (R. J. Smith); 36 CLJ 227 (D. J. Hayton); 40 MLR 602 (S. Anderson). See p. 214, ante.

and wife. They get a house; but it is put in his name alone. Then, before they get married, the relationship breaks down. In strict law she has no claim on him whatever. She is not his wife. He is not bound to provide a roof over her head. He can turn her into the street. She is not entitled to any maintenance from him for herself. All she can do is to go to the magistrates and ask for an affiliation order against him on the footing that she is a 'single woman': and get an order for him to pay maintenance for the children. If he does not pay, she may have great difficulty in getting any money out of him, even for the children. Such is the strict law. And a few years ago even equity would not have helped her. But things have altered now. Equity is not past the age of child bearing. One of her latest progeny is a constructive trust of a new model. Lord Diplock brought it into the world and we have nourished it. In *Gissing v Gissing* [1971] AC 886 at 905, Lord Diplock said:

> 'A resulting, implied or constructive trust—and it is unnecessary for present purposes to distinguish between these three classes of trust—is created by a transaction between the trustee and the cestui que trust in connection with the acquisition by the trustee of a legal estate in land, whenever the trustee has so conducted himself that it would be inequitable to allow him to deny to the cestui que trust a beneficial interest in the land acquired. And he will be held so to have conducted himself if by his words or conduct he has induced the cestui que trust to act to his own detriment in the reasonable belief that by so acting he was acquiring a beneficial interest in the land.'

We have followed this advice in several cases, notably in *Binions v Evans* [1972] Ch 359, [1972] 2 All ER 70; *Cooke v Head* [1972] 1 WLR 518, [1972] 2 All ER 38 and *Hussey v Palmer* [1972] 1 WLR 1286, [1972] 3 All ER 744. I would specially mention *Cooke v Head* because there too a man and woman set up home without being married. I ventured to suggest, at p. 520:

> '. . . whenever two parties by their joint efforts acquire property to be used for their joint benefit, the courts may impose or impute a constructive or resulting trust. The legal owner is bound to hold the property on trust for them both. This trust does not need any writing. It can be enforced by an order for sale, but in a proper case the sale can be postponed indefinitely. It applies to husband and wife, to engaged couples, and to man and mistress, and maybe to other relationships too.'

This principle was considered by Walton J in *Richards v Dove* [1974] 1 All ER 888. But that case turned on its own special circumstances and is not of any general application.

The principle does apply in the present case. Although Janet did not make any financial contribution, it seems to me that this property was acquired and maintained by both by their joint efforts with the intention that it should be used for their joint benefit until they were married and thereafter as long as the marriage continued. At any rate, Stuart Eves cannot be heard to say to the contrary. He told her that it was to be their home for them and their children. He gained her confidence by telling her that he intended to put it in their joint names (just as married couples often do) but that it was not possible until she was 21. The judge described this as a 'trick', and said that it 'did not do him much credit as a man of honour'. The man never intended to put it in joint names but always determined to have it in his own name. It seems to me that he should be judged by what he told her—by what he led her to believe—and not by his own intent which he kept to himself. Lord Diplock made this clear in *Gissing v Gissing* [1971] AC 886 at 906.

It seems to me that this conduct by Mr. Eves amounted to a recognition by him that, in all fairness, she was entitled to a share in the house, equivalent in some way to a declaration of trust; not for a particular share, but for such share as was fair in view of all she had done and was doing for him and the children and would thereafter do. By so doing he gained her confidence. She trusted him. She did not make any financial contribution but she contributed in many other ways. She did much work in the house and garden. She looked after him and cared for the children. It is clear that her contribution was such that if she had been a wife she would have had a good claim to have a share in it on a divorce: see *Wachtel v Wachtel* [1973] Fam 72 at 92–94.

In view of his conduct, it would, I think, be most inequitable for him to deny her any share in the house. The law will impute or impose a constructive trust by which he was to hold it in trust for them both. But what should be the shares? I think one half would be too much. I suggest it should be one quarter of the equity. But seeing that she is now remarried, this share would I hope be regarded by her as more in the nature of a provision for the children than for her. The parties may negotiate so that he buys out her interest now by a lump sum charged on the property. The administration of her share must be left for further application; but, if the parties cannot agree on a lump sum, it would seem desirable to postpone any order for sale of the house so long as he makes reasonable payments of maintenance for the children and also a reasonable amount off the arrears and such further sum as would seem reasonable in respect of her share. He is in good work. He tells us his basic wage is £50 a week. So his take-home pay may be more. At any rate, there is no possible excuse for him not paying the maintenance for the children.

I would therefore allow the appeal and declare that the defendant holds the legal estate on trust for sale but the benefit in proportion of the shares of one quarter to Janet and three quarters to Mr. Eves."[15]

In *Hussey v Palmer* ([1972] 1 WLR 1286, [1972] 3 All ER 744)[16] Mrs. Hussey, an elderly widow, was invited to live with her daughter and son-in-law. The house was too small, and an additional bedroom was added, at a cost of £607, which Mrs. Hussey paid.

Differences arose, and Mrs. Hussey left the house. She claimed the £607 on the basis of a resulting trust.

Lord DENNING MR said at p. 1289: "Although the plaintiff alleged that there was a resulting trust, I should have thought that the trust in

[15] For a different reasoning leading to the same conclusion, see the judgments of BROWNE LJ and BRIGHTMAN J.

[16] (1973) 89 LQR 2; 37 Conv (NS) 65 (D. J. Hayton).

this case, if there was one, was more in the nature of a constructive trust; but that is more a matter of words than anything else. The two run together. By whatever name it is described, it is a trust imposed by law whenever justice and good conscience require it. It is a liberal process, founded upon large principles of equity, to be applied in cases where the legal owner cannot conscientiously keep the property for himself alone, but ought to allow another to have the property or the benefit of it or a share in it. The trust may arise at the outset when the property is acquired, or later on, as the circumstances may require. It is an equitable remedy by which the court can enable an aggrieved party to obtain restitution. It is comparable to the legal remedy of money had and received which, as Lord Mansfield said, is 'very beneficial and therefore, much encouraged' [*Moses v MacFerlan* (1760) 2 Burr 1005 at 1012]. Thus we have repeatedly held that, when one person contributes towards the purchase price of a house, the owner holds it on a constructive trust for him, proportionate to his contribution, even though there is no agreement between them, and no declaration of trust to be found, and no evidence of any intention to create a trust. Instances are numerous where a wife has contributed money to the initial purchase of a house or property; or later on to the payment of mortgage instalments; or has helped in business: see *Falconer v Falconer* [1970] 1 WLR 1333, [1970] 3 All ER 449, *Heseltine v Heseltine* [1971] 1 WLR 342, [1971] 1 All ER 952 and *Re Cummins* [1972] Ch 62, [1971] 3 All ER 782. Similarly, when a mistress has contributed money, or money's worth, to the building of a house: *Cooke v Head* [1972] 1 WLR 518, [1972] 2 All ER 38. Very recently we held that a purchaser, who bought a cottage subject to the rights of an occupier, held it on trust for her benefit: *Binions v Evans* [1972] Ch 359, [1972] 2 All ER 70. In all those cases it would have been quite inequitable for the legal owner to take the property for himself and exclude the other from it. So the law imputed or imposed a trust for his or her benefit.

The present case is well within the principles of those cases. Just as a person, who pays part of the purchase price, acquires an equitable interest in the house, so also he does when he pays for an extension to be added to it. Mr. Owen has done a lot of research and has found a case in 1858 to that very effect. It is *Unity Joint Stock Mutual Banking Association v King* (1858) 25 Beav 72. A father had land on which he built a granary. His two sons built two other granaries on it at a cost of £1,200. Sir John Romilly MR held that the two sons had a lien or charge on the property as against the father, and any person claiming through him. The father had never promised to pay the sons £1,200. He was not indebted to them in that sum. He had never engaged or promised to make over the land to them or to give them a charge on it. Yet they had a lien or charge on the land. That case was approved by the Privy Council in *Chalmers v Pardoe* [1963] 1 WLR 677 at 681–682, where it was said to be based on the "general equitable principle that . . . it would be against conscience" for the owner to take the land without repaying the sums expended on the buildings. To this I would add *Inwards v Baker* [1965] 2 QB 29, [1965] 1 All ER 446, when a son built a bungalow on his father's land in the expectation that he would be allowed to stay there as his home, though there was no promise to that effect. After the father's death, his trustees sought to turn the son out. It was held that he had an equitable interest which was good against the trustees. In those cases it was emphasised that the court must look at the circumstances of each case to decide in what way the equity can be satisfied. In some by an equitable lien. In others by a constructive trust. But in either case it is because justice and good conscience so require.

In the present case Mrs. Hussey paid £607 to a builder for the erection of this extension. It may well be, as the defendant says, that there was no contract to repay it at all. It was not a loan to the son-in-law. She could not sue him for repayment. He could not have turned her out. If she had stayed there until she died, the extension would undoubtedly have belonged beneficially to the son-in-law. If, during her lifetime, he had sold the house, together with the extension, she would be entitled to be repaid the £607 out of the proceeds. He admits this himself. But he has not sold the house. She has left, and the son-in-law has the extension for his own benefit and could sell the whole if he so desired. It seems to me to be entirely against conscience that he should retain the whole house and not allow Mrs. Hussey any interest in it, or any charge upon it. The court should, and will, impose or impute a trust by which Mr. Palmer is to hold the property on terms under which, in the cirumstances that have happened, she has an interest in the property proportionate to the £607 which she put into it. She is quite content if he repays her the £607. If he does not repay the £607, she can apply for an order for sale, so that the sum can be paid to her. But the simplest way for him would be to raise the £607 on mortgage and pay it to her. But, on the legal point raised, I have no doubt there was a resulting trust, or, more accurately, a constructive trust, for her, and I would so declare. I would allow the appeal, accordingly."[17]

(1973) Current Legal Problems, at p. 38 (A. J. Oakley)

"The Recent Decisions Assessed

In each of the recent decisions which have been considered, the Court of Appeal has imposed a constructive trust in order to prevent a result which would, otherwise, have been inequitable. It is clear that, in the field of matrimonial property, such practice is contrary to the most recent decisions of the House of Lords. This apart, the practice has, in principle, little to commend it; it makes the operation of the law totally uncertain and enables one spouse to acquire rights over property which could never have been obtained under existing equitable principles[18]. Outside the field of matrimonial property, the practice is even more undesirable, since the implications of the imposition of constructive trusts to do justice *inter partes* may well seriously undermine established principles of property law[19]. Recent developments in the field of constructive trusts in English law have been towards imposing a constructive trust only where there is some

[17] Phillimore LJ held that a resulting trust arose; Cairns LJ dissented.
[18] See *Heseltine v Heseltine* [1971] 1 WLR 342, [1971] 1 All ER 953.
[19] See *Binions v Evans* [1972] Ch 359, [1972] 2 All ER 70.

conscious unconscionable act by the trustee. Among the many examples of this approach are *Holder v Holder*[20], where an executor who purchased trust property was held not liable to account for it to the trust in the absence of actual abuse of position, and *Carl-Zeiss Stiftung v Herbert Smith & Co (No. 2)*[1], where it was stated that agents handling trust property in the ordinary course of their agency would be liable to account for that property to the trust only where they had actual notice of a breach of trust. The use of the constructive trust to do justice *inter partes* must, in some cases, involve the imposition of constructive trusts upon parties not in any way guilty of a legal wrong. The practice, therefore, is not in accordance with recent developments in English law. This is not to say that the categories of situations in which English courts will impose a constructive trust should not be extended. But they should only be extended where the courts are prepared to lay down a new principle which will apply generally. It is unsatisfactory for a constructive trust to be imposed whenever the courts feel, on their own individual ideas of justice, that such a remedy will bring about the 'right' result.

What, then, can be said by way of conclusion? It cannot be denied that the cases discussed in this paper have built up a formidable body of case law in support of the proposition that the constructive trust may be used to prevent a result which would, otherwise, be inequitable. Nevertheless, it is submitted that the imposition of a constructive trust on such a basis in these cases cannot be justified on the criteria that should be a prerequisite of the imposition of a constructive trust. It is hoped, therefore, that should the House of Lords have an opportunity of considering these recent developments, some certainty will be restored to this area of the law."

III. The Principle

The question remains, whether the law relating to constructive trusts should be regarded as a catalogue of situations, or as a single principle with various manifestations.

(1955) 71 LQR 39 (A. W. Scott)

"It is, I think, coming to be recognised, particularly in the United States, that the constructive trust is a concept of a wide scope, of a scope which is gradually growing wider.

It is sometimes said that a constructive trust is imposed in case of fraud. It is sometimes said that it is imposed in case of a breach of a fiduciary relation. It seems clear, however, that not only may a constructive trust be imposed in both of these cases, but it may be imposed in others too. How then shall we define a constructive trust? It is my belief that an exact definition cannot be framed. Indeed, I do not know that any legal concept can be exactly defined, that is, defined in such a way that it includes

[20] [1968] Ch 353, [1968] 1 All ER 665, p. 594, post.
[1] [1969] 2 Ch 276, [1969] 2 All ER 367, p. 222, ante.

all that falls within the concept and excludes everything else. This is true not only of juridical concepts but is largely true of physical objects. We can, to be sure, define a parallelogram with perfect accuracy, but the reason is that there never was a parallelogram, except as we have in our own minds given it characteristics. And even the definition of a parallelogram is incomplete without further definition; we have to define a plane figure and state what is meant by parallel lines. As to the concept of a constructive trust, I think that the best that we can do is to give a rough working description of it.

This we attempted to do in the *Restatement of Restitution* which was promulgated by The American Law Institute in 1936. It is stated (§160):

> 'Where a person holding title to property is subject to an equitable duty to convey it to another on the ground that he would be unjustly enriched if he were permitted to retain it, a constructive trust arises.'

Certainly this is a pretty broad statement. It is not, perhaps, as broad as that which Judge Cardozo made when sitting on the Court of Appeals in New York, who said: 'A constructive trust is the formula through which the conscience of equity finds expression'[2]. The provision in the *Restatement* does not purport to define a constructive trust but purports to state the circumstances under which a constructive trust arises. It arises where the circumstances are such that the holder of the title to property would be unjustly enriched if he were permitted to retain it, and where, therefore, a court of equity (or a court having the powers of a court of equity) will compel him to convey the property to another."

QUESTIONS

1. What subject matter would you include in a chapter on Constructive Trusts?

   Consider now whether:

   a) secret trusts (pp. 114-129, ante)
   b) mutual wills
   c) land subject to a contract for sale
   d) a power of sale exercised by a mortgagee
   e) cases like *Bannister v Bannister* ([1948] 2 All ER 133, p. 129, ante); *Hodgson v Marks* ([1971] Ch 892, [1971] 2 All ER 684, p. 198, ante); *Binions v Evans*, ([1972] Ch 359, [1972] 2 All ER 70), and *Hussey v Palmer* ([1972] 1 WLR 1286, [1972] 3 All ER 744, p. 236, ante)
   f) benefits acquired by a felonious killer

   are instances of constructive trusts.

2. Consider the distinction made above (p. 213, ante) between accountability and liability on a constructive trustee. Is the distinction important? Are *Karak Rubber Co Ltd v Burden (No. 2)* [1972] 1 WLR 602, [1972] 1 All ER 1210, p. 219, ante, and *Boardman v Phipps* [1967] 2 AC 46, [1966] 3 All ER 721, p. 600, post, cases on constructive trusts?

[2] *Beatty v Guggenheim Exploration Co* (1919) 225 NY 380 at 386.

3. Do you think that the recent developments in the law of constructive trusts as shown by the material in section G are to be encouraged? Could justice otherwise be done? (1973) CLP 17 (A. J. Oakley); (1977) 28 NILQ 123 (R. H. Maudsley).

9. Non-Charitable Purpose Trusts[1]

I. General Principles

The orthodox view is that a private trust can only exist if the trustees hold the trust property on trust for ascertainable individuals—or for such as will be ascertained during the period of perpetuity[2]. Various reasons are given. The beneficial interest must be vested in somebody within the period of perpetuity. The court must be able to enforce a trust, and there must therefore be ascertainable persons in whose favour the court can decree performance. A trust is obligatory; and there cannot be an obligation unless there is a corresponding right. And, of course, a purpose must be sufficiently certain. "Benevolent" or "patriotic" or "public" purposes are too vague. None of these reasons applies of course to charitable trusts. Charitable trusts are a special type of purpose trust[3], one which is of special importance to society, and one which is therefore given special privileges in terms of perpetuity, taxation and enforcement. The Attorney-General is charged with the duty of enforcement of charitable trusts.

The reasons given for disallowing non-charitable purpose trusts can all be challenged[4]. Supporters of such trusts point out that enforcement should be no problem; for in every case which has been litigated, the trustees have been willing to perform. Those entitled in default could complain in a case of misapplication. If a question of enforcement should arise, this is no more of a problem than the enforcement of charitable trusts; if it is a matter of social importance to enforce a particular purpose trust, an officer or Department of State could be instructed to undertake it. Further, the requirement of ascertainable beneficiaries is a rule of *private* trusts in favour of *beneficiaries*. That rule should not be relevant to a purpose trust. If it is insisted that, charitable trusts always excepted, a trust *must* have a beneficiary who can enforce the trust, then purpose trusts could

[1] H & M, pp. 346–365; K & S, pp. 133–141; P & M, pp. 161–167; Pettit, pp. 38–43; Snell, pp. 99–100; Morris and Leach, *Rule Against Perpetuities* (2nd Edn, 1962), Ch 12; (1953) 17 Conv (NS) 46 (L. A. Sheridan); (1953) 6 CLP 151 (O. R. Marshall); (1958) 4 University of Western Australia LR 235 (L. A. Sheridan); (1970) 34 Conv (NS) 77 (P. A. Lovell); (1971) 87 LQR 31 (J. W. Harris); (1973) 37 Conv (NS) 420 (L. McKay).

[2] *Re Flavel's Will Trusts* [1969] 1 WLR 444, especially pp. 446–447.

[3] See Part II, pp. 273 at seq., post.

[4] See Morris and Leach, op. cit., p. 307, note 1; H & M, pp. 348–351; (1977) 40 MLR 397 (N. P. Gravells).

be treated as powers[5]. It is not asking very much to suggest that a disposition which calls itself a trust but fails to provide persons capable of enforcing the obligation should be treated as a power. To say that trustees cannot be *compelled* to perform, is not to say that they *must not* perform[6].

Some cases at first instance have upheld non-charitable purpose trusts. The modern trend however is to declare them void; and the court will not extend the confines of existing decisions. Even those have been described by HARMAN LJ as "troublesome, anomalous and aberrant"[7]. We will consider in Section VII the ways in which it is possible to achieve a non-charitable purpose without setting up a trust.

In *Morice v Bishop of Durham* ((1804) 9 Ves 399, affd. (1805) 10 Ves 522) there was a bequest to the Bishop upon trust for "such objects of benevolence and liberality as the Bishop of Durham in his own discretion shall most approve of". This was held not to be a charitable trust. As there were no ascertainable beneficiaries the trust failed. Sir William GRANT MR said (at p. 404): "The only question is whether the Trust, upon which the residue of the personal Estate is bequeathed, be a trust for charitable purposes. That it is upon some trust, and not for the personal benefit of the Bishop is clear from the words of the Will; and is admitted by his Lordship; who expressly disclaims any beneficial interest. That it is a Trust, unless it be of a charitable nature, too indefinite to be executed by this Court, has not been, and cannot be denied. There can be no Trust over the exercise of which this Court will not assume a control; for an uncontrollable power of disposition would be Ownership, and not Trust. If there be a clear Trust, but for uncertain objects, the property, that is the subject of the trust, is undisposed of, and the benefit of such Trust must result to those, to whom the Law gives Ownership in default of disposition by the former owner. But this doctrine does not hold good with regard to Trusts for Charity. Every other Trust must have a definite object. There must be somebody, in whose favour the Court can decree performance."

It must not however be assumed that it is always a simple matter to *classify* a trust as being a trust for persons, or a trust for purposes. The problem has been seen in the earlier discussion[8] of unincorporated associations. A gift of property to an unincorporated association raises the question of the identification of the beneficial ownership. We saw that such a gift may be construed as a gift to the present members beneficially, or to those persons who may be members at any particular time; and that the claim of each member may be based upon the contractual rights controlling his membership, or upon rights arising under trusts on which the property

[5] Ames, *Lectures on Legal History*, p. 285; Morris and Leach, op. cit., pp. 319–321.

[6] Scott, *Trusts* (3rd Edn) §§. 123, 124. *IRC v Broadway Cottages Trust* [1955] Ch 20, [1954] 3 All ER 120, is Court of Appeal authority against this view.

[7] *Re Endacott* [1960] Ch 232 at 251, [1959] 3 All ER 562 at 571; *Re Wood* [1949] Ch 498, [1949] 1 All ER 1100 (The Week's Good Cause).

[8] See p. 61, ante.

is held. If the rights are based upon a trust, there are, as we have seen, problems relating to the nature of the ownership among the members; whether each one can sever and claim his share[9], and problems of perpetuity. The real problem arises however where the gift cannot be construed as one to which the members are entitled; as where the gift was not intended to be for their personal benefit[10], or where there is no list kept of the members; or, more especially, where the object of the association is the promotion of a purpose, as opposed to the benefit of the members. Then the problem is the same as that of an express trust for purposes. "It is at this point that the cases on gifts to unincorporated associations become relevant to the question whether there can be a trust without a *cestui que trust*. It would certainly seem strange if a testator could give property to an unincorporated anti-vivisection society to be applied for its purposes, but could not give property to an individual trustee to be applied by him for the purpose of anti-vivisection."[11] But a gift to an anti-vivisection society may be construed as a gift to its members[12]. And a gift which is to benefit specified persons by the use of property in a particular manner may be construed as a trust for those persons and not a trust for purposes[13]. This question is discussed in Section IV. The non-charitable purpose trust will first be examined.

II. Anomalous Cases of Purpose Trusts being Enforced

Most of the successful purpose trusts in England have been concerned with the care of particular animals[14], and a few for the erection or maintenance of tombs or monuments[15].

RE DEAN
(1889) 41 ChD 552 (ChD, NORTH J)

A testator charged his freehold estates with the payment of £750 per annum to his trustees for the period of fifty years if any of his horses and hounds should so long live, and declared that the trustees should apply the money in the maintenance of his horses and hounds; but without imposing upon them any obligation to render any account.

Held. This was a valid non-charitable trust, although there was no one who could enforce it.

[9] See p. 61, ante. *Neville Estates Ltd v Madden* [1962] Ch 832, [1961] 3 All ER 769.
[10] *Leahy v A-G of New South Wales* [1959] AC 457, [1959] 2 All ER 300; p. 63, ante; *Re Smith* [1914] 1 Ch 937.
[11] Morris and Leach, op. cit., p. 317.
[12] *Re Recher's Will Trusts* [1971] WLR 321, [1971] 3 All ER 401, p. 71, ante.
[13] *Re Denley's Trust Deed* [1969] 1 Ch 373, [1968] 3 All ER 65 (recreation ground for benefit of employees); (1968) ASCL 437 (J. D. Davies); (1969) 32 MLR 96 (J. M. Evans); (1970) 34 Conv (NS) 77 (P. A. Lowell); *Re Lipinski's Will Trusts* [1976] Ch 235, [1977] 1 All ER 33 (buildings for Jewish Association for benefit of members); (1977) 93 LQR 167, p. 256, post.
[14] *Pettingall v Pettingall* (1842) LJ Ch 176; *Re Dean* (1889) 41 ChD 552; *Re Haines* (1952) Times, 7th November. See also *Re Thompson* [1934] Ch 342, p. 247, post.
[15] *Trimmer v Danby* (1856) 25 LJ Ch 424, p. 247, post; *Musset v Bingle* [1876] WN 170, p. 247, post; *Pirbright v Salwey* [1896] WN 86; *Re Hooper* [1932] 1 Ch 38, p. 246, post.

NORTH J: The first question is as to the validity of the provision made by the testator in favour of his horses and dogs. It is said that it is not valid; because (for this is the principal ground upon which it is put) neither a horse nor a dog could enforce the trust; and there is no person who could enforce it. It is obviously not a charity, because it is intended for the benefit of the particular animals mentioned and not for the benefit of animals generally, and it is quite distinguishable from the gift made in a subsequent part of the will to the *Royal Society for the Prevention of Cruelty to Animals,* which may well be a charity. In my opinion this provision for the particular horses and hounds referred to in the will is not, in any sense, a charity, . . .

Then it is said, that there is no *cestui que trust* who can enforce the trust, and that the Court will not recognise a trust unless it is capable of being enforced by some one. I do not assent to that view. There is not the least doubt that a man may if he pleases, give a legacy to trustees, upon trust to apply it in erecting a monument to himself, either in a church or in a churchyard, or even in unconsecrated ground, and I am not aware that such a trust is in any way invalid, although it is difficult to say who would be the *cestui que trust* of the monument. In the same way I know of nothing to prevent a gift of a sum of money to trustees, upon trust to apply it for the repair of such a monument. In my opinion such a trust would be good, although the testator must be careful to limit the time for which it is to last, because, as it is not a charitable trust, unless it is to come to an end within the limits fixed by the rule against perpetuities, it would be illegal. But a trust to lay out a certain sum in building a monument, and the gift of another sum in trust to apply the same to keeping that monument in repair, say, for ten years, is in my opinion, a perfectly good trust, although I do not see who could ask the Court to enforce it. If persons beneficially interested in the estate could do so, then the present Plaintiff can do so; but, if such persons could not enforce the trust, still it cannot be said that the trust must fail because there is no one who can actively enforce it.

Is there then anything illegal or obnoxious to the law in the nature of the provision, that is, in the fact that it is not for human beings, but for horses and dogs? It is clearly settled by authority that a charity may be established for the benefit of horses and dogs, and, therefore, the making of a provision for horses and dogs, which is not a charity, cannot of itself be obnoxious to the law, provided, of course, that it is not to last for too long a period. Then there is what I consider an express authority upon this point in *Mitford v Reynolds* ((1848) 16 Sim 105). . . .

RE HOOPER

[1932] 1 Ch 38 (ChD, MAUGHAM J)

A testator gave a sum of money to trustees for the care and upkeep of certain family graves and monuments, and a tablet and a window in a church for "so far as [the trustees] legally can do so". The question was whether the gift was valid.

Held. The trust for the upkeep of the graves and monuments, not being charitable, was valid for 21 years.

MAUGHAM J: This point is one to my mind of doubt, and I should have felt some difficulty in deciding it if it were not for *Pirbright v Salwey* ([1896] WN 86) a decision of Stirling J, which unfortunately is reported, as far as I know, only in the Weekly Notes. The report is as follows: "A testator, after expressing his wish to be buried in the inclosure in which his child lay in the churchyard of E., bequeathed to the rector and churchwardens for the time being of the parish church 800*l*. Consols, to be invested in their joint names, the interest and dividends to be derived therefrom to be applied, so long as the law for the time being permitted, in keeping up the inclosure and decorating the same with flowers: *Held*, that the gift was valid for at least a period of 21 years from the testator's death, and *semble* that it was not charitable."

That was a decision arrived at by Stirling J, after argument by very eminent counsel. The case does not appear to have attracted much attention in text-books, but it does not appear to have been commented upon adversely, and I shall follow it.

The trustees here have the sum of 1000*l*. which they have to hold upon trust to "invest the same and to the intent that so far as they legally can do so and in any manner that they may in their discretion arrange they will out of the annual income thereof" do substantially four things: first, provide for the care and upkeep of the grave and monument in the Torquay cemetery; secondly, for the care and upkeep of a vault and monument there in which lie the remains of the testator's wife and daughter; thirdly, for the care and upkeep of a grave and monument in Shotley churchyard near Ipswich, where the testator's son lies buried; and, fourthly, for the care and upkeep of the tablet in Saint Matthias' Church at Ilsham to the memories of the testator's wife and children and the window in the same church to the memory of his late father. All those four things have to be done expressly according to an arrangement made in the discretion of the trustees and so far as they legally can do so. I do not think that is distinguishable from the phrase "so long as the law for the time being permits," and the conclusion at which I arrive, following the decision I have mentioned, is that this trust is valid for a period of twenty-one years from the testator's death so far as regards the three matters which involve the upkeep of graves or vaults or monuments in the churchyard or in the cemetery. As regards the tablet in St. Matthias' Church and the window in the same church there is no question but that that is a good charitable gift, and, therefore, the rule against perpetuities does not apply.

Something has been said with regard to apportionment. To my mind there is no room for a legal apportionment, because it is left to the discretion of the trustees to arrange how much they will out of this income apply during the twenty-one years to the four objects in question. At the end of the twenty-one years any part which is not applied for the upkeep of the tablet and the window in St. Matthias' Church will, of course, be undisposed of and will fall, unless some other event happens, into residue.

In *Trimmer v Danby* ((1856) 25 LJ Ch 424) the testator gave £1,000 to his executors, "and I do direct them to lay out and expend the same to erect a monument to my memory in St. Paul's Cathedral, among those of my brothers in art." The bequest was upheld by KINDERSLEY V-C, who said (at p. 427): "I do not suppose that there would be anyone who could compel the executors to carry out this bequest and raise the monument; but if the residuary legatees or the trustees insist upon the trust being executed, my opinion is that this Court is bound to see it carried out. I think, therefore, that as the trustees insist upon the sum of 1000*l*. being laid out according to the directions in the will, that sum must be set apart for the purpose."

In *Mussett v Bingle* ([1876] WN 170) the testator gave £300 to be applied in the erection of a monument to his wife's first husband, and £200 the interest of which was to be applied in keeping up the monument. It was admitted that the latter direction was void for perpetuity. The former was upheld; Hall V-C saying that the direction was one which the executors "were ready to perform, and it must be performed accordingly".

PARISH COUNCILS AND BURIAL AUTHORITIES (MISCELLANEOUS PROVISIONS) ACT 1970

1. Maintenance of private graves.—(1) A burial authority or a local authority may agree with any person in consideration of the payment of a sum by him, to maintain—

(*a*) a grave, vault, tombstone, or other memorial in a burial ground or crematorium provided or maintained by the authority;

(*b*) a monument or other memorial to any person situated in any place within the area of the authority to which the authority have a right of access;

so, however, that no agreement . . . made under this subsection by any authority with respect to a particular grave, vault, tombstone, monument or other memorial may impose on the authority an obligation with respect to maintenance for a period exceeding 99 years from the date of that agreement.

In *Re Thompson* ([1934] Ch 342) the testator, an alumnus of Trinity Hall, Cambridge, gave a legacy of £1,000 to a friend George William Lloyd, to be applied by him towards the promotion and furthering of fox-hunting. Trinity Hall was the residuary legatee. Both parties desired to carry out the testator's wishes, so far as they could legally do so, but Trinity Hall felt obligated, as a charity, to make objections to the enforcement of the trust. CLAUSON J upheld the gift; "following the example of Knight Bruce V-C in *Pettingall v Pettingall* (1842) 11 LJ Ch 176, to order that, upon the defendant Mr. Lloyd giving an undertaking (which I understand he is willing to give) to apply the legacy when received by him towards the object expressed in the testator's will, the plaintiffs do pay to the defendant Mr. Lloyd the legacy of 1000*l*.; and that, in case the legacy should be applied by him otherwise than towards the promotion and furthering of fox-hunting, the residuary legatees are to be at liberty to apply".

III. The Requirement of Ascertainable Beneficiaries

RE ASTOR'S SETTLEMENT TRUSTS[16]

[1952] Ch 534, [1952 1 All ER 1067 (ChD, ROXBURGH J)

An *inter vivos* settlement was made in 1945, expressly limited to the perpetuity period, under which substantially all the issued shares in The Observer Ltd were held by the trustees upon trust for various non-charitable purposes; which included, among others, 1. The maintenance . . . of good understanding sympathy and co-operation between nations. 2. The preservation of the independence and integrity of newspapers. 4. The control publication . . . financing or management of any newspapers periodicals books pamphlets or publications. 5. The protection of newspapers . . . from being absorbed . . . by combines or being tied by finance or otherwise to special . . . views . . . inconsistent with the highest integrity and independence. It was conceded that the trusts were not charitable.

Held. The trusts were invalid; because (i) they were non-charitable purpose trusts which no-one could enforce; (ii) the trusts included objects which were too uncertain.

ROXBURGH J: The question upon which I am giving this reserved judgment is whether the non-charitable trusts of income during "the specified period" declared by clause 5 and the third schedule of the settlement of 1945 are void. Mr. Jennings and Mr. Buckley have submitted that they are void on two grounds: (1) that they are not trusts for the benefit of individuals; (2) that they are void for uncertainty.

Lord Parker considered the first of these two questions in his speech in *Bowman v Secular Society Ltd* ([1917] AC 406) and I will cite two important passages. The first is (at p. 437): "The question whether a trust be legal or illegal or be in accordance with or contrary to the policy of the law, only arises when it has been determined that a trust has been created, and is then only part of the larger question whether the trust is enforceable. For, as will presently appear, trusts may be unenforceable and therefore void, not only because they are illegal or contrary to the policy of the law, but for other reasons." The second is (at p. 441): "A trust to be valid must be for the benefit of individuals, which this is certainly not, or must be in that class of gifts for the benefit of the public which the courts in this country recognize as charitable in the legal as opposed to the popular sense of that term."

Commenting on those passages Mr. Gray observed that *Bowman v Secular Society Ltd* arose out of a will and he asked me to hold that Lord Parker intended them to be confined to cases arising under a will. But they were,

[16] (1952) 68 LQR 449 (R.E.M.); (1953) 6 CLP 151 (O. R. Marshall); (1953) 17 Conv (NS) 46 (L. A. Sheridan); (1955) 18 MLR 120 (L. H. Leigh).

I think, intended to be quite general in character. Further, Mr. Gray pointed out that Lord Parker made no mention of the exceptions or apparent exceptions which undoubtedly exist, and from this he asked me to infer that no such general principle can be laid down. The question is whether those cases are to be regarded as exceptional and anomalous or whether they are destructive of the supposed principle. I must later analyse them. But I will first consider whether Lord Parker's propositions can be attacked from a base of principle.

The typical case of a trust is one in which the legal owner of property is constrained by a court of equity so to deal with it as to give effect to the equitable rights of another. These equitable rights have been hammered out in the process of litigation in which a claimant on equitable grounds has successfully asserted rights against a legal owner or other person in control of property. Prima facie, therefore, a trustee would not be expected to be subject to an equitable obligation unless there was somebody who could enforce a correlative equitable right, and the nature and extent of that obligation would be worked out in proceedings for enforcement. This is what I understand by Lord Parker's first proposition. At an early stage, however, the courts were confronted with attempts to create trusts for charitable purposes which there was no equitable owner to enforce. Lord Eldon explained in *A-G v Brown* ((1818) 1 Swan 265 at 290) how this difficulty was dealt with: "It is the duty of a court of equity, a main part, originally almost the whole, of its jurisdiction, to administer trusts; to protect not the visible owner, who alone can proceed at law, but the individual equitably, though not legally, entitled. From this principle has arisen the practice of administering the trust of a public charity: persons possessed of funds appropriate to such purposes are within the general rule; but no one being entitled by an immediate and peculiar interest to prefer a complaint, who is to compel the performance of their obligations, and to enforce their responsibility? It is the duty of the King, as parens patriae, to protect property devoted to charitable uses; and that duty is executed by the officer who represents the Crown for all forensic purposes. On this foundation rests the right of the Attorney-General in such cases to obtain by information the interposition of a court of equity. . . ." But if the purposes are not charitable, great difficulties arise both in theory and in practice. In theory, because having regard to the historical origins of equity it is difficult to visualize the growth of equitable obligations which nobody can enforce, and in practice, because it is not possible to contemplate with equanimity the creation of large funds devoted to non-charitable purposes which no court and no department of state can control, or in the case of maladministration reform. Therefore, Lord Parker's second proposition would prima facie appear to be well founded. Moreover, it gains no little support from the practical considerations that no officer has ever been constituted to take, in the case of non-charitable purposes, the position held by the Attorney-General in connexion with charitable purposes, and no case has been found in the reports in which the court has ever directly enforced a non-charitable purpose against a trustee. Indeed where, as in the present case, the only beneficiaries are purposes and an at present unascertainable person, it is difficult to see who could initiate such proceedings. If the purposes are valid trusts, the settlors have retained no beneficial interest and could not initiate them. It was suggested that the trustees might proceed ex parte to enforce the trusts against themselves. I doubt that, but at any rate nobody could enforce the trusts against them. This point, in my judgment, is of importance, because in most of the cases which are put forward to disprove Lord Parker's propositions the court had indirect means of enforcing the execution of the non-charitable purpose.

These cases I must now consider. First of all, there is a group relating to horses, dogs, graves and monuments, among which I was referred to *Pettingall v Pettingall* ((1842) 11 LJ Ch 176), *Mitford v Reynolds* ((1848) 16 Sim 105), *Re Dean* ((1889) 41 ChD 552), *Pirbright v Salwey* ([1896] WN 86); and *Re Hooper* ([1931] 1 Ch 38).

[His Lordship examined these cases, and also *Re Thompson* [1934] Ch 342, and *Re Price* [1943] Ch 422, [1943] 2 All ER 505, and continued]

Let me then sum up the position so far. On the one side there are Lord Parker's two propositions with which I began. These were not new, but merely re-echoed what Sir William Grant had said as Master of the Rolls in *Morice v The Bishop of Durham* ((1804) 9 Ves 399 at 405) as long ago as 1804: "There must be somebody, in whose favour the court can decree performance." The position was recently restated by Harman J in *Re Wood* ([1949] Ch 498 at 501). "A gift on trust must have a cestui que trust", and this seems to be in accord with principle. On the other side is a group of cases relating to horses and dogs, graves and monuments—matters arising under wills and intimately connected with the deceased—in which the courts have found means of escape from these general propositions and also *Re Thompson* ([1934] Ch 342) and *Re Price* ([1943] Ch 422, [1943] 2 All ER 505) which I have endeavoured to explain. *Re Price* belongs to another field. The rest may, I think, properly be regarded as anomalous and exceptional and in no way destructive of the proposition which traces descent from or through Sir William Grant through Lord Parker to Harman J. Perhaps the late Sir Arthur Underhill was right in suggesting that they may be concessions to human weakness or sentiment (see Law of Trusts, 8th Ed, p. 79). They cannot, in my judgment, of themselves (and no other justification has been suggested to me) justify the conclusion that a Court of Equity will recognize as an equitable obligation affecting the income of large funds in the hands of trustees a direction to apply it in furtherance of enumerated non-charitable purposes in a manner which no court or department can control or enforce. I hold that the trusts here in question are void on the first of the grounds submitted by Mr. Jennings and Mr. Buckley.

The second ground upon which the relevant trusts are challenged is uncertainty. If (contrary to my view) an enumeration of purposes outside the realm of charities can take the place of an enumeration of beneficiaries, the purposes must, in my judgment, be stated in phrases which embody definite concepts and the means by which the trustees are to try to attain them must also be prescribed with a sufficient degree of certainty. The test to be applied is stated by Lord Eldon in *Morice v Bishop of Durham* ((1805) 10 Ves 522) as follows (at p. 539): "As it is a maxim, that the execution of a trust shall be under the control of the court, it must be of such a nature, that it can be under that control; so that the administration of it can be reviewed by the court; or, if the trustee dies, the court itself can execute the trust: a trust therefore, which, in case of mal-administration could be reformed; and a due administration directed; and then, unless the subject and the objects can be ascertained, upon principles, familiar in other cases, it must be decided, that the court can neither reform mal-administration, nor direct a due administration." See also *Re Macduff* ([1896] 2 Ch 451 at 463).

Mr. Gray argued that this test was not properly applicable to trusts declared by deed, but I can see no distinction between a will and a deed in this respect.

Applying this test, I find many uncertain phrases in the enumeration of purposes, for example, "different sections of people in any nation or community" in paragraph 1 of the third schedule, "constructive policies" in paragraph 2, "integrity of the press" in paragraph 3, "combines" in paragraph 5, "the restoration . . . of the independence of . . . writers in newspapers" in paragraph 6, and "benevolent schemes" in paragraph 7. Mr. Gray suggested that in view of the unlimited discretion bestowed upon the trustees (subject only to directions from the settlors) the trustees would be justified in excluding from their purview purposes indicated by the settlors but insufficiently defined by them. But I cannot accept this argument. The purposes must be so defined that if the trustees surrendered their discretion, the court could carry out the purposes declared, not a selection of them arrived at by eliminating those which are too uncertain to be carried out. If, for example, I were to eliminate all the purposes except those declared in paragraph 4, but to decree that those declared in paragraph 4 ought to be performed, should I be executing the trusts of this settlement?

But how in any case could I decree in what manner the trusts applicable to income were to be performed? The settlement gives no guidance at all. Mr. Hunt suggested that the trustees might apply to the court ex parte for a scheme. It is not, I think, a mere coincidence that no case has been found outside the realm of charity in which the court has yet devised a scheme of ways and means for attaining enumerated trust purposes. If it were to assume this (as I think) novel jurisdiction over public but not charitable trusts it would, I believe, necessarily require the assistance of a custodian of the public interest analogous to the Attorney-General in charity cases, who would not only help to formulate schemes but could be charged with the duty of enforcing them and preventing maladministration. There is no such person. Accordingly, in my judgment, the trusts for the application of income during "the specified period" are also void for uncertainty.

But while I have reached my decision on two separate grounds, both, I think, have their origin in a single principle, namely, that a court of equity does not recognize as valid a trust which it cannot both enforce and control. This seems to me to be good equity and good sense.

I dealt at the hearing with the trusts for accumulation and the trusts to take effect at the end of "the specified period", and the order will be drawn up accordingly.

RE ENDACOTT

[1960] Ch 232, [1959] 3 All ER 562 (CA, Lord Evershed MR, Sellers and Harman LJJ)

The testator gave his residuary estate "to North Tawton Devon Parish Council for the purpose of providing some useful memorial to myself . . ." The value of the residuary estate was approximately £20,000. The question was whether the gift was valid.

Held. The gift, not being beneficial to the Council, nor to the inhabitants, and not being charitable, was void.

Lord Evershed MR [Having held that the language of the will showed an intention to impose a trust; and that the trust was not charitable]:

I now turn to Mr. Arnold's alternative argument based on the view that there is here a trust and a trust of a public character, but not a charitable trust. What he says is, that the trust is in line with the trusts which were rendered effective in those cases which I have called "anomalous", and many of which are referred to in Roxburgh J's decision, beginning with *Pettingall v Pettingall* ((1842) 11 LJ Ch 176). I include in that list cases such as the three to which we have had our attention particularly drawn today. The argument is that assuming the non-charitable but public nature of this trust, still it is of a character which the court can efficiently, and will, enforce. It must be said that these cases are of a somewhat anomalous kind. They are classified in the recent book written by Mr. J. H. C. Morris and Professor Barton Leach, The Rule Against Perpetuities (1956) (p. 298). "We proceed", say the authors, "to examine these 'anomalous' exceptions. It will be found that they fall into the following groups: (1) trusts for the erection or maintenance of monuments or graves; (2) trusts for the saying of masses, in jurisdictions where such trusts are not regarded as charitable; (3) trusts for the maintenance of particular animals; (4) trusts for the benefit of unincorporated associations (though this group is more doubtful); (5) miscellaneous cases." I am prepared to accept, for the purposes of the argument, that it does not matter that the trusts here are attached to residue and not to a legacy; that is to say, it does not matter that the persons who would come to the court and either complain if the trusts were not being carried out, or claim the money on the footing that they had not been carried out, are next-of-kin rather than residuary legatees. Still, in my judgment, the scope of these cases . . . ought not to be extended. So to do would be to validate almost limitless heads of non-charitable trusts, even though they were not (strictly speaking) public trusts, so long only as the question of perpetuities did not arise; and, in my judgment, that result would be out of harmony with the principles of our law. No principle perhaps has greater sanction of authority behind it than the general proposition that a trust by English law, not being a charitable trust, in order to be effective, must have ascertained or ascertainable beneficiaries. These cases constitute an exception to that general rule. The general rule, having such authority as that of Lord Eldon, Lord Parker and my predecessor, Lord Greene MR, behind it, was most recently referred to in the Privy Council in *Leahy v A-G for New South Wales* ([1959] AC 457, [1959] 2 All ER 300). I add also that, in my judgment, the proposition stated in Mr. Morris and Professor Barton Leach's book (p. 308) that if these trusts should fail as trusts they may survive as powers, is not one which I think can be treated as accepted in English law.

I therefore, so far as this case is concerned, conclude (having already stated my view of the meaning of the words) that, though this trust is specific, in the sense that it indicates a purpose capable of expression, yet it is of far too wide and uncertain a nature to qualify within the class of cases cited. It would go far beyond any fair analogy to any of those decisions.

HARMAN LJ: I cannot think that charity has anything to do with this bequest. As for establishing it without the crutch of charity, I applaud the orthodox sentiments expressed by Roxburgh J in the *Astor* case ([1952] Ch 534, [1952] 1 All ER 1067), and I think, as I think he did, that though one knows there have been decisions at times which are not really to be satisfactorily classified, but are perhaps merely occasions when Homer has nodded, at any rate these cases stand by themselves and ought not to be increased in number, nor indeed followed, except where the one is exactly like another. Whether it would be better that some authority now should say those cases were wrong, this perhaps is not the moment to consider. At any rate, I cannot think a case of this kind, the case of providing outside a church an unspecified and unidentified memorial, is the kind of instance which should be allowed to add to those troublesome, anomalous and aberrant cases.

In my judgment, Danckwerts J came to the right conclusion, and this appeal ought to be dismissed.

In *Re Shaw* ([1957] 1 WLR 729, [1957] 1 All ER 745) the question arose as to the validity of a residuary gift under the will of George Bernard Shaw, which provided that the residue of his estate should be applied towards the institution of a 40-letter alphabet in the place of the present 26-letter alphabet. HARMAN J decided that the trusts were not charitable; nor could they be enforced as purpose trusts or as powers[17].

By way of background, HARMAN J said: "All his long life Bernard Shaw was an indefatigable reformer. He was already well known when the present century dawned, as novelist, critic, pamphleteer, playwright, and during the ensuing half-century he continued to act as a kind of itching powder to the British public, to the English-speaking peoples, and, indeed to an even wider audience, castigating their follies, their foibles and their fallacies, and bombarding them with a combination of paradox and wit that earned him in the course of years the status of an oracle: the Shavian oracle; and the rare distinction of adding a word to the language. Many of his projects he lived to see gain acceptance and carried into effect and become normal. It was natural that he should be interested in English orthography and pronunciation. These are obvious targets for the reformer. It is as difficult for the native to defend the one as it is for the foreigner

[17] Mrs. Shaw's will was held to be valid, p. 300, post.

to compass the other. The evidence shows that Shaw had for many years been interested in the subject. Perhaps his best known excursion in this field is 'Pygmalion', in which the protagonist is a professor of phonetics: this was produced as a play in 1914 and has held the stage ever since and invaded the world of the film. It is, indeed, a curious reflection that this same work, tagged with versicles which I suppose Shaw would have detested, and tricked out with music which he would have eschewed (see the preface to the 'Admirable Bashville'), is now charming huge audiences on the other side of the Atlantic and has given birth to the present proceedings. I am told that the receipts from this source have enabled the executor to get on terms with the existing death duties payable on the estate, thus bringing the interpretation of the will into the realm of practical politics.

The testator, whatever his other qualifications, was the master of a pellucid style, and the reader embarks on his will confident of finding no difficulty in understanding the objects which the testator had in mind. This document, moreover, was evidently originally the work of a skilled equity draftsman. As such I doubt not it was easily to be understood if not of the vulgar at any rate by the initiate. Unfortunately the will bears ample internal evidence of being in part the testator's own work. The two styles, as ever, make an unfortunate mixture. It is always a marriage of incompatibles: the delicate testamentary machinery devised by the conveyancer can but suffer when subjected to the cacoethes scribendi of the author, even though the latter's language, if it stood alone, might be a literary masterpiece."

[And on purpose trusts:] "The principle has been recently restated by Roxburgh J in *Re Astor Settlement Trusts* ([1952] Ch 534, [1952] 1 All ER 1067) where the authorities are elaborately reviewed. An object cannot complain to the court, which therefore cannot control the trust, and, therefore, will not allow it to continue. I must confess that I feel some reluctance to come to this conclusion. I agree at once that, if the persons to take in remainder are unascertainable, the court is deprived of any means of controlling such a trust, but if, as here, the persons taking the ultimate residue are ascertained, I do not feel the force of this objection. They are entitled to the estate except in so far as it has been devoted to the indicated purposes, and in so far as it is not devoted to those purposes, the money being spent is the money of the residuary legatees of the ultimate remaindermen, and they can come to the court and sue the executor for a devastavit, or the trustee for a breach of trust, and thus, though not themselves interested in the purposes, enable the court indirectly to control them. This line of reasoning is not, I think, open to me. See, for instance, the statement by Lord Greene MR in *Re Diplock* ([1941] Ch 253 at 259). 'Those principles,' he says, dealing with uncertainty, 'I apprehend are really nothing more than the application of a fundamental principle of the law relating to trusts. In order that a trust may be properly constituted, there must be a beneficiary. The beneficiary must be ascertained or must be ascertainable. In the case of what I may call impersonal trusts, such as a gift to charitable purposes, or to benevolent purposes, there is no class of beneficiary which can be defined in the same sense as a class of beneficiaries such as a class of relatives. In the latter case, although no particular person in the class may be able to say that at any given moment he is entitled to anything out of the trust, the class as a whole can enforce the trust. Now in the case of charitable trusts in which no defined class is specified, nevertheless owing to the particular principles which have come to be applied to charitable gifts, the courts have not treated the trust as failing for that reason. There is a very good ground for that, namely that the Crown, as parens patriae taking all charities under its protection, is in a position to enforce the trust; and therefore, although there may be no specified charitable beneficiary who can come to the court and insist on having the trust performed, nevertheless the Attorney-General can appear and is entitled to insist on the trust being carried out, if necessary, by a scheme cy près. But that exception to the general rule, that there must be beneficiaries ascertained or ascertainable—if I may call it an exception—does not extend beyond what falls within the legal class of charity. It does not extend to other public spirited purposes.' The same view is taken in the judgment of Jenkins LJ in *IRC v Broadway Cottages Trust* ([1955] Ch 20, [1954] 3 All ER 120).

I should have wished to regard this bequest as a gift to the ultimate residuary legatees subject to a condition by which they cannot complain of income during the first 21 years after the testator's death being devoted to the alphabet project. This apparently might be the way in which the matter would be viewed in the United States, for I find in Morris and Leach's work on the Rule against Perpetuities (1956), at p. 308, the following passage quoted from the American Law Institute's Restatement of Trusts[18]. 'Where the owner of property transfers it upon an intended trust for a specific non-charitable purpose, and there is no definite or definitely ascertainable beneficiary designated, no trust is created; but the transferee has power to apply the property to the designated purpose, unless he is authorized so to apply the property beyond the period of the rule against perpetuities, or the purpose is capricious'. As the authors point out, this is to treat a trust of this sort as a power, for clearly there is no one who can directly enforce the trust, and if the trustees choose to pay the whole moneys to the residuary legatees, no one can complain. All that can be done is to control the trustees indirectly in the exercise of their power. In my judgment, I am not at liberty to validate this trust, by treating it as a power. (See per Jenkins LJ in *Sunnylands* case above ([1955] Ch at 36, [1954] 3 All ER at 128). 'We do not think that a valid power is to be spelt out of an invalid trust'. This also was the view of the learned author of Gray on Perpetuities (4th edn), the leading work on the subject (See Appendix H), and I feel bound to accept it).

The result is that the alphabet trusts are, in my judgment, invalid, and must fail. It seems that their begotter suspected as much, hence his jibe about failure by judicial decision. I answer that it is not the fault of the law, but of the testator, who failed almost for the first time in his life to grasp the legal problem or to make up his mind what he wanted."[19]

[18] 1st Edn. For 2nd Edn. § 124, see p. 266, post.

[19] "It is understood that the case was compromised on appeal and that the alphabet trusts are being carried out; see [1958] 1 All ER 245." Morris and Leach, op. cit., p. 310. See (1957) 73 LR 305 (R.E.M.).

IV. Trusts for Persons or Purposes

A gift which is to benefit specified persons by the use of property in a particular manner may be construed as a trust for persons and not for purposes.

RE LIPINSKI'S WILL TRUSTS[20]

[1976] Ch 235, [1977] 1 All ER 33 (Ch D, OLIVER J)

In 1967 the testator bequeathed his residuary estate to trustees on trust as to one half for the Hull Judeans (Maccabi) Association "in memory of my late wife to be used solely in the work of constructing the new buildings for the association and/or improvements to the said buildings". The objects of the Association included "(a) To promote the interest, and the active participation of Anglo-Jewish youth, of both sexes, in amateur sports, in all forms of cultural, and in non-political, communal activities. (b) To inculcate within its ranks a team spirit, a conception of fair play, good citizenship and self-discipline. . . . (d) To promote and foster the interest to cultivate a knowledge of Jewish history, of the Hebrew language and national traditions". On a summons to determine the effect of the trust.

Held. It was valid. It was a trust for the members of the Association, who were ascertained or ascertainable.

OLIVER J: I approach question 1 of the summons, therefore, on the footing that this is a gift to an unincorporated non-charitable association. Such a gift, if it is an absolute and beneficial one, is of course perfectly good: see, for instance, the gift to the Corps of Commissionaires in *Re Clarke* [1901] 2 Ch 110. What I have to consider, however, is the effect of the specification by the testator of the purposes for which the legacy was to be applied.

The principles applicable to this type of case were stated by Cross J in *Neville Estates Ltd v Madden* [1962] Ch 832 at 849 [see p. 68, ante], and they are conveniently summarised in *Tudor, Charities*, 6th Edn (1967), p. 150, where it is said:

> "In *Neville Estates Ltd v Madden* Cross J expressed the opinion (which is respectfully accepted as correct) that every such gift might, according to the actual words used, be construed in one of three quite different ways: (*a*) As a gift to the members of the association at the date of the gift as joint tenants so that any member could sever his share and claim it whether or not he continued to be a member. (*b*) As a gift to the members of the association at the date of the gift not as joint tenants, but subject to their contractual rights and liabilities towards one another as members of the association. In such a case a member cannot sever his share. It will accrue to the other members on his death or resignation, even though such members include persons who become members after the gift took effect. If this is the effect of the gift, it will not be open to objection on the score of perpetuity or uncertainty unless there is something in its terms or circumstances or in the rules

[20] (1977) 93 LQR 167; (1977) 41 Conv (NS) 139 (F. R. Crane), 179 (K. Widdows); (1977) 40 MLR 231 (N. P. Gravells).

> of the association which precludes the members at any given time from dividing the subject of the gift between them on the footing that they are solely entitled to it in equity. (*c*) The terms or circumstances of the gift or the rules of the association may show that the property in question—i.e., the subject of the gift—is not to be at the disposal of the members for the time being but is to be held in trust for or applied for the purposes of the association as a quasi-corporate entity. In this case the gift will fail unless the association is a charitable body."

That summary may require, I think, a certain amount of qualification in the light of subsequent authority, but for present purposes I can adopt it as a working guide. Mr. Blackburne, for the next-of-kin, argues that the gift in the present case clearly does not fall within the first category, and that the addition of the specific direction as to its employment by the association prevents it from falling into the second category. This is, therefore, he says, a purpose trust and fails both for that reason and because the purpose is perpetuitous. He relies upon this passage from the judgment of the Board in *Leahy v A-G for New South Wales* [1959] AC 457 at 478:

> "If the words 'for the general purposes of the association' were held to import a trust, the question would have to be asked, what is the trust and who are the beneficiaries? A gift can be made to persons (including a corporation) but it cannot be made to a purpose or to an object: so also, a trust may be created for the benefit of persons as cestuis que trust but not for a purpose or object unless the purpose or object be charitable. For a purpose or object cannot sue, but, if it be charitable, the Attorney-General can sue to enforce it."...

I accept Mr. Blackburne's submission that the designation of the sole purpose of the gift makes it impossible to construe the gift as one falling into the first of Cross J's categories, even if that were otherwise possible. But I am not impressed by the argument that the gift shows an intention of continuity. Mr. Blackburne prays in aid *Re Macaulay's Estate* [1943] Ch 435 which is reported as a note to *Re Price* [1943] Ch 422, [1943] 2 All ER 505, where the gift was for the "maintenance and improvement of the Theosophical Lodge at Folkestone". The House of Lords held that it failed for perpetuity, the donee being a non-charitable body. But it is clear from the speeches of both Lord Buckmaster and Lord Tomlin that their Lordships derived the intention of continuity from the reference to "maintenance". Here it is quite evident that the association was to be free to spend the capital of the legacy. As Lord Buckmaster said in *Re Macaulay's Estate* at p. 436:

> "In the first place it is clear that the mere fact that the beneficiary is an unincorporated society in no way affects the validity of the gift.... The real question is what is the actual purpose for which the gift is made. There is no perpetuity if the gift were for the individual members for their own benefit, but that, I think, is clearly not the meaning of this gift. Nor again is there a perpetuity if the society is at liberty in accordance with the terms of the gift, to spend both capital and income as they think fit."

Re Price itself is authority for the proposition that a gift to an unincorporated non-charitable association for objects upon which the association is at liberty to spend both capital and income will not fail for perpetuity, although the actual conclusion in that case has been criticised—the point that the trust there (the carrying on of the teachings of Rudolf Steiner) was a "purpose trust" and thus unenforceable on that ground was not argued. It does not seem to me, therefore, that in the present case there is a valid ground for saying that the gift fails for perpetuity.

But that is not the end of the matter. If the gift were to the association simpliciter, it would, I think, clearly fall within the second category of Cross J's categories. At first sight, however, there appears to be a difficulty in arguing that the gift is to members of the association subject to their contractual rights inter se when there is a specific direction or limitation sought to be imposed upon those contractual rights as to the manner in which the subject matter of the gift is to be dealt with. This, says Mr. Blackburne, is a pure "purpose trust" and is invalid on that ground, quite apart from any question of perpetuity. I am not sure, however, that it is sufficient merely to demonstrate that a trust is a "purpose" trust. With the greatest deference, I wonder whether the dichotomy postulated in the passage which I have referred to in the judgment of the Board in *Leahy's* case [1959] AC 457 at 478 is not an over-simplification. Indeed, I am not convinced that it was intended as an exhaustive statement or to do more than indicate the broad division of trusts into those where there are ascertainable beneficiaries (whether for particular purposes or not) and trusts where there are none. . . .

There would seem to me to be, as a matter of common sense, a clear distinction between the case where a purpose is prescribed which is clearly intended for the benefit of ascertained or ascertainable beneficiaries, particularly where those beneficiaries have the power to make the capital their own, and the case where no beneficiary at all is intended (for instance, a memorial to a favourite pet) or where the beneficiaries are unascertainable: as in the case, for instance, of *Re Price* [1943] Ch 422, [1943] 2 All ER 505. If a valid gift may be made to an unincorporated body as a simple accretion to the funds which are the subject matter of the contract which the members have made inter se—and *Neville Estates Ltd v Madden* [1962] Ch 832, [1961] 3 All ER 769, and *Re Recher's Will Trusts* [1972] Ch 526, [1971] 3 All ER 401, show that it may—I do not really see why such a gift, which specifies a purpose which is within the powers of the association and of which the members of the association are the beneficiaries, should fail. Why are not the beneficiaries able to enforce the trust or, indeed, in the exercise of their contractual rights, to terminate the trust for their own benefit? Where the donee association is itself the beneficiary of the prescribed purpose, there seems to me to be the strongest argument in common sense for saying that the gift should be construed as an absolute one within the second category—the more so where, if the purpose is carried out, the members can by appropriate action vest the resulting property in themselves, for here the trustees and the beneficiaries are the same persons.

Is such a distinction as I have suggested borne out by the authorities? The answer is, I think, "not in terms," until recently. But the cases appear to me to be at least consistent with this. For instance *Re Clarke*[1901] 2

Ch 110 (the case of the Corps of Commissionaires); *Re Drummond* [1914] 2 Ch 90 (the case of the Old Bradfordians) and *Re Taylor* [1940] Ch 481, [1940] 2 All ER 637 (the case of the Midland Bank Staff Association), in all of which the testator had prescribed purposes for which the gifts were to be used, and in all of which the gifts were upheld, were all cases where there were ascertainable beneficiaries; whereas in *Re Wood* [1949] Ch 498, [1949] 1 All ER 1100, and *Leahy's* case (where the gifts failed) there were none. *Re Price* is perhaps out of line, because there was no ascertained beneficiary and yet Cohen J was prepared to uphold the gift even on the supposition that (contrary to his own conclusion) the purpose was non-charitable. But, as I have mentioned, the point about the trust being a purpose trust was not argued before him.

A striking case which seems to be not far from the present is *Re Turkington* [1937] 4 All ER 501, where the gift was to a masonic lodge "as a fund to build a suitable temple in Stafford". The members of the lodge being both the trustees and the beneficiaries of the temple, Luxmoore J construed the gift as an absolute one to the members of the lodge for the time being.

Directly in point is the more recent decision of Goff J in *Re Denley's Trust Deed* [1969] 1 Ch 373, [1968] 3 All ER 65, where the question arose as to the validity of a deed under which land was held by trustees as a sports ground:

> "primarily for the benefit of employees of [a particular company] and secondarily for the benefit of such other person or persons . . . as the trustees may allow to use the same . . ."

The latter provision was construed by Goff J as a power and not a trust. The same deed conferred on the employees a right to use and enjoy the land subject to regulations made by the trustees. Goff J held that the rule against enforceability of non-charitable "purpose or object" trusts was confined to those which were abstract or impersonal in nature where there was no beneficiary or cestui que trust. A trust which, though expressed as a purpose, was directly or indirectly for the benefit of an individual or individuals was valid provided that those individuals were ascertainable at any one time and the trust was not otherwise void for uncertainty. Goff J said at p. 382:

> "I think there may be a purpose or object trust, the carrying out of which would benefit an individual or individuals, where that benefit is so indirect or intangible or which is otherwise so framed as not to give those persons any locus standi to apply to the court to enforce the trust, in which case the beneficiary principle would, as it seems to me, apply to invalidate the trust, quite apart from any question of uncertainty or perpetuity. Such cases can be considered if and when they arise. The present is not, in my judgment, of that character, and it will be seen that clause 2 (d) of the trust deed expressly states that, subject to any rules and regulations made by the trustees, the employees of the company shall be entitled to the use and enjoyment of the land. Apart from this possible exception, in my judgment the beneficiary principle of *Re Astor's Settlement Trusts* [1952] Ch 534, [1952] 1 All ER 1067, which was approved in *Re Endacott* [1960] Ch 232—see particularly

by Harman LJ, at p. 250—is confined to purpose or object trusts which are abstract or impersonal. The objection is not that the trust is for a purpose or object per se, but that there is no beneficiary or cestui que trust . . . . Where, then, the trust, though expressed as a purpose, is directly or indirectly for the benefit of an individual or individuals, it seems to me that it is in general outside the mischief of the beneficiary principle."

I respectfully adopt this, as it seems to me to accord both with authority and with common sense.

If this is the right principle, then on which side of the line does the present case fall? Mr. Morritt has submitted in the course of his argument in favour of charity that the testator's express purpose "solely in the work of constructing the new buildings for the association" referred and could only refer to the youth centre project, which was the only project for the erection of buildings which was under consideration at the material time. If this is right, then the trust must, I think, fail, for it is quite clear that the project as ultimately conceived embraced not only the members of the association, but the whole Jewish community in Hull, and it would be difficult to argue that there was any ascertainable beneficiary. I do not, however, so construe the testator's intention. The evidence is that the testator knew the association's position and that he took a keen interest in it. I infer that he was kept informed of its current plans. The one thing that is quite clear from the minutes is that from 1965 right up to the testator's death there was great uncertainty about what was going to be done. There was a specific project for the purchase of a house in 1965. By early 1966 the youth centre was back in favour. By October 1966 it was being suggested that the association should stay where they were in their rented premises. The meeting of March 21 is, I think, very significant because it shows that they were again thinking in terms of their own exclusive building and that the patrons (of whom the testator was one) would donate the money when it was needed. At the date of the will, the association had rejected the youth centre plans and were contemplating again the purchase of premises of their own; and thereafter interest shifted to the community centre. I am unable to conclude that the testator had any specific building in mind; and, in my judgment, the reference to "the" buildings for the association means no more than whatever buildings the association may have or may choose to erect or acquire. The reference to improvements reflects, I think, the testator's contemplation that the association might purchase or might, at his death, already have purchased an existing structure which might require improvement or conversion, or even that they might, as had at one time been suggested, expend money in improving the premises which they rented from the Jewish Institute. The association was to have the legacy to spend in this way for the benefit of its members.

I have already said that, in my judgment, no question of perpetuity arises here, and accordingly the case appears to me to be one of the specification of a particular purpose for the benefit of ascertained beneficiaries, the members of the association for the time being. There is an additional factor. This is a case in which, under the constitution of the association, the members could, by the appropriate majority, alter their constitution so as to provide, if they wished, for the division of the association's assets among themselves. This has, I think, a significance. I have considered whether anything turns in this case upon the testator's direction that the legacy shall be used "solely" for one or other of the specified purposes. Mr. Rossdale has referred me to a number of cases where legacies have been bequeathed for particular purposes and in which the beneficiaries have been held entitled to override the purpose, even though expressed in mandatory terms.

Perhaps the most striking in the present context is *Re Bowes* [1896] 1 Ch 507, where money was directed to be laid out in the planting of trees on a settled estate. That was a "purpose" trust, but there were ascertainable beneficiaries, the owners for the time being of the estate; and North J. held that the persons entitled to the settled estate were entitled to have the money whether or not it was laid out as directed by the testator. . . .

I can see no reason why the same reasoning should not apply in the present case simply because the beneficiary is an unincorporated non-charitable association. I do not think the fact that the testator has directed the application "solely" for the specified purpose adds any legal force to the direction. The beneficiaries, the members of the association for the time being, are the persons who could enforce the purpose and they must, as it seems to me, be entitled not to enforce it or, indeed, to vary it.

Thus, it seems to me that whether one treats the gift as a "purpose" trust or as an absolute gift with a superadded direction or, on the analogy of *Re Turkington* [1937] 4 All ER 501 as a gift where the trustees and the beneficiaries are the same persons, all roads lead to the same conclusion.

In my judgment, the gift is a valid gift.

v. Useless or Capricious Purposes

If there is a theory upon which purpose trusts are valid, will this cover trusts for every purpose? Or will there be exceptions for illegal, immoral, wasteful or useless purposes?

In *Brown v Burdett* ((1882) 21 ChD 667) the testratrix devised a freehold house upon trust to block up all the rooms of the house[1], except four which were to be set aside for a house-keeper and his wife for twenty years, and subject thereto upon trust for Richard Burdett for life and after his death to Thomas Baxter in fee. BACON V-C had no difficulty in holding that the provisions for blocking up the house were void. The whole judgment states: "I think I must 'unseal' this useless, undisposed of property. There will be a declaration that the house and premises were undisposed of by the will, for the term of twenty years from the testratrix's death."

The M'Caigs of Oban could not resist the attractions of posthumous

[1] The method is described in some detail at pp. 668–670 of the report.

greatness. John Stuart M'Caig provided in his will that the income of his whole estate should be used for the purpose of building statues of himself and his family and the building of "artistic towers" at prominent points on his estates. Miss Catherine M'Caig, who was his sister and also his heir, succeeded in having the trust set aside on the ground that, under Scots law, an heir can only be disinherited by a beneficial gift to someone else (*M'Caig v University of Glasgow,* 1907 SC 231). On the question whether the doctrine of public policy would have destroyed the trust, Lord KYLLACHY said (at p. 242): "I have, I confess, much sympathy with that argument. For I consider that if it is not unlawful, it ought to be unlawful, to dedicate by testamentary disposition, for all time, or for a length of time, the whole income of a large estate—real and personal—to objects of no utility, private or public, objects which benefit nobody, and which have no other purpose or use than that of perpetuating at great cost, and in an absurd manner, the idiosyncracies of an eccentric testator. I doubt much whether a bequest of that character is a lawful exercise of the *testamenti factio.* Indeed, I suppose it would be hardly contended to be so if the purposes, say of the trust here, were to be slightly varied, and the trustees were, for instance, directed to lay the truster's estate waste, and to keep it so; or to turn the income of the estate into money, and throw the money yearly into the sea; or to expend income in annual or monthly funeral services in the testator's memory; or to expend it in discharging from prominent points upon the estate, salvoes of artillery upon the birthdays of the testator, and his brothers and sisters. Such purposes would hardly, I think, be alleged to be consistent with public policy; and I am by no means satisfied that the purposes which we have here before us are in a better position."

In her turn, Miss Catherine M'Caig provided in her will for the erection of eleven bronze statues of her parents and their nine children, each to cost not less than £1,000. This failed (*M'Caig's Trustees v Kirk-Session of United Free Church of Lismore,* 1915 SC 426). Lord SALVESEN declared it void on grounds of public policy (at p. 434): "In the first place, I think it is so because it involves a sheer waste of money, and not the less so that the expenditure would give employment to a number of sculptors and workmen, for it must be assumed that their labour could be usefully employed in other ways. I think, further, that it would be a dangerous thing to support a bequest of this kind which can only gratify the vanity of testators, who have no claim to be immortalised, but who possess the means by which they can provide for more substantial monuments to themselves than many that are erected to famous persons by public subscription. A man may, of course, do with his money what he pleases while he is alive, but he is generally restrained from wasteful expenditure by a desire to enjoy his property, or to accumulate it, during his lifetime. The actings of the two M'Caigs form an excellent illustration of this principle of human conduct. For many years they had apparently contemplated the erection of similar statues, but they could not bring themselves to part with the money during their own lifetimes . . . The prospect of Scotland being dotted with monuments to obscure persons who happened to have amassed a sufficiency of means, and cumbered with trusts for the purposes of maintaining these monuments in all time coming, appears to me to be little less than appalling . . ."[2]

VI. Rule against Perpetuities

The rule against perpetuities may affect the duration as well as the commencement of purpose trusts. Thus, a purpose trust is void, not only if it fails to vest within the perpetuity period, but also if, by its terms, the income or capital are required to be tied up for a time in excess of the perpetuity period[3]. The latter is the rule against excessive duration. It is not applicable to trusts for charitable purposes; the community interest is that charitable trusts should last for ever.

There seems to be no reason why purpose trusts should not be drafted so as to continue for the full period of lives in being plus 21 years. No English case, however, has upheld a purpose trust for more than 21 years[4]. The trust in *Re Astor's Settlement Trusts*[5] was designed to continue for lives in being plus 21 years; and, though the trust failed, no objection was taken on this point; indeed, counsel pointed out that "such a trust could continue for 100 years". If the trust provides for its continuation "so long as the law allows", or for some similar period, it will be valid for 21 years[6]. In *Re Dean*[7], a trust for the maintenance of the testator's horses and hounds "for the period of 50 years if any should so long live" was upheld, presumably on the ground that it must end within 21 years. Certainly, the animals could not be used as lives in being: as MEREDITH J said in *Re Kelly*[8]: "There can be no doubt that 'lives' means lives of human beings, not animals or trees in California."

In *Re Khoo Cheng Teow* ([1932] Straits Settlement Reports 226) a Chinese testator devised No. 56 Church Street, Singapore to the British Malaya Trustee and Executor Co. Ltd. as trustees, with a direction to let the premises and to apply the net rents "in the performance of the religious ceremonies according to the custom of the Chinese called *Sin Chew* to perpetuate my memory". The period specified was "during the lives of Her Majesty Queen Victoria and her descendants now living and during the lives and life of the survivors and survivor of them and during the period of

[2] See also *Aitken's Trustee v Aitken*, 1927 SC 374 (massive bronze equestrian statue of artistic merit); *Mackintosh's Judicial Factor v Lord Advocate* 1935 SC 406 (erection of vault); *Lindsay's Executor v Forsyth*, 1940 SC 458 (£1,000 on trust to provide a weekly supply of fresh flowers on the grave of my mother and my own).

[3] Before 1964, the rule was that it was void unless it must vest, if it vest at all, within the period. See generally H & M, pp. 332–336; Cheshire, *Modern Law of Real Property* (11th Edn, 1976) pp. 312 et seq.; Megarry & Wade, *Law of Real Property* (4th Edn, 1975), pp. 207 et seq.; Morris & Leach, *Rule against Perpetuities* (2nd Edn, 1962 and Supplement). Perpetuities and Accumulations Act 1964.

[4] See *Re Khoo Cheng Teow* [1932] Straits Settlements Reports 226, infra.

[5] [1952] Ch 534, [1952] 1 All ER 1067, p. 248, ante.

[6] *Re Hooper* [1932] 1 Ch 38, p. 245, ante.

[7] (1889) 41 ChD 552, p. 244, ante.

[8] [1932] IR 255 at 260–261; Maudsley and Burn, *Land Law, Cases and Materials* (3rd Edn, 1975), p. 291.

twenty-one years after the death of such survivor." TERRELL J, in declaring the trust valid, held that the rule against perpetuities applied to the Straits Settlements, and that the gift for Sin Chew ceremonies was not charitable, and said at p. 228: "It is clear that the devise does not offend the rule against perpetuities".

PERPETUITIES AND ACCUMULATIONS ACT 1964

15. Short title, interpretation and extent.—. . .

(4) Nothing in this Act shall affect the operation of the rule of law rendering void for remoteness certain dispositions under which property is limited to be applied for purposes other than the benefit of any person or class of persons in cases where the property may be so applied after the end of the perpetuity period.

Hanbury & Maudsley: *Modern Equity* (10th Edn, 1976), p. 360

"The provision is susceptible of two constructions. First, the orthodox view, that it means, in short, that the Act is to make no change to the law relating to the duration of purpose trusts. On the other hand, under the terms of the section, what is unaffected is the 'operation of the rule of law rendering void . . . certain dispositions . . . where the property may be so applied after the end of the perpetuity period.' In short, a purpose trust still remains void if it may last beyond the perpetuity period. But, what is the perpetuity period? Section 1 says that the perpetuity period 'applicable to [a] disposition . . . shall be of a duration equal to such number of years not exceeding eighty as is specified . . . in the instrument.'

So construed, the subsection means that purpose trusts existing beyond the perpetuity period are void; but the perpetuity period may be either the usual period measured by life in being plus 21 years; or a period of years not exceeding 80 as may be specified in the instrument; and it would seem therefore that a testator could specify such a period. Eighty years is of course longer than many would think to be the ideal period. But it is an improvement on royal lives; and it is submitted that the second interpretation is open to the courts, and that it should be applied."[9]

NEW ZEALAND PERPETUITIES ACT 1964[10]

20. Rule against inalienability.—(1) Except as provided in subsection (2) of this section, nothing in this Act shall affect the operation of the rule of law rendering non-charitable purpose trusts void for remoteness in cases where the trust property may be applied for the purposes of the trusts after the end of the perpetuity period.

(2) If any such trust is not otherwise void, the provision of section 8 of this Act [Necessity to wait and see] shall apply to it, and the property

[9] (1965) 29 Conv (NS) 165 (J. A. Andrews).

[10] Cf. Victoria Perpetuities and Accumulations Act 1968, s. 18.

subject to the trust may be applied for the purposes of the trust during the perpetuity period, but not thereafter.

VII. How to Achieve a Non-Charitable Purpose

A. By Incorporation

Report of the Goodman Committee on Charity Law and Voluntary Organisations (1976, para. 24.

"**Purpose Trusts**

24. The point made about those trusts whose purposes are held not to be charitable because they fail on grounds of legal uncertainty is one of substance. The legal argument is that these trusts fail because the beneficiaries are a fluctuating class and therefore uncertain, or because their objects are uncertain. This can in fact be obviated by careful drafting through the medium of a company. A simple and common course is to form a company limited by guarantee with the desired non-charitable objects and this will be perfectly valid. The long-standing invalidity of non-charitable purpose trusts now serves as a trap for the unwary and has led to much litigation. A will which provides money for the fulfilment of a purpose the testator has in mind may be attacked by disappointed beneficiaries on the grounds that the gift is void. The question before the court is whether the declared purpose is charitable, or whether the testator has declared a charitable intent. If so, the gift is valid but, if not, void. This involves the trustees in much expense and if the gift is held invalid, the clearly stated intentions of the testator will have been defeated. Since the testator's object could have been achieved by adopting a different technique, there seems no purpose in maintaining the rule as it stands. Accordingly, our recommendation is that further consideration be given by government to the validation of such 'purpose trusts'."

B. By Legislation

ONTARIO PERPETUITIES ACT 1966[11]

16. Specific non-charitable trusts.—(1) A trust for a specific non-charitable purpose that creates no enforceable equitable interest in a specific person shall be construed as a power to appoint the income or the capital, as the case may be, and, unless the trust is created for an illegal purpose or a purpose contrary to public policy, the trust is valid so long as and to the extent that it is exercised either by the original trustee or his successor, within a period of twenty-one years, notwithstanding that the limitation creating the trust manifested an intention, either expressly or by implication, that the trust should or might continue for a period in excess of that

[11] See (1967) ASCL, pp. 378–380 (J. D. Davies).

period, but, in the case of such a trust that is expressed to be of perpetual duration, the court may declare the limitation to be void if the court is of opinion that by so doing the result would more closely approximate the intention of the creator of the trust than the period of validity provided by this section.

(2) To the extent that the income or capital of a trust for a specific non-charitable purpose is not fully expended within a period of twenty-one years, or within any annual or other recurring period within which the limitation creating the trust provided for the expenditure of all or a specified portion of the income or the capital, the person or persons, or his or their successors, who would have been entitled to the property comprised in the trust if the trust had been invalid from the time of its creation, are entitled to such unexpended income or capital.

C. Construe or Draft as a Power

Restatement of the Law of Trusts (2d) §124

"Where the owner of property transfers it in trust for a specific non-charitable purpose, and there is no definite or definitely ascertainable beneficiary designated, no enforceable trust is created; but the transferee has power to apply the property to the designated purpose, unless such application is authorized or directed to be made beyond the period of the rule against perpetuities, or the purpose is capricious."

Although the courts have ruled[12] that "a valid power is not to be spelt out of an invalid trust", there appears to be no objection to drafting the purpose as a power instead of as a trust i.e., by giving the property not to a trustee upon trust, but to the ultimate beneficiary subject to a power in a third party to apply the property for the non-charitable purpose for the perpetuity period.

Morris and Leach: *Rule Against Perpetuities* (2nd Edn, 1965), p. 320

"No case decides that a power to apply property towards a specific non-charitable purpose must be treated as void. Such authority as exists suggests that it may well be valid. It is now clear that the law recognises the validity of powers of appointment which cannot be described as either general or special powers. Moreover, a power to appoint to such charitable institutions (including two named unincorporated associations) as the donee should nominate has been upheld, notwithstanding that the two named institutions were not charitable[13]. It is not a long step from this to hold that a power to appoint for a specific non-charitable purpose is valid, even though a trust for such a purpose is void. . . . It may well be, therefore, that if testators or settlors express their wishes in the form of a power and not in the form of a trust, they may be able to accomplish

[12] *IRC v Broadway Cottages Trust* [1955] Ch 20, [1954] 3 All ER 120, per JENKINS LJ. See also *Re Shaw* [1957] 1 WLR 729 at 746, [1957] 1 All ER 745, where HARMAN J followed the Court of Appeal with apparent reluctance.

[13] *Re Douglas* (1887) 35 ChD 472.

their non-charitable purposes. No question of enforcement would arise, for to the extent that the power was not exercised, there would be a resulting trust for the persons entitled in default of appointment. Of course the power, being more analogous to a special than to a general power of appointment, would have to be exercisable only within the limits of perpetuity. But subject to this, the only question would be one of policy. It is not desirable that eccentric or vainglorious testators should be allowed to give large sums of money for the purpose of erecting costly monuments to themselves or to seal up their houses for twenty years or to order their property to be thrown into the sea. But is there anything contrary to public policy in permitting testators to indulge such human desires as to bequeath a moderate sum of money for the maintenance of their pet animals or the repair of their graves within the period of perpetuities? The present authors conclude that there is not."

D. Draft as a Gift to a Group of Persons, such as an Unincorporated Association

Re Recher's Will Trusts [1972] Ch 526, [1971] 3 All ER 401, p. 71, ante. *Re Denley's Trust Deed* [1969] 1 Ch 373, [1968] 3 All ER 65, p. 259, ante. *Re Lipinski's Will Trusts* [1976] Ch 235, [1977] 1 All ER 33, p. 256, ante.

E. Conveyancing Device

If there is a gift to one charity followed by a gift over to another charity upon an event which may happen outside the perpetuity period, the gift over to the second charity is valid. Advantage was taken of this rule to achieve a non-charitable purpose in

RE TYLER

[1891] 3 Ch 252 (CA, Lindley, Fry and Lopes LJJ)

Sir James Tyler, who died in 1890, bequeathed £42,000 Russian 5 per cent. stock to the trustees of the London Missionary Society and committed to their care and charge the keys of his family vault at Highgate Cemetery "the same to be kept in good repair, and name legible, and to rebuild when it shall require: failing to comply with this request, the money to go to the Blue Coat School, Newgate Street, London".

Held. The gift and gift over were valid.

Fry LJ: In this case the testator has given a sum of money to one charity with a gift over to another charity upon the happening of a certain event. That event, no doubt, is such as to create an inducement or motive on the part of the first donee, the *London Missionary Society,* to repair the family tomb of the testator. Inasmuch as both the donees of this fund, the first donee and the second, are charitable bodies, and are created for the purposes of charity, the rule of law against perpetuities has nothing whatever to do with the donees. Does the rule of law against perpetuities create any objection to the nature of the condition? If the testator had required the first donee, the *London Missionary Society*, to apply any portions of the fund towards the repair of the family tomb, that would, in all probability, at any rate, to the extent of the sum required, have been void as a perpetuity which was not charity. But he has done nothing of the sort. He has given the first donee no power to apply any part of the money. He has only created a condition that the sum shall go over to *Christ's Hospital* if the *London Missionary Society* do not keep the tomb in repair. Keeping the tomb in repair is not an illegal object. If it were, the condition tending to bring about an illegal act would itself be illegal; but to repair the tomb is a perfectly lawful thing. All that can be said is that it is not lawful to tie up property for that purpose. But the rule of law against perpetuities applies to property, not motives; and I know of no rule which says that you may not try to enforce a condition creating a perpetual inducement to do a thing which is lawful. That is this case.

Then it is said by Mr. *Buckley*, "But if the gift had been to the *London Missionary Society* simply, they might have spent the money; by imposing this condition you require them to keep that invested, because it may have to go over at any moment to *Christ's Hospital*." What is the harm of that? Being a charity, and not affected by the rule against perpetuities, whether you direct them to keep the money invested in plain words, or whether you impose the condition which renders it necessary to keep it invested, seems to me the same thing and to be equally harmless, and not affected by the law against perpetuities.

I think the learned Judge in the Court below was quite right, and that this appeal must be dismissed.

In *Re Dalziel* ([1943] Ch 277, [1943] 2 All ER 656) a testatrix gave £20,000 to the governors of St. Bartholomew's Hospital "subject to the condition that they shall use the income" for the upkeep and repair of the mausoleum and surrounding garden in Highgate Cemetery, with a gift over to another charity "subject to the above conditions" if they failed to do so.

COHEN J held that both the gift and the gift over were void, and said at p. 282: "Lady Dalziel has not only given power, but directed the trustees to apply part of this gift or, if necessary, the whole of this gift in the maintenance of the tomb".

QUESTIONS

1. "There are, however, difficulties in reconciling *Re Denley's Trust Deed* with dicta in *Leahy v A-G for New South Wales*." (Pettit, p. 42). Should we now add *Re Recher's Will Trusts* [1972] Ch 526, [1971] 3 All ER 401, p. 71, ante?

   What would you say of the following purpose in *Re Astor's Settlement Trusts* [1952] Ch 534, [1952] 1 All ER 1067. "7. The establishment . . . or support of any charitable public or benevolent schemes . . . for or in connection with (a) the improvement of newspapers or journalism or (b) the relief or benefit of persons (or the families or dependents of persons) actually or formerly engaged in journalism or in the newspaper business."?

2. Consider *Oppenheim v Tobacco Securities Trust Co Ltd* [1951] AC 297, [1951] 1 All ER 31, p. 310, post. Must such a gift be void, whether as a charitable or a non-charitable purpose trust?
3. How would you advise a client who wanted to provide for the application of money to encourage the sport of fishing?
4. Assuming that purpose trusts are enforceable upon one theory or another, do you consider that it will be necessary to determine a dividing line between those which are useful to the public and those which are useless or harmful? How would you draw such a line? Is the theory of *Brown v Burdett* ((1882) 21 ChD 667, p. 261, ante) adequate? Before finally reaching a conclusion on this, read the material on the definition of legal charity (pp. 276, et seq., post), and observe the difficulties that have been experienced in drawing a line between "charitable purposes" and "useful" or "benevolent purposes". Royal Commission on the Taxation of Profits and Income, paras. 168–175 (1955) Cmd 9474; (1956) 72 LQR 187 (G. Cross); *Dingle v Turner* [1972] AC 601, [1972] 1 All ER 878, p. 287, post, per Lord Cross.
5. Consider the perpetuity problem raised in *Re Dean* ((1889) 41 ChD 552, p. 244, ante). How would this be affected by the Perpetuities and Accumulations Act 1964? Morris and Leach, p. 322. *Re Kelly* [1932] IR 255. *Re Searight's Estate*, 87 Ohio App 417, 95 NE 2d 779 (1950); Scott, *Cases on Trusts* (5th Edn), p. 351; H & M, pp. 358–361.

Part Two. Charities

10. Charitable Trusts[1]

I. Introduction

A trust by the terms of which the income is to be applied exclusively for charitable purposes is treated with special favour by the law. Such

[1] H & M, pp. 366–432; K & S, pp. 156–172; P & M, pp. 168–216; Pettit, pp. 157–225; Snell pp. 142–171. See generally *Tudor on Charities* (6th Edn, 1967); Cracknell, *Law Relating to Charities* (1973); Keeton and Sheridan, *The Modern Law of Charities* (2nd Edn, 1971); Picarda, *The Law and Practice Relating to Charities* (1977); Nightingale, *Charities* (1973); Whitaker, *The Foundations* (1974). See also the Annual Reports of the Charity Commissioners for England and Wales; the annual Charity Appeals Supplement of the Solicitors' Journal and the Annual Charities Review of the New Law Journal. For important reviews of the law and practice, see 10th Report from the Expenditure Committee of the House of Commons: Charity Commissioners and their Accountability 1974–1975, vol. I, Report, vol. II, Minutes of Evidence and Appendices; the Goodman Committee Report on Charity Law and Voluntary Organisations (1976); Annual Report of Charity Commissioners for 1976, paras. 7–14; (1976) 39 MLR 77 (M. Partington); (1976) 5 Anglo-American Law Review 153 (L. A. Sheridan). A committee under Lord Wolfenden is examining the role and functions of voluntary organisations in the last quarter of the 20th century. On the history of charity, see Jones, *History of the Law of Charity* (1969).

a trust is valid, although it is a purpose trust; the Attorney-General is charged with the duty of enforcing it. It may exist perpetually; indeed, many trusts currently in existence were founded some 500 years ago. It is no objection that the trust fails to provide with reasonable certainty what are the charitable purposes for which the money must be applied; certainty of intention to apply it for charitable purposes is sufficient. If there is doubt as to the particular charitable purposes, the Charity Commissioners or the court, or in some cases the Crown, will prepare a scheme. And, last but by no means least, a charitable trust is free from liability to income tax[2] and corporation tax, and from capital gains tax[3]; it is also entitled to relief in respect of half of the normal liability to rates; further relief being at the discretion of the Rating Authority[4]. A charity also enjoys certain advantages under the Community Land Act 1975[5], and is entitled to certain exemptions and reliefs in respect of development land tax[6], value added tax[7], national insurance surcharge[8] and stamp duty[9]. There are reliefs given to donors to charity; gifts of any amount in favour of a charity are exempt from capital gains tax[10], and, if made by way of gift by an individual more than one year before death, from capital transfer tax. If made on death or within a year of death, the gift is exempt up to £100,000[11], but there is no limit if made in favour of a number of National Institutions[12]. This is a formidable list of fiscal advantages[13]. The more significant it becomes, the more insistent is the Revenue to challenge particular claims to relief. It is by no mere chance that the bulk of the cases on charitable trusts in the years leading up to 1960 were Revenue cases. Nor should it occasion any surprise that the courts have become less inclined to find a construction in favour of charity. Lord LOREBURN could say in 1908[14]: "Now there is no better rule than that a benignant construction will be placed upon charitable bequests." That is not so today. The increase in the rate of income tax from one shilling in the £ in 1908 to 34p at the present day is sufficient to explain the change[15].

[2] I.C.T.A. 1970, s. 360. Profits from a trade are not exempt, unless the trade is exercised in the course of the actual carrying out of a primary purpose of the charity, or the work in connection with the trade is mainly carried out by beneficiaries of the charity. Ibid., s. 360 (1) (e).

[3] F.A. 1965, s. 35 (1), (2) as amended by I.C.T.A. 1970, s. 538 (1) and Sch. 15. I.C.T.A. 1970, s. 360 (2).

[4] General Rate Act 1967, s. 40; Rating (Charity Shops) Act 1976 (reversing *Oxfam v Birmingham City District Council* [1976] AC 126, [1975] 2 All ER 289). Tudor, pp. 393–400; [1971] BTR 86 (G. N. Glover).

[5] Sections 4 (1) (*b*), 6 (1), 25 (5), (6), (7); Annual Report for 1975, paras. 13–15.

[6] Development Land Tax Act 1976, ss. 24, 25.

[7] F.A. 1972, ss. 12, 13, Schs. 4, 5. *Customs and Excise Comrs v Automobile Association* [1974] 1 WLR 1447, [1974] 1 All ER 1257; Annual Report for 1974, paras. 17–21. Charges for admission to charity balls, dances, first nights in aid of charities, and similar fund-raising functions are within the scope of V.A.T.: H. M. Customs and Excise (1977) VAT News No. 13, p. 13.

[8] F.A. 1977, s. 57.

[9] F.A. 1974, 49 (2), Sch. 11.

[10] F.A. 1972, s. 119.

[11] F.A. 1975, s. 29, Sch. 6, para. 10.

[12] Ibid., Sch. 6, para. 12., e.g., The National Gallery, the British Museum, the National Trust and any university or university college in the United Kingdom.

[13] For a review and criticism of fiscal advantages, see Goodman Committee, chap. 5; [1972] BTR 346 (G. N. Glover).

[14] *Weir v Crum-Brown* [1908] AC 162 at 167.

[15] See the different views expressed in the House of Lords on this question in *Dingle v Turner* [1972] AC 601, [1972] 1 All ER 878, p. 287, post.

A study of the material in this Part will indicate the many problems which are faced in keeping this area of the law in line with modern developments. Much of the work previously done by voluntary bodies is now undertaken by the Government. It is no small problem to make the law of charity adjust to the pattern of the modern welfare state.

10th Report from the Expenditure Committee of the House of Commons (1975), vol. I, paras. 15, 16, 86, 87[16].

"*The number of Charities and their resources*

15. One of our difficulties has been the lack of reliable statistics in this area. There are some 115,000[17] Charities registered with the Charity Commissioners, and some 2,500 Charities are added to the register each year, nearly one half of those being newly-established Charities (Ev. p. 23). The value of investments in the custody of the Commissioners is around £250 million, and this does not include land values. There are thousands of other Charities excepted or exempt from registration . . .There is no reliable information on the total wealth of all these Charities. It is estimated that their annual income is well over £300 million (Q. 826) and that repayments of tax to Charities are in the region of £70 million to £75 million per annum (Q. 461). This does not include the amount exempted from tax on untaxed income of various kinds, e.g., gilt-edged securities, capital gains, trading profits.

16. The Inland Revenue were reluctant to provide even a rough estimate but they hazarded a guess that the total annual exemption must run into 'well over three figures' (in terms of millions of pounds) (Q. 462). . . . Using the 'guesstimate' of the Inland Revenue it would not appear to be extravagant to put the value of charitable assets at a minimum of £2,500 million—£3,000 million (App. 18). The total amount of the nation's resources owned by Charities must be very considerable indeed.

The Inland Revenue and Tax Privileges

86. Charities enjoy substantial financial privileges through freedom from income tax, corporation tax, capital gains tax, estate duty (subject to a limitation of £100,000), capital transfer and from seven year covenants (Ev. p. 84). The latter continue to gain in popularity and amount at present to over £20 million in terms of tax exemption (Q. 464)[18].

87. They also benefit from other fiscal reliefs in the field of rating and of V.A.T., though these are not matters within the purview of the Board of Inland Revenue. The total amount of tax repaid by Inland Revenue is annually around £70 to £75 million[19]. Remission from rates is roughly around £10 million (App. 13): that from V.A.T., again very approximately, about £1 million (House of Commons Official Report, 17th April 1975 Col. 146). As has already been stated in paragraph 16,

16 See also vol. II, pp. 84–102 (memorandum and evidence from Board of Inland Revenue), 106, 118, 252, 287–292, 332–337, 368–369, 390.

17 112, 715 at the end of 1976. Annual Report for 1975–6, para. 37.

18 £30 million in 1975–1976; £35 million in 1976–1977.

19 £80 million in 1975–1976.

the total annual exemption must, according to the Inland Revenue, easily exceed £100 million (Q. 462)."

II. Definition of Charity[20]

A. The Preamble to the Charitable Uses Act 1601

With so much at stake, one would hope for a precise definition of charity. Instead, the courts have sought a satisfactory one for nearly 400 years. The recommendation of the Nathan Committee in 1952 that a new statutory definition of charity should be enacted was not implemented[21]. In 1976 the Goodman Committee recommended that the categories of charities should be re-stated in simple and modern language replacing that of the Charitable Uses Act of 1601 and extending these to include objects now considered to be within the scope of charity[1]. The scope of charity today is based upon a large number of decisions, themselves based on the spirit and intendment of the preamble to the Charitable Uses Act 1601. These decisions may be either those of the courts or of the Charity Commissioners[2].

Tudor on Charities (6th Edn, 1967) p. 2

"The Charitable Uses Act, 1601[3]. This Act will usually be referred to in this work as 'the Statute of Elizabeth I'. The Statute of Elizabeth I was not directed so much to the definition of charity as to the correction of abuses which had grown up in the administration of trusts of a charitable nature. But the Court of Chancery used the preamble to the statute in order to simplify its task of determining what purposes were charitable and what were not. The preamble to the statute contained a comprehensive list of objects which in 1601 were recognised as charitable. The court never regarded the list as exhaustive. It treated the objects enumerated in the preamble as particular instances to which additions might properly be made from time to time. It became the practice of the court to refer to the preamble as a sort of index or chart[4] in order to determine whether or not a given purpose was charitable. That which began as a rule of practice became in course of time a rule of law, and in 1805 Sir William Grant MR was able to declare that 'those purposes are charitable which that Statute enumerates

[20] H & M, pp. 373–376; K & S, pp. 159–162; K & S (Charities), pp. 22–51; P & M, pp. 171–178; Pettit, pp. 167–170; Snell, pp. 141–145; Tudor, pp. 1–8; Picarda, pp. 3–16. See also (1945) 61 LQR 268 (J. Brunyate); (1956) 72 LQR 187 (G. Cross).

[21] Report of the Committee on the Law and Practice relating to Charitable Trusts (1952 Cmd. 8710), paras. 120–140. See also SACHS LJ IN *Incorporated Council of Law Reporting for England and Wales v A-G* [1972] Ch 73 at 94 ("Any statutory definition might well merely produce a fresh spate of litigation and provide a set of undesirable artificial distinctions"); Annual Report for 1970, para. 25; 1973, paras. 1–3.

[1] Page 16; p. 281, post. See also the House of Commons Report, Vol. 1, paras. 24–34; Vol. II, pp. 13, 23–25, 48–56, 67, 116–117, 149, 155–156, 172–175, 287; Annual Report for 1973, paras. 2–5.

[2] Charities Act 1960, s. 4; p. 400, post.

[3] 43 Eliz. 1, c. 4.

[4] *Income Tax Comrs v Pemsel* [1891] AC 531 at 581, per Lord MACNAGHTEN.

or which by analogies are deemed within its spirit and intendment.'[5] But objects which are neither enumerated in the preamble nor by analogy deemed to be within its spirit and intendment are not charitable, even though such objects are beneficial to the public.[6]"

---

43 Eliz. I, c. 4: The Preamble

WHEREAS Lands, Tenements, Rents, Annuities, Profits, Hereditaments, Goods, Chattels, Money and Stocks of Money, have been heretofore given, limited, appointed and assigned, as well by the Queen's most excellent Majesty, and her most noble Progenitors, as by sundry other well disposed Persons; some for Relief of aged, impotent and poor People, some for Maintenance of sick and maimed Soldiers and Mariners, Schools of Learning, Free Schools, and Scholars in Universities, some for Repair of Bridges, Ports, Havens, Causways, Churches, Sea-Banks and Highways, some for Education and Preferment of Orphans, some for or towards Relief, Stock or Maintenance for Houses of Correction, some for Marriages of poor Maids, some for Supportation, Aid and Help of young Tradesmen, Handicraftsmen and Persons decayed, and others for Relief or Redemption of Prisoners or Captives, and for Aid or Ease of any poor Inhabitants concerning Payments of Fifteens[7], setting out of Soldiers and other Taxes; which Lands, Tenements, Rents, Annuities, Profits, Hereditaments, Goods, Chattels, Money and Stocks of Money, nevertheless have not been employed according to the charitable Intent of the givers and Founders thereof, by reason of Frauds, Breaches of Trust, and Negligence in those that should pay, deliver and employ the same: For Redress and Remedy whereof, Be it enacted . . ."

In *Commissioners for Special Purposes of Income Tax v Pemsel* ([1891] AC 531 at 583) Lord MACNAGHTEN summarized the scope of charity[8]: "No doubt the popular meaning of the words 'charity' and 'charitable' does not coincide with their legal meaning; and no doubt it is easy enough to collect from the books a few decisions which seem to push the doctrine of the court to the extreme, and to present a contrast between the two meanings in an aspect almost ludicrous. But still it is difficult to fix the point of divergence, and no one as yet succeeded in defining the popular meaning of the word 'charity'. . . . How far then, it may be asked, does the popular meaning of the word 'charity' correspond with its legal meaning? 'Charity' in its legal sense comprises four principal divisions: trusts for the relief of poverty; trusts for

[5] *Morice v Bishop of Durham* (1805) 9 Ves 399 at 405.

[6] *Gilmour v Coats* [1949] AC 426 at 443, per Viscount SIMONDS; *A-G v National Provincial and Union Bank of England* [1924] AC 262 at 265, per Viscount CAVE LC; *Houston v Burns* [1918] AC 337; *Re Macduff* [1896] 2 Ch 451 at 466, per LINDLEY LJ; *Dunne v Byrne* [1912] AC 407 at 411, per Lord MACNAGHTEN; *Farley v Westminster Bank Ltd* [1939] AC 430, [1939] 3 All ER 491. This is only a selection from among the many cases that might have been cited.

[7] A tax on movable property originating in the twelfth century and last heard of in the reign of James I. See I Bl Com. 309. Jowitt, *Dictionary of English Law* (1976) Vol. I, p. 789.

[8] The classification originated in the argument of Sir Samuel Romilly in *Morice v Bishop of Durham* (1805) 10 Ves 522 at 523; *Ashfield Municipal Council v Joyce* [1978] AC 122.

the advancement of education; trusts for the advancement of religion; and trusts for other puposes beneficial to the community, not falling under any of the preceding heads."

The preamble to 43 Eliz. I, c. 4, was repealed by s. 38 (1)[9] of the Charities Act 1960; however, for a trust to be charitable, its purposes must still be within the spirit and intendment of the preamble. In *Scottish Burial Reform and Cremation Society v Glasgow Corporation* ([1968] AC 138), Lord WILBERFORCE spoke of the legal test of charitable purposes (at p. 154): "On this subject, the law of England, though no doubt not very satisfactory and in need of rationalisation, is tolerably clear. The purposes in question, to be charitable, must be shown to be for the benefit of the public, or the community, in a sense or manner within the intendment of the preamble to the statute 43 Eliz. 1, c. 4. The latter requirement does not mean quite what it says; for it is now accepted that what must be regarded is not the wording of the preamble itself, but the effect of decisions given by the courts as to its scope, decisions which have endeavoured to keep the law as to charities moving according as new social needs arise or old ones become obsolete or satisfied. Lord Macnaghten's grouping of the heads of recognised charity in *Pemsel's* case[10] is one that has proved to be of value and there are many problems which it solves. But three things may be said about it, which its author would surely not have denied: first that, since it is a classification of convenience, there may well be purposes which do not fit neatly into one or other of the headings; secondly, that the words used must not be given the force of a statute to be construed; and thirdly, that the law of charity is a moving subject which may well have evolved even since 1891."[11]

B. Criteria for Charitable Status

For a trust to be charitable it must not only be within the spirit and intendment of the preamble to the Act of 1601; it must also satisfy the requirement of public benefit[12]. It will be seen that each of the four heads of Lord MACNAGHTEN's classification involves two elements; that of benefit, and that of public benefit. There is no need to prove that the relief of poverty, the advancement of education, or the advancement of religion are beneficial. They are. The question of proving that the purposes of a trust are beneficial arises only under the fourth head. A trust for the

[9] Itself repealed by Education Act 1973, Sch. 2, Part I. See also Charities Act 1960 ss. 38 (4), 45 (1) and 46 (1).

[10] [1891] AC 531 at 583.

[11] See also Lord REID at p. 146 and Lord UPJOHN at p. 153, p. 337, post; and RUSSELL LJ in *Incorporated Council of Law Reporting for England and Wales v A-G* [1972] Ch 73 at 88–89, p. 354, post.

[12] H & M, pp. 398–408; K & S, pp. 161–162; K & S (Charities), pp. 29–34; P & M, pp. 174–180; Pettit, pp. 187–194; Snell, pp. 150–152; Tudor, pp. 2–3; Picarda, pp. 16–27. (1953) 31 Can BR 537 (G. H. L. Fridman); (1956) 72 LQR 187 (G. Cross); (1958) 21 MLR 138 (P. S. Atiyah); (1947) CLJ 63 (G. H. Jones); (1975) 39 Conv (NS) 183 (S. Plowright); (1976) 27 NILQ 198 (J. C. Brady); (1977) 40 MLR 397 (N. P. Gravells); Goodman Report, chap. 2 (Benefit to the "Community"), chap. 3 ("Benefit" to the Community).

advancement of education, or advancement of religion among a selected few, is not charitable. The problem is to determine the proper test for the identification of the public; or that part of the public which the law requires to be benefited.

This requirement of public benefit will be illustrated in the context of each of the four heads. It varies from head to head. The variation is most marked in the context of trusts for the relief of poverty.

Report of the Goodman Committee: Charity Law and Voluntary Organisations (1976), paras. 16–32[13].

Importance of Charitable Status

16. One of the questions to which we have given a great deal of attention is whether there is a better way of defining the scope and ambit of charity but before we can come to that we have to consider whether the result of the cases is satisfactory; whether there should be amendments in detail; or whether the whole concept is wrong and charity should either be narrowed or expanded in some more fundamental way. . . .

17. On the one hand, we had evidence suggesting that the scope of charities should be restricted to what is said to be its meaning as generally understood in its ordinary sense. In short, that it should be restricted to the relief of the poor and of people suffering from deprivation of one sort or another. On the other hand, we have had evidence suggesting that the benefits accorded to charities should be extended to other voluntary bodies which have not so far been considered to come at all within the ambit of charities. Such bodies include pressure groups and, in fact, any voluntary organisation, political or otherwise. We do not agree with either of these views and we feel that at the outset we should make clear our reasons.

21. There are many fields where the control which tends to go with state assistance can be unwelcome and this applies especially to the arts and provision for cultural and recreational facilities. Charity is increasingly moving into these fields and this is a development which in our opinion is to be welcomed.

Should the Concept of Charity be Expanded?

22. But then comes the question where is it to stop? Parallel to the pressure to restrict the ambit of charity, there is also the desire to extend it and to afford to all 'Non-Profit Distributing Organisations' (NPDOs) the privileges afforded to charities[14]. There would have to be stringent provisions to avoid abuse but otherwise the objects and activities of the NPDO would be irrelevant. Thus professional bodies, political parties and pressure groups of all sorts could be accorded the privileges now

[13] See also House of Commons Report (1975) vol. I, paras. 24–62, which proposes that the head "Beneficial to the Community" should be made the governing criterion in all cases. Nightingale, *Charities*, pp. 34–68.

[14] This approach was advocated by the Charity Law Reform Committee. See a similar rejection in House of Commons Report, vol. I, paras. 31–32, vol. II, pp. 48 et seq.

confined to charities. . . . While, therefore, we believe that the ambit of charity should remain flexible and capable of growth (and as a corollary that some objects may with time cease to be charitable), we think that the existing concept should remain despite the difficulties of definition.

Criteria for Charitable Status

26. We have now reached the position that the scope of charity should not be restricted (except perhaps in so far as objects which once were accepted as charitable may have in the course of time ceased to have the relevant characteristics of charity); that it should continue its natural process of development, but that it should not include all voluntary activities. How then can we distinguish charitable objects from other objects? Is it possible to frame the definition which will neatly include every object which ought to be regarded as charitable and as neatly exclude everything which ought not to be so regarded, or can we at least point to the general criteria which should govern the decision whether an object is charitable or not and leave it to the Charity Commissioners and the courts to develop the concept as they have done in the past, or is there any other way?

Benefit to the Community

27. It is clear that there must be a desire to benefit the community but many things which are far removed from charity may benefit the community. For instance, a highly successful commercial venture, generating exports and providing massive employment is of immense benefit to the community but it is not charitable. Conversely, the importance of the tax factors to charities has led some to suggest that one should first consider what purposes or activities should be subsidised and to define charity to conform to the answer so found. To argue thus turns the argument upside down. If the field open for tax benefits is undefined, it follows that any purpose which some may consider deserving of subsidy would qualify to be regarded as charitable. But the government may choose to subsidise certain types of industry and lame ducks and public utilities which cannot be run at a profit and although these might in 1601, when they were provided, if at all, by private enterprise have been regarded as charitable, they cannot now be so regarded. It would seem therefore that the concept of charity must be confined to an object to benefit the community in certain particular ways, such as relief of distress, or deprivation, and, in its more modern manifestations, the improvement of the quality of life in relation to the arts, recreation, amenities and our national heritage.

Altruism

28. Although altruism is not definable in legal terms it is nevertheless an important element in our social thinking which makes for a better quality of life. Generally speaking, it may be said that charity and the private profit of the donor are mutually exclusive and it is for this reason that at a later part in this report we have suggested that gifts to relatives or to employees of the donor even for the relief of poverty should no longer be regarded as charitable. . . .

Definition of Charity

29. Given these two criteria of benefit to the community and altruism, the decision in particular cases is at present left to the Charity Commissioners and the court, who refer to the preamble to the Act of 1601 as summarised by Lord Macnaghten in the Pemsel case and to as many of the hundreds of decided cases as they may feel to be relevant to the case before them. There has never been a definition of charity and many people believe that the time has come to formulate one. Others point out that to define is to confine believing the very flexibility of the law in relation to charities is, and should continue to be, its strength. They emphasise the difficulty of finding a definition in sufficiently wide terms to encompass all that is now considered charitable, or may in the future be so considered and nothing else. There has been much concern too that if any new definition were adopted, the entire body of case law established over the centuries would cease to be relevant. On the other hand, it is said that the cases have established law which is unsatisfactory in that it is out of tune with modern modes of thought and social needs and that it is inflexible. . . We do not believe that it is possible to formulate a definition of this sort, and we are comforted by the fact that the same conclusion was reached in the debates leading to the passing of the 1960 Act. For instance, in relation to the element of public benefit, there are a large number of cases which consider the degree of public benefit required and the nature of that public benefit whether direct or indirect. We do not think that all these cases should be swept aside, nor would it be possible without a complete codification to incorporate them in a statute. What we have done in the succeeding chapters is to consider some of the fields in which the existing case law is the subject of criticism and to suggest a number of amendments of a specific nature which could be made.

Categories of Charity

32. We have also given particular consideration to the question whether a greater degree of certainty can be introduced in relation to the categories of objects which should qualify as charitable. The preamble to the Act of 1601 is written in language inappropriate to contemporary concepts and it has led, and will lead, to mental gymnastics if it is to encompass within its terms the many forms of human endeavour now or hereafter deserving to fall within the scope of charity, while excluding those which should lie outside. What we suggest therefore would be beneficial would be to produce an updated version of the preamble to the Act of 1601 and we have therefore produced a list, in general terms, of objects deemed to be charitable (see Appendix 1)[15]. It is based upon the Pemsel classification extended by references in relation to the fourth head to objects which are now considered to be within the scope of charity. It is, we hope, formulated in modern and simple language. We place particular emphasis on ensuring the continued flexibility of the law in this respect and propose that the formulation should be such as not to close the categories of charity and thus crystallise and prevent the future development of the

[15] Which is too long for inclusion here.

scope of charity. As it would be made clear that this new classification is an updated version of the old classification, we do not think that the existing case law would become irrelevant[16]."

The Tenth Report from the Expenditure Committee of the House of Commons recommended, in 1975, as follows:

"34. We recommend, therefore, that legislation should be introduced whereby all Charities should be required to satisfy the test of purposes beneficial to the community. In the case of those Charities formerly admitted under one of the other heads, namely, the relief of poverty, the advancement of education and the advancement of religion, they should continue to qualify only if they also satisfy the main criterion. We do not believe such a change would affect the great majority of Charities in any way; but we do believe it would act as a check to abuse at the fringe."

III. The Four Heads of Charity

A. The Relief of Aged Impotent and Poor People[17]

I. DISJUNCTIVE CONSTRUCTION

It is not necessary that the trust should be for the relief of persons in all three categories. Any one category will do. But the trust must be within the spirit and intendment of the Preamble.

(*a*) *Impotent*

In *Re Lewis* ([1955] Ch 104, [1954] 3 All ER 257) the testator left to 10 blind girls and 10 blind boys "Tottenham residents if possible the sum of £100 each". ROXBURGH J held that the bequest constituted a valid charitable trust. It was not necessary that there should also be a requirement of poverty.

(*b*) *Aged*

In *Re Glyn's Will Trusts* ([1950] 2 All ER 1150n.) DANCKWERTS J upheld a residuary gift which established a trust to build and endow free cottages for old women of the working classes of the age of sixty or upwards. The words of the preamble were to be read disjunctively; aged people did not need also to be poor to come within the preamble.

In *Re Bradbury* ([1950] 2 All ER 1150n) VAISEY J upheld as charitable a gift to pay money from a fund "for the maintenance of an aged person or persons in a nursing home approved by my trustees . . ."

In *Re Robinson* ([1951] Ch 198, [1950] 2 All ER 1148) the testator

[16] See also the Minority Report, pp. 143 et seq.

[17] H & M, pp. 376–378, 389–391, 399–400; K & S, p. 164; K & S (Charities), pp. 99–113; P & M, pp. 178–182; Pettit, pp. 170–171, 193; Snell, pp. 144, 145–146, 152; Tudor, pp. 9–26; Picarda, pp. 29–37; Goodman Report, paras. 45 (Self-Help Organisations), 55–59 (Poverty Prevention).

gave his residuary estate, *inter alia*, to "the old people over sixty-five years of Hazel Slade near Hednesford to be given as my trustees think best". VAISEY J upheld the gift. He said (at p. 201): "Here I think that 'the old people over sixty-five years[18] in a particular parish are a class of persons just as much objects of charity, having regard to the preamble of the statute, as the poor of the parish or the sick of the parish. They are, I think, proper objects of the charitable purposes of the testator. . . ."

Tudor on Charities (6th Edn, 1967), p. 12

"Thus the gifts for the benefit of the blind[19], the sick and wounded[20], and the prevention of cruelty to children[1] and (so it has been held) faith-healing[2], are charitable.

It is considered that gifts for the benefit of patients in hospitals or to establish homes for persons in need of rest are charitable as being for the relief of impotent persons."

(1955) 71 LQR 16 (R.E.M.)

"[*Re Lewis*] revives the question whether a trust for the relief of 'aged peers' or 'impotent millionaires' would be charitable: see (1951) 67 LQR 164. Escape from the conclusion that charity embraces these objects may lie in holding that such a trust would not 'promote a public benefit'."[3]

In *Re Payling's Will Trusts* ([1969] 1 WLR 1595, [1969] 3 All ER 498) BUCKLEY J upheld a gift of a house "to be used as a home for aged persons . . . as Mansfield Corporation in their absolute discretion may decide". The accommodation was to be free, but the occupiers had to provide for their own maintenance. A similar trust to provide flats for persons over 65 years of age to be let at economic rents was upheld by DANCKWERTS J in *Re Cottam* ([1955] 1 WLR 1299, [1955] 3 All ER 704)[4].

Report of the Charity Commissioners for England and Wales for the year 1967, para. 29.

"*Homes for Old People*

29. To sum up, the charitable status of a society or institution which provides a home for old people, or some other service calculated to alleviate the special needs of old people, cannot be called into question

[18] In *Re Wall* (1889) 42 ChD 510, the age of 50 years was accepted as a qualification for "aged".
[19] *Re Fraser* (1883) 22 ChD 827; *Re Lewis* [1955] Ch 104, [1954] 3 All ER 257; and see *Re Elliott* (1910) 102 LT 528 at 530; *Barber v Chudley* (1922) 128 LT 766.
[20] *Re Hillier* [1944] 1 All ER 480; and see *Re Robinson* [1931] 2 Ch 122 (gift for disabled German soldiers charitable).
[1] *Income Tax Comrs v Pemsel* [1891] AC 531 at 572.
[2] *Re Kerin* (1966) Times, 24th May (GOFF J held faith-healing was for the relief of impotent persons or for the advancement of religion or both).
[3] See p. 287, post. And see on this especially (1958) 21 MLR at pp. 140–141 (P. S. Atiyah).
[4] Cf. *Re Martin* (1977) 121 Sol Jo 828. See also *Re Neal* (1966) 110 Sol Jo 549.

merely because the benefits of that home or institution are not confined to old people who are poor or because that home or institution makes charges on a scale reasonably calculated to meet all its outgoings but not to produce a profit. Furthermore, there is a need today for homes able to accommodate old people who have some money of their own and if new homes of this sort are to be founded they will probably not be able to carry on and maintain a good standard without making quite high charges."

(*c*) *Poor*

Tudor on Charities (6th Edn, 1967), p. 150

"**Meaning of 'poor'.** 'Poor' is a relative term and an individual need not be destitute in order to qualify as a poor person within the meaning of the preamble. The adjective 'poor' has never been defined by the courts: its meaning has to be ascertained from the reported cases, which show clearly enough that an individual is considered to be poor if he is in genuinely straitened circumstances and is unable to maintain a very modest standard of living for himself and the persons (if any) dependent upon him[5]. It would be convenient if there were a satisfactory statutory definition of 'poor', but the difficulties of framing one are very great."[6]

(1956) 72 LQR 187 at pp. 206–207 (G. Cross)

"Poverty . . . is a vague word which has meant different things at different times and in different places . . ."

In *Re Coulthurst* ([1951] Ch 661) Sir Raymond EVERSHED said, (at p. 665): "It is quite clearly established that poverty does not mean destitution; it is a word of wide and somewhat indefinite import; it may not unfairly be paraphrased for present purposes as meaning persons who have to 'go short' in the ordinary acceptation of that term, due regard being had to their status in life, and so forth."

Tudor on Charities (6th Edn, 1967), p. 16

"A charitable gift for the poor may be expressed in general and indefinite language[7], or may be for the poor of a particular defined area (parish, town or other place)[8], or poor persons of a particular religious denomi-

[5] *Mary Clark Home Trustees v Anderson* [1904] 2 KB 645; *Re Gardom* [1914] 1 Ch 662 (reversed, but not on this point, by the House of Lords (1915) 84 LJ Ch 749); *Shaw v Halifax Corpn* [1915] 2 KB 170; *Re Clarke* [1923] 2 Ch 407; *Re De Carteret* [1933] Ch 103.

[6] See (1956) 72 LQR 182 at 206, 207 (G. Cross).

[7] *A-G v Peacock* (1676) Finch 245 (for the good of poor people for ever); *A-G v Rance* (1728) cited in (1762) Amb 422; *Nash v Morley* (1842) 5 Beav 177; *Re Darling* [1896] 1 Ch 50 (to the poor and the service of God, following *Powerscourt v Powerscourt* (1824) 1 Mol 616).

[8] *Woodford (Inhabitants) v Parkhurst* (1639) Duke 70; *A-G v Pearce* (1740) 2 Atk 87; *A-G v Clarke* (1762) Amb 422; *A-G v Exeter Corpn* (1826) 2 Russ 45; (1827) 3 Russ 395; *A-G v Wilkinson* (1839) 1 Beav 370; *A-G v Bovill* (1840) 1 Ph 762; *Salter v Farey* (1848) 7 Jur 831; *Re Lambeth Charities* (1853) 22 LJ Ch 959; *A-G v Blizard* (1855) 21 Beav 233; *Russell v Kellett* (1855) 3 Sm & G 264; *Re Lousada* (1887) 82 LT Jo 358 (London Poor); *Re St Alphage, London Wall* (1888) 59 LT 614; *Re Lucas* [1922] 2 Ch 52 (poor inhabitants of G., a small town); *Re Monk* [1927] 2 Ch 197 (gift of income of a fund set aside out of residue to buy coal for distribution among poor and deserving inhabitants of a particular parish and to apply the rest of the residue, capital and income, in making loans of interest to poor and deserving inhabitants of that parish); *Re Roadley* [1930] 1 Ch 524 (poor of two named parishes).

nation attending a specified chapel or chapels[9], or the poor of a particular regiment[10], or a particular class of poor people, such as poor gentlewomen[11], distressed gentlefolk[12], or persons of moderate[13] or limited[14] means, who are not self-supporting[15], or housekeepers[16], or tradesmen of a particular kind[17], or unsuccessful literary men[18], or servants[19], or 'poor struggling youths of merit[20]', or poor pious persons[1], or poor emigrants[2], or persons descended from residents of a named borough (Hastings) in a particular year needing assistance to improve their condition in life by emigrating[3], or inmates of a workhouse[4], or patients in a hospital[5], or debtors[6], or fifty needy and deserving old men and fifty needy and deserving old women of a particular place[7], or widows and orphans of poor clergymen[8], or seamen of a particular port[9], or victims of a particular disaster[10], or widows and orphans of a particular parish[11], or indigent bachelors and widowers 'who have shown sympathy with science'[12], or the relief of domestic distress.[13]"

In *Re De Carteret* ([1933] Ch 103) a trust, created by the will of a Bishop of Jamaica, provided for the payment of "annual allowances of forty

[9] *Re Wall* (1889) 42 ChD 510.

[10] *Re Donald* [1909] 2 Ch 410.

[11] *A-G v Power* (1809) 1 Ball & B 145; *Mary Clark Home Trustees v Anderson* [1904] 2 KB 645; *Re Gardom* [1914] 1 Ch 662; *Shaw v Halifax Corpn* [1915] 2 KB 170.

[12] *Re Young* [1951] Ch 344.

[13] *Re Clarke* [1923] 2 Ch 407.

[14] *Re De Carteret* [1933] Ch 103. In this case, as in *Re Clarke* (supra), the potential beneficiaries, though not destitute, were poor people within the meaning of the preamble to the statute 43 Eliz. I, c. 4. Only people of very limited means would have needed the benefits provided.

[15] *Re Central Employment Bureau for Women and Students' Careers Association* [1942] 1 All ER 232.

[16] *A-G v Pearce* (1740) 2 Atk 87.

[17] *Re White's Trusts* (1886) 33 ChD 449.

[18] *Thompson v Thompson* (1844) 1 Coll 381 at 395.

[19] *Reeve v A-G* (1843) 3 Hare 191; *Loscombe v Wintringham* (1850) 13 Beav 87.

[20] *Milne's Executors v Aberdeen University Court* 1905 7 F (Ct of Sess) 642.

[1] *Nash v Morley* (1842) 5 Beav 177.

[2] *Barclay v Maskelyne* (1858) 32 LTOS 205. But a gift "for emigration uses" is not charitable: see *Re Sidney* [1908] 1 Ch 488.

[3] *Re Tree* [1945] Ch 325, [1945] 2 All ER 65. For the grounds on which EVERSHED J distinguished *Re Compton* [1945] Ch 123, [1945] 1 All ER 198, see [1945] Ch 328–332; and see (1956) 72 LQR (G. Cross), at p. 190, note 8. In *Re Tree* [1945] Ch 325, [1945] 2 All ER 65, the element of poverty was present. It is doubtful whether the decision could have been justified if that element had been absent: see *Davies v Perpetual Trustee Co* [1959] AC 439 at 456.

[4] *A-G v Vint* (1850) 3 De G & Sm 704.

[5] *Reading Corpn v Lane* (1601) Toth 32; see also *Re Roadley* [1930] 1 Ch 524.

[6] *A-G v Painter-Stainers Co* (1788) 2 Cox Eq Cas 51; *A-G v Ironmongers Co* (1834) 2 My & K 576.

[7] *Re Reed* (1893) 10 TLR 87; and see also Re Wall (1889) 42 ChD 510.

[8] *Waldo v Caley* (1809) 16 Ves 206; and see *Re Friend of the Clergy's Charters* [1921] 1 Ch 409, where this was assumed without argument.

[9] *Powell v A-G* (1817) 3 Mer 48.

[10] *Pease v Pattinson* (1886) 32 ChD 154; *Re Hartley Colliery Accident Relief Fund* (1908) 102 LT 165n; *Cross v Lloyd-Greame* (1909) 102 LT 163 (where there were only six victims; *Re North Devon and West Somerset Relief Fund Trusts* [1953] 1 WLR 1260, [1953] 2 All ER 1032 (flood disaster).

[11] *A-G v Comber* (1824) 2 Sim & St 93; *Russell v Kellett* (1855) 3 Sm & G 264.

[12] *Weir v Crum-Brown*, [1908] AC 162 (on appeal from the Court of Session).

[13] *Kendall v Granger* (1842) 5 Beav 300 at 303.

pounds each to widows or spinsters in England whose income otherwise shall not be less than eighty or more than one hundred and twenty pounds per annum". Preference was to "be given to widows with young children dependent on them". This was held to be a valid charitable trust for the relief of poverty. It was no objection that there was a minimum income qualification for the persons to be benefited[14]. Emphasis was placed by MAUGHAM J on the fact that the preference was to be given to widows with young children dependent upon them. "I should have hesitated to hold that it was a good charitable gift had it merely been for "widows and spinsters"; but I think that, in confining it, as I do, in effect, to widows with young children dependent on them, I am within the decisions to which I have referred."

In *Re Sanders' Will Trusts* ([1954] Ch 265, [1954] 1 All ER 667) a codicil gave money "to provide or assist in providing dwellings for the working classes and their families resident in the area of Pembroke Dock . . . or within a radius of five miles therefrom . . ."

HARMAN J held that the gift was not a charitable trust because the expression "the working classes" did not indicate poor persons[15].

In *Biscoe v Jackson* ((1887) 35 ChD 460) the testator gave a sum of money out of his residuary estate to be applied in the establishment of a soup kitchen for the parish of Shoreditch and of a cottage hospital adjoining thereto. This was held to be a charitable trust for the relief of poverty.

In *Re Coulthurst* ([1951] Ch 661, [1951] 1 All ER 774) a testator provided a fund to be applied "to or for the benefit of such . . . of the . . . widows and orphaned children of deceased officers and deceased ex-officers of Coutts & Co . . . as the bank shall in its absolute discretion consider by reason of his her or their financial circumstances to be most deserving of such assistance". This was held by the Court of Appeal to create a valid trust for the relief of poverty[16].

In *Re Gwyon* ([1930] 1 Ch 255) the testator established a fund, to be

14 Following *Spiller v Maude* (1881) 32 ChD 158 ("incapacitated actors"); *Re Lacy* [1899] 2 Ch 149; *Re Gardom* [1914] 1 Ch 662 (where the gift was "for the maintenance of a temporary house of residence for ladies of limited means"); cf. *Over Seventies Housing Association v Westminster London Borough Council* (1974) 230 Estates Gazette 1593.

15 Cf. *Re Niyazi's Will Trusts* (1978) Times, 8th February (gift for "the construction of a working men's hostel" in Famagusta, Cyprus, held charitable). Some homes for working classes have been registered as charities: Annual Report for 1965, App. C, paras. I. A. 9; Goodman Report, paras. 75–78 (Housing).

16 On the element of public benefit in the definition of the class to be benefited, cf. *Re Compton* [1945] Ch 123, [1945] 1 All ER 198; *Oppenheim v Tobacco Securities Trust Co Ltd* [1951] AC 297, [1951] 1 All ER 31, p. 310, post; Gibson v South American Stores (Gath and Chaves) Ltd [1950] Ch 177, [1949] 2 All ER 895; (necessitous and deserving employees, ex-employees and their dependents): *Dingle v Turner* [1972] AC 601, [1972] 1 All ER 878, p. 287, post; *Re Denison* (1974) 42 DLR (3d) 652 ("relief of impoverished or indigent members of the Law Society of Upper Canada and of their wives, widows and children" held charitable).

called "Gwyon's Boys Clothing Foundation". The income of the fund was to be applied in providing knickers ("loose fitting breeches, gathered in at the knee"[17]) for boys of Farnham and district, with certain qualifications expressed by EVE J in the extract below. No preference was indicated in favour of children of poor parents. In holding that the trust was not charitable, but void, EVE J said: ". . . . The question is whether the testator has effectively created such a charity as he contemplated, a charity in the legal sense of the word. Is the object of his benefaction the relief of poverty, are the gifts for the benefit of the poor and needy? I do not think they are. Apart from residential and age qualifications, the only conditions imposed on a recipient are (1) that he shall not belong to or be supported by any charitable institution, (2) that neither he nor his parents shall be in receipt of parochial relief, (3) that he shall not be black, (4) that on a second or subsequent application he shall not have disposed of any garment received within the then preceding year from the Foundation and that when he comes for a new pair of knickers or trousers the legend 'Gwyon's Present' shall still be decipherable on the waistband of his old ones.

None of these conditions necessarily imports poverty nor could the recipients be accurately described as a class of aged, impotent or poor persons. The references to the receipt of parochial relief and to the possibility of last year's garment having been disposed of show, no doubt, that the testator contemplated that candidates might be forthcoming from a class of society where incidents of this nature might occur, but although a gift to or for the poor other than those who were in receipt of parochial relief—that is, paupers—would be a good charitable gift, it does not follow that a gift to all and sundry in a particular locality and not expressed to be for the poor ought to be construed as evidencing an intention to relieve poverty merely because the testator is minded to exclude paupers. I think that according to the true construction of these testamenttary documents the benevolence of the testator was intended for all eligible boys other than paupers, and I cannot spell out of them any indication which would justify the Foundation Trustees refusing an applicant otherwise eligible on the ground that his material circumstances were of too affluent a character. In these circumstances I cannot hold this trust to be within the description of a legal charitable trust."

ii. PUBLIC BENEFIT

DINGLE v TURNER[18]

[1972] AC 601, [1972] 1 All ER 878 (HL, Viscount DILHORNE, Lords MACDERMOTT, HODSON, SIMON OF GLAISDALE and CROSS OF CHELSEA)

Frank Hanscombe Dingle, the testator, directed the trustees of his will to pay the income of his residuary estate to his wife for her life, and

[17] *Shorter Oxford English Dictionary*.

[18] (1974) CLJ 63 (G. H. Jones); (1972) 36 Conv (NS) 209 (D. J. Hayton); (1973) 36 MLR 532 (S. E. A. Johnson); Goodman Report, para. 37 (Poor Relations Cases), 38–39 (Trusts for Employees). As a background to the problem discussed in this case by Lord CROSS, see p. 290, post.

after her death to invest a capital sum in the names of the "pension fund trustees" upon trust "to apply the income thereof in paying pensions to poor employees of E. Dingle and Co Ltd" who were aged or incapacitated. The ultimate residue of the estate was to be held on similar trusts. At the date of the testator's death in 1950, the company had over 600 employees and there was a substantial number of ex-employees. The widow died in 1966.

Held (affirming MEGARRY J). The will created a valid charitable trust.

LORD CROSS OF CHELSEA: By his judgment given on April 2, 1971, Megarry J held inter alia, following the decision of the Court of Appeal in *Gibson v South American Stores (Gath and Chaves) Ltd* [1950] Ch 177, [1949] 2 All ER 985, that the trust declared by clause 8 (e) was a valid charitable trust but, on the application of the appellant Betty Mary Dingle, one of the persons interested under an intestacy, he granted a certificate under section 12 of the Administration of Justice Act 1969 enabling her to apply to this House directly for leave to appeal against that part of his judgment and on May 17, 1971, the House gave her leave to appeal.

Your Lordships, therefore, are now called upon to give to the old "poor relations" cases and the more modern "poor employees" cases that careful consideration which, in his speech in *Oppenheim v Tobacco Securities Trust Co Ltd* [1951] AC 297 at 313, Lord Morton of Henryton said that they might one day require.

The contentions of the appellant and the respondents may be stated broadly as follows. The appellant says that in the *Oppenheim* case this House decided that in principle a trust ought not to be regarded as charitable if the benefits under it are confined either to the descendants of a named individual or individuals or to the employees of a given individual or company and that though the "poor relations" cases may have to be left standing as an anomalous exception to the general rule because their validity has been recognised for so long the exception ought not to be extended to "poor employees" trusts which had not been recognised for long before their status as charitable trusts began to be called in question. The respondents, on the other hand, say, first, that the rule laid down in the *Oppenheim* case with regard to educational trusts ought not to be regarded as a rule applicable in principle to all kinds of charitable trust, and, secondly, that in any case it is impossible to draw any logical distinction between "poor relations" trusts and "poor employees" trusts, and that, as the former cannot be held invalid today after having been recognised as valid for so long, the latter must be regarded as valid also. . . .

Most of the cases on the subject were decided in the 18th or early 19th centuries and are very inadequately reported, but two things at least were clear. First, that it never occurred to the judges who decided them that in the field of "poverty" a trust could not be a charitable trust if the class of beneficiaries was defined by reference to descent from a common ancestor. Secondly, that the courts did not treat a gift or trust as necessarily charitable because the objects of it had to be poor in order to qualify, for in some of the cases the trust was treated as a private trust and not a charity. The problem in *Re Scarisbrick's Will Trusts* ([1951] Ch 622, [1951]

1 All ER 822) was to determine on what basis the distinction was drawn. . . . The Court of Appeal . . . held that in this field the distinction between a public or charitable trust and a private trust depended on whether as a matter of construction the gift was for the relief of poverty amongst a particular description of poor people or was merely a gift to particular poor persons, the relief of poverty among them being the motive of the gift. The fact that the gift took the form of a perpetual trust would no doubt indicate that the intention of the donor could not have been to confer private benefits on particular people whose possible necessities he had in mind; but the fact that the capital of the gift was to be distributed at once did not necessarily show that the gift was a private trust.

[His Lordship reviewed the earlier cases, referring to *Spiller v Maude* (1881) reported at (1886) 32 ChD 158n; *Pease v Pattinson* (1886) 32 ChD 154; *Re Buck* [1896] 2 Ch 727; *Re Gosling* (1900) 48 WR 300; *Re Drummond* [1914] 2 Ch 90; *Re Sir Robert Laidlaw*, unreported, but explained at [1950] Ch 177 at 195; *Re Compton* [1945] Ch 123, [1945] 1 All ER 198; *Re Hobourn Aero Components Ltd's Air Raid Distress Fund* [1946] Ch 194, [1945] 2 All ER 711; *Gibson v South American Stores (Gath and Chaves) Ltd* [1950] Ch 177, [1949] 2 All ER 985; *Oppenheim v Tobacco Securities Trust Co Ltd* [1951] AC 297, [1951] 1 All ER 31; *Re Cox* [1955] AC 627, [1955] 2 All ER 550; *Re Young decd.* [1955] 1 WLR 1269, [1955] 3 All ER 689 and *Davies v Perpetual Trustee Co. Ltd* [1959] AC 439, [1959] 2 All ER 128 and continued:] After this long—but I hope not unduly long—recital of the decided cases, I turn to consider the arguments advanced by the appellant in support of the appeal. Even on [the assumption that the "poor relations" cases, the "poor members" cases and the "poor employees" cases are all anomalous] the appeal must fail. The status of some of the "poor relations" trusts as valid charitable trusts was recognized more than 200 years ago and a few of those then recognised are still being administered as charities today. In *Re Compton* Lord Greene MR said, at p. 139, that it was "quite impossible" for the Court of Appeal to overrule such old decisions and in *Oppenheim* [1951] AC 297 Lord Simonds in speaking of them remarked, at p. 309, on the unwisdom of casting doubt on "decisions of respectable antiquity in order to introduce a greater harmony into the law of charity as a whole". Indeed, counsel for the appellant hardly ventured to suggest that we should overrule the "poor relations" cases. His submission was that which was accepted by the Court of Appeal for Ontario in *Re Cox* [1951] OR 205—namely that while the "poor relations" cases might have to be left as long standing anomalies there was no good reason for sparing the "poor employees" cases which only date from *Re Gosling* (1900) 48 WR 300 and which have been under suspicion ever since the decision in *Re Compton* [1945] Ch 123, [1945] 1 All ER 198. But the "poor members" and the "poor employees" decisions were a natural development of the "poor relations" decisions and to draw a distinction between different sorts of "poverty" trusts would be quite illogical and could certainly not be said to be introducing "greater harmony" into the law of charity. Moreover, though not as old as the "poor relations" trusts "poor employees" trusts have been recognised as charities for many years; there are now a large number of such trusts in existence; and assuming, as one must, that they are properly administered in the sense that benefits under them are only given to people who can fairly be said to be, according to current standards, "poor persons", to treat such trusts as charities is not open to any practical objection. So as it seems to me it must be accepted that wherever else it may hold sway the *Compton* rule has no application in the field of trusts for the relief of poverty and that there the dividing line between a charitable trust and a private trust lies where the Court of Appeal drew it in *Re Scarisbrick's Will Trusts* [1951] Ch 622, [1951] 1 All ER 822.

Oppenheim [1951] AC 297, [1951] 1 All ER 31 was a case of an educational trust and though the majority evidently agreed with the view expressed by the Court of Appeal in the *Hobourn Aero* case [1946] Ch 194 that the *Compton* rule [1945] Ch 123 was of universal application outside the field of poverty it would no doubt be open to this House without overruling *Oppenheim* to hold that the scope of the rule was more limited. If ever I should be called upon to pronounce on this question—which does not arise in this appeal—I would as at present advised be inclined to draw a distinction between the practical merits of the *Compton* rule and the reasoning by which Lord Greene MR sought to justify it. That reasoning—based on the distinction between personal and impersonal relationships—has never seemed to me very satisfactory and I have always—if I may say so—felt the force of the criticism to which my noble and learned friend Lord MacDermott subjected it in his dissenting speech in *Oppenheim*. For my part I would prefer to approach the problem on far broader lines. The phrase a "section of the public" is in truth a vague phrase which may mean different things to different people. In the law of charity judges have sought to elucidate its meaning by contrasting it with another phrase: "a fluctuating body of private individuals". But I get little help from the supposed contrast for as I see it one and the same aggregate of persons may well be describable both as a section of the public and as a fluctuating body of private individuals. The ratepayers of the Royal Borough of Kensington and Chelsea, for example, certainly constitute a section of the public; but would it be a misuse of language to describe them as a "fluctuating body of private individuals"? After all, every part of the public is composed of individuals and being susceptible of increase or decrease is fluctuating. So at the end of the day one is left where one started with the bare contrast between "public" and "private". No doubt some classes are more naturally describable as sections of the public than as private classes while other classes are more naturally describable as private classes than as sections of the public. The blind, for example, can naturally be described as a section of the public; but what they have in common—their blindness—does not join them together in such a way that they could be called a private class. On the other hand, the descendants of Mr. Gladstone might more reasonably be described as a "private class" than as a section of the public, and in the field of common employment the same might well be said of the employees in some fairly small firm. But if one turns to large companies employing many thousands of men and women most of whom are quite unknown to one another and to the directors the answer is by no means so clear. One might say that in such a case the distinction between a section of the public and a private class is not applicable at all or even that the employees in such concerns as I.C.I. or G.E.C. are just as much "sections of the public" as the residents in some geographical area. In truth the question whether or not the potential beneficiaries of a trust can fairly be said to constitute a section of the public is a question of degree and cannot be by itself decisive of the question whether the trust is a charity. Much must depend on the purpose of the trust. It may well be that, on the one hand, a trust to promote some purpose, prima facie charitable, will constitute a charity even though the class of potential beneficiaries might fairly be called a private class and that, on the other hand, a trust to promote another purpose, also prima facie charitable, will not constitute a charity even though the class of potential beneficiaries might seem to some people fairly describable as a section of the public. In answering the question whether any given trust is a charitable trust the courts—as I see it—cannot avoid having regard to the fiscal privileges accorded to charities. As counsel for the Attorney-General remarked in the course of the argument the law of charity is bedevilled by the fact that charitable trusts enjoy two quite different sorts of privilege. On the one hand, they enjoy immunity from the rules against perpetuity and uncertainty and though individual potential beneficiaries cannot sue to enforce them the public interest arising under them is protected by the Attorney-General. If this was all there would be no reason for the courts not to look favourably on the claim of any "purpose" trust to be considered as a charity if it seemed calculated to confer some real benefit on those intended to benefit by it whoever they might be and if it would fail if not held to be a charity. But that is not all. Charities automatically enjoy fiscal privileges which with the increased burden of taxation have become more and more important and in deciding that such and such a trust is a charitable trust the court is endowing it with a substantial annual subsidy at the expense of the taxpayer[19]. Indeed, claims of trusts to rank as charities are just as often challenged by the revenue as by those who would take the fund if the trust was invalid. It is, of course, unfortunate that the recognition of any trust as a valid charitable trust should automatically attract fiscal privileges, for the question whether a trust to further some purpose is so little likely to benefit the public that it ought to be declared invalid and the question whether it is likely to confer such great benefits on the public that it should enjoy fiscal immunity are really two quite different questions. The logical solution would be to separate them and to say—as the Radcliffe Commission[20] proposed—that only some charities should enjoy fiscal privileges. But, as things are, validity and fiscal immunity march hand in hand and the decisions in the *Compton* [1945] Ch 123, [1945] 1 All ER 198 and *Oppenheim* [1951] AC 297, [1951] 1 All ER 31 cases were pretty obviously influenced by the consideration that if such trusts as were there in question were held valid they would enjoy an undeserved

[19] See at p. 610, where counsel for the Attorney-General stated that in 1972 the annual estimated income of trusts for poor employees, poor members of associations, or professional groups was £4,690,000, and the income for poor relations was £3,400.

[20] Royal Commission on the Taxation of Profits and Income (1955) Cmd. 9474, Ch. 7; see also (1956) 72 LQR 187 (G. Cross); (1977) 40 MLR 397 (N. P. Gravells).

fiscal immunity. To establish a trust for the education of the children of employees in a company in which you are interested is no doubt a meritorious act; but however numerous the employees may be the purpose which you are seeking to achieve is not a public purpose. It is a company purpose and there is no reason why your fellow taxpayers should contribute to a scheme which by providing "fringe benefits" for your employees will benefit the company by making their conditions of employment more attractive. The temptation to enlist the assistance of the law of charity in private endeavours of this sort is considerable—witness the recent case of the Metal Box scholarships—*IRC v Educational Grants Association Ltd* [1967] Ch 993, [1967] 2 All ER 893—and the courts must do what they can to discourage such attempts. In the field of poverty the danger is not so great as in the field of education—for while people are keenly alive to the need to give their children a good education and to the expense of doing so they are generally optimistic enough not to entertain serious fears of falling on evil days much before they fall on them. Consequently the existence of company "benevolent funds" the income of which is free of tax does not constitute a very attractive "fringe benefit". This is a practical justification—though not, of course, the historical explanation—for the special treatment accorded to poverty trusts in charity law. For the same sort of reason a trust to promote some religion among the employees of a company might perhaps safely be held to be charitable provided that it was clear that the benefits were to be purely spiritual. On the other hand, many "purpose" trusts falling under Lord Macnaghten's fourth head [*Income Tax Special Purposes Comrs v Pemsel* [1891] AC 531 at 583] if confined to a class of employees would clearly be open to the same sort of objection as educational trusts. As I see it, it is on these broad lines rather than for the reasons actually given by Lord Greene MR that the *Compton* rule [1945] Ch 123, [1945] 1 All ER 198 can best be justified.

My Lords, for the reasons given earlier in this speech I would dismiss this appeal; but as the view was expressed in the *Oppenheim* case [1951] AC 297, [1951] 1 All ER 31 that the question of the validity of trusts for poor relations and poor employees ought some day to be considered by this House and as the fund in dispute in this case is substantial your Lordships may perhaps think it proper to direct that the cost of all parties to the appeal be paid out of it.

LORD HODSON: My Lords, I agree with my noble and learned friend, Lord Cross of Chelsea, that this appeal should be dismissed and with his reasons for that conclusion. With this reservation: that I share the doubts expressed by my noble and learned friends, Lord MacDermott and Viscount Dilhorne, as to the relevance of fiscal considerations in deciding whether a gift or trust is charitable.

iii. IMMEDIATE DISTRIBUTION

In *Re Scarisbrick* ([1951] Ch 622, [1951] 1 All ER 822) a testatrix provided that, after the death of her children, the residue of her estate should be held upon trust "for such relations of my said son and daughters as in the opinion of the survivor of my said son and daughters shall be in needy circumstances and for such charitable objects either in Germany or . . . Great Britain . . . for such interests and in such proportions. . . . as the survivor of my said son and daughters shall by deed or will appoint."

The parties agreed that one half of the fund was effectively devoted to charity. The question arose in respect of the gifts in favour of the relations. No appointment was ever made by the survivor of the children. The Court of Appeal (reversing ROXBURGH J) upheld the gift.

JENKINS LJ, after laying down a number of general propositions relating to the requirement of public benefit in charitable trusts, and referring to the exceptional case of a trust for poor relations, said (at p. 650): "Applying these general propositions to the present case, I ask myself whether the trust in cl. 11 for 'such relations . . . as in the opinion of the survivor of' the testatrix's 'son and daughters shall be in needy circumstances for such interests and in such proportions . . . as the survivor . . . shall by deed or will appoint' is a trust for the relief of poverty. If it is such a trust, then, as I understand the exception above referred to, it matters not that the potential objects of such trust are confined to relations of the son and daughters. If language means anything, a person in needy circumstances is a person who is poor and as such a proper object of charity, and no one can take under this trust who is not in needy circumstances. I do not think that the effect of the expression in 'needy circumstances' is materially altered by the qualifying words 'in the opinion of the survivor. . . .'

'Poverty' is necessarily to some extent a relative matter, a matter of opinion, and it is not to be assumed that the person made the judge of 'needy circumstances' in the present case would have acted otherwise than in accordance with an opinion fairly and honestly formed as to the circumstances, needy or otherwise, of anyone coming into consideration as a potential object of the power. Under a similar trust which did not expressly make the appointor's opinion the test of eligibility, the appointor would in practice have to make the selection according to the best of his or her opinion or judgment. The express reference to the appointor's opinion merely serves to reduce the possibility of dispute as to the eligibility or otherwise of any particular individual on the score of needy circumstances. Accordingly, I dismiss the words 'in the opinion of the survivor' as having no material bearing on the character of this trust. In so doing, I am fortified by the similar conclusion reached in this court as to the effect of the words 'in the opinion of the London Board' in *Gibson v South American Stores (Gath and Chaves) Ltd* ([1950] Ch 177 at 185)".

His Lordship discussed the cases relating to the requirement of public benefit in relation to gifts in favour of poor relations, and continued (at p. 652): "Accordingly, in the view I take, this is a trust for the relief of poverty in the charitable sense amongst the class of relations described, and, being a trust for the relief of poverty, is in view of the exception above stated, not disqualified from ranking as a legally charitable trust by the circumstance that its application is confined to a class of relations (albeit a wide class), with the result that its potential beneficiaries do not comprise the public or a section thereof under the decisions to which I have referred.

I am accordingly of opinion that as the law now stands the trust in question should be upheld as a valid charitable trust for the relief of poverty.

The judge took a different view . . .

I find myself unable to accept the judge's view as to the effect of the authorities. I think the true question in each case has really been whether the gift was for the relief of poverty amongst a class of persons, or rather, as Sir William Grant MR put it[1], a particular description of poor, or was merely a gift to individuals, albeit with relief of poverty amongst those individuals as the motive of the gift, or with a selective preference for the poor or poorest amongst those individuals. If the gift is perpetual in character, that no doubt is an important circumstance as demonstrating that the intention cannot have been merely to benefit the statutory next of kin of the propositus or other particular individuals identified by the gift. Moreover, the gift, if perpetual, can only be supported on the footing that it is charitable—an illogical though in past practice probably a persuasive reason for holding it such.

But I see no sufficient ground in the authorities for holding that a gift for the benefit of poor relations qualifies as charitable only if it is perpetual in character. I do not think that the observation of Sir William Grant MR above referred to goes by any means as far as that. It is fully satisfied if taken as meaning that an immediate bequest of a sum to be distributed among poor relations may on its true construction be no more than a gift to particular individuals (i.e., the next of kin of the propositus), whereas a gift having perpetual continuance cannot be so confined. If a gift or trust on its true construction does extend to those in need amongst relations in every degree, even though it provides for immediate distribution, then, inasmuch as the class of potential beneficiaries becomes so wide as to be incapable of exhaustive ascertainment, the impersonal quality, if I may so describe it, supplied in continuing gifts by the element of perpetuity, is equally present."[2]

QUESTION

Can you formulate a satisfactory definition of Poverty?

Should this be sought in terms of persons who pay no income tax, receive public assistance, or are entitled to legal aid? (Tudor, p. 15; (1965) 72 LQR 187 at pp. 206–207; Nathan Report, paras. 120–140).

Or should it be limited to persons who, for one reason or another, are ineligible to obtain relief from the State?

B. The Advancement of Education[3]

i. GENERAL

The concept of Education has progressed a long way since the Preamble

[1] In *A-G v Price* (1810) 17 Ves 371 at 374.

[2] *Re Cohen* [1973] 1 WLR 415, [1973] 1 All ER 889 (trust "for or towards the maintenance and benefit of any relative of mine whom my trustees shall consider to be in special need" held charitable).

[3] H & M, pp. 378–384, 400–404; K & S, pp. 163–164; K & S (Charities), pp. 72–86; P & M, pp. 176–177, 182–186; Pettit, pp. 171–174, 188–192; Snell, pp. 146–147, 150–152; Tudor, pp. 26–38; Picarda, pp. 38–53; Goodman Report, paras. 62 (The Arts), 63 (Research), 64–67 (Learned Societies), 68 (Propaganda).

to the Statute of Elizabeth I spoke of "the maintenance of schools of learning, free schools and scholars in universities" and "the education and preferment of orphans". As BUCKLEY LJ said in *Incorporated Council of Law Reporting for England and Wales v A-G*[4], it now extends "to the improvement of a useful branch of human knowledge and its public dissemination."[5] The main areas of controversy in the modern law will be discussed in the cases which follow. The concept includes of course "satellite" purposes such as the payment of teachers and administrative staff[6], and an educational institution may be charitable, although a private company, so long as it does not operate for profit[7].

It was in this area that the modern emphasis on the necessity for "public benefit" first came to the fore. Apart from the fourth category (p. 331, post), the question was hardly material in the low-tax days before 1939. If it was charitable to advance education among the many, why was it not charitable to advance education among the few? Indeed, the highly selective system of British education assumes this. Scholarships for boys born in particular villages, or for boys to be educated at particular schools, have been upheld for centuries, as have "closed" scholarships to individual Colleges at Oxford or Cambridge. The fiscal exemptions which charities enjoy and the dramatic increase in the rates of taxation from 1939 and the emphasis upon equality in education rather than selectivity prompt the asking of a different question: Even if the provision of money for the education of a selected few is to be encouraged, how is it possible to justify the tax free status of such money? In short, the law of charity must not be allowed to develop into a tax-planning device for the tax free education of the children of the wealthy[8]; nor must employers be able, by setting up educational trusts for the children of their employees, to be allowed to use it for commercial advantage. The same sort of concept carried over to religious trusts. We have seen that the problem has been avoided in the case of trusts for the relief of poverty.

ii. EDUCATION IS NOT LIMITED TO TEACHING

In *Royal Choral Society v Inland Revenue Commissioners* ([1943] 2 All ER 101) the question was whether the appellants were a society "established for charitable purposes only" and thus entitled to exemption from income tax. The objects of the society were "to form and maintain a choir in order to promote the practice and performance of choral works, whether by way of concerts or choral pageants in the Royal Albert Hall or as otherwise decided from time to time".

The Court of Appeal held that the Society was charitable as being established for the purposes of the advancement of aesthetic education. Lord

[4] [1972] Ch 73, [1971] 3 All ER 1029.

[5] [1972] Ch at 102.

[6] *Case of Christ's College, Cambridge* (1757) 1 Wm Bl 90.

[7] *Abbey Malvern Wells Ltd v Ministry of Local Government and Planning* [1951] Ch 728, [1951] 2 All ER 154; *Re Girls' Public Day School Trust* [1951] Ch 400, where a girls' school carried on by private company was held not to be a charity because profits could benefit the shareholders. See *Butterworth v Keeler* (1916) 219 NY 446, 114 NE 308; Scott, *Cases on Trusts* (5th Edn) pp. 678–679.

[8] Goodman Report, paras. 47 (Costly Services), 60–61 (Education), p. 145; House of Commons Report, vol. I, paras. 45–52, vol. II, pp. 39–43, 93, 164–165, 249–271.

GREENE MR said (at p. 104): "Dealing with the educational aspect from the point of view of the public who hear music, the Solicitor-General argued that nothing could be educational which did not involve teaching—as I understood him, teaching in the sense of a master teaching a class. He said that in the domain of art the only thing that could be educational in a charitable sense would be the education of the executants: the teaching of the painter, the training of the musician, and so forth. I protest against that narrow conception of education when one is dealing with aesthetic education. Very few people can become executants, or at any rate executants who can give pleasure either to themselves or to others; but a very large number of people can become instructed listeners with a trained and cultivated taste. In my opinion, a body of persons established for the purpose of raising the artistic taste of the country and established by an appropriate document which confines them to that purpose, is established for educational purposes, because the education of artistic taste is one of the most important things in the development of a civilised human being."

In *Re Dupree's Deed Trusts* ([1945] Ch 16, [1944] 2 All ER 443) a trust with a capital of £5,000 was established for the purpose of providing an annual chess tournament for boys and young men under the age of 21 resident in the city of Portsmouth[9]. In spite of the argument of counsel for the next-of-kin that the encouragement of "the playing of chess in schools would not be altogether desirable. It might take pupils away from cricket, football and athletic pursuits generally", the trust was upheld as an educational charitable trust. VAISEY J however had some anxiety as to the problem of drawing the right line in these cases. He said (at p. 20): "One feels, perhaps, that one is on rather a slippery slope. If chess, why not draughts? If draughts, why not bezique, and so on, through to bridge and whist, and, by another route, to stamp collecting and the acquisition of birds' eggs? Those pursuits will have to be dealt with if and when they come up for consideration. . . ."

RE HOPKINS' WILL TRUSTS[10]

[1965] Ch 669, [1964] 3 All ER 46 (ChD, WILBERFORCE J)

The testatrix gave one third part of her estate to "the Francis Bacon Society Inc. . . . to be earmarked and applied towards finding the Bacon-Shakespeare manuscripts and in the event of the same having been discovered by the date of my death then for the general purposes of the work and propaganda of the society".

The objects of the Society were: "(1) To encourage the study of the works of Francis Bacon as philosopher, lawyer, statesman and poet; also his character, genius and life; his influence on his own and succeeding times, and the tendencies and results of his writings. (2) To encourage the general

[9] This is not contrary to Sex Discrimination Act 1975. Charities are expressly excepted, s. 43; Sex Discrimination Act 1975 (Amendment of Section 43) Order 1977, S.I. 1977 No. 528. In 1976 a Phyllis Loe Chess Tournament for Girls Trust was established for girls below the age of 18 educated in Portsmouth. See (1977) 41 Conv (NS) 8.

[10] (1965) 29 Conv (NS) 368 (M. Newark and A. Samuels).

study of evidence in favour of Francis Bacon's authorship of the plays commonly ascribed to Shakespeare, and to investigate his connection with other works of the Elizabethan period." The Society was registered as a charity under the Charities Act 1960.

Held. A valid educational charitable trust.

WILBERFORCE J [commenting that the society was a registered charity under Charities Act 1960 and so was conclusively presumed to be a charity[11] continued:] Miss Hopkins could have given the money to the society during her life and the society under its constitution could have spent it for the purposes stated in the will. But the validity of her testamentary disposition is questioned. The basis for the challenge is that this is a gift to the society not absolutely but upon a stated trust, so that it is necessary to see whether the trust is valid. It cannot be upheld as a gift upon valid but non-charitable trusts, and the society does not seek so to uphold it. It can only be supported if it is a valid charitable trust. Whether it is so is what the court has to decide . . .

Let me say at once that no determination of the authorship of the "Shakespeare" plays, or even of any subsidiary question relating to it, falls to be made in the present proceedings. The court is only concerned, at this point, with the practicability and later with the legality of carrying Miss Hopkins' wishes into effect, and it must decide this, one way or the other, upon the evidence of the experts which is before it.

[His Lordship reviewed the evidence and continued:] On this evidence, should the conclusion be reached that the search for the Bacon-Shakespeare manuscripts is so manifestly futile that the court should not allow this bequest to be spent upon it as upon an object devoid of the possibility of any result? I think not. The evidence shows that the discovery of any manuscript of the plays is unlikely; but so are many discoveries before they are made (one may think of the Codex Sinaiticus, or the Tomb of Tutankhamen, or the Dead Sea Scrolls); I do not think that that degree of improbability has been reached which justifies the court in placing an initial interdict on the testatrix's benefaction.

I come, then, to the only question of law: is the gift of a charitable character? The society has put its case in the alternative under the two headings of education and of general benefit to the community and has argued separately for each. This compartmentalisation is derived from the accepted classification into four groups of the miscellany found in the Statute of Elizabeth (43 Eliz. I, c. 4). That statute, preserved as to the preamble only by the Mortmain and Charitable Uses Act, 1888, lost even that precarious hold on the Statute Book when the Act of 1888 was repealed by the Charities Act, 1960, but the somewhat ossificatory classification to which it gave rise survives in the decided cases. It is unsatisfactory because the frontiers of "educational purposes" (as of the other divisions) have been extended and are not easy to trace with precision, and because, under the fourth head, it has been held necessary for the court to find a benefit to the public within the spirit and intendment of the obsolete Elizabethan statute. The difficulty of achieving that, while at the same time keeping

[11] See p. 403, post.

the law's view of what is charitable reasonably in line with modern requirements, explains what Lord Simonds accepted as the case-to-case approach of the courts: see *National Anti-Vivisection Society v IRC* ([1948] AC 31, [1947] 2 All ER 217). There are, in fact, examples of accepted charities which do not decisively fit into one rather than the other category. Examples are institutes for scientific research (see the *National Anti-Vivisection* case, per Lord Wright ([1948] AC at 42)), museums (see *Re Pinion* ([1965] Ch 85 at 104)), the preservation of ancient cottages (*Re Cranstoun* ([1932] 1 Ch 537)), and even the promotion of Shakespearian drama (*Re Shakespeare Memorial Theatre Trust* ([1923] 2 Ch 398)). The present may be such a case.

Accepting, as I have the authority of Lord Simonds for so doing, that the court must decide each case as best it can, on the evidence available to it, as to benefit, and within the moving spirit of decided cases, it would seem to me that a bequest for the purpose of search, or research, for the original manuscripts of England's greatest dramatist (whoever he was) would be well within the law's conception of charitable purposes. The discovery of such manuscripts, or of one such manuscript, would be of the highest value to history and to literature. It is objected, against this, that as we already have the text of the plays, from an almost contemporary date, the discovery of a manuscript would add nothing worth while. This I utterly decline to accept. Without any undue exercise of the imagination, it would surely be a reasonable expectation that the revelation of a manuscript would contribute, probably decisively, to a solution of the authorship problem, and this alone is benefit enough. It might also lead to improvements in the text. It might lead to more accurate dating.

Is there any authority, then, which should lead me to hold that a bequest to achieve this objective is not charitable? By Mr. Fox, for the next-of-kin, much reliance was placed on the decision on Bernard Shaw's will, the *"British Alphabet"* case (*Re Shaw* ([1957] 1 WLR 729, [1957] 1 All ER 745))[12]. Harman J held that the gift was not educational because it merely tended to the increase of knowledge and that it was not within the fourth charitable category because it was not itself for a beneficial purpose but for the purpose of persuading the public by propaganda that it was beneficial. The gift was very different from the gift here. But the judge did say this ([1957] 1 WLR at 737): "if the object be merely the increase of knowledge, that is not in itself a charitable object unless it be combined with teaching or education"; and he referred to the House of Lords decision, *Whicker v Hume* ((1858) 7 HL Cas 124), where, in relation to a gift for advancement of education and learning, two of the Lords read "learning" as equivalent to "teaching", thereby in his view implying that learning, in its ordinary meaning, is not a charitable purpose.

This decision certainly seems to place some limits upon the extent to which a gift for research may be regarded as charitable. Those limits are that either it must be "combined with teaching or education", if it is to fall under the third head, or it must be beneficial to the community in a way regarded by the law as charitable, if it is to fall within the fourth category. The words "combined with teaching or education", though

12 See p. 253, ante.

well explaining what the judge had in mind when he rejected the gift in *Shaw's* case ([1957] 1 WLR 729, [1957] 1 All ER 745), are not easy to interpret in relation to other facts. I should be unwilling to treat them as meaning that the promotion of academic research is not a charitable purpose unless the researcher were engaged in teaching or education in the conventional meaning; and I am encouraged in this view by some words of Lord Greene MR in *Re Compton* ([1945] Ch 123 at 127). The testatrix there had forbidden the income of the bequest to be used for research, and Lord Greene MR treated this as a negative definition of the education to be provided. It would, he said, exclude a grant to enable a beneficiary to conduct research on some point of history or science. This shows that Lord Greene MR considered that historic research might fall within the description of "education". I think, therefore, that the word "education" as used by Harman J in *Re Shaw* ([1957] 1 WLR 729, [1957] 1 All ER 745) must be used in a wide sense, certainly extending beyond teaching, and that the requirement is that, in order to be charitable, research must either be of educational value to the researcher or must be so directed as to lead to something which will pass into the store of educational material, or so as to improve the sum of communicable knowledge in an area which education may cover—education in this last context extending to the formation of literary taste and appreciation (compare *Royal Choral Society v IRC* ([1943] 2 All ER 101)). Whether or not the test is wider than this, it is, as I have stated it, amply wide enough to include the purposes of the gift in this case.

As regards the fourth category, Harman J is evidently leaving it open to the court to hold, on the facts, that research of a particular kind may be beneficial to the community in a way which the law regards as charitable, "beneficial" here not being limited to the production of material benefit (as through medical or scientific research) but including at least benefit in the intellectual or artistic fields.

So I find nothing in this authority to prevent me from finding that the gift falls under either the third or fourth head of the classification of charitable purposes.

On the other side there is *Re British School of Egyptian Archaeology* ([1954] 1 WLR 546, [1954] 1 All ER 887) also a decision of Harman J, a case much closer to the present. The trusts there were to excavate, to discover antiquities, to hold exhibitions, to publish works and to promote the training and assistance of students—all in relation to Egypt. Harman J held that the purposes were charitable, as being educational. The society was one for the diffusion of a certain branch of knowledge, namely, knowledge of the ancient past of Egypt; and it also had a direct educational purpose, namely, to train students. The conclusion reached that there was an educational charity was greatly helped by the reference to students, but it seems that Harman J must have accepted that the other objects—those of archaeological research—were charitable, too. They were quite independent objects on which the whole of the society's funds could have been spent, and the language "the school has a direct educational purpose, namely, to train students" seems to show that the judge was independently upholding each set of objects.

Mr. Fox correctly pointed out that in that case there was a direct obligation to diffuse the results of the society's research and said that it was this that justified the finding that the archaeological purposes were charitable. I accept that research of a private character, for the benefit only of the members of a society, would not normally be educational—or otherwise charitable—as did Harman J ([1954] 1 WLR at 551), but I do not think that the research in the present case can be said to be of a private character, for it is inherently inevitable, and manifestly intended, that the result of any discovery should be published to the world. I think, therefore, that the *British School of Egyptian Archaeology* case supports the society's contentions.

A number of other authorities were referred to as illustrating the wide variety of objects which have been accepted as educational or as falling under the fourth category but, since none of them is close to the present, I shall not refer to them. They are well enough listed in the standard authorities.

One final reference is appropriate: to *Re Shakespeare Memorial Trust* ([1923] 2 Ch 398). The scheme there was for a number of objects which included the performance of Shakespearian and other classical English plays, and stimulating the art of acting. I refer to it for two purposes, first as an example of a case where the court upheld the gift either as educational or as for purposes beneficial to the community—an approach which commends itself to me here—and secondly as illustrative of the educational and public benefit accepted by the court as flowing from a scheme designed to spread the influence of Shakespeare as the author of the plays. This gift is not that, but it lies in the same field, for the improving of our literary heritage, and my judgment is for upholding it.

In *Re Shaw's Will Trusts* ([1952] Ch 163, [1952] 1 All ER 49) the testatrix, who was the widow of George Bernard Shaw, bequeathed the residue of her estate upon the following trusts: "The making of grants contributions and payments to any foundation . . . having for its objects the bringing of the masterpieces of fine art within the reach of the people of Ireland of all classes in their own country. . . . The teaching promotion and encouragement in Ireland of self control, elocution, oratory, deportment, the arts of personal contact, of social intercourse, and the other arts of public, private, professional and business life . . ."

Vaisey J upheld the gift as an educational charitable trust. It was "a sort of finishing school for the Irish people". "I think" he said (at p. 172) "that 'education' includes . . . not only teaching, but the promotion or encouragement of these arts and graces of life which are, after all, perhaps the finest and best part of the human character . . . It is education of a desirable sort, and which, if corrected and augmented and amplified by other kinds of teaching and instruction, might have most beneficial results."

In *Incorporated Council of Law Reporting for England and Wales v Attorney-General*[13] ([1972] Ch 73, [1971] 3 All ER 1029) the Court of Appeal

[13] See pp. 354, 369, post.

unanimously held that the Council was charitable under the fourth head of Lord MACNAGHTEN's classification[14]. Two of the judges, SACHS and BUCKLEY LJJ held that it was charitable also as being for the advancement of education. BUCKLEY LJ said (at p. 101): "Foster J declined to accept the view that the council's objects are educational, mainly, I think, upon the ground that in many respects they are not used for instructional purposes. He did, however, take the view that they are charitable on the ground that the purpose of the publication of The Law Reports is to enable judge-made law to be properly developed and administered by the courts, a purpose beneficial to the community and within the spirit of the preamble.

What then does the evidence establish about the need for reliable law reports and the reasons for publishing them? As the uncontradicted evidence of Professor Goodhart makes clear, in a legal system such as ours, in which judges' decisions are governed by precedents, reported decisions are the means by which legal principles (other than those laid down by statutes) are developed, established and made known, and by which the application of those legal principles to particular kinds of facts are illustrated and explained. Reported decisions may be said to be the tissue of the body of our non-statutory law. Whoever, therefore, would carry out any anatomical researches upon our non-statutory corpus juris must do so by research amongst, and study of, reported cases.

Professor Goodhart recalls that Sir Frederick Pollock in his paper entitled *The Science of Case Law* published in 1882 pointed out that the study of law is a science in the same sense as physics or chemistry are sciences, and that the material with which it is concerned consists of individual cases which must be analysed and measured as carefully as is the material in the other sciences. At about the same time the 'case system' of teaching law was introduced at the Harvard Law School, which has since become generally adopted. Accurate and authoritative law reports are thus seen to be essential both for the advancement of legal education and the proper administration of justice. As Professor Goodhart says: 'Accuracy in The Law Reports is, therefore, as important for the science of law as is the accuracy of instruments in the physical sciences.'

The legal profession has from times long past been termed a learned profession, and rightly so, for no man can properly practise or apply the law who is not learned in that field of law with which he is concerned. He must have more than an aptitude and more than a skill. He must be learned in a sense importing true scholarship. In a system of law such as we have in this country this scholarship can only be acquired and maintained by a continual study of case law.

I agree with Foster J in thinking that, when counsel in court cites a case to a judge, counsel is not in any real sense 'educating' the judge, counsel performing the role of a teacher and the judge filling the role of a pupil; but I do not agree with him that the process should not be regarded as falling under the charitable head of 'the advancement of education'.

In a number of cases learned societies have been held to be charitable.

[14] See also *Incorporated Council of Law Reporting of the State of Queensland v Commissioner of Taxation* (1971) 45 ALJR 552; (1972) 88 LQR 171.

Sometimes the case has been classified under Lord Macnaghten's fourth head, sometimes under the second. It does not really matter under which head such a case is placed, but for my own part I prefer to treat the present case as falling within the class of purposes for the advancement of education rather than within the final class of other purposes for the benefit of the community. For the present purpose the second head should be regarded as extending to the improvement of a useful branch of human knowledge and its public dissemination.

[His Lordship referred to (a) *Beaumont v Oliveira* ((1869) 4 Ch App 309), where bequests to the Royal Society whose object is 'improving natural knowledge' and the Royal Geographical Society 'the improvement and diffusion of geographical knowledge' were held charitable under the fourth head of charity; (b) *Royal College of Surgeons of England v National Provincial Bank Ltd* ([1952] AC 631, [1952] 1 All ER 984), where the objects were 'the encouragement of the study and practice of the art and science of surgery'; (c) *Re Lopes* ([1931] 2 Ch 130), a gift to the Zoological Society of London whose objects are 'the advancement of zoology and animal physiology and the introduction of new and curious subjects of the animal kingdom'; and (d) *Re British School of Egyptian Archaeology* ([1954] 1 WLR 546, [1954] 1 All ER 887 (p. 299, ante)), where gifts were upheld as being for the advancement of education; and continued:]

The fact that the council's publications can be regarded as a necessary part of a practising lawyer's equipment does not prevent the council from being established exclusively for charitable purposes. The practising lawyer and the judge must both be lifelong students in that field of scholarship for the study of which The Law Reports provide essential material and a necessary service. The benefit which the council confers upon members of the legal profession in making accurate reports available is that it facilitates the study and ascertainment of the law. It also helps the lawyer to earn his livelihood, but that is incidental to or consequential on the primary scholastic function of advancing and disseminating knowledge of the law, and does not detract from the exclusively charitable character of the council's objects: compare *Royal College of Surgeons of England v National Provincial Bank Ltd* ([1952] AC 631, [1952] 1 All ER 984) and *Royal College of Nursing v St Marylebone Borough Council* ([1959] 1 WLR 1077, [1959] 3 All ER 663).

The service which publication of The Law Reports provides benefits not only those actively engaged in the practice and administration of the law, but also those whose business it is to study and teach law academically, and many others who need to study the law for the purposes of their trades, businesses, professions or affairs. In all these fields, however, the nature of the service is the same: it enables the reader to study, and by study to acquaint himself with and instruct himself in the law of this country. There is nothing here which negatives an exclusively charitable purpose.

Although the objects of the council are commercial in the sense that the council exists to publish and sell its publications, they are unself-regarding. The members are prohibited from deriving any profit from the council's activities, and the council itself, although not debarred from making a profit out of its business, can only apply any such profit in the further pursuit of its objects. The council is consequently not prevented from being a charity by reason of any commercial element in its activities.

I therefore reach the conclusion that the council is a body established exclusively for charitable purposes and is entitled to be registered under the Act of 1960."

iii. SPECIAL SCHOOL ACTIVITIES

Some activities, not otherwise educational, are treated as being for the advancement of education if they are carried out as part of school activities[15].

RE MARIETTE

[1915] 2 Ch 284 (ChD, EVE J)

A testator bequeathed "£1000 to the Governing Body of Aldenham School for the purpose of building Eton fives courts or squash rackets courts, or for some similar purpose that shall be decided by a majority of the housemasters at the time of my death" and "£100 to the headmaster . . . upon trust to use the interest to provide a prize for some event in the school athletic sports. . . ."

Held. Both legacies were valid charitable gifts.

EVE J: The admonition with which Mr. Clayton commenced his argument is by no means to be disregarded. One must be careful not to allow one's natural inclination to give effect to a gift of this sort to lead one to disregard well-established principles. The gift in question is a gift by a gentleman who had served this school for twenty-four years as an assistant master and who had obviously come to entertain for it in a marked degree that affection which most men feel for the old school, and which would certainly tend to increase in the case of a man who had given the best part of his life to its services. The amount is to be laid out in the erection of additional fives courts at the school, and the question is whether it is a gift which in law can be supported or whether it is void as not being charitable and tending to a perpetuity. It is a gift to an institution which admittedly is a charity within the Statute of Elizabeth, but I accede to the argument of the residuary legatees that it is quite possible that a gift to a charity may be of such a character as not to be in itself a charitable gift. On the other hand I think in considering whether a gift is charitable or not one must not confine oneself to the character of the gift itself, but must pay regard also to the character and objects of the charity who are the intended recipients of the gift.

The object of this charity is the education, in the widest sense, of boys and young men between the ages of ten and nineteen. No one of sense could be found to suggest that between those ages any boy can be properly educated unless at least as much attention is given to the development of his body as is given to the development of his mind. It is necessary,

[15] The Kent Youth Cricket Association, providing facilities for coaching and playing cricket among school and university students, was registered as a charity. Subsequently, applications by similar Associations in Essex and Surrey have been challenged. Annual Report for 1973, paras. 80–82; 1974, paras. 63–64. The Football Association Youth Trust was held not to be charitable: *IRC v McMullen* [1978] 1 All ER 230. It is understood that there will be further litigation on these matters.

therefore, in any satisfactory system of education to provide for both mental and bodily occupation, mental occupation by means of the classics and those other less inviting studies to which a portion of the day is devoted, and bodily occupation by means of regular and organized games. To leave 200 boys at large and to their own devices during their leisure hours would be to court catastrophe; it would not be educating them, but would probably result in their quickly relapsing into something approaching barbarism. For these reasons I think it is essential that in a school of learning of this description, a school receiving and retaining as boarders boys of these ages, there should be organized games as part of the daily routine, and I do not see how the other part of the education can be successfully carried on without them. It is not disputed that if this sum—I am dealing now with the 1000*l.*—had been left to the charity, for the general purposes of the charity, it might have been applied to any of the purposes to which moneys coming to the hands of the governing body are in fact applied; it might have been expended in the repair or in additions to the class-rooms, laboratory, and other buildings of that sort; or it might equally, as it seems to me, have been applied to the repair or enlargement of the swimming bath, the gymnasium, the fives courts, or other buildings employed in those branches of education which have exclusively to do with the bodily welfare of the students. I cannot, in these circumstances, bring myself to think, because the testator has indicated his intention that in the hands of the charity this money shall be used for the particular purposes stated in his will, that the gift is thereby vitiated. On the contrary I think the gift is a good charitable gift. It is a gift to a charity for purposes which seem to me to be included in the objects of the charity.

The same reasoning applies to the 100*l.* It is given not to the charity but to the headmaster, but it is given for a purpose which, though not quite so specific as the purpose for which the 1000*l.* is given, is in my opinion within the objects of the charity, that is to say, the advancement of that part of the educational work of the charity which has to do with the bodily and physical development of the students. I think both legacies are valid charitable legacies, and I so hold.

I have said nothing about the 100*l.* for the classical prize; that is clearly good, and the contrary has not really been argued[16].

In *Re Mellody* ([1918] 1 Ch 228) a testator provided for an annual treat or field day for the school children of Turton. Eve J upheld this as a gift for the advancement of education and also as a gift under the fourth head[17].

In *Re Webber* ([1954] 1 WLR 1500, [1954] 3 All ER 712) Vaisey J upheld, as a valid educational charitable trust, a gift for the furthering of the Boy

[16] Similarly *Re Gray* [1925] Ch 362, p. 352, post (sport in the Army). See also *Re Lipinski's Will Trusts* [1976] Ch 235 at 242, [1977] 1 All ER 33.

[17] See p. 331, post.

Scouts Movement, whose purpose was stated in its Charter to be the instruction of "boys of all classes in the principles of discipline, loyalty, and good citizenship".

---

iv. EVALUATION OF AESTHETIC MERIT

Even within a school curriculum, there may be doubt whether a particular subject is educational in the legal sense. The question is all the more difficult outside the school context. The acceptance of aesthetic and artistic subjects as being educational brings the court face to face with the problem of selecting which activities qualify. Not all noise-making qualifies as educational music; not every collection of junk as a museum of art. And what qualifies in one age may fail in the next, and *vice-versa*. The policy of the law is to encourage the promotion of artistic work of quality; but it is an extreme step to permit the promotion, free of tax and permanently, of the work of a particular artist. The same problem arises in other fields of charity. Indeed it is at the back of many of the decisions under the fourth head[18]. How should the selection be determined, and by whom? In *Re Shaw's Will Trusts* ([1952] Ch 163 at 168) VAISEY J said: "The court ought not to weigh the respective merits of particular educational methods"; and at p. 172: "Whatever may be my own personal views about this type of education, they have nothing to do with the case."

RE DELIUS

[1957] Ch 299, [1957] 1 All ER 854 (ChD, ROXBURGH J)

The widow of the composer Frederick Delius gave her residuary estate upon various trusts for the advancement of Delius's musical works. The most significant clause was clause 12 by which the trustees were to "apply the royalties income and the income of my residuary trust fund for or towards the advancement . . . of the musical works of my late husband . . . under conditions in which the making of profit is not the object to be attained and which might be economically impossible by any concert operatic or other organisation . . ." and then suggested ways in which this should be achieved. The question was whether the will created a charitable trust.

Held. A valid charitable trust for the advancement of education.

ROXBURGH J: First of all, I have to decide what is the purpose of this trust. In arriving at a conclusion on that point, I must have regard not only to the language in which the purpose is expressed (and, indeed, that is of itself reasonably clear) but also to the means which are indicated for achieving that purpose, which make the position even clearer. It seems to me that in very truth the purpose is the spreading and establishment of knowledge and appreciation of Delius's works amongst the public of the world. It is, indeed, remarkable to what extent that objective has been achieved in the 21 years or so since the widow died. The copyrights in

[18] Cf. *National Anti-Vivisection Society v IRC* [1948] AC 31, [1947] 2 All ER 217, p. 331, post.

Delius's works were valued at the date of her death at £1,483, and at that time formed a comparatively small portion of his residuary estate. The royalties received in the year ending April 5, 1936, amounted to £103, in the year 1946 they amounted to £2,233, and in the year 1956 they amounted to £7,278; which is no doubt largely to be attributed to Sir Thomas Beecham.

The position is now that certain of Delius's works are so well known that no guarantee is required by the recording companies in respect thereof, but the trustees are now advised that some of the lesser-known works which were recorded in the early history of the trust should be re-recorded if the work of the trust can continue to be carried on. Sir Thomas Beecham has been engaged for some years on the task of editing the whole of the compositions of Delius, with a view to the publication and issue of a uniform edition of the whole body of his musical works in accordance with the provisions of clause 12 of the will, but the printing and publication of the major portion of this edition has been held in abeyance pending the decision of this court whether after the period of 21 years from the death of the testatrix the trusts declared in clause 12 constitute valid and effectual charitable trusts, or are void as infringing the rule against perpetuities or otherwise.

I have stated what I understand to be the purpose of the trusts, and the question is whether that purpose is charitable in the eye of the law? I can do no better in this connexion than to read certain passages from the judgment of Lord Greene MR in *Royal Choral Society v IRC* ([1943] 2 All ER 101). There are, of course, certain points which necessarily occur to the mind in connexion with a musical composition. It might be suggested as regards some music, at any rate, that its purpose was limited to giving pleasure, and as regards all music it must be said that it gives pleasure. That is a feature about music. When I say "all music", I mean all that can be truly called music. Indeed, a lot of pleasure is derived by some from something which can hardly be truly called music, but, at any rate, pleasure is a circumstance intimately connected with music. But that in itself does not operate to destroy the charitable character of a bequest for the advancement of the art of music. I adopt, with great satisfaction, the words of Lord Greene ([1943] 2 All ER 101 at 104): "Curiously enough, some people find pleasure in providing education. Still more curiously, some people find pleasure in being educated: but the element of pleasure in those processes is not the purpose of them, but what may be called a by-product which is necessarily there." That seems to me to be all that need be said about the aspect of pleasure connected with the music of Delius.

Lord Greene proceeded: [His Lordship quoted the extract at p. 296, ante; and continued:] Those words have been freely adopted in subsequent cases, and I adopt them and also hold that they are directly applicable to this trust.

I do not find it necessary to consider what the position might be if the trusts were for the promotion of the works of some inadequate composer. It has been suggested that perhaps I should have no option but to give effect even to such a trust. I do not know, but I need not investigate that problem, because counsel who have argued before me have been unanimous in the view that the standard of Delius's work is so high that that question does not arise in the present case.

The point which has been made—and it is one of interest and importance —is, that first of all this trust is not a trust for the promotion of music in general but the music of a particular individual composer. That could not of itself vitiate the charitable nature of the trust, because, after all, aesthetic appreciation of music in a broad sense can only be derived from aesthetic appreciation of the works of a large number of composers. It is the aggregate of the work of a large number of composers which is the basis of the aesthetic appreciation, and, therefore, if it is charitable to promote music in general it must be charitable to promote the music of a particular composer, presupposing (as in this case I can assume) that the composer is one whose music is worth appreciating.

In order to make that plain, I would refer to *Re Shakespeare Memorial Trust* ([1923] 2 Ch 398), where the charitable trust was, to put it shortly, to promote the works of Shakespeare. I cannot conceive that anybody would doubt that a trust to promote the works of Beethoven would be charitable, but the real strength of the point put in this case arises from the fact that this trust was created by the widow of Delius, and nobody would doubt that, amongst the many motives which actuated her, affection for her deceased husband was to be found. But one must be careful to distinguish motive from purpose, because motive is not relevant in these cases except in so far as it is incorporated into the purpose. Considering the purposes, it is possible to approach the purposes upon the hypothesis that their intention was, as Mr. Browne-Wilkinson put it, to enhance her husband's reputation.

This is, of course, rather subtle. It is a question which is the cart and which is the horse, because, of course, the more aesthetic appreciation of Delius's music is achieved the more Delius's reputation will necessarily be enhanced. The two things fit together, and there is no doubt whatever that both objects have in fact already been to a large extent achieved. But, in my judgment, it is not fair to approach the problem from that point of view. I think that there is every reason to suppose that the testatrix took the view, and was well advised to take it, that if the work of Delius was brought before the public in an efficient manner, the aesthetic appreciation of the public would grow and, inherent in that growth, would be the enhancement of Delius's reputation, which was in itself a desirable thing, and I for my part refuse to disentangle it. There is no reliable evidence on which I can disentangle it. What is quite clear to me is that these purposes would plainly be charitable if for the name "Delius" the name "Beethoven" were substituted and, in my judgment, they do not cease to be charitable because in this context the name is "Delius" and not "Beethoven".

RE PINION

[1965] Ch 85, [1964] 1 All ER 890 (CA, Harman, Davies and Russell LJJ)

By his will, the testator, Arthur Watson Hyde Pinion, gave the income of the residue of his estate to his sister Edith for her life and after her death provided that his studio and contents, which included pictures, furniture, china, glass and objets d'art should be offered to the National Trust and kept intact in the studio and displayed to the public. A custodian was appointed, the post to be offered to Edith and after her death to a blood relation. Goods and chattels not of an antique nature could be disposed of. By a codicil he revoked his sister's life interest and provided that if, as happened, the National Trust was not prepared to observe the provisions of the will, his executors should maintain the studio and contents as a museum.

Held (reversing WILBERFORCE J). The trust was not for the advancement of education and was void.

HARMAN LJ: This appeal concerns the testamentary dispositions of Arthur Watson Hyde Pinion, who died in the year 1961, having, by his will made in 1956 as varied by a codicil made in 1961, sought to devote almost the whole of his not inconsiderable estate to a project designed to keep himself and his family for all time before the public eye by allowing the public to view without cost his studio, situate at 22A, Pembridge Villas, Notting Hill, intact with its entire contents. These treasures are to be entrusted to a custodian, first his sister and subsequently a blood relation of his, who are to be paid and housed out of his estate. The question is whether he was entitled to saddle his property with this chimaera to the deprivation of his next-of-kin and this, the judge has held, he was entitled to do at the instance of the Attorney-General, who persuaded him, though hardly, that the testator has created a valid charitable trust.

The will and codicil are rambling and half coherent documents reduced to some semblance of order by the judge but his summary is, I think, perhaps too neat and logical and the actual words should be read to convey its authentic flavour. It starts by conferring a life interest in the whole estate on his sister, the first defendant, who is also his sole next-of-kin, and proceeds. [His Lordship then read passages of the will and codicils and continued:] I construe this farrago as meaning that the entire contents of the studio, which housed all the articles referred to, are to be exhibited as a whole and, as he says, "to be kept intact in the studio". The only exception is that articles "not of an antique nature" may be disposed of. I assume that the revocation of the sister's life interest accelerated the gift to the National Trust, which has refused the bequest, and that the authority to his executors to appoint a trust to carry out the bequest is in fact mandatory, the contrary not having been argued.

In this court the Attorney-General did not seek to support the gift as being beneficial in a general sense to the public, but confined his plea to that head of charity which is characterised as the advancement of education. He argued both here and below that no evidence was receivable on this subject. A museum, he said, is a place which the law assumes to have an educational value and purpose. The cases on this subject to be found in Tudor on Charities, 5th edition (1929), are not very satisfactory. It would appear that a gift to an established museum is charitable: see *British Museum Trustees v White* ((1826) 2 Sim & St 594). In *Re Holburne* ((1885) 53 LT 212) a gift to trustees of objects of art to form an art museum in Bath open to the public and a fund to endow it was held a valid charitable gift as being of public utility or benefit. No question was there raised as to the merit of the collection. It must have been agreed that such merit existed, for everyone assumed it, including the judge. I conclude that a gift to found a public museum may be assumed to be charitable as of public utility if no one questions it. So in a case about religion, such as *Thornton v Howe* ((1862) 31 Beav 14), the case about Joanna Southcote, the court will assume without inquiry that the teaching may do some good if not shown to be subversive of morality. Where the object is to found a school the court will not study the methods of education provided that on the face of them they are proper: *Re Shaw's Will Trusts* ([1952] Ch 163, [1952] 1 All ER 49). A school for prostitutes or pickpockets would obviously fail. A case about education is *Re Hummeltenberg* ([1923] 1 Ch 237), where the headnote reads: "To be valid a charitable bequest must be for the public benefit, and the trust must be capable of being adminstered and controlled by the court. The opinion of the donor of a gift or the creator of a trust that the gift or trust is for the public benefit does not make it so, the matter is one to be determined by the court on the evidence before it."

The bequest in that case was connected with spiritualism and the point to which I draw attention is that the judge (the late Lord Russell of Killowen, then Russell J) said it must be decided on the evidence. There is a passage in his judgment as follows ([1923] 1 Ch at 242): "It was contended" (says he) "that the court was not the tribunal to determine whether a gift or trust was or was not a gift or a trust for the benefit of the public. It was said that the only judge of this was the donor of the gift or the creator of the trust. For this view reliance was placed on the views expressed by the Master of the Rolls [Porter MR] and by some members of the Court of Appeal in Ireland in *Re Cranston* ([1898] 1 IR 431 at 446). Reliance was also placed on a sentence in the judgment of Chitty J in *Re Foveaux* ([1895] 2 Ch 501). So far as the views so expressed declare that the personal or private opinion of the judge is immaterial, I agree; but so far as they lay down or suggest that the donor of the gift or the creator of the trust is to determine whether the purpose is beneficial to the public, I respectfully disagree. If a testator by stating or indicating his view that a trust is beneficial to the public can establish that fact beyond question, trusts might be established in perpetuity for the promotion of all kinds of fantastic (though not unlawful) objects, of which the training of poodles to dance might be a mild example. In my opinion the question whether a gift is or may be operative for the public benefit is a question to be answered by the court by forming an opinion upon the evidence before it."

Where a museum is concerned and the utility of the gift is brought in question it is, in my opinion, and herein I agree with the judge, essential to know at least something of the quality of the proposed exhibits in order to judge whether they will be conducive to the education of the public. So I think with a public library, such a place if found to be devoted entirely to works of pornography or of a corrupting nature, would not be allowable. Here it is suggested that education in the fine arts is the object. For myself a reading of the will leads me rather to the view that the testator's object was not to educate anyone, but to perpetuate his own name and the repute of his family, hence perhaps the direction that the custodian should be a blood relation of his. However that may be, there is a strong body of evidence here that as a means of education this collection is worthless. The testator's own paintings, of which there are over 50, are said by competent persons to be in an academic style and "atrociously bad" and the other pictures without exception worthless. Even the so-called "Lely" turns out to be a 20th century copy.

Apart from pictures there is a haphazard assembly—it does not merit the name collection, for no purpose emerges, no time nor style is illustrated—of furniture and objects of so-called "art" about which expert opinion is unanimous that nothing beyond the third-rate is to be found. Indeed one of the experts expresses his surprise that so voracious a collector should not by hazard have picked up even one meritorious object. The most that skilful cross-examination extracted from the expert witnesses was that there were a dozen chairs which might perhaps be acceptable to a minor provincial museum and perhaps another dozen not altogether worthless, but two dozen chairs do not make a museum and they must, to accord with the will, be exhibited stifled by a large number of absolutely worthless pictures and objects.

It was said that this is a matter of taste, and de gustibus non est disputandum, but here I agree with the judge that there is an accepted canon of taste on which the court must rely, for it has itself no judicial knowledge of such matters, and the unanimous verdict of the experts is as I have stated. The judge with great hesitation concluded that there was that scintilla of merit which was sufficient to save the rest. I find myself on the other side of the line. I can conceive of no useful object to be served in foisting upon the public this mass of junk. It has neither public utility nor educative value. I would hold that the testator's project ought not to be carried into effect and that his next-of-kin is entitled to the residue of his estate.

V. PUBLIC BENEFIT

OPPENHEIM v TOBACCO SECURITIES TRUST CO LTD[19]

[1951] AC 297, [1951] 1 All ER 31 (HL, Lords SIMONDS, NORMAND, OAKSEY, MORTON OF HENRYTON and MACDERMOTT)

The income of a trust fund was directed to be applied "in providing for . . . the education of children of employees or former employees of the British-American Tobacco Co., Ltd. . . . or any of its subsidiary or allied companies in such manner . . . as the acting trustees shall in their absolute discretion . . . think fit" with power also to apply the capital for the like purposes.

The number of employees of the company and their subsidiary and allied companies exceeded 110,000.

[19] (1951) 67 LQR 162 (R.E.M.), 164 (A.L.G.); *Caffoor v Income Tax Comr, Colombo* [1961] AC 584 at 602, per Lord RADCLIFFE. See also *Davies v Perpetual Trustee Co Ltd* [1959] AC 439, [1959] 2 All ER 128 (a gift of land in Sydney, New South Wales "to the Presbyterians the descendants of those settled in the Colony hailing from or born in the North of Ireland to be held in trust for the purpose of establishing a college for the education and tuition of their youth in the standards of the Westminster Divines as taught in the Holy Scriptures" held void by Privy Council. The class of persons was "a fluctuating body of private individuals", and in no sense "a section of the community").

The question was whether the class to be benefited was a sufficient section of the public.

Held. (Lord MacDermott dissenting). Because the qualification to benefit was based upon a personal nexus, the class of beneficiaries was not a section of the public; and the trust was void.

Lord Simonds: My Lords, once more your Lordships have to consider the difficult subject of charitable trusts, and this time a question is asked to which no wholly satisfactory answer can be given.

Before I turn to the authorities I will make some preliminary observations. It is a clearly established principle of the law of charity that a trust is not charitable unless it is directed to the public benefit. This is sometimes stated in the proposition that it must benefit the community or a section of the community. Negatively it is said that a trust is not charitable if it confers only private benefits. In the recent case of *Gilmour v Coats* ([1949] AC 426, [1949] 1 All ER 848) this principle was reasserted. It is easy to state and has been stated in a variety of ways, the earliest statement that I find being in *Jones v Williams* ((1767) 2 Amb 651) in which Lord Hardwicke LC is briefly reported as follows: "Definition of charity: a gift to a general public use, which extends to the poor as well as to the rich . . .". With a single exception, to which I shall refer, this applies to all charities. We are apt now to classify them by reference to Lord Macnaghten's division in *Income Tax Comrs v Pemsel* ([1891] AC 531 at 538), and, as I have elsewhere pointed out, it was at one time suggested that the element of public benefit was not essential except for charities falling within the fourth class, "other purposes beneficial to the community". This is certainly wrong except in the anomalous case of trusts for the relief of poverty with which I must specifically deal. In the case of trusts for educational purposes the condition of public benefit must be satisfied. The difficulty lies in determining what is sufficient to satisfy the test, and there is little to help your Lordships to solve it.

If I may begin at the bottom of the scale, a trust established by a father for the education of his son is not a charity. The public element, as I will call it, is not supplied by the fact that from that son's education all may benefit. At the other end of the scale the establishment of a college or universtiy is beyond doubt a charity. "Schools of learning and free schools and scholars of universities" are the very words of the preamble to the Statute of Elizabeth. So also the endowment of a college, university or school by the creation of scholarships or bursaries is a charity and none the less because competition may be limited to a particular class of persons. It is upon this ground, as Lord Greene MR pointed out in *Re Compton* ([1945] Ch 123 at 136) that the so-called Founder's Kin cases can be rested. The difficulty arises where the trust is not for the benefit of any institution either then existing or by the terms of the trust to be brought into existence, but for the benefit of a class of persons at large. Then the question is whether that class of persons can be regarded as such a "section of the community" as to satisfy the test of public benefit. These words "section of the community" have no special sanctity, but they conveniently indicate first, that the possible (I emphasize the word "possible") beneficiaries must not be numerically negligible, and secondly, that the quality which distinguishes them from other members of the community, so that they form by themselves a section of it, must be a quality which does not depend on their relationship to a particular individual. It is for this reason that a trust for the education of members of a family or, as in *Re Compton* ([1945] Ch 123, [1945] 1 All ER 198), of a number of families cannot be regarded as charitable. A group of persons may be numerous but, if the nexus between them is their personal relationship to a single propositus or to several propositi, they are neither the community nor a section of the community for charitable purposes.

I come, then, to the present case where the class of beneficiaries is numerous but the difficulty arises in regard to their common and distinguishing quality. That quality is being children of employees of one or other of a group of companies. I can make no distinction between children of employees and the employees themselves. In both cases the common quality is found in employment by particular employers. The latter of the two cases by which the Court of Appeal held itself to be bound, *Re Hobourn Aero Components Ltd's Air Raid Distress Fund* ([1946] Ch 194, [1946] 1 All ER 501), is a direct authority for saying that such a common quality does not constitute its possessors a section of the public for charitable purposes. In the former case, *Re Compton*, Lord Greene MR had by way of illustration placed members of a family and employees of a particular employer on the same footing, finding neither in common kinship nor in common employment the sort of nexus which is sufficient. My Lords, I am so fully in agreement with what was said by Lord Greene in both cases and by my noble and learned friend, then Morton LJ in the *Hobourn* case, that I am in danger of repeating without improving upon their words. No one who has been versed for many years in this difficult and very artificial branch of the law can be unaware of its illogicalities, but I join with my noble and learned friend in echoing the observations which he cited ([1946] Ch at 208) from the judgment of Russell LJ in *Re Grove-Grady* ([1929] 1 Ch 557 at 582), and I agree with him that the decision in *Re Drummond* ([1914] 2 Ch 90) "imposed a very healthy check upon the extension of the legal definition of 'charity' ". It appears to me that it would be an extension, for which there is no justification in principle or authority, to regard common employment as a quality which constitutes those employed a section of the community. It must not, I think, be forgotten that charitable institutions enjoy rare and increasing privileges, and that the claim to come within that privileged class should be clearly established. With the single exception of *Re Rayner* ((1920) 89 LJCh 369), which I must regard as of doubtful authority, no case has been brought to the notice of the House in which such a claim as this has been made, where there is no element of poverty in the beneficiaries, but just this and no more, that they are the children of those in a common employment.

Learned counsel for the appellant sought to fortify his case by pointing to the anomalies that would ensue from the rejection of his argument. For, he said, admittedly those who follow a profession or calling, clergymen, lawyers, colliers, tobacco-workers and so on, are a section of the public; how strange then it would be if, as in the case of railwaymen, those who follow a particular calling are all employed by one employer. Would a trust for the education of railwaymen be charitable, but a trust for the education of men employed on the railways by the Transport Board not be charitable? And what of service of the Crown whether in the civil service or the armed forces? Is there a difference between soldiers and soldiers of the King? My Lords, I am not impressed by this sort of argument and will consider on its merits, if the occasion should arise, the case where the description of the occupation and the employment is in effect the same, where in a word, if you know what a man does, you know who employs him to do it. It is to me a far more cogent argument, as it was to my noble and learned friend in the *Hobourn* case, that if a section of the public is constituted by the personal relation of employment, it is impossible to say that it is not constituted by 1,000 as by 100,000 employees, and, if by 1,000, then by 100, and, if by 100, then by 10. I do not mean merely that there is a difficulty in drawing the line, though that too is significant: I have it also in mind that, though the actual number of employees at any one moment might be small, it might increase to any extent, just as, being large, it might decrease to any extent. If the number of employees is the test of validity, must the court take into account potential increase or decrease, and, if so, as at what date? . . .

I would also, as I have previously indicated, say a word about the so called "poor relations" cases. I do so only because they have once more been brought forward as an argument in favour of a more generous view of what may be charitable. It would not be right for me to affirm or to denounce or to justify these decisions: I am concerned only to say that the law of charity, so far as it relates to "the relief of aged, impotent and poor people" (I quote from the statute) and to poverty in general, has followed its own line, and that it is not useful to try to harmonize decisions on that branch of the law with the broad proposition on which the determination of this case must rest. It is not for me to say what fate might await those cases if in a poverty case this House had to consider them[20] . . . .

The appeal should in my opinion be dismissed with costs.

Lord MacDermott (dissenting): My Lords, it is not disputed that this trust is for the advancement of education. The question is whether it is of a public nature, whether, in the words of Lord Wrenbury in *Verge v Somerville* ([1924] AC 496 at 499), "it is for the benefit of the community or of an appreciably important class of the community". The relevant class here is that from which those to be educated are to be selected. The appellant contends that this class is public in character; the respondent bank (as personal representative of the last surviving settlor) denies this and says that the class is no more than a group of private individuals.

Until comparatively recently the usual way of approaching an issue of this sort, at any rate where educational trusts were concerned, was, I believe, to regard the facts of each case and to treat the matter very much as one of degree. No definition of what constituted a sufficient section of the public for the purpose was applied, for none existed; and the process seems to have been one of reaching a conclusion on a general survey of the circumstances and considerations regarded as relevant rather than of making a single, conclusive test. The investigation left the course

[20] See *Dingle v Turner* [1972] AC 601, [1972] 1 All ER 878, p. 287, ante.

of the dividing line between what was and what was not a section of the community unexplored, and was concluded when it had gone far enough to establish to the satisfaction of the court whether or not the trust was public; and the decision as to that was, I think, very often reached by determining whether or not the trust was private.

If it is still permissible to conduct the present inquiry on these broad if imprecise lines, I would hold with the appellant. The numerical strength of the class is considerable on any showing. The employees concerned number over 110,000, and it may reasonably be assumed that the children, who constitute the class in question, are no fewer. The large size of the class is not, of course, decisive but in my view it cannot be left out of account when the problem is approached in this way. Then it must be observed that the propositi are not limited to those presently employed. They include former employees (not reckoned in the figure I have given) and are, therefore, a more stable category than would otherwise be the case. And, further, the employees concerned are not limited to those in the service of the "British American Tobacco Co., Ltd. or any of its subsidiary or allied companies"—itself a description of great width—but include the employees, in the event of the British American Tobacco Co., Ltd. being reconstructed or merged on amalgamation, of the reconstructed or amalgamated company or any of its subsidiary companies. No doubt the settlors here had a special interest in the welfare of the class they described, but, apart from the fact that this may serve to explain the particular form of their bounty, I do not think it material to the question in hand. What is material, as I regard the matter, is that they have chosen to benefit a class which is, in fact, substantial in point of size and importance and have done so in a manner which, to my mind, manifests an intention to advance the interests of the class described as a class rather than as a collection or succession of particular individuals. . . .

The respondent bank, however, contends that the inquiry should be of quite a different character to that which I have been discussing. It advances as the sole criterion a narrower test derived from the decisions of the Court of Appeal in *Re Compton* ([1945] Ch 123, [1945] 1 All ER 198), and *Re Hobourn Aero Components Ltd's Air Raid Distress Fund* ([1946] Ch 194, [1946] 1 All ER 501). . . .

The test [there] propounded focuses upon the common quality which unites those within the class concerned and asks whether that quality is essentially impersonal or essentially personal. If the former, the class will rank as a section of the public and the trust will have the element common to and necessary for all legal charities; but, if the latter, the trust will be private and not charitable. It is suggested in the passage just quoted, and made clear beyond doubt in *Re Hobourn* that in the opinion of the Court of Appeal employment by a designated employer must be regarded for this purpose as a personal and not as an impersonal bond of union. In this connexion and as illustrating the discriminating character of what I may call "the *Compton* test" reference should be made to that part of the judgment of the learned Master of the Rolls in *Re Hobourn* ([1946] Ch at 206 in which he speaks of the decision in *Hall v Derby Borough Urban Sanitary Authority* ((1885) 16 QBD 163). The passage runs thus: "That related to a trust for railway servants. It is said that if a trust for railway servants can be a good charity, so too a trust for railway servants in the employment of a particular railway company is a good charity. That is not so. The reason, I think, is that in the one case the trust is for railway servants in general and in the other case it is for employees of a particular company, a fact which limits the potential beneficiaries to a class ascertained on a purely personal basis."

My Lords, I do not quarrel with the result arrived at in the *Compton* and *Hobourn* cases, and I do not doubt that the *Compton* test may often prove of value and lead to a correct determination. But, with the great respect due to those who have formulated this test, I find myself unable to regard it as a criterion of general applicability and conclusiveness. In the first place I see much difficulty in dividing the qualities or attributes, which may serve to bind human beings into classes, into two mutually exclusive groups, the one involving individual status and purely personal, the other disregarding such status and quite impersonal. As a task this seems to me no less baffling and elusive than the problem to which it is directed, namely, the determination of what is and what is not a section of the public for the purposes of this branch of the law. After all, what is more personal than poverty or blindness or ignorance? Yet none would deny that a gift for the education of the children of the poor or blind was charitable; and I doubt if there is any less certainty about the charitable nature of a gift for, say, the education of children who satisfy a specified examining body that they need and would benefit by a course of special instruction designed to remedy their educational defects.

But can any really fundamental distinction, as respects the personal or impersonal nature of the common link, be drawn between those employed, for example, by a particular university and those whom the same university has put in a certain category as the result of individual examination and assessment? Again, if the bond between those employed by a particular railway is purely personal, why should the bond between those who are employed as railway men be so essentially different? Is a distinction to be drawn in this respect between those who are employed in a particular industry before it is nationalized and those who are employed therein after that process has been completed and one employer has taken the place of many? Are miners in the service of the National Coal Board now in one category and miners at a particular pit or of a particular district in another? Is the relationship between those in the service of the Crown to be distinguished from that obtaining between those in the service of some other employer? Or, if not, are the children of, say, soldiers or civil servants to be regarded as not constituting a sufficient section of the public to make a trust for their education charitable?

It was conceded in the course of the argument that, had the present trust been framed so as to provide for the education of the children of those engaged in the tobacco industry in a named county or town, it would have been a good charitable disposition, and that even though the class to be benefited would have been appreciably smaller and no more important than is the class here. That concession follows from what the Court of Appeal has said. But if it is sound and a personal or impersonal relationship remains the universal criterion I think it shows, no less than the queries I have just raised in indicating some of the difficulties of the problem, that the *Compton* test is a very arbitrary and artificial rule. This leads me to the second difficulty that I have regarding it. If I understand it aright it necessarily makes the quantum of public benefit a consideration of little moment; the size of the class becomes immaterial and the need of its members and the public advantage of having that need met appear alike to be irrelevant. To my mind these are considerations of some account in the sphere of educational trusts for, as already indicated, I think the educational value and scope of the work actually to be done must have a bearing on the question of public benefit.

Finally, it seems to me that, far from settling the state of the law on this particular subject, the *Compton* test is more likely to create confusion and doubt in the case of many trusts and institutions of a character whose legal standing as charities has never been in question. I have particularly in mind gifts for the education of certain special classes such, for example, as the daughters of missionaries, the children of those professing a particular faith or accepted as ministers of a particular denomination, or those whose parents have sent them to a particular school for the earlier stages of their training. I cannot but think that in cases of this sort an analysis of the common quality binding the class to be benefited may reveal a relationship no less personal than that existing between an employer and those in his service. Take, for instance, a trust for the provision of university education for boys coming from a particular school. The common quality binding the members of that class seems to reside in the fact that their parents or guardians all contracted for their schooling with the same establishment or body. That the school in such a case may itself be a charitable foundation seems altogether beside the point and quite insufficient to hold the *Compton* test at bay if it is well founded in law.

My Lords, counsel for the appellant and for the Attorney-General adumbrated several other tests for establishing the presence or absence of the necessary public element. I have given these my careful consideration and I do not find them any more sound or satisfactory than the *Compton* test. I therefore return to what I think was the process followed before the decision in *Compton's* case, and, for the reasons already given, I would hold the present trust charitable and allow the appeal. I have only to add that I recognize the imperfections and uncertainties of that process. They are as evident as the difficulties of finding something better. But I venture to doubt if it is in the power of the courts to resolve those difficulties satisfactorily as matters stand. It is a long cry to the age of Elizabeth and I think what is needed is a fresh start from a new statute.

INLAND REVENUE COMMISSIONERS v EDUCATIONAL GRANTS ASSOCIATION LTD[21]

[1967] Ch 123, [1966] 3 All ER 708 (ChD, Pennycuick J)

The Educational Grants Association Ltd. was an association established for the advancement of education. It had a close relation with the Metal

[21] See Annual Report for 1976, paras. 45–49 (The Cowen Charitable Trust).

Box Co. Ltd., and the bulk of its income came from a deed of covenant executed in its favour by the Metal Box Co. Ltd.

In the years relevant to the present claim for repayment of income tax, between 76 per cent. and 85 per cent. of the income of the Association was applied for the education of children of persons connected with the Metal Box Co. Ltd.

The claim for repayment raised the question whether the Association was established for charitable purposes only, and whether the income was applied "for charitable purposes only" within s. 447 (1) (*b*) of the Income Tax Act 1952[21a].

Held. The claim failed because the income was not applied for charitable purposes only.

PENNYCUICK J: . . . . The objects of the corporation, in order that they may be exclusively charitable, must be confined to objects for the public benefit. Equally, the application of the income, if it is to be within those objects, must be for the public benefit. Conversely, the application of income otherwise than for the public benefit must be outside the objects and ultra vires. For example, under an object for the advancement of education, once that is accepted as an exclusively charitable object, the income must be applied for the advancement of education by way of public benefit. An application of income for the advancement of education by way of private benefit would be ultra vires, and nonetheless so by reason that, in the nature of things, the members of a private class are included in the public as a whole. This may perhaps explain the repetition of the words "for charitable purposes only" in the second requirement of the subsection.

Mr. Talbot, for the association, advanced a simple and formidable argument: namely, (i) the association is established for specified educational purposes; (ii) those purposes are admittedly charitable purposes, so the first requirement is satisfied; (iii) the income has been applied for the specified educational purposes; and (iv) therefore the income has been applied for charitable purposes, and the second requirement is satisfied. It seems to me that this argument leaves out of account the element of public benefit. It is true that it is claimed by the association and admitted by the revenue that the educational purposes specified in the association's memorandum are charitable purposes, but this by definition implies that the purposes are for the public benefit. In order that the second requirement may be satisfied, it must equally be shown that its income has been applied not merely for educational purposes as expressed in the memorandum but for those educational purposes by way of public benefit. An application of income by way of private benefit would be ultra vires. It is not open to the association first to set up a claim which can only be sustained on the basis that the purposes expressed in the memorandum are for the public benefit, and then, when it comes to the application of income, to look only to the purposes expressed in the memorandum, leaving the element of public benefit out of account. This point may be illustrated by considering the familiar example of a case in which a fund

[21a] See now I.C.T.A. 1970, s. 360 (1) (*c*).

is settled upon trust for the advancement of education in general terms and the income is applied for the education of the settlor's children. Mr. Talbot does not shrink from the conclusion that such an application comes within the terms of the trust and satisfies the second requirement of the subsection. I think it does neither.

I understand from Mr. Talbot that he advanced the foregoing contention—and, I think, only this contention—before the special commissioners, although it is not very clearly reflected in their findings. The special commissioners were evidently much pre-occupied by *Re Koettgen's Will Trusts,* ([1954] Ch 252, [1954] 1 All ER 581), to which I shall refer in a moment. It was substantially the only argument which Mr. Talbot advanced before me as to the construction of the section.

Mr. Goulding, for the Inland Revenue Commissioners, based his argument upon construction broadly on the lines which I have indicated above as being correct. He devoted much of his argument to repelling the application of the *Koettgen* case to the present one. The headnote in the *Koettgen* case is as follows:

> "A testatrix bequeathed her residuary estate on trust 'for the promotion and furtherance of commerical education. . . .' The will provided that 'The persons eligible as beneficiaries under the fund shall be persons of either sex who are British-born subjects and who are desirous of educating themselves or obtaining tuition for a higher commercial career but whose means are insufficient or will not allow of their obtaining such education or tuition at their own expense. . . .' She further directed that in selecting the beneficiaries 'it is my wish that the . . . trustees shall give a preference to any employees of John Batt & Co. (London) Ltd. or any members of the families of such employees; failing a sufficient number of beneficiaries under such description then the persons eligible shall be any persons of British birth as the . . . trustees may select Provided that the total income to be available for benefiting the preferred beneficiaries shall not in any one year be more than 75 per cent. of the total available income for that year.' In the event of the failure of those trusts there was a gift over to a named charity. It was admitted that the trust was for the advancement of education, but it was contended for the charity that having regard to the direction to prefer a limited class of persons the trusts were not of a sufficiently public nature to constitute valid charitable trusts:—
>
> "*Held*, that the gift to the primary class from whom the trustees could select beneficiaries contained the necessary element of benefit to the public, and that it was when that class was ascertained that the validity of the trust had to be determined; so that the subsequent direction to prefer, as to 75 per cent. of the income, a limited class did not affect the validity of the trust, which was accordingly a valid and effective charitable trust. *Oppenheim v Tobacco Securities Trust Co Ltd* ([1951] AC 297, [1951] 1 All ER 31) distinguished."

That headnote, I think, accurately represents the effect of what the judge decided.

The other case considered by the special commissioners was *Caffoor v*

Income Tax Comr, Colombo ([1961] AC 584, [1961] 2 All ER 436), in the Privy Council. The headnote, so far as now relevant, is as follows:

"By the terms of a trust deed executed in Ceylon in 1942 the trust income after the death of the grantor was to be applied by the board of trustees, the appellants, in their absolute discretion for all or any of a number of purposes which included '(2) . . . (b) the education instruction or training in England or elsewhere abroad of deserving youths of the Islamic Faith' in any department of human activity. 'The recipients of the benefits . . . shall be selected by the board from the following classes of persons and in the following order:—(i) male descendants along either the male or female line of the grantor or of any of his brothers or sisters failing whom' youths of the Islamic faith born of Moslem parents of the Ceylon Moorish community permanently resident in Colombo or elsewhere in Ceylon. . . .

"*Held*, . . . (2) that in view of what was in effect the absolute priority to the benefit of the trust income which was conferred on the grantor's own family by clause (2) (b) (i) of the trust deed this was a family trust and not a trust of a public character solely for charitable purposes, and the income thereof was accordingly not entitled to the exemption claimed. . . ." *Re Compton* ([1945] Ch 123, [1945] 1 All ER 198), *Oppenheim v Tobacco Securities Trusts Co Ltd* ([1951] AC 297, [1951] 1 All ER 31) and *Re Koettgen's Will Trusts* ([1954] Ch 252, [1954] 1 All ER 581) considered. . . .

I think it right, however, to add that for myself I find considerable difficulty in the *Koettgen* decision. I should have thought that a trust for the public with preference for a private class comprised in the public might be regarded as a trust for the application of income at the discretion of the trustees between charitable and non-charitable objects. However, I am not concerned here to dispute the validity of the *Koettgen* decision. I only mention the difficulty I feel as affording some additional reason for not applying the *Koettgen* decision by analogy in connection with the second requirement of the subsection[1].

I return now to the present case. The association has claimed that the purposes of the association are exclusively charitable, which imports that the purposes must be for the public benefit. The revenue have admitted that claim. I have then to consider whether the association has applied its income within its expressed objects and by way of public benefit. There is no doubt that the application has been within its expressed objects, but has it been by way of public benefit? In order to answer this question, I must, I think, look at the individuals and institutions for whose benefit the income has been applied, and seek to discern whether these individuals and institutions possess any, and, if so, what, relevant characteristics by virtue of which the income has been applied for their benefit. One may for this purpose look at the minutes of the council, circular letters and so forth. Mr. Goulding at one time appeared to suggest that one might look at the actual intention of the members of the council. I do not think that is so.

When one makes this inquiry, one finds that between 75 per cent. and 85 per cent. of the income of the association has been expended upon

[1] See also *Re Martin* (1977) 121 Sol Jo 828.

the education of children connected with Metal Box. The association is intimately connected with Metal Box in the many respects found in the case stated. It derives most of its income from Metal Box. The council of management, as the special commissioners found, has followed a policy of seeking applications for grants from employees and ex-employees of Metal Box, though these applications are not, of course, always successful. The inference is inescapable that this part of the association's income—i.e., 75 per cent. to 85 per cent.—has been expended for the benefit of these children by virtue of a private characteristic; i.e., their connection with Metal Box. Such an application is not by way of public benefit. It is on all fours with an application of 75 per cent. to 85 per cent. of the income of a trust fund upon the education of a settlor's children. It follows, in my judgment, that, as regards the income which has been applied for the education of children connected with Metal Box, the association has failed to satisfy the second requirement in the subsection, and that the claim for relief fails. No reason has been suggested why the association should not obtain relief in respect of income applied for the benefit of institutions and outside individuals: see the words "so far as" in the section.

I recognise that this conclusion involves a finding that the council of management has acted ultra vires in applying the income of the association as it has done, albeit within the expressed objects of the association memorandum. This conclusion follows from the basis on which the association has framed its objects and based its claim. It is of course open to a comparable body to frame its objects so as to make clear that its income may be applied for private as well as public purposes, but in that case it may not obtain tax relief. It does not seem to me that such a body can have it both ways. I propose, therefore, to allow this appeal.

QUESTIONS

1. Consider the difficulties with which a court is faced when compelled to make a value judgment upon artistic matters. What would you say of a gift
   (*a*) to promote the music of the "Blithe Spirits" (an unknown but promising Pop Group)?
   (*b*) to the Plantagenet Society for the purpose of establishing that Henry VII was responsible for the deaths of the Princes in the Tower?
   (*c*) for sex education in primary schools?
   (*d*) for the provision in schools of instruction on driving automobiles?
2. The disagreement between Lord Simonds and Lord MacDermott on the question of the ascertainment of the test of public benefit was discussed by Lord Cross in *Dingle v Turner* (p. 287, ante). Where do you stand on this controversy? How would *Oppenheim v Tobacco Securities Trust Co Ltd* (p. 310, ante) be decided if it arose today? [1974] CLJ 63 (G. H. Jones); Annual Report for 1971, para. 21.
3. (After reading Section C) Compare the test of public benefit in trusts for the advancement of education and trusts for the advancement of religion.

C. The Advancement of Religion[2]

i. GENERAL

The charitable nature of the third head of charity is based on nothing more specific than the inclusion in the Preamble of "the repair of churches". The concept has widened with the spread of religious toleration. It is not confined to the Established Church; or even to the Christian religion[3]. The boundaries are ill-defined, and many of the cases are conflicting. The extracts which follow are chosen as illustrations of significant issues which arise in this field.

Again, it is necessary to show a benefit to the public or a section of the public. This must be proved by evidence which is acceptable to the court; the faith of a particular religion that prayer and intercession will confer a benefit on the public is not sufficient. It seems that the concept of public benefit under this head is similar to that in the case of education; but not identical; for while the pupils of a private school form a section of the public for the purposes of education, the same is not true of the members of a cloistered order in the context of religion.

ii. WHAT IS RELIGION?

Tudor on Charities (6th Edn, 1967), p.47

"The Meanings of 'Religion' and 'Religious'

It seems that any form of monotheistic theism is a religion within the meaning of Lord Macnaghten's third head of charity[4], and that a trust for the advancement of any form of monotheistic religion may be a good charitable trust[5], provided that the court is satisfied by evidence of which it can take cognisance that the purposes of the trust are beneficial to the public or to a sufficiently important section of the public[6].

A trust for the advancement of any form of monotheism may be upheld as a trust for the advancement of religion[7], provided that the purposes of the trust satisfy the overriding requirement of public benefit[8], and that the doctrines of the particular form of monotheism are not subversive of all religion and morality[9]. If the doctrines are subversive of all religion and morality, the purposes cannot be beneficial to the community.

The definitions of 'the promotion of religion' by Lord Hanworth MR in *Keren Kayemeth Le Jisroel Ltd v IRC*[10] and of 'advancement of religion' by Donovan J in *United Grand Lodge of Ancient Free and Accepted Masons of England*

[2] H & M, pp. 174–178, 187–188, 190; K & S, pp. 163–164; K & S (Charities), pp. 52–71; P & M, pp. 186–189; Pettit, pp. 384–387, 404–406; Snell, pp. 147–148, 151; Tudor, pp. 38–68; Picarda, pp. 54–77; Goodman Report, paras. 40–41, 51–57; House of Commons Report, vol. I, paras. 53–58, 60, vol. II, pp. 191–217, 313–316, 362–364. See generally Crowther, *Religious Trusts* (1954).

[3] *Gilmour v Coats* [1949] AC 426 at 457, 458, per Lord REID; *Neville Estates Ltd v Madden* [1962] Ch 832 at 853, per CROSS J.

[4] *Income Tax Special Purposes Comrs v Pemsel* [1891] AC 531 at 583.

[5] See *Bowman v Secular Society Ltd* [1917] AC 406 at 449, per Lord PARKER OF WADDINGTON.

[6] *Gilmour v Coats* [1949] AC 426, [1949] 1 All ER 848.

[7] *Bowman v Secular Society Ltd* [1917] AC 406 at 449.

[8] See p. 324, post.

[9] *Thornton v Howe* (1862) 31 Beav 14, cf. *Re Price* [1943] Ch 422, [1943] 2 All ER 505.

[10] [1931] 2 KB 465 at 477.

and Wales v Holborn Borough Council[11] and the numerous decided cases concerned with gifts or trusts for the advancement of religion show that the court uses the word 'religion' as meaning 'a particular system of faith and worship which involves the recognition on the part of a man of some higher unseen power as having control of his destiny which is entitled to reverence and worship.' "[12]

In the *United Grand Lodge* case, DONOVAN J, in holding that the objects of freemasonry were not "charitable or otherwise concerned with the advancement of religion" within Rating and Valuation (Miscellaneous Provisions) Act 1955, s. 8 (1) (*a*), said (at p. 1090):

"Accordingly, one cannot really begin to argue that the main object of freemasonry is to advance religion, except perhaps by saying that religion can be advanced by example as well as by precept, so that the spectacle of a man leading an upright moral life may persuade others to do likewise. The appellants did not in fact advance this argument, but even if it were accepted, it leads to no useful conclusion here. For a man may persuade his neighbour by example to lead a good life without at the same time leading him to religion. And there is nothing in the constitution, nor, apparently, in the evidence tendered to the appeals committee, to support the view that the main object of masonry is to encourage masons to go out in the world and by their example lead persons to some religion or another.

When one considers the work done by organizations which admittedly do set out to advance religion, the contrast with masonry is striking. To advance religion means to promote it, to spread its message ever wider among mankind; to take some positive steps to sustain and increase religious belief; and these things are done in a variety of ways which may be comprehensively described as pastoral and missionary. There is nothing comparable to that in masonry. This is not said by way of criticism. For masonry really does something different. It says to a man, 'Whatever your religion or your mode of worship, believe in a Supreme Creator and lead a good moral life.' Laudable as this precept is, it does not appear to us to be the same thing as the advancement of religion. There is no religious instruction, no programme for the persuasion of unbelievers, no religious supervision to see that its members remain active and constant in the various religions they may profess, no holding of religious services, no pastoral or missionary work of any kind."

Pettit: *Equity and the Law of Trusts* (3rd Edn, 1974), pp. 174-175

"It is generally accepted that 'the Court of Chancery makes no distinction between one religion and another, . . . [or] one sect and another . . . [unless] the tenets of a particular sect inculcate doctrines adverse to the

[11] [1957] 1 WLR 1080 at 1090. In *Re Thackrah* [1939] 2 All ER 4 it was held that the objects of the "Oxford Group", which had not then been incorporated, were not for the advancement of religion.

[12] See the *Shorter Oxford English Dictionary*.

very foundations of all religion and . . . subversive of all morality. . . . If the tendency were not immoral and although this Court might consider the opinions sought to be propagated foolish or even devoid of foundation' the trust would nevertheless be charitable[13]. As between different religions the law stands neutral, but assumes that any religion is at least likely to be better than none[14].' These propositions are undoubtedly true so far as the various Christian denominations are concerned; there is no doubt as to the charitable character of religious trusts not only for the established church, but also for non-conformist bodies[15], Unitarians,[16] Roman Catholics[17], and, it has been held, even for the publication of the works of Joanna Southcote[18]. Similarly with regard to organisations which exist for the advancement of religion, such as the Church Army[19], the Salvation Army[20], the Church Missionary Society[1], the Society for the Propagation of the Gospel in Foreign Parts[2], the Sunday School Association[3], the Protestant Alliance and kindred institutions[4], and even, it has been held, a society of clergymen, in connection with a trust to provide dinners, on the ground that the free meals would increase the usefulness of the society by attracting a greater number of clergymen to the meeting[5]. But not, it has been decided, the Oxford Group Movement[6].

Beyond the Christian religion, trusts for the advancement of the Jewish religion are undoubtedly charitable[7], but there seems to be no authority on wholly distinct religions such as Mohammedism or Buddhism, though regulations[8] made under the Charities Act 1960 assume that a trust for the advancement of a religion other than Christianity is charitable. The objects

[13] Per ROMILLY MR in *Thornton v Howe* (1862) 31 Beav 14 at 19; *Gilmour v Coats* [1949] AC 426, [1949] 1 All ER 848; *Re Watson* [1973] 1 WLR 1472, [1973] 3 All ER 678, p. 324, post.

[14] Per CROSS J in *Neville Estates Ltd v Madden* [1962] Ch 832 at 853, [1961] 3 All ER 769 at 781.

[15] Since the Toleration Act 1688. See, e.g., *Re Strickland's Will Trusts* [1936] 3 All ER 1027, appeal dismissed by consent [1937] 3 All ER 676 (Baptist); *Re Manser* [1905] 1 Ch 68 (Quakers).

[16] Since the Unitarian Relief Act 1813. E.g. *Re Nesbitt's Will Trusts* [1953] 1 All ER 936.

[17] Since the Roman Catholic Charities Act 1832. E.g. *Dunne v Byrne* [1912] AC 407; *Re Flinn* [1948] Ch 241, [1948] 1 All ER 541.

[18] *Thornton v Howe*, supra. Joanna Southcote claimed that she was with child by the Holy Ghost, and would give birth to a second Messiah.

[19] *Re Smith* (1938) 54 TLR 851.

[20] *Re Fowler* (1914) 31 TLR 102; *Re Smith,* supra.

[1] *Re The Clergy Society* (1856) 2 K & J 615.

[2] *Re Maguire* (1870) LR 9 Eq 632.

[3] *R v Income Tax, Special Comrs* [1911] 2 KB 434.

[4] *Re Delmar Charitable Trust* [1897] 2 Ch 163 (societies having as their object "to maintain and defend the doctrines of the Reformation, and the principles of civil and religious liberty against the advance of Popery").

[5] *Re Charlesworth* (1910) 26 TLR 214.

[6] *Re Thackrah* [1939] 2 All ER 4; *Oxford Group v IRC* [1949] 2 All ER 537 (the movement is probably a social movement founded on Christian ethics rather than a movement for the advancement of religion).

[7] Since the Religious Disabilities Act 1846, according, *inter alia*, to *Neville Estates Ltd v Madden* [1962] Ch 832, [1961] 3 All ER 769, But a Jewish religious trust was held charitable in *Straus v Goldsmid* (1837) 8 Sim 614, not following Lord HARDWICKE's decision in *De Costa v De Paz* (1754) 2 Swan 487n.

[8] S.I. 1962 No. 1421; S.I. 1963 No. 2074. [Many immigrant religious organisations have been recognised as charitable. However, "many Hindu, Sikh, and Moslem organisations which are basically religious also have social, cultural and educational functions which have a greater importance than is the case with comparable Christian communities". Annual Report for 1976, para. 109.]

of the Theosophical Society are not charitable[9], as being for the advancement of religion or otherwise, and it has not been thought arguable that gifts for the maintenance of a masonic temple[10] or a college for training spiritualistic mediums[11] are charitable, and the same must surely be true of an atheistic society."[12]

In *Re Watson* ([1973] 1 WLR 1472, [1973] 3 All ER 678)[13], PLOWMAN J had to consider the validity of a gift in a will "for the continuance of the work of God as it has been maintained by Mr. H. G. Hobbs and myself since 1942 by God's enabling . . . in propagating the truth as given in the Holy Bible". The testatrix and Mr. Hobbs were members of a very small group of undenominational Christians, who met at Long Melford, Suffolk, and which apparently contained no member outside their immediate families. Mr. Hobbs had written and distributed a large number of religious books and tracts mainly at the expense of the testatrix. Expert evidence was given that their intrinsic worth was nil. The trust was upheld.

iii. PUBLIC BENEFIT

GILMOUR v COATS

[1949] AC 426, [1949] 1 All ER 848 (HL, Lords SIMONDS, DU PARCQ, NORMAND, MORTON OF HENRYTON and REID)

A gift of £500 was made in trust for the purposes of the Carmelite Priory, St Charles' Square, Notting Hill, if those purposes were charitable.

The Priory was a community of strictly cloistered nuns, who devoted their lives to prayer, contemplation, penance and self-sanctification. They engaged in no works outside the convent.

An affidavit of Cardinal Griffin, Roman Catholic Archbishop of Westminster, stated that, according to the doctrine of the Roman Catholic Church, the work of such a community conferred benefits, not only upon the participants, but upon the public generally.

Held. The purposes of the Priory lacked the element of public benefit which was necessary to make them charitable.

LORD SIMONDS: It is the established belief of the Roman Catholic Church, as appears from the Apostolic Constitution "Umbratilem," that the prayers and other spiritual penances and exercises, in which the nuns engage for the benefit of the public, in fact benefit the public by drawing down upon them grace from God, which enables those who are not yet Christians

[9] *Re Macaulay's Estate* [1943] Ch 435n ("to form a nucleus of Universal Brotherhood of Humanity without distinction of race, creed, caste or colour"). Cf. *Re Price* [1943] Ch 422, [1943] 2 All ER 505 (Anthroposophical Society).

[10] *Re Porter* [1925] Ch 746.

[11] *Re Hummeltenberg* [1923] 1 Ch 237.

[12] The point did not arise in *Bowman v Secular Society Ltd* [1917] AC 406; where it was held that there is nothing contrary to law in an attack on or a denial of the truth of Christianity unaccompanied by vilification, ridicule or irreverence. Christianity is not a part of the law of England.

[13] (1974) 90 LQR 4; (1973) ASCL 468 (J. Hackney). On Fringe Religious Organizations, see Annual Report for 1976, paras. 103–108; and on Exorcism, paras. 65–67.

to embrace the Christian religion and those who are already Christians to practice Christianity more fully and fruitfully, and, further that the prayers and other spiritual exercises of the nuns are the more efficacious by virtue of the fact that they devote their lives with especial devotion to the service of God. It is this benefit to all the world, arising from the value of their intercessory prayers, that the appellant puts in the forefront of her case in urging the charitable purpose of the trust.

Nor is it only on the intercessory value of prayer that the appellant relies for the element of public benefit in their lives. For it is the evidence of Cardinal Griffin—and I do not pause to ask whether it is evidence of fact or opinion—that the practice of the religious life by the Carmelite nuns and other religions is a source of great edification to other Catholics—and indeed in innumerable cases to non-Catholics—leading them to a higher estimation of spiritual things and to a greater striving after their own spiritual perfection and that the knowledge that there are men and women who are prepared to sacrifice all that the worldly in man holds dear in order to attain a greater love of God and union with Him inculcates in them a greater estimation of the value and importance of the things which are eternal than they would have if they had not these examples before them. Here then is the second element of public benefit on which the appellant relies, the edification of a wider public by the example of lives devoted to prayer.

I will reserve for final consideration an argument which was not urged in the courts below; that the trusts declared by the settlement are beneficial to the public, in that qualification for admission to the community is not limited to any private group of persons but any person being a female Roman Catholic may be accepted, and therefore those trusts provide facilities for the intensified and most complete practice of religion by those members of the public who have a vocation for it. Your Lordships were reluctant to listen to an argument on which you have not the advantage of the opinions of the learned judges in the courts below, but in the special circumstances of this case thought fit to admit it.

I turn then to the question whether, apart from this final consideration, the appellant has established that there is in the trusts which govern this community the element of public benefit which is the necessary condition of legal charity . . .

I need not go beyond the case of *Cocks v Manners* ((1871) LR 12 Eq 574) which was decided nearly eighty years ago by Wickens V-C. In that case the testatrix left her residuary estate between a number of religious institutions, one of them being the Dominican Convent at Carisbrooke, a community not differing in any material respect from the community of nuns now under consideration. The learned judge who was, I suppose, as deeply versed in this branch of the law as any judge before or since (for he had been for many years junior counsel to the Attorney-General in equity cases), used these words, which I venture to repeat, though they have already been cited in the courts below ((1871) LR 12 Eq at 585). "On the Act [sc. the Statute of Elizabeth] unaffected by authority I should certainly hold that the gift to the Dominican Convent is neither within the letter nor the spirit of it; and no decision has been referred to which compels me to adopt a different conclusion. A voluntary association of women for the purpose of working out their own salvation by religious exercises and self-denial seems to me to have none of the requisites of a charitable institution, whether the word 'charitable' is used in its popular sense or in its legal sense. It is said, in some of the cases, that religious purposes are charitable, but that can only be true as to religious services tending directly or indirectly towards the instruction or the edification of the public; an annuity to an individual, so long as he spent his time in retirement and constant devotion, would not be charitable, nor would a gift to ten persons, so long as they lived together in retirement and performed acts of devotion, be charitable. Therefore the gift to the Dominican Convent is not, in my opinion, a gift on a charitable trust." No case, said the learned Vice-Chancellor, had been cited to compel him to come to a contrary conclusion, nor has any such case been cited to your Lordships. Nor have my own researches discovered one. But since that date the decision in *Cocks v Manners* has been accepted and approved in numerous cases. They are referred to in the judgment of Jenkins J and I need only remind your Lordships, first, that Lindley LJ in *Re White* ([1893] 2 Ch 41 at 51) used these words: "A society for the promotion of private prayer and devotion by its own members, and which has no wider scope, no public element, no purposes of general utility would be a 'religious' society, but not a 'charitable' one: see *Cocks v Manners,*" and, secondly, that in *Dunn v Byrne* ([1912] AC 407 at 410) Lord Macnaghten in delivering the judgment of the Privy Council refers to *Cocks v Manners* as the exemplar of a case in which the purpose would be considered by a devout Catholic to be conducive to the good of religion but which is "certainly not charitable". I have thus stated the law as it was universally accepted in case-law (except some recent Irish cases) and also in all text-books of authority at the date when these proceedings were begun, and I now ask what is the argument upon which your Lordships are invited to unsettle it.

Apart from what I have called the final argument, which I will deal with later, the contention of the appellant rests not on any change in the lives of the members of such a community as this nor, from a wider aspect, on the emergence of any new conception of the public good, but solely on the fact that for the first time certain evidence of the value of such lives to a wider public together with new arguments based upon that evidence has been presented to the court. Never before, it was urged, has the benefit to be derived from intercessory prayer and from edification been brought to the attention of the court; if it had been, the decision in *Cocks v Manners* ((1871) LR 12 Eq 574) would, or at least should, have been otherwise. I have examined the records of *Cocks v Manners* which were supplied to me by the Record Office and I find that the case has been fully and accurately reported. There was no such evidence as was adduced in this case by the appellant and Cardinal Griffin. Nor, as appears from the report, was any argument addressed to this specific point nor any judgment on it. What weight is to be attributed to this, which is the mainstay of the appellant's case? To me, my Lords, despite the admirable argument of Mr. Charles Russell, the weight is negligible. True it is that Wickens

V-C emphasized that aspect of the religious life which is admittedly its more important aim, "the love and contemplation of divine things" ((1871) LR 12 Eq at 585). But "its secondary aim the apostolate, particularly all that pertains to our neighbour's salvation" (I use the appellant's words) is no new thing and I cannot suppose that it was absent from the learned judge's mind that those, who devote their lives to prayer, pray not for themselves alone, or that they believe that their prayers are not in vain. Nor, as I think, can he have been unaware of the effect which the example of their lives may have upon others. As I venture to think, these aspects of the case were neither insisted on in evidence or argument nor discussed by the learned judge because they do not afford any real support for the contention that there is in the purpose of the community the element of public benefit which is the condition of legal charity.

My Lords, I would speak with all respect and reverence of those who spend their lives in cloistered piety, and in this House of Lords Spiritual and Temporal, which daily commences its proceedings with intercessory prayers, how can I deny that the Divine Being may in His wisdom think fit to answer them? But, my Lords, whether I affirm or deny, whether I believe or disbelieve, what has that to do with the proof which the court demands that a particular purpose satisfies the test of benefit to the community? Here is something which is manifestly not susceptible of proof. But, then it is said, this is a matter not of proof but of belief: for the value of intercessory prayer is a tenet of the Catholic faith, therefore in such prayer there is benefit to the community. But it is just at this "therefore" that I must pause. It is, no doubt, true that the advancement of religion is, generally speaking, one of the heads of charity. But it does not follow from this that the court must accept as proved whatever a particular church believes. The faithful must embrace their faith believing where they cannot prove: the court can act only on proof. A gift to two or ten or a hundred cloistered nuns in the belief that their prayers will benefit the world at large does not from that belief alone derive validity any more than does the belief of any other donor for any other purpose. The importance of this case leads me to state my opinion in my own words but, having read again the judgment of the learned Master of the Rolls, I will add that I am in full agreement with what he says on this part of the case[14].

I turn to the second of the alleged elements of public benefit, edification by example. And I think that this argument can be dealt with very shortly. It is in my opinion sufficient to say that this is something too vague and intangible to satisfy the prescribed test. The test of public benefit has, I think, been developed in the last two centuries. To-day it is beyond doubt that that element must be present. No court would be rash enough to attempt to define precisely or exhaustively what its content must be. But it would assume a burden which it could not discharge if now for the first time it admitted into the category of public benefit something so indirect, remote, imponderable and, I would add, controversial as the benefit which may be derived by others from the example of pious lives. The appellant

[14] [1948] Ch 340, [1948] 1 All ER 521. "They are to be paid, not to do good, but to be good", at p. 353, per GREENE MR.

called in aid the use by Wickens V-C of the word "indirectly" in the passage that I have cited from his judgment in *Cocks v Manners* ((1871) LR 12 Eq 574 at 585), but I see no reason to suppose that that learned judge had in mind any such question as your Lordships have to determine. . . .

It remains finally to deal with an argument which, as I have said, was not presented to the Court of Appeal but appears in the appellant's formal case. It is that the element of public benefit is supplied by the fact that qualification for admission to membership of the community is not limited to any group of persons but is open to any woman in the wide world who has the necessary vocation. Thus, it is said, just as the endowment of a scholarship open to public competition is a charity, so also is a gift to enable any woman (or, presumably, any man) to enter a fuller religious life a charity. To this argument which, it must be admitted, has a speciously logical appearance, the first answer is that which I have indicated earlier in this opinion. There is no novelty in the idea that a community of nuns must, if it is to continue, from time to time obtain fresh recruits from the outside world. That is why a perpetuity is involved in a gift for the benefit of such a community and it is not to be supposed that, to mention only three masters of this branch of the law, Wickens V-C, Lord Lindley, or Lord Macnaghten failed to appreciate the point. Yet by direct decision or by way of emphatic example a community such as this is by them regarded as the very type of religious institution which is not charitable. I know of no consideration applicable to this case which would justify this House in unsettling a rule of law which has been established so long and by such high authority. But that is not the only, nor indeed the most cogent, reason why I cannot accede to the appellant's argument. It is a trite saying that the law is life, not logic. But it is, I think, conspicuously true of the law of charity that it has been built up not logically but empirically. It would not, therefore, be surprising to find that, while in every category of legal charity some element of public benefit must be present, the court had not adopted the same measure in regard to different categories, but had accepted one standard in regard to those gifts which are alleged to be for the advancement of education and another for those which are alleged to be for the advancement of religion, and it may be yet another in regard to the relief of poverty. To argue by a method of syllogism or analogy from the category of education to that of religion ignores the historical process of the law. Nor would there be lack of justification for the divergence of treatment which is here assumed. For there is a legislative and political background peculiar to so-called religious trusts, which has I think influenced the development of the law in this matter. Thus, even if the simple argument that, if education is a good thing, then the more education the better, may appear to be irrefutable, to repeat that argument substituting "religion" for "education" is to ignore the principle which I understand to be conceded that not all religious purposes are charitable purposes. It was, no doubt, this consideration which led Wickens V-C to say ((1871) LR 12 Eq 574 at 585) that a gift to a Dominican convent was "one of the last gifts which the legislature which passed the Act would have thought of including in it". Upon this final argument I would add this observation. I have stressed the empirical development of the law of charity and your Lordships may detect some inconsistency in an attempt to rationalize it. But it appears to me that it would be irrational to the point of absurdity on the one hand to deny to a community of contemplative nuns the character of a charitable institution but on the other to accept as a charitable trust a gift which had no other object than to enable it to be maintained in perpetuity by recruitment from the outside world.

Finally I would say this. I have assumed for the purpose of testing this argument that it is a valid contention that a gift for the advancement of education is necessarily charitable if it is not confined within too narrow limits. But that assumption is itself difficult to justify. It may well be that the generality of the proposition is subject to at least two limitations. The first of them is implicit in the decision of Russell J in *Re Hummeltenberg* ([1923] 1 Ch 237): the second is one that is not in the nature of things likely to occur, but, if it can be imagined that it was made a condition of a gift for the advancement of education that its beneficiaries should lead a cloistered life and communicate to no one, and leave no record of, the fruits of their study, I do not think that the charitable character of the gift could be sustained.

For the reasons that I have given I am of opinion that this appeal should be dismissed.

In *Neville Estates Ltd v Madden* ([1962] Ch 832, [1961] 3 All ER 769) the trustees of the Catford Synagogue entered into a contract to sell two plots of land to the plaintiffs for £10,000. The plaintiffs obtained detailed planning permission for the building thereon of flats and garages. The value of the land increased and the Charity Commissioners refused their permission to sell.

The plaintiffs brought an action for specific performance arguing, *inter alia,* that the land was not held on charitable trusts, and that the permission of the Charity Commissioners was not therefore necessary.

The argument was that the trustees held the land upon trust for the advancement of religion among a private group of persons only. In holding that the purposes were charitable, Cross J said: "I turn now to the argument that this is a private, not a public trust . . . The trust with which I am concerned resembles that in *Gilmour v Coats* ([1949] AC 426, [1949] 1 All ER 848) in this, that the persons immediately benefited by it are not a section of the public but the members of a private body. All persons of the Jewish faith living in or about Catford might well constitute a section of the public, but the members for the time being of the Catford Synagogue are no more a section of the public than the members for the time being of a Carmelite Priory. The two cases, however, differ from one another in that the members of the Catford Synagogue spend their lives in the world, whereas the members of a Carmelite Priory live secluded from the world. If once one refuses to pay any regard—as the courts refused to pay any regard—to the influence which these nuns living in seclusion might have on the outside world, then it must follow that no public benefit is involved in a trust to support a Carmelite Priory. As Lord

Greene said in the Court of Appeal ([1948] Ch 340 at 345, [1948] 1 All ER 521 at 525): 'Having regard to the way in which the lives of the members are spent, the benefit is a purely private one.' But the court is, I think, entitled to assume that some benefit accrues to the public from the attendance at places of worship of persons who live in this world and mix with their fellow citizens. As between different religions the law stands neutral, but it assumes that any religion is at least likely to be better than none.

But then it is said—and it is this part of the argument that has caused me the greatest difficulty: 'But this is a case of self-help.' Suppose that a body of persons, being dissatisfied with the facilities for the education of small children provided in their district, form an association for the education of the children of members. A committee is formed; each member pays a subscription; the funds of the society are employed in hiring premises and paying a teacher; and the rules provide that the association cannot be dissolved by the members at any given moment but is to continue for the benefit of the members existing from time to time. No doubt the public benefits by the fact that the children of the members receive an education. But could it possibly be argued that the association was a charity and was entitled to the great fiscal advantages which a charity enjoys? Or would it make any difference if the committee allowed the children of non-members to attend the classes free of charge if there was room for them, in the same way as members of the public, though having no right to enter the synagogue, are not in practice refused admission?

I feel the force of this analogy; but, as Lord Simonds pointed out in *Gilmour v Coats* ([1949] AC 426 at 449), it is dangerous to reason by analogy from one head of charity to another. After the passing of the Toleration Acts, dissenting chapels sprang up all over the country. As can be deduced from the language of section 1 of the Trustees Appointment Act, 1850 (see Sir Morton Peto's Act), the chapel was normally vested in trustees for the particular congregation or society of dissenters in question. In course of time disputes sometimes arose between rival groups, some members alleging that others had ceased to hold the tenets laid down in the trust deed and were not entitled to its benefits. A typical example of such a dispute is to be found in *A-G v Bunce* ((1868) LR 6 Eq 563). No one, so far as I know, ever questioned that trusts for such dissenting bodies were charitable trusts provided that the members for the time being could not put an end to them. What the position would be if the members for the time being could divide the property among themselves was expressly left open by Sir George Jessel MR in *Bunting v Sargent* ((1879) 13 ChD 330 at 337).

Section 4 of the Religious Disabilities Act, 1846, provided that Her Majesty's subjects professing the Jewish religion in respect of their schools, places of religious worship, education and charitable purposes and the property held therewith, should be subject to the same laws as Her Majesty's Protestant subjects dissenting from the Church of England were subject to and not further or otherwise. From that time it has, I think, always been assumed by lawyers that trusts for the benefit of a congregation of Jews attending a synagogue were charitable trusts. It is, for example, obvious that Parliament and the Charity Commissioners assumed in 1870 that the four synagogues which became the constituent synagogues of the United Synagogue were charitable bodies. Yet it is equally clear from clause 6a of this scheme that the constituent synagogues have not been open to all persons of the Jewish faith, but were unincorporated associations with a list of members.

Generally speaking, no doubt, an association which is supported by its members for the purposes of providing benefits for themselves will not be a charity. But I do not think that this principle can apply with full force in the case of trusts for religious purposes. As Lord Simonds pointed out, the law of charity has been built up not logically but empirically, and there is a political background peculiar to religious trusts which may well have influenced the development of the law with regard to them.

In my judgment, this trust with which I am concerned in this case is a charitable trust".

QUESTION

Now compare the differences in the requirements of public benefit between religious and educational trusts.

What would you say of

a) a trust for the provision of a private chapel in a preparatory school?

b) a trust to provide religious services for long-term prisoners in the maximum security wing of a prison?

c) a trust to provide a church for Methodists and for persons likely to become Methodists in West Ham? (see *IRC v Baddeley* [1955] AC 572, [1955] 1 All ER 525, p. 342, post).

Would there have been a different result in *Gilmour v Coats* if it had been shown that a number of nuns retired periodically and returned to life outside the convent? See Cross J in *Neville Estates Ltd v Madden* [1962] Ch 832 at 853.

D. Other Purposes Beneficial to the Community[15]

i. GENERAL

(a) The Test is what the Law treats as Charitable

The test is what the law treats as charitable, and not what the testator thought was charitable. This question may however make it necessary for the court to make a subjective decision in the determination of what is beneficial.

NATIONAL ANTI-VIVISECTION SOCIETY v INLAND REVENUE COMMISSIONERS

[1948] AC 31, [1947] 2 All ER 217 (HL, Viscount Simon, Lords Wright, Simonds, Normand and Porter)

The appellants were a society whose object was the suppression of vivisection. They claimed exemption from income tax on the ground that they

[15] H & M, pp. 387–398, 406–408; K & S, pp. 164–165; K & S (Charities), pp. 25–26, 87–98, 114–133; P & M, pp. 189–195; Pettit, pp. 179–192; Snell, pp. 148–152; Tudor, pp. 68–125; Picarda, pp. 78–119.

were "a body of persons . . . established for charitable purposes only" within the Income Tax Act 1918, s. 37 (1) (*b*) [16].

Held. (Lord PORTER dissenting.) The Society was not established for charitable purposes only, and was not therefore within this exemption.

LORD SIMONDS: My Lords, the question raised in this appeal is whether the National Anti-Vivisection Society, which I will call "the society," is a body of persons established for charitable purposes only within the meaning of s. 37 of the Income Tax Act, 1918, and, accordingly, entitled to exemption from income tax on the income of its investments. Before I refer to the cases and to the judgments in the courts below I will state the two questions which appear to me to be raised in this appeal. The first and shorter point is whether a main purpose of the society is of such a political character that the court cannot regard it as charitable. To this point little attention was directed in the courts below. It is mentioned only in the judgment of the learned Master of the Rolls. As will appear in the course of this opinion, it is worthy of more serious debate[17]. The second point is fundamental. It is at the very root of the law of charity as administered by the Court of Chancery and its successor, the Chancery Division of the High Court of Justice. It is whether the court, for the purpose of determining whether the object of the society is charitable may disregard the finding of fact that any assumed public benefit in the direction of the advancement of morals and education was far outweighed by the detriment to medical science and research and consequently to the public health which would result if the society succeeded in achieving its object, and that on balance, the object of the society, so far from being for the public benefit, was gravely injurious thereto. The society says that the court must disregard this fact, arguing that evidence of disadvantages or evils which would or might result from the stopping of vivisection is irrelevant and inadmissible.

The second question raised in this appeal, which I have already tried to formulate, is of wider importance, and I must say at once that I cannot reconcile it with my conception of a court of equity that it should take under its care and administer a trust, however well-intentioned its creator, of which the consequence would be calamitous to the community. I would not weary your Lordships with a historical excursion into the origin of the equitable jurisdiction in matters of charity, one of the "heads of equity" as Lord Macnaghten called it in *Pemsel's* case ([1891] AC 531) . . .

My Lords, this then being the position, that the court determined "one by one" whether particular named purposes were charitable, applying always the overriding test whether the purpose was for the public benefit, and that the King as parens patriae intervened pro bono publico for the protection of charities, what room is there for the doctrine which has found favour with the learned Master of the Rolls and has been so vigorously supported at the bar of the House, that the court may disregard the evils that will ensue from the achievement by the society of its ends? It is to me a strange and bewildering idea that the court must look so far and no farther, must see a charitable purpose in the intention of the

[16] See now I.C.T.A. 1970, s. 360 (1) (*c*).
[17] See p. 358, post.

society to benefit animals and thus elevate the moral character of men but must shut its eyes to the injurious results to the whole human and animal creation. I will readily concede that, if the purpose is within one of the heads of charity forming the first three classes in the classification which Lord Macnaghten borrowed from Sir Samuel Romilly's argument in *Morice v Bishop of Durham* ((1805) 10 Ves 522), the court will easily conclude that it is a charitable purpose. But even here to give the purpose the name of "religious" or "education" is not to conclude the matter. It may yet not be charitable, if the religious purpose is illegal or the educational purpose is contrary to public policy. Still there remains the overriding question: Is it pro bono publico? It would be another strange mis-reading of Lord Macnaghten's speech in *Pemsel's* case ([1891] AC 531) (one was pointed out in *Re Macduff* ([1896] 2 Ch 451)) to suggest that he intended anything to the contrary. I would rather say that, when a purpose appears broadly to fall within one of the familiar categories of charity, the court will assume it to be for the benefit of the community and, therefore, charitable, unless the contrary is shown, and further that the court will not be astute in such a case to defeat on doubtful evidence the avowed benevolent intention of a donor. But, my Lords, the next step is one that I cannot take. Where on the evidence before it the court concludes that, however well-intentioned the donor, the achievement of his object will be greatly to the public disadvantage, there can be no justification for saying that it is a charitable object. If and so far as there is any judicial decision to the contrary, it must, in my opinion, be regarded as inconsistent with principle and be overruled. This proposition is clearly stated by Russell J in *Re Hummeltenberg* ([1923] 1 Ch 237 at 242). "In my opinion," he said, "the question whether a gift is or may be operative for the public benefit is a question to be answered by the court forming an opinion upon the evidence before it." This statement of that very learned judge follows immediately upon some observations on the cases of *Re Foveaux* ([1895] 2 Ch 501) and *Re Cranston* ([1898] 1 IR 431) which were the mainstay of the appellant's argument. . . .

[His Lordship examined these cases and *A-G v Marchant* (1866) LR 3 Eq 424 and *Re Campden Charities* (1881) 18 ChD 310, and continued:]

My Lords, what I have said is enough to conclude this case. But there is an important passage in the judgment of the Master of the Rolls, which I ought not to ignore. "I do not see," he says ([1946] KB 185, 205), "how at this time of day it can be asserted that a particular exemplification of those objects is not beneficial merely because in that particular case the achievement of those objects would deprive mankind of certain consequential benefits however important those benefits may be. If this were not so, it would always be possible, by adducing evidence which was not before the court on the original occasion to attack the status of an established charitable object to the great confusion of trustees and all others concerned. Many existing charities would no doubt fall if such a criterion were to be adopted." I venture with great respect to think that this confuses two things. A purpose regarded in one age as charitable may in another be regarded differently. I need not repeat what was said by Jessel MR in *Re Campden Charities* ((1881) 18 ChD 310). A bequest in the will of a testator dying in 1700 might be held valid on the evidence then before the court but on different evidence held invalid if he died in 1900. So, too, I conceive that an anti-vivisection society might at different times be differently regarded. But this is not to say that a charitable trust, when it has once been established can ever fail. If by a change in social habits and needs, or, it may be, by a change in the law the purpose of an established charity becomes superfluous or even illegal, or if with increasing knowledge it appears that a purpose once thought beneficial is truly detrimental to the community, it is the duty of trustees of an established charity to apply to the court or in suitable cases to the charity commissioners . . . and ask that a cy-près scheme may be established. And I can well conceive that there might be cases in which the Attorney-General would think it his duty to intervene to that end. A charity once established does not die, though its nature may be changed. But it is wholly consistent with this that in a later age the court should decline to regard as charitable a purpose, to which in an earlier age that quality would have been ascribed, with the result that (unless a general charitable intention could be found) a gift for that purpose would fail. I cannot share the apprehension of the Master of the Rolls that great confusion will be caused if the court declines to be bound by the beliefs and knowledge of a past age in considering whether a particular purpose is to-day for the benefit of the community. But if it is so, then I say that it is the lesser of two evils.

Restatement of the Law of Trusts (2nd Edn) § 374, Comment 1

"The Courts do not take sides or attempt to decide which of two conflicting views of promoting the social interest of the community is the better adapted to the purpose, even though the views are opposed to each other. Thus, a trust to promote peace by disarmament, as well as a trust to promote peace by preparedness for war, is charitable (see Comment d)."

(b) The Spirit and Intendment of the Preamble

The benefit to the public must be within the spirit and intendment of the Preamble; or at least within the cases previously decided. It is easier of course for a trust to qualify if its purpose is one expressly mentioned in the Preamble.

WILLIAMS' TRUSTEES v INLAND REVENUE COMMISSIONERS

[1947] AC 447, [1947] 1 All ER 513 (HL, Viscount SIMON, Lords WRIGHT, PORTER, SIMONDS and NORMAND)

A trust was established for the purpose of promoting Welsh interests in London by various methods: by social contacts, the study of the Welsh language, literature, and art, the maintenance of a library of literature in the Welsh language or relating to Wales. The trustees were also empowered to maintain an institute for the benefit of the Welsh people in London "with a view to creating a centre in London for promoting the moral social spiritual and educational welfare of Welsh people and fostering the study of the Welsh language and of Welsh history literature music and art." No alcoholic liquor was to be sold or consumed on any part of the premises.

The question was whether the trust was exempt from income tax.

Held. Not being charitable, the trust was liable to pay income tax.

LORD SIMONDS: My Lords, there are, I think, two propositions which must ever be borne in mind in any case in which the question is whether a trust is charitable. The first is that it is still the general law that a trust is not charitable and entitled to the privileges which charity confers, unless it is within the spirit and intendment of the preamble to the statute of Elizabeth (43 Eliz. c. 4), which is expressly preserved by s. 13, sub-s. 3 of the Mortmain and Charitable Uses Act, 1888[18]. The second is that the classification of charity in its legal sense into four principal divisions by Lord Macnaghten in *Income Tax Commissioners v Pemsel* ([1891] AC 531 at 583) must always be read subject to the qualification appearing in the judgment of Lindley LJ in *Re Macduff* ([1896] 2 Ch 451 at 466): "Now Sir Samuel Romilly did not mean, and I am certain Lord Macnaghten did not mean, to say that every object of public general utility must necessarily be a charity. Some may be, and some may not be." This observation has been expanded by Lord Cave LC in this House in these words: "Lord Macnaghten did not mean that all trusts for purposes beneficial to the community are charitable, but that there were certain beneficial trusts which fell within that category; and accordingly to argue that because a trust is for a purpose beneficial to the community it is therefore a charitable trust is to turn round his sentence and to give it a different meaning. So here it is not enough to say that the trust in question is for public purposes beneficial to the community or for the public welfare; you must also show it to be a charitable trust. See *A-G v National Provincial and Union Bank of England* ([1924] AC 262 at 265)". But it is just because the purpose of the trust deed in this case is said to be beneficial to the community or a section of the community and for no other reason that its charitable character is asserted. It is not alleged that the trust is (*a*) for the benefit of the community and (*b*) beneficial in a way which the law regards as charitable. Therefore, as it seems to me, in its mere statement the claim is imperfect and must fail.

My Lords, the cases in which the question of charity has come before the courts are legion and no one who is versed in them will pretend that all the decisions even of the highest authority are easy to reconcile, but I will venture to refer to one or two of them to make good the importance of my two general propositions. In *Houston v Burns* ([1918] AC 337) the question was as to the validity of a gift "for such public, benevolent, or charitable purposes in connexion with the parish of Lesmahagow or the neighbourhood" as might be thought proper. This was a Scotch case but upon the point now under consideration there is no difference between English and Scotch law. It was argued that the limitation of the purpose to a particular locality was sufficient to validate the gift, that is to say, though purposes beneficial to the community might fail, yet purposes beneficial to a localized section of the community were charitable. That argument was rejected by this House. If the purposes are not charitable per se, the localization of them will not make them charitable. It is noticeable that Lord Finlay LC expressly overrules a decision or dictum

[18] Now repealed by the Charities Act 1960, s. 38 (1), p. 278, ante.

of Lord Romilly ([1918] AC 337 at 341) to the contrary effect in *Dolan v Macdermot* ((1867) LR 5 Eq 60). Next I will refer to a case in the Privy Council which is the more valuable because Lord Macnaghten himself delivered the judgment of the Board. In that case the question was of the validity of a residuary gift "to the Roman Catholic Archbishop of Brisbane and his successors to be used and expended wholly or in part as such Archbishop may judge most conducive to the good of religion in this diocese." What could have been easier than to say that such a trust was beneficial to the community, and moreover to a section of the community sufficiently defined by a reference to the diocese, and was therefore charitable? Yet the only argument was that the benefit to the community was of a character which fell within the preamble to the Statute of Elizabeth, i.e., for religious purposes, and therefore was charitable. And it is to be observed that this contention was rejected on the narrow ground that the terms of the bequest were not identical with religious purposes. "The language of the bequest" said Lord Macnaghten "would (to quote Lord Langdale's words) be open to such latitude of construction as to raise no trust which a Court of Equity could carry into execution": *Dunne v Byrne* ([1912] AC 407 at 411). One more decision out of many to the same effect may be cited. In *Farley v Westminster Bank* ([1939] AC 430, [1939] 3 All ER 491) a testatrix had bequeathed the residue of her estate in equal shares to the respective vicars and churchwardens of two named churches "for parish work". Could it be doubted that the purpose of the gift was beneficial to the community? It could fairly be described in the very words in which the appellants here assert the charitable nature of their trust. Yet the gift failed. It was, in the words of Lord Russell of Killowen ([1939] AC 437) "for the assistance and furtherance of those various activities connected with the parish church which are to be found in . . . every parish". It would be unduly cynical to say that that is not a purpose beneficial to the community. Yet it failed. And it failed because it did not fall within the spirit and intendment of the preamble to the Statute of Elizabeth.

My Lords, I must mention another aspect of this case, which was discussed in the Court of Appeal and in the argument at your Lordships' bar. It is not expressly stated in the preamble to the statute, but it was established in the Court of Chancery, and, so far as I am aware, the principle has been consistently maintained, that a trust in order to be charitable must be of a public character. It must not be merely for the benefit of particular private individuals: if it is, it will not be in law a charity though the benefit taken by those individuals is of the very character stated in the preamble. The rule is thus stated by Lord Wrenbury in *Verge v Somerville* ([1924] AC 496 at 499): "To ascertain whether a gift constitutes a valid charitable trust so as to escape being void on the ground of perpetuity, a first inquiry must be whether it is public—whether it is for the benefit of the community or of an appreciably important class of the community. The inhabitants of a parish or town, or any particular class of such inhabitants, may for instance, be the objects of such a gift, but private individuals, or a fluctuating body of private individuals, cannot." It is, I think, obvious that this rule, necessary as it is, must often be difficult of application and so the courts have found.

Fortunately perhaps, though Lord Wrenbury put it first, the question does not arise at all, if the purpose of the gift whether for the benefit of a class of inhabitants or of a fluctuating body of private individuals is not itself charitable. I may however refer to a recent case in this House which in some aspects resembles the present case. In *Keren Kayemeth le Jisroel Ltd v IRC* ([1932] AC 650) a company had been formed which had as its main object (to put it shortly) the purchase of land in Palestine, Syria or other parts of Turkey in Asia and the peninsula of Sinai for the purpose of settling Jews on such lands. In its memorandum it took numerous other powers which were to be exercised only in such a way as should in the opinion of the company be conducive to the attainment of the primary object. No part of the income of the company was distributable among its members. It was urged that the company was established for charitable purposes for numerous reasons, with only one of which I will trouble your Lordships, namely, that it was established for the benefit of the community or of a section of the community, namely, Jews, whether the association was for the benefit of Jews all over the world or of the Jews repatriated in the Promised Land. Lord Tomlin dealing with the argument that I have just mentioned upon the footing that, if benefit to "a community" could be established the purpose might be charitable, proceeded to examine the problem in that aspect and sought to identify the community. He failed to do so, finding it neither in the community of all Jews throughout the world nor in that of the Jews in the region prescribed for settlement. It is perhaps unnecessary to pursue the matter. Each case must be judged on its own facts and the dividing line is not easily drawn. But the difficulty of finding the community in the present case, when the definition of "Welsh people" in the first deed is remembered, would not I think be less than that of finding the community of Jews in *Keren's* case.

In *Scottish Burial Reform and Cremation Society v Glasgow Corporation* ([1968] AC 138, [1967] 3 All ER 215) the question was whether the appellant Society was a charity and therefore entitled to partial exemption from rates under the Local Government (Financial Provisions, etc.) (Scotland) Act 1962, s. 4 (2) (*a*). The objects of the Society so far as relevant were:

"(*a*) To promote reform in the present methods of burial in Scotland both as regards the expense involved and the dangerous effects on the public health.

(*b*) To promote inexpensive and at the same time sanitary methods of disposal of the dead, which shall best tend to render the remains innocuous; and, in particular, to promote the method known as cremation."

The Society charged fees, but was non-profit making.

The House of Lords held that the objects were for the benefit of the public and also within the spirit and intendment of the statute of Elizabeth, and were charitable. On the latter point Lord Reid said (at p. 146): "But the appellants must also show that the public benefit is of a kind within the spirit and intendment of the Statute of Elizabeth I. The preamble specifies a number of objects which were then recognised as charitable. But in more recent times a wide variety of other objects have come to be recognised as also being charitable. The courts appear to have proceeded first by seeking some analogy between an object mentioned in the preamble and the object with regard to which they had to reach a decision. And then they appear to have gone further and to have been satisfied if they could find an analogy between an object already held to be charitable and the new object claimed to be charitable. And this gradual extension has proceeded so far that there are few modern reported cases where a bequest or donation was made or an institution was being carried on for a clearly specified object which was for the benefit of the public at large and not of individuals, and yet the object was held not to be within the spirit and intendment of the Statute of Elizabeth I. Counsel in the present case were invited to search for any case having even the remotest resemblance to this case in which an object was held to be for the public benefit but yet not to be within that spirit and intendment. But no such case could be found.

There is, however, another line of cases where the bequest did not clearly specify the precise object to which it was to be applied but left a discretion to trustees or others to choose objects within a certain field. There the courts have been much more strict, so that if it is possible that those entrusted with the discretion could, without infringing the testator's directions, apply the bequest in any way which would not be charitable (for example, because it did not benefit a sufficiently large section of the public) then the claim that the bequest is charitable fails. But that line of cases can have no application to the present case, and it is easy to fall into error if one tries to apply to a case like the present judicial observations made in a case where there was a discretion which could go beyond objects strictly charitable."

And Lord UPJOHN (at p.153): "My Lords, I conclude by saying that the authorities show that the 'spirit and intendment' of the preamble to the Statute of Elizabeth have been stretched almost to breaking point. In the nineteenth and early twentieth centuries this was often due to a desire on the part of the courts to save the intentions of the settlor or testator from failure from some technical rule of law. Now that it is used so frequently to avoid the common man's liability to rates or taxes, this generous trend of the law may one day require reconsideration."[19]

ii. ANIMALS[20]

In *Re Wedgwood* ([1915] 1 Ch 113) the testatrix gave the residue of her estate to her brother Cecil upon an oral understanding that he would apply it for the protection and benefit of animals. One aspect of such work—and one in which the testatrix was particularly interested—was the improvement of methods of slaughtering animals.

The Court of Appeal held this to be a valid charitable trust. The protection of animals was calculated to protect public morality by checking the innate tendency to cruelty.

[19] See also *Incorporated Council of Law Reporting for England and Wales v A-G* [1972] Ch 73 at 88, per RUSSELL LJ, p. 354, post.

[20] Goodman Report, paras. 72–73 (Animal Charities); House of Commons Report, vol. II, pp. 133–134, 140–144 (Memorandum of Evidence of RSPCA).

In *Re Moss* ([1949] 1 All ER 495) the testatrix made gifts to a friend, Miss Harvey, "for her to use at her discretion for her work for the welfare of cats and kittens needing care and attention". ROMER J held this to be a valid charitable trust[1].

RE GROVE-GRADY[2]

[1929] 1 Ch. 557 (CA, Lord HANWORTH MR, LAWRENCE and RUSSELL LJJ)

The testatrix gave her residuary estate upon trust to found the "Beaumont Animals Benevolent Society", whose objects included (object No. 1) the acquisition of land "for the purpose of providing a refuge or refuges for the preservation of all animals birds or other creatures not human . . . and so that all such animals birds or other creatures not human shall there be safe from molestation or destruction by man . . ."

Held (LAWRENCE LJ dissenting; and reversing ROMER J).The trust was not charitable because it lacked the necessary element of benefit to the community.

RUSSELL LJ: There can be no doubt that upon the authorities as they stand a trust in perpetuity for the benefit of animals may be a valid charitable trust if in the execution of the trust there is necessarily involved benefit to the public; for if this be a necessary result of the execution of the trust, the trust will fall within Lord Macnaghten's fourth class in *Pemsel's* case ([1891] AC 531 at 583)—namely, "trusts for other purposes beneficial to the community."

So far as I know there is no decision which upholds a trust in perpetuity in favour of animals upon any other ground than this, that the execution of the trust in the manner defined by the creator of the trust must produce some benefit to mankind. I cannot help feeling that in some instances matters have been stretched in favour of charities almost to bursting point: and that a decision benevolent to one doubtful charity has too often been the basis of a subsequent decision still more benevolent in favour of another.

The cases have accordingly run to fine distinctions, and speaking for myself I doubt whether some dispositions in favour of animals held to be charitable under former decisions would be held charitable to-day. For instance, anti-vivisection societies, which were held to be charities by Chitty J in *Re Foveaux*[3], and were described by him as near the border line, might possibly in the light of later knowledge in regard to the benefits accruing to mankind from vivisection be held not to be charities.

The difficulty arises when you apply the test of benefit to the public to each particular case. The will of Mrs. Grove-Grady is no exception, for it presents a very difficult problem. . . .

1 *Re Douglas* (1887) 35 ChD 472 (home for lost dogs); *Re Cranston* [1898] 1 IR 431 (to promote vegetarianism); *Marsh v Means* (1857) 3 Jur NS 790 (to finance propaganda against cruelty to animals); *Tatham v Drummond* (1864) 4 De GJ & Sm 484 (society for prevention of cruelty to animals); *University of London v Yarrow* (1857) 1 De G & J 72 (hospital for animals useful to mankind); *National Anti-Vivisection Society v IRC* [1948] AC 31 at 45, per Lord WRIGHT.

2 Compromised in the House of Lords sub nom. *A-G v Plowden*, [1931] WN 89.

3 [1895] 2 Ch 501 at 507; overruled in *National Anti-Vivisection Society v IRC* [1948] AC 31, [1947] 2 All ER 217, p. 331, ante.

Assuming that I have correctly interpreted object No. 1, it comes down to this, that the residuary estate may be applied in acquiring a tract of land, in turning it into an animal sanctuary, and keeping a staff of employees to ensure that no human being shall ever molest or destroy any of the animals there. Is that a good charitable trust within the authorities?

In my opinion it is not. It is merely a trust to secure that all animals within the area shall be free from molestation or destruction by man. It is not a trust directed to ensure absence or diminution of pain or cruelty in the destruction of animal life. If this trust is carried out according to its tenor, no animal within the area may be destroyed by man no matter how necessary that destruction may be in the interests of mankind or in the interests of the other denizens of the area or in the interests of the animal itself; and no matter how painlessly such destruction may be brought about. It seems to me impossible to say that the carrying out of such a trust necessarily involves benefit to the public. Beyond perhaps hearing of the existence of the enclosure the public does not come into the matter at all. Consistently with the trust the public could be excluded from entering the area or even looking into it. All that the public need know about the matter would be that one or more areas existed in which all animals (whether good or bad from mankind's point of view) were allowed to live free from any risk of being molested or killed by man; though liable to be molested and killed by other denizens of the area. For myself I feel quite unable to say that any benefit to the community will necessarily result from applying the trust fund to the purposes indicated in the first object.

If then benefit to the community as a necessary result of the execution of the trust is essential, this trust is not charitable. It is well settled that if consistently with the trust the funds may be applied for a purpose not charitable, the trust will fail for perpetuity notwithstanding that the funds might under the trust have been applied for purposes strictly charitable

[His Lordship referred to *Re Wedgwood* [1915] 1 Ch 113 and continued:]

It was a peculiar case in this, that the trust was a secret trust declared orally. To ascertain the scope of the trust all the verbal statements made by the testatrix had to be regarded. The testatrix had explained the nature of the methods by which she desired her estate to be applied for the protection and benefit of animals—namely, in obtaining for them the benefit of humane slaughtering, i.e. avoidance of cruelty. All the members of the Court refer to that fact in their judgments; and from that they were able to spell out public benefit. Except for that purpose, there was no occasion to refer to that fact at all. Lord Cozens-Hardy says ([1915] 1 Ch 113 at 117): "It tends to promote public morality by checking the innate tendency to cruelty." Kennedy LJ (at 120, 121), in reviewing what he calls the particularly pertinent decisions, relies on those in which it is pointed out that the prevention of cruelty to animals is for the benefit of the public. Swinfen Eady LJ seems quite clear on the point. After referring to the explanation of the testatrix above mentioned he uses this language (at 122): "The object of the trust being thus ascertained and defined, the question arises, is this a valid charitable trust?" He says that it is, because it is a gift for a general public purpose beneficial to the community. He arrives at that view, because (amongst other things) the discouragement of cruelty promotes humane sentiments in man towards the lower animals and elevates the human race. It seems to me that the decision in *Re Wedgwood* is definitely based on the view that the object of the trust being discouragement of cruelty to lower animals, that, upon the existing authorities, involved benefit to the community.

The Court in *Re Wedgwood* was certainly not purporting to lay down any new law. It is not, in my opinion, a decision either (1) that every trust for the benefit of animals necessarily involves benefit to the community, or (2) that a trust for the benefit of animals which involves no such benefit is a charitable trust.

In my opinion, the Court must determine in each case whether the trusts are such that benefit to the community must necessarily result from their execution.

In the present case I cannot persuade myself that the trusts described by the testatrix under the head of the first object fulfil that description. To do so would go beyond any decided case. The authorities have, in my opinion, reached the furthest admissible point of benevolence in construing, as charitable, gifts in favour of animals, and for myself, I am not prepared to go any further.

In *Re Murawski's Will Trust* ([1971] 1 WLR 707, [1971] 2 All ER 328) a gift to the Bleakholt Animal Sanctuary, whose objects were "the provision of care and shelter for stray, neglected and unwanted animals of all kinds and the protection of animals from ill-usage, cruelty and suffering." was held to be charitable[4].

Purposes connected with animals may be charitable if expressed in terms of education[5] or of environmental preservation[6].

Report of the Charity Commissioners for England and Wales for the year 1973, para. 40.

"40. Concern for the protection of the environment was the motive for the establishment of a number of new charities. As an example, the Advisory Committee on Oil Pollution of the Sea was registered in October. Its objects include the preservation of the seas of the world in general and the seas adjacent to the United Kingdom in particular from pollution by human activities and the promotion of research into the causes and effects of such pollution and the means by which the injurious effects of pollution may be prevented or reduced. The establishment of the original Committee in 1952 was due to concern about the plight of oiled sea birds but the Committee are now proposing to increase the scope of their activities and money has been raised for research into the causes of pollution as well as the rehabilitation of sea birds."

[4] See Annual Report for 1971, para. 26 (Home of Rest for Horses).
[5] *Re Lopes* [1931] 2 Ch 130.
[6] *Re Verrall* [1916] 1 Ch 100 (National Trust).

iii. SOCIAL AND RECREATIONAL TRUSTS

In *Inland Revenue Commissioners v City of Glasgow Police Athletic Association* ([1953] AC 380, [1953] 1 All ER 747) the question was whether the Association was entitled to exemption from income tax on the ground that it was a body of persons established for charitable purposes only.

The object of the Association was "to encourage and promote all forms of athletic sports and general pastimes".

Nearly every member of the Glasgow police force was a member. The Association provided athletic, social and recreational facilities. It played a valuable part in maintaining health, morale and *esprit de corps* in the force, promoted good relations between the force and the public and increased the efficiency of the force generally.

The House of Lords (Lords NORMAND, MORTON OF HENRYTON, REID and COHEN, with Lord OAKSEY dissenting) held that the Association was not entitled to exemption. A trust for the promotion of the efficiency of the force would be charitable; but the provision of recreation was not.

Lord NORMAND said (at p. 395): "The Special Commissioners had evidence before them which entitled them to find that, among its purposes, were the encouragement of recruiting, the improvement of the efficiency of the force, and the public advantage. This is a purpose which the Special Commissioners were entitled to hold in law to be a public charitable purpose. But there remains the non-charitable purpose of providing recreation to the members. The question is whether this non-charitable purpose is incidental to the public charitable purpose. If not, it cannot be said that the association was a body established for charitable purposes only . . . The private advantage of members is a purpose for which the association is established and it therefore cannot be said that this is an association established for a public charitable purpose only."

INLAND REVENUE COMMISSIONERS v BADDELEY[7]

[1955] AC 572, [1955] 1 All ER 525 (HL, Viscount SIMONDS, Lords PORTER, REID, TUCKER and SOMERVELL OF HARROW)

Two conveyances of land were made to the respondent trustees on similar but not identical terms. In the first deed land, on which were a mission church, lecture room and store, was conveyed upon trust to permit the property to be "used by the leaders for the time being of the Stratford Newtown Methodist Mission for the promotion of the religious social and physical well-being of persons resident in the County Boroughs of West Ham and Leyton . . . by the provision of facilities for religious services and instruction and for the social and physical training and recreation of such aforementioned persons who for the time being are in the opinion of such leaders members or likely to become members of the Methodist Church and of insufficient means otherwise to enjoy the advantages provided . . . and by promoting and encouraging all forms of such activities as are calculated to contribute to the health and well-being of such persons".

[7] See also *D'Aguiar v Guyana Commissioner of Inland Revenue* [1970] TR 31 (Citizens' Advice and Aid Service of Georgetown held non-charitable by Privy Council).

(Clause 2 (a)). In the second deed four pieces of land laid out as playing-fields were conveyed upon similar trusts, the main difference being that the trustees were to permit them to be used for the moral (instead of religious) social and physical well-being of the same class of persons.

The question was whether the conveyances could be stamped at the reduced rate on the ground that the purposes were charitable.

Held. (Lord REID dissenting). The purposes were not charitable, because: (i) The purposes were wide enough to include non-charitable purposes; (ii) (Lords TUCKER and PORTER expressing no opinion) The requirement of public benefit was not satisfied.

VISCOUNT SIMONDS: I find it convenient, my Lords, to examine the two deeds separately, and take first a deed of conveyance to the respondents as trustees of certain land at Stratford, in the county of Essex, of an area of about 680 square yards with a mission church, lecture room and store erected on some part thereof. So far as relevant (omitting certain words which admittedly were inserted in error) the trusts of this property were as follows: [His Lordship read clause 2 (*a*) and continued:] This main trust is followed by certain ancillary provisions which cannot, I think, affect the question whether it is a charitable trust. It is at once apparent that the document is not skilfully drawn. It is presumably *all* the persons resident in the specified boroughs whose religious, social and physical well-being is to be promoted, but this is to be achieved by providing certain facilities for religious services and instruction and for the social and physical training and recreation of "such aforementioned persons," i.e., such residents, as are for the time being "in the opinion of such leaders members or likely to become members of the Methodist Church and of insufficient means . . . to enjoy the advantages provided by these presents". This awkward phraseology leaves me in doubt whether the beneficiaries under this trust are to be all the residents in a certain area or only such of the residents as satisfy two conditions, first that they are Methodists or in the opinion of the leaders potential Methodists, and secondly, that they are of limited means. It might even be that upon a true interpretation of the deed some benefits are open to all the residents, others to a more limited class. Fortunately I do not find it necessary to determine this question, for I think that, whatever view may be taken of it, this case is governed by the recent decision of this House in *Williams' Trustees v IRC* ([1947] AC 447)[8] . . . .

Other aspects of the trust established by the first deed were discussed and it is right that I should make some observations upon them, but before doing so I will turn to the second deed. . . . . [His Lordship held that this trust also failed for vagueness and generality, and continued:].

This brings me to another aspect of the case, which was argued at great length and to me at least presents the most difficult of the many difficult problems in this branch of the law. Suppose that, contrary to the view that I have expressed, the trust would be a valid charitable trust, if the beneficiaries were the community at large or a section of the community defined by some geographical limits, is it the less a valid trust if it is

[8] See p. 334, ante.

confined to members or potential members of a particular church within a limited geographical area?

The starting point of the argument must be, that this charity (if it be a charity) falls within the fourth class in Lord Macnaghten's classification. It must therefore be a trust which is, to use the words of Sir Samuel Romilly in *Morice v Bishop of Durham* ((1805) 10 Ves 522 at 532), of "general public utility," and the question is what these words mean. It is, indeed, an essential feature of all "charity" in the legal sense that there must be in it some element of public benefit, whether the purpose is educational, religious or eleemosynary: see the recent case of *Oppenheim v Tobacco Securities Trust Co Ltd* ([1951] AC 297, [1951] 1 All ER 31)[9], and, as I have said elsewhere, it is possible, particularly in view of the so-called "poor relations' cases," the scope of which may one day have to be considered, that a different degree of public benefit is requisite according to the class in which the charity is said to fall. But it is said that if a charity falls within the fourth class, it must be for the benefit of the whole community or at least of all the inhabitants of a sufficient area. And it has been urged with much force that, if, as Lord Greene said in *Re Strakosch* ([1949] Ch 529, [1949] 2 All ER 6)[10], this fourth class is represented in the preamble to the Statute of Elizabeth by the repair of bridges, etc., and possibly by the maintenance of Houses of Correction, the class of beneficiaries or potential beneficiaries cannot be further narrowed down. Some confusion has arisen from the fact that a trust of general public utility, however general and however public, cannot be of equal utility to all and may be of immediate utility to few. A sea wall, the prototype of this class in the preamble, is of remote, if any, utility to those who live in the heart of the Midlands. But there is no doubt that a trust for the maintenance of sea walls generally or along a particular stretch of coast is a good charitable trust. Nor, as it appears to me, is the validity of a trust affected by the fact that by its very nature only a limited number of people are likely to avail themselves, or are perhaps even capable of availing themselves, of its benefits. It is easy, for instance, to imagine a charity which has for its object some form of child welfare, of which the immediate beneficiaries could only be persons of tender age. Yet this would satisfy any test of general public utility. It may be said that it would satisfy the test because the indirect benefit of such a charity would extend far beyond its direct beneficiaries, and that aspect of the matter has probably not been out of sight. Indirect benefit is certainly an aspect which must have influenced the decision of the "cruelty to animal" cases. But, I doubt whether this sort of rationalization helps to explain a branch of the law which has developed empirically and by analogy upon analogy.

It is, however, in my opinion, particularly important in cases falling within the fourth category to keep firmly in mind the necessity of the element of general public utility, and I would not relax this rule. For here is a slippery slope. In the case under appeal the intended beneficiaries are a class within a class; they are those of the inhabitants of a particular area who are members of a particular church: the area is comparatively

[9] See p. 310, ante.
[10] See p. 357, post.

large and populous and the members may be numerous. But, if this trust is charitable for them, does it cease to be charitable as the area narrows down and the numbers diminish? Suppose the area is confined to a single street and the beneficiaries to those whose creed commands few adherents: or suppose the class is one that is determined not by religious belief but by membership of a particular profession or by pursuit of a particular trade. These were considerations which influenced the House in the recent case of *Oppenheim* ([1951] AC 297, [1951] 1 All ER 31). That was a case of an educational trust, but I think that they have even greater weight in the case of trusts which by their nominal classification depend for their validity upon general public utility.

It is pertinent, then, to ask how far your Lordships might regard yourselves bound by authority to hold the trusts now under review valid charitable trusts, if the only question in issue was the sufficiency of the public element. I do not repeat what I said in the case of *Williams' Trustees v IRC* ([1947] AC 447, [1947] 1 All ER 513) about *Goodman v Mayor of Saltash* ((1882) 7 App Cas 633) and the cases that closely followed it. Further consideration of them does not change the view that I then expressed, which in effect indorsed the opinion of the learned editor of the last edition of Tudor on Charities. More relevant is the case of *Verge v Somerville* ([1924] AC 496). In that case, in which the issue was as to the validity of a gift "to the trustees of the Repatriation Fund or other similar fund for the benefit of New South Wales returned soldiers," Lord Wrenbury, delivering the judgment of the Judicial Committee, said ([1924] AC at 499) that, to be a charity, a trust must be "for the benefit of the community or of an appreciably important class of the community. The inhabitants", he said, "of a parish or town or any particular class of such inhabitants, may, for instance, be the objects of such a gift, but private individuals, or a flutuating body of private individuals, cannot." Here, my Lords, are two expressions: "an appreciably important class of the community" and "any particular class of such inhabitants," to which in any case it is not easy to give a precise quantitative or qualitative meaning. But I think that in the consideration of them the difficulty has sometimes been increased by failing to observe the distinction, at which I hinted earlier in this opinion, between a form of relief extended to the whole community yet by its very nature advantageous only to the few and a form of relief accorded to a selected few out of a larger number equally willing and able to take advantage of it. Of the former type repatriated New South Wales soldiers would serve as a clear example. To me it would not seem arguable that they did not form an adequate class of the community for the purpose of the particular charity that was being established. It was with this type of case that Lord Wrenbury was dealing, and his words are apt to deal with it. Somewhat different considerations arise if the form, which the purporting charity takes, is something of general utility which is nevertheless made available not to the whole public but only to a selected body of the public—an important class of the public it may be. For example, a bridge which is available for all the public may undoubtedly be a charity and it is indifferent how many people use it. But confine its use to a selected number of persons, however numerous and important: it is then clearly not a charity. It is not of general public utility: for it does not serve the public purpose which its nature qualifies it to serve.

Bearing this distinction in mind, though I am well aware that in its application it may often be very difficult to draw the line between public and private purposes, I should in the present case conclude that a trust cannot qualify as a charity within the fourth class in *Income Tax Commissioners v Pemsel* ([1891] AC 531) if the beneficiaries are a class of persons not only confined to a particular area but selected from within it by reference to a particular creed. The Master of the Rolls in his judgment cites a rhetorical question asked by Mr. Stamp in argument ([1953] Ch 504 at 519, [1953] 2 All ER 233). "Who has ever heard of a bridge to be crossed only by impecunious Methodists?'" The reductio ad absurdum is sometimes a cogent form of argument, and this illustration serves to show the danger of conceding the quality of charity to a purpose which is not a public purpose. What is true of a bridge for Methodists is equally true of any other public purpose falling within the fourth class and of the adherents of any other creed.

The passage that I have cited from *Verge v Somerville* ([1924] AC 496 at 499) refers also (not, I think, for the first time) to "private individuals" or a "fluctuating body of private individuals" in contradistinction to a class of the community or of the inhabitants of a locality. This is a difficult conception to grasp: the distinction between a class of the community and the private individuals from time to time composing it is elusive. But, if it has any bearing on the present case, I would suppose that the beneficiaries, a body of persons arbitrarily chosen and impermanent, fall more easily into the latter than the former category.

I conclude that on this ground also I should decide this case against the respondents even if I were otherwise in their favour, and will only add that in coming to this conclusion I find myself in agreement with Babington LJ in the *Londonderry* case[11] to which I have already referred.

I move that the appeals be allowed accordingly. The costs of all parties will be paid by the appellants in accordance with the undertaking previously given.

The charitable status of various associations, such as Women's Institutes, Boys' Clubs and the National Playing Fields Association, which had for many years been assumed to be charitable, was put in doubt as a result of these decisions.

The Recreational Charities Act 1958 soon followed; but it may well be thought to have created as many problems as it solved.

RECREATIONAL CHARITIES ACT 1958[12]

1. General provision as to recreational and similar trusts, etc.—(1) Subject to the provisions of this Act, it shall be and be deemed always

[11] *Londonderry Presbyterian Church House Trustees v IRC* [1946] NI 178.

[12] (1959) 23 Conv (NS) 15 (S. G. Maurice); (1958) 21 MLR 534 (L. Price); Goodman Report, paras. 69–71 (Sport).

to have been charitable to provide, or assist in the provision of, facilities for recreation or other leisure-time occupation, if the facilities are provided in the interests of social welfare:

Provided that nothing in this section shall be taken to derogate from the principle that a trust or institution to be charitable must be for the public benefit.

(2) The requirement of the foregoing subsection that the facilities are provided in the interests of social welfare shall not be treated as satisfied unless—

(*a*) the facilities are provided with the object of improving the conditions of life for the persons for whom the facilities are primarily intended; and

(*b*) either—

(i) those persons have need of such facilities as aforesaid by reason of their youth, age, infirmity or disablement, poverty or social and economic circumstances[13]; or

(ii) the facilities are to be available to the members or female members of the public at large.

(3) Subject to the said requirement, subsection (1) of this section applies in particular to the provision of facilities at village halls, community centres and women's institutes, and to the provision and maintenance of grounds and buildings to be used for purposes of recreation or leisure-time occupation, and extends to the provision of facilities for those purposes by the organising of any activity.

2. Miners' welfare trusts.—(1) Where trusts declared before the seventeenth day of December, nineteen hundred and fifty-seven, required or purported to require property to be held for the purpose of activities which are social welfare activities within the meaning of the Miners' Welfare Act, 1952, and at that date the whole or part of the property held on those trusts or of any property held with that property represented an application of moneys standing to the credit of the miners' welfare fund or moneys provided by the Coal Industry Social Welfare Organisation, those trusts shall be treated as if they were and always had been charitable.

(2) For the purposes of this section property held on the same trusts as other property shall be deemed to be held with it, though vested in different trustees[13a].

QUESTION

What is the effect of the Recreational Charities Act 1958 on the *Glasgow Police* and *Baddeley* cases? H & M, pp. 393–394.

[13] *IRC v McMullen* [1978] 1 All ER 230.

[13a] Section 3 provides a number of savings and other provisions relating to past transactions.

iv. HOSPITALS[14]

RE RESCH'S WILL TRUSTS

[1969] 1 AC 514, [1967] 3 All ER 915 (PC, Lords HODSON, GUEST, DONOVAN, WILBERFORCE and Sir Alfred NORTH)

A number of questions arose under the will of Edmund Resch, who died in 1963, leaving a residuary estate worth A $8,000,000. The relevant question was whether a gift to a private non-profit-making hospital was a charitable gift. The gift was of income "to the Sisters of Charity for a period of 200 years or for so long as they shall conduct St Vincent's Private Hospital whichever shall be the shorter period, to be applied for the general purposes of such hospital and upon the expiration of the said period of 200 years or upon the said Sisters of Charity ceasing to conduct such hospital" to pay the income to named charities.

Held. A valid charitable gift.

LORD WILBERFORCE: St Vincent's Private Hospital was inaugurated in 1909, when the present building, called by that name, was converted to that purpose, having previously been used as a Hospice for the Dying. The hospital was established and has since 1909 been conducted by the Sisters of Charity, a voluntary association or congregation of women, governed by their constitution under which they devote themselves without reward to good works. The Sisters also conducted in 1909 and still conduct the adjacent St Vincent's Hospital which is a public hospital within the Public Hospitals Act, 1929–59. The evidence shows that the reason for the establishment of the private hospital was to relieve the pressing demand of the public for admission to the general hospital which was quite inadequate to the demand upon it. Another reason was that there were many persons who needed hospital nursing and attention who were not willing to enter a public hospital but were willing and desirous of having hospital accommodation with more privacy and comfort than would be possible in the general hospital. The establishment of an adjacent private hospital would enable the honorary medical staff in the general hospital to admit for treatment under their care in the private hospital patients who were reluctant to enter the general hospital and were able and willing to pay reasonable and proper fees for admission and treatment in a private hospital. The private hospital has 82 beds as compared with over 500 in the general hospital. . . .

A gift for the purposes of a hospital is prima facie a good charitable gift. This is now clearly established both in Australia and in England, not merely because of the use of the word "impotent" in the preamble to 43 Eliz. c. 4, though the process of referring to the preamble is one often used for reassurance, but because the provision of medical care for the sick is, in modern times, accepted as a public benefit suitable to attract the privileges given to charitable institutions. This has been recognised in the High Court in Australia in *Taylor v Taylor*[15] and *Kytherian Association of Queensland v Sklavos* ((1958) 101 CLR 56): in England in *Re Smith* ([1962] 1 WLR 763, [1962] 2 All ER 563).

In spite of this general proposition, there may be certain hospitals, or

[14] Goodman Report, pp. 47 (Costly Services), 48–49 (Hospitals).
[15] (1910) 10 CLR 218 at 227, per GRIFFITH CJ.

categories of hospitals, which are not charitable institutions (see *Re Smith*). Disqualifying indicia may be either that the hospital is carried on commercially, i.e., with a view to making profits for private individuals, or that the benefits it provides are not for the public, or a sufficiently large class of the public to satisfy the necessary tests of public character. Each class of objection is taken in the present case. As regards the first, it is accepted that the private hospital is not run for the profit, in any ordinary sense, of individuals. Moreover, if the purposes of the hospital are otherwise charitable, they do not lose this character merely because charges are made to the recipients of benefits—see *IRC v Falkirk Temperance Café Trust* (1927 SC 261), *Salvation Army (Victoria) Property Trust v Fern Tree Gully Corpn* ((1951) 85 CLR 159 at 173). But what is said is that surpluses are made and are used for the general purposes of the Sisters of Charity. This association, while in a broad sense philanthropic, has objects which may not be charitable in the legal sense. Furthermore its purposes, though stated in its "constitutions" are not limited by law, other than the canon law of the Roman Catholic Church, and under this, they are empowered, and may be obliged, to alter their purposes so as to include other objects which may not be strictly charitable.

Their Lordships do not consider it necessary to enter upon these latter considerations. For whatever the Sisters of Charity may be empowered to do with regard to their general property, as regards the share of income of the residuary estate, given to them as trustees, they are bound by the trusts declared in the will under which any money received by them must be applied exclusively for the general purposes of the private hospital as above defined. As regards these purposes, it appears, from the evidence already summarised, that the making of profits for the benefit of individuals is not among them. The most that is shown is that, on a cash basis, and without making such adjustments as would be required for commercial accounting, a net surplus is produced over the years which in fact has been applied largely, though not exclusively for hospital purposes. The share of income given by the will must be devoted entirely to the purposes of the private hospital. The character, charitable or otherwise, of the general activities of the Sisters, is not therefore a material consideration . . .

Their Lordships turn to the second objection. This, in substance, is that the private hospital is not carried on for purposes "beneficial to the community" because it provides only for persons of means who are capable of paying the substantial fees required as a condition of admission.

In dealing with this objection, it is necessary first to dispose of a misapprehension. It is not a condition of validity of a trust for the relief of the sick that it should be limited to the poor sick. Whether one regards the charitable character of trusts for the relief of the sick as flowing from the word "impotent" ("aged, impotent and poor people") in the preamble to 43 Eliz. c. 4 or more broadly as derived from the conception of benefit to the community, there is no warrant for adding to the condition of sickness that of poverty. As early as *IRC v Pemsel* Lord Herschell was able to say ([1891] AC 531 at 571):

"I am unable to agree with the view that the sense in which 'charities' and 'charitable purpose' are popularly used is so restricted as this. I

> certainly cannot think that they are limited to the relief of wants occasioned by lack of pecuniary means. Many examples may, I think, be given of endowments for the relief of human necessities, which would be as generally termed charities as hospitals or almshouses, where, nevertheless, the necessities to be relieved do not result from poverty in its limited sense of the lack of money."

Similarly in *Verge v Somerville* ([1924] AC 496) Lord Wrenbury, delivering the judgment of this Board on an appeal from New South Wales, pointed out that trusts for education and religion do not require any qualification of poverty to be introduced to give them validity and held generally that poverty is not a necessary qualification in trusts beneficial to the community. The proposition that relief of sickness was a sufficient purpose without adding poverty was accepted by the Court of Appeal in *Re Smith* ([1962] 1 WLR 763, [1962] 2 All ER 563). The appellants did not really contest this. They based their argument on the narrower proposition that a trust could not be charitable which excluded the poor from participation in its benefits. The purposes of the private hospital were, they said, to provide facilities for the well-to-do: an important section of the community was excluded: the trusts could not therefore be said to be for the benefit of the community. There was not sufficient "public element".

To support this, they appealed to some well-known authorities. [His Lordship referred to *Jones v Williams* ((1767) Amb 651) and *Re Macduff* ([1896] 2 Ch 451), where] in a general discussion of such expressions as "charitable" or "philanthropic", Lindley LJ said (at p. 464):

> "I am quite aware that a trust may be charitable though not confined to the poor; but I doubt very much whether a trust would be declared to be charitable which excluded the poor."

. . . Their Lordships accept the correctness of what has been said in those cases, but they must be rightly understood. It would be a wrong conclusion from them to state that a trust for the provision of medical facilities would necessarily fail to be charitable merely because by reason of expense they could only be made use of by persons of some means. To provide, in response to public need, medical treatment otherwise inaccessible but in its nature expensive, without any profit motive, might well be charitable: on the other hand to limit admission to a nursing home to the rich would not be so. The test is essentially one of public benefit, and indirect as well as direct benefit enters into the account. In the present case, the element of public benefit is strongly present. It is not disputed that a need exists to provide accommodation and medical treatment in conditions of greater privacy and relaxation than would be possible in a general hospital and as a supplement to the facilities of a general hospital. This is what the private hospital does and it does so at, approximately, cost price. The service is needed by all, not only by the well-to-do. So far as its nature permits it is open to all: the charges are not low, but the evidence shows that it cannot be said that the poor are excluded: such exclusion as there is, is of some of the poor—namely, those who have (a) not contributed sufficiently to a medical benefit scheme or (b) need to stay longer in the hospital than their benefit will cover or (c) cannot get a reduction of or exemption from the charges. The general benefit to the community of such facilities results from the beds and medical staff of the general hospital, the availability of a particular type of nursing and treatment which supplements that provided by the general hospital and the benefit to the standard of medical care in the general hospital which arises from the juxtaposition of the two institutions . . .

[Their Lordships] . . . hold . . . that the gift in favour of the Sisters of Charity is a valid charitable bequest.

Report of the Charity Commissioners for England and Wales for the year 1975, para. 70.

"*Charities engaged in fringe medicine*

70. As a result of our consideration of the New Age Healing Trust mentioned in paragraphs 68 and 69 above[16] we considered the practical difficulties involved and the principles which should be followed in considering applications for the registration of institutions set up to promote and/or practice unorthodox methods of healing. The main problem was the need to make value judgments in such cases. For this purpose we would require evidence to satisfy us that an unusual form of treatment had some merit, in the same way as the court would require evidence if the case had been brought before them. An organisation proposing to engage in such well known therapeutic activities as acupuncture, osteopathy and faith healing would not necessarily be required to submit evidence concerning the effectiveness of its activities. In other cases, however, evidence would be required concerning the nature of the healing method proposed and the therapeutic result of that method. The effectiveness of proposed treatment could be a matter of special knowledge derived from a study of cases or from other sources. It could also be provided by evidence that the treatment was generally acceptable to the medical profession. This did not mean that every institution practising in the field of fringe medicine must necessarily use methods acceptable to the generality of the medical profession if it were to obtain charitable status, but there might be grounds for reasonable doubt if no medically qualified persons were prepared to testify to the beneficial results of the treatment. We concluded that where therapeutic methods and results were common knowledge evidence on these points would not be required before registration but, where they were not, the applicant should be required to submit evidence, and a decision whether to register the institution should be based on a study of that evidence as well as of the stated objects."

V. MISCELLANEOUS

It is impossible to include or even to foresee all the areas which could be included under the fourth head. This section will present a miscellaneous collection of cases which help to illustrate the borderlines of this class.

[16] An application to register a trust for "the practising for the public benefit of New Age Healing for the relief of the sick and persons in ill-health" was rejected.

(a) The Services[17]

In *Re Gray* ([1925] Ch 362) the testator gave sums of money for the establishment of a regimental fund for the Carabiniers to be called "the Gray Fund". Its objects were "the promotion of sport (including in that term only shooting fishing cricket football and polo)".

ROMER J held that the gifts were charitable, as they promoted the physical efficiency of the Army. He said (at p. 365): "It is contended on behalf of the persons entitled to the residue that those two legacies were given on trusts which are not charitable. It is said that the object of the testator was merely to encourage sport. If that were so the gifts would no doubt be given on trusts which were not charitable: see *Re Nottage* ([1895] 2 Ch 649), where a gift for purposes of encouraging yacht racing was held not to be a charitable legacy. But in my opinion it was not the object of the testator in the present case to encourage or promote either sport in general or any sport in particular. I think it is reasonably clear that it was his intention to benefit the officers and men of the Carabiniers by giving them an opportunity of indulging in healthy sport. It is to be observed that the particular sports specified were all healthy outdoor sports, indulgence in which might reasonably be supposed to encourage physical efficiency. That I think was his object even though he refers to the fund as the 'Sporting Fund.' This case, therefore, does not, in my opinion, fall within *Re Nottage*.

I realize the truth of what Eve J said in *Re Mariette* ([1915] 2 Ch 284)[18] as to the natural inclination of the Court, if possible, to give effect to a gift of this sort and the danger of allowing that natural inclination to induce one to disregard established principles. But I am glad to find that there is an established principle enabling me to give effect to the gifts in the present case. This principle was established by Farwell J in *Re Good* ([1905] 2 Ch 60 at 66, 67) in 1905, a case that as far as I know has never been questioned in any way. In that case the testator gave his residuary personalty upon trust for the officers' mess of his regiment, to be invested and the income to be applied in maintaining a library for the officers' mess for ever, any surplus to be expended in the purchase of plate for the mess. According to the headnote of the report of that case it was held that the gift to maintain the library and to purchase plate for the officers' mess, being for a general public purpose tending to increase the efficiency of the army and aid taxation, was a good charitable bequest.

[17] *Re Stephens* (1892) 8 TLR 792 (gift to the National Rifle Association "for the teaching of shooting at moving objects so as to prevent as far as possible a catastrophe similar to that at Majuba Hill" held charitable); *Re Lord Stratheden and Campbell* [1894] 3 Ch 265 ("an annuity of £100 to be provided to the Central London Rangers on the appointment of the next lieutenant-colonel." The gift was held to be charitable but void for perpetuity; H & M, p. 370); *Re Donald* [1909] 2 Ch 410 (gift "to the officer commanding the Northamptonshire Militia for the mess of that regiment or for the poor of the regiment" held charitable); *Re Barker* (1909) 25 TLR 753 (gift to the Royal Engineers' Institute to provide prizes for competition among Royal Engineer cadets or officers held charitable); *Re Corbyn* [1941] Ch 400, [1941] 2 All ER 160 (trust for the benefit of boys from the training ship Exmouth "to be trained to become officers in His Majesty's Navy (Britannic) or the British Mercantile Marine" held charitable); *Re Driffill* [1950] Ch 92, [1949] 2 All ER 933 (trust to be applied "in whatever manner the trustees may consider desirable to promote the defence of the United Kingdom against the attack of hostile aircraft' held charitable).

[18] See p. 303, ante.

It was also held that the gift might be supported as a 'setting out of soldiers' within the meaning of those words in the statute of Elizabeth. But the judgment of Farwell J was based primarily on the ground that the gift on trust for the maintenance of the library was a gift tending to increase the efficiency of the army, and he referred, only as a possible alternative ground, to the fact that the trust tended to aid taxation.

In the course of his judgment he said, referring to the argument for the Attorney-General: 'Now Mr. Parker has put his argument on two grounds. First, he says that anything that improves the efficiency of the army is charitable within the meaning of the Act, because it is for a public purpose—a purpose in which the public are interested. Secondly, he says that it also comes within the last clause of the preamble of the statute of Elizabeth: "The aid or ease of any poor inhabitants concerning payments of fifteens, setting out of soldiers and other taxes," because it will relieve the taxation of the public. . . . I think it would be difficult to say that money given to be expended in terms in some specific way in order to increase the efficiency of a regiment in a particular mode is not a good charity. This gift, to my mind, does tend to increase the efficiency of the army by giving the officers greater opportunities of providing themselves with literature.' Then, after dealing with the suggestion that the money might conceivably be applied in the purchase of books which were unlikely to increase the efficiency of the army, he says: 'An officer is all the better equipped if he can speak several languages, and if he knows the history and geography of his own nation as well as many other nations, as well as being instructed in the military art, I should be sorry to have to hold that any gift which tends to educational equipment in that way is not a charitable gift.' . . .

In the case before Farwell J the efficiency was mental efficiency, and the only distinction between that case and the present case is that in the present case the efficiency is physical as opposed to mental efficiency. But it is obviously for the benefit of the public that those entrusted with the defence of the realm should be not only mentally but also physically efficient, and I think I am justified in coming to the conclusion that there is no difference between mental and physical efficiency for the present purpose."

(b) The Police

In *Inland Revenue Commissioners v City of Glasgow Police Athletic Association* ([1953] AC 380, [1953] 1 All ER 747, p. 342, ante) Lord Normand said (at p. 391): "The Special Commissioners, having found these facts, rejected the only contention then put forward on behalf of the Crown that, by reason of the wide nature and extent of the objects of the association, it was not a body of persons established for charitable purposes only. They were aided in arriving at this conclusion by such cases as *Re Good* ([1905] 2 Ch 60)[19] and *Re Gray* ([1925] Ch 362)[20]. As I shall not have occasion to refer to these cases again I will say now that so far as they are founded on the principle that gifts exclusively for the purpose of promoting the efficiency of the armed forces

[19] See p. 352, ante.
[20] See p. 352, ante.

are good charitable gifts, they are, in my opinion, unassailable, but that the decision that the actual gifts were of that nature is more doubtful. I would hold further that gifts or contributions exclusively for the purpose of promoting the efficiency of the police forces and the preservation of public order are by analogy charitable gifts."

(c) Miscellaneous Public Purposes

In *Re Wokingham Fire Brigade Trusts* ([1951] Ch 373, [1951] 1 All ER 454) a voluntary fire brigade was purchased by the National Fire Service in 1942. DANCKWERTS J held that the provision of a fire brigade was a charitable purpose and that the assets should be applied *cy-près*.

INCORPORATED COUNCIL OF LAW REPORTING FOR ENGLAND AND WALES v ATTORNEY-GENERAL[1]

[1972] Ch 73, [1971] 3 All ER 1029 (CA, RUSSELL, SACHS AND BUCKLEY LJJ)

The Incorporated Council of Law Reporting for England and Wales was incorporated in 1870 with the primary object of "the preparation and publication in a convenient form, at a moderate price, and under gratuitous professional control, of reports of judicial decisions of the superior and appellate courts in England". All income and property were to be applied solely towards the promotion of the Council's objects, and no portion could be paid by way of profit to its members. Payment of remuneration was authorised for editors, reporters and other persons for services rendered.

In 1966 the Council applied to be registered as a charity under s. 4 of the Charities Act 1960. In 1967 the Charity Commissioners refused to register it as a charity. The Council appealed to the High Court under s. 5 (3)[2], joining as parties the Commissioners of Inland Revenue and the Attorney-General.

Held. The Council was entitled to be registered as a charity under the fourth head; and also (RUSSELL LJ dissenting) as a trust for the advancement of education.

RUSSELL LJ: I come now to the question whether, if the main purpose of the council is, as I think it is, to further the sound development and administration of the law in this country, and if, as I think it is, that is a purpose beneficial to the community or of general public utility, that purpose is charitable according to the law of England and Wales.

On this point the law is rooted in the Statute of Elizabeth I, a statute the object of which was the oversight and reform of abuses in the administration of property devoted by donors to purposes which were regarded as worthy of such protection as being charitable. The preamble to the

[1] (1972) 88 LQR 171; *Incorporated Council of Law Reporting of the State of Queensland v Commissioner of Taxation of the Commonwealth* (1971) 45 ALJ 552, where the High Court of Australia held that the council was a charitable institution within the Income Tax and Social Services Contribution Assessment Act 1936–62, s. 23 (e). BARWICK CJ said at p. 555: "the production of law reports is clearly beneficial to the whole community because of the universal importance of maintaining the socially sustaining fabric of the law".

[2] This was the first such application under the Act. Annual Report for 1970, para. 27.

Statute listed certain examples of purposes worthy of such protection. These were from an early stage regarded merely as examples, and have through the centuries been regarded as examples or guideposts for the courts in the differing circumstances of a developing civilisation and economy. Sometimes recourse has been had by the courts to the instances given in the preamble in order to see whether in a given case sufficient analogy may be found with something specifically stated in the preamble, or sufficient analogy with some decided case in which already a previous sufficient analogy has been found. Of this approach perhaps the most obvious example is the provision of crematoria by analogy with the provisions of burial grounds by analogy with the upkeep of churchyards by analogy with the repair of churches. On other occasions a decision in favour or against a purpose being charitable has been based in terms upon a more general question whether the purpose is or is not within "the spirit and intendment" of the Statute of Elizabeth I and in particular its preamble. Again (and at an early stage in development) whether the purpose is within "the equity" or within "the mischief" of the Statute. Again whether the purpose is charitable "in the same sense" as purposes within the preview of the Statute. I have much sympathy with those who say that these phrases do little of themselves to elucidate any particular problem. "Tell me", they say, "what you define when you speak of spirit, intendment, equity, mischief, the same sense, and I will tell you whether a purpose is charitable according to law. But you never define. All you do is sometimes to say that a purpose is none of these things. I can understand it when you say that the preservation of sea walls is for the safety of lives and property, and therefore by analogy the voluntary provision of lifeboats and fire brigades are charitable. I can even follow you as far as crematoria. But these other generalities teach me nothing."

I say I have much sympathy for such approach: but it seems to me to be unduly and improperly restrictive. The Statute of Elizabeth I was a statute to reform abuses: in such circumstances and in that age the courts of this country were not inclined to be restricted in their implementation of Parliament's desire for reform to particular examples given by the Statute: and they deliberately kept open their ability to intervene when they thought necessary in cases not specifically mentioned, by applying as the test whether any particular case of abuse of funds or property was within the "mischief" or the "equity" of the Statute.

For myself I believe that this rather vague and undefined approach is the correct one, with analogy, its handmaid, and that when considering Lord Macnaghten's fourth category in *Pemsel's* case [1891] AC 531 at 583 of "other purposes beneficial to the community" (or as phrased by Sir Samuel Romilly (then Mr. Romilly) in argument in *Morice v Bishop of Durham* (1805) 10 Ves 522 at 531: "objects of general public utility") the courts, in consistently saying that not all such are necessarily charitable in law, are in substance accepting that if a purpose is shown to be so beneficial or of such utility it is prima facie charitable in law, but have left open a line of retreat based on the equity of the Statute in case they are faced with a purpose (e.g., a political purpose) which could not have been within the contemplation of the Statute even if the then legislators had been endowed with the gift of foresight into the circumstances of later centuries.

In a case such as the present, in which in my view the object cannot be thought otherwise than beneficial to the community and of general public utility, I believe the proper question to ask is whether there are any grounds for holding it to be outside the equity of the Statute[3]: and I think the answer to that is here in the negative. I have already touched upon its essential importance to our rule of law. If I look at the somewhat random examples in the preamble to the Statute I find in the repair of bridges, havens, causeways, sea banks and highways examples of matters which if not looked after by private enterprise must be a proper function and responsibility of government, which would afford strong ground for a statutory expression by Parliament of anxiety to prevent misappropriation of funds voluntarily dedicated to such matters. It cannot I think be doubted that if there were not a competent and reliable set of reports of judicial decisions, it would be a proper function and responsibility of government to secure their provision for the due administration of the law. It was argued that the specific topics in the preamble that I have mentioned are all concerned with concrete matters, and that so also is the judicially accepted opinion that the provision of a court house is a charitable purpose. But whether the search be for analogy or for the equity of the Statute this seems to me to be too narrow or refined an approach. I cannot accept that the provision, in order to facilitate the proper administration of the law, of the walls and other physical facilities of a court house is a charitable purpose, but that the dissemination by accurate and selective reporting of knowledge of a most important part of the law to be there administered is not.

Accordingly the purpose for which the association is established is exclusively charitable in the sense of Lord Macnaghten's fourth category. I would not hold that the purpose is purely the advancement of education: but in determining that the purpose is within the equity of the Statute I by no means ignore the function of the purpose in furthering knowledge in legal science.

I would dismiss the appeal.

Report of the Charity Commissioners for England and Wales for the year 1973, paras 69–70.

"*Council of Industrial Design*

The object of the council of improving the design of industrial products was in our view clearly of benefit to the public not only in the general sense of making industry more efficient and competitive but also more directly in encouraging the production of safer, more effective and more pleasing articles. The spread of knowledge of such articles was also of public benefit. On the other hand the council's activities, through its design

[3] Cf. the approach of the High Court of Australia in *Incorporated Council of Law Reporting of the State of Queensland v Commissioner of Taxation of the Commonwealth* (1971) 45 ALJR 552 at 555; *Royal National Agricultural and Industrial Association v Chester* (1974) 48 ALJR 304 at 305 ("improving the breeding and racing of Homer pigeons" held not charitable); (1975) 91 LQR 167.

centres with their catalogues describing approved products and displaying goods with the manufacturer's name attached, must provide some commercial benefit to the individual firms concerned. Moreover, the advantage was something more than mere advertisement in the sense of publicity: there was the additional publicised advantage of approval by the council, a body subsidised by public funds and so semi-official. However, the industrial firms whose products were exhibited were not members of the institution. Moreover the members of the council were not self-regarding industrialists but the nominees of a Minister of the Crown who had an absolute power to remove them from office. It accordingly appeared to us that it was not a purpose of the council to benefit the firms concerned and we decided that the council was a charity and should be registered.

[The Commissioners referred in para. 70 to the judgment of RUSSELL LJ in *Incorporated Council of Law Reporting for England and Wales v A-G* (p. 354, ante), and continued:]

We were satisfied that in the case of the Council of Industrial Design there was a substantial public benefit which raised a *prima facie* assumption of charitability and that, applying Lord Justice Russell's test mentioned above, there was nothing in the circumstances of the case to negative the assumption."

In *Re Strakosch* ([1949] Ch 529) a testator provided a fund "for any purpose which in [the trustees'] opinion is designed to strengthen the bonds of unity between the Union of South Africa and the Mother Country, and which incidentally will conduce to the appeasement of racial feeling between the Dutch and English speaking sections of the South African community".

The Court of Appeal held that this was not a charitable trust. Lord GREENE said (at p. 536): "Roxburgh J held that it was not a good charitable gift. Before us further evidence was produced consisting of an affidavit by Field Marshal Smuts. We have given this affidavit most careful consideration but we are unable to regard it as affording a reason for coming to a conclusion different from that at which Roxburgh J arrived. We realize the truth of the contention that the objects to which the gift is to be devoted are matters of great public concern both in the Union of South Africa and in the Mother Country. In particular the appeasement of racial feeling in the Union cannot but benefit all inhabitants of the Union, not merely the members of the two sections of the community expressly referred to. But the very wide and vague scope of the gift and the unrestricted latitude of application which its language permits make it impossible in our opinion to find that it falls within the spirit and intendment of the preamble to the Statute of Elizabeth. . . ."

(*d*) *Politics*[4]

Political activity is not charitable. Indeed the rule appears to be that an activity whose objective is to change the law is thereby disabled from

[4] Goodman Report, Ch 4; House of Commons Report, vol. I, paras. 35–44, vol II, pp. 23, 25–26, 48–83, 117–119, 129–154, 156–159, 214–215, 313–314, 316–317, 349–350, 361–362.

being a charity. How, it is said, can a trust to change the law be regarded by the law as so beneficial to the community that it deserves the privileges of charity?

A trust for a political party is not charitable. Attempts have been made to establish trusts for political purposes in the form of educational trusts. The dividing line between education in certain political principles and support of a political party is sometimes difficult to draw. A trust for "the furtherance of Conservative principles and religious and mental improvement" was upheld as charitable in *Re Scowcroft* ([1898] 2 Ch 638). Since then however, the courts have been quick to find a political object disguised as education. In the present century, the courts have at least been consistent between the parties[5]. The latest reported case is *Re Hopkinson* ([1949] 1 All ER 346), where the testator gave his residuary estate to found an educational fund "for the advancement of adult education with particular reference to . . . the education of men and women of all classes (on the lines of the Labour Party's memorandum headed 'A Note on Education in the Labour Party' . . .) to a higher conception of social, political and economic ideas and values and of the personal obligations of duty and service which are necessary for the realisation of an improved and enlightened social civilisation."

VAISEY J held that the trust was not charitable. He said (at p. 348): "In my judgment, there are two ways of reading the words which I have quoted. They may be read, first, as equivalent to a general trust for the advancement of adult education which, standing alone, would admittedly be charitable, the super-added purpose being treated merely as a rough guide to be followed or as a hint to be taken as to the kind of adult education which the testator had in mind, the strictly educational main purpose always being adhered to, or, secondly, they may be read as indicating that the first part is to be taken as a general direction and the second part beginning with the words 'with particular reference to' as the particular direction dominating the whole of the trust. The second of these alternative views seems to me to be the right one. I think that the particular purpose is the main purpose of the trust, that is to say, while every or any other kind of adult education is within the discretion reposed in the residuary legatees, the particular purpose referred to is, so to speak, the overriding and essential purpose, on the nature of which the validity of the whole trust depends . . .

Political propaganda masquerading—I do not use the word in any sinister sense—as education is not education within the Statute of Elizabeth (43 Eliz., c. 4). In other words, it is not charitable."

In *National Anti-Vivisection Society v Inland Revenue Commissioners* ([1948] AC 31) Lord SIMONDS said (at p. 61): "The learned Master of the Rolls cites in his judgment ([1946] KB 185 at 207) a passage from the speech of Lord Parker in *Bowman v Secular Society Ltd* ([1917] AC 406 at 442): 'A trust for the attainment of political objects has always been held invalid, not because it

[5] *Bonar Law Memorial Trust v IRC* (1933) 49 TLR 220 (Conservative); *Re Ogden* [1933] Ch 878 (Liberal); *Re Hopkinson* [1949] 1 All ER 346 (Labour).

is illegal . . . but because the court has no means of judging whether a proposed change in the law will or will not be for the public benefit.' Lord Parker is here considering the possibility of a valid charitable trust and nothing else and when he says 'has always been held invalid' he means 'has always been held not to be a valid charitable trust'. The learned Master of the Rolls found this authoritative statement upon a branch of the law, with which no one was more familiar than Lord Parker, to be inapplicable to the present case for two reasons, first, because he felt difficulty in applying the words to 'a change in the law which is in common parlance a "non-political" question,' and secondly, because he thought they could not in any case apply, when the desired legislation is 'merely ancillary to the attainment of what is ex hypothesi a good charitable object'.

My Lords, if I may deal with this second reason first, I cannot agree that in this case an alteration in the law is merely ancillary to the attainment of a good charitable object. In a sense no doubt, since legislation is not an end in itself, every law may be regarded as ancillary to the object which its provisions are intended to achieve. But that is not the sense in which it is said that a society has a political object. Here the finding of the commissioners is itself conclusive. 'We are satisfied,' they say, 'that the main object of the society is the total abolition of vivisection . . . and (for that purpose) the repeal of the Cruelty to Animals Act, 1876, and the substitution of a new enactment prohibiting vivisection altogether.' . . . Coming to the conclusion that it is a main object, if not the main object, of the society, to obtain an alteration of the law, I ask whether that can be a charitable object, even if its purposes might otherwise be regarded as charitable.

My Lords, I see no reason for supposing that Lord Parker in the cited passage used the expression 'political objects' in any narrow sense or was confining it to objects of acute political controversy. On the contrary he was, I think, propounding familiar doctrine, nowhere better stated than in a text-book, which has long been regarded as of high authority but appears not to have been cited for this purpose to the courts below (as it certainly was not to your Lordships), Tyssen on Charitable Bequests, 1st ed. The passage which is at p. 176, is worth repeating at length: 'It is a common practice for a number of individuals amongst us to form an association for the purpose of promoting some change in the law, and it is worth our while to consider the effect of a gift to such an association. It is clear that such an association is not of a charitable nature. However desirable the change may really be, the law could not stultify itself by holding that it was for the public benefit that the law itself should be changed. Each court in deciding on the validity of a gift must decide on the principle that the law is right as it stands. On the other hand, such a gift could not be held void for illegality.' Lord Parker uses slightly different language but means the same thing, when he says that the court has no means of judging whether a proposed change in the law will or will not be for the public benefit. It is not for the court to judge and the court has no means of judging. The same question may be looked at from a slightly different angle. One of the tests, and a crucial test, whether a trust is charitable, lies in the competence of the court to control and reform it. I would remind your Lordships that it is the King as parens patriae who is the guardian of charity and that it is the right and duty of his Attorney-General to intervene and inform the court, if the trustees of a charitable trust fall short of their duty. So too it is his duty to assist the court, if need be, in the formulation of a scheme for the execution of a charitable trust. But, my Lords, is it for a moment to be supposed that it is the function of the Attorney-General on behalf of the Crown to intervene and demand that a trust shall be established and administered by the court, the object of which is to alter the law in a manner highly prejudicial, as he and His Majesty's Government may think, to the welfare of the state? This very case would serve as an example, if upon the footing that it was a charitable trust it became the duty of the Attorney-General on account of its maladministration to intervene. There is undoubtedly a paucity of judicial authority on this point. It may fairly be said that *De Themmines v De Bonneval* ((1828) 5 Russ 288), to which Lord Parker referred in *Bowman's* case ([1917] AC 406), turned on the fact that the trust there in question was held to be against public policy. In *IRC v Temperance Council of the Christian Churches of England and Wales* ((1926) 136 LT 27), the principle was clearly recognized by Rowlatt J, as it was in *Re Hood* ([1931] 1 Ch 240 at 250, 252). But in truth the reason of the thing appears to me so clear that I neither expect nor require much authority. I conclude upon this part of the case that a main object of the society is political and for that reason the society is not established for charitable purposes only. I would only add that I would reserve my opinion on the hypothetical example of a private enabling Act, which was suggested in the course of the argument. I do not regard *Re Villers-Wilkes* ((1895) 72 LT 323) as a decision that a legacy which had for its main purpose the passing of such an Act is charitable."[6]

In *Re Bushnell* ([1975] 1 WLR 1596, [1975] 1 All ER 721)[7] a testator who died in 1941 gave the residue of his estate, subject to a life interest for his wife, who died in 1972, on trust to apply the income towards "furthering the knowledge of the socialised application of medicine to public and personal health and well-being and to demonstrating that the full advantage of socialised medicine can only be enjoyed in a socialist state" by means of lectures and by publishing and distributing books and literature on socialised medicine. GOULDING J held that the trust was not charitable.

Report of the Charity Commissioners for England and Wales for the year 1969, paras. 8–16; reprinted as Appendix "A" to the Report for the year 1973[8].

[6] Lord PORTER thought that the rule should apply only to trusts which are purely political. Lord NORMAND would have excluded only trusts whose predominant purpose was political. See also *Re Shaw* [1957] 1 WLR 729, [1957] 1 All ER 745.

[7] (1975) 38 MLR 471 (R. M. B. Cotterrell).

[8] See also Annual Report for 1973, paras. 7–10.

"8. One contemporary development which has given us some concern has been the increasing desire of voluntary organisations for 'involvement' in the causes with which their work is connected. Many organisations now feel that it is not sufficient simply to alleviate distress arising from particular social conditions or even to go further and collect and disseminate information about the problems they encounter. They feel compelled also to draw attention as forcibly as possible to the needs which they think are not being met, to rouse the conscience of the public to demand action and to press for effective official provision to be made to meet those needs. As a result 'pressure groups', 'action groups' or 'lobbies' come into being. But when a voluntary organisation which is a charity seeks to develop such activities it nearly always runs into difficulties through going beyond its declared purposes and powers. No charity should, of course, undertake any activity unless it is reasonably directed to achieving its purposes and is within the powers conferred by the charity's governing instrument[9].

9. This development has resulted in our having to consider in a number of different contexts the extent to which individual charities may properly engage in activities which may be described generally as of a political nature, and further whether it is possible for us to indicate in a general way what in our view are the pitfalls for which charities must be on the lookout. We endeavour in the following paragraphs to give some guidance on this matter, but we would emphasise that the law is based on a limited number of decided cases and there is some danger in trying to stretch them to cover the whole of the ground. In the last resort any particular case must be judged on all the circumstances pertaining to it, and what we say below must be regarded as guidance of only the most general kind which may well need to be modified when applied to individual cases. We are always ready to give our opinion on any particular case where the trustees are in doubt, although many charities likely to come into contact with this problem will have their own legal advisers to whom they should turn for advice in the first instance.

10. It is a well-established principle of charity law that a trust for the attainment of a political object is not a valid charitable trust and that any purpose with the object of influencing the legislature is a political purpose. Thus no organisation can be a charity and at the same time include among its purposes the object of bringing influence to bear directly or indirectly on Parliament to change the general law of the land. If the governing instrument of an organisation were to give it power, other than in a way merely ancillary to some charitable purpose, to play a part in bringing political pressure to bear, that by itself would throw serious doubt on the organisation's claim to be a charity. Thus it is very unlikely that it will lie within any charity's purposes and powers to sponsor action groups or bring pressure to bear on the government to adopt or alter a particular line of action. In the past it was recognised that such activity lay well outside the true field of charity although, as will be mentioned below, there are other more traditional approaches to Parliament and to the government

[9] In *Baldry v Feintuck* [1972] 1 WLR 552, [1972] 2 All ER 81 the Students' Union of Sussex University was restrained from making payment to a publicity campaign against the abolition of free milk.

that have long been accepted as perfectly proper for a charity. Today, however, it seems that the limitations on action of this kind are not always recognised by those responsible for running charities.

11. Those trustees who feel that their charity should become involved in the political field frequently seek to justify such action as coming within the field of "education". In our report for 1966 we mentioned the misuse of this word in the governing instruments of some organisations applying for registration as charities. Increasingly we are confronted by attempts to represent as educational a variety of activities which are primarily of a propagandist nature and which accordingly cannot be accepted as coming within the meaning of the "advancement of education" as it is used in charity law. There is a similar tendency for those registered charities which have as a subsidiary object the education of the public in the particular aspect of charity with which the organisation is concerned (for instance the need for the relief of poverty in under-developed countries) to overstep the boundary of what might properly be described as education and pass outside their declared purposes into the field of propaganda. There is obvious difficulty in determining exactly where this boundary lies but if a charity with general objects, such as the relief of poverty or distress, issues literature urging the government to take a particular course or organises sympathisers to apply pressure for that purpose to their elected representatives, we think it is clear that the boundary has been overstepped.

12. We would emphasise that it is not for us to judge whether the object of a propagandist or political activity is morally or socially right or wrong although we can appreciate the reasons why some charities feel a moral obligation to attempt to influence policies. We are concerned simply with the law of charity and with seeking to ensure that funds which are impressed with charitable trusts are used for the purposes of those trusts and not for other purposes which could not be recognised as charitable. However small the proportion of the income of a charity which may be used in this way, we believe that the charity will be led into difficulties if it appears to be giving its support to any objects that are not strictly within its charitable purposes.

13. We have, where it has seemed to us to be necessary, brought these considerations to the notice of individual charities. We are aware, however, that there may be other charities, which have perhaps not yet discussed their problems with us, and which are hesitating about promoting their objects by activities which might perhaps be considered to be political activities. We believe that it might help charities to realise what they have power to do if we point the contrast by giving some examples of such activities which we believe can justifiably be regarded as being proper for a charity. These examples fall into three classes, the first and third of which present little difficulty. The first class comprises those examples in which it is the government itself which is investigating or has propounded proposals for changes in the law. Government officials frequently seek advice and information from those who are responsible for running charities and the charities quite properly respond. Similarly by publishing a green or white paper the government may impliedly invite comments from the public generally and a charity may justifiably avail itself of such an

invitation to make any comments which may appear to be useful. Again when a parliamentary bill has been published a charity will be justified in supplying relevant information to a member of either House and such arguments to be used in debate as it believes will assist the furtherance of its purposes. So also there can be other cases, not involving legislation, in which a charity is entitled to persuade a Member to support its cause in Parliament, for instance, where the question arises whether a government grant is to be made or continued to a particular charity.

14. The second class of examples, which includes those in which the charity itself or with others wishes to put forward proposals for changes in the law, can be more difficult to justify. It is probably unobjectionable for a charity to present to a government department a reasoned memorandum advocating changes in the law provided that in doing so the charity is acting in furtherance of its purposes. On the other hand, a charity can only spend its funds on the promotion of public general legislation if in doing so it is exercising a power that is merely ancillary to its charitable purposes. But here again difficulty arises in defining the boundary between what is merely ancillary and what amounts to adopting a new purpose in itself. A charity would be well advised to seek advice either from its legal advisers or from us before undertaking any such activities.

15. Finally, the third class of examples comprises cases where, although Parliament is involved, it appears to us that the reason for approaching it is not to be regarded as political. This, for instance, includes legislation that is only intended to confer enabling powers, such as the Sharing of Church Buildings Act which is mentioned in paragraphs 36 to 39 of this report. By supporting the passage of this Act the various charities involved were seeking to obtain wider powers to carry out their purposes. Similarly, virtually all private bills are free from taint of political activities. A private bill is in the nature of litigation as much as of legislation and the action of supporting or opposing such a bill resembles a court action and nearly always has no political tinge. We feel, therefore, that the principle laid down by the courts that a political object is not a charitable purpose should not be extended in such a way as to deny to a charity that right to promote or oppose private legislation which is enjoyed by public and private bodies in general. Thus in every session some charities, with our consent under section 19 (7) of the Charities Act, promote private bills which may set out to alter the constitution of the charity or to give it powers which only Parliament can confer. An example of such a bill in the present session is the National Trust Bill. The case mentioned in paragraphs 23 and 24 of this report provides an example of a charity which in order to realise its charitable purposes played a part in opposing a private bill.

16. There are two general points which we should like to mention in concluding this section of our report. First, if the trustees of a charity do stray into the field of political activity their action will be in breach of trust and those responsible for the action could be called on at law to recoup to the charity any of its funds which have been spent outside its purposes. Moreover a charity is not entitled to tax relief on income which is not applied to charitable purposes. But the fact that political

action had been taken in the name of the charity would not affect its status as a charity nor constitute a reason for removing it from the register of charities. If, however, doubt had been cast on the correctness of the original registration removal might be considered by us or by the High Court on an appeal by any other body interested. Secondly we think it should also be borne in mind that if charities step outside the sphere of activities to which the law confines them they may not only prejudice the support they receive from some people, who could resent the new activities, but they may also eventually endanger the privileged position which charities as a whole have been accorded by the state. The attempts now being made in the United States to curtail the privileges enjoyed by charitable foundations there result in part from allegations that some of those foundations have been using their funds for purposes which are essentially political."

Report of the Goodman Committee on Charity Law and Voluntary Organisations (1976), paras. 104–105.

"*Conclusions and Recommendations*

104. In considering this matter the Committee attempted to make a distinction between on the one hand advocating or promoting the continuance or change in the law or government policy or action and support on the other hand directly or indirectly to a political party or assistance to an individual or group to obtain elective office. The Committee rejected any step which would enable charities to give financial or other support to political parties or to individuals or groups seeking elective office. With regard to other political activity ancillary to the object of a charity, the Committee considered that there was a general lack of knowledge and understanding of the present law, many charities being under the impression that all political activity was prohibited to charities notwithstanding the contents of the Charity Commissioners' Reports referred to in paras. 95 and 96 above. There is, however, no doubt that the dearth of case law and the general nature of the guidance given by the Charity Commissioners has resulted in great uncertainty which should, if practicable, be dispelled. It is clear that a rigid approach to this problem would be inappropriate. Rather than attempting some definition of permissible political activity we believe, as at present, that each case should be considered individually but in the context of newly formulated guidelines and that political activity should be subject to review, as in other cases, as recommended in Chapters VI and VII of this report. We envisage that the guidelines should prescribe:

(a) that political activity should not be an object of the charity nor a principal activity such that its charitable object is in effect displaced by the extent of its political activity

(b) that political activity should be and be seen to be ancillary to the object of the charity

(c) that political activity should not include direct or indirect financial or other support for or opposition to any political party or individual or group seeking elective office, or any organisation having a political object . . .

105. We recognise that by maintaining a distinction between charitable and political institutions there may remain for certain bodies a problem relating to duality of function in cases where the political activity is outside the guidelines. This is, in our view, one which has to be accepted. Where a group of people promotes a body with charitable objects and another body with political objects it is said that the division is artificial. We disagree. The two institutions have different functions which should not be confused. We would indeed prefer to see greater separation rather than unification under a charitable banner.

In reaching our conclusions, we have naturally borne in mind that the word 'charity' has a moral connotation which itself attracts support and that some are concerned that the notion of a charity being permitted to become involved in political activity may detract from the special status accorded in the minds of many to charities. We recognise, also, that the liberty to undertake political activity within the limits we envisage has for many a moral connotation. Accordingly, provided those charities which choose to embark on such activity in the context we envisage make clear to the public what the context is in relation to that charity, we believe this may enhance rather than detract from the high regard in which charities are presently held. We stress in Chapter VII of this report the need for an annual statement by charities of their activities and we consider that a statement of political activity is no less important than other activities[10].

IV. The Trust Must be Exclusively Charitable[11]

To be charitable, the purpose of a trust must not merely include purposes which are charitable. The purposes must be exclusively charitable. This requirement has appeared in cases previously discussed. It appears dramatically in cases where the purposes are for charitable or some alternative purpose which is wider than legal charity. Thus, "charitable or benevolent" purposes are wider than legal charity. "Charitable and benevolent purposes" are however charitable, because, even though "benevolent" is wider than "charitable"[10a], the purposes here must be not only "benevolent" but "charitable" as well.

Where the purposes of a trust extend beyond the limits of legal charity, the court may, on construing the language, reach one of several possible solutions.

(i) That the trust is void. This result seems inevitable if it is possible, consistently with the terms of the trust, to apply the whole of the fund to non-charitable purposes.

(ii) That the non-charitable purposes are incidental only.

(iii) That the fund should be divided into parts; some being applicable to charity and some not. Such a solution can only be reached where the language of the trust instrument can be construed as directing such a division.

[10] See also paras. 81–82, 85 (Environment); and the Minority Report, pp. 148–150.

[10a] See also *Re Atkinson's Will Trusts* [1978] 1 WLR 586, [1978] 1 All ER 1275, "worthy causes" held not to be exclusively charitable).

[11] H & M, pp. 410–415; K & S, pp. 165–168; K & S (Charities), pp. 179–201; P & M, pp. 195–200; 204; Pettit, pp. 157–164; Snell, pp. 152–157; Tudor, pp. 171–187; Picarda, pp. 140–165.

A. And/Or Cases[12]

CHICHESTER DIOCESAN FUND AND BOARD OF FINANCE (INCORPORATED) v SIMPSON

[1944] AC 341, [1944] 2 All ER 60 (HL, Viscount SIMON LC, Lords MACMILLAN, PORTER and SIMONDS, Lord WRIGHT dissenting)

Caleb Diplock, the testator, directed his executors to apply the residue of his estate, amounting to more than £250,000 "for such charitable institution or institutions or other charitable or benevolent object or objects in England" as they should in their absolute discretion select.

Held. The gift was void[13].

LORD SIMONDS: My Lords, the words for your consideration are "charitable or benevolent". The question is whether, in the context in which they are found in this will, these words give to the executors a choice of objects extending beyond that which the law recognizes as charitable. If they do not, that is the end of the matter. The trust is a good charitable trust. If they do, it appears to be conceded by counsel for the appellant institution that the trust is invalid, but, in deference to the argument of the Attorney-General, who invited your Lordships to take a different view, I must say a few words at a later stage. My Lords, of those three words your Lordships will have no doubt what the first, "charitable", means. It is a term of art with a technical meaning and that is the meaning which the testator must be assumed to have intended. If it were not so, if in this will "charitable" were to be given, not its legal, but some popular, meaning, it would not be possible to establish the validity of the bequest. The last of the three words "benevolent" is not a term of art. In its ordinary meaning it has a range in some respects far less wide than legal charity, in others somewhat wider. It is, at least, clear that the two words, the one here used in its technical meaning, the other having only, and, accordingly, here used in, a popular meaning, are by no means coterminous. These two words are joined or separated by the word "or", a particle, of which the primary function is to co-ordinate two or more words between which there is an alternative. It is, I think, the only word in our language apt to have this effect. Its primary and ordinary meaning is the same, whether or not the first alternative is preceded by the word "either".

12 (a) Cases of *Or*: *Blair v Duncan* [1902] AC 37 ("such charitable or public purposes as my trustee thinks proper"); *Houston v Burns* [1918] AC 337 ("public, benevolent or charitable purposes"); *Re Macduff* [1896] 2 Ch 451 ("some one or more purposes, charitable, philanthropic or . . ."). These purposes were all held not charitable. Cf. *Re Bennett* [1920] 1 Ch 305 ("charity, or any other public objects in the parish of Faringdon").

(b) Cases of *And*: *Blair v Duncan*, supra, at p. 44, per Lord DAVEY: "If the words were 'charitable and public purposes', I think effect might be given to them, the words . . . being construed to mean charitable purposes of a public character."); *Re Sutton* (1885) 28 ChD 464 ("charitable and deserving objects"); *Re Best* [1904] 2 Ch 354 ("charitable and benevolent institutions"). These purposes were held to be charitable. Cf. *Williams v Kershaw* (1835) 5 Cl & F 111n ("benevolent, charitable and religious purposes"); *Re Eades* [1920] 2 Ch 353 ("such religious, charitable and philanthropic objects as X Y and Z shall jointly appoint"). See also *A-G v National Provincial and Union Bank of England* [1924] AC 262 ("such patriotic purposes or objects and such charitable institution or institutions or charitable object or objects in the British Empire as my trustees may select" held void).

13 For the sequel, see *Ministry of Health v Simpson* [1951] AC 251, [1950] 2 All ER 1137, p. 643, post.

My Lords, averting my mind from the possible ill effects of an alternative choice between objects "charitable" and objects "benevolent", I cannot doubt that the plain meaning of the testator's words is that he has given this choice, and that, if he intended to give it, he could have used no words more apt to do so. Is there, then, anything in the context which narrows the area of choice by giving to the words "or benevolent" some other meaning than that which they primarily and naturally have? And if so, what is the other meaning which is to be given to them? Let me examine the second question first. Since the test of validity depends on the area of choice not being extended beyond the bounds of legal charity, a meaning must be given to the words "or benevolent" which retains them within these bounds. This result, it has been contended, may be reached by giving to the word "or" not its primary disjunctive meaning but a secondary meaning which may, perhaps, be called exegetical or explanatory. Undoubtedly "or" is capable of this meaning. So used, it is equivalent to "alias" or "otherwise called". The dictionary examples of this use will generally be found to be topographical, as "Papua or New Guinea", but, my Lords, this use of the word "or" is only possible if the words or phrases which it joins connote the same thing and are interchangeable the one with the other. In this case the testator is assumed to use the word "charitable" in its legal sense. I see no possible ground for supposing that he proceeds to explain it by another word which has another meaning and by no means can have that meaning. I must reject the exegetical "or". Then it was suggested that the words "or benevolent" should be construed as equivalent to "provided such objects are also of a benevolent character", that is to say, the objects must be charitable but of that order of charity which is commonly called benevolent. I think that this is only a roundabout way of saying that "or" should be read as "and," that the objects of choice must have the two characteristics of charitable and benevolent. It is possible that a context may justify so drastic a change as that involved in reading the disjunctive as conjunctive. I turn then to the context to see what justification it affords for reading the relevant words in any but their natural meaning. Reading and re-reading them, as your Lordships have so often done in the course of this case, I can find nothing which justifies such a departure. It is true that the word "other" introduces the phrase "charitable or benevolent object or objects" and to this the appellants attached some importance, suggesting that since "other" looked back to "charitable institution or institutions", so all that followed must be of the genus charitable. There can be no substance in this, for in the phrase so introduced the word "charitable" is itself repeated and is followed by the alternative "or benevolent". Apart from this slender point it seemed that the appellants relied on what is called a general, a dominant, an overriding, charitable intention, giving charitable content to a word or phrase which might otherwise not have that quality. That such a result is possible there are cases in the books to show. Some of them have been cited to your Lordships, but here again I look in vain for any such context. On the plain reading of this will I could only come to the conclusion that the testator intended exclusively to benefit charitable objects if I excised the words "or benevolent" which he has used. That I cannot do.

B. Main and Subsidiary Objects

In *Oxford Group v Inland Revenue Commissioners* ([1949] 2 All ER 537) the question was whether the Oxford Group, a company limited by guarantee, was exempt from income tax. The objects of the movement, as laid down in its memorandum of association, included—

"3 (A) The advancement of the Christian religion, and, in particular, by the means and in accordance with the principles of the Oxford Group Movement, founded in or about the year 1921 by Frank Nathan Daniel Buchman. (B) The maintenance, support, development and assistance of the Oxford Group Movement in every way . . . (C) (9) To establish and support or aid in the establishment and support of any charitable or benevolent associations or institutions, and to subscribe or guarantee money for charitable or benevolent purposes in any way connected with the purposes of the association or calculated to further its objects. (10) To do all such other things as are incidental, or the association may think conducive, to the attainment of the above objects or any of them."

No question arose under 3 (A). The Court of Appeal held however that 3 (B) and 3 (C) (9) and (10) included purposes which were outside the scope of legal charity, and that the Company was not exempt from income tax.

In *General Nursing Council for England and Wales v St Marylebone Borough Council* ([1959] AC 540, [1959] 1 All ER 325) the House of Lords, by a majority of 3-2, decided that the General Nursing Council for England and Wales, a body whose main object was the regulation of the nursing profession, was not a charity, nor was it "otherwise concerned with the advancement of . . . social welfare". (Rating and Valuation (Miscellaneous Provisions) Act 1955, s. 8 (1) (*a*)). It was not therefore entitled to rating relief under s. 8 (2).

There may, however, be incidental non-charitable purposes.

In *Re Bernstein's Will Trusts* ((1971) 115 Sol Jo 808) the testator, after a life interest to his widow, gave his residuary estate on trust for the Eye, Ear and Throat Infirmary, Liverpool, one quarter of which was to form a nursing staff fund, "for the purpose of providing extra comforts at Christmas time for the nursing staff". UNGOED-THOMAS J held that the trust for the nursing staff was charitable, being subservient to the gift to the hospital.

In *Royal College of Surgeons of England v National Provincial Bank Ltd* ([1952] AC 631, [1952] 1 All ER 984) the House of Lords decided, by a majority of 3–2, that the Royal College of Surgeons was a charity. Its object was "the due promotion and encouragement of the study and practice of the . . . art and science [of surgery]". The other activities, which included the professional protection of the members of the profession, were merely ancillary.

In *Re Coxen* ([1948] Ch 747, [1948] 2 All ER 492) a trust fund, amounting to some £200,000, was held upon trust for medical charities and provided expressly for the payment of £100 towards a dinner for the Court of Aldermen of the City of London upon their meeting upon the business of the trust, and the payment of one guinea to each Alderman who attended during the whole of a Committee meeting. The trust was upheld on the ground, either that such payments should be treated as being made for the better administration of the trust; or as being incidental and ancillary to it.

In *Incorporated Council of Law Reporting for England and Wales v Attorney-General*[14] ([1972] Ch 73, [1971] 3 All ER 1029, see p. 300, ante) the Court of Appeal held that the activities of the Council were charitable. BUCKLEY LJ said (at p. 876): "The subsidiary objects, such as printing and publishing statutes, the provision of a noting-up service and so forth, are ancillary to this primary object and do not detract from its exclusively charitable character. Indeed, the publication of the statutes of the realm is itself, I think, a charitable purpose for reasons analogous to those applicable to reporting judicial decisions."[15]

C. Severance

In *Salusbury v Denton* ((1857) 3 K & J 529) Lynch Burrows bequeathed a fund to his widow to be applied by her in her will, "part to the foundation of a charity school, or such other charitable endowment for the benefit of the poor of Offley as she may prefer . . . and the remainder . . . to be at her disposal among my relatives, in such proportions as she may be pleased to direct". The widow died without having made a will or appointment. One question was whether the fund was divisible. PAGE-WOOD V-C held that the fund was divisible into two equal parts, one for charitable purposes, and the other for the plaintiff absolutely, as the only person entitled under the Statutes of Distribution. He said (at p. 539): "Here there is a plain direction to the widow to give a part to the charitable purposes referred to in the will as she may think fit, and the remainder among the testator's relatives as she may direct. And the widow having died without exercising that discretion, the moiety in question must be divided equally."

---

[14] Followed by the Charity Commissioners, in deciding that the Commonwealth Magistrates Association should be entered on the register of charities. Annual Report for 1975, para. 63.

[15] See also *IRC v City of Glasgow Police Athletic Association* [1953] AC 380, [1953] 1 All ER 747; p. 342, ante; *Re Lipinski's Will Trusts* [1976] Ch 235, [1976] 1 All ER 33, p. 256, ante; cf. *London Hospital Medical College v IRC* [1976] 1 WLR 613, [1976] 2 All ER 113.

Equal division may however be inappropriate (*Re Coxen* [1948] Ch 747, [1948] 2 All ER 492, see p. 369, ante).

D. Limited Reform

The Charitable Trusts (Validation) Act 1954[16] provided retrospective validation for instruments coming into effect before December 16, 1952[17], where, "consistently with the terms of the [trust] provision, the property could be used exclusively for charitable purposes, but could nevertheless be used for purposes which are not charitable". The Act is complex, and produced much litigation[18]. It has no application upon trusts coming into effect after 15 December 1952. More comprehensive legislation has been enacted in some Commonwealth countries[19].

v. Charitable Purposes Overseas[20]

Report of the Charity Commissioners for England and Wales for the year 1963, paras. 72, 73.

"72. The following extracts [are] from a letter recently sent to the principal charities concerned with overseas relief work:—

Relief Work

'4. The Commissioners have entertained no doubt that the advancement of religion, the advancement of education[1] and the relief of poverty (the first three heads of charity as classified in the well-known *Pemsel* judgment) are charitable purposes in whatever part of the world they are carried out; but charities must be satisfied in the last case that the poverty to be relieved actually exists in observable cases and is not merely inferred from statistics, and that the measures designed to relieve it, e.g., irrigation, will have a reasonably direct result. (The relief of poverty in this context should be interpreted throughout this letter as including the relief, e.g., of poor refugees or victims of natural disasters). If, however, the measures are directed merely to improving the general economy or standard of living of an overseas community, they probably would be charitable, subject to what is said below about public works within the British Commonwealth.

[16] (1954) 18 Conv (NS) 532; (1962) 26 Conv (NS) 200 (S. G. Maurice).

[17] The date of the publication of the Report of the Committee on the Law and Practice relating to Charitable Trusts (1952 Cmd. 8710), see chap. 12.

[18] *Vernon v IRC* [1956] 1 WLR 1169, [1956] 3 All ER 14; *Re Gillingam Bus Disaster Fund* [1959] Ch 62, [1958] 2 All ER 749; (1958) 74 LQR 190, 489 (P. S. Atiyah); (1959) CLJ 41 (S. J. Bailey); *Re Wykes* [1961] Ch 229, [1961] 1 All ER 470; *Re Mead's Trust Deed* [1961] 1 WLR 1244, [1961] 2 All ER 836; *Re Harpur's Will Trusts* [1962] Ch 78, [1961] 3 All ER 588; *Re Chitty's Will Trusts* [1970] Ch 254, [1969] 3 All ER 1492.

[19] (New South Wales) Conveyancing Act 1919–1969, s. 37D; (New Zealand) Trustee Act 1956, s. 82; (Victoria) Property Law Act 1958, s. 131; (Western Australia) Trustees Act 1962, s. 102; (1940) 14 ALJ 58; (1946) 62 LQR 23; (1950) 24 ALJ 239 (E. H. Coghill); (1967) 16 ICLQ 464 (M. C. Cullity); (1973) 47 ALJ 68 (I. J. Hardingham); Charities Act (Northern Ireland) 1964, s. 24.

[20] (1965) 29 Conv (NS) 123 (D. M. Emrys Evans); Goodman Report, paras. 86–88 (International Activity); 89–92 (Foreign Charities).

[1] Annual Report for 1976, paras. 43–44 (Centre for British Teachers in Europe Ltd).

Other work for the benefit of the community

5. Charities within the fourth head of the classification in the *Pemsel* case, i.e., for other purposes beneficial to the community, will be charitable only if of benefit to the community of the United Kingdom. Benefit to the United Kingdom need not be material or direct, but must not be too remote. Charities with general humanitarian objects (e.g., cancer research) can benefit the community of the United Kingdom even if carried on in foreign countries. But where the purposes are the local provision of public works or development projects such as roads and irrigation, these will generally be charitable only if (as I have already said) they are a reasonably direct means to the end of relieving existing poverty in observable cases; but they appear not to be charitable if the purpose is the general economic improvement of another country.

6. Benefit to the United Kingdom community, however, might arise from charitable purposes for the general benefit of a British Commonwealth country which is in close association with the United Kingdom. But the provision of public works for the general benefit of such a country seemingly could not be charitable if the works were of a class (e.g., a commercial factory) that it would not be charitable to provide in the United Kingdom. It must be repeated that opinions on the law in this field can only be speculative since the decided cases give no clear guidance; but it would appear that the distinction drawn between the Commonwealth countries and foreign sovereign states is based on relationship with the community of the United Kingdom, and it may therefore be charitable to continue to promote the general benefit of countries which are in the process of emerging from dependent to sovereign status. The relief of poverty in foreign states is, of course, charitable if carried out in accordance with para. 4 above.

9. It is recognized that these principles may not be easy to apply in practice. In particular, where projects for the indirect benefit of poverty are concerned, trustees should take all reasonable steps to satisfy themselves, on the best evidence available before expending charity funds on a particular project, first, that the poverty demonstrably exists, and second that its relief will not be too remote an effect of the particular project; but even so, there will be borderline cases. In cases of doubt, the Commissioners will be prepared in consultation with the Inland Revenue to do what they can to advise trustees who consult them regarding their duties.'

73. It will be seen that expenditure on measures linked reasonably directly with the relief of demonstrably existing poverty, including physical hardship, in any part of the world, is charitable, whether or not the measures are carried out in co-operation with the territorial government. On the other hand, it is apparently not within the field of charity at law to contribute to the cost of public works or other measures designed merely to develop or increase the general prosperity of foreign countries, although this may be charitable as regards countries within the British Commonwealth."

In *Re Robinson* ([1931] 2 Ch 122) MAUGHAM J held that a gift "to the German Government for the time being for the benefit of its soldiers disabled in the late war" was charitable. He said at p. 126: "It is abundantly clear that, whatever the construction which might have been placed upon the Statute of Elizabeth when that statute was passed in the forty-third year of that Queen's reign, for at least 200 years the Courts have been in the habit of treating the phrase 'charitable purposes' as not confined to charitable purposes within this realm."[2]

QUESTIONS

1. Does fiscal immunity play too large a part in the law of Charities? Should provision be made to validate certain useful and beneficial trusts without giving to them tax-free status? Consider what is said by the House of Lords in *Dingle v Turner* [1972] AC 601, [1972] 1 All ER 878, p. 287, ante; (1956) 72 LQR 187 (G. Cross); Royal Commission on the Taxation of Profits and Income (1955) Cmd. 9474, Chap. 7; (1977) 40 MLR 397 (N. P. Gravells); and tie this in with your thoughts on Purpose Trusts in Chapter 9.
2. Note the difference in the requirement of Public Benefit in each of the heads of Charity.
3. To what extent should relief for the population of developing counties be provided through charitable trusts; and to what extent through foreign aid? Appreciate that the domestic taxpayer contributes in either case.

[2] See also *Keren Kayemeth Le Jisroel Ltd v IRC* [1932] AC 650 (trust for the purchase of land in "Palestine, Syria, or other parts of Turkey, in Asia and the peninsula of Sinai for the purpose of settling Jews on such lands" held not charitable); *Re Jacobs* (1970) 114 Sol Jo 515 (trust "for the purpose of planting a grove of trees in Israel to perpetuate my name on the eternal soil of the Holy Land" held charitable. Annual Report for 1970, para. 78); *Re Niyazi's Will Trusts* (1978) Times, 8th February (trust for "the construction of a working men's hostel" in Famagusta, Cyprus, held charitable)

11. Cy-près[1]

I. General

If it should be impossible or impracticable to apply funds for the precise charitable purpose intended by the donor, the question arises whether the trust should fail, or whether the funds should be applied for a slightly different charitable purpose. If the gift is to charity for a determinable period, the gift will terminate on the happening of the determining event —so long as the event occurs within the perpetuity period[2]. The intention to terminate the gift must be clearly stated; for, generally, the resulting trust doctrines do not apply to property once dedicated to charity. In the situation in which it applies, the *cy-près* doctrine makes possible the application of funds to purposes as near as possible to those selected by the donor.

Before the Charities Act 1960 came into force, the *cy-près* doctrine could only be applied if it was "impossible or impracticable" to carry out the purposes of the trust. This requirement, although the word "impossible" was widely construed, caused a number of difficulties; for nothing could be done in cases where the continued administration of the trust was highly inconvenient, but not "impossible"; nor where, perhaps through changes in the needs of society or the value of money, an old charity served no useful purpose in modern times. The whole matter has been modernised by the Charities Act 1960, ss. 13 and 14.

Before that matter is examined in detail, however, it will be convenient to look at another requirement for the application of the doctrine, namely that, in a case where the problem arises *at the commencement* of the trust, the language of the instrument must show that there was a paramount charitable intention. There is no such requirement in a case of subsequent failure.

It is necessary therefore to distinguish between an intent to benefit charity generally—though by the means indicated by the donor; and an intent to apply the funds to the one purpose or institution selected by the donor, and no other. This distinction is only made in the case of *initial failure*.

[1] H & M, pp. 421–432; K & S, pp. 168–172; K & S (Charities), pp. 134–164; P & M, pp. 201–209; Pettit, pp. 215–224; Snell, pp. 160–165; Tudor, pp. 219–301; Picarda, pp. 219–308. See, generally, Sheridan and Delany, *The Cy-près Doctrine* (1959); Report of the Committee on the Law and Practice relating to Charitable Trusts (1952 Cmd. 8710), chap. 9; Goodman Report, paras. 188–192; House of Commons Report, vol I, paras. 63–71, vol. II, pp. 122, 177–178, 200–201, and, in the context of local reviews of charities, pp. 218–225, 228–248, 364–368.

[2] *Re Peel's Release* [1921] 2 Ch 218; *Re Randell* (1888) 38 ChD 213; *Re Cooper's Conveyance Trusts* [1956] 1 WLR 1096, [1956] 3 All ER 28; Perpetuities and Accumulations Act 1964, ss. 3, 12.

If the trust has once operated as a charitable trust, the problem no longer arises. "Once money is effectually dedicated to charity, whether in pursuance of a general or a particular charitable intent, the testator's next-of-kin or residuary legatees are for ever excluded."[3]

II. Initial Failure[4]

RE RYMER

[1895] 1 Ch 19 (CA, Lord HERSCHELL LC, LINDLEY and A. L. SMITH LJJ)

Horatio Rymer bequeathed a legacy of £5,000 "to the rector for the time being of St. Thomas' Seminary for the education of priests in the diocese of Westminster". The testator died in 1893.

At the date of the will St. Thomas' Seminary was in existence and provided education for priests for the diocese of Westminster. But at the date of the testator's death, the seminary ceased to exist, and the students were transferred to a seminary near Birmingham.

The question was whether the legacy lapsed or whether it should be applied *cy-près*.

Held (affirming CHITTY J). There being no general charitable intent, the legacy lapsed and fell into the testator's estate.

LINDLEY LJ: I think the result at which Mr. Justice Chitty has arrived is right. I have attended to and followed the arguments both of Mr. *Cozens-Hardy* and of Mr. *Ingle Joyce*, and in a great many of those arguments I concur. I think, with Mr. *Joyce*, that it does not do to approach a will of this kind by a short cut by saying there is a lapse, and there is an end of it. It is begging the question whether there is a lapse or not. You must construe the will and see what the real object of the language which you have to interpret is. I will not read the words of this gift again; I have read them very often, and studied them with care. I cannot arrive at the conclusion at which the Appellant's counsel ask me to arrive, that this is in substance and in truth a bequest of £5,000 for the education of the priests in the diocese of *Westminster*. I do not think it is. It is a gift of £5,000 to a particular seminary for the purposes thereof, and I do not think it is possible to get out of that. I think the context shews it. I refer to the masses, the choice of candidates, and so on. If once you get thus far the question arises, Does that seminary exist? The answer is, It does not. Then you arrive at the result that there is a lapse; and if there is a lapse, is there anything in the doctrine of *cy-près* to prevent the ordinary doctrine of lapse from applying? I think not. Once you arrive at the conclusion that there is a lapse, then all the authorities which are of any value shew that the residuary legatee takes the lapsed gift. We are asked to overrule that doctrine, laid down by Vice-Chancellor *Kindersley* in *Clark v Taylor* ((1853) 1 Drew 642) and followed in *Fisk v A-G* ((1867) LR 4 Eq 521). I think that the doctrine is perfectly right. There may be a difficulty in arriving at the conclusion that there is a lapse. But when once you arrive at the conclusion that a gift to a particular seminary or institution, or whatever

[3] *Re Wright* [1954] Ch 347 at 362, per ROMER LJ.

[4] See generally (1969) 32 MLR 283 (J. B. E. Hulton).

you may call it, is "for the purposes thereof", and for no other purpose—if you once get to that, and it is proved that that institution or seminary, or whatever it is, has ceased to exist in the lifetime of the testator, you are driven to arrive at the conclusion that there is a lapse, and then the doctrine of *cy-près* is inapplicable. That is in accordance with the law, and in accordance with all the cases that can be cited. I quite agree that in coming to that conclusion you have to consider whether the mode of attaining the object is only machinery, or whether the mode is not the substance of the gift. Here it appears to me the gift to the seminary is the substance of the whole thing. It is the object of the testator. I think that is plain from the language used.

Those are the short grounds of my judgment. I do not comment upon the decisions, because the Lord Chancellor has done that sufficiently.

In *Re Wilson* ([1913] 1 Ch 314) a testator, who died in 1870, provided a sum of money as a salary for a school-master, who was to teach at a school to be erected by voluntary subscriptions from landowners in the neighbourhood. There was no reasonable likelihood of such a school being established.

PARKER J was unable to find any general charitable intent. The particular purpose failed, and the gift fell into residue.

In *Re Packe* ([1918] 1 Ch 437) the testatrix gave to the Poor Clergy Relief Corporation a cottage and £1,000 upon trust to provide "a holiday home or house of rest for clergymen of the Church of England and their wives"; and provided that if the Corporation should refuse the gift, then the property was to be given to any other society selected by her executors "as a holiday home or house of rest for ladies or gentlemen of limited means". The Corporation renounced the gift, and it was not possible to find any other society willing to carry out the wishes of the testatrix. NEVILLE J held that the gift failed.

In *Re Good's Will Trusts* ([1950] 2 All ER 653) the testator provided funds for the purpose of purchasing land, erecting thereon "six more rest homes each home consisting of a living-room, sleep apartment (sic) and usual outside domestic conveniences all to be on the ground floor and all on one level", and money for paying for the upkeep of the homes. The money was insufficient for the purpose. WYNN-PARRY J held that the language was so particular as to exclude the possibility of finding a general charitable intention. The gift failed.

BISCOE v JACKSON
(1887) 35 ChD 460 (CA, COTTON, LINDLEY and FRY LJJ)

A testator provided that his trustees should set aside, out of such of his personal estate as might by law be bequeathed for charitable purposes, a sum of £10,000, of which £4,000 was to be applied "in the establishment of a soup kitchen for the parish of *Shoreditch*, and of a cottage hospital adjoining thereto . . ." and the provision of various related services. It was impossible to obtain the land necessary to carry out the provisions of the will. The next of kin claimed the fund.

Held. The will showed a general charitable intention. A scheme for the application of the funds *cy-près* was directed.

COTTON LJ: This is an appeal from an order made in November by Mr. Justice *Kay*, which directed a reference to settle a scheme to apply a sum of £10,000. For the purpose of this appeal we must assume that the bequest contained in the will could not be carried into effect in accordance with the particular directions contained in the will as was found by the certificate. That certificate was excepted to, and Mr. Justice *Kay* disallowed the exception. For the present purpose the Attorney-General does not press his appeal against the decision of Mr. Justice *Kay*. The real question, therefore, is whether or not the Court can, in a legacy like this, apply the doctrine of *cy-près*? It is clear that when there is a legacy given to a particular legatee, and that legatee fails before the death of the testator—there being only the gift to the particular legatee, even though that legatee is an institution—the legacy fails. But the question which we have now to consider is this, is this to be considered as a legacy to a particular institution which cannot be carried into effect, or do we see here an expressed intention by the testator to benefit the poor of the parish of *Shoreditch*, pointing out a particular mode in which he desires that benefit to be effected? For if the latter be the true view, then if that particular mode cannot have effect given to it, the Court will take hold of the charitable intention to benefit the poor of the parish and will apply the legacy in the best way *cy-près* for their benefit.

Now, in my opinion, notwithstanding the argument which has been addressed to us, I think there is that general intention. It is very true that the testator leaves certain things to be done by the trustees to whom he is giving the sum of £10,000, and if that is to be considered as a gift to an existing institution, or as a gift for that purpose only, it has failed. But then, in my opinion, looking at this whole clause, we see an intention on the part of the testator to give £10,000 to the sick and poor of the parish of *Shoreditch*, pointing out how he desires that to be applied; and that particular mode having failed, as we must for the purposes of this appeal assume to be the case, then the intention to benefit the poor of *Shoreditch,* being a good charitable object, will have effect given to it according to the general principle laid down long ago by this Court, by applying it *cy-près*. If the will had said that the trustees must build the particular building within the parish of *Shoreditch* there might be some difficulty, but what the testator desires to do is to provide a particular kind of hospital and a soup kitchen for the poor of the parish of *Shoreditch*. To my mind that shews that he intends not that it is to be located in a particular place, though that would be a proper mode of giving effect to the particular directions contained, if a place in the parish could be found; but that it is for the benefit of the parish, that is of the poor in the parish of *Shoreditch*. The testator directs that this shall be done by providing them with soup in this kitchen, by providing them with relief in a cottage hospital, and then by a direction that there is to be a woman living in the hospital to look after the inmates in the hospital, and that a sum of money is to be paid to a medical man to attend to them; and then he directs his trustees "to apply the residue of such annual income towards the necessities and for the benefit thereof, and of the patients who shall from time to time be taken into such hospital in such manner in all respects as my trustees or trustee in their or his absolute discretion think fit". Of course we have to determine what is the effect, looking fairly at the words used by the testator, to see what his intention was. To my mind the clear result is that he intended here to provide for the benefit of the poor, which is a good charitable bequest, and to provide for that primarily in the particular way he points out. If that fails then the doctrine applies, and Mr. Justice *Kay* was right in directing a reference to ascertain what was the best means for giving effect to his intentions, having regard to what the testator has said in the will as to the particular mode in which he desires his intentions should have effect given to them. In my opinion this appeal must fail; and that being our decision the other appeal is of course abandoned by the Attorney-General.

In *Re Harwood*[4a] ([1936] Ch 285) a testatrix, by a will made in 1925, left *inter alia* £200 to the Wisbech Peace Society, Cambridge, and £300 to the Peace Society of Belfast. She died in 1934. The Wisbech Peace Society had existed before 1934 but had ceased to exist by that date; there was no evidence that the Peace Society of Belfast had ever existed. FARWELL J held the second legacy was applicable *cy-près*, but not the first legacy. He said (at p. 286): "The first question that I have to determine is whether a gift of 200*l*. 'to the Wisbech Peace Society, Cambridge' fails. The evidence is that this particular society ceased to exist in the testatrix's lifetime. It is said that it is being still carried on as part of the work of the Peace Committee of the Society of Friends. The onus is upon them to show that they are the persons entitled to take. The evidence in this case is so unsatisfactory that I cannot say that that onus has been discharged.

That leaves the question whether there is any general charitable intent, so as to admit of the application of the cy-près doctrine. In that will there is a long list of various charitable societies including charities whose work is devoted to peace. It is said that as this is one of a long list of charitable legacies there is a general charitable intent. On the other hand, it is said that where there is a gift to a particular society, which once existed but ceased to exist before the death of the testator or testatrix, the gift lapses and there is no room for the cy-près doctrine. I have been referred to *Re Davis* ([1902] 1 Ch 876). In that case the learned judge was able to come to the conclusion that as to one particular gift there was a general charitable intent; but in that case no such society as that named in the will had ever existed. It was not a case of a society which had been in existence and had ceased to exist. I do not propose to decide that it can never be possible for the Court to hold that there is a general charitable

4a *Re Spence* (1978) Times, 18th, April.

intent in a case where the charity named in the will once existed but ceased to exist before the death. Without deciding that, it is enough for me to say that, where the testator selects as the object of his bounty a particular charity and shows in the will itself some care to identify the particular society which he desires to benefit, the difficulty of finding any general charitable intent in such case if the named society once existed, but ceased to exist before the death of the testator, is very great. Here the testatrix has gone out of her way to identify the object of her bounty. In this particular case she has identified it as being 'the Wisbech Peace Society Cambridge (which is a branch of the London Peace Society)'. Under those circumstances, I do not think it is open to me to hold that there is in this case any such general charitable intent as to allow the application of the cy-près doctrine.

Accordingly, in my judgment, the legacy of 200*l*. fails and is undisposed of.

Then there is the gift to the 'Peace Society of Belfast'.

The claimant for this legacy is the Belfast Branch of the League of Nations Union. I am quite unable on the evidence to say that that was the society which this lady intended to benefit, and I doubt whether the lady herself knew exactly what society she did mean to benefit. I think she had a desire to benefit any society which was formed for the purpose of promoting peace and was connected with Belfast. Beyond that, I do not think that she had any very clear idea in her mind. That is rather indicated by the pencil note which was found after her death. At any rate I cannot say that by the description, 'the Peace Society of Belfast,' the lady meant the Belfast Branch of the League of Nations Union; but there is enough in this case to enable me to say that, although there is no gift to any existing society, the gift does not fail. It is a good charitable gift and must be applied cy-près. The evidence suggests that at some time or other, possibly before the late War, there may have been a society called the Peace Society of Belfast. It is all hearsay evidence; there is nothing in the least definite about it, and it does not satisfy me that there ever was any society in existence which exactly fits the description in this case, and there being a clear intention on the part of the lady, as expressed in her will, to benefit societies whose object was the promotion of peace, and there being no such society as that named in her will, in this case there is a general charitable intent, and, accordingly, the doctrine of cy-près applies."

Although a particular charity no longer exists in its original form, the court may find that it continues elsewhere.

RE FARAKER[5]

[1912] 2 Ch 488 (CA, COZENS-HARDY MR, FARWELL and KENNEDY LJJ)

Mrs. Faraker, the testatrix, who died in 1911, bequeathed a legacy of £200 to "Mrs Bailey's Charity, Rotherhithe".

[5] *Re Lucas* [1948] Ch 424, [1948] 2 All ER 22; cf. *Re Stemson's Will Trusts* [1970] Ch 16, [1969] 2 All ER 517; *Re Slatter's Will Trusts* [1964] Ch 512, [1964] 2 All ER 469; (1964) 28 Conv (NS) 313 (J. T. Farrand).

A charity, known as Hannah Bayly's Charity, had been founded in 1756 by a Mrs. Hannah Bayly for the benefit of poor widows who were resident in and parishioners of Rotherhithe.

A scheme had been made in 1905 by the Charity Commissioners which had consolidated this and a number of charities in Rotherhithe. The funds were to be held upon various trusts for the benefit of the poor of Rotherhithe, no mention being made of widows.

No question was raised as to the spelling of the name Bayly, and it was admitted that the testatrix referred to Hannah Bayly's Charity.

The question was whether the legacy had lapsed.

Held (reversing NEVILLE J). The consolidated charities were entitled to the legacy.

FARWELL LJ: . . . Neville J has held that Hannah Bayly's Charity is no longer in existence. If that be so, I ask myself, How did it come to an end? and the answer suggested is, By the scheme of the Charity Commissioners. The jurisdiction given to the Charity Commissioners is given by the Act of 1860, and they have amongst other authorities the same power that the Court of Chancery had and the Chancery Division has for establishing schemes for the administration of any charity. That administration may, under proper circumstances, be cy-près, but the jurisdiction is for the establishment, encouragement, and continuance of a charity—even going beyond the actual words of the will, if there be an impossibility of carrying out literally the trusts—and a jurisdiction to administer cy-près. In the present case there is no question of a cy-près execution. Nobody suggests that there has been a failure of poor widows in Rotherhithe, and unless and until that happy event happens there will be no case for any cy-près administration. What is said is this: the Commissioners have in fact destroyed this trust because in the scheme which they have issued dealing with the amalgamation of the several charities the objects are stated to be poor persons of good character resident in Rotherhithe, not mentioning widows in particular—not of course excluding them, but not giving them that preference which I agree with the Master of the Rolls in thinking ought to have been given. But to say that this omission has incidentally destroyed the Bayly Trust is a very strained construction of the language and one that entirely fails, because the Charity Commissioners had no jurisdiction whatever to destroy the charity. Suppose the Charity Commissioners or this Court were to declare that a particular existing charitable trust was at an end and extinct, in my opinion they would go beyond their jurisdiction in so doing. They cannot take an existing charity and destroy it; they are obliged to administer it. To say that this pardonable slip (I use the word with all respect to the draftsman) has the effect of destroying the charity appears to me extravagant. In all these cases one has to consider not so much the means to the end as the charitable end which is in view, and so long as that charitable end is well established the means are only machinery, and no alteration of the machinery can destroy the charitable trust for the benefit of which the machinery is provided.

In my opinion it is quite impossible to say here that the widows are excluded, or even if they were in terms excluded, that that would destroy the trust: it could only give grounds for an application to set right that which in any event could only be put in per incuriam. I agree that the appeal must be allowed.

In *Re Finger's Will Trusts*[6] ([1972] Ch 286, [1971] 3 All ER 1050) GOFF J pointed out that where there was a gift to a charitable institution, and that institution failed before the death of the testator, it was easier to find a general charitable intent if the gift was to an unincorporated charitable association, than if it was a gift to a charitable corporation. He relied on a dictum of BUCKLEY J in *Re Vernon's Will Trusts* [1972] Ch 300n at 303, [1971] 3 All ER 1061n at 1064.

"Every bequest to an unincorporated charity by name without more must take effect as a gift for a charitable purpose. No individual or aggregate of individuals could claim to take such a bequest beneficially. If the gift is to be permitted to take effect at all, it must be as a bequest for a purpose, viz., that charitable purpose which the named charity exists to serve. A bequest which is in terms made for a charitable purpose will not fail for lack of a trustee but will be carried into effect either under the Sign Manual or by means of a scheme. A bequest to a named unincorporated charity, however, may on its true interpretation show that the testator's intention to make the gift at all was dependent upon the named charitable organisation being available at the time when the gift takes effect to serve as the instrument for applying the subject-matter of the gift to the charitable purpose for which it is by inference given. If so and the named charity ceases to exist in the lifetime of the testator, the gift fails (*Re Ovey* (1885) 29 ChD 560). A bequest to a corporate body, on the other hand, takes effect simply as a gift to that body beneficially, unless there are circumstances which show that the recipient is to take the gift as a trustee. There is no need in such a case to infer a trust for any particular purpose. The objects to which the corporate body can properly apply its funds may be restricted by its constitution, but this does not necessitate inferring as a matter of construction of the testator's will a direction that the bequest is to be held in trust to be applied for those purposes: the natural construction is that the bequest is made to the corporate body as part of its general funds, that is to say, beneficially and without the imposition of any trust. That the testator's motive in making the bequest may have undoubtedly been to assist the work of the incorporated body would be insufficient to create a trust."

In *Re Jenkins's Will Trusts* ([1966] Ch 249, [1966] 1 All ER 926) the testatrix bequeathed her residuary estate to be divided into seven equal parts, one of which was to be held in trust for six charitable institutions and the seventh in trust for the British Union for the Abolition of Vivisection. The question was whether the seventh share should be held upon charitable trusts on the ground that the will disclosed a general charitable intention. BUCKLEY J held that the gift of the seventh share failed. He said at p. 256:

[6] (1972) 36 Conv (NS) 198 (R. B. M. Cotterrell); (1974) 38 Conv (NS) 187 (J. Martin); *Re Edis's Declaration of Trust* [1972] 1 WLR 1135, [1972] 2 All ER 769.

"the principle of noscitur a sociis does not in my judgment entitle one to overlook self-evident facts. If you meet seven men with black hair and one with red hair you are not entitled to say that here are eight men with black hair. Finding one gift for a non-charitable purpose among a number of gifts for charitable purposes the court cannot infer that the testator or testatrix meant the non-charitable gift to take effect as a charitable gift when in the terms it is not charitable, even though the non-charitable gift may have a close relation to the purposes for which the charitable gifts are made."

In *Re Satterthwaite's Will Trusts*[7] ([1966] 1 WLR 277, [1966] 1 All ER 919) the testatrix announced to an official of the Bond Street branch of the Midland Bank that she hated the whole human race and wished to leave her estate to animal charities. Nine were selected, apparently from the London telephone directory. Seven of them were animal charities, and the other two were an anti-vivisectionist society and the London Animal Hospital. It was not possible to identify an institution of that name which was in existence at the date of the will. The Court of Appeal (HARMAN, DIPLOCK and RUSSELL LJJ) held that the share for the hospital was to be applied *cy-près*. RUSSELL LJ said at p. 286: "What is the result in law of this? I have already indicated that [the testatrix] is to be taken as intending to benefit a charitable activity. But the organisation picked by name was not such. Prima facie, therefore, the bequest would fail and there would be a lapse, with the result in this case in fact—owing to the incidence of liabilities and death duties—of mere relief of other residuary objects. But my assumption is that the testatrix was pointing to a particular charitable application of this one-ninth of residue. If a particular mode of charitable application is incapable of being performed as such, but it can be discerned from his will that the testator has a charitable intention (commonly referred to as a general charitable intention) which transcends the particular mode of application indicated, the court has jurisdiction to direct application of the bequest to charitable purposes cy-près. Here I have no doubt from the nature of the other dispositions by this testatrix of her residuary estate that a general intention can be discerned in favour of charity through the medium of kindness to animals. I am not in any way deterred from this conclusion by the fact that one-ninth of residue was given to an anti-vivisection society which in law—unknown to the average testator—is not charitable."

III. Subsequent Failure

As has been seen, once money is absolutely and effectively dedicated to charity, the next of kin are for ever excluded. Thus, *cy-près* may apply even if a general charitable intent is lacking.

[7] Decided twelve days earlier than, but apparently not cited in *Re Jenkins's Will Trusts*, supra.

RE SLEVIN

[1891] 2 Ch 236 (CA, LINDLEY, BOWEN and KAY LJJ)

The testator by his will bequeathed "the pecuniary legacies following", one of which was a legacy of "£200 to the Orphanage of St. Dominic's, Newcastle-on-Tyne". That Orphanage was in existence at the testator's death; but it came to an end soon afterwards, and before the legacy was paid.

Held (reversing STIRLING J). The money was applicable *cy-près*.

KAY LJ: The orphanage did come to an end before the legacy was paid over. In the case of a legacy to an individual, if he survived the testator it could not be argued that the legacy would fall into the residue. Even if the legatee died intestate and without next of kin, still the money was his, and the residuary legatee would have no right whatever against the Crown. So, if the legatee were a corporation which was dissolved after the testator's death, the residuary legatee would have no claim.

Obviously it can make no difference that the legatee ceased to exist immediately after the death of the testator. The same law must be applicable whether it was a day, or month, or year, or, as might well happen, ten years after; the legacy not having been paid either from delay occasioned by the administration of the estate or owing to part of the estate not having been got in. The legacy became the property of the legatee upon the death of the testator, though he might not, for some reason, obtain the receipt of it till long after. When once it became the absolute property of the legatee, that is equivalent to saying that it must be provided for; and the residue is only what remains after making such provision. It does not for all purposes cease to be part of the testator's estate until the executors admit assets and appropriate and pay it over; but that is merely for their convenience and that of the estate. The rights as between the particular legatee and the residue are fixed at the testator's death.

These propositions are so obvious that it would seem impossible to dispute them without some authority to the contrary. Is there any such authority?

[Having found no such authority, his Lordship continued:] In the present case we think that the Attorney-General must succeed, not on the ground that there is such a general charitable intention that the fund should be administered *cy-près* even if the charity had failed in the testator's lifetime, but because, as the charity existed at the testator's death, this legacy became the property of that charity, and on its ceasing to exist its property falls to be administered by the Crown, who will apply it, according to custom, for some analogous purpose of charity: *A-G v Ironmongers' Co* ((1834) 2 My & K 576); *Wilson v Barnes* ((1886) 38 Ch D 507), *Tyssen* on Charitable Bequests (at p. 440).

In *Re Wright*[8] ([1954] Ch 347, [1954] 2 All ER 98) the testatrix, who died in 1933, provided that her residuary estate, subject to a life interest, should be held on trust to provide and maintain a convalescent home. This would

[8] *Re Tacon* [1958] Ch 447, [1958] 1 All ER 163.

have been practicable in 1933. But, on the death of the life tenant in 1942, the balance of probabilities was against it. The question was whether the test of practicability should be applied at the date of the testatrix's death or at the date when the funds became available. The Court of Appeal, DENNING and ROMER LJJ following *Re Slevin* ([1891] 2 Ch 236), held that the material date was that of the death of the testatrix. ROMER LJ said: at p. 359 "Mr. Dillon's argument, on behalf of the testatrix's next-of-kin, was to the effect that the gift in the will was for a special charitable purpose: namely, for the establishment and maintenance of the convalescent home which the testatrix had in mind and which she described with such particularity; and that the gift was dependent and conditional upon it being practicable to carry the purpose, as so described, into effect when the death of the life tenant, Mrs. Webb, made the fund available for the home. It is not so much a question of lapse, he said, as a condition of practicability being attached to the gift, so that if the condition could not be satisfied the bequest would fail. Mr. Buckley, on the other hand, contended that no such condition or contingency as suggested attached to the bequest. He argued that in the case of any charitable gift by will, whether immediate or future, no question of impracticability supervening after the testator's death is of any materiality, provided that the object or purpose to which the gift is to be applied is practicable when the testator died. That is the time, he argued, when the rights of the parties, charity on the one hand and the next-of-kin or other persons taking in default on the other, are to be ascertained and they are to be ascertained at that time once and for all.

In the present case Roxburgh J followed, on the point now under consideration, his earlier decision in *Re Moon* ([1948] 1 All ER 300). In that case a testator directed that after the death of his wife his trustees should pay a legacy of '£3,000 to the Trustees of the Gloucester Street Wesleyan Methodist Church at Devonport on trust to invest the same in some Government security and to apply the income thereof to mission work in the district served by the said Gloucester Street Wesleyan Methodist Church including particularly John Street and Moon Street'. When the testator's widow died, it had become impracticable to carry out the mission work which the testator envisaged. Roxburgh J held that the gift was charitable and held further that, although the legacy was a future legacy, the question whether or not the charitable purpose lapsed for impracticability had to be ascertained at the moment when the charity trustees became absolutely entitled to the legacy, that was, at the moment of the testator's death and not at the moment when it became payable. The judge was guided to this conclusion by the reasoning of the judgment of this court in *Re Slevin* ([1891] 2 Ch 236), which was delivered by Kay LJ. The testator in that case bequeathed, amongst other 'charitable legacies', a legacy to an orphanage which was in existence at the time of the testator's death but which was discontinued before his assets had been administered and therefore before the legacy was or properly could be paid. The question was whether, in those circumstances, the legacy failed and fell into residue. In the course of the argument Kay LJ rhetorically asked ([1891] 2 Ch at 237): . . . where the charity, the legatee, is in existence at the death of the testator, and has received, or might have received the legacy, does not the legacy by that very fact become impressed with charity which the residuary legatee cannot get rid of?' The judgment of the court gave an affirmative answer to that question."

In *Re King* ([1923] 1 Ch 243) a testatrix left residue for the purpose of providing a stained glass window in the church of Irminster to the memory of herself and her relatives. The net residue was £1,094 14s 4d. and the estimate for the window was between £750 and £800. ROMER J held that the whole residue had been dedicated to charity and directed that the surplus be applied *cy-près*. He said (at p. 246): "In cases of a gift to a charitable institution, where such institution ceases to exist before the death of the testator the cy-près doctrine does not apply unless a general charitable intention can be found, and it is contended by the next of kin that there is not any difference between such a case and the present case, where a sum is left over after a particular intention has been fulfilled, there being no general charitable intention shown. But in the case of a legacy to a charitable institution that exists at the death of the testator, but ceases to exist after his death and before the legacy is paid over, the legacy is applied cy-près, even in the absence of a general charitable intention: see *Re Slevin* ([1891] 2 Ch 236). In Tyssen's Charitable Bequests, 2nd Ed, p. 202, I find the following statement: 'Where a gift is made for a particular charitable purpose which is sufficiently provided for without the gift, the gift will be applied cy-près,' and various authorities are cited in support of this principle. Such authorities and the other authorities cited to me show that the contention of the Attorney-General is well founded, and I therefore hold that the contention on behalf of the next of kin fails, and that the surplus must be applied cy-près. The Attorney-General consenting, this surplus will be applied in the erection of a further stained-glass window or windows in the same church."

IV. Impossibility and Impracticability

A. Before Charities Act 1960

Even if there was a paramount charitable intent or if a charitable trust had once operated, the *cy-près* doctrine could only be applied if the object of the trust became impossible or impracticable in whole or in part. If it became impossible or impracticable to apply the whole of the fund for the charitable purpose, the surplus may be applied *cy-près*. *Cy-près* application was not available where the fund could be more usefully or conveniently applied for other purposes, nor where the objects were outmoded in the sense that they concerned purposes which were once of significance, but which are unrelated to present day conditions; or for purposes which are provided for from other sources. In order to move with the times, the test of impossibility or impracticability was given an increasingly wide construction.

In *Attorney-General v City of London* ((1790) 3 Bro CC 171) there was a trust for "the advancement and propagation of the Christian religion among the Infidels in Virginia". Lord THURLOW LC said (at p. 177): "The trusts to the corporation to convert infidels ceasing for want of objects (there being now no infidels) the charity must be applied *de novo*."

In *Ironmonger's Co v Attorney-General* ((1844) 10 Cl & Fin 908) Thomas Belton, by his will of 1723, left the residue of his estate to the Worshipful Company or Corporation of Ironmongers of the City of London upon trust to pay half of the income "unto the redemption of British slaves in Turkey or Barbary". In 1833 "the altered circumstances of those countries left little or no demand for the bounty of the testator" and Lord BROUGHAM LC decreed that the fund be applied *cy-près*.

In *Re Weir Hospital* ([1910] 2 Ch 124) Benjamin Weir died in 1902 the owner of two freehold houses, No. 12 Devonshire Road, Balham and The Hawthorns, Streatham. The Hawthorns was subject to a restrictive covenant (which prevented its use as a hospital); but this expired in 1907. The testator devised the houses upon trust; to use No. 12 Devonshire Road as a hospital or convalescent home, to be called the Weir Hospital, and to use The Hawthorns for the same purpose after the expiration of the restrictive covenant, either independently or in conjunction with No. 12 Devonshire Road. The residuary estate was given for the maintenance of the hospital.

In 1907 expert opinion was agreed that The Hawthorns was not a suitable site for a hospital. The Charity Commissioners approved a scheme whereby The Hawthorns would be turned into a home for nurses, and the bulk of the fund applied in enlarging and maintaining the Bolingbroke Hospital, to be renamed the Weir and Bolingbroke Hospital. The Court of Appeal, reversing Eve J, held that the Commissioners had acted *ultra vires*. It was not impracticable to carry out the provisions of the will.

In *Re Robinson* ([1923] 2 Ch 332) a testatrix bequeathed £1,500 towards the endowment of an evangelical church in Bournemouth, subject to various conditions, one of which was that a black gown should always be worn (by the preacher) in the pulpit. On a showing that the observance of this condition was likely to alienate the congregation and to defeat the testatrix's main object, P. O. LAWRENCE J deleted the condition on the ground of impracticability.

In *Re Dominion Students' Hall Trust*[9] ([1947] Ch 183) a company, limited

[9] "[The Race Relations Act 1976, s. 34 (1)] provides that any discrimination necessary to comply with the terms of the governing instrument of a charity established to confer benefits on persons of a particular racial group shall not be unlawful, but it specifically excludes from this exception any provision which restricts the benefits by reference to colour. Any provision of this latter kind is to operate so as to confer benefits on the class of person which results if the restriction as to colour is disregarded." Annual Report for 1976, para. 20.

by guarantee, was established for various charitable purposes, one of which was to promote community of citizenship, culture and tradition among all members of the British Commonwealth of Nations. It maintained a hostel for students in Bloomsbury. The benefit of the charity was restricted to Dominion students of European origin. The court was asked to approve an alteration of the memorandum of the company, deleting the words "of European origin". EVERSHED J, in approving the application, said: "The purpose of both the petition and the summons is that a restriction which has hitherto been characteristic of the charity, limiting its objects so as to exclude coloured students of the British Empire, should be removed and that the benefits of the charity should be open to all citizens from the Empire without what is commonly known as the 'colour bar.' Having regard to the interest of the Inns of Court in Imperial students, I have thought it right to be particularly careful to see that I have jurisdiction to authorize the scheme and to sanction the petition. The proposed removal of the 'colour bar' restriction has been put to a substantial number of the subscribers. Owing to the necessities of the case, it has not been possible to put it to all, but those to whom it has been put represent over 75 per cent. in value of the subscription and none dissents from what is now proposed.

It is plain that I have to bear in mind the general proposition contained in the headnote to *Re Weir Hospital* ([1910] 2 Ch 124), which is to the effect that funds given by a testator for a particular charitable purpose. cannot be applied cy-près by the court unless it has been shown to be impossible to carry out the testator's intention. True, the present is not a case of a testator and the court is, perhaps, not quite so strictly limited as in the case of a will. It is true, also, that the word 'impossible' should be given a wide significance: see *Re Campden Charities* ((1881) 18 ChD 310); *Re Robinson* ([1923] 2 Ch 332). It is not necessary to go to the length of saying that the original scheme is absolutely impracticable. Were that so, it would not be possible to establish in the present case that the charity could not be carried on at all if it continued to be so limited as to exclude coloured members of the Empire.

I have, however, to consider the primary intention of the charity. At the time when it came into being, the objects of promoting community of citizenship, culture and tradition among all members of the British Commonwealth of Nations might best have been attained by confining the Hall to members of the Empire of European origin. But times have changed, particularly as a result of the war; and it is said that to retain the condition, so far from furthering the charity's main object, might defeat it and would be liable to antagonize those students, both white and coloured, whose support and goodwill it is the purpose of the charity to sustain. The case, therefore, can be said to fall within the broad description of impossibility illustrated by *Re Campden Charities* ((1881) 18 ChD 310) and *Re Robinson* ([1923] 2 Ch 332)."

In *Re Lysaght* ([1966] Ch 191, [1965] 2 All ER 888) the testatrix provided funds to found medical studentships within the gift of the

Royal College of Surgeons of England. One of the qualifications, Clause 11, was that "any such student shall be of the male sex and the son of a duly qualified British born medical man . . . and must be a British born subject and not of the Jewish or Roman Catholic faith".

The Royal College of Surgeons declined to accept the gift since the exclusion of those of the Jewish or Roman Catholic faith was "so invidious and so alien to the spirit of the College's work as to make the gift inoperable in its present form". It was however willing to accept it with that paragraph deleted.

BUCKLEY J held that the testatrix's intention was that the gift was conditional upon the College accepting the office of trustee. Their refusal to act would defeat the paramount intention. A scheme should be ordered to provide for the payment of the money to the College to be held on the trusts declared by the will, but omitting the religious disqualification.

BUCKLEY J said at p. 202: "A general charitable intention, then, may be said to be a paramount intention on the part of a donor to effect some charitable purpose which the court can find a method of putting into operation, notwithstanding that it is impracticable to give effect to some direction by the donor which is not an essential part of his true intention—not, that is to say, part of his paramount intention.

In contrast, a particular charitable intention exists where the donor means his charitable disposition to take effect if, but only if, it can be carried into effect in a particular specified way, for example, in connection with a particular school to be established at a particular place, *Re Wilson* ([1913] 1 Ch 314)[10] or by establishing a home in a particular house: *Re Packe* ([1918] 1 Ch 437). The alternatives are neatly stated by Younger LJ in *Re Willis* ([1921] 1 Ch 44 at 54):

> 'The problem which in this case we have to solve is to say by which of two different principles the construction of this gift has to be controlled. The first of these principles is that if a testator has manifested a general intention to give to charity, whether in general terms or to charities of a defined character or quality, the failure of the particular mode in which the charitable intention is to be effectuated shall not imperil the charitable gift. If the substantial intention is charitable the court will substitute some other mode of carrying it into effect. The other principle which I paraphrase from the judgment of Kay J in *Biscoe v Jackson* ((1887) 35 Ch D 460 at 463)[11] is this. If on the proper construction of the will the mode of application is such an essential part of the gift that you cannot distinguish any general purpose of charity but are obliged to say that the prescribed mode of doing that charitable act is the only one the testator intended or at all contemplated, then, the court cannot, if that mode fails, apply the money cy-près.'

When, therefore, the Attorney-General submits that the primary intention of the testatrix in the present case was to found a medical studentship and that the detailed directions contained in clause 11 are not essential to that intention, he is, I think, contending, notwithstanding his concession

[10] See p. 375, ante.
[11] See p. 375, ante.

to the contrary, that the testatrix had a general charitable intention, that is to say, a paramount intention to which the court can give effect, notwithstanding that it may be impracticable or, as Mr. Clauson suggests, impolitic to give effect to that part of those detailed directions which requires religious discrimination. I proceed, therefore, to consider how far (a) the selection of the college as the trustee of the endowment fund and (b) the provision for religious discrimination, are essential parts of the testatrix's intention . . ."

B. Charities Act 1960

The Nathan Committee[12] recommended the relaxation of the requirements of impracticability.

CHARITIES ACT 1960

13. Occasions for applying property cy-près.[13]—(1) Subject to subsection (2) below, the circumstances in which the original purposes of a charitable gift can be altered to allow the property given or part of it to be applied cy-près shall be as follows:—

(*a*) where the original purposes, in whole or in part,—

(i) have been as far as may be fulfilled; or

(ii) cannot be carried out, or not according to the directions given and to the spirit of the gift; or

(*b*) where the original purposes provide a use for part only of the property available by virtue of the gift; or

(*c*) where the property available by virtue of the gift and other property applicable for similar purposes can be more effectively used in conjunction, and to that end can suitably, regard being had to the spirit of the gift, be made applicable to common purposes;[14] or

(*d*) where the original purposes were laid down by reference to an area which then was but has since ceased to be a unit for some other purpose, or by reference to a class of persons or to an area which has for any reason since ceased to be suitable, regard being had to the spirit of the gift, or to be practical in administering the gift; or

(*e*) where the original purposes, in whole or in part, have, since they were laid down—

(i) been adequately provided for by other means; or

(ii) ceased, as being useless or harmful to the community or for other reasons, to be in law charitable;[15] or

(iii) ceased in any other way to provide a suitable and effective method of using the property available by virtue of the gift, regard being had to the spirit of the gift.

[12] Report of the Committee on the Law and Practice relating to Charitable Trusts (1952 Cmd. 8710), para. 365.

[13] See Annual Report for 1970, paras. 37–46.

[14] For the previous powers concerning amalgamation, see T.A. 1925, s. 57; *Re Harvey* [1941] 3 All ER 284.

[15] *National Anti-Vivisection Society v IRC* [1948] AC 31, [1947] 2 All ER 217.

(2) Subsection (1) above shall not affect the conditions which must be satisfied in order that property given for charitable purposes may be applied cy-près, except in so far as those conditions require a failure of the original purposes.

(3) References in the foregoing subsections to the original purposes of a gift shall be construed, where the application of the property given has been altered or regulated by a scheme or otherwise, as referring to the purposes for which the property is for the time being applicable.

(4) Without prejudice to the power to make schemes in circumstances falling within subsection (1) above, the court may by scheme made under the court's jurisdiction with respect to charities, in any case where the purposes for which the property is held are laid down by reference to any such area as is mentioned in the first column in the Third Schedule[16] to this Act, provide for enlarging the area to any such area as is mentioned in the second column in the same entry in that Schedule.

(5) It is hereby declared that a trust for charitable purposes places a trustee under a duty, where the case permits and requires the property or some part of it to be applied cy-près, to secure its effective use for charity by taking steps to enable it to be so applied.

RE LEPTON'S CHARITY

[1972] Ch 276, [1971] 1 All ER 799 (Ch D, PENNYCUICK V-C)

By his will of November 26, 1715, Joseph Lepton devised land known as "Dickroyd" in Pudsey, Yorkshire, to trustees upon trust to pay £3 per annum "unto such Protestant dissenting minister whether he be Presbiterian or Independant as shall statedly preach at the Protestant dissenting meeting place at Pudsey soe long as such minister shall preach there" and to distribute "the overplus of the profitts . . . unto such poor aged and necessitouse people legally settled within the town of Pudsey as shall subsist without the town allowance" at the discretion of the trustees. Lepton died in 1716 when the total income from the rents and profits was £5 per annum. The land was sold and the income in 1970 was £791 14s. 6d. There was one Protestant dissenting meeting place, the Pudsey Congregational Chapel.

The question arose whether the court had jurisdiction to vary the will by scheme under Charities Act 1960, s. 13 so as to raise the annual payment to £100.

Held. Scheme so ordered.

PENNYCUICK V-C: The occasions for applying property cy-près are now set out in section 13 of the Charities Act 1960. It is clear that this section in part restates the principles applied under the existing law, but also extends those principles. The section should be read as a whole, but for the present purpose it will be sufficient to refer specifically only to a few sentences. Section 13 reads:

> "(1) Subject to subsection (2) below, the circumstances in which the original purposes of a charitable gift can be altered to allow the

[16] As amended by Local Government Act 1972, s. 210 (9) (f).

property given or part of it to be applied cy-près shall be as follows:—(*a*) where the original purposes, in whole or in part,— . . . (ii) cannot be carried out, or not according to the directions given and to the spirit of the gift; . . . (*e*) where the original purposes, in whole or in part, have, since they were laid down,— . . . (iii) ceased in any other way to provide a suitable and effective method of using the property available by virtue of the gift, regard being had to the spirit of the gift.(2) Subsection (1) above shall not affect the conditions which must be satisfied in order that property given for charitable purposes may be applied cy-près, except in so far as those conditions require a failure of the original purposes."

Subsection (1) (*e*) (iii) appears to be no more than a final writing out large of paragraph (*a*) (ii). The expression "spirit of the gift" may be an echo of words used in the *Campden Charities* case ((1881) 18 ChD 310). It must, I think, be equivalent in meaning to the basic intention underlying the gift, that intention being ascertainable from the terms of the relevant instrument read in the light of admissible evidence.

One must next consider whether in relation to a trust for payment of a fixed annual sum out of the income of a fund to charity A and payment of the residue of that income to charity B the expression "the original purposes of a charitable gift" in section 13 (1) should be construed as referring to the trusts as a whole or must be related severally to the trust for payment of the fixed annual sum and the trust for payment of residuary income. Mr. Browne-Wilkinson contends that the former is the correct view. Mr. Griffith contends that the latter is the correct view.

It seems to me that the words "the original purposes of a charitable gift" are apt to apply to the trusts as a whole in such a case. Where a testator or settlor disposes of the entire income of a fund for charitable purposes, it is natural to speak of the disposition as a single charitable gift, albeit the gift is for more than one charitable purpose. Conversely, it would be rather unnatural to speak of the disposition as constituting two or more several charitable gifts each for a single purpose. Nor, I think, is there any reason why one should put this rather artificial construction on the words. The point can, so far as I can see, only arise as a practical issue in regard to a trust of the present character. A trust for division of income between charities in aliquot shares would give rise to different considerations, inasmuch as even if one treats it as a single gift the possibility or otherwise of carrying out the trusts of one share according to the spirit of the gift could hardly react upon the possibility or otherwise of carrying out the trusts of the other share according to the spirit of the gift. The same is true, mutatis mutandis, of trusts for charities in succession. But in a trust of the present character there is an obvious inter-relation between the two trusts in that changes in the amount of the income and the value of money may completely distort the relative benefits taken under the respective trusts. The point is familiar in other instances of fixed annuity and residual income.

Once it is accepted that the words "the original purposes of a charitable gift" bear the meaning which I have put upon them it is to my mind clear that in the circumstances of the present case the original purposes of the gift of Dickroyd cannot be carried out according to the spirit of the gift, or to use the words of paragraph (*e*) (iii) "have ceased . . . to provide a suitable and effective method of using the property . . . regard being had to the spirit of the gift". The intention underlying the gift was to divide a sum which, according to the values of 1715, was modest but not negligible, in such a manner that the minister took what was then a clear three fifths of it. This intention is plainly defeated when in the conditions of today the minister takes a derisory £3 out of a total of £791.

It is not suggested that subsection (2) has any significant bearing upon the present question, for it is precisely the condition requiring the failure of the original purposes that subsection (1) (*a*) (ii) and subsection (1) (*e*) (iii) are concerned to modify.

If, contrary to my view, the words "the original purposes of a charitable gift" must be read severally in relation to the trust for payment of the fixed annual sum and to the trust for payment of residuary income, I think it is no less clear that paragraphs (*a*) (ii) and (*e*) (iii) would have no application. On this footing it would be impossible to maintain in respect of either trust that the original purposes cannot be carried out in the spirit of the gift. The minister is available to receive £3 a year, for what it is worth, and it is conceded by Mr. Browne-Wilkinson that there are sufficient poor, aged and necessitious people in Pudsey to absorb £788 a year.

Neither counsel sought to derive any assistance from the definitions in sections 45 and 46 of the Act.

I conclude that the new conditions for cy-près applications introduced by section 13 of the Act of 1960 have been satisfied. Mr. Griffith concedes that if it is legitimate to alter the purposes at all then £100 a year is a reasonable amount to be paid to the minister. There was some expert evidence on the value of money into which, for this reason, it is unnecessary to enter.

I propose to make an order by way of scheme accordingly. I should perhaps add, to avoid misunderstanding—and this is not in dispute—that should there cease to be a minister at the chapel with the consequence that the income becomes applicable in accordance with the provisions of the will, limited to take effect upon that event, section 13 will have no application as between the poor of Pudsey and the heirs of the testator.

CHARITIES ACT 1960

14. Application cy-près of gifts of donors unknown or disclaiming.—(1) Property given for specific charitable purposes which fail shall be applicable cy-près as if given for charitable purposes generally, where it belongs—

(*a*) to a donor who, after such advertisements and inquiries as are reasonable, cannot be identified or cannot be found[17], or

(*b*) to a donor who has executed a written disclaimer of his right to have the property returned.

(2) For the purposes of this section property shall be conclusively presumed (without any advertisement or inquiry) to belong to donors who cannot be identified, in so far as it consists—

[17] *Re Henry Wood National Memorial Trust* [1966] 1 WLR 1601, [1967] 1 All ER 238n.

(*a*) of the proceeds of cash collections made by means of collecting boxes or by other means not adapted for distinguishing one gift from another; or

(*b*) of the proceeds of any lottery, competition, entertainment, sale or similar money-raising activity, after allowing for property given to provide prizes or articles for sale or otherwise to enable the activity to be undertaken.

(3) The court may by order direct that property not falling within subsection (2) above shall for the purposes of this section be treated (without any advertisement or inquiry) as belonging to donors who cannot be identified, where it appears to the court either—

(*a*) that it would be unreasonable, having regard to the amounts likely to be returned to the donors, to incur expense with a view to returning the property; or

(*b*) that it would be unreasonable, having regard to the nature, circumstances and amount of the gifts, and to the lapse of time since the gifts were made, for the donors to expect the property to be returned.

(4) Where property is applied cy-près by virtue of this section, the donor shall be deemed to have parted with all his interest at the time when the gift was made; but where property is so applied as belonging to donors who cannot be identified or cannot be found, and is not so applied by virtue of subsection (2) or (3) above,—

(*a*) the scheme shall specify the total amount of that property; and

(*b*) the donor of any part of that amount shall be entitled, if he makes a claim not later than twelve months after the date on which the scheme is made, to recover from the charity for which the property is applied a sum equal to that part, less any expenses properly incurred by the charity trustees after that date in connection with claims relating to his gift; and

(*c*) the scheme may include directions as to the provision to be made for meeting any such claim.

(5) For the purposes of this section, charitable purposes shall be deemed to "fail" where any difficulty in applying property to those purposes makes that property or the part not applicable cy-près available to be returned to the donors.

(6) In this section, except in so far as the context otherwise requires, references to a donor include persons claiming through or under the original donor, and references to property given include the property for the time being representing the property originally given or property derived from it.

(7) This section shall apply to property given for charitable purposes, notwithstanding that it was so given before the commencement of this Act.

Report of the Charity Commissioners for England and Wales for the year 1970, paras. 42–44, 46.

"42. The relaxation of the rule relating to failure has enabled us over the last 10 years to assist many charities which wish to serve the local community in more modern and effective ways. As we have indicated above, this process had started 100 years before the Charities Act; but many of the schemes which our predecessors made during that time have in their turn grown out-of-date. The process of modifying the objects of charities, whether local or national, is an ever-continuing process. Thus the original terms of a charitable gift of the 18th century or earlier may have required the trustees to distribute to poor persons loaves of bread, candles or particular kinds of clothing. Even by the end of the 19th century many such trusts had failed, but the schemes which we then made prescribed in narrow terms the amounts of income which could be given in direct grants, or the particular institutions (e.g. a hospital or a clothing club) to which subscriptions might be granted, or the particular purposes (e.g., the cost of an outfit on entering a trade or the provision of passage money to aid emigration) to which contributions might be made. The amount of money which might be granted by way of temporary relief in cases of unexpected loss or sudden destitution was always most carefully limited as our predecessors were concerned lest the indiscriminate distribution of gifts by a charity might have the effect of pauperizing the beneficiaries. Only too often neither the terms of the original gift nor the terms of the subsequent scheme appear to us to be achieving the basic intention of the donor, which was usually to make a real contribution towards relieving distress. In such cases we substitute more general provisions allowing the trustees to use the charity's resources in ways which will relieve need in whatever form it may still be found to exist. It is therefore our practice to make the provisions of the scheme as wide as possible, but we also add an explanatory note, which is strictly not part of the scheme, to draw the trustees' attention to those ways which we know of at present in which the income may be usefully applied.

43. We have made good use of the power contained in section 13 (1) (*e*) (i) which makes it clear that a cy-près scheme can be made where the original purposes in whole or in part have, since they have been laid down, been adequately provided for by other means. For example, we have made schemes for a number of charities established for the repair of roads and bridges, substituting for those purposes other general purposes for the benefit of local inhabitants which could include, for instance, the promotion of the arts, the provision of seats or shelters, the preservation of old buildings, or the improvement of local amenities.

44. Although we have been able to do much in these ways to help charities to re-orientate themselves in modern conditions, much undoubtedly still remains to be done. There can be no doubt that the publicity given to the Charities Act and the need to register charities has made many aware also of our readiness to help them; and the actual process of supplying the information on registration has drawn the attention of some trustees to the extent to which the trusts they should be following are now out-of-date. The local reviews of charities, to which we have already referred[18], are also performing a useful function in helping to stimulate trustees to make the applications for schemes without which we cannot normally move. But even where reviews are being undertaken there are always some

[18] See p. 410, post.

trustees who, despite the obvious need for the trusts of their charities to be modernised, are not willing to make application to us. It may be that trustees sometimes hesitate to approach us for fear that they will be penalised for not having followed their trusts to the letter. If, however, trustees have departed from their trusts in the honest belief that what they were doing was better for the community they serve, they need have no fear of approaching us to ask for a scheme to alter the purposes of their charities. Failure to keep within the trusts may often be evidence of the need to alter the purposes of the charity rather than of dereliction of duty on the part of the trustees.

46. Section 14 of the Act was designed to overcome the difficulties which previously arose when money was collected for a particular charitable purpose and that purpose then turned out to be unattainable. Mention was made in the debates on this provision in Committee in the House of Commons of a fund which was raised to provide a new hospital, but when the project had to be abandoned it was held that the money should be returned to the subscribers, who had to be regarded as having a particular, as distinct from a general, charitable intention in making their gifts. Section 14 provides that if the donors of funds for a purpose which is no longer practical cannot be identified or found or, if they can be found, they execute a disclaimer of their right to have the property returned, they can be deemed to have had a general charitable intention so that the money they contributed can be applied cy-près. We have been able to make a number of schemes under this provision enabling money to be used for other charitable purposes which previously could not have been used[19]."

Report of the Charity Commissioners for England and Wales for the year 1973, para. 11.

"11. A criticism of a different kind which is sometimes levelled against us is that we do not interpret sufficiently widely the powers given to us by section 13 of the Charities Act to make schemes for the application of charitable funds cy-près. We explained the scope of these powers and our use of them in paragraphs 37 to 43 of our report for 1970. The important point, which often seems to be overlooked by trustees or others who wish to see the purposes of a charity altered, is that the basic consideration remains that the object which the donor wished to promote should be carried out unless the circumstances referred to in section 13 apply. It is not sufficient that a better way of using the money under some quite different head of charity should have occurred to the trustees, or that some pressing new need substantially different from the original purposes should have emerged to which it may be desired to divert the money; so long as the donor's general intentions can effectively be carried out they must continue to be respected. This principle must apply even where there is no donor as such and the original source of a charity's property may have been, for instance, an inclosure award."

[19] See, e.g. Annual Report for 1965, paras. 19, 20, 21 (Mile End Memorial Hall Fund (Colchester)); Annual Report 1971, paras. 72–75 (Church Hall Fund, Hartstone St Peter, Derbyshire).

QUESTIONS

1. Would it now be possible for gifts such as those in *National Anti-Vivisection Society v IRC* [1948] AC 31, [1947] 2 All ER 217, p. 331, ante, and *Oppenheim v Tobacco Securities Trust Co Ltd* [1951] AC 297, [1951] 1 All ER 31, p. 310, ante, to be saved by Charities Act 1960, s. 13 (1) (*e*) (ii)? H & M, pp. 431–432; (1974) 38 Conv (NS) at p. 233.
2. In what circumstances is proof of a general charitable intent still necessary? Charities Act 1960, s. 13 (2), s. 14. Pettit, p. 217.

12. The Administration of Charities[1]

I. General

The administration of charities is being effected more and more through the control and supervision of the Charity Commissioners and less and less by the courts. Prior to 1960 the powers of the administrative authorities were inadequate; but, as we have seen, major reforms in the law relating to *cy-près* were introduced by the Charities Act 1960. The bulk of the Act is concerned with the administration of charities. These matters receive inadequate treatment in some of the books, but they form the lifeblood of the modern law. Little of this appears in the law reports. Most of this chapter will consist of extracts from the statute and from the valuable Reports produced annually by the Charity Commissioners.

II. The Authorities

CHARITIES ACT 1960

1. The Charity Commissioners.—(1) There shall continue to be a body of Charity Commissioners for England and Wales, and they shall have such functions as are conferred on them by this Act in addition to any functions under any other enactment not repealed by this Act.

(2) The provisions of the First Schedule to this Act shall have effect with respect to the constitution and proceedings of the Commissioners and other matters relating to the Commissioners and their officers and servants.

(3) The Commissioners shall (without prejudice to their specific powers and duties under other enactments) have the general function of promoting the effective use of charitable resources by encouraging the development of better methods of administration, by giving charity trustees information

[1] H & M, pp. 415–421; K & S (Charities), pp. 207–230; P & M, pp. 209–216; Pettit, pp. 197–214; Snell, pp. 165–171; Tudor, pp. 332–370; Picarda, pp. 311–493. See also Hill, *A Guide for Charity Trustees* (2nd Edn, 1974).

or advice on any matter affecting the charity and by investigating and checking abuses.

(4) It shall be the general object of the Commissioners so to act in the case of any charity (unless it is a matter of altering its purposes) as best to promote and make effective the work of the charity in meeting the needs designated by its trusts; but the Commissioners shall not themselves have power to act in the administration of a charity.

(5) The Commissioners shall, as soon as possible after the end of every year, make to the Secretary of State a report on their operations during that year, and he shall lay a copy of the report before each House of Parliament[2].

FIRST SCHEDULE Section 1.

CONSTITUTION, ETC., OF CHARITY COMMISSIONERS

1.—(1) There shall be a Chief Charity Commissioner, and two other commissioners.

(2) Two at least of the commissioners shall be barristers or solicitors.

(3) . . . the chief commissioner and the other commissioners shall be appointed by the Secretary of State, and shall be deemed for all purposes to be employed in the civil service of the Crown.

(4) There may be paid to each of the commissioners such salary and allowances as the Secretary of State may with the approval of the Treasury determine.

(5) If at any time it appears to the Secretary of State that there should be more than three commissioners, he may with the approval of the Treasury appoint not more than two additional commissioners.

3. The official custodian for charities.—(1) There shall be an "official custodian for charities", whose function it shall be to act as trustee for charities in the cases provided for by this Act[3], and the official custodian for charities shall be by that name a corporation sole having perpetual succession and using an official seal, which shall be officially and judicially noticed.

(2) Such officer of the Commissioners as they may from time to time designate shall be the official custodian for charities.

10th Report from the Expenditure Committee of the House of Commons (1975), vol. II, pp. 21–22. Memorandum of the Charity Commissioners.

"THE OFFICIAL CUSTODIAN FOR CHARITIES AND CHARITY INVESTMENT[4]

29. The Official Custodian for Charities is a member of the Commissioners' staff. His powers derive from section 3 of the Act of 1960, as successor to the Official Trustees of Charitable Funds and the Official Trustee of Charity Lands of the early Charitable Trusts legislation. The Official

[2] See the Annual Reports of the Charity Commissioners for England and Wales. The Report for the year 1970 contains a detailed review of the operation of the Charities Act 1960 during its first ten years.

[3] See, e.g., ss. 16, 17, 20 (1), (2), 22 (6).

[4] See also Annual Report for 1970, paras. 75–76; 1974, paras. 107–108; 1976, para. 150.

Custodian acts as a permanent holder of charity land or other property vested in him, thus avoiding the need to alter title wherever there is a change of trustee. Where shares are vested in him he collects dividends and remits them free of tax to the trustees. He acts only as a custodian trustee (except that he has no power to charge fees) and has no power of management, so that the trustees retain the responsibility for ensuring that the charity's property is invested to the best advantage and that real property is properly maintained and rents are collected. Besides holding numerous fixed interest stocks, the Official Custodian holds well over a thousand different equity shares and is involved in work whenever any of those holdings are changed by the charities to which they belong. No charge is made to charities for the Official Custodian's services. The Official Custodian's accounts are published each year in the Commissioners' annual report[5].

30. In 1962 the Commissioners, under the powers given them by section 22 of the Act of 1960, established the Charities Official Investment Fund to enable charities which, usually because of their small size, were unable to take full advantage of the wider powers of investment given to trustees by the Trustee Investments Act 1961. The Fund is in effect a unit trust limited to registered charities only and with a wide spread of investment. It is managed by trustees appointed by the Commissioners. The value of the Fund has suffered a setback in recent times, in common with other investments, but the dividends on income shares (which account for the great bulk of the Fund) have increased from 4·96p in the first year, on a share purchased in 1962 to 6·96 on the same share in 1973[6].

31. The Commissioners have made other schemes under section 22 of the Act of 1960 pooling the funds of groups of closely related charities so that they can have the benefit of a larger investment portfolio and expert management.

32. Many charities, particularly smaller ones, have not acted to take advantage of the wider powers of investment given them by the Trustee Investments Act 1961, often because they could not face the immediate drop in income which reinvestment would entail. As a result such charities often still have their endowment invested in un-dated stocks such as 2 per cent. Consols and 3 per cent. War Stock."

III. The Work of the Charity Commission

Report of the Charity Commissioners for England and Wales for the year 1966, paras. 18–26[7].

"18. We are often asked by those who are interested in charity matters what the Charity Commission actually does and what kind of work our staff are engaged on. It seems appropriate to give here a brief answer to this question.

[5] The nominal values of investments other than land held by the Official custodian in January 1975 was about £250,000,000: House of Commons Report, vol. II, p. 47.

[6] This increased to 8.23p in 1976. Annual Report for 1976, para. 154. See also Annual Report for 1970, paras. 68–72, p. 417, post.

[7] See also House of Commons Report, vol. II, pp. 337–338.

19. The main bulk of our work originates from the charities themselves, whose trustees may seek our guidance or authority either because they are troubled by some problem of administration or because they wish to undertake some new activity or carry out some transaction to which our prior sanction is needed. Three divisions of our office, each in the charge of a Deputy Commissioner (the title recently adopted for members of our staff who hold the civil service rank of assistant solicitor), are responsible for dealing with problems put up in this way by charities. One case may call for short advice on the effect of a trust deed or will, another may involve protracted consideration of means of overcoming by scheme or order made under the provisions of the Charities Act difficulties arising from proposals to use the funds or property of a charity in a way not covered by the existing trusts. From day to day new questions of complexity come up for consideration, involving perhaps relations between trustees and their servants or beneficiaries, complaints from beneficiaries or members of the public, disputes between fellow trustees, appointments of new trustees, requests for merger or combination of separate trusts, proposals for the winding up or distribution of funds, plans for the augmentation of endowments, ambitious projects for the improvement or construction of almshouses or other property used for the purpose of the charity, advice on accounting procedures or powers of investment and other problems of a very varied character arising in the administration of the charity.

20. This work is usually dealt with by correspondence. Our senior staff however are always glad to discuss more complex problems round the table with trustees or their representatives and many trustees do in fact call at the Charity Commission. Sometimes members of our staff are able to visit the trustees on their own ground and see the charity's buildings.

21. The solution that emerges from these discussions will very often require either a scheme or order under the powers in the Charities Act. These documents are drafted by our staff. Although some of the routine orders mentioned in the next paragraph do not present difficulties which require the attention of lawyers, the drafts of many orders and practically all schemes need to be settled by a lawyer. More complex schemes and orders are referred to lawyers who are whole-time draftsmen. In 1966 we made 669 orders establishing schemes[8] and 434 other orders were made in the three divisions mentioned in paragraph 19.

22. We have devolved on a separate division, not staffed by lawyers, some of the more routine work involved in giving the sanction required by the Charities Act before property forming part of the permanent endowment of a charity may be mortgaged, sold, leased or otherwise disposed of. This division handles the correspondence relating to these and similar transactions, sometimes including quite acrimonious letters of objection and complaint. This division was responsible in 1966 for 2,334 orders, of which 1,426 concerned the sale or exchange of charity land[9].

23. Another division is responsible for the maintenance of the register

[8] In 1976 this had risen to 943: Annual Report for 1976, para. 69. See p. 413, post.

[9] See p. 419, post. In 1976 the figures were 3,781 and 2,234 respectively. Annual Report for 1976, para. 71.

of charities under section 4 of the Charities Act and, with legal advice from within the office, for the registration of charities and for advising on the formation of new charities. They are prepared to say whether proposed trust instruments are considered to be technically charitable and, if asked, they will give advice on the efficacy of the administrative provisions and on the suitability of the proposed organisation and suggest other bodies who might usefully be consulted. In regard to registration and all questions of charitable status, our staff keep in close touch with the Inland Revenue authorities[10]. Now that most existing charities have been registered and the work of registration is less than formerly it is convenient for the same division to undertake the task of scrutinising charity accounts (described at paragraph 95 of this report). The same staff are also responsible for discharging duties laid upon us by other statutes, such as the maintenance of the central register of charities for disabled persons and the issue of certificates to enable charities to reclaim selective employment tax payments[11].

24. Another division of our office serves the Official Custodian for Charities who acts as custodian of charity property. His functions . . . include providing advice to and carrying out the instructions of charity trustees as to the investment of charity funds which he holds, distributing dividends and interest payments arising from such funds, free of deduction of income tax, and making arrangements for investment in the Charities Official Investment Fund[12].

25. A certain amount of work also arises from enquiries and complaints about charities in general, charities of a particular kind or individual charities. Although we are always ready to examine any well founded allegation of abuse by a charity, we have found that it is only rarely necessary for us to make use of the powers given us by the Act to require charities to provide us with information, or to institute a formal inquiry into the administration of a charity[13].

26. It is, finally, necessary for us to maintain liaison with Government departments responsible for social services, with those responsible for promoting legislation which may affect the interests of charities, with local authorities and with the major charitable organisations[14]."

IV. The Register[15]

CHARITIES ACT 1960

4. Register of Charities.—(1) There shall be a register of charities which shall be established and maintained by the Commissioners and in which there shall be entered such particulars as the Commissioners may from time to time determine of any charity there registered.

[10] House of Commons Report, vol. II, pp. 87–88, 95–97; Goodman Report, paras. 149–152.
[11] See infra.
[12] See p. 398, ante, p. 416, post.
[13] See p. 422, post.
[14] See p. 409, post.
[15] See Annual Report for 1970, paras. 17–27; Goodman Report, chap. 6; House of Commons Report, vol. I, paras. 93–104, 115–117.

(2) There shall be entered in the register every charity not excepted by subsection (4) below; and a charity so excepted may be entered in the register at the request of the charity, but (whether or not it was excepted at the time of registration) may at any time, and shall at the request of the charity, be removed from the register.

(3) Any institution which no longer appears to the Commissioners to be a charity shall be removed from the register, with effect, where the removal is due to any change in its purposes or trusts, from the date of that change; and there shall also be removed from the register any charity which ceases to exist or does not operate.

(4) The following charities are not required to be registered, that is to say,—

(*a*) any charity comprised in the Second Schedule to this Act (in this Act referred to as an "exempt charity");

(*b*) any charity which is excepted by order or regulations[16];

(*c*) any charity having neither any permanent endowment, nor any income from property amounting to more than fifteen pounds a year, nor the use and occupation of any land;

and no charity is required to be registered in respect of any registered place of worship.

(5) With any application for a charity to be registered there shall be supplied to the Commissioners copies of its trusts (or, if they are not set out in any extant document, particulars of them), and such other documents or information as may be prescribed or as the Commissioners may require for the purpose of the application.

(6) It shall be the duty—

(*a*) of the charity trustees of any charity which is not registered nor excepted from registration to apply for it to be registered, and to supply the documents and information required by subsection (5) above; and

(*b*) of the charity trustees (or last charity trustees) of any institution which is for the time being registered to notify the Commissioners if it ceases to exist, or if there is any change in its trusts, or in the particulars of it entered in the register, and to supply to the Commissioners particulars of any such change and copies of any new trusts or alterations of the trusts;

and any person who makes default in carrying out any of the duties imposed by this subsection may be required by order of the Commissioners to make good that default.

(7) The register (including the entries cancelled when institutions are removed from the register) shall be open to public inspection at all reasonable times[17]; and copies (or particulars) of the trusts of any registered charity as supplied to the Commissioners under this section shall, so long as it remains on the register, be kept by them and be open to public

[16] S.I. 1963 No. 2074; S.I. 1964 No. 1825 (Religious Charities); S.I. 1961 No. 1044 (Boy Scouts and Girl Guides); S.I. 1965 No. 1056 (Armed Forces); S.I. 1966 No. 965 (Non-Exempt Universities).

[17] At St. Alban's House, Haymarket, London, and Graeme House, Derby Square, Liverpool.

inspection at all reasonable times, except in so far as regulations otherwise provide.

45. Construction of references to a "charity" or to particular classes of charity.—(4) References in this Act to a charity not having income from property to a specified amount shall be construed by reference to the gross revenues of the charity, but without bringing into account anything for the yearly value of land occupied by the charity apart from the pecuniary income (if any) received from that land; any question as to the application of any such reference to a charity shall be determined by the Commissioners, whose decision shall be final.

Sections 4 & 45. SECOND SCHEDULE

EXEMPT CHARITIES

The following institutions, so far as they are charities, are exempt charities within the meaning of this Act, that is to say—

(*a*) any institution which, if this Act had not been passed, would be exempted from the powers and jurisdiction under the Charitable Trusts Acts, 1853 to 1939, of the Commissioners or Minister of Education (apart from any power of the Commissioners or Minister to apply those Acts in whole or in part to charities otherwise exempt) by the terms of any enactment not contained in those Acts[18] other than section nine of the Places of Worship Registration Act, 1855;

(*b*) the universities of Oxford, Cambridge, London and Durham, the colleges and halls in the universities of Oxford, Cambridge and Durham and the colleges of Winchester and Eton;

(*c*) any university, university college, or institution connected with a university or university college, which Her Majesty declares by Order in Council to be an exempt charity for the purposes of this Act[19];

(*d*) the British Museum;

(*e*) any institution which is administered by or on behalf of an institution included above and is established for the general purposes of, or for any special purpose of or in connection with, the last-mentioned institution;

(*f*) the Church Commissioners and any institution which is administered by them;

(*g*) any registered society within the meaning of the Industrial and Provident Societies Act, 1893, and any registered society or branch within the meaning of the Friendly Societies Act, 1896.

(*h*) the Board of Governors of the Museum of London[20];

(*i*) the British Library Board[21].

---

[18] E.g. Imperial War Museum Act 1929, s. 5; National Maritime Museum Act 1934, s. 7.

[19] Further universities were added by Exempt Charities Orders 1962 (S.I. No. 1343), 1965 (S.I. No. 1715), 1966 (S.I. No. 1460), 1967 (S.I. No. 821), 1969 (S.I. No. 1496) (The Open University), 1978 (S.I. No. 453).

[20] Added by Museum of London Act 1965, s. 11.

[21] Added by British Library Act 1972, s. 4 (2).

CHARITIES ACT 1960

5. Effect of, and claims and objections to registration.—(1) An institution shall for all purposes other than rectification of the register be conclusively presumed to be or have been a charity at any time when it is or was on the register of charities[22].

(2) Any person who is or may be affected by the registration of an institution as a charity may, on the ground that it is not a charity, object to its being entered by the Commissioners in the register, or apply to them for it to be removed from the register; and provision may be made by regulations as to the manner in which any such objection or application is to be made, prosecuted or dealt with[1].

(3) An appeal against any decision of the Commissioners to enter or not to enter an institution in the register of charities, or to remove or not to remove an institution from the register, may be brought in the High Court by the Attorney General, or by the persons who are or claim to be the charity trustees of the institution, or by any person whose objection or application under subsection (2) above is disallowed by the decision.

(5) Any question affecting the registration or removal from the register of an institution may, notwithstanding that it has been determined by a decision on appeal under subsection (3) above, be considered afresh by the Commissioners and shall not be concluded by that decision, if it appears to the Commissioners that there has been a change of circumstances or that the decision is inconsistent with a later judicial decision, whether given on such an appeal or not.

Report of the Charity Commissioners for England and Wales for the year 1970, paras. 17, 20, 22.

"*The Establishment of a Central Register of Charities*

17. The requirement that all charities should be registered, subject to certain exceptions and exemptions, was one of the main new provisions of the Act of 1960. As we remarked in our report on our work in 1961, the primary purpose of establishing a central register of charities was to facilitate communication. The register contains essential information about the purposes for which charities exist, how to get into touch with them and, if known, the approximate income available. This information is reproduced in classified form in three indexes, one containing index slips filed on a geographical basis, another slips filed alphabetically, and the third slips filed in accordance with the purposes of the charity. Local authorities are also supplied with copies of the slips for charities operating in their areas, to be kept in a local index of charities, and copies of slips for national charities are held at 10 regional centres."

---

[22] *Re Murawski's Will Trust* [1971] 1 WLR 707, [1971] 2 All ER 328, p. 341, ante.

[1] An application for the removal of the Oxford Literary and Debating Union Charitable Trust was refused. The Family Planning Association was also under consideration. Annual Report for 1976, paras., 54–64.

Report of the Goodman Committee on Charity Law and Voluntary Organisations (1976), para, 137–138.

"*New Registrations*

137. About 3,000 charities are registered each year at present by the Charity Commissioners. Many of these are old charities, i.e., those created before 1960. In 1975, 2,859 charities were registered, of which 2,388 were post-1960 charities. We were given a breakdown of these by the Charity Commissioners, classified according to objects, as follows:

Objects	**Number**
General Charitable Purposes	192
Relief of Poverty	136
Children and Young People	126
Old People	95
Health and Sickness	243
Social Welfare and Culture	572
Moral Welfare and Reform	57
Religion	133
Education	319
Misc. purposes for Benefit of the Community	74
Multiple Objects (2 or more)*	441
Total	2,388

*including many 'for general charitable purposes and in particular' . . .

The usefulness of this table in giving a picture of new trends in charities is limited. The Commissioners themselves subdivide these categories into a large number of sub-categories and some information as to trends could be gleaned from a breakdown of these sub-categories.

Modern Developments

138. Some of the more unusual types of new charities recently established according to the Commissioners have been in the field of social welfare, to meet current social problems relating to drug addiction and the consequences of the break-up of family life, and cultural matters. The formation of charities for the conservation of the environment has also become increasingly popular including, on the one hand, the prevention of pollution and, on the other, the preservation of industrial relics. Particular new developments in the charity field in the past few years have included the establishment of organisations to help battered wives and their children by providing them with alternative accommodation and in other ways; a charity for artificial kidney users; a disabled drivers' motor club; a charity for providing recorded tapes for the disabled and toy libraries. Another significant new development is the general purposes foundation or trust which collects money for distribution to other charities. Two registered in 1974 were the Charities Aid Foundation and the Charity Stamp Fund. The less fortunate in our community remain the concern of a high proportion of the newly established charities. But the Charity

Commissioners note that a changing pattern is evolving. In the past the most usual way of expressing this concern has been for people to give of their personal fortune, often by will, with instructions to trustees to apply the income for these purposes. Now there is an increasing tendency for institutions to be established with little or no permanent endowment, as a result of a small group of people joining together to pursue charitable objects which are of concern to them. The founders bring to the new charities their enthusiasm and perhaps their expertise in a particular subject, but few, or no, funds. They have to depend on the ability of the trustees to raise funds by appeals to the public or to grant-making charities or agencies. One of the fields in which this change is evident is in the number of charities for religious and social welfare purposes which are founded for immigrant communities, pioneered and administered by members of these communities themselves. These examples illustrate how charities arise to meet new needs and carry on pioneering work in fields where the welfare services do not operate or are inadequate. This is a development to be welcomed as explained in Chapter 1[2]."

Report of the Charity Commissioners for England and Wales for the year 1966, paras. 27–41.

"*The Commissioners' Decisions on Charitable Purposes*[3]

27. Now that the registration of charities has been in progress for nearly six years, it seems opportune to consider some of the problems that have emerged and to give a brief explanation of our practice. By the end of 1966 we had registered 63,500 charities[4] and had rejected 800 applications for registration, but during this period there has been no appeal to the High Court under section 5 (3) of the Charities Act against our decisions either to register or to reject[5]. It is not suggested that the lack of any appeal against us implies that everyone has been happy with our decisions: appeals to the High Court cost money[6]. It appears that those, such as rating authorities, who might have an interest to deny that an institution is a charity, feel that there are no cases in which the point at issue is of sufficient importance to warrant the spending of money in challenging our decision. On the other hand, the institution whose claim to be a charity has been rejected has often made representations to the effect that it cannot afford to go to the court and is also afraid of damaging publicity: it prefers to put forward proposed amendments to its objects in the hope of satisfying us that words have been found which are charitable in law.

[2] For detail, see Annual Report for 1974, para. 34–36; 1975, paras. 32–34; 1976, paras. 38–41.

[3] House of Commons Report 1975, vol. II, pp. 18, 23–24.

[4] Some 122,000 are now on the Register; Annual Report for 1976, para. 37. Since 1961, 1,760 charities have been removed from the Register, mainly because they have been wound up or have ceased to operate.

[5] The first appeal under this section was heard on November 18, 1970, *Incorporated Council of Law Reporting for England and Wales v A-G* [1971] Ch 626, [1971] 1 All ER 436; affd. [1972] Ch 73, [1971] 3 All ER 1029. See also *Re Murawski's Will Trust* [1971] 1 WLR 707, [1971] 2 All ER 328; *Re Construction Industry Training Board* [1973] Ch 173, [1972] 2 All ER 1339; Annual Report for 1973, para. 39; *IRC v McMullen* [1978] 1 All ER 230.

[6] For recommendations that appeals be financed from public funds, see Annual Report for 1973, para. 6; Goodman Report, para. 151; House of Commons Report, vol. I, paras. 84–85.

28. Section 5 (1) of the Charities Act provides that an institution which is on the register shall be conclusively presumed to be a charity and this has given us power in effect to decide that an institution is a charity, subject only to an appeal to the High Court. We have no similar power to decide that an institution is not a charity, because no conclusive presumptions are to be drawn from its absence from the register, but experience has shown that a decision not to register an institution is likely to result in its losing many of the advantages enjoyed by charities. Thus in the absence of appeals to the court, it has, over the past six years, fallen to us . . . to decide whether an existing institution is a charity. Cases not involving existing institutions continue to come before the courts, usually on the construction of a will, in which a decision is reached affecting the law of charitable purposes.

29. It has long been recognised that the court has treated the concept of charity flexibly and has been ready to extend the meaning of "charitable purposes" to meet changed circumstances. It is our belief that when Parliament entrusted us with the duty of registering charities and thereby of determining the charitable status of applicant institutions it expected us to bring to this task the flexibility which the court has already shown. Since Parliament has provided that appeal from our decision lies to the High Court, it is clear that we must reach our decision on charitable status as a matter of law, applying the principles adopted by the court. In doing so, however, we believe that we are entitled and expected to follow the court in extending the field of charity by analogy from cases already decided. It would surely have been a serious and unintended result of the passing of the Charities Act if the field of charity had become fixed and limited by the decisions already reached in the courts and consequently capable of enlargement only on the few occasions when one of the class of cases mentioned at the end of the last paragraph or an appeal against a decision of ours comes before the court.

30. Many cases have already come before us in which new voluntary and non-profit-making bodies have been founded to meet new problems thrown up by changing social needs. Acting on analogy with court decisions in broadly similar cases we have felt it right to regard the field of charity as extending to some of these bodies. We have had as an example the practice of the Chief Inspector of Taxes (Claims Division) in allowing relief from tax to organisations whose claims to be charities did not fall into a category originally recognised as charitable although analogous to a case in some such category. In this the Chief Inspector of Taxes has doubtless been guided by the confidential decisions of the Special Commissioners of Inland Revenue. There have been many instances in which it would have been unreasonable for us not to have followed the line already adopted by these authorities especially where an institution had long enjoyed relief from income tax.

31. The problem whether a newly formed society is a charity when its purposes are unlike any which the court has already considered can on occasion prove extremely difficult. As the judges themselves have admitted charity law is not always governed by logic nor are the decisions entirely consistent. For instance, it has more than once been stated in

judgments that if a purpose is to be regarded as charitable it must fall within the spirit and intendment of the preamble to the Elizabethan Statute of Charitable Uses of 1601 (see, for example, Lord Simonds in *William's Trustees v IRC* [1947] AC 447 at page 455); nor can it be argued that this doctrine is affected by the fact that the Charities Act, in repealing the Mortmain and Charitable Uses Act, 1888, has removed the express preservation of this preamble to which Lord Simonds drew attention. It does appear, however, that almost all the cases in which this doctrine has been mentioned have been cases in which the court decided that the institution before it was not a charity. There are many other cases in which the court, when deciding that some society was a charity, did not pause to trace its connection with the Elizabethan preamble. We believe, that, although we must never lose sight of the list of charitable instances in the preamble, we are entitled to enter in the register organisations whose connection with any of them may seem tenuous, provided that the court has given us a lead in a decision about a comparable organisation.

32. Another doctrine in charity law which causes many problems is expressed in the statement that although a charity must be for the benefit of the community, not all purposes that are for the benefit of the community are necessarily charitable: if an institution is to be charitable its purposes must be for the benefit of the community in a way which the law recognises as charitable. This can, however, be interpreted indifferently either as restricting the field of charity within the limits of previous decisions or as permitting an almost unrestricted flexibility. We do not believe that either of these extremes is right; and it is our hope that by constant attention to previous court decisions, we shall succeed in developing from them, with the approval of the court if there is an appeal, such a concept of the field of charity as may meet the needs of the community.

33. We think it important to mention these matters not only by way of explaining how we interpret our duties in deciding whether or not to register organisations as charities, but also because it is clear that in the absence of any regular flow of appeals from our decisions we shall inevitably move further and further away from cases decided by the court. In considering future applications we must necessarily take account of what, acting as a Board of Commissioners, we have previously decided, as the court takes account of its previous decisions, and this cannot but gradually extend the field of charity. Such continual development appears to us to be inevitable as attempts are made within the concept of charity progressively to meet the needs of a society which is not itself static.

34. It may be useful to mention one or two other matters that arise in connexion with our consideration of charitable purposes. We consider that we are bound by the decisions of the courts to base our decision whether an institution is a charity upon the words used in its constitution or other instrument of government, particularly where the words appear in a deed or in the memorandum of association of a company. Words to define a charitable purpose must be clear and certain. Many organisations have applied to us to register objects expressed in terms so obscure and containing so much that is merely emotive that the objects were uncertain or unenforceable.

35. There have been a few cases in which it has become apparent that an institution's activities are in conflict with the words used and are in no sense charitable; in such cases we have preferred, whenever possible, to put a construction on the words which will permit the known activities, even though this has inevitably involved our rejecting the application for registration as a charity. But there have been times when the words have been so free from doubt that we have had no option but to register the institution with the caution that in future its objects must be strictly observed.

36. Some of our non-legal correspondents have questioned the justification for the importance which the law attaches to the words used rather than to the institution's activities. It is felt by such correspondents that it should be enough to examine the activities of the institution to decide whether it is a charity and that two organisations both doing the same things should be equally qualified for registration. But this fails to take account of the fact that the law must be concerned principally with the obligation imposed on the institution to pursue certain objects. It is this obligation which establishes it as a charity; and so long as an institution is free to pursue any activities it wishes it cannot be treated as an established charity, however much its current activities may resemble those of other recognised charities.

37. The problem of interpreting words presents a somewhat different aspect when we are asked to consider draft documents intended to set up proposed charities. It is not unusual to find an attempt to dress up the purposes of the proposed institution in words which it is hoped will be accepted as charitable even though the purposes, so phrased, are quite remote from the true intentions of the promoters. We are convinced that this is a highly unsatisfactory course and that the governing instrument of every institution should show unequivocally what the instituion really sets out to achieve. Three particular devices call for comment.

38. The first is the over-working of the word "education". Ingenious draftsmen have found it possible to embrace within this word a vast variety of activities, mainly propagandist, which do not come within the meaning of the "advancement of education" as it is used in charity law. A purpose which is not charitable cannot be made charitable merely by representing it to be a form of education.

39. The second device is the use of very wide general terms. It is of course true that there are some founders of charities, particularly those who are settling part of their own personal fortune, who genuinely expect to apply the settled property for all manner of charitable purposes; in such a case the general words are not intended to conceal a more limited true purpose. But, nonetheless, they may be difficult to interpret and it is undesirable that they should be used in any case where the proposed charity has a more limited purpose, particularly if the charity is intending to appeal to the public and not be merely the vehicle for the founder's own benevolence.

40. The third device is that of enumerating a number of objects, some perhaps charitable and others less obviously so, and then declaring that the institution is to be confined to carrying out such of the listed objects as are charitable. We have already commented on this device in paragraph

25 of our report for 1964. This approach begs the question, prevents the real purpose of the institution from being readily recognised and quite unnecessarily introduces difficulty in construing and acting upon the documents in which it is used. If a proposed charity shows us a draft instrument incorporating such a phrase we consider ourselves entitled to enquire what are intended to be its activities, with a view to seeing whether those activities can be authorised in terms of clearly defined charitable purposes.

41. As in our reports for the last two years we give a list, in Appendix A, of the cases in which decisions on or affecting charitable status have been reached by us, sitting as a Board. As was to be expected, there were fewer cases considered last year at this level than in previous years, and this reflects both a reduction in the number of institutions applying for registration and the fact that a great deal more work is now done in advising on draft documents. We find that advice given by our staff on a document still in draft is usually readily accepted by those concerned with the foundation of the charity. No problem then arises when the institution applies for registration."

V. Co-Ordination of Charitable and State Welfare Activities[7]

CHARITIES ACT 1960

10. Local authority's index of local charities.—(1) The council of a county or of a district or London[8] borough may maintain an index of local charities or of any class of local charities in the council's area, and may publish information contained in the index, or summaries or extracts taken from it.

11. Reviews of local charities by local authority.—(1) The council of a county or of a district or London[8] borough may, subject to the following provisions of this section, initiate, and carry out in co-operation with the charity trustees, a review of the working of any group of local charities with the same or similar purposes in the council's area, and may make to the Commissioners such report on the review and such recommendations arising from it as the council after consultation with the trustees think fit.

12. Co-operation between charities and between charities and local authorities.—(1) Any local council and any joint board discharging any functions of such a council may make, with any charity established for purposes similar or complementary to services provided by the council or board, arrangements for co-ordinating the activities of the council or board and those of the charity in the interests of persons who may benefit from

[7] See Annual Report for 1970, paras. 28–36; 1971, paras. 101–107; 1972, para. 49; 1976, paras. 78–84 (an example of co-operation between a charity and a local authority); Local Authority Social Services Act 1970; Goodman Report, pp. 81–100; House of Commons Report, vol. I, paras. 72–78; vol. II, pp. 20–21, 37, 58, 76, 163–164; 218–248 (criticism by Oxfordshire Charities Review Organiser), 297, 303–304, 351–358, 364–368 (The Charity Commissioners' Reply), 371–372, 382–390.

[8] As amended by Local Government Act 1972, s. 210 (9).

those services or from the charity, and shall be at liberty to disclose to any such charity in the interests of those persons any information obtained in connection with the services provided by the council or board, whether or not arrangements have been made with the charity under this subsection.

In this subsection "local council" means the council of a county, of a London borough, of a county district, of a rural parish, and includes also the Common Council of the City of London and the Council of the Isles of Scilly.

(2) Charity trustees shall, notwithstanding anything in the trusts of the charity, have power by virtue of this subsection to do all or any of the following things, where it appears to them likely to promote or make more effective the work of the charity, and may defray the expense of so doing out of any income or moneys applicable as income of the charity, that is to say,—

(*a*) they may co-operate in any review undertaken under the last foregoing section or otherwise of the working of charities or any class of charities;

(*b*) they may make arrangements with an authority acting under subsection (1) above, or with another charity for co-ordinating their activities and those of the authority or of the other charity;

(*c*) they may publish information of other charities with a view to bringing them to the notice of those for whose benefit they are intended.

10th Report from the Expenditure Committee of the House of Commons (1975), vol. II, pp. 20–21. Memorandum submitted by the Charity Commissioners.

"*Local Reveiws of Charities*

23. The general conclusion reached as a result of the post-war debate on the part which charities should play in the welfare state was that while charities should not withdraw from fields in which they were performing useful services, their special function should be to seek out gaps in the statutory services and to pioneer new services. With these principles in mind sections 10 to 12 of the Act of 1960 contain powers for closer co-ordination of the work of local charities, and for encouraging co-operation between charities and local authorities, the latter, of course, being responsible for many statutory services which parallel or overlap the work of some charities.

24. In order to enable the situation in each area to be assessed and the necessary steps to achieve these objectives to be formulated, provision was made, in section 11 of the Act, for a review of local charities by the local authority. There is, however, no obligation on local authorities to carry out such a review or on trustees of charities to take part in a review. At the end of a review the local authority can make recommendations to the Charity Commissioners, but the Commissioners can normally make a scheme for a charity only if they receive an application for that purpose from the trustees of that charity.

25. The starting of local reviews of charities was not possible until

the registration of existing charities had reached some degree of finality, but the first reviews started in 1964. At the present time the position as regards reviews in the 57 former counties (i.e., pre-April 1974 counties, but counting each Riding of Yorkshire and the three parts of Lincoln as separate counties) is as follows:—

Review completed in	16 counties
Review active in	18 counties
Review terminated before completion in	14 counties
Review not started in	9[9] counties
Total	57

Reviews had also been carried out, before April 1974, in some 30 county boroughs.

26. The quality of reviews has varied greatly, according to the interest shown by the local authority and the calibre of person appointed to conduct the review. In some areas intensive reviews have continued over a period of years, resulting in fairly extensive changes in the working of many local charities, while in other areas the review has been superficial and has had much less impact. The Charity Commissioners have endeavoured to give the persons carrying out the reviews—who are usually employed by an agent acting for the local authority, such as the local council of social service—all the assistance and encouragement they can and have usually established direct contact with them for that purpose.

27. In general the results of local reviews have been useful but not perhaps as far-reaching as the Nathan Committee envisaged. However, it has to be remembered that the whole process depends on persuading local authorities and charity trustees to move. Pressure on local authority finances and local government reorganisation have not made things easier.

28. One or two of the persons appointed to carry out reviews of local charities have expressed disappointment that the Commissioners have not always been prepared to go as far in altering charity trusts as the trustees would have liked to go. This has occasionally happened where it has been proposed to amalgamate charities with different purposes, to alter the objects of a charity to a different class of object or to extend areas of benefit. The Commissioners have, since long before 1960, been favourably disposed to grouping local charities which exist for similar circumstances, and to giving them new objects more appropriate to modern conditions, but they have still to keep within the accepted scope of the doctrine of cy-près and to try to ensure that they do not go beyond what they think the court would approve in a similar case[10]."

---

[9] One or two small areas may have been covered in some of these counties.

[10] 969 schemes have been made as a result of local reviews. Annual Report for 1976, para. 118.

Report of the Goodman Committee on Charity Law and Voluntary Organisations (1976), paras. 184–185.

"*Conclusions*

184. The impression we get from these varied review reports and the other evidence is that the review procedure can perform and in many cases, is performing a useful service as regards local endowed charities in promoting co-operation among charities and between charities and the public services and that this work should be continued as speedily as possible. The review director often has to contend with intense initial suspicion that the object of the exercise is a takeover by the local authority or the body conducting the review on its behalf such as the Community Council. The review works best when it is carried out under the auspices of a Council for Voluntary Service or a Community Council or other local voluntary body. There does seem to be a strong current of opinion emerging from all the reviews that while they are in progress, active support and encouragement should be given on the spot by a representative of the Charity Commissioners and their advice and encouragement would contribute greatly to the success of the process. It is also clear that much will remain to be done when the review has been completed to ensure that co-operation among local endowed charities and between them and the public services continues to be fostered.

185. We are disappointed that after 16 years comparatively little progress has been made in dealing with the problem of the small endowed charities and one can understand the suggestion which has been made to us from several sources that compulsory powers should be used to compel amalgamation of charities whose funds are so small as to prevent them from making a useful contribution to the welfare of their area. The administration of some of them, it is said, is in the hands of elderly trustees who resist change and who do not even know the source of income of the trust and sometimes have stock certificates in the names of people long dead. On the other hand, many of these charities are ancient. They cost the country nothing in the sense that the services of the trustees are given free of charge and in most cases with a genuine desire to do the most good with the money available. The comparative lack of success of reviews has been due, in our view, to a number of factors. Many local authorities who are charged with the conduct of local reviews are too busy particularly following reorganisation to take much interest. The Charity Commissioners have taken the view that they should not themselves intervene except where their advice is specifically sought or if they are asked to make schemes while the review officers and trustees on their side sometimes complain of the lack of interest by the Charity Commissioners. On the whole we think that the solution, at any rate for the next ten years or so, lies not in compulsion but in a more enthusiastic form of persuasion. We think that the idea of collecting the small charities together into Neighbourhood Trusts is a good one. It would make administration much easier. It would enable the welfare services to have access to funds of reasonable size to cover cases where the public services do not apply or are inadequate for one good reason or another. It would be most

important, in our view, that any such fund should be entirely independent of central or local government control and no doubt it could invite the services of the trustees of trusts which were amalgamated in the Neighbourhood Trust. To preserve this independence and having regard to the lack of interest on the part of many local authorities we feel that the whole review procedure should now be directed by representatives of the Charity Commissioners assisted by the local voluntary services and then on completion some permanent arrangement should be made between local co-ordinating bodies to continue to foster co-operation between local endowed charities. The Expenditure Committee of the House of Commons recommended a sort of roving task force for review but we prefer our own solution."

VI. Scheme Making Powers[11]

CHARITIES ACT 1960

18. Concurrent jurisdiction with High Court for certain purposes.—(1) Subject to the provisions of this Act, the Commissioners may by order exercise the same jurisdiction and powers as are exercisable by the High Court in charity proceedings for the following purposes, that is to say:—

(*a*) establishing a scheme for the administration of a charity;

(*b*) appointing, discharging or removing a charity trustee or trustee for a charity, or removing an officer or servant;

(*c*) vesting or transferring property, or requiring or entitling any person to call for or make any transfer of property or any payment.

(2) Where the court directs a scheme for the administration of a charity to be established, the court may by order refer the matter to the Commissioners for them to prepare or settle a scheme in accordance with such directions (if any) as the court sees fit to give, and any such order may provide for the scheme to be put into effect by order of the Commissioners as if prepared under subsection (1) above and without any further order of the court.

(3) The Commissioners shall not have jurisdiction under this section to try or determine the title at law or in equity to any property as between a charity or trustee for a charity and a person holding or claiming the property or an interest in it adversely to the charity, or to try or determine any question as to the existence or extent of any charge or trust.

(4) Subject to the following subsections, the Commissioners shall not exercise their jurisdiction under this section as respects any charity, except—

(*a*) on the application of the charity; or

(*b*) on an order of the court under subsection (2) above.

(5) In the case of a charity not having any income from property amounting to more than fifty pounds a year, and not being an exempt charity,

[11] See Annual Report for 1970, paras. 47–49; 1976, paras. 69–75; Charities Act 1960, ss. 15 (schemes for charities established or regulated by Royal Charter), 19 (schemes for charities established by statute), 22 (schemes to establish common investment funds, p. 416, post). For examples, see Annual Report for 1975, paras. 51–61; 1976, paras. 76–95.

the Commissioners may exercise their jurisdiction under this section on the application—

(*a*) of the Attorney General; or

(*b*) of any one or more of the charity trustees, or of any person interested in the charity, or of any two or more inhabitants of the area of the charity, if it is a local charity.

(6) Where in the case of a charity, other than an exempt charity, the Commissioners are satisfied that the charity trustees ought in the interests of the charity to apply for a scheme, but have unreasonably refused or neglected to do so, the Commissioners may apply to the Secretary of State for him to refer the case to them with a view to a scheme, and if, after giving the charity trustees an opportunity to make representations to him, the Secretary of State does so, the Commissioners may proceed accordingly without the application required by subsection (4) or (5) above:

Provided that the Commissioners shall not have power in a case where they act by virtue of this subsection to alter the purposes of a charity, unless forty years have elapsed from the date of its foundation.

(7) The Commissioners may on the application of any charity trustee or trustee for a charity exercise their jurisdiction under this section for the purpose of discharging him from his trusteeship.

(10) An appeal against any order of the Commissioners under this section may be brought in the High Court by the Attorney General.

(11) An appeal against any order of the Commissioners under this section may also, at any time within the three months beginning with the day following that on which the order is published, be brought in the High Court by the charity or any of the charity trustees, or by any person removed from any office or employment by the order (unless he is removed with the concurrence of the charity trustees or with the approval of the special visitor, if any, of the charity):

Provided that no appeal shall be brought under this subsection except with a certificate of the Commissioners that it is a proper case for an appeal or with the leave of one of the judges of the High Court attached to the Chancery Division.

(12) Where an order of the Commissioners under this section establishes a scheme for the administration of a charity, any person interested in the charity shall have the like right of appeal under subsection (11) above as a charity trustee, and so also, in the case of a charity which is a local charity in any area, shall any two or more inhabitants of the area and the parish council of any rural parish comprising the area or any part of it[12].

23. Power to authorise dealings with charity property, etc[13].—(1) Subject to the provisions of this section, where it appears to the Commissioners that any action proposed or contemplated in the administration of a charity is expedient in the interests of the charity, they may by order sanction that action, whether or not it would otherwise be within the powers exercisable by the charity trustees in the administration of the charity; and any-

[12] See *Childs v A-G* [1973] 1 WLR 497, [1973] 2 All ER 108.

[13] See Annual Report for 1970, para. 63. Between 2,000 and 3,000 orders are made each year under this section.

thing done under the authority of such an order shall be deemed to be properly done in the exercise of those powers.

(2) An order under this section may be made so as to authorise a particular transaction, compromise or the like, or a particular application of property, or so as to give a more general authority, and (without prejudice to the generality of subsection (1) above) may authorise a charity to use common premises, or employ a common staff, or otherwise combine for any purpose of administration, with any other charity.

Report of the Charity Commissioners for England and Wales for the year 1976, paras. 69–71, 74.

"*Schemes and Orders*

69. One of our main tasks is the making of schemes and orders to help trustees to administer their charities more efficiently, and to utilise their funds and property more effectively. During the year we established 943 schemes, 24 fewer than in 1975.

70. These schemes may deal with all or any of such subjects as the appointment of new bodies of trustees, the vesting of property in new trustees, or in a custodian trustee, the provision of new *cy près* objects in place of objects which are no longer practicable, the amalgamation of charities, the erection or improvement of almshouses, or the extension of powers of investment. Schemes which only deal with one or two of these subjects may be short and comparatively simple; other schemes may be long and complicated and involve much correspondence and discussion with the trustees. . . .

71. We also made during the year 3,781 orders relating to charities, six more than in 1975. A large proportion of these orders related to transactions in land. Orders authorising the charity trustees to sell their property numbered 1,809, 78 fewer than in 1975, while a further 425 orders were made authorising the exchange or the purchase of real estate or the grant of leases or easements, 66 more than in 1975. This side of our work continued to be affected by the depressed state of the property market.

Amalgamating Schemes

74. We have referred elsewhere in this and previous reports to schemes which group or amalgamate charities. The grouping of charities under a single body of trustees may be effected in one of three ways depending on the circumstances in each case. Some schemes consolidate the charities into a single new charity, so that the constituent charities thereafter lose their identity for all practical purposes. In other schemes the individual charities retain their identity but are all given the same objects so that they can be managed together efficiently with a single set of minute books, books of account, etc. In other cases again it may be inappropriate, or indeed beyond our powers, to give all the charities identical objects and while most of the grouped charities may be given similar purposes the income of one or two of them may have to be made applicable for other purposes and accounted for separately. This might happen, for instance, where a scheme is being made to group a number of charities for the

relief of the needy but the income of one of the charities is applicable partly for the relief of the needy and partly for the advancement of education or of religion.

75. It is perhaps not generally known how extensively charities are grouped or amalgamated in one or other of these ways. During the last seven years we have made 1,233 schemes involving 6,322 charities. So an annual average of 900 charities have been grouped during this period."

VII. Provision of Advice

CHARITIES ACT 1960

24. Power to advise charity trustees[14]—(1) The Commissioners may on the written application of any charity trustee give him their opinion or advice on any matter affecting the performance of his duties as such.

(2) A charity trustee or trustee for a charity acting in accordance with the opinion or advice of the Commissioners given under this section with respect to the charity shall be deemed, as regards his responsibility for so acting, to have acted in accordance with his trust, unless, when he does so, either—

(*a*) he knows or has reasonable cause to suspect that the opinion or advice was given in ignorance of material facts; or

(*b*) the decision of the court has been obtained on the matter or proceedings are pending to obtain one.

VIII. Investment[15]

CHARITIES ACT 1960

22. Schemes to establish common investment funds.—(1) The court or the Commissioners may by order make and bring into effect schemes (in this section referred to as "common investment schemes") for the establishment of common investment funds under trusts which provide—

(*a*) for property transferred to the fund by or on behalf of a charity participating in the scheme to be invested under the control of trustees appointed to manage the fund; and

(*b*) for the participating charities to be entitled (subject to the provisions of the scheme) to the capital and income of the fund in shares determined by reference to the amount or value of the property transferred to it by or on behalf of each of them and to the value of the fund at the time of the transfers.

(2) The court or the Commissioners may make a common investment scheme on the application of any two or more charities[16].

[14] See Annual Report for 1970, para. 64.

[15] See Annual Report for 1970, paras. 68–74. See also the Trustee Investments Act 1961, p. 479, post.

[16] Even though the trustees of the trust funds are the same. *Re London University's Charitable Trust* [1964] Ch 282, [1963] 3 All ER 859.

(3) A common investment scheme may be made in terms admitting any charity to participate, or the scheme may restrict the right to participate in any manner.

(4) A common investment scheme may make provision for, and for all matters connected with, the establishment, investment, management and winding up of the common investment fund, and may in particular include provision—

(*a*) for remunerating persons appointed trustees to hold or manage the fund or any part of it, with or without provision authorising a person to receive the remuneration notwithstanding that he is also a charity trustee of or trustee for a participating charity;

(*b*) for restricting the size of the fund, and for regulating as to time, amount or otherwise the right to transfer property to or withdraw it from the fund, and for enabling sums to be advanced out of the fund by way of loan to a participating charity pending the withdrawal of property from the fund by the charity;

(*c*) for enabling income to be withheld from distribution with a view to avoiding fluctuations in the amounts distributed, and generally for regulating distributions of income;

(*d*) for enabling moneys to be borrowed temporarily for the purpose of meeting payments to be made out of the fund;

(*e*) for enabling questions arising under the scheme as to the right of a charity to participate, or as to the rights of participating charities, or as to any other matter, to be conclusively determined by the decision of the trustees managing the fund or in any other manner;

(*f*) for regulating the accounts and information to be supplied to participating charities.

(6) A common investment scheme may provide for the assets of the common investment fund or any of them to be vested in the official custodian for charities, and, if made by the Commissioners or if they consent, may also appoint him or authorise him to be appointed trustee to manage the fund or any part of it, and as managing trustee he shall, subject to section three of this Act, have the same powers, duties and liabilities as other managing trustees; but where a common investment scheme provides for the official custodian for charities to exercise any discretion with respect to the investment of the fund it shall make provision for him to be advised by a committee of persons who have special experience of investment and finance or of the administration of trusts, or who represent or are nominated by bodies having that experience.

Report of the Charity Commissioners for England and Wales for the year 1970, paras. 69–72[17].

"*Investment Policy for Charities*

69. The Trustee Investments Act 1961 in general enabled trustees to seek a remedy for this situation by allowing them to invest up to one half of the trust's property in a wide range of industrial and commercial ordinary

[17] See House of Commons Report, vol II, pp. 21–22, p. 397, ante.

shares, the value of which, and the income from which, might be expected in the long run to rise, thus off-setting the effects of any further inflation. This, however, still left a problem for the many charities which had insufficient property to enable them to achieve a sufficient spread of their investments over a number of different enterprises. It was primarily to meet this need that section 22 of the Charities Act had provided for the establishment by us or the court of common investment funds. Such a fund is essentially a combination of the resources of a group of charities for the purpose of forming a pool of a reasonable size which can be managed with the advice of investment experts.

70. The first fund to be established by us under section 22 was the National Association of Almshouses Common Investment Fund set up by a scheme in May 1962. The fund was, as its name implies, established to serve almshouse charities and its value at the end of 1970 was approximately £3½ million[18]. This was followed by the Charities Official Investment Fund which was established by our scheme of December 1962[19]. This fund is open to all charities, unless by their trust instruments they are specifically excluded from investing in it. Any charity entitled to participate in either of these funds may invest the whole of its capital in the fund. The Charities Official Investment Fund started to operate on 3rd January 1963 with total assets, contributed by 5,344 charities, of just over £6 million. There has been steady growth since then as more charities have joined the fund and its total value at the end of 1970 was just over £41 million[20]. The period since 1962 has been a difficult one for investment and the value of individual shares in the Charities Official Investment Fund has fluctuated considerably, but the income has increased steadily from 11.90d. (4.95p) on each income share in the first year to 14.45d. (6.02p) in the fund's last financial year. An account of the fund's performance in its last financial year will be found in paragraphs 107 and 108 of this report[21].

71. Although we have made a number of schemes for the pooling of the resources of groups of charities having the same body of trustees, so that the assets can be managed as a single fund, we have made only the two schemes mentioned above establishing common investment funds with bodies of expert trustees separate from those responsible for the administration of the contributing charities.

72. Several authorised unit trusts operating on a commercial basis have also been set up in recent years catering only for charities or for charities and other tax-exempt organisations such as pension funds. Under the Trustee Investments Act, however, only the wider-range part of the trust property may be invested in authorised unit trusts. A recent development in this field has been the formation of a number of unit trusts investing mainly in real property. These are not authorised unit trusts and a charity has no power under the 1961 Act to invest in them. If a charity of sufficient size does not have the necessary power under its governing instrument we

[18] See Annual Report for 1976, paras. 146–148, for the establishment of two common funds for narrower-range investment.
[19] For the text of the Scheme, see Tudor, pp. 721–735; Annual Report for 1962, App. B.
[20] £58,735,904 at the end of 1976; Annual Report for 1976, para. 153.
[21] This increased to 8.23p in 1976. Annual Report for 1976, para. 154.

are prepared to make an order under section 23 of the Charities Act authorising it to invest a specified amount in property unit trusts."

IX. Dealings with Charity Property[22]

A. Charities Act 1960

CHARITIES ACT 1960

29. Restrictions on dealing with charity property.—(1) Subject to the exceptions provided for by this section, no property forming part of the permanent endowment of a charity shall, without an order of the court or of the Commissioners, be mortgaged or charged by way of security for the repayment of money borrowed, nor, in the case of land in England or Wales, be sold, leased or otherwise disposed of[23].

(2) Subsection (1) above shall apply to any land which is held by or in trust for a charity and is or has at any time been occupied for the purposes of the charity, as it applies to land forming part of the permanent endowment of a charity; but a transaction for which the sanction of an order under subsection (1) above is required by virtue only of this subsection shall, notwithstanding that it is entered into without such an order, be valid in favour of a person who (then or afterwards) in good faith acquires an interest in or charge on the land for money or money's worth.

(3) This section shall apply notwithstanding anything in the trusts of a charity, but shall not require the sanction of an order—

(*a*) for any transaction for which general or special authority is expressly given (without the authority being made subject to the sanction of an order) by any statutory provision contained in or having effect under an Act of Parliament or by any scheme legally established; or

(*b*) for the granting of a lease for a term ending not more than twenty-two years after it is granted, not being a lease granted wholly or partly in consideration of a fine; or

(*c*) for any disposition of an advowson.

(4) This section shall not apply to an exempt charity[1], nor to any charity which is excepted by order or regulations[2].

B. Ex Gratia Payments

Report of the Charity Commissioners for England and Wales for the year 1969, paras. 26–31.

"26. We have frequently been asked by the trustees of charities to allow them to make voluntary payments out of their funds to meet what seems

[22] See Annual Report for 1970, para. 67; House of Commons Report, vol. I, paras. 105, 108–109; vol. II, pp. 192–198, 214–215, 303–305, 319, 369–371, 375–390.

[23] *Michael Richards Properties Ltd v Corpn of Wardens of St. Saviour's Parish, Southwark* [1975] 3 All ER 416 (contract for sale of charity land subject to approval of Commissioners held valid).

[1] See p. 402, ante.

[2] See Annual Report for 1970, paras. 90–91; S.I. 1961, Nos. 225, 1282; S.I. 1963 No. 1062, excepting certain land of religious charities of various denominations.

to them to be a valid moral obligation even though it has no legal basis. Charity trustees have, for instance, wished to make an ex-gratia payment where the intentions of a testator have been frustrated by the operation of some facet of the law of wills, with the result that the charity received a large legacy at the expense of some person who had lost his claim to a legacy obviously intended for him. In spite of the strength of the moral obligations in such cases we have had to reply that not only have the trustees no power under their trusts to make an ex-gratia payment, but also that there was no way in which we could provide authority for them to do so. Similarly, for a very long time it has been the settled practice adopted by the junior counsel advising the Attorney-General in charity matters to say that no authority can be given to charities to make these voluntary payments. There was, however, no reported case in which the court had laid down this rule and the practice had come to be questioned in recent years.

27. While it was felt that a change of practice might be desirable it was considered that a new practice ought not to be adopted without authority from the court. Two cases in which the Attorney-General encouraged the plaintiffs to submit the facts to the court so that they could be treated as test cases were eventually heard together in the Chancery Division during the year. They were *Re Snowden*, and *Re Henderson* [1970] Ch 700, [1969] 3 All ER 208. Briefly summarised the facts in the *Snowden* case were that a testator gave to close relatives all his shares in certain companies with which he had been connected and, after making other legacies, left his residuary estate to a number of charities. Those companies were, however, taken over by a much larger company and all the testator's shares were sold and at the date of his death were represented in his estate by cash. The result was that nothing passed under the gift to the relatives, but the legacies received by the charities under the residuary gift were enhanced to an extent that the testator obviously had not anticipated. Most, but not all, of the charities felt that they were under an obligation to make a payment out of the residuary legacies to the relatives to go some way towards achieving the obvious intention of the testator. It was argued on their behalf that since charities rely for their subscriptions on the recognition by the public of a moral duty to support charities, so also charities cannot and must not ignore moral obligations that are laid on them and should behave in this respect at least as well as a responsible individual.

28. The facts in the Henderson case were different because there were no specific named charities which benefited and which could consider whether or not an ex-gratia payment should be made. In this case the testatrix made a holograph will to which certain words had been added in her handwriting but in a different colour. It was uncertain whether these words had been added before execution and they were not admitted to probate; but in the circumstances they would have had a considerable effect in increasing the size of legacies that were payable to a nephew and niece. The will ended with the words: "Anything over to Charitys" (*sic*). The proceedings were brought by the executrix who asked that she might be allowed to make some reasonable payment to provide increased legacies for the nephew and niece to meet the wishes expressed in

the written words even though this would reduce the size of the residue falling to be distributed to charities.

29. Mr. Justice Cross delivered a considered judgment in which he reviewed other instances in which persons under disability are expected to recognise moral obligations and considered some old cases where charities were authorised not to press to their full legal claims arising from breaches of trust. He then reached the important conclusion that the court and the Attorney-General had power to give authority to charity trustees to make ex-gratia payments out of funds held on charitable trusts. It is to be noted, however, that the Judge did not suggest that trustees have any power themselves to make such payments without authority. The Judge emphasised that the power to give this authority is not to be exercised on slender grounds but only in cases where it can be fairly said that if the charity were an individual it would be morally wrong for him to refuse to make the payment. He drew the distinction between cases like those which were before him in which the testator never intended the charity to receive so large a gift as it did receive and other cases in which the testator did intend the charity to receive exactly what came to it but the testator's relatives considered that he was not morally justified in leaving his money to a charity rather than to them. In the latter case there would as a rule be no moral obligation resting on the charity and no authority should be given for it to make a payment. There might be some cases where an ex-gratia payment could be justified even though the intentions of the testator had been carried out; for instance the testator in making the gift to the charity might have been breaking a solemn, though not legally enforceable, promise to leave a legacy to someone else. The judge, however, said he thought that instances in which an ex-gratia payment would be justified would be rarer in the cases where the testator clearly intended to leave the money to charity and not to the claimant, than in those in which the testator's obvious intention to benefit the claimant had been frustrated through some oversight or legal technicality.

30. The Judge also discussed the practice that should be followed. In cases like the Snowden case in which individual charities are concerned it is in the first place for the charity trustees to decide whether or not they wish to make an ex-gratia payment having regard to the strength of any supposed moral obligation. If they decide to do so they should apply to us . . . . The approach to us should not be made by the claimant asking for the payment who must put his case to the charity concerned. We shall consider the facts which the trustees submit to us and perhaps ask for more information. We shall then make a report to the Attorney-General who will decide whether or not the trustees are to be given authority to make a payment. If, however, the case put up seems to us to be ill-founded, we shall usually explain to the trustees why we consider that the Attorney-General should not be troubled with it. In those cases where no individual charity is concerned but, as in the Henderson case, there is a legacy to charity generally, the approach should be made normally on behalf of the executors to the Treasury Solicitor who will report to the Attorney-General.

31. In 1969, after the decision in *Re Snowden*, there were five cases in which charities asked for authority to make ex-gratia payments and in which

we made reports to the Attorney-General. The facts in these cases were not considerably different from those in the two cases before the Judge and in all of them the Attorney-General gave authority[3]."

x. Inquiries

CHARITIES ACT 1960

6. General power to institute inquiries.—(1) The Commissioners may from time to time institute inquiries with regard to charities or a particular charity or class of charities, either generally or for particular purposes:

Provided that no such inquiry shall extend to any exempt charity.

(2) The Commissioners may either conduct such an inquiry themselves or appoint a person to conduct it and make a report to them.

(7) Where the Commissioners propose to take any action in consequence of an inquiry under this section, they may publish the report of the person conducting the inquiry, or such other statement of the results of the inquiry as they think fit, in any manner calculated in their opinion to bring it to the attention of persons who may wish to make representations to them about the action to be taken.

Report of the Charity Commissioners for England and Wales for the year 1970, paras. 50–52.

"*Power to institute inquiries and act for the protection of charities*

50. As mentioned in paragraph 10, one of the ways in which we are required under section 1 (3) of the Act to carry out our general function of promoting the effective use of charitable resources is by the investigation and checking of abuses. The Commissioners have power under section 6 of the Act to institute inquiries with regard to charities or a particular charity or class of charities, either generally or for particular purposes. We can either conduct such an inquiry ourselves or appoint a person to conduct it. Section 8(3) of the Act further empowers us to require that the condition and accounts of a charity shall be investigated and audited by a qualified accountant. Under section 20(1)[4], following an inquiry under section 6, we can act to suspend or remove a trustee or servant of a charity and to prevent the charity's property from being misused.

51. It has not been our practice to make use of the powers conferred under section 6 to institute a formal inquiry in every case which seems to merit some investigation. It is often preferable to resolve doubts which have arisen by friendly and informal discussion with the charity trustees concerned, although the fact that formal powers of inquiry are available if needed may well not be without its influence. We have found it necessary to make formal use of our powers under section 6 only sparingly[5]. There

[3] See Annual Report for 1970, para. 84; 1976, paras. 114–116.

[4] See p. 425, post.

[5] See Annual Report for 1973, paras. 87–97; 1974, paras. 78–97; 1975, paras. 74–94; 1976, paras. 125–142.

have been a fair number of cases in which, with the co-operation of the charity trustees concerned, we have been able to remove causes of complaint brought to our notice by members of the public or members or ex-members of the charity anxious about the way in which it was being administered. Some of the complaints have arisen because the governing instruments, though well enough drafted in themselves, were unsuited to the charitable purposes which in practice the trustees really wished to serve. Others have arisen from a disregard or misunderstanding of the purposes of the charity or of the administrative provisions set out in the governing instrument. There have been other cases in which the trustees have found themselves in difficulty through inexperience in financial matters or the pursuit of projects which were too ambitious for the slender resources found to be available in practice. At the opposite end of the scale there have been charities whose trustees have concentrated too exclusively on maintaining a large annual surplus, considering that the administration was efficient if this surplus was continually increasing, and tending to neglect or unreasonably defer the distribution of benefits. Some complaints can be dealt with simply by sending a copy of the complaint, with the writer's consent, to the charity in question for the trustees' comments, or by asking the trustees for information required to clarify the situation. In most other cases discussion with the trustees has been sufficient to set the administration on the right path and it has not been necessary even to suggest the possibility of a formal inquiry. We have, however, no power to act in those cases where the complaints relate to the way in which charity trustees are properly exercising their discretion in carrying out the purposes of their charity.

52. Up to the end of 1970 we had instituted seven formal inquiries under the provisions of section 6. In only two cases did we appoint an auditor to investigate the charity's accounts, the remainder of the inquiries being carried out by members of our staff. In only one case has it so far been necessary to use the powers conferred by section 20 (1)[6]. As these figures indicate, the number of cases coming to our notice in which serious doubt arises as to the way in which a charity is being run is small."

XI. Trustees[7]

A. Number

TRUSTEE ACT 1925

34. Limitation of the number of trustees.—(3) This section[8] only applies to settlements and dispositions of land, and the restrictions imposed on the number of trustees do not apply—

(*a*) in the case of land vested in trustees for charitable, ecclesiastical, or public purposes.

[6] For another case, see *Jones v A-G* (1976) Times, 10th November; Annual Report for 1977, paras. 25–29, p. 452, post.

[7] Goodman Report, paras. 143–146, 159–162; House of Commons Report, vol. I, paras. 105–106. Helpful advice to trustees in dealing with financial matters is given in Annual Report for 1976, para. 127.

[8] See p. 432, post.

B. Acting by Majority

In *Re Whiteley* ([1910] 1 Ch 600) one question was whether a decision of the majority of charitable trustees was binding on the whole. Earlier cases[9] had held that the decision of the majority was binding in matters of a public nature. EVE J held that the rule covered decisions of charitable trustees generally (at p. 608): "It is true that the authorities referred to by the applicants are both concerned with the appointment of a person to discharge the duties of an office of a public nature, but I cannot read the observations of Lord Lyndurst[10] as limiting the principle there stated to the particular class of case with which he was there dealing; and I think when he speaks of a 'trust of a public nature' he is using an expression equivalent for all practical purposes to 'a trust of a charitable nature'. In other words, I regard the words 'public' and 'charitable' in this connection as synonymous, and, so regarding them, I think that the rule on which the applicants rely is of general application . . ."

C. Appointment

CHARITIES ACT 1960

20. Power to act for protection of charities.—(4) The Commissioners may by order made of their own motion appoint a person to be a charity trustee—[11]

(*a*) in place of a charity trustee removed by them under this section or otherwise;

(*b*) where there are no charity trustees, or where by reason of vacancies in their number or the absence or incapacity of any of their number the charity cannot apply for the appointment;

(*c*) where there is a single charity trustee, not being a corporation aggregate, and the Commissioners are of opinion that it is necessary to increase the number for the proper administration of the charity;

(*d*) where the Commissioners are of opinion that it is necessary for the proper administration of the charity to have an additional charity trustee, because one of the existing charity trustees who ought nevertheless to remain a charity trustee either cannot be found or does not act or is outside England and Wales.

(5) The powers of the Commissioners under this section to remove or appoint charity trustees of their own motion shall include power to make any such order with respect to the vesting in or transfer to the charity trustees of any property as the Commissioners could make on the removal or appointment of a charity trustee by them under section eighteen of this Act[12].

(6) Any order under this section for the removal or appointment of a charity trustee or trustee for a charity, or for the vesting or transfer of

[9] *Wilkinson v Malin* (1832) 2 Tyr 544; *Perry v Shipway* (1859) 4 De G & J 353.

[10] *Wilkinson v Malin*, supra, at 571.

[11] "Means the persons having the general control and management of the administration of a charity", s. 46.

[12] See p. 413, ante.

any property, shall be of the like effect as an order made under section eighteen of this Act[13].

(9) Before exercising any jurisdiction under this section, the Commissioners shall give notice of their intention to do so to each of the charity trustees, except any that cannot be found or has no known address in the United Kingdom; and any such notice may be given by post and, if given by post, may be addressed to the recipient's last known address in the United Kingdom.

(12) This section shall not apply to an exempt charity.

35. Transfer and evidence of title to property vested in trustees.—(1) Where, under the trusts of a charity, trustees of property held for the purposes of the charity may be appointed or discharged by resolution of a meeting of the charity trustees, members or other persons, a memorandum declaring a trustee to have been so appointed or discharged shall be sufficient evidence of that fact, if the memorandum is signed either at the meeting by the person presiding or in some other manner directed by the meeting, and is attested by two persons present at the meeting.

(2) A memorandum evidencing the appointment or discharge of a trustee under subsection (1) above, if executed as a deed, shall have the like operation under section forty of the Trustee Act, 1925[14] (which relates to vesting declarations as respects trust property in deeds appointing or discharging trustees), as if the appointment or discharge were effected by the deed.

D. Removal

CHARITIES ACT 1960

20. Power to act for protection of charities.—(1) Where the Commissioners are satisfied as the result of an inquiry instituted by them under section six of this Act—

(*a*) that there has been in the administration of a charity any misconduct or mismanagement; and

(*b*) that it is necessary or desirable to act for the purpose of protecting the property of the charity or securing a proper application for the purposes of the charity of that property or of property coming to the charity;

then for that purpose the Commissioners may of their own motion do all or any of the following things:—

(i) they may by order remove any trustee[15], charity trustee, officer, agent or servant of the charity who has been responsible for or privy to the misconduct or mismanagement or has by his conduct contributed to it or facilitated it;

[13] See p. 413, ante.
[14] See p. 440, post.
[15] This power was first exercised in 1964 as a result of the report of an accountant appointed under Charities Act 1960, ss. 6, 8; Annual Report for 1964, paras. 12, 57, 58. See also Annual Report for 1971, paras. 90–96; 1972, paras. 78–81; 1976, paras. 25–29; *Jones v A-G* (1976) Times, 10th November; Annual Report for 1976, paras. 25–29, p. 452, post.

(ii) they may make any such order as is authorised by subsection (1) of section sixteen of this Act with respect to the vesting in or transfer to the official custodian for charities of property held by or in trust for the charity;

(iii) they may order any bank or other person who holds money or securities on behalf of the charity or of any trustee for it not to part with the money or securities without the approval of the Commissioners;

(iv) they may, notwithstanding anything in the trusts of the charity, by order restrict the transactions which may be entered into, or the nature or amount of the payments which may be made, in the administration of the charity without the approval of the Commissioners[16].

(3) The Commissioners may also remove a charity trustee by order made of their own motion—

(*a*) where the trustee[17] . . . is a bankrupt or a corporation in liquidation, or is incapable of acting by reason of mental disorder within the meaning of the Mental Health Act, 1959;

(*b*) where the trustee has not acted, and will not declare his willingness or unwillingness to act;

(*c*) where the trustee is outside England and Wales or cannot be found or does not act and his absence or failure to act impedes the proper administration of the charity.

(5) [*See p.* 424, *ante.*]

(7) Subsections (10) and (11) of section eighteen of this Act shall apply to orders under this section as they apply to orders under that, save that where the Commissioners have by order removed a trustee, charity trustee, officer, agent, or servant of a charity under the power conferred by subsection (1) of this section, an appeal against such an order may be brought by any person so removed without a certificate of the Commissioners and without the leave of one of the judges of the High Court attached to the Chancery Division[18].

(8) The power of the Commissioners under subsection (1) above to remove a trustee, charity trustee, officer, agent or servant of a charity shall include power to suspend him from the exercise of his office or employment pending the consideration of his removal (but not for a period longer than three months), and to make provision as respects the period of the suspension for matters arising out of it, and in particular for enabling any person to execute any instrument in his name or otherwise act for him and, in the case of a charity trustee, for adjusting any rules governing the proceedings of the charity trustees to take account of the reduction in the number capable of acting.

18. Concurrent jurisdiction with High Court for certain purposes.—(7) [*See p. 413, ante.*]

16 The powers conferred by this section have so far only been used once; Annual Report for 1970, para. 52.

17 As amended by Criminal Law Act 1967, s. 10 (2) and Sch. 3, Part III.

18 *Jones v A-G* [1974] Ch 148, [1973] 3 All ER 518. It is for the appellant to show that the order was wrongly made.

XII Land held by Charitable Trustees is Settled Land[19]

SETTLED LAND ACT 1925

29. Charitable and public trusts.—(1) For the purposes of this section, all land vested or to be vested in trustees on or for charitable, ecclesiastical, or public trusts or purposes shall be deemed to be settled land, and the trustees shall, without constituting them statutory owners, have in reference to the land, all the powers which are by this Act conferred on a tenant for life and on the trustees of a settlement.

In connexion only with the exercise of those powers, and not so as to impose any obligation in respect of or to affect—

(*a*) the mode of creation or the administration of such trusts; or

(*b*) the appointment or number of trustees of such trusts;

the statute or other instrument creating the trust or under which it is administered shall be deemed the settlement, and the trustees shall be deemed the trustees of the settlement, and, save where the trust is created by a will coming into operation after the commencement of this Act, a separate instrument shall not be necessary for giving effect to the settlement.

Any conveyance of land held on charitable, ecclesiastical or public trusts shall state that the land is held on such trusts, and, where a purchaser has notice that the land is held on charitable, ecclesiastical, or public trusts, he shall be bound to see that any consents or orders requisite for authorising the transaction have been obtained.

[19] See Cheshire, *Modern Law of Real Property* (12th Edn. 1976), pp. 932–933; *Re Booth and Southend-on-Sea Co's Contract* [1927] 1 Ch 579.

Part Three. Trustees

13. General Principles Relating to Trustees[1]

I. Duties and Discretions[2]

A trustee's duties are imperative. Equity requires strict compliance. The standard required is that of *exacta diligentia*. Failure to comply may render a trustee liable for breach of trust; even though he thought that what he did was right, and even if it was done with the intention of benefiting the beneficiaries. Trustees can be faced with difficult decisions when it seems that the requirements of the law are contrary to the interests of the beneficiaries. Such a situation often arose in the 1950s in the case of a trust which contained no special investment power. The stock market was rising, and it was in the interest of the fund to be invested in equities. But it would be a breach of trust if investments outside the permitted range were purchased[3]. More recently, there have been fiscal advantages in having the trustees resident overseas, and the management of the trust carried on overseas. Yet many English trustees have been reluctant to retire and make way for overseas resident trustees, because there is some doubt concerning the propriety of appointing persons resident overseas to be trustees of an English trust[4].

Powers are discretionary, and there can be no rule of strict compliance. This is also true where the discretion is coupled with a duty to exercise it; as with the selection of beneficiaries of a discretionary trust, and with

[1] For a general commentary on the Trustee Act 1925, see Wolstenholme & Cherry, *Conveyancing Statutes* (13th Edn, 1972) vol. 4. See also Mellows, *The Trustee's Handbook* (2nd Edn, 1971); Sladen, *Practical Trust Administration* (1977). The Law Reform Committee is considering the existing statutory and other powers, rights and obligations of trustees and personal representatives in the light of existing conditions.

[2] H & M, pp. 434–436; P & M, pp. 273–277; Pettit, pp. 262–263; Snell, pp. 204–205.

[3] See pp. 479 et seq. post.

[4] See p. 437, post; H & M, pp. 247–252.

the selection of investments in performance of the duty to invest in a particular type of investment. In exercising a power or discretion the rule is that a trustee must use the same due diligence and care as an ordinary, prudent man of business would use in the management of his own affairs.

In *Learoyd v Whiteley,* Lord WATSON said[5]: "As a general rule the law requires of a trustee no higher degree of diligence in the execution of his office than a man of ordinary prudence would exercise in the management of his own private affairs. Yet he is not allowed the same discretion in investing the moneys of the trust as if he were a person sui juris dealing with his own estate.

Businessmen of ordinary prudence, may, and frequently do, select investments which are more or less of a speculative character; but it is the duty of a trustee to confine himself to the class of investments which are permitted by the trust, and likewise to avoid all investments of that class which are attended with hazard. So, so long as he acts in honest observance of these limitations, the general rule already stated will apply."

Hanbury & Maudsley: *Modern Equity* (10th Edn, 1976), p. 435

"It is sometimes said that a higher standard is set for paid trustees than for amateurs. In *Re Waterman's Will Trusts*[6], Harman J said: 'I do not forget that a paid trustee is expected to exercise a higher standard of diligence and knowledge than an unpaid trustee.' It is submitted that this statement may be misleading. A paid trustee is usually a professional trustee, and a professional who holds himself out as possessing special skill will be expected to apply it[7]. Further, a paid trustee will be expected to do more of the work himself and to delegate less; and a paid trustee will be given less opportunity to shelter behind section 61[8]. It may well be that a paid or professional trustee will be expected to have greater personal knowledge and skill. But it is submitted that there is no difference in the standard of diligence expected; indeed, it would be a brave amateur trustee who attempted to excuse himself for lack of diligence on the ground that he was not being paid."[9]

II. Appointment[10]

A. Appointment by Donee of Power to Appoint

i. NUMBER OF TRUSTEES

TRUSTEE ACT 1925

34. Limitation of the number of trustees[11]—(1) Where, at the com-

[5] (1887) 12 App Cas 727 at 733.

[6] [1952] 2 All ER 1054 at 1055; cf. *Jobson v Palmer* [1893] 1 Ch 71; (1969) 33 Conv (NS) 179 (M. Davies); (1973) 37 Conv (NS) 48 (D. S. Paling).

[7] *Re Rosenthal* [1972] 1 WLR 1273, [1972] 3 All ER 552.

[8] T.A. 1925, p. 622, post; *National Trustee Co of Australasia v General Finance Co of Australasia* [1905] AC 373; *Re Pauling's Settlement Trusts* [1964] Ch 303 at 338, 339, [1963] 3 All ER 1.

[9] For a contrary view, see P & M, p. 275.

[10] H & M, pp. 440–449; K & S, pp. 219–236; P & M, 223–234; Pettit, pp. 226–244; Snell, pp. 191–197.

[11] The restrictions affecting the number of persons entitled to hold land on trust for sale and the number of trustees of a settlement apply to registered land; L.R.A. 1925, s. 95.

mencement of this Act, there are more than four trustees of a settlement of land, or more than four trustees holding land on trust for sale, no new trustees shall (except where as a result of the appointment the number is reduced to four or less) be capable of being appointed until the number is reduced to less than four, and thereafter the number shall not be increased beyond four.

(2) In the case of settlements and dispositions on trust for sale of land made or coming into operation after the commencement of this Act—

(*a*) the number of trustees thereof shall not in any case exceed four, and where more than four persons are named as such trustees, the four first named (who are able and willing to act) shall alone be the trustees, and the other persons named shall not be trustees unless appointed on the occurrence of a vacancy;

(*b*) the number of the trustees shall not be increased beyond four.

(3) This section only applies to settlements and dispositions of land, and the restrictions imposed on the number of trustees do not apply—

(*a*) in the case of land vested in trustees for charitable, ecclesiastical, or public purposes; or

(*b*) where the net proceeds of the sale of the land are held for like purposes; or

(*c*) to the trustees of a term of years absolute limited by a settlement on trusts for raising money, or of a like term created under the statutory remedies relating to annual sums charged on land.

ii. APPOINTMENT OF NEW OR ADDITIONAL TRUSTEES

TRUSTEE ACT 1925

36. Power of appointing new or additional trustees.—(1) Where a trustee, either original or substituted, and whether appointed by a court or otherwise, is dead, or remains out of the United Kingdom for more than twelve months, or desires to be discharged from all or any of the trusts or powers reposed in or conferred on him, or refuses or is unfit to act therein, or is incapable of acting therein, or is an infant, then, subject to the restrictions imposed by this Act on the number of trustees,—

(*a*) the person or persons nominated for the purpose of appointing new trustees by the instrument, if any, creating the trust; or

(*b*) if there is no such person, or no such person able and willing to act, then the surviving or continuing trustees or trustee for the time being, or the personal representatives of the last surviving or continuing trustee[12];

may, by writing, appoint one or more other persons (whether or not being the persons exercising the power) to be a trustee or trustees in the place of the trustee so deceased, remaining out of the United Kingdom, desiring

[12] Or the executor of a deceased sole trustee (*Re Shafto's Trusts* (1885) 29 ChD 247). A personal representative may exercise the power without having obtained probate (*Re Crowhurst Park* [1974] 1 WLR 583, [1974] 1 All ER 991); but a trustee so appointed will be unable to prove his title unless a grant is obtained. Apart from the circumstances covered by the sub-para., executors do not have power to appoint new trustees; see *Re King's Will Trusts* [1964] Ch 542, [1964] 1 All ER 833.

to be discharged, refusing, or being unfit or being incapable, or being an infant, as aforesaid.

(2) Where a trustee has been removed under a power contained in the instrument creating the trust, a new trustee or new trustees may be appointed in the place of the trustee who is removed, as if he were dead, or, in the case of a corporation, as if the corporation desired to be discharged from the trust, and the provisions of this section shall apply accordingly, but subject to the restrictions imposed by this Act on the number of trustees.

(3) Where a corporation being a trustee is or has been dissolved, either before or after the commencement of this Act, then, for the purposes of this section and of any enactment replaced thereby, the corporation shall be deemed to be and to have been from the date of the dissolution incapable of acting in the trusts or powers reposed in or conferred on the corporation.

(4) The power of appointment given by subsection (1) of this section or any similar previous enactment to the personal representatives of a last surviving or continuing trustee shall be and shall be deemed always to have been exercisable by the executors for the time being (whether original or by representation) of such surviving or continuing trustee who have proved the will of their testator or by the administrators for the time being of such trustee without the concurrence of any executor who has renounced or has not proved.

(5) But a sole or last surviving executor intending to renounce, or all the executors where they all intend to renounce, shall have and shall be deemed always to have had power, at any time before renouncing probate, to exercise the power of appointment given by this section, or by any similar previous enactment, if willing to act for that purpose and without thereby accepting the office of executor.

(6) Where a sole trustee, other than a trust corporation, is or has been originally appointed to act in a trust, or where, in the case of any trust, there are not more than three trustees (none of them being a trust corporation) either original or substituted and whether appointed by the court or otherwise, then and in any such case—

(*a*) the person or persons nominated for the purpose of appointing new trustees by the instrument, if any, creating the trust; or

(*b*) if there is no such person, or no such person able and willing to act, then the trustee or trustees for the time being;

may, by writing, appoint another person or other persons[13] to be an additional trustee or additional trustees, but it shall not be obligatory to appoint any additional trustee, unless the instrument, if any, creating the trust, or any statutory enactment provides to the contrary, nor shall the number of trustees be increased beyond four by virtue of any such appointment.

(7) Every new trustee appointed under this section as well before as after all the trust property becomes by law, or by assurance, or otherwise, vested in him, shall have the same powers, authorities, and

[13] And not therefore himself; *Re Power's Settlement Trusts* [1951] Ch 1074, [1951] 2 All ER 513. Under sub-s. (1) the donee may appoint himself.

discretions, and may in all respects act as if he had been originally appointed a trustee by the instrument, if any, creating the trust.

(8) The provisions of this section relating to a trustee who is dead include the case of a person nominated trustee in a will but dying before the testator, and those relative to a continuing trustee include a refusing or retiring trustee, if willing to act in the execution of the provisions of this section.

(9) Where a trustee is incapable, by reason of mental disorder within the meaning of the Mental Health Act, 1959, of exercising his functions as trustee and is also entitled in possession to some beneficial interest in the trust property, no appointment of a new trustee in his place shall be made by virtue of paragraph (*b*) of subsection (1) of this section unless leave to make the appointment has been given by the authority having jurisdiction under Part VIII of the Mental Health Act, 1959[14].

iii. "INCAPABLE" OR "UNFIT"

In *Re Wheeler and De Rochow* ([1896] 1 Ch 315)[15] a marriage settlement gave to the husband and wife, or the survivor of them, the power to appoint new trustees in certain specified circumstances, including that of a trustee becoming "incapable". One of the trustees became bankrupt. This rendered him "unfit" but not "incapable". The question was whether a new trustee should be appointed by the husband (as the survivor), under para. (*a*) of s. 36 (1), or by the continuing trustees under para. (*b*)[16]. KEKEWICH J held that the husband and wife (or the survivor) were the "persons nominated for the purpose of appointing new trustees by the instrument" only in the circumstances specified in the settlement. No such circumstances had occurred, and the new trustee must therefore be appointed by the continuing trustees.

iv. "SURVIVING" OR "CONTINUING"

Section 36 (8) enables a retiring sole trustee or a retiring group of trustees to appoint their successors. It is usual for retiring trustees to participate in the appointment of new trustees. But it is not essential. In *Re Coates to Parsons* ((1886) 34 ChD 370) the title to a Methodist chapel at Thrapston, Northamptonshire, was vested in eleven trustees. One died, and another, W. R. Dearlove, remained out of the United Kingdom for twelve months. The nine remaining trustees purported to appoint T. M. Coleman a trustee, acting under the statutory power[17].

A purchaser under a contract for sale of the land by the trustees objected to the title, one of the grounds being that W. R. Dearlove had not participated in the appointment of new trustees. NORTH J upheld the appointment, saying (at p. 377): "I hold, therefore, that under the terms of the Act the nine trustees, who were clearly continuing trustees were competent to make the appointment, unless it was shewn that the person who had

[14] As substituted by Mental Health Act 1959, Sch. 7.
[15] Followed reluctantly in *Re Sichel's Settlements* [1916] 1 Ch 358.
[16] The section applicable was T.A. 1893, s. 10 (1), which was substantially the same as T.A. 1925, s. 36 (1).
[17] Given by Conveyancing Act 1881, s. 31 (1).

been absent for so long, and in whose place there was a clear right to substitute a new trustee, was willing and competent to act. This has not been shewn, and it seems to me, therefore, that the first objection, viz. that *W. R. Dearlove* ought to have concurred in making the appointment, is not established."

In *Re Stoneham Settlement Trusts* ([1953] Ch 59, [1952] 2 All ER 694) one trustee, Stoneham, who had absented himself from the United Kingdom for over twelve months, was willing to continue to act. His co-trustee, intending to retire, appointed two others in place of Stoneham and himself. Stoneham wished to continue. DANCKWERTS J held that the appointments were valid. The co-trustee could make them as a retiring trustee. Stoneham's participation was not necessary. "I come to the conclusion quite plainly that a trustee who is removed against his will is not a refusing or retiring trustee, not, at any rate, in the case of a trustee removed because of his absence outside the United Kingdom for consecutive periods of more than 12 months."

V. INFLUENCE OF BENEFICIARIES

In *Re Higginbottom* ([1892] 3 Ch 132) Mary Jane Broadbent, an illiterate person of no means, and having no beneficial interest in the trust property, was sole executrix of the surviving trustee of a trust fund, and entitled to exercise the statutory power of appointing new trustees. A large majority of the beneficiairies desired the Court to appoint William Wood and Ralph Rupert Wood as trustees. Mary Jane wished to exercise the power herself. KEKEWICH J refused to make an appointment at the request of the majority of beneficiaries.

In *Re Brockbank* ([1948] Ch 206, [1948] 1 All ER 287) the testator's residuary estate was held on trust for his widow for life and after her death for his children. Ward and Bates were the trustees. Ward wished to retire. The widow and all the children wished that Lloyds Bank Ltd. should be appointed trustee. Bates thought that this would impose an unnecessary charge upon the small estate. Ward, the widow and the children brought this summons, asking that Lloyds Bank Ltd. should be appointed sole trustee in the place of Ward and Bates. VAISEY J refused. "This case," he said, "involves a question which is said to be novel. It is possible, I think, that the reason for the novelty is that the courage required for the raising of it has hitherto been lacking.

The two alternative grounds of relief claimed are sought to be justified by the following argument: It is said that where all the beneficiaries concur, they may force a trustee to retire, compel his removal and direct the trustees, having the power to nominate their successors, to appoint as such successors such persons or person or corporation as may be indicated by the beneficiaries, and it is suggested that the trustees have no option but to comply.

I do not follow this. The power of nominating a new trustee is a discretionary power, and, in my opinion is no longer exercisable and, indeed, can no longer exist if it has become one of which the exercise can be dictated by others. But then it is said that the beneficiaries could direct the trustees to transfer the trust property either to themselves absolutely, or to any other person or persons or corporation, upon trusts identical with or corresponding to the trusts of the testator's will. I agree, provided that the trustees are adequately protected against any possible claim for future death duties and are fully indemnified as regards their costs, charges and expenses. . . .

It seems to me that the beneficiaries must choose between two alternatives. Either they must keep the trusts of the will on foot, in which case those trusts must continue to be executed by trustees duly appointed pursuant either to the original instrument or to the powers of s. 36 of the Trustee Act, 1925, and not by trustees arbitrarily selected by themselves; or they must, by mutual agreement, extinguish and put an end to the trusts . . .

The claim of the beneficiaries to control the exercise of the defendant's fiduciary power of making or compelling an appointment of the trustees is, in my judgment, untenable. The court itself regards such a power as deserving of the greatest respect and as one with which it will not interfere."

vi. SELECTION OF TRUSTEES[18]

The selection of the right trustees is a matter of the greatest importance. Modern settlements usually give many discretionary powers to the trustees. In selecting the original trustees, the settlor will select persons who can be relied on to exercise these powers in a manner of which he would himself approve. He cannot, however, control the trustees in the exercise of their powers and discretions. Nor, unless he retains the power to appoint new trustees, can he determine future appointments.

The question has been raised whether the statutory power enables a donee of the power to appoint a person resident outside the United Kingdom. Such an appointment may produce certain fiscal advantages, especially in respect of capital gains tax.

There is no absolute bar against the appointment of a foreign resident trustee of an English trust. Where, however, the beneficiaries have no connection with the foreign country, the court may regard such an appointment as not being a "proper" appointment; and may, if approached in time, take steps to restrain it. Once made, however, such an appointment, whether made under an express[19] or statutory power, is valid. The court, however, will only appoint foreign resident trustees in special circumstances[20].

In *Re Whitehead's Will Trusts* ([1971] 1 WLR 833, [1971] 2 All ER 1334) the question was whether Barclay's Bank, Ltd., and Mrs. Burke, the existing English resident trustees, could properly appoint trustees resident in Jersey and retire. The beneficiaries had for many years been resident in Jersey

[18] Potter and Monroe, *Tax Planning* (8th Edn, 1978), pp. 60–70.

[19] *Meinertzhagen v Davis* (1844) 1 Coll 335; *Re Smith's Trusts* (1872) 26 LT 820; (1969) 85 LQR 15 (P.V.B.); (1976) 40 Conv (NS) 295 (T. G. Watkins); Morcom & Parry, *Capital Transfer Tax* (1975), p. 80.

[20] See p. 445, post; *Precedents from the Conveyancer*, p. 5569.

and intended to remain there. PENNYCUICK V-C held that the appointment was proper in the circumstances. He said (at p. 836): "The deed was, I imagine, executed in something of a hurry and the bank insisted, evidently, as a term of appointing the new trustees, on this provision that an application should be made to this division for a declaration that the new appointment was effective. That is the application which now comes before me.

Upon the present summons Mr. Burke himself is the plaintiff. The defendants are his mother, Mrs. Dorothy Burke, Barclays Bank Ltd., the three infant children of Mr. Burke, representatives of the collaterals who would be interested should Mr. Burke's family die out, and finally, the new trustees resident in Jersey. All the parties were represented by counsel except the new trustees, who were not represented.

The set-up is rather a curious one. None of the beneficiaries were concerned to argue, or were desirious of arguing, against the validity of the appointment, but Mr. Johnston, who appeared for the retiring trustees very properly thought it right to put before the court such objections as there might be to the validity of the appointment which those trustees had themselves made. They wished to be assured that what they had done was proper and that they had been effectively discharged from the trusts.

It is not in dispute that Mr. Burke and his family are genuinely and indefinitely settled in Jersey. It is not in dispute that the new trustees are fit and proper persons to act as such. Then there was evidence on the summons by a Mr. Bailhache, who is an advocate practising in Jersey, to the effect that the Jersey court would execute these trusts in accordance with the law of England rather than that of Jersey, that is to say, although the local law of Jersey itself is quite different from that of England, should any question arise in connection with these trusts the court in Jersey would apply the law of England. Mr. Bailhache is a well-known advocate, and it is accepted that the beneficiaries would be adequately protected by the Jersey court. Mr. Johnston for the retiring trustees based his contention entirely on the proper construction of section 36 of the Trustee Act 1925, to which I will return in a moment. Leaving aside that point, the law has been quite well established for upwards of a century that there is no absolute bar to the appointment of persons resident abroad as trustees of an English trust. I say "no absolute bar", in the sense that such an appointment would be prohibited by law and would consequently be invalid. On the other hand, apart from exceptional circumstances, it is not proper to make such an appointment, that is to say, the court would not, apart from exceptional circumstances, make such an appointment; nor would it be right for the donees of the power to make such an appointment out of court. If they did, presumably the court would be likely to interfere at the instance of the beneficiaries. There do, however, exist exceptional circumstances in which such an appointment can properly be made. The most obvious exceptional circumstances are those in which the benefcaries have settled permanently in some country outside the United Kingdom and what is proposed to be done is to appoint new trustees in that country. In those exceptional circumstances it has, I believe, almost uniformly been accepted as the law that trustees in the country where the beneficiaries have settled can properly be appointed. . . .

The point made by Mr. Johnston is this: this provision now contained in section 36 of the Act of 1925 provides that in a number of instances the persons possessing the power of appointing new trustees may appoint one or more other persons to be trustees in their place. He points out that the trustee to be supplanted is enumerated in these terms:

> '. . . is dead, or remains out of the United Kingdom for more than twelve months, or desires to be discharged from all or any of the trusts or powers reposed in or conferred on him, or refuses or is unfit to act therein, or is incapable of acting therein, or is an infant, . . .'

and then those categories of persons are repeated after words 'in place of'. Mr. Johnston points out that the person possessing the power of appointment could not validly appoint any of these categories of person, apart from the trustee, who remains out of the United Kingdom for more than twelve months, to be a new trustee. Obviously he could not appoint a dead trustee to be a new trustee. Nor could he appoint a person who desired to be discharged from the trust, who refused to act, who was unfit to act, was incapable of acting or was an infant. So Mr. Johnston says that by necessary implication one must also treat the section as excluding from the power of appointment a person who resides out of the United Kingdom. With all respect to Mr. Johnston, I think that is a non sequitur. The other categories of person are obviously ineligible to be appointed as new trustees under the general law either because they are unfit or because they are unwilling to act. On the other hand, there is no such disability under the general law in the case of a person who resides out of the United Kingdom, and I do not think there is any reason why one should by implication include him amongst the persons disqualified from appointment.

It seems to me that, bearing in mind the state of the law as it was when this Act and its statutory predecessors in 1881 to 1893 were enacted, if Parliament had intended to render ineligible for appointment persons resident outside the United Kingdom, Parliament would inevitably have inserted an express provision to that effect. It cannot be right that Parliament should be regarded as having intended to make this important change in the law by implication.

I conclude, therefore, that the words of section 36 are not apt to prevent the appointment of a person residing out of the United Kingdom. I should add that if that had been otherwise, it would be very strange that the cases determined in the last few years under the Act of 1958[1] should have been so determined without any reference to the bar imposed, as it is said, by section 36 of the Act of 1925. It seems to me, therefore, that section 36 has not altered the law in this respect. The persons having the power of appointing new trustees can still in exceptional circumstances properly and validly appoint new trustees residing out of the United Kingdom. Again, it seems to me that this is such a case.

I should, perhaps, add that one of the purposes of this appointment is unquestionably to escape the burden of certain United Kingdom fiscal liabilities. It has, however, long been established that that is no reason why

[1] Variation of Trusts Act 1958, p. 564, post.

the court should not lend its assistance in connection with a particular transaction, and so far as the appointment of new trustees out of court is concerned, it is, I think, an absolutely irrelevant consideration. Those possessing the power are clearly entitled to exercise it as they think best in the interest of the trust estate."

vii. VESTING OF THE PROPERTY IN THE TRUSTEES

TRUSTEE ACT 1925

40. Vesting of trust property in new or continuing trustees.—(1) Where by a deed a new trustee is appointed to perform any trust, then—

(*a*) if the deed contains a declaration by the appointor to the effect that any estate or interest in any land subject to the trust, or in any chattel so subject, or the right to recover or receive any debt or other thing in action so subject, shall vest in the persons who by virtue of the deed become or are the trustees for performing the trust, the deed shall operate, without any conveyance or assignment, to vest in those persons as joint tenants and for the purposes of the trust the estate interest or right to which the declaration relates; and

(*b*) if the deed is made after the commencement of this Act and does not contain such a declaration, the deed shall, subject to any express provision to the contrary therein contained, operate as if it had contained such a declaration by the appointor extending to all the estates interests and rights with respect to which a declaration could have been made.

(2) Where by a deed a retiring trustee is discharged under the statutory power without a new trustee being appointed, then—

(*a*) if the deed contains such a declaration as aforesaid by the retiring and continuing trustees, and by the other person, if any, empowered to appoint trustees, the deed shall, without any conveyance or assignment, operate to vest in the continuing trustees alone, as joint tenants, and for the purposes of the trust, the estate, interest, or right to which the declaration relates; and

(*b*) if the deed is made after the commencement of this Act and does not contain such a declaration, the deed shall, subject to any express provision to the contrary therein contained, operate as if it had contained such a declaration by such persons as aforesaid extending to all the estates, interests and rights with respect to which a declaration could have been made.

(3) An express vesting declaration, whether made before or after the commencement of this Act, shall, notwithstanding that the estate, interest or right to be vested is not expressly referred to, and provided that the other statutory requirements were or are complied with, operate and be deemed always to have operated (but without prejudice to any express provision to the contrary contained in the deed of appointment or discharge) to vest in the persons respectively referred to in subsections (1) and (2) of this section, as the case may require, such estate, interests and rights as are capable of being and ought to be vested in those persons.

(4) This section does not extend—

(*a*) to land conveyed by way of mortgage for securing money subject to the trust, except land conveyed on trust for securing debentures or debenture stock;

(*b*) to land held under a lease which contains any covenant, condition or agreement against assignment or disposing of the land without licence or consent, unless, prior to the execution of the deed containing expressly or impliedly the vesting declaration, the requisite licence or consent has been obtained, or unless, by virtue of any statute or rule of law, the vesting declaration, express or implied, would not operate as a breach of covenant or give rise to a forfeiture;

(*c*) to any share, stock, annuity or property which is only transferable in books kept by a company or other body, or in a manner directed by or under an Act of Parliament.

In this subsection "lease" includes an underlease and an agreement for a lease or underlease.

(5) For purposes of registration of the deed in any registry, the person or persons making the declaraion expressly or impliedly, shall be deemed the conveying party or parties, and the conveyance shall be deemed to be made by him or them under a power conferred by this Act.

(6) This section applies to deeds of appointment or discharge executed on or after the first day of January, eighteen hundred and eighty-two.

LAND REGISTRATION ACT 1925

47. Vesting instruments and dispositions in name of proprietor.[2]—(1) The registrar shall give effect on the register to any vesting order or vesting declaration (express or implied) made on the appointment or discharge of a trustee or otherwise, and to dispositions made in the name and on behalf of a proprietor by a person authorised to make the disposition; and the provisions of the Trustee Act, 1925, relating to the appointment and discharge of trustees and the vesting of trust property, shall apply to registered land subject to the proper entry being made on the register.

(2) The registrar shall also give effect on the register in the prescribed manner to any vesting instrument which may be made pursuant to any statutory power.

B. Appointment by the Court[3]

i. THE POWER TO APPOINT

TRUSTEE ACT 1925

41. Power of court to appoint new trustees.—(1) The court may, whenever it is expedient to appoint a new trustee or new trustees, and it is found inexpedient difficult or impracticable so to do without the assistance of

[2] See Registered Land Practice Notes (1972), pp. 35–36.

[3] H & M, pp. 445–449; K & S, p. 231; P & M, pp. 232–234; Pettit, pp. 235–237; Snell, pp. 196–197.

the court[4], make an order appointing a new trustee or new trustees either in substitution for or in addition to any existing trustee or trustees, or although there is no existing trustee.

In particular and without prejudice to the generality of the foregoing provision, the court may make an order appointing a new trustee in substitution for a trustee who is incapable, by reason of mental disorder within the meaning of the Mental Health Act, 1959, of exercising his functions as trustee or is a bankrupt, or is a corporation which is in liquidation or has been dissolved[5].

(4) Nothing in this section gives power to appoint an executor or administrator.

43. Powers of new trustee appointed by the court.—Every trustee appointed by a court of competent jurisdiction shall, as well before as after the trust property becomes by law, or by assurance, or otherwise, vested in him, have the same powers, authorities, and discretions, and may in all respects act as if he had been originally appointed a trustee by the instrument, if any, creating the trust.

ii. SELECTION OF TRUSTEES

RE TEMPEST
(1866) LR 1 Ch App 485 (CA in Ch, TURNER and KNIGHT-BRUCE LJJ)

A family settlement was created by the will of Sir Charles Robert Tempest, Bart., appointing the Hon. T. E. Stonor and Mr. J. Fleming as trustees. Mr. Stonor predeceased the testator. The persons to whom the power of appointing new trustees was given were unable to agree upon a selection. A petition was presented, asking the court to appoint the Hon. Edward Petre. One beneficiary opposed, on the ground that Mr. Petre was connected with, and proposed by, a branch of the family with which the testator was not on friendly terms, and which he had excluded from participation in the management of his property. The Master of the Rolls appointed Mr. Petre and Lord Camoys "hoping to satisfy both parties".

Held. Mr. Petre was not a person whom the Court would appoint.

TURNER LJ: There are two questions raised by this appeal. First, whether the order of the Master of the Rolls ought to be reversed in so far as it appoints Mr. *Petre* to be a trustee of the testator's will; and secondly, whether assuming that the order ought to be reversed in this respect, Lord *Camoys* ought to be appointed the trustee. The first of these questions has not seemed to me to be altogether free from difficulty, and in my view of this case it is by no means an unimportant question. It involves, as I think, to no inconsiderable extent the principles on which this Court ought to act in the appointment of new trustees.

It was said in argument, and has been frequently said, that in making such appointments the Court acts upon and exercises its discretion; and this, no doubt, is generally true; but the discretion which the Court has

4 If the power of appointment given by T.A. 1925, s. 36, can be exercised, the court should not be asked to make an appointment; *Re Gibbon's Trusts* (1882) 30 WR 287; see also *Re May's Will Trusts* [1941] Ch 109.

5 As amended by Mental Health Act 1959, s. 149 (1), Sch. 7, Part I.

and exercises in making such appointments, is not, as I conceive, a mere arbitrary discretion, but a discretion in the exercise of which the Court is, and ought to be, guided by some general rules and principles, and, in my opinion, the difficulty which the Court has to encounter in these cases lies not so much in ascertaining the rules and principles by which it ought to be guided, as in applying those rules and principles to the varying circumstances of each particular case. The following rules and principles may, I think, safely be laid down as applying to all cases of appointments by the Court of new trustees.

First, the Court will have regard to the wishes of the persons by whom the trust has been created, if expressed in the instrument creating the trust, or clearly to be collected from it. I think this rule may be safely laid down, because if the author of the trust has in terms declared that a particular person, or a person filling a particular character, should not be a trustee of the instrument, there cannot, as I apprehend, be the least doubt that the Court would not appoint to the office a person whose appointment was so prohibited, and I do not think that upon a question of this description any distinction can be drawn between express declarations and demonstrated intention. The analogy of the course which the Court pursues in the appointment of guardians affords, I think, some support to this rule. The Court in those cases attends to the wishes of the parents, however informally they may be expressed.

Another rule which may, I think, safely be laid down is this—that the Court will not appoint a person to be trustee with a view to the interest of some of the persons interested under the trust, in opposition either to the wishes of the testator or to the interests of others of the *cestuis que trusts*. I think so for this reason, that it is of the essence of the duty of every trustee to hold an even hand between the parties interested under the trust. Every trustee is in duty bound to look to the interests of all, and not of any particular member or class of members of his *cestuis que trusts*.

A third rule which, I think, may safely be laid down is,—that the Court in appointing a trustee will have regard to the question, whether his appointment will promote or impede the execution of the trust, for the very purpose of the appointment is that the trust may be better carried into execution.

These are the principles by which, in my judgment, we ought to be guided in determining whether Mr. *Petre* ought to be appointed to be a trustee of this will, and, in my opinion, there are substantial objections to his appointment on each of the three grounds to which I have referred. There is not, of course, and cannot be, any possible objection to Mr. *Petre* in point of character, position, or ability, and I desire most anxiously to be understood as not intending, in disapproving his appointment, to cast the slightest possible reflection upon him. I have not for one moment doubted that he is a gentleman of most unexceptionable character, and well qualified in every respect to fill the office of trustee; but I think that the principles to which I have referred are opposed to his appointment.

First, as to the wishes of this testator, it is impossible, I think, to read this will without being fully satisfied that the great object and purpose of the testator was to exclude Mr. *Charles Henry Tempest* not only from all interest in, but from all connection with his estate. A more complete exclusion of him, both from any interest in and from any power over the estate, could not, as it seems to me, have been devised. Is it then consistent with this purpose of the testator that a trustee should be appointed who, upon the evidence before us, I cannot doubt is the nominee of Mr. *Charles Henry Tempest*, and is proposed for the purpose of carrying into effect his wishes and intentions? The facts, I think, prove that this is the position of Mr. *Petre*. He is proposed by Mr. *Washington Hibbert*, the father-in-law of Mr. *C. H. Tempest*, and the very person the connection with whom led to the making of this will, by which he was excluded. He is supported, and I desire not to be understood as saying, in any other than a legal sense, improperly, by Mr. *A. C. Tempest* his brother, who it appears upon the evidence declined to attend the testator's funeral on account of the dispositions of the will; and one of the principal witnesses in support of his appointment, and the person most active in these proceedings is Mr. *Broadbent*, the solicitor of Sir *C. H. Tempest*, under whose advice we find that Mr. *Petre* adopted that most unfortunate and, I must say, ill-advised step of declining to meet his co-trustees. Looking to all these circumstances, and to the whole of the evidence before us, I have as little doubt as to what led to the proposal of Mr. *Petre* as I have as to the intentions of this testator, and upon this ground, therefore, I think that Mr. *Petre* ought not to be appointed to be a trustee of this will.

It was said for the respondents, that the testator's dispositions were captious and absurd, and ought not therefore to be regarded, but much as we may regret that such dispositions were made, we cannot disregard them.

Then, as to the second ground, the objection to the appointment of Mr. *Petre* seems to me to be still more decisive. The evidence, in my opinion, very plainly shews that Mr. *Petre* has been proposed as trustee, and has accepted that office, with a view to his acting in the trust in the interests of some only of the objects of it, and in opposition to the wishes of the testator, and not with a view to his acting as an independent trustee for the benefit of all the objects of the trusts, and I do not hestitate to say that, in my opinion, this fact is alone sufficient to prevent us from confirming his appointment. It was objected on the part of the respondents, that the proof of this fact rests upon evidence of what has occurred since the order under appeal was pronounced, and ought not, therefore, to be attended to; but this is a re-hearing of the Petition under which Mr. *Petre* has been appointed. The question before us, therefore, is, whether he ought now to be appointed or not—a question of his present fitness or unfitness—and I am aware of no rule which precludes us from receiving upon such a question evidence of what has occurred since the original hearing. Supposing however, that there was any difficulty upon that point, I apprehend there can be no doubt that the evidence of what has so occurred ought to be looked at as shewing the purpose for which he was proposed, and that it was not proper that he should be appointed at the time when the order appointing him was made.

It was also argued on the part of the respondents, that their interests ought to be considered in the appointment to be made by the Court, and there would have been great force in this argument, if it could have been considered that Mr. *Petre* was proposed as an independent trustee to act on behalf of, and with a view to, the interests of all the *cestui que trusts*; but when the purpose for which he is proposed is seen, this argument loses all weight and cannot be attended to. It is the appointment of a trustee for the benefit of all, and not with a view to the interests of some, that the wishes of *cestui que trusts* are to be consulted, for the trustee to be appointed must represent and consult the interests of all, and not of some only of the *cestui que trusts*. It was indeed with this view, that in the course of the argument I suggested to the parties the expediency of their agreeing upon the appointment of an independent trustee.

The third and remaining ground of objection to the appointment of Mr. *Petre* is, I think, open to more difficulty. On the one hand, there cannot, I think, be any doubt that the Court ought not to appoint a trustee whose appointment will impede the due execution of the trust; but, on the other hand, if the continuing or surviving trustee refuses to act with a trustee who may be proposed to be appointed—and I make this observation with reference to what appears to have been said by Mr. *Fleming*, as to Mr. *Petre* having come forward in opposition to his wishes—I think it would be going too far to say that the Court ought, on that ground alone, to refuse to appoint the proposed trustee; for this would, as suggested in the argument, be to give the continuing or surviving trustee a veto upon the appointment of the new trustee. In such a case, I think it must be the duty of the Court to inquire and ascertain whether the objection of the surviving or continuing trustee is well founded or not, and to act or refuse to act upon it accordingly. If the surviving or continuing trustee has improperly refused to act with the proposed trustee, it might be a ground for removing him from the trust. Upon the facts of this case, however, it seems to me that the objections taken by Mr. *Fleming* to the appointment of Mr. *Petre* were and are well founded, and upon the whole case, therefore, my opinion is, that the order under appeal, so far as it appoints Mr. *Petre*, ought to be discharged. . .

The order upon this appeal should, I think, be to discharge the order at the Rolls, to appoint Lord *Camoys* to be the trustee in the place of Mr. *Stonor*, and to vest the estate in him and Mr. *Fleming*.

Two recent cases indicate, in a modern context, the way in which the court's discretion will be exercised. In *Re Weston's Settlements* ([1969] 1 Ch 223, [1968] 3 All ER 338)[6] and *Re Windeatt's Will Trusts* ([1969] 1 WLR 692, [1969] 2 All ER 324) applications were made to the court to vary the provisions of English trusts by appointing two persons resident in Jersey as trustees in the place of the English trustees, and to transfer the trust fund to them to be held on the trusts of a new Jersey settlement, the trusts corresponding to those of the English settlement. In each case the reasons for the application were fiscal. In reaching its conclusions, the court had to consider the exercise of its discretion both in respect of the

[6] See p. 581, post

appointment of new trustees and in respect of the variation of the settlements. In acceding to the application in *Re Windeatt's Will Trusts*, PENNYCUICK J said at p. 696: "[*Re Seale's Marriage Settlement* [1961] Ch 574, [1961] 3 All ER 136] covers the matter of jurisdiction. I am told, also, that in at least two subsequent cases other judges have made comparable orders. The only difficulty results from *Re Weston's Settlements* [1969] 1 Ch 223 before Stamp J, and [1969] 1 Ch 223 at 234 before the Court of Appeal. On the particular facts of the case Stamp J exercised his discretion under the Act to refuse to sanction an arrangement, and the Court of Appeal affirmed his decision. Stamp J, in *Re Weston's Settlements,* referred to *Re Seale's Marriage Settlement*, as did the Court of Appeal, without disapproval. *Re Weston's Settlements* went on its own facts entirely, which were extremely striking. There the settlor, with his family, had moved to Jersey only a very short time before the application to the court was made. It might well be inferred that the whole object of moving to Jersey was to escape a particular fiscal liability, and it appeared that their stay in that country might well be transitory. These facts are brought out in the judgment of Lord Denning MR in the Court of Appeal, [1969] 1 Ch 223 at 245:

> 'But here the family had only been in Jersey three months when they presented this scheme to the court. The inference is irresistible: the underlying purpose was to go there in order to avoid tax. . . . I cannot help wondering how long these young people will stay in Jersey. It may be to their financial interest at present to make their home there permanently. But will they remain there once the capital gains are safely in hand, clear of tax? They may well change their minds and come back to enjoy their untaxed gains.'

Similarly, Harman LJ says at p. 247:

> 'The two young men who alone may be considered cannot be said to have proved that they truly intend to make Jersey their home.'

It seems to me that *Re Weston's Settlements* [1969] 1 Ch 223 was decided upon its own particular facts, and on those facts it is a decision with which I am, if I may respectfully say so, in the most complete agreement. The facts of the case now before me are quite different. Here, the family has been in Jersey for 19 years and has made a genuine and permanent home in Jersey. The children were born there. There is no other reason why it would not be right to exercise the jurisdiction in the present case."[7]

---

iii. VESTING ORDERS

TRUSTEE ACT 1925

44. Vesting orders of land.—In any of the following cases, namely:—

(i) Where the court appoints or has appointed a trustee, or where a trustee has been appointed out of court under any statutory or express power;

(ii) Where a trustee entitled to or possessed of any land or interest therein, whether by way of mortgage or otherwise, or entitled to a

[7] *Re Guibert's Trust Estate* (1852) 16 Jur 852; *Re Simpson* [1897] 1 Ch 256.

contingent right therein, either solely or jointly with any other person—

(*a*) is under disability; or

(*b*) is out of the jurisdiction of the High Court; or

(*c*) cannot be found, or being a corporation, has been dissolved;

(iii) Where it is uncertain who was the survivor of two or more trustees jointly entitled to or possessed of any interest in land;

(iv) Where it is uncertain whether the last trustee known to have been entitled to or possessed of any interest in land is living or dead;

(v) Where there is no personal representative of a deceased trustee who was entitled to or possessed of any interest in land, or where it is uncertain who is the personal representative of a deceased trustee who was entitled to or possessed of any interest in land;

(vi) Where a trustee jointly or solely entitled to or possessed of any interest in land, or entitled to a contingent right therein, has been required, by or on behalf of a person entitled to require a conveyance of the land or interest or a release of the right, to convey the land or interest or to release the right, and has wilfully refused or neglected to convey the land or interest or release the right for twenty-eight days after the date of the requirement;

(vii) Where land or any interest therein is vested in a trustee whether by way of mortgage or otherwise, and it appears to the court to be expedient;

the court may make an order (in this Act called a vesting order) vesting the land or interest therein in any such person in any such manner and for any such estate or interest as the court may direct, or releasing or disposing of the contingent right to such person as the court may direct:

Provided that—

(*a*) Where the order is consequential on the appointment of a trustee the land or interest therein shall be vested for such estate as the court may direct in the persons who on the appointment are the trustees; and

(*b*) Where the order relates to a trustee entitled or formerly entitled jointly with another person, and such trustee is under disability or out of the jurisdiction of the High Court or cannot be found, or being a corporation has been dissolved, the land interest or right shall be vested in such other person who remains entitled, either alone or with any other person the court may appoint[8].

III. Retirement[9]

TRUSTEE ACT 1925

39. Retirement of trustee without a new appointment.—(1) Where a trustee is desirous of being discharged from the trust, and after his discharge there

[8] See also ss. 45–56 and M.H.A. 1959, s. 141 (1), Sch. 7, replacing T.A. 1925, s. 54, for further provisions relating to orders made by the court.

[9] H & M, pp. 449–450; K & S, pp. 231–233; P & M, pp. 234–235; Pettit, pp. 250–252; Snell, pp. 201–202.

will be either a trust corporation or at least two individuals to act as trustees to perform the trust, then, if such trustee as aforesaid by deed declares that he is desirous of being discharged from the trust, and if his co-trustees and such other person, if any, as is empowered to appoint trustees, by deed consent to the discharge of the trustee, and to the vesting in the co-trustees alone of the trust property, the trustee desirous of being discharged shall be deemed to have retired from the trust, and shall, by the deed, be discharged therefrom under this Act, without any new trustee being appointed in his place.

(2) Any assurance or thing requisite for vesting the trust property in the continuing trustees alone shall be executed or done.

A trustee who retires, whether by replacement under s. 36 or under this section should seek from the beneficiaries a formal discharge from liability. Even without this, he will incur no liability in respect of future breaches of trust, unless he resigned in order to facilitate a breach[10].

A personal representative is unable to retire.

IV. Removal[11]

TRUSTEE ACT 1925

36. Power of appointing new or additional trustees: see p. 433, ante.
41. Power of court to appoint new trustees: see p. 441, ante.

In *Letterstedt v Broers* ((1884) 9 App Cas 371) the Privy Council had to consider whether, independently of statute, it should remove the Board of Executors of Cape Town, the sole surviving executors and trustees of the will of Jacob Letterstedt, against whom the appellant, a beneficiary, made allegations of misconduct in the administration of the trust. The Board was removed; but the allegations were not substantiated, and no costs were awarded. Lord BLACKBURN described as follows the principles upon which the court's discretion should be exercised: "The whole case has been argued here, and, as far as their Lordships can perceive, in the Court below, as depending on the principles which should guide an English Court of Equity when called upon to remove old trustees and substitute new ones. It is not disputed that there is a jurisdiction 'in cases requiring such a remedy,' as is said in Story's Equity Jurisprudence, s. 1287, but there is very little to be found to guide us in saying what are the cases requiring such a remedy; so little that their Lordships are compelled to have recourse to general principles.

Story says, s. 1289, 'But in cases of positive misconduct, Courts of Equity have no difficulty in interposing to remove trustees who have abused their trust; it is not indeed every mistake or neglect of duty, or inaccuracy of

[10] *Head v Gould* [1898] 2 Ch 250 at 272, p. 621, post.
[11] H & M, pp. 450–451; K & S, p. 231; P & M, pp. 235–236; Pettit, pp. 252–253; Snell, p. 202.

conduct of trustees, which will induce Courts of Equity to adopt such a course. But the acts or omissions must be such as to endanger the trust property or to shew a want of honesty, or a want of proper capacity to execute the duties, or a want of reasonable fidelity.'

It seems to their Lordships that the jurisdiction which a Court of Equity has no difficulty in exercising under the circumstances indicated by Story is merely ancillary to its principal duty, to see that the trusts are properly executed. This duty is constantly being performed by the substitution of new trustees in the place of original trustees for a variety of reasons in non-contentious cases. And therefore, though it should appear that the charges of misconduct were either not made out, or were greatly exaggerated, so that the trustee was justified in resisting them, and the Court might consider that in awarding costs, yet if satisfied that the continuance of the trustee would prevent the trusts being properly executed, the trustee might be removed. It must always be borne in mind that trustees exist for the benefit of those to whom the creator of the trust has given the trust estate.

The reason why there is so little to be found in the books on this subject is probably that suggested by Mr. Davey in his argument. As soon as all questions of character are as far settled as the nature of the case admits, if it appears clear that the continuance of the trustee would be detrimental to the execution of the trusts, even if for no other reason than that human infirmity would prevent those beneficially interested, or those who act for them, from working in harmony with the trustee, and if there is no reason to the contrary from the intentions of the framer of the trust to give this trustee a benefit or otherwise, the trustee is always advised by his own counsel to resign, and does so. If, without any reasonable ground, he refused to do so, it seems to their Lordships that the Court might think it proper to remove him; but cases involving the necessity of deciding this, if they ever arise, do so without getting reported. It is to be lamented that the case was not considered in this light by the parties in the Court below, for, as far as their Lordships can see, the Board would have little or no profit from continuing to be trustees, and as such coming into continual conflict with the appellant and her legal advisers, and would probably have been glad to resign, and get out of an onerous and disagreeable position. But the case was not so treated.

In exercising so delicate a jurisdiction as that of removing trustees, their Lordships do not venture to lay down any general rule beyond the very broad principle above enunciated, that their main guide must be the welfare of the beneficiaries. Probably it is not possible to lay down any more definite rule in a matter so essentially dependent on details often of great nicety. But they proceed to look carefully into the circumstances of the case. . . .

It is quite true that friction or hostility between trustees and the immediate possessor of the trust estate is not of itself a reason for the removal of the trustees. But where the hostility is grounded on the mode in which the trust has been administered, where it has been caused wholly or partially by substantial overcharges against the trust estate, it is certainly not to be disregarded.

Looking therefore at the whole circumstances of this very peculiar case, the complete change of position, the unfortunate hostility that has arisen, and the difficult and delicate duties that may yet have to be performed, their Lordships can come to no other conclusion than that it is necessary, for the welfare of the beneficiaries, that the Board should no longer be trustees.

Probably if it had been put in this way below they would have consented. But for the benefit of the trust they should cease to be trustees, whether they consent or not.

Their Lordships think therefore that the portion of the final judgment which is, 'That the prayer for removal of the executors be refused,' should be reversed, and that in lieu of it the Court below should be directed to remove the Board from the further execution of the trusts created by the will, and to take all necessary and proper proceedings for the appointment of other and proper persons to execute such trusts in future, and to transfer to them the trust property in so far as it remains vested in the Board. The rest of the judgment should stand."

In *Re Wrightson* ([1908] 1 Ch 789) the trustees had been guilty of a breach of trust, in connection with an advance of a part of the trust funds upon mortgage. In an administration action, one question was whether the trustees should be removed.

WARRINGTON J said: "The next question is, Ought I to make an order for the removal of the trustees upon the materials which were before the Court at the trial, which, in my judgment, are the only materials at which I can look? That raises a somewhat troublesome question. The trustees admitted that they were guilty of a breach of trust. The statement to which I have already referred, together with the proposals of the trustees, was remarked upon in strong language by the judge at the trial,and I desire to associate myself with the remarks which he made without further explanation that that statement is one which the trustees ought not to have made, and I think that the learned judge intended that an application for the removal of the trustees founded on that statement should prima facie be one which would at all events receive the favourable attention of the Court. But I have now before me not only the plaintiffs, but other beneficiaries representing somewhere about one-half of the estate. The plaintiffs' interest, if you are to count heads, predominates to some extent, but I have a very substantial proportion of the beneficiaries who object to the removal of the trustees, and who say there is no ground for it. Now, what are the grounds on which the Court removes trustees? The only case that I can find which helps one at all in this matter is the case of *Letterstedt v Broers* (1884) 9 App Cas 371, in the Privy Council. There some very valuable remarks were made by Lord Blackburn, who delivered the judgment of the Judicial Committee (at p. 385). [His Lordship quoted from the extract on p. 448, ante, and continued:] And then [Lord Blackburn] thus sums up what he regards as expressing the general principle guiding the Court in these cases (at p. 387): 'In exercising so delicate a jurisdiction as that of removing trustees, their Lordships do not venture to lay down any general rule beyond the very broad principle enunciated, that their main guide must be the welfare of the beneficiaries. Probably it is not possible to lay down any more definite rule in a matter so essentially dependent on details often of great nicety. But they proceed to look carefully into the circumstances of the case.' Is it necessary here, having regard to the welfare of the beneficiaries and for the protection of this trust, to remove the trustees? At the present moment nothing remains for the trustees to do except to wind up the estate; the testator's widow is dead; the whole of the estate is divisible amongst a number of persons who are sui juris. But the summons was taken out on February 27, 1906, two years ago, at a time when the widow was alive and the estate was not immediately divisible, and therefore I must, with a view at any rate of dealing with the costs, look at the state of things as they existed at the date when the summons was issued. Is it necessary for the welfare of the trust now to remove the trustees on the grounds alleged in the statement of claim? There is one contention on the part of the plaintiffs to which I think I ought to refer. Mr. Cave as one argument, or as one reason for the removal of the trustees, said, in effect, 'We do not like to have these persons who have been charged with a breach of trust and have admitted it, and who have made that statement which is set out in the pleadings, in custody of our trust estate.' That is not enough, especially when there are other cestuis que trust entitled. A somewhat similar question arose in the case of *Forster v Davies* ((1861) 4 De F & J 133 at 139), in which Turner LJ expressed the view, which I have just expressed, that disagreement between the cestuis que trust and the trustees, or the disinclination on the part of the cestuis que trust to have the trust property remain in the hands of a particular individual, is not a sufficient ground for the removal of the trustees. You must find something which induces the court to think either that the trust property will not be safe, or that the trust will not be properly executed in the interests of the beneficiaries. Is that so here, and is it for the welfare of the trust generally, and not merely of the plaintiffs, that these trustees should be removed? I think it is not. The trustees were undoubtedly guilty of a breach of trust, and they undoubtedly in the statement to which I have referred expressed views which have occasioned the blame which has been attached to the trustees both by Buckley J and myself, but, having regard to the fact that the Court has now the power of seeing that the trust is properly executed, to the fact that a large proportion of the beneficiaries do not require the trustees to be removed, and further (and this is of great importance), to the extra expense and loss to the trust estate which must be occasioned by the change of trustees, I think it would not be for the welfare of the cestuis que trust generally, or necessary for the protection of the trust estate, that these trustees should be removed. I must therefore refuse the application for their removal as well as the application for the further accounts and inquiries."

In *Moore v M'Glynn* ([1894] 1 IR 74) William M'Glynn appointed his brother Edward and his son Patrick as trustees of his estate for the benefit of his widow and children. After his death, Edward managed the testator's business of shop-keeper and local postmaster. Subsequently Edward was appointed postmaster, and later started his own business which was similar to that of the trust. CHATTERTON V-C held that Edward had committed no breach of trust; but that the conflict required that he should be discharged from his office as trustee.

Report of the Charity Commissioners for England and Wales for the year 1976, paras. 25–29.

"*Sanctuary*

25. In paragraphs 90 to 96 of our report for 1971 we mentioned that, following an inquiry and report under section 6 of the Charities Act 1960, we had made an order removing Mr. Robert Jones and his sister from being trustees of the charity called Sanctuary, that Mr. Jones' appeal to the High Court against our order had been dismissed by Mr. Justice Ungoed-Thomas and that Mr. Jones was appealing to the Court of Appeal. In 1973 the Court of Appeal resolved that the case should be remitted for a rehearing in the Court of first instance on the grounds that the Judge might have attributed too little weight to the appellant's affidavit evidence in which he sought to challenge some of the findings in the report of the inquiry. The Court of Appeal held that it was for an appellant who appeals against such an order to show that it had been wrongly made, but the report of the inquiry, to the extent that it was not challenged by him, should be treated as evidence in the appeal (*Jones v A-G* [1974] 1 Ch 148, [1973] 3 All ER 518).

26. The rehearing took place before Mr. Justice Brightman, and Mr. Jones' application was dismissed. In his Judgment dated the 9th November 1976 the Judge noted that out of a sum exceeding £10,000 collected from the public over a period of some three years not one penny was ever spent on any charitable purpose; that collecting boxes left in public places were frequently abandoned because it was uneconomic to collect them; that most of the personal collectors for the charity, but not Mr. Jones himself, received a percentage remuneration sometimes as high as 35 per cent., and probably even as high as 50 per cent.; and that the administrative expenses of the charity were so high that between January 1970 and May 1971 only 11 pennies out of each pound remained available for charitable purposes.

27. The Judge commented on the fact that during the three years that Mr. Jones ran the charity he was living on social security and had indicated that he would probably have tried to stay on social security for the rest of his life so as to carry on the charity. The Judge found it disturbing that a person could draw public funds for his maintenance while engaged in charitable activities selected by himself.

28. Another point which troubled Mr. Justice Brightman was the legality of commissions charged by people who took round charity collecting boxes. A collecting box which named a charity as the recipient of a donation represented that money placed in the box went to the charity, and if the collector retained commission this was contrary to the representation on

the collecting box and to the belief of most contributors. Furthermore, a person who solicited money for a charity was a trustee of the contribution and unless he made it known to the donor that he intended to retain a percentage of the contribution for himself it seemed to the Judge that he had no title to that percentage.

29. The Judge also referred to the use of deceptive labels and letter-headings, failure to check the credentials of area organisers, an untruthful application for a licence under the House to House Collections Act, a failure to maintain proper books of account over part of the period, misuse of charity money, and lack of security in regard to the issue and sealing of collecting boxes. In his judgment there was overwhelming evidence to support the allegations of misconduct and mismanagement which had been made against Mr. Jones, and he found the allegations proved. In his judgment it was out of the question to set aside our order removing Mr. Jones from the trusteeship of Sanctuary."[11a]

v. Particular Trustees[12]

A. Judicial Trustees

JUDICIAL TRUSTEES ACT 1896

1. Power of court on application to appoint judicial trustee.—(1) Where application is made to the court by or on behalf of the person creating or intending to create a trust, or by or on behalf of a trustee or beneficiary, the court may, in its discretion, appoint a person (in this Act called a judicial trustee) to be a trustee of that trust, either jointly with any other person or as sole trustee, and, if sufficient cause is shown, in place of all or any existing trustees.

(2) The administration of the property of a deceased person, whether a testator or intestate, shall be a trust, and the executor or administrator a trustee, within the meaning of this Act.

(3) Any fit and proper person nominated for the purpose in the application may be appointed a judicial trustee, and, in the absence of such nomination, or if the court is not satisfied of the fitness of a person so nominated, an official of the court may be appointed, and in any case a judicial trustee shall be subject to the control and supervision of the court as an officer thereof.

(4) The court may, either on request or without request, give to a judicial trustee any general or special directions in regard to the trust or the administration thereof.

(5) There may be paid to a judicial trustee out of the trust property such remuneration, not exceeding the prescribed limits, as the court may assign in each case, subject to any rules under this Act respecting the application of such remuneration where the judicial trustee is an official of the court, and the remuneration so assigned to any judicial trustee shall, save as

[11a] The plaintiff's appeal was dismissed on December 14, 1977. (1978) CL; March, p. 2.

[12] H & M, pp. 437–440; K & S, pp. 55–61; P & M, pp. 222–223; Pettit, pp. 256–261; Snell, pp. 197–201. See also Keeton: *Modern Developments of the Law of Trusts* (1971) pp. 16–27.

the court may for special reasons otherwise order, cover all his work and personal outlay.

(6) Once in every year the accounts of every trust of which a judicial trustee has been appointed shall be audited, and a report thereon made to the court by the prescribed persons, and, in any case where the court shall so direct, an inquiry into the administration by a judicial trustee of any trust, or into any dealing or transaction of a judicial trustee, shall be made in the prescribed manner.

In *Re Ridsdel* ([1947] Ch 597, [1947] 2 All ER 312) the question arose whether r. 12 of the Judicial Trustee Rules 1897[13], under which the judicial trustee may at any time request the court to give him directions as to the trust or its administration, by implication deprived him of the power of compromise under s. 15 of the Trustee Act 1925. JENKINS J held that it did not, and said (at p. 605): "I cannot think that that is the effect of this rule. After all, the object of the Judicial Trustees Act, 1896, as I understand it, was to provide a middle course in cases where the administration of the estate by the ordinary trustees had broken down and it was not desired to put the estate to the expense of a full administration. In those circumstances, a solution was found in the appointment of a judicial trustee, who acts in close concert with the court and under conditions enabling the court to supervise his transactions. I cannot think that it was intended to complicate the matter by prohibiting such a trustee from exercising any discretion without first going to the court and asking for directions. That, as Mr. Stamp points out, involves this, that whenever the trustee wanted to exercise some discretion, such as the power of compromise under s. 15 of the Trustee Act, 1925, he would perforce have to come to the court for directions; but (to give only one instance) the court would give no directions without summoning before it all persons interested in the exercise of the discretion in order that the matter might be argued and decided in the presence of all parties. One would thus reduce the administration of an estate by a judicial trustee to very much the same position as where an estate is being administered by the court and every step has to be taken in pursuance of the court's directions. It does not seem to me to be right or necessary to construe the Judicial Trustee Rules, 1897, as having any such effect."

B. The Public Trustee

The powers and duties of the Public Trustee Office, which was set up in 1906, appear below[14]. In 1977 it was responsible for 8,660 separate trusts and estates, the combined value amounting to £201 million[15]. It now receives only a minimal and declining proportion of the total work in the field of executorships and trusteeships. "The work of the Office will continue to decrease as the older Trusts are distributed and it is too soon to forecast at what level we shall regain equilibrium"[16].

---

[13] See now Judicial Trustee Rules 1972, S.I. 1972 No. 1096.
[14] (1974) 71 LS Gaz 1068 (J. O'Sullivan).
[15] 69th Annual Report of the Public Trustee 1976–1977, p. 5.
[16] 68th Annual Report of the Public Trustee 1975–1976, p. 3.

PUBLIC TRUSTEE ACT 1906

1. Office of public trustee.—(1) There shall be established the office of public trustee.

(2) The public trustee shall be a corporation sole under that name, with perpetual succession and an official seal, and may sue and be sued under the above name like any other corporation sole, but any instruments sealed by him shall not, by reason of his using a seal, be rendered liable to a higher stamp duty than if he were an individual.

POWERS AND DUTIES OF PUBLIC TRUSTEE

2. General powers and duties of public trustee.—(1) Subject to and in accordance with the provisions of this Act and rules made thereunder, the public trustee may, if he thinks fit—

(*a*) act in the administration of estates of small value;

(*b*) act as custodian trustee;

(*c*) act as an ordinary trustee;

(*d*) be appointed to be a judicial trustee; . . .

(2) Subject to the provisions of this Act, and to the rules made thereunder, the public trustee may act either alone or jointly with any person or body of persons in any capacity to which he may be appointed in pursuance of this Act, and shall have all the same powers, duties, and liabilities, and be entitled to the same rights and immunities and be subject to the control and orders of the court, as a private trustee acting in the same capacity.

(3) The public trustee may decline, either absolutely or except on the prescribed conditions, to accept any trust, but he shall not decline to accept any trust on the ground only of the small value of the trust property.

(4) The public trustee shall not accept any trust which involves the management or carrying on of any business, except in the cases in which he may be authorised to do so by rules made under this Act, nor any trust under a deed of arrangement for the benefit of creditors, nor the administration of any estate known or believed by him to be insolvent.

(5) The public trustee shall not accept any trust exclusively for religious or charitable purposes, and nothing in this Act contained, or in the rules to be made under the powers in this Act contained, shall abridge or affect the powers or duties of the official trustee of charity lands or official trustees of charitable funds[17].

(1) In the Administration of small Estates

3. Administration of small estates.—(1) Any person who in the opinion of the public trustee would be entitled to apply to the court for an order for the administration by the court of an estate, the gross capital value whereof is proved to the satisfaction of the public trustee to be less than one thousand pounds, may apply to the public trustee to administer the estate, and, where any such application is made and it appears to the public trustee that the persons beneficially entitled are persons of small means, the public trustee shall administer the estate, unless he sees good reason for refusing to do so.

[17] Now the Official Custodian for Charities.

(2) On the public trustee undertaking, by declaration in writing signed and sealed by him, to administer the estate the trust property other than stock shall, by virtue of this Act, vest in him, and the right to transfer or call for the transfer of any stock forming part of the estate shall also vest in him, in like manner as if vesting orders had been made for the purpose by the High Court under the Trustee Act, 1893[18], and that Act shall apply accordingly. As from such vesting any trustee entitled under the trust to administer the estate shall be discharged from all liability attaching to the administration, except in respect of past acts: . . .

(5) Where proceedings have been instituted in any court for the administration of an estate, and by reason of the small value of the estate it appears to the court that the estate can be more economically administered by the public trustee than by the court, or that for any other reason it is expedient that the estate should be administered by the public trustee instead of the court, the court may order that the estate shall be administered by the public trustee, and thereupon (subject to any directions by the court) this section shall apply as if the administration of the estate had been undertaken by the public trustee in pursuance of this section.

(2) *As Custodian Trustee*

4. Custodian trustee.—(1) Subject to rules under this Act the public trustee may, if he consents to act as such, and whether or not the number of trustees has been reduced below the original number, be appointed to be custodian trustee of any trust—

(*a*) by order of the court made on the application of any person on whose application the court may order the appointment of a new trustee; or

(*b*) by the testator, settlor, or other creator of any trust; or

(*c*) by the person having power to appoint new trustees.

(2) Where the public trustee is appointed to be custodian trustee of any trust—

(*a*) The trust property shall be transferred to the custodian trustee as if he were sole trustee, and for that purpose vesting orders may, where necessary, be made under the Trustee Act, 1893[19]:

(*b*) The management of the trust property and the exercise of any power or discretion exercisable by the trustees under the trust shall remain vested in the trustees other than the custodian trustee (which trustees are herein-after referred to as the managing trustees):

(*c*) As between the custodian trustee and the managing trustees, and subject and without prejudice to the rights of any other persons, the custodian trustee shall have the custody of all securities and documents of title relating to the trust property, but the managing trustee shall have free access thereto and be entitled to take copies thereof or extracts therefrom:

(*d*) The custodian trustee shall concur in and perform all acts necessary to enable the managing trustees to exercise their powers of management or any other power or discretion vested in them (including the power

[18] Now T.A. 1925.
[19] Now T.A. 1925.

to pay money or securities into court), unless the matter in which he is requested to concur is a breach of trust, or involves a personal liability upon him in respect of calls or otherwise, but, unless he so concurs, the custodian trustee shall not be liable for any act or default on the part of the managing trustees or any of them:

(*e*) All sums payable to or out of the income or capital of the trust property shall be paid to or by the custodian trustee: Provided that the custodian trustee may allow the dividends and other income derived from the trust property to be paid to the managing trustees or to such person as they direct, or into such bank to the credit of such person as they may direct, and in such case shall be exonerated from seeing to the application thereof and shall not be answerable for any loss or misapplication thereof:

(*f*) The power of appointing new trustees, when exerciseable by the trustees, shall be exerciseable by the managing trustees alone, but the custodian trustee shall have the same power of applying to the court for the appointment of a new trustee as any other trustee:

(*g*) In determining the number of trustees for the purposes of the Trustee Act, 1893[20], the custodian trustee shall not be reckoned as a trustee.

(*h*) The custodian trustee, if he acts in good faith, shall not be liable for accepting as correct and acting upon the faith of any written statement by the managing trustees as to any birth, death, marriage, or other matter of pedigree or relationship, or other matter of fact, upon which the title to the trust property or any part thereof may depend, nor for acting upon any legal advice obtained by the managing trustees independently of the custodian trustee:

(*i*) The court may, on the application of either the custodian trustee, or any of the managing trustees, or of any beneficiary, and on proof to their satisfaction that it is the general wish of the beneficiaries, or that on other grounds it is expedient, to terminate the custodian trusteeship, make an order for that purpose, and the court may thereupon make such vesting orders and give such directions as under the circumstances may seem to the court to be necessary or expedient.

(3) The provisions of this section shall apply in like manner as to the public trustee to any banking or insurance company or other body corporate entitled by rules made under this Act to act as custodian trustee[21], with power for such company or body corporate to charge and retain or pay out of the trust property fees not exceeding the fees chargeable by the public trustee as custodian trustee.

(3) *As an ordinary Trustee*

5. Appointment of public trustee to be trustee, executor, &c.—(1) The public trustee may by that name, or any other sufficient description, be appointed to be trustee of any will or settlement or other instrument creating a trust or to perform any trust or duty belonging to a class which he

[20] Now T.A. 1925.

[21] Section 14; Public Trustee Rules 1912, r. 30, as substituted by the Public Trustee (Custodian Trustee) Rules 1975, S.I. 1975 No. 1189), p. 459, post.

is authorised by the rules made under this Act to accept, and may be so appointed whether the will or settlement or instrument creating the trust or duty was made or came into operation before or after the passing of this Act, and either as an original or as a new trustee, or as an additional trustee, in the same cases, and in the same manner, and by the same persons or court, as if he were a private trustee, with this addition, that, though the trustees originally appointed were two or more, the public trustee may be appointed sole trustee.

(2) Where the public trustee has been appointed a trustee of any trust, a co-trustee may retire from the trust under and in accordance with section eleven of the Trustee Act, 1893[1], notwithstanding that there are not more than two trustees, and without such consents as are required by that section.

(3) The public trustee shall not be appointed either as a new or additional trustee where the will, settlement, or other instrument creating the trust or duty contains a direction to the contrary, unless the court otherwise order.

7. Liability of Consolidated Fund.—(1) The Consolidated Fund of the United Kingdom shall be liable to make good all sums required to discharge any liability which the public trustee, if he were a private trustee, would be personally liable to discharge, except where the liability is one to which neither the public trustee nor any of his officers has in any way contributed, and which neither he nor any of his officers could by the exercise of reasonable diligence have averted, and in that case the public trustee shall not nor shall the Consolidated Fund, be subject to any liability.

9. Fees charged by public trustee.—(1) There shall be charged in respect of the duties of the public trustee such fees, whether by way of percentage or otherwise, as the Treasury with the sanction of the Lord Chancellor may fix, and such fees shall be collected and accounted for by such persons, and in such manner, and shall be paid to such account, as the Treasury direct[2].

10. Appeal to the court.—(1) A person aggrieved by any act or omission or decision of the public trustee in relation to any trust may apply to the court, and the court may make such order in the matter as the court thinks just.

(2) Subject to rules of court, an application under this section to the High Court shall be made to a judge of the Chancery Division of the High Court in Chambers.

C. Custodian Trustees[3]

PUBLIC TRUSTEE ACT 1906

4. Custodian Trustee, (2), (3): see p. 456, ante.

[1] Now T.A. 1925, s. 39.

[2] See Public Trustee (Fees) Act 1957; Administration of Justice Act 1965, s. 2; Public Trustee (Fees) Order 1977, S.I. 1977 No. 508, as amended by Public Trustee (Fees) (Amendment) Order 1978, S.I. 1978 No. 373.

[3] See generally (1960) 24 Conv (NS) 196 (S. G. Maurice).

PUBLIC TRUSTEE RULES 1912[4]

30. Corporate Bodies as Custodian Trustees.—The following corporations shall be entitled to act as custodian trustees:—

(*a*) the Treasury Solicitor;

(*b*) any corporation which:—

(i) is constituted under the law of the United Kingdom or of any part thereof, or under the law of any other Member State of the European Economic Community or of any part thereof;

(ii) is empowered by its constitution to undertake trust business (which for the purpose of this rule means the business of acting as trustee under wills and settlements and as executor and administrator) in England and Wales[5];

(iii) has one or more places of business in the United Kingdom; and

(iv) is—

a company incorporated by special Act of Parliament or Royal Charter, or

a company registered (with or without limited liability) in the United Kingdom under the Companies Act 1948 or under the Companies Act (Northern Ireland) 1960 or in another Member State of the European Economic Community and having a capital (in stock or shares) for the time being issued of not less than £250,000 (or its equivalent in the currency of the State where the company is registered), of which not less than £100,000 (or its equivalent) has been paid up in cash, or

a company which is registered without limited liability in the United Kingdom under the Companies Act 1948 or the Companies Act (Northern Ireland) 1960 or in another Member State of the European Economic Community and of which one of the members is a company within any of the classes defined in this sub-paragraph;

(*c*) any corporation which is incorporated by special Act or Royal Charter or under the Charitable Trustees Incorporation Act 1872 which is empowered by its constitution to act as a trustee for any charitable purposes, but only in relation to trusts in which its constitution empowers it to act;

(*d*) any corporation which is constituted under the law of the United Kingdom or of any part thereof and having its place of business there, and which is either:—

(i) established for the purpose of undertaking trust business for the benefit of Her Majesty's Navy, Army, Air Force or Civil Service or of any unit, department, member or association of members thereof, and having among its directors or members any persons appointed or nominated by the Defence Council or any Department of State or any one or more of those Departments, or

[4] As substituted by the Public Trustee (Custodian Trustee) Rules 1975, S.I. 1975 No. 1189, r. 2.

[5] *Re Bigger* [1977] 2 WLR 773, [1977] 2 All ER 644 (Bank of Ireland).

(ii) authorised by the Lord Chancellor to act in relation to any charitable, ecclesiastical or public trusts as a trust corporation, but only in connection with any such trust as is so authorised;

(*e*) (i) any Regional Health Authority, Area Health Authority or special health authority, but only in relation to any trust which the authority is authorised to accept or hold by virtue of section 21 of the National Health Service Reorganisation Act 1973;

(ii) any preserved Board as defined by section 15 (6) of that Act, but only in relation to any trust which the Board is authorised to accept or hold by virtue of an order made under that section;

(*f*) the British Gas Corporation, but only in relation to a pension scheme or pension fund established or maintained by the Corporation by virtue of section 36 of the Gas Act 1972;

(*g*) the London Transport Executive, but only in relation to a pension scheme or pension fund—

(i) which is established or administered by the Executive by virtue of section 6 of the Transport (London) Act 1969, or

(ii) in relation to which rights, liabilities and functions have been transferred to the Executive by an order under section 74 of the Transport Act 1962 as applied by section 18 of the Transport (London) Act 1969;

(*h*) any of the following, namely:—

(i) the Greater London Council,

(ii) the corporation of any London borough (acting by the council),

(iii) a county council, district council, parish council or community council,

(iv) the Council of the Isles of Scilly,

but only in relation to charitable or public trusts (and not trusts for an ecclesiastical charity or for a charity for the relief of poverty) for the benefit of the inhabitants of the area of the local authority concerned and its neighbourhood, or any part of that area.

In *Re Brooke Bond & Co Ltd's Trust Deed* ([1963] Ch 357, [1963] 1 All ER 454)[6] the Welfare Insurance Co. Ltd. were custodian trustee under a trust deed which secured the pension fund of the employees of Brooke Bond & Co. Ltd. Its managing trustees had powers to take out a group insurance policy and they desired to take it out with Welfare Insurance Co. Ltd., the cutodian trustee. The question was whether, without leave of the court, the custodian trustee could enter into the policy with the managing trustees and retain for their own benefit any profit which they might make. CROSS J held that they could not and said (at p. 363): "It is apparent that the duties of a custodian trustee differ substantially from those of an ordinary trustee. If the trust instrument or the general law gives the trustees power to do this, that or the other, it is not for the custodian trustee to consider whether it should be done. The exercise of powers or discretions is a

[6] (1963) 79 LQR 177 (R.E.M.). See also *Forster v Williams Deacon's Bank Ltd* [1935] Ch 359 (bank may not be appointed both managing trustee and custodian trustee in order to allow it to charge fees as custodian trustee).

matter for the managing trustees with which the custodian trustee has no concern, and he is bound to deal with the trust property so as to give effect to the decisions and actions taken by the managing trustees unless what he is requested to do by them would be a breach of trust or would involve him in personal liability. On the other hand, it is plain that he is a trustee holding the trust property and its income on trust for the beneficiaries according to the terms of the trust instrument and he is prima facie liable to the beneficiaries for any dealing with capital or income which is a breach of trust. In practice this liability may be considerably qualified as regards income by the provisions of subsection (2) (*e*)[7] and as regards capital or income by the provisions of subsection (2) (*h*); but subject to the protection provided by those subsections the custodian trustee, as I understand the matter, is as liable as an ordinary trustee to be sued by a beneficiary for the misapplication of the trust property. His position is quite unlike that of a third party—a bailee of the trust property, for instance—who is in contractual relationship with the trustee but owes no duty to the beneficiaries.

It is, however, argued that the fact that a custodian trustee is not concerned with the management of the trust makes the rule that a trustee may not make a profit out of his trust inapplicable to him. If trustees have power to sell or lease the trust property or to invest it in some way, the custodian trustee is not concerned with the question whether the power should be exercised and is not concerned with any negotiations which take place between the managing trustees and the other contracting parties. All the custodian trustee is concerned to do is to be satisfied that the managing trustees have the power to enter into the transaction which they call on him to carry out.

That being the position, it is said how can there be any conflict between his interest and duty if he himself is the other contracting party? He must indeed satisfy himself that the proposed transaction is one which the managing trustees have power to enter into just as he would have to do if they had contracted with a third party, but once he is satisfied as to that, his duty in the matter is at an end and he can properly look only to his own interests in negotiating the terms of the contract in question with the managing trustees.

This argument is ingenious but in my judgment it is unsound. In the first place, it presupposes that a hard and fast line can always be drawn between the power to enter into a contract of a certain character and the terms of the contract. I do not think that this is always the case. For example, the managing trustees may have power to lease the trust property but only on the terms that they obtain the best rent reasonably obtainable. In such a case if the proposal was to grant a lease to a nominee of the custodian trustee, the custodian trustee would be under a duty to see that the best rent was obtained so that no breach of trust was committed, but it would be to his interest as the prospective lessee to have the rent fixed at as low a figure as possible. Again it is prima facie the duty of a trustee to place at the disposal of the beneficiaries any special knowledge he

[7] Public Trustee Act 1906, s. 4 (2), p. 456, ante.

has of the value of the trust property or of any advantages or disadvantages of any contract which is in contemplation with regard to it. It may be that if the contract is being made by the managing trustees with a third party, a custodian trustee is under no positive duty to communicate any such knowledge which he may have to the managing trustees. I do not say whether that is so or not, but assuming it is so it does not follow by any means that if the custodian trustee was himself the other contracting party he could properly refrain from disclosing any such special knowledge to the managing trustees as a third party would be entitled to refrain from disclosing it. I appreciate that it may well be that the chances of there being a conflict between interest and duty are less in the case of transactions between a custodian trustee and managing trustees than they are in the case of transactions between an ordinary trustee and his co-trustees. But the possibility of conflict is still there and the rule, as Lord Herschell pointed out in *Bray v Ford* ([1896] AC 44), is an inflexible one unless the trust instrument provides for a profit being made by the trustees or the court makes a special order in a particular case.

For the reasons I have tried to give, I can see no sound reason for saying that the rule does not apply to a custodian trustee as much as to an ordinary trustee."

D. Trustees of Charitable Trusts

TRUSTEE ACT 1925

34 (3). Limitation of the number of trustees: see p. 423, ante.

CHARITIES ACT 1960

18 (7). Concurrent jurisdiction with High Court for certain purposes: see p. 414, ante.

20. Power to act for protection of charities: see p. 425, ante.

35 (1). Transfer and evidence of title to property vested in trustees: see p. 425, ante.

E. Trust Corporations

TRUSTEE ACT 1925[8]

68 (18). Definitions.—(1) In this Act, unless the context otherwise requires, the following expressions have the meanings hereby assigned to them respectively, that is to say:—

(xxx) "Trust corporation" means the Public Trustee or a corporation either appointed by the court in any particular case to be a trustee or entitled by rules made under subsection (3) of section four of the Public Trustee Act, 1906, to act as custodian trustee . . .[9]

[8] See also S.L.A. 1925, s. 117 (xxx); L.P.A. 1925, s. 205 (1) (xxviii); A.E.A. 1925, s. 55 (1) (xxvi); Supreme Court of Judicature (Consolidation) Act 1925, s. 175 (1).

[9] See p. 457, ante.

LAW OF PROPERTY (AMENDMENT) ACT 1926

3. Meaning of "trust corporation".—(1) For the purposes of the Law of Property Act, 1925, the Settled Land Act, 1925, the Trustee Act, 1925, the Administration of Estates Act, 1925, and the Supreme Court of Judicature (Consolidation) Act, 1925, the expression "Trust Corporation" includes the Treasury Solicitor, the Official Solicitor and any person holding any other official position prescribed by the Lord Chancellor, and, in relation to the property of a bankrupt and property subject to a deed of arrangement, includes the trustee in bankruptcy and the trustee under the deed respectively, and, in relation to charitable ecclesiastical and public trusts, also includes any local or public authority so prescribed, and any other corporation constituted under the laws of the United Kingdom or any part thereof which satisfies the Lord Chancellor that it undertakes the administration of any such trusts without remuneration, or that by its constitution it is required to apply the whole of its net income after payment of outgoings for charitable, ecclesiastical or public purposes, and is prohibited from distributing, directly or indirectly, any part thereof by way of profits amongst any of its members, and is authorised by him to act in relation to such trusts as a trust corporation.

(2) For the purposes of this provision, the expression "Treasury Solicitor" means the solicitor for the affairs of His Majesty's Treasury, and includes the solicitor for the affairs of the Duchy of Lancaster.

VI. Control of Trustees[10]

Although the court will compel a trustee to carry out a specific duty, there are difficulties in determining what is the right course to take in respect of powers and discretions. Generally the court will not intervene, in the absence of *mala fides*, in the exercise of a power. But the trustee may, as in the case of a discretionary trust, be under an obligation to exercise a discretion. If he does not exercise it, the court may in appropriate circumstances, as has been seen, exercise it for him[11]. But if he does exercise it within the terms of the power or discretion, how can the court interfere? The discretion is that of the trustee, not that of the court. The court can interfere in the case of fraud; or if the trustees show that they reached a conclusion for wrong reasons. But if they say nothing, there is little that the court can do. The problem is particularly acute if a complainant suspects fraud or *mala fides* on the part of the trustees; but cannot prove this unless the trustees disclose their deliberations.

TEMPEST v LORD CAMOYS

(1882) 21 ChD 571 (CA, JESSEL MR, BRETT and COTTON LJJ)

Under the will of Sir Charles Robert Tempest, Bart. Mr. James Fleming,

[10] H & M, pp. 451–453; P & M, pp. 276–277; Pettit, pp. 360–362; Snell pp. 226–228.

[11] *McPhail v Doulton* [1971] AC 424, [1970] 2 All ER 228, p. 48, ante; *Re Locker's Settlement* [1977] 1 WLR 1323, [1978] 1 All ER 216.

and Mr. Wilfred Tempest, the trustees, had power at their absolute discretion, to sell land, to apply the purchase money in the purchase of other land, and to raise money by mortgage for the purpose.

Some of the family wished to purchase Bracewell Hall for £60,000, using £30,000 of available money, and raising the balance by mortgage. Tempest supported the suggestion, Fleming opposed. Tempest brought this petition, asking that the purchase might be ordered.

Held (affirming CHITTY J). The Court would not interfere with the *bona fide* exercise of his discretion by a trustee.

JESSEL MR: It is very important that the law of the Court on this subject should be understood. It is settled law that when a testator has given a pure discretion to trustees as to the exercise of a power, the Court does not enforce the exercise of the power against the wish of the trustees, but it does prevent them from exercising it improperly. The Court says that the power, if exercised at all, is to be properly exercised. This may be illustrated by the case of persons having a power of appointing new trustees. Even after a decree in a suit for administering the trusts has been made they may still exercise the power, but the Court will see that they do not appoint improper persons.

But in all cases where there is a trust or duty coupled with the power the Court will then compel the trustees to carry it out in a proper manner and within a reasonable time. In the present case there was a power which amounts to a trust to invest the fund in question in the purchase of land. The trustees would not be allowed by the Court to disregard that trust, and if Mr. *Fleming* had refused to invest the money in land at all the Court would have found no difficulty in interfering. But that is a very different thing from saying that the Court ought to take from the trustees their uncontrolled discretion as to the particular time for the investment and the particular property which should be purchased. In this particular case it appears to me that the testator in his will has carefully distinguished between what is to be at the discretion of his trustees and what is obligatory on them.

There is another difficulty in this case. The estate proposed to be purchased will cost £60,000, and only £30,000 is available for the purchase, and the trustees will have to borrow the remaining £30,000. There is power to raise money by mortgage at the absolute discretion of the trustees, and assuming that such a transaction as this is within the power, and that the trustees can mortgage the estate before they have actually bought it, there is no trust to mortgage, it is purely discretionary. The Court cannot force Mr. *Fleming* to take the view that it is proper to mortgage the estate in this way; he may very well have a different opinion from the other trustee. Here again the Court cannot interfere with his discretion. The appeal must therefore be dismissed.

RE BELOVED WILKES'S CHARITY
(1851) 3 Mac & G 440 (Lord TRURO LC)

Trustees of a charitable trust were to select a boy to be educated at Oxford in preparation for him to become a Minister of the Church of England.

Preference was to be given to boys from four named parishes if, in the judgment of the trustees, a fit and proper candidate therefrom could be found.

In 1848 the trustees selected Charles Joyce, who did not come from one of the four parishes. They gave no reasons for their choice, but stated that they had considered the candidates impartially. It appeared however that Joyce's brother was a Minister, who had sought the assistance of one of the trustees in favour of Charles. The court was asked to set aside the selection, and to select William Gale, whose father was a respectable farmer residing in one of the specified parishes.

Held. In the absence of evidence that the trustees had exercised their discretion unfairly or dishonestly, the Court would not interfere.

LORD TRURO LC: The question, therefore, is, whether it was the duty of the trustees to enter into particulars, or whether the law is not, that trustees who are appointed to execute a trust according to discretion, that discretion to be influenced by a variety of circumstances (as, in this instance, by those particular circumstances which should be connected with the fitness of a lad to be brought up as a minister of the Church of England), are not bound to go into a detail of the grounds upon which they come to their conclusion, their duty being satisfied by shewing that they have considered the cirumstances of the case, and have come to their conclusion accordingly. Without occupying time by going into a lengthened examination of the decisions, the result of them appears to me so clear and reasonable, that it will be sufficient to state my conclusion in point of law to be, that in such cases as I have mentioned it is to the discretion of the trustees that the execution of the trust is confided, that discretion being exercised with an entire absence of indirect motive, with honesty of intention, and with a fair consideration of the subject. The duty of supervision on the part of this Court will thus be confined to the question of the honesty, integrity, and fairness with which the deliberation has been conducted, and will not be extended to the accuracy of the conclusion arrived at, except in particular cases. If, however, as stated by Lord Ellenborough in *The King v Archbishop of Canterbury* ((1812) 15 East 117), trustees think fit to state a reason, and the reason is one which does not justify their conclusion, then the Court may say that they have acted by mistake and in error, and that it will correct their decision; but if, without entering into details, they simply state, as in many cases it would be most prudent and judicious for them to do, that they have met and considered and come to a conclusion, the Court has then no means of saying that they have failed in their duty, or to consider the accuracy of their conclusion[12]. It seems, therefore, to me, that having in the present case to look to the motives of the trustees as developed in the affidavits, no ground exists for imputing bad motives. The Petitioners, indeed, candidly state, on the face of their petition, that they do not impute such motives, they merely charge the trustees with a miscarriage as regards the duty which they had to perform. I cannot, therefore, deal with the case as if the petition had contained a statement of a different kind, and if I could, still I should say, having read the

[12] See *Re Londonderry's Settlement* [1965] Ch 918, [1964] 3 All ER 855, p. 516, post.

affidavits, that I see nothing whatever which can lay the foundation for any judicial conclusion that the trustees intentionally and from bad motives failed in their duty, if they failed at all.

KLUG v KLUG
[1918] 2 Ch 67 (ChD, NEVILLE J)

Madame Moro (as Frida Klug) became entitled, on attaining the age of 21 in August, 1915, to a share in her father's estate. Legacy duty had to be paid, and it was agreed with the Inland Revenue that this should be paid by four equal instalments. Owing to the fall in income of the investments and the rise in the cost of living after the war, she was unable to make the payments out of income, and asked the trustees of her father's will to make an advancement to her out of the capital of her share, as they had power to do under the advancement clause of the will.

The trustees were the Public Trustee, and Mrs. Klug, the mother of Madame Moro. The Public Trustee wished to make an advancement; but Mrs. Klug refused, on the ground that Madame Moro had married without her approval.

Held. Payment out of the capital was ordered.

NEVILLE J: In this case Madame Moro is entitled to a life interest in one third of her father's residuary estate with remainder to her children, and has to pay a legacy duty of 10 per cent. because, according to English law, she is to be considered a stranger to her father. But that is not material, the real question here being when and how far the Court will interfere with the discretion given to trustees. I should be sorry by anything I may say to be thought to diminish the jurisdiction and control which the Court has over trustees in exercising their discretion, but on the other hand I should be loth to say that, where trustees have honestly exercised their discretion, the Court will interfere in the absence of special circumstances. Here the trustees are the Public Trustee and the testator's widow, and they have power to advance not more than a moiety of the capital of Madame Moro's settled share for her advancement and benefit, and the question is whether it will be for her benefit that the instalments of the legacy duty that have been paid and the two remaining instalments that are due should be paid out of the corpus instead of out of the income of her settled share. She is in difficulties owing to the times in which we are living. When the summons was previously before me I decided that the trustees could in the exercise of their discretion under the powers of advancement, if they thought fit, advance out of capital a sum sufficient to pay this legacy duty. The Public Trustee thinks that their discretion should be so exercised, but his co-trustee, the mother, declines to join him in so doing, not because she has considered whether or not it would be for her daughter's welfare that the advance should be made, but because her daughter has married without her consent, and her letters show, in my opinion, that she has not exercised her discretion at all. What, then, ought the Court to do when one trustee very properly desires to exercise his discretion under a power for the benefit of a beneficiary and his co-trustee will not exercise her discretion? I think that in such circumstances it is the duty of the Court to interfere and, in the exercise of its control over the discretion given to the trustees, to direct a sum to be raised out of the capital sufficient to pay off the mortgage of 250*l.* and two remaining instalments of the legacy duty, and that is the order I now make.

Hanbury & Maudsley: *Modern Equity* (10th Edn, 1976), p. 452.

"Some cases in the nineteenth century reserve to the courts a jurisdiction to investigate the exercise of a discretion that has already been made and that, on external evidence only, appears to have been 'mischievously and ruinously exercised'. And Lord Normand, in a Scottish appeal to the House of Lords, thought that 'The principles on which the courts must proceed are the same whether the trustees' reasons for their decision are disclosed or not[13], but it is not clear whether all the propositions in this case are acceptable as part of the English law of trusts. A conclusion can only be drawn in the form that it will never be easy to persuade a court to review the exercise of a discretion by trustees in the absence of some clear facts from which it is not difficult to discern that the discretion has been irregularly exercised."

VII. Power of Decision[14]

A settlor or testator sometimes gives to his trustees express power to make decisions concerning certain issues relating to the trust. The dividing line between what is permitted and what is not is very obscure. Certainly, "a testator cannot confide to another the right to make a will for him."[15] Nor can the jurisdiction of the court be excluded.

RE COXEN

[1948] Ch 747, [1948] 2 All ER 492 (ChD, JENKINS J)

The testator devised a dwelling-house to trustees upon trust to permit his wife to reside therein; and he declared that, "if in the opinion of my trustees she shall have ceased permanently to reside therein", the house was to fall into residue. The question was whether this proviso constituted a valid limitation upon the gift.

Held. The condition was not void for uncertainty. The decision of the trustees would be sufficient to determine the widow's interest.

JENKINS J: I have so far treated the condition as if it was simply in the terms "if she shall have ceased permanently to reside," whereas its actual terms are "if in the opinion of my trustees she shall have ceased permanently to reside." That I think makes a very material difference. The opinion of the trustees that the double event has happened, and not simply the

[13] *Dundee General Hospitals v Walker* [1952] 1 All ER 896 at 900; cf. *Padfield v Minister of Agriculture* [1968] AC 997 at 1033.

[14] H & M, p. 453; K & S, p. 289; Pettit, p. 359; Snell, p. 228.

[15] Per Lord PENZANCE in *In Bonis Smith* (1869) LR 1 P & D 717; (1953) 69 LQR 334 (D. M. Gordon).

happening of the double event, is what brings about the cesser of Lady Coxen's interest. If the testator had insufficiently defined the state of affairs on which the trustees were to form their opinion, he would not I think have saved the condition from invalidity on the ground of uncertainty merely by making their opinion the criterion, although the declaration by the trustees of this or that opinion would be an event about which in itself there could be no uncertainty. But as I have already indicated, I think the relevant double event is sufficiently defined to make it perfectly possible for the trustees (as the judges of fact for this purpose) to decide whether it has happened or not, and in my view the testator by making the trustees' opinion the criterion has removed the difficulties which might otherwise have ensued from a gift over in a double event the happening of which, though in itself sufficiently defined, may necessarily be a matter of inference involving nice questions of fact and degree.

In *Re Wynn* ([1952] Ch 271, [1952] 1 All ER 341) the question was whether a clause in a will in the following terms was valid: "I authorize and empower my trustees to determine what articles pass under any specific bequest contained in this my will . . . and whether any moneys are to be considered as capital or income and how valuations are to be made and/or value determined for any purpose in connexion with the trusts and provisions of this my will . . . and to apportion blended trust funds and to determine all questions and matters of doubt arising in the execution of the trusts of this my will . . . and I declare that every such determination whether made upon a question actually raised or only implied in the acts and proceedings of . . . my trustees shall be conclusive and binding upon all persons interested under this my will."

Danckwerts J held it void. He said at p. 279: "Not doubt it may be said that it is convenient to have matters regarding the apportionment of capital moneys and the application of moneys in the payment of expenses referred to some informal decision, and that in that way expense may be saved which would be necessarily incurred if the matters had to be referred to the court; but in my view a clause of this kind has no effect if it is attempted to use it so as to prevent the beneficiaries requiring the matter to be decided by the court. As long as the clause is not contested, it may be that the beneficiaries will be content to have the matters dealt with by the trustees in the course of their operations in the administration of the estate; and it may, of course, be that the trustees have applied their minds and carried out their duties in a perfectly proper manner in the way in which they deal with matters connected with the estate; but it seems to me that the result is that any beneficiary is entitled to go to the court to have his rights considered and, if necessary, upheld; and that a testator may not by the provisions of his will exclude the right of the court to decide the matters, even though the trustees have considered them and reached a certain decision."

In *Re Jones* ([1953] Ch 125, [1953] 1 All ER 357) a testator directed his trustees to hold his residuary trust fund after the death of his wife upon trust to purchase an annuity for his daughter Doris Mabel, and he directed that "if at any time . . . my . . . daughter Doris . . . shall in the uncontrolled opinion of the company [the trustees] have social or other relationship with [a certain named person] . . . then in such case as from the occurrence of such event my said daughter . . . shall absolutely forfeit and lose one half of the annuity payments hereinbefore directed to be paid to her . . ." On the question whether the forfeiture clause was valid, DANCKWERTS J held (a) that it was void for uncertainty and (b) that the reference to the opinion of the trustees did not prevent that invalidity. He said (at p. 128): "Unless [the difficulty] is cured by reference to the opinion of the trustees, it seems to me that this clause cannot be regarded as sufficiently certain to be upheld as a forfeiture clause or a condition subsequent. The words in the present case are 'shall in the uncontrolled opinion of the company have social or other relationship'. Mr. Albery has submitted that that surmounts the difficulty, because the guiding factor is not the existence of 'social or other relationship', but the existence of 'the uncontrolled opinion' on the part of the executor company, the bank.

He has referred me to a decision of the House of Lords, which certainly is of great interest in regard to the matter: *Dundee General Hospitals Board of Management v Walker* ([1952] 1 All ER 896 at 898). In that case, in order that a named body should qualify for a legacy, the trustees had to be satisfied as regarded a certain hospital, the Dundee Royal Infirmary, that 'the said infirmary has not been taken over wholly or partly by or otherwise placed under the control of the State or of a local authority or of a body directly or indirectly responsible to the State and/or a local authority'. As Mr. Albery perfectly correctly said, after quoting a well-known observation of Bowen LJ that the state of a man's mind was as much a fact as the state of his digestion, it is the existence of an opinion or the non-existence of a particular opinion on the part of the company, the trustees, which is the test of forfeiture or otherwise in the present case.

In the present case, however, the opinion of the trustees is substituted for the opinion of the court, and it is the trustees who have to decide whether or not a certain obscure and difficult state of facts has occurred; the trustees might be unable to decide the question just as the court might be unable to decide it, and further the court might have to decide the matter or to attempt to decide the matter upon a reference to it by the trustees."

In *Re Tuck's Settlement Trusts* ([1978] 2 WLR 411, [1978] 1 All ER 1047) the settlor provided an income for the holder for the time being of the family baronetcy if and when and so long as he should be of the Jewish faith and married and living with "an approved wife" or, if separated, being so separated through no fault of his. An "approved wife" was defined as a wife of Jewish blood by one or both of her parents, who had been brought up in the Jewish faith, had never departed from it, and, who, at the date of the marriage, continued to worship according to the Jewish faith. The Chief Rabbi in London of either the Portuguese or the Anglo-German community was designated to decide any question as to who was an approved wife, and whether any separation was or was not due to the fault of the baronet.

The question was whether the trusts were void for uncertainty; and whether the reference to the Chief Rabbi was effective, or void as an ouster of the jurisdiction of the court. The Court of Appeal held that the condition was sufficiently certain. On the question whether, if it had been void for uncertainty, the trust would have been saved by the provision making the Chief Rabbi's decision conclusive, Lord DENNING MR referred to *Dundee General Hospitals Board of Management v Walker* [1952] 1 All ER 896 as being a decision "of the highest persuasive value", and continued at p. 417: "I see no reason why a testator or settlor should not provide that any dispute or doubt should be resolved by his executors or trustees, or even by a third person. To prove this, I will first state the law in regard to contracts. Here the general principle is that whenever persons agree together to refer a matter to a third person for decision, and further agree that his decision is to be final and binding upon them, then, so long as he arrives at his decision honestly and in good faith, the two parties are bound by it. . . .

If two contracting parties can by agreement leave a doubt or difficulty to be decided by a third person, I see no reason why a testator or settlor should not leave the decision to his trustees or to a third party. He does not thereby oust the jurisdiction of the court. If the appointed person should find difficulty in the actual wording of the will or settlement, the executors or trustees can always apply to the court for directions so as to assist in the interpretation of it. But if the appointed person is ready and willing to resolve the doubt or difficulty, I see no reason why he should not do so. So long as he does not misconduct himself or come to a decision which is wholly unreasonable, I think his decision should stand. After all, that was plainly the intention of the testator or settlor."

QUESTIONS

1. Consider the dilemma of a disappointed beneficiary, such as the plaintiff in *Re Beloved Wilkes's Charity* ((1851) 3 Mac & G 440, p. 464, ante), who suspects that the trustees' discretion has been wrongly, or even fraudulently, exercised, but can only establish such fact if he can compel the trustees to give their reasons.

   Is this problem insoluble? Compare *Re Londonderry's Settlement* ([1965] Ch 918, [1964] 3 All ER 855, p. 516, post).

2. Assume that you are:
   a) The owner of £100,000 more than you can ever need, and you decide to make a settlement. Whom would you choose as your trustees?
   b) The trustee of a family trust. You are old and doddery, and out of touch with finance and investment. But you are very conscientious and loyal, and in spite of the wish of the other trustees and all the beneficiaries that you resign, you insist on keeping your last

promise to the deceased, made in 1926, that you will look after his affairs. What, if anything, can the other trustees or the beneficiaries do about you?

c) The trustee of a family trust, whose value has quadrupled since 1965. The beneficiaries wish you to resign from the trust, so that some Jersey resident trustees can be appointed, and the trust managed in Jersey. The beneficiaries are all resident in England. What would you do?

14. Duties of Trustees

I. Duty on Becoming Trustee[1]

Parker and Mellows: *Modern Law of Trusts* (3rd Edn, 1975), p. 271

"When a person accepts a trusteeship, he should do four things, and if he fails to do any he may make himself liable for an action for breach of trust. These things are:

(a) acquaint himself with the terms of the trust;

(b) inspect the trust instrument and any other trust deeds;

(c) procure that all the property subject to the trust is vested in the joint names of himself and his co-trustees, and that all title deeds are placed under their joint control; and

(d) in the case of an appointment as a new trustee of an existing trust, to investigate any suspicious circumstances which indicate a prior breach of trust, and to take action to recoup the trust fund if any breach has in fact taken place."

[1] H & M, pp. 454–456; K & S, pp. 230, 242–246; P & M, pp. 271–273; Pettit, pp. 263–265; Snell, pp. 204–206; *Re Strahan* (1856) 8 De GM & G 291; *Harvey v Olliver* (1887) 57 LT 239; *Hallows v Lloyd* (1888) 39 ChD 686; *Re Chapman* (1895) 72 LT 66; *Re Lucking's Will Trusts* [1968] 1 WLR 866, [1967] 3 All ER 726.

RE BROGDEN[2]

(1888) 38 ChD 546 (ChD, NORTH J; CA, COTTON, FRY and LOPES LJJ)

By his will, John Brogden, a successful contractor in Manchester, left substantial legacies to members of his family, and provided that none of them should be payable until five years after his death, nor should money be paid out of the partnership between him and his sons for five years thereafter, unless his sons so required. He also covenanted to pay £10,000 to the trustees of his daughter's (Mrs. Billing's) marriage settlement, within five years of his death. This sum and the legacies were to carry interest meanwhile. John Brogden died on December 9, 1869.

Samuel Budgett was one of the trustees of Mrs. Billing's marriage settlement. He pressed the Brogden brothers on many occasions for payment, before and after the expiration of the five year period. On several occasions security for the payment was given, one of these being in response to an action started by Budgett for the administration of the estate.

The Brogden partnership became increasingly unprosperous. Budgett throughout was trying to avoid disturbances within the family, and any crisis which would upset the solvency of the firm. Eventually the firm became insolvent, and the securities were inadequate. The question was whether Budgett was liable to Mrs. Billing for breach of trust.

Held. Budgett was liable, as he had not taken all possible steps to obtain payment of the £10,000.

COTTON LJ: Now what was the duty of the trustee, Mr. *Budgett*? It was his duty, in my opinion, at the expiration of five years, to call for payment and to take reasonable means of enforcing payment if the executors did not pay the debt and the legacy. And there having been a postponed period during which no steps were to be taken against the partners or against the executors, it was the more his duty at the expiration of that period to assume that the executors had done what it was their duty to do by preparing for paying the debts and paying the legacies of the testator. . . . And, in my opinion, in the case here, it became the duty of Mr. *Budgett* to take active measures immediately after the expiration of the five years—that is immediately the legacy became payable and immediately the debt became payable.

We must therefore consider what he did. The five years expired in the beginning of December, 1874. I do not suggest that during the remainder of that month of December he should have taken any legal proceedings. That would hardly be expected, but what in my opinion he ought to have done, if not in December, 1874, early in the year 1875, was to have demanded payment, and if payment was not made, then he ought to have taken effectual proceedings in order to recover payment both of the legacy and of the debt. I do not say it was his duty to recover them, because that assumes that he could have done so: but in my opinion it was his duty to demand payment of them, and to take effectual proceedings for the purpose of recovering them.

Now, what did he do? On the 12th of December, 1874, Mr. *Billing*, who was anxious, subject to what I shall hereafter mention, to recover

[2] Cf. *Ward v Ward* (1843) 2 HL Cas 777.

payment of the sum settled on his wife and children, wrote to him urging him to see about getting payment of these sums of money. That was on the 12th of December, 1874, and he did nothing as far as one can see—nothing in the way of taking any proceedings at all, till some time in March, 1875. On the 18th of March, 1875, he had an interview with Mr. *Alexander Brogden*, who was the eldest son, and was the senior surviving partner in the firm, and who apparently had the command which his position gave him. Then there is a letter from Mr. *Holmes*. . . . Mr. *Holmes* of Messrs. *Ingle, Cooper & Holmes*, writes a letter on the 18th of March, 1875, to Mr. *Alexander Brogden*, he says this:—[His Lordship read the letter and proceeded:] In my opinion this points to what was the great blot in the proceedings taken by Mr. *Budgett*. He did not say "you must pay". He was willing to enter into negotiations for the purpose of getting security. And what seems to have been proposed—we have not got very satisfactory evidence as to what took place at the interview—was that they should have a charge upon certain shares in order to secure the money. I gather from that letter that he did not direct Mr. *Holmes* to demand the payment: he did not say "do not make any doubt about it: have payment. If you cannot have payment, then let the partners see that I am determined, as being the only independent trustee, to do my duty, and to enforce payment from them by such means as are open to me".

Then we come to two other letters, which are the only other ones I shall read, namely, those from Mr. *Budgett* to Mrs. *Billing* of the 27th of May, 1875, and from Mr. *Budgett* to his solicitors of the 29th June, 1875:—[His Lordship read portions of these letters.] I do not at all say that I have any suspicion that Mr. *Budgett* acted from any self-interested motives, I think it was suggested that his wife had a legacy left to her, and her interests were looked after better than Mrs. *Billing's* interests. I have no such suspicion. What I think is this: it was natural that he should be unwilling to take any active proceedings against his brother-in-law; he trusted him in the belief that this firm, which then stood in good credit, was a perfectly solvent firm, and that the money was safe; and that being so he did not take those proceedings which he ought to have taken to make them understand that it was his duty to obtain payment, and that he must obtain payment from them. He did not take that course, and he takes the risk of whatever the consequences may be.

To proceed with the story. In October, 1875, proceedings were taken, but they were not taken by him. They were taken by his brother, who was a trustee for Mrs. *Budgett*. As I say, I do not at all suggest that that was done to get her any benefit rather than Mrs. *Billing*, but that left the control of the proceedings not in Mr. *Budgett's* hands, and when a settlement was made in March of the following year, it was a settlement only to give security for the legacy and the debt which was due to his brother, the trustee for his wife.

Then, again in May, 1876, he does take proceedings, and does not get any security which can excuse him for the loss of the money, because he took in September, 1876, the security of a leasehold colliery, and although it is possible that if he had at once realized that security in the then state of the market he might have got money enough to pay everything of which he was trustee, yet it was a leasehold colliery; coals went down; there was a difficulty about the rent; the landlord took proceedings; there had to be a large sum paid in order to get that colliery; and when it was realized it realized a sum insufficient to provide for the payment of these sums for which Mr. *Budgett* was trustee. That being so it is said that a trustee who is acting as he was, and not without consulting his solicitor, has never been held liable for what must be considered as an error of judgment.

In my opinion that is not the true way to state the case. If he had determined to get payment for this—if he had applied for payment in such a way as to shew that he meant to have it, and had consulted solicitors as to the best mode of proceeding, that might have been an error of judgment. But the conclusion to which I come, having regard to those letters, is this, that he did not do his duty in requiring payment—demanding it, and taking what he was advised were the best means of enforcing payment at least till the period of October, 1876—a late period, when we consider the state of the market as regards coal and iron. In regard to that the evidence is this; that in 1874 coal was in a very good state, collieries were very valuable property. But, although they were good in 1875, and not quite so good in 1876, both coal and iron then went rapidly down; and although in 1874 and 1875 there was a good state of coal and iron, unhappily at a later period that was not the case.

That decides the first question, with regard to which the rule is well laid down by Lord *Cottenham* in the case of *Clough v Bond* ((1838) 3 My & Cr 490 at 496), that where a trustee does not do that which it is his duty to do, *prima facie* he is answerable for any loss occasioned thereby.

Then comes this question, if any loss is occasioned, on whom does it lie to shew whether any good would have resulted if the trustee had taken proceedings? Is that for the *cestuis que trust*, who are seeking to make Mr. *Budgett* liable, or is it for Mr. *Budgett* to shew that no good would have resulted? Is it for the *cestuis que trust* to shew that he could have got the money, or for Mr. *Budgett* to shew that he could not have got it if he had taken such proceedings as it was his duty to take?

In my opinion it is not for the *cestuis que trust* seeking to make the trustee liable, to shew that if he had done his duty he would have got the money for which they are seeking to make him answerable. It is the trustee who is seeking to excuse himself for the consequences of his breach of duty. It was his duty to take active proceedings if necessary earlier—to take active proceedings by way of action at law, if necessary; and if the trustee is to excuse himself, it is for him to shew that if he had taken proceedings no good would have resulted from it. Once shew that he has neglected his duty and *prima facie* he is answerable for all the consequences of that neglect; and in this case the result has been that only a very small sum could be recovered from the security which he took in the year 1876. That being so, has the trustee made out that if he had taken proceedings against the executors—against those who were carrying on the business, he would not have got any good from it? In my opinion he has not made that out, and my reason for thinking so is this—that at the time of the expiration of the five years, and certainly during the early part of the year 1875—probably up to the autumn of that year, the firm of *Brogden & Sons* was in very good credit. Immediately before the expiration of the five years, as I say, coal and iron had both been, as regards vendors, in a very satisfactory state. Coal was at an extraordinarily high price, and iron was good in the market. . . .

I have therefore come to the conclusion that the decision of Mr. Justice *North* must be affirmed. It is an unfortunate position no doubt for Mr. *Budgett*, and I quite think that he believed that the firm were perfectly solvent, and that he was incurring no risk in letting the money remain with them. He ought not to have trusted them; as he did that and his expectations and those of the family have turned out to be wrong, and he has not shewn that no good would have resulted from his performing his duty by pressing for payment, and if necessary by taking proceedings to enforce payment, he must be held liable.

In *Buttle v Saunders* ([1950] 2 All ER 193)[3] trustees for sale of land had orally agreed to sell it to Mrs. Simpson for £6,142. One of the beneficiaries, Canon Buttle, wished to purchase it for a charity. After all the documents had been prepared for the sale to Mrs. Simpson, but before the contract was signed, Canon Buttle offered £6,500. The trustees felt that they had reached a stage in the negotiation with Mrs. Simpson from which they could not honourably withdraw. Canon Buttle brought this action to restrain the trustees from selling for any price below that which he offered. By a counterclaim, the trustees asked for the directions of the court. WYNN-PARRY J held that the trustees must accept Canon Buttle's offer. He said (at p. 195): "It has been argued on behalf of the trustees that they were justified in the circumstances in not pursuing the offer made by Canon Buttle and in deciding to go forward with the transaction with Mrs. Simpson. It is true that persons who are not in the position of trustees are entitled, if they so desire, to accept a lesser price than that which they might obtain on the sale of property, and not infrequently a vendor, who has gone some lengths in negotiating with a prospective purchaser, decides to close the deal with that purchaser, notwithstanding that he is presented with a higher offer. It redounds to the credit of a man who acts like that in such circumstances. Trustees, however, are not vested with such complete freedom. They have an overriding duty to obtain the best price which they can for their beneficiaries. It would, however, be an unfortunate simplification of the problem if one were to take the view that the mere production of an increased offer at any stage, however late in the negotiations, should throw on the trustees a duty to accept the higher offer and resile from the existing offer. For myself, I think that trustees have such a discretion in the matter as will allow them to act with proper prudence. I can see no reason why trustees should not pray in aid the common-sense rule underlying the old proverb: 'A bird in the hand is worth two in the bush.' I can imagine cases where trustees could

[3] (1950) 14 Conv (NS) 228 (E. H. Bodkin); (1975) 39 Conv (NS) 177 (A. Samuels); *Cuckmere Brick Co Ltd v Mutual Finance Ltd* [1971] Ch 949, [1971] 2 All ER 633; Building Societies Act 1962, s. 36 (1) (a).

properly refuse a higher offer and proceed with a lower offer. Each case must, of necessity, depend on its own facts. In regard to the case now before me, my view is that the trustees and their solicitors acted on an incorrect principle. The only consideration which was present to their minds was that they had gone so far in the negotiations with Mrs. Simpson that they could not properly, from the point of view of commercial morality, resile from those negotiations. That being so, they did not, to any extent, probe Canon Buttle's offer as, in my view, they should have done. It was urged on me that, by pausing to probe his offer, they ran the risk of losing the contract with Mrs. Simpson. On the view of the facts which I take, I do not consider that that was much of a risk. Mrs. Simpson had bought the leasehold term, which was nearing its end, and she was a very anxious purchaser. Equally, Canon Buttle had demonstrated beyond a peradventure that he was a very anxious buyer, and, as it seems to me, the least the trustees should have done would have been to have said to him: 'You have come on the scene at a late stage. You have made this offer well past the eleventh hour. We have advanced negotiations with Mrs. Simpson which can be concluded within a matter of hours. If you are really serious in your offer, you must submit in the circumstances to somewhat stringent terms, and you must be prepared to bind yourself at once to purchase the property for the sum of £6,500 on the terms, so far as applicable, of the draft contract which otherwise would be entered into with Mrs. Simpson.' I have not the slightest doubt but that in the circumstances Canon Buttle would have agreed to those stringent terms and that the matter would have been carried out. The trustees, however, perfectly *bona fide*, maintained their attitude . . ."[4]

QUESTION

What would you have done in Mr. Budgett's place in 1875–76? To what extent would his position have been eased if the Trustee Act 1925, s. 15 (or its predecessor) had been in operation at that time? See p. 525, post. *Re Greenwood* (1911) 105 LT 509; *Re Ezekiel's Settlement Trusts* [1942] Ch 230, [1942] 2 All ER 224.

II. Duty to Invest[5]

A. Express Power of Investment

It is common to give to trustees a wide power of investment.

I. CONSTRUCTION

In *Re Harari's Settlement Trusts* ([1949] 1 All ER 430)[6] a settlement made by Sir Victor Harari, Pasha, gave power to the trustees to retain, or, with his daughter's consent, to sell and invest the proceeds and all other capital moneys subject to the trust "in or upon such investments as to

[4] The property was subsequently ordered to be sold to Mrs. Simpson for £6,600.

[5] H & M, pp. 456–468; K & S, pp. 246–257; P & M, pp. 286–304; Pettit, pp. 265–281; Snell, pp. 206–217.

[6] *Re Peczenik's Settlement Trusts* [1964] 1 WLR 720, [1964] 2 All ER 339.

them may seem fit". The existing investments were certain Egyptian bonds and securities; none was a trustee investment.

The question was whether the provision gave to the trustees power to invest outside the usual range of trustee investments; or whether the power authorised the trustees to exercise their discretion only within the authorised range. JENKINS J held that the trustees were authorised to invest in any investments which they honestly thought to be desirable. He said (at p. 432): "There is, however, a good deal of authority . . . to the effect that investment clauses should be strictly construed and should not be construed as authorising investments outside the trustee range unless they clearly and unambiguously indicate an intention to that effect." He then referred to a number of cases and continued: "That, I think, is a representative collection of the authorities bearing on this topic, and, having given them the best consideration I can, it seems to me that I am left free to construe this settlement according to what I consider to be the natural and proper meaning of the words used in their context, and, so construing the words 'in or upon such investments as to them may seem fit', I see no justification for implying any restriction. I think the trustees have power, under the plain meaning of those words, to invest in any investments which, to adopt Kekewich J's observation, they 'honestly think' are desirable investments for the investment of moneys subject to the trusts of the settlement. To hold otherwise would really be to read words into the settlement which are not there. The wide construction which the words themselves are, in my view, sufficient to bear, is, I think, to some extent, supported by the fact that the investments brought in, in the first place, are non-trustee investments, and also to some small extent by the reference in para. 2 to 'investments money or property representing' the trust fund. There is nothing in those words that one can say is really inconsistent with a limitation on the range of investment to trustee investments, but there is, perhaps, more likelihood of something which in common parlance would be described as 'property' rather than an 'investment' coming into the hands of the trustees in the course of exercising their powers of investment if the range is the unrestricted one rather than the narrow one. The real ground, however, for my decision is the plain and ordinary meaning of the words 'in or upon such investments as to them may seem fit'. Having found nothing in the authorities to constrain me to construe those words otherwise than in accordance with their plain meaning, that is the meaning I propose to place on them".

ii. PRECEDENT

Encyclopaedia of Forms and Precedents (4th Edn) vol. 20, p. 678

"Any capital monies or other monies required to be invested under the trusts hereof may be invested in the names or under the control of the trustees in the purchase of or at interest upon the security of such stocks funds shares securities or other investments or property or interests (whether in possession or in remainder and whether vested or contingent) or in any property of whatsoever nature and wheresoever situate and whether or not involving liability and whether or not producing income (including the purchase of any chattels for use with any of the settled land) and also including the purchase of or (subject to the rules of law as to insurable interest) the effecting and (without prejudice to the powers contained in clause 4 hereof) the keeping up of any policy or policies of insurance (including an endowment policy or endowment policies) on the life or lives of any person or persons as the trustees shall from time to time in their absolute discretion think fit or may be placed and left on deposit with the National Savings Bank or with any bank or building society or other institution carrying on business in the United Kingdom whose business includes the receipt of money on deposit for such period or periods and on such terms as to interest and otherwise in all respects as the trustees shall in the like discretion from time to time think fit PROVIDED that where any such monies are invested in the purchase of any interest in any property which is contingent on any event the trustees may at the same time apply a further sufficient part of the capital monies in purchasing or effecting a policy or policies of insurance against such event for such amount as the trustees shall in their absolute discretion consider appropriate in all the circumstances."[7]

B. Statutory Power

i. AUTHORISED INVESTMENTS

TRUSTEE INVESTMENTS ACT 1961[8]

1. New powers of investment of trustees.—(1) A trustee may invest any property in his hands, whether at the time in a state of investment or not, in any manner specified in Part I or II of the First Schedule to this Act or, subject to the next following section, in any manner specified in Part III of that Schedule, and may also from time to time vary any such investments.

(2) The supplemental provisions contained in Part IV of that Schedule shall have effect for the interpretation and for restricting the operation of the said Parts I to III.

(3) No provision relating to the powers of the trustee contained in any instrument (not being an enactment or an instrument made under an enactment) made before the passing of this Act shall limit the powers conferred by this section, but those powers are exerciseable only in so far as a contrary intention is not expressed in any Act or instrument made under an enactment, whenever passed or made, and so relating or in any other instrument so relating which is made after the passing of this Act.

For the purposes of this subsection any rule of the law of Scotland whereby a testamentary writing may be deemed to be made on a date other than that on which it was actually executed shall be disregarded.

(4) In this Act "narrower-range investment" means an investment falling

[7] For alternative forms of investment clauses, see Forms 1:F:1 to 1:F:20.

[8] See (1961) 25 Conv (NS) 372 (A. Samuels); and, for an American view, 1954 CLP 139 (V. Latham); (1974) 23 ICLQ 748 (D. Grash); Model Prudent Man Investment Act (1961), reproduced in (1974) 23 ICLQ at pp. 767–8; (1975) 39 Conv (NS) 327 (D. Paling); see also (1976) American Bar Foundation Research Journal 1 (J. H. Langbein and R. A. Posner). For the application of the Act to the investment of a superannuation fund's moneys under the Local Government Superannuation Regulations 1974, see S.I. 1974 No. 520, Part B, reg. B6 (1), Sch. 2.

within Part I or II of the First Schedule to this Act and "wider-range investment" means an investment falling within Part III of that Schedule.

2. Restrictions on wider-range investment.—(1) A trustee shall not have power by virtue of the foregoing section to make or retain any wider-range investment unless the trust fund has been divided into two parts (hereinafter referred to as the narrower-range part and the wider-range part), the parts being, subject to the provisions of this Act, equal in value at the time of the division; and where such a division has been made no subsequent division of the same fund shall be made for the purposes of this section, and no property shall be transferred from one part of the fund to the other unless either—

(*a*) the transfer is authorised or required by the following provisions of this Act, or

(*b*) a compensating transfer is made at the same time.

In this section "compensating transfer", in relation to any transferred property, means a transfer in the opposite direction of property of equal value.

(2) Property belonging to the narrower-range part of a trust fund shall not by virtue of the foregoing section be invested except in narrower-range investments, and any property invested in any other manner which is or becomes comprised in that part of the trust fund shall either be transferred to the wider-range part of the fund, with a compensating transfer, or be reinvested in narrower-range investments as soon as may be.

(3) Where any property accrues to a trust fund after the fund has been divided in pursuance of subsection (1) of this section, then—

(*a*) if the property accrues to the trustee as owner or former owner of property comprised in either part of the fund[9], it shall be treated as belonging to that part of the fund;

(*b*) in any other case, the trustee shall secure, by apportionment of the accruing property or the transfer of property from one part of the fund to the other, or both, that the value of each part of the fund is increased by the same amount.

Where a trustee acquires property in consideration of a money payment the acquisition of the property shall be treated for the purposes of this section as investment and not as the accrual of property to the trust fund, notwithstanding that the amount of the consideration is less than the value of the property acquired[10]; and paragraph (*a*) of this subsection shall not include the case of a dividend or interest becoming part of a trust fund.

(4) Where in the exercise of any power or duty of a trustee property falls to be taken out of the trust fund, nothing in this section shall restrict his discretion as to the choice of property to be taken out.

[9] As a "bonus issue" of shares.

[10] As a "rights issue": which is thus added to the part of the fund which makes the purchase.

FIRST SCHEDULE

Section 1.

Manner of Investment

Part I

Narrower-Range Investments not Requiring Advice

1. In Defence Bonds, National Savings Certificates and Ulster Savings Certificates, Ulster Development Bonds[11], National Development Bonds[12] and British Savings Bonds[13].

2. In deposits in the National Savings Bank[14], and deposits in a bank or department thereof certified under subsection (3) of section nine of the Finance Act, 1956[15].

Part II

Narrower-Range Investments Requiring Advice

1. In securities issued by Her Majesty's Government in the United Kingdom, the Government of Northern Ireland or the Government of the Isle of Man, not being securities falling within Part I of this Schedule and being fixed-interest securities registered in the United Kingdom or the Isle of Man, Treasury Bills or Tax Reserve Certificates or any variable interest securities issued by Her Majesty's Government in the United Kingdom and registered in the United Kingdom[16].

2. In any securities the payment of interest on which is guaranteed by Her Majesty's Government in the United Kingdom or the Government of Northern Ireland.

3. In fixed-interest securities issued in the United Kingdom by any public authority or nationalised industry or undertaking in the United Kingdom.

4. In fixed-interest securities issued in the United Kingdom by the government of any overseas territory within the Commonwealth or by any public or local authority within such a territory, being securities registered in the United Kingdom.

References in this paragraph to an overseas territory or to the government of such a territory shall be construed as if they occurred in the Overseas Service Act, 1958.

4A. In securities issued in the United Kingdom by the government of an overseas territory within the Commonwealth or by any public or local authority within such a territory, being securities registered in the United Kingdom and in respect of which the rate of interest is variable by reference to one or more of the following:—

(*a*) the Bank of England's minimum lending rate;
(*b*) the average rate of discount on allotment on 91-day Treasury bills;
(*c*) a yield on 91-day Treasury bills;
(*d*) a London sterling inter-bank offered rate;

[11] Trustee Investments (Additional Powers) (No. 2) Order 1962, S.I. 1962 No. 2611.
[12] Trustee Investments (Additional Powers) Order 1964, S.I. 1964 No. 703.
[13] Trustee Investments (Additional Powers) Order 1968, S.I. 1968 No. 470.
[14] Post Office Act 1969, ss. 94, 114, Sch. 6, Part III.
[15] See now I.C.T.A. 1970, s. 414 (3), (5); Birmingham Municipal Bank S.I. 1958 No. 932, S.I. 1959 No. 300; S.I. 1970 No. 1742.
[16] Trustee Investments (Additional Powers) Order 1977, S.I. 1977 No. 831.

(*e*) a London sterling certificate of deposit rate.

References in this paragraph to an overseas territory or to the government of such a territory shall be construed as if they occurred in the Overseas Service Act, 1958[17].

5. In fixed-interest securities issued in the United Kingdom by the International Bank for Reconstruction and Development, being securities registered in the United Kingdom, and in fixed-interest securities issued in the United Kingdom by the Inter-American Development Bank[18], and in fixed-interest securities issued in the United Kingdom by the European Investment Bank, or by the European Coal and Steel Community[19], being securities registered in the United Kingdom.

5A. In securities issued in the United Kingdom by

(i) the International Bank for Reconstruction and Development or by the European Investment Bank or by the European Coal and Steel Community, being securities registered in the United Kingdom or

(ii) the Inter-American Development Bank

being securities in respect of which the rate of interest is variable by reference to one or more of the following:—

(*a*) the Bank of England's minimum lending rate;

(*b*) the average rate of discount on allotment on 91-day Treasury bills;

(*c*) a yield on 91-day Treasury bills;

(*d*) a London sterling inter-bank offered rate;

(*e*) a London sterling certificate of deposit rate[20].

6. In debentures issued in the United Kingdom by a company incorporated in the United Kingdom, being debentures registered in the United Kingdom.

7. In stock of the Bank of Ireland and in Bank of Ireland 7 per cent. Loan Stock 1986/91[21].

8. In debentures issued by the Agricultural Mortgage Corporation Limited or the Scottish Agricultural Securities Corporation Limited.

9. In loans to any authority to which this paragraph applies charged on all or any of the revenues of the authority or on a fund into which all or any of those revenues are payable, in any fixed-interest securities issued in the United Kingdom by any such authority for the purpose of borrowing money so charged, and in deposits with any such authority by way of temporary loan made on the giving of a receipt for the loan by the treasurer or other similar officer of the authority and on the giving of an undertaking by the authority that, if requested to charge the loan as aforesaid, it will either comply with the request or repay the loan.

This paragraph applies to the following authorities, that is to say—

(*a*) any local authority in the United Kingdom;

[17] Trustee Investments (Additional Powers) (No. 2) Order 1977, S.I. 1977 No. 1878.

[18] Trustee Investments (Additional Powers) (No. 2) Order 1964, S.I. 1964 No. 1404.

[19] Trustee Investments (Additional Powers) Order 1972, S.I. 1972 No. 1818.

[20] Trustee Investments (Additional Powers) (No. 2) Order 1977, S.I. 1977 No. 1878.

[21] Trustee Investments (Additional Powers) Order 1966, S.I. 1966 No. 401.

(*b*) any authority all the members of which are appointed or elected by one or more local authorities in the United Kingdom;

(*c*) any authority the majority of the members of which are appointed or elected by one or more local authorities in the United Kingdom, being an authority which by virtue of any enactment has power to issue a precept to a local authority in England and Wales, or a requisition to a local authority in Scotland, or to the expenses of which, by virtue of any enactment, a local authority in the United Kingdom is or can be required to contribute;

(*d*) the Receiver for the Metropolitan Police District or a combined police authority (within the meaning of the Police Act, 1946[22]);

(*e*) the Belfast City and District Water Commissioners;

(*f*) the Great Ouse Water Authority[23];

(*g*) any district council in Northern Ireland[1].

9A. In any securities issued in the United Kingdom by any authority to which paragraph 9 applies for the purpose of borrowing money charged on all or any of the revenues of the authority or on a fund into which all or any of those revenues are payable and being securities in respect of which the rate of interest is variable by reference to one or more of the following:—

(*a*) the Bank of England's minimum lending rate;

(*b*) the average rate of discount on allotment on 91-day Treasury bills;

(*c*) a yield on 91-day Treasury bills;

(*d*) a London sterling inter-bank offered rate;

(*e*) a London sterling certificate of deposit rate[2];

10. In debentures or in the guaranteed or preference stock of any incorporated company, being statutory water undertakers within the meaning of the Water Act, 1945[3], or any corresponding enactment in force in Northern Ireland, and having during each of the ten years immediately preceding the calendar year in which the investment was made paid a dividend of not less than 3½ per cent.[4] on its ordinary shares.

12. In deposits in a building society designated under section one of the House Purchase and Housing Act, 1959[5].

13. In mortgages of freehold property in England and Wales or Northern Ireland and of leasehold property in those countries of which the unexpired term at the time of investment is not less than sixty years, and in loans on heritable security in Scotland.

14. In perpetual rent-charges charged on land in England and Wales

[22] See now the Police Act 1964.

[23] Trustee Investments (Additional Powers) Order 1962, S.I. 1962 No. 658. By the Water Resources Act 1963, s. 6 (6) and Sch. 4, para. 33, any river which, apart from that para., would not be included among the authorities to which para. 9 applies is, by virtue of that Act, included among those authorities.

[1] Trustee Investments (Additional Powers) Order 1973, S.I. 1973 No. 1332.

[2] Trustee Investments (Additional Powers) (No. 2) Order 1977, S.I. 1977 No. 1878.

[3] As amended by Water Act 1948, s. 1.

[4] Replacing 5 per cent. from 1973. (Trustee Investments (Water Companies) Order 1973, S.I. 1973 No. 1393).

[5] See Building Societies (Designation for Trustee Investment) Regulations 1964, S.I. 1964 No. 1354, 1972, S.I. 1972 No. 1577 and 1977, S.I. 1977 No. 1207. At the end of 1976, there were 211 designated societies representing over 99 per cent. of the total assets of the Building Society Movement: Report of the Chief Registrar of Friendly Societies 1976, Part II, p. 21.

or Northern Ireland and fee-farm rents (not being rent-charges) issuing out of such land, and in feu-duties or ground annuals in Scotland.

15. In certificates of tax deposit[6].

PART III

WIDER-RANGE INVESTMENTS

1. In any securities issued in the United Kingdom by a company incorporated in the United Kingdom, being securities registered in the United Kingdom and not being securities falling within Part II of this Schedule.

2. In shares in any building society designated under section one of the House Purchase and Housing Act, 1959.

3. In any units, or other shares of the investments subject to the trusts, of a unit trust scheme in the case of which there is in force at the time of investment an order of the Board of Trade under section seventeen of the Prevention of Fraud (Investments) Act, 1958, or of the Ministry of Commerce for Northern Ireland under section sixteen of the Prevention of Fraud (Investments) Act (Northern Ireland), 1940.

PART IV

SUPPLEMENTAL

1. The securities mentioned in Parts I to III of this Schedule do not include any securities where the holder can be required to accept repayment of the principal, or the payment of any interest, otherwise than in sterling.

2. The securities mentioned in paragraphs 1 to 8 of Part II, other than Treasury Bills or Tax Reserve Certificates, securities issued before the passing of this Act by the Government of the Isle of Man, securities falling within paragraph 4 of the said Part II issued before the passing of this Act or securities falling within paragraph 9 of that Part, and the securities mentioned in paragraph 1 of Part III of this Schedule, do not include—

(*a*) securities the price of which is not quoted on a recognised stock exchange within the meaning of the Prevention of Fraud (Investments) Act, 1958, or the Belfast stock exchange;

(*b*) shares or debenture stock not fully paid up (except shares or debenture stock which by the terms of issue are required to be fully paid up within nine months of the date of issue).

3. The securities mentioned in paragraph 6 of Part II and paragraph 1 of Part III of this Schedule do not include—

(*a*) shares or debentures of an incorporated company of which the total issued and paid up share capital is less than one million pounds;

(*b*) shares or debentures of an incorporated company which has not in each of the five years immediately preceding the calendar year in which the investment is made paid a dividend on all the shares issued by the company, excluding any shares issued after the dividend was declared and any shares which by their terms of issue did not rank for the dividend for that year.

For the purposes of sub-paragraph (*b*) of this paragraph a company formed—

[6] Trustee Investments (Additional Powers) Order 1975, S.I. 1975 No. 1710.

(i) to take over the business of another company or other companies, or

(ii) to acquire the securities of, or control of, another company or other companies,

or for either of those purposes and for other purposes shall be deemed to have paid a dividend as mentioned in that sub-paragraph in any year in which such a dividend has been paid by the other company or all the other companies, as the case may be[7].

ii. SPECIAL RANGE

TRUSTEE INVESTMENTS ACT 1961

3. Relationship between Act and other powers of investment.—(1) The powers conferred by section one of this Act are in addition to and not in derogation from any power conferred otherwise than by this Act of investment or postponing conversion exerciseable by a trustee (hereinafter referred to as a "special power").

(2) Any special power (however expressed) to invest property in any investment for the time being authorised by law for the investment of trust property, being a power conferred on a trustee before the passing of this Act or conferred on him under any enactment passed before the passing of this Act, shall have effect as a power to invest property in like manner and subject to the like provisions as under the foregoing provisions of this Act.

(3) In relation to property, including wider-range but not including narrower-range investments,—

(*a*) which a trustee is authorised to hold apart from—

(i) the provisions of section one of this Act or any of the provisions of Part I of the Trustee Act, 1925, or any of the provisions of the Trusts (Scotland) Act, 1921, or

(ii) any such power to invest in authorised investments as is mentioned in the foregoing subsection, or

(*b*) which became part of a trust fund in consequence of the exercise by the trustee, as owner of property falling within this subsection, of any power conferred by subsection (3) or (4) of section ten of the Trustee Act, 1925, or paragraph (*o*) or (*p*) of subsection (1) of section four of the Trusts (Scotland) Act, 1921,

the foregoing section shall have effect subject to the modifications set out in the Second Schedule to this Act.

SECOND SCHEDULE Section 3.

MODIFICATION OF S. 2 IN RELATION TO PROPERTY FALLING WITHIN S. 3 (3)

1. In this Schedule "special-range property" means property falling within subsection (3) of section three of this Act.

2.—(1) Where a trust fund includes special-range property, subsection (1) of section two of this Act shall have effect as if references to the trust

[7] For further details and definitions, see paras. 4–7.

fund were references to so much thereof as does not consist of special-range property, and the special-range property shall be carried to a separate part of the fund.

(2) Any property which—

(*a*) being property belonging to the narrower-range or wider-range part of a trust fund, is converted into special-range property, or

(*b*) being special-range property, accrues to a trust fund after the division of the fund or part thereof in pursuance of subsection (1) of section two of this Act or of that subsection as modified by sub-paragraph (1) of this paragraph,

shall be carried to such a separate part of the fund as aforesaid; and subsections (2) and (3) of the said section two shall have effect subject to this sub-paragraph.

(3) Where property carried to such a separate part as aforesaid is converted into property other than special-range property,—

(*a*) it shall be transferred to the narrower-range part of the fund or the wider-range part of the fund or apportioned between them, and

(*b*) any transfer of property from one of those parts to the other shall be made which is necessary to secure that the value of each of those parts of the fund is increased by the same amount.

3. Relationship between Act and other powers of investment.—(4) The foregoing subsection[8] shall not apply where the powers of the trustee to invest or postpone conversion have been conferred or varied—

(*a*) by an order of any court made within the period of ten years ending with the passing of this Act, or

(*b*) by any enactment passed, or instrument having effect under an enactment made, within that period, being an enactment or instrument relating specifically to the trusts in question; or

(*c*) by an enactment contained in a local Act of the present Session;

but the provisions of the Third Schedule to this Act shall have effect in a case falling within this subsection.

THIRD SCHEDULE

Section 3.

Provisions Supplementary to s. 3 (4)

1. Where in a case falling within subsection (4) of section three of this Act, property belonging to the narrower-range part of a trust fund—

(*a*) is invested otherwise than in a narrower-range investment, or

(*b*) being so invested, is retained and not transferred or as soon as may be reinvested as mentioned in subsection (2) of section two of this Act,

then, so long as the property continues so invested and comprised in the narrower-range part of the fund, section one of this Act shall not authorise the making or retention of any wider-range investment.

2. Section four of the Trustee Act, 1925, or section thirty-three of the Trusts (Scotland) Act, 1921 (which relieve a trustee from liability for retaining an investment which has ceased to be authorised), shall not apply

[8] Section 3 (3), p. 485, ante.

where an investment ceases to be authorised in consequence of the foregoing paragraph.

iii. VALUATION FOR PURPOSES OF SECTIONS 2–4

TRUSTEE INVESTMENTS ACT 1961

5. Certain valuations to be conclusive for purposes of division of trust fund.—(1) If for the purposes of section two or four of this Act or the Second Schedule thereto a trustee obtains, from a person reasonably believed by the trustee to be qualified to make it, a valuation in writing of any property, the valuation shall be conclusive in determining whether the division of the trust fund in pursuance of subsection (1) of the said section two, or any transfer or apportionment of property under that section or the said Second Schedule, has been duly made.

(2) The foregoing subsection applies to any such valuation notwithstanding that it is made by a person in the course of his employment as an officer or servant.

iv. METHOD OF SELECTION

TRUSTEE INVESTMENTS ACT 1961

4. Interpretation of references to trust property and trust funds.—(1) In this Act "property" includes real or personal property of any description, including money and things in action:

Provided that it does not include an interest in expectancy, but the falling into possession of such an interest, or the receipt of proceeds of the sale thereof, shall be treated for the purposes of this Act as an accrual of property to the trust fund.

(2) So much of the property in the hands of a trustee shall for the purposes of this Act constitute one trust fund as is held on trusts which (as respects the beneficiaries or their respective interests or the purposes of the trust or as respects the powers of the trustee) are not identical with those on which any other property in his hands is held.

(3) Where property is taken out of a trust fund by way of appropriation so as to form a separate fund, and at the time of the appropriation the trust fund had (as to the whole or a part thereof) been divided in pursuance of subsection (1) of section two of this Act, or that subsection as modified by the Second Schedule to this Act, then if the separate fund is so divided the narrower-range and wider-range parts of the separate fund may be constituted so as either to be equal, or to bear to each other the same proportion as the two corresponding parts of the fund out of which it was so appropriated (the values of those parts of those funds being ascertained as at the time of appropriation), or some intermediate proportion.

(4) In the application of this section to Scotland the following subsection shall be substituted for subsection (1) thereof:—

"(1) In this Act 'property' includes property of any description (whether heritable or moveable, corporeal or incorporeal) which is presently enjoyable, but does not include a future interest, whether vested or contingent."

6. Duty of trustees in choosing investments.—(1) In the exercise of his powers of investment a trustee shall have regard—

(*a*) to the need for diversification of investments of the trust, in so far as is appropriate to the circumstances of the trust;

(*b*) to the suitability to the trust of investments of the description of investment proposed and of the investment proposed as an investment of that description.

(2) Before exercising any power conferred by section one of this Act to invest in a manner specified in Part II or III of the First Schedule to this Act, or before investing in any such manner in the exercise of a power falling within subsection (2) of section three of this Act, a trustee shall obtain and consider proper advice on the question whether the investment is satisfactory having regard to the matters mentioned in paragraphs (*a*) and (*b*) of the foregoing subsection.

(3) A trustee retaining any investment made in the exercise of such a power and in such a manner as aforesaid shall determine at what intervals the circumstances, and in particular the nature of the investment, make it desirable to obtain such advice as aforesaid, and shall obtain and consider such advice accordingly.

(4) For the purposes of the two foregoing subsections, proper advice is the advice of a person who is reasonably believed by the trustee to be qualified by his ability in and practical experience of financial matters; and such advice may be given by a person notwithstanding that he gives it in the course of his employment as an officer or servant.

(5) A trustee shall not be treated as having complied with subsection (2) or (3) of this section unless the advice was given or has been subsequently confirmed in writing.

(6) Subsections (2) and (3) of this section shall not apply to one of two or more trustees where he is the person giving the advice required by this section to his co-trustee or co-trustees, and shall not apply where powers of a trustee are lawfully exercised by an officer or servant competent under subsection (4) of this section to give proper advice.

(7) Without prejudice to section eight of the Trustee Act, 1925, or section thirty of the Trusts (Scotland) Act, 1921 (which relate to valuation, and the proportion of the value to be lent, where a trustee lends on the security of property) the advice required by this section shall not include, in the case of a loan on the security of freehold or leasehold property in England and Wales or Northern Ireland or on heritable security in Scotland, advice on the suitability of the particular loan.

15. Saving for powers of court.—The enlargement of the investment powers of trustees by this Act shall not lessen any power of a court to confer wider powers of investment on trustees, or affect the extent to which any such power is to be exercised[9].

---

[9] But in the absence of special circumstances, the court will not confer wider investment powers than those contained in the Act: *Re Cooper's Settlement* [1962] Ch 826, [1961] 3 All ER 636; *Re Kolb's Will Trusts* [1962] Ch 531, [1961] 3 All ER 811; *Re Clarke's Will Trusts* [1961] 1 WLR 1471, [1961] 3 All ER 1133; *Re University of London Charitable Trusts* [1964] Ch 282, [1963] 3 All ER 859.

The trustee's duty in the selection of authorised investments was explained by Lord WATSON in *Learoyd v Whiteley* (1887) 12 App Cas 727, p. 432, ante.

C. Mortgages of Land[10]

i. AUTHORISED INVESTMENTS

TRUSTEE INVESTMENTS ACT 1961

FIRST SCHEDULE

Part II, para. 13, see p. 481, ante.

Lewin on Trusts (16th Edn, 1964) pp. 370–371

"Before August 3, 1961, the rule was that trustees should not invest on second, contributory or equitable mortgages, . . . but it is at least doubtful whether this rule has survived the commencement of the Trustee Investments Act, 1961, on the above date. For investment 'in mortgages of freehold property . . . and of leasehold property' with sixty years to run is a narrower-range investment not requiring advice under that Act, and, unless the context otherwise requires, 'mortgage' has the same meaning as in the Trustee Act, 1925[11], in which it relates to 'every estate and interest regarded in equity as merely a security for money'[12]. There does not seem to be anything in the context of the Act of 1961 (whose object is plainly to increase trustees' powers) to require a more limited meaning to be put on 'mortgages' in the relevant provision, and it is submitted that the effect of the Act is to sweep away the old provisions on inferior types of mortgage.

But if the legislature intended this, it was a strong thing to do with a referential interpretation section, and in case the above submission is wrong as well as to cover pre-1961 mortgages the old rules are now discussed. . . ."

ii. VALUATION

TRUSTEE ACT 1925

8. Loans and investments by trustees not chargeable as breaches of trust. —(1) A trustee lending money on the security of any property on which he can properly lend shall not be chargeable with breach of trust by reason only of the proportion borne by the amount of the loan to the value of the property at the time when the loan was made, if it appears to the court—

(*a*) that in making the loan the trustee was acting upon a report as to the value of the property made by a person whom he reasonably believed to be an able practical surveyor or valuer instructed and employed independently of any owner of the property, whether such surveyor or

[10] H & M, pp. 466–468; K & S, pp. 251–254; P & M, pp. 304–308; Pettit, pp. 274–277; Snell, pp. 211–213.

[11] See Trustee Investments Act 1961, s. 17 (4).

[12] See T.A. 1925, s. 68 (7).

valuer carried on business in the locality where the property is situate or elsewhere; and

(*b*) that the amount of the loan does not exceed two third parts of the value of the property as stated in the report; and

(*c*) that the loan was made under the advice of the surveyor or valuer expressed in the report.

(2) A trustee lending money on the security of any leasehold property shall not be chargeable with breach of trust only upon the ground that in making such loan he dispensed either wholly or partly with the production or investigation of the lessor's title.

10. Powers supplementary to powers of investment.—(1) Trustees lending money on the security of any property on which they can lawfully lend may contract that such money shall not be called in during any period not exceeding seven years from the time when the loan was made, provided interest be paid within a specified time not exceeding thirty days after every half-yearly or other day on which it becomes due, and provided there be no breach of any covenant by the mortgagor contained in the instrument of mortgage or charge for the maintenance and protection of the property.

(2) On a sale of land for an estate in fee simple or for a term having at least five hundred years to run by trustees or by a tenant for life or statutory owner, the trustees, or the tenant for life or statutory owner on behalf of the trustees of the settlement, may, where the proceeds are liable to be invested, contract that the payment of any part, not exceeding two-thirds, of the purchase money shall be secured by a charge by way of legal mortgage or a mortgage by demise or sub-demise for a term of at least five hundred years (less a nominal reversion when by sub-demise), of the land sold, with or without the security of any other property, such charge or mortgage, if any buildings are comprised in the mortgage, to contain a covenant by the mortgagor to keep them insured against loss or damage by fire to the full value thereof.

The trustees shall not be bound to obtain any report as to the value of the land or other property to be comprised in such charge or mortgage, or any advice as to the making of the loan, and shall not be liable for any loss which may be incurred by reason only of the security being insufficient at the date of the charge or mortgage; and the trustees of the settlement shall be bound to give effect to such contract made by the tenant for life or statutory owner.

iii. EXTENT OF LIABILITY

TRUSTEE ACT 1925

9. Liability for loss by reason of improper investment.—(1) Where a trustee improperly advances trust money on a mortgage security which would at the time of the investment be a proper investment in all respects for a smaller sum than is actually advanced thereon, the security shall be deemed an authorised investment for the smaller sum, and the trustee shall only be liable to make good the sum advanced in excess thereof with interest.

(2) This section applies to investments made before as well as after the commencement of this Act.

SHAW v CATES
[1909] 1 Ch 389 (ChD, Parker J)

A valuation was made of land in Folkestone which contained two houses which were built and occupied, and two others in the course of construction. They were valued at £9,180 by one Barton, and recommended as suitable for a mortgage up to two-thirds of that sum. A schedule to the report gave the separate values of the four properties. After inspection the trustees, without further consulting the valuer, lent £4,400 on the security of the partially constructed houses, the sum being exactly two-thirds of the value as shown in the schedule.

Barton was also the rent-collector of the mortgagor. No covenant was given by the mortgagor to keep the premises in repair. The premises deteriorated, and, on the bankruptcy of the mortgagor, proved to be an inadequate security.

The beneficiaries sought to hold the trustees liable for the whole sum involved.

Held. The trustees were liable for the excess.

PARKER J: In this action the beneficiaries under the will of a Mrs. Davis, who died in June, 1891, ask to have the defendant Cates, a trustee of the will, and the estate of Mildred Whiteley, deceased, a former trustee of the will, declared liable for breach of trust in respect of the investment on October 22, 1897, of 4400*l*., part of the trust moneys on the security of a legal mortgage of certain freehold houses in Shorncliffe Road, Folkestone. The beneficiaries contend (1) that this investment was altogether improper, because, having regard to the nature of the property, it was too hazardous to be accepted as a trust investment; and (2) that, even if otherwise proper to be accepted as a trust investment, it was not a proper investment for so large a sum as 4400*l*.

The defendants join issue on both these contentions, and, as to the second contention, further say that they are entitled to the protection of s. 8 of the Trustee Act, 1893,[13] or at any rate that the defendant Cates and Mildred Whiteley, in making the investment in question, acted honestly and reasonably, taking all the precautions which a man of ordinary prudence might have been expected to take in the conduct of his own affairs, and relying, as they were entitled to rely, on expert advice as to values; and further, if those defences fail, they ask to be wholly relieved from liability for breach of trust under s. 3 of the Judicial Trustees Act, 1896[14], or to be partially relieved from such liability by virtue of s. 9 of the Trustee Act, 1893[15].

It is clear that the trustees had in the present case power to invest upon the security of freehold hereditaments. The onus, therefore, of proving that the investment in question was altogether too hazardous to be accepted

[13] T.A. 1925, s. 8, p. 489, ante.
[14] T.A. 1925, s. 61, p. 622, post.
[15] T.A. 1925, s. 9, p. 490, ante.

as a trust investment lies upon the plaintiffs. In my opinion they have not discharged this onus. . . .

Section 4 of the Trustee Act, 1888[16] somewhat modified the law as above stated. It provided as follows: "No trustee lending money upon the security of any property shall be chargeable with breach of trust by reason only of the proportion borne by the amount of the loan to the value of such property at the time when the loan was made, provided that it shall appear to the Court that in making such loan the trustee was acting upon a report as to the value of the property made by a person whom the trustee reasonably believed to be an able practical surveyor or valuer, instructed and employed independently of any owner of the property, whether such surveyor or valuer carried on business in the locality where the property is situate or elsewhere, and that the amount of the loan does not exceed two equal third parts of the value of the property as stated in such report, and that the loan was made under the advice of such surveyor or valuer expressed in such report." Since the Act, therefore, a trustee has been, and is, justified in acting on expert advice, not only as to the value of the property, but also as to the amount he may properly advance thereon, provided the advice be given in such manner, and by such person, as is contemplated in the section, and that, whatever be the nature of the property, the amount advanced is not more than two thirds of its value. The principle involved seems to be that within the limits of what is often called the "two thirds" rule a prudent man may, as to the amount which can properly be advanced on any proposed security, whether the property be agricultural land or houses or buildings used for trade purposes, rely on expert advice obtained with certain precautions, it being of course assumed that in giving the advice the expert will consider all the circumstances of the case, including the nature of the property, and will not advise a larger advance than under all the circumstances can be prudently made. I dissent entirely from the position taken up by some of the defendants' expert witnesses, that when once they have ascertained the value of the property they are, whatever its nature and whatever method of valuation they have adopted, at least prima facie justified in advising an advance of two thirds of its value. Such a position in my opinion defeats the object of the section by making what the Legislature has recognized as the standard of the minimum protection which a prudent man will require into a standard of the normal risk which, whatever the nature of the property, a prudent man will be prepared to run; and it deprives the expert advice on which the trustee is to rely as to the margin of protection to be required of all its value. It is as true now as it was before the Act that the maximum sum which a prudent man can be advised to lend upon a mortgage depends on the nature of the property and upon all the circumstances of the case. If the property is liable to deteriorate or is specially subject to fluctuations in value, or depends for its value on circumstances the continual existence of which is precarious, a prudent man will now, as much as before the Act, require a larger margin for his protection than he would in the case of property attended by no such

[16] T.A. 1925, s. 8, p. 489, ante.

disadvantages, and an expert who does his duty will take this into consideration. . . .

I have come to the conclusion that, under the circumstances which I have shortly stated, Mr. Barton's report is not such a report as was contemplated by the Act. To advise an advance of two thirds of the value of four properties is not the same thing as advising an advance of two thirds of the value of any one or more of the properties apart from the others or other. This is more especially the case where one of the properties is not at the date of the report an income-bearing property. As I have already pointed out, the amount of income which a property is producing is material in considering what amount can properly be advanced thereon. In the present case the income of three of the four properties originally proposed to be mortgaged was sufficient to provide, with a considerable margin, for the payment of interest on the amount proposed to be advanced, although the other property was unlet. The importance of this point was fully recognized by Beckingsale & Co. when considering the propriety of an advance on the first three properties mentioned in the report only, the income of which was more than sufficient to provide for the interest. I cannot explain why they no longer thought it of consequence when they came to consider the propriety of an advance on the first two properties, the existing income from which did not amount to the interest on the proposed advance.

In my opinion the advance which was actually made was not the advance which Mr. Barton advised, and his report, therefore, cannot be relied on as within s. 8 of the Trustee Act, 1893. Again, I do not think that Mr. Barton was in fact instructed and employed independently of the mortgagor. He was suggested by the mortgagor, instructed by the mortgagor's solicitors, referred to the mortgagor both as to his fee and as to the properties he was to value, and was accompanied by the mortgagor when he made his survey. I am not suggesting that he was consciously influenced by the mortgagor or that he acted otherwise than honestly in the matter, but I do not think that he in fact fulfilled the conditions mentioned in the section as to his instructions and employment. If, according to the true meaning of the section, the belief of the trustees is the material point, I am unable to hold that the trustees did reasonably believe that Mr. Barton was instructed and employed independently of the mortgagor. They left the instructions to be given by Beckingsale & Co., who were also the mortgagor's solicitors, and after ascertaining that Mr. Barton was a competent person took no further trouble in the matter.

Lastly, it appears that one of the properties which Mr. Barton in fact valued differed from that actually comprised in the mortgage, because Mr. Barton valued a property with an easement of access across other land of the mortgagor, whereas the mortgage contained no such easement. I need not express an opinion whether this alone would, under the circumstances, have prevented the trustees from relying on the section. I mention it because the fact seems to me to illustrate the importance of the surveyor who makes the valuation being independently instructed and employed. In valuing for the mortgagor, and on information supplied by the mortgagor, it might have been immaterial to mention this suggested easement, the proposed dominant and proposed servient tenement being in the same hands. In valuing for a mortgage of the proposed dominant tenement it was a point of great importance, and yet there is no mention of it in Mr. Barton's report, and because of this omission, coupled with the subsequent readiness of the solicitors to accept the mortgagor's statement of the property to be included in the mortgage, the mortgagees have got a property without an easement, whereas Mr. Barton valued it with an easement. I very much doubt whether this could have happened if the surveyor who made the valuation had been instructed and employed independently of the mortgagor, and had not in talking matters over with the mortgagor been influenced by the mortgagor's view of how he could deal with his various properties to the best advantage, as opposed to the question what the mortgagee of one of these properties could make of it.

If, apart from s. 8 of the Trustee Act, 1893, I ask myself whether in the matter of this mortgage the trustees acted reasonably and took all the precautions which a prudent man acting in his own affairs might be expected to have taken, I can only answer the question in the negative. In leaving Mr. Barton to be instructed by their solicitors, whom they knew to be acting for the mortgagor, in taking no means to see that he was properly instructed or that he was instructed and employed independently of the mortgagor, in not themselves considering the surveyor's report when made, but leaving it to their solicitors to decide whether the report might be acted on, in making an advance not advised in the report to two thirds of the value of two only of the properties mentioned in the report, notwithstanding that one of the properties consisted of unfinished houses—in all this it seems to me that they failed to act as a prudent man might reasonably be expected to act in the management of his own affairs.

I am of opinion also that under the circumstances, however honestly they acted—and no one has suggested or could suggest that they did not act honestly—they cannot be said to have acted reasonably within the meaning of s. 3 of the Judicial Trustees Act, 1896, if only because they neglected to do what a reasonable man would do in the prudent management of his own business.

It remains, therefore, to consider whether the three houses comprised in the mortgage were in fact of sufficient value to justify an advance of trust money to the amount of 4400*l*., and, if not, for what amount they might properly have been accepted as security by the trustees; for having decided that there was nothing hazardous in advancing trust moneys thereon the trustees are, in my opinion, entitled to the benefit of s. 9 of the Trustee Act, 1893.

For the purpose of considering these questions it seems to me that the Court ought to be guided by the same general considerations which would have guided it prior to the Trustee Act, 1888. Section 8[17] of that Act merely protects trustees who within certain limits and under certain circumstances act on expert opinions as to the amount they may advance. It does not, as has been suggested, abrogate all distinction between agricultural land

[17] Presumably s. 4 of the 1888 Act was intended.

and houses or buildings used for trade in determining the margin of protection to be required by a prudent man, or indicate that a prudent man may, prima facie, be content in all cases with a margin of one third the value of the property. At most it suggests that the extra margin of protection beyond one third the value depends on the particular circumstances of each case, and assumes that whatever may be the nature of the property the expert employed will give the matter his bona fide consideration, advising with a view to the security of the trust money, and not only in such a way as to protect the trustees from liability for breach of trust. In cases not within the section it perhaps suggests that the rule which the Courts had laid down in the case of houses and buildings used for trade is less stringent than the two thirds rule laid down in the case of agricultural land, and this I believe to have been the case before the Act. As well since the Act as before it, it is therefore necessary to consider not only the value of the property proposed to be mortgaged, but also the margin of protection which a prudent man would require remembering that the margin of protection to be required must depend on the nature of the property and all the circumstances of the case. . . .

Considering all the facts of this case, I have come to the conclusion that the largest sum for which the property could be considered a good security in 1897 is 3400*l*. and therefore, under s. 9 of the Act, the trustees' liability is confined to making good the excess of the amount actually advanced over this amount and with interest.

Re Solomon ([1912] 1 Ch 261) was another case in which a mortgage security, made on the advice of valuers, proved to be insufficient, and the beneficiaries sought to make the trustees account. WARRINGTON J reviewed the facts in great detail and continued:

"Now, do [the trustees] make out that they are within the second part of the sub-section?[18] The second part is, first, that in making the loan the trustee is acting upon a certain report. That the trustees in this case acted on the report of Messrs. Toplis & Harding is abundantly clear, and I need say no more about that. Then, that report must be a report as to the value of the property; and that of course it was, and it was to be made by a person whom the trustee reasonably believed to be an able practical surveyor. As to that there can be no question. Messrs. Toplis & Harding were surveyors and valuers of long standing and of good reputation. They had been employed by the trustees for years in making such valuations; they had been employed by the defendant Meyer himself in making valuations on his own behalf. It seems to me beyond question that the trustees in this case believed Mr. Harding, who attended to the business, to be an able practical surveyor or valuer. Next, he must be, or be believed to be,—there is a question about that—instructed and employed independently of any owner of the property. Now, what is meant by 'instructed and employed independently of any owner of the property'? I think it means this: that the relation existing between employer and

[18] T.A. 1893, s. 8 (1), now T.A. 1925, s. 8 (1), p. 489, ante.

employed must exist as between the trustees and the valuer, and between them only—that the valuer must be entitled to look for his remuneration to the person who employs him, and, on the other hand, must be responsible to that person and to that person only for the due performance of his duty as valuer. When you have that, he is instructed and employed by the trustee, and he is instructed and employed by him independently of the owner[19]. I do not think it is incumbent on the trustee to inquire into all the previous business transactions of the valuer and to find out whether he has at any time recently or long before advised or acted for the mortgagor. He must in this matter be instructed and employed independently of the mortgagor, and, if that is made out, then I think the provisions of the sub-section are satisfied. Is that made out in the present case? The plaintiffs say it is not. I think it is. The trustees, through their solicitors, gave the instructions to the surveyor, and, but for the fact that certain particulars appended to those instructions had, as must necessarily be the case, been furnished by the mortgagor, the mortgagor had nothing whatever to do with the instructions given to Messrs. Toplis & Harding. Then, were they employed by, or partly by, the mortgagor? There again the mortgagor, it seems to me, had nothing to do with their employment. He was not responsible to them for their fee. The contract to value was made between the trustees and the valuers. The duty which the valuers owed they owed to the trustees, and to them alone, and it was the trustees and the trustees alone who were responsible to them for their remuneration. I think it is abundantly made out that that was the true relation between the trustees and the valuers, and that therefore the trustees have, in this case, established that they have acted on a report of a valuer instructed and employed independently of the owner of the property.

The next point is that the sub-section further requires the amount of the loan not to exceed two equal third parts of the value of the property as stated in the report. As to that, there is no question; there is no doubt that the amount advanced did not exceed two third parts of the value of the property as stated in the report.

Now, on that, I think it is desirable to add my opinion to that of other judges who have dealt with this question of valuers' reports made to trustees. It has, I think, undoubtedly become the practice of valuers, thinking that they are thereby complying with the requirements of the Act, to advise practically in every case that trustees may safely advance two-thirds of the value, and that practice appears to be based on the fact that, so far as the liabilities of the trustees are concerned, the Act makes no distinction between one kind of property and another; it only requires that they shall not advance more than two third parts of the value of the property. That, I think, is a mistake. It is the duty of the valuer to consider not only the value of the property, but the proportion which, in his opinion, as an expert and practical man, the trustees would, in each particular case, be justified in advancing. But the fact that the valuer has advised a loan of two-thirds of the value does not make the report a bad one. He has

[19] In *Re Somerset* [1894] 1 Ch 321, KEKEWICH J held that the valuer must *in fact* be instructed and employed independently. It was not sufficient that the trustee believed him to have been so employed.

reported that the trustees may safely advance that amount, and that is sufficient for them. I think valuers should bear in mind that it is their duty, in advising trustees, to advise them not only as to what they consider the actual value, but what proportion of that value the trustees may safely advance upon the security quite independently of any supposed rule relating to the two-thirds; only, of course, if the valuers were so satisfied with the security as to advise the advance, say, of three-fourths, the trustees would not be justified in acting on that advice, because the Act confines them to two-thirds. The trustees, therefore, have not advanced more than two-thirds of the value of the property as stated in the report.

The next requirement of the sub-section is 'that the loan was made under the advice of the surveyor or valuer expressed in the report'. It is said that that condition has not been complied with because the surveyor and valuer in this case did not in so many words say 'I advise the trustees to advance so much money'. In my opinion, to so hold would be to cast away the substance for the shadow. The surveyors are told, in their instructions, that a certain security is offered to the trustees, and they are asked to survey that property and to report what, in their opinion, is the value of the security offered, and what amount can be advanced by trustees thereon; and in answer to those instructions they tell the trustees what they consider to be the value of the property, and that that property forms a sufficient security for the amount which they are told in the instructions the trustees are asking them to advise upon. What can that mean except that the surveyors are telling the trustees that they may, in their opinion, properly advance that sum—in other words that they are advising the trustees to make that advance? Could it possibly be contended by the surveyors that the trustees, acting on that report and making the advance, if there were circumstances of negligence or misconduct on the part of the surveyors, could not claim that they were misled by the report and induced to make the advance by it? Of course it could not. The surveyor making this report in answer to such instructions as those must be taken to have known that if his report was favourable the trustees would make the advance, and make the advance to the amount for which he advised the property was sufficient security.

I think, therefore, that the trustees in the present case have complied also with the final requirement of the sub-section, and sufficiently made it appear to the Court that the loan was made under the advice of the surveyor or valuer, and that the advice was expressed in the report.

That being the conclusion at which I have arrived, it follows that the trustees in the present case are not chargeable with the breach of trust which is alleged against them, and the result is that I must dismiss this action against all the defendants with costs."

In *Re Walker* ((1890) 62 LT 449) trustees made an improper investment of trust funds on a mortgage of land. The security proved insufficient. The trustees claimed to be protected under Trustee Act 1888, s. 5 (now Trustee Act 1925, s. 9). KEKEWICH J, having held that the investment was improper, said: "Then, as regards the 5th section of the Act, a different question arises. That is a beneficial section, the object of which is to provide that, when a trustee has advanced more money on mortgage of the property than was reasonably prudent, and the estate fails, then he is not to be chargeable with the whole, but only with so much as would have been a loss if you take the real value at the time of investment, not the value he put upon it. That is the substance of it. Supposing, for instance, a man invests 100 *l* on property that would bear only 80 *l*; he is not to lose the whole 100 *l* because of that. That is a reasonable provision on behalf of trustees. But the whole section depends on this: 'When a trustee shall have improperly advanced trust money on a mortgage security which would, at the time of the investment, have been a proper investment in all respects for a less sum than was actually advanced thereon'. That I understood to mean that the impropriety consists in the amount invested. If the investment is otherwise improper—as, for instance, if a man invests on mortgage of trade buildings when he is only entitled to invest on mortgage of agricultural land—he cannot claim the benefit of the section, and say, 'I might take the value at two-thirds of the advance, although not the whole'. He must establish the propriety of the investment independently of value, and then he has the benefit of the section to save him from any loss greater than that which would have been incurred by advancing too large a sum on what otherwise would be a proper security."

In *Re Stuart* ([1897] 2 Ch 583) a trustee acted on a valuation which stated merely the amount for which the property was a good security, without stating the value of the property, and advanced more than two-thirds of the amount stated in the valuation. The valuer was employed by the solicitor who acted for the mortgagor. Liability was admitted and the question was whether the trustee should be relieved under the predecessor to Trustee Act 1925, s. 61[20]. In refusing relief, STIRLING J said (at pp. 591–592): "As to the valuations, which have been produced, they do not satisfy the requirements of s. 4 of the Trustee Act, 1888, which has now been replaced by s. 8 of the Trustee Act, 1893. It was contended, and in my opinion rightly contended, that this was not necessarily a fatal obstacle to the application of the section. Still, I think that those requirements cannot be left out of consideration. The Legislature in 1888 dealt with the duties of trustees with regard to investments, and laid down certain rules for their guidance which in some respects relaxed those previously existing and are in themselves reasonable, and they appear to me to constitute a standard by which reasonable conduct is to be judged."

In *Re Chapman* ([1896] 2 Ch 763) the estate of the testator included several mortgages. Because of a general agricultural depression, the value of the properties had decreased and become insufficient to cover the mortgages. The trustees decided to hold the securities, and wait for a more favourable time for realisation. The question was whether the defendants

[20] See p. 622, post.

were liable as executors because of their failure to call in the mortgage within twelve months of the testator's death, or as trustees for the subsequent retention. The Court of Appeal found for the defendants. LINDLEY LJ said (at p. 776): "There is no rule of law which compels the Court to hold that an honest trustee is liable to make good loss sustained by retaining an authorized security in a falling market, if he did so honestly and prudently, in the belief that it was the best course to take in the interest of all parties. Trustees acting honestly, with ordinary prudence and within the limits of their trust, are not liable for mere errors of judgment. Any loss sustained by the trust estate under such circumstances falls upon and must be borne by the owners of the property—i.e., the cestuis que trust—and cannot be thrown by them on their trustees, who have done no wrong, though the result may prove that they possibly might have done better. *Learoyd v Whiteley* ((1887) 12 App Cas 727) is a clear authority to this effect; so are *Buxton v Buxton* ((1835) 1 My & Cr 80) and *Marsden v Kent* ((1877) 5 ChD 598).

The case is an important one not only to the trustees of this particular will, but to trustees of mortgages generally. Owing to the great fall in the value of agricultural land trustees of mortgage securities have been placed in a position of great difficulty. To throw on the trustees the loss sustained by the fall in value of securities authorized by the trust, wilful default, which includes want of ordinary prudence on the part of the trustees, must be proved; but it is not proved in this case. In my opinion, wilful default is disproved in all the important cases and is not proved in the doubtful ones.

The appeals must be allowed."

D. Purchase of Land

Unless expressly authorised, trustees, other than tenants for life under the Settled Land Act 1925 and trustees for sale, are not permitted to invest in the purchase of land. Tenants for life are authorised by Settled Land Act 1925, s. 73, to apply capital money in the purchase of land in fee simple or of leasehold land with at least 60 years unexpired. And trustees for sale are by Law of Property Act 1925, s. 28, given the same powers as tenants for life of settled land[1].

It is common to give to other trustees express powers to purchase land; enabling them, for example, to purchase a house for a widow.

QUESTION

You are trustee of a new trust and the investment clause provides for investment in securities authorised by law. The fund is worth £100,000, all in cash. What would you do? If you cannot answer this question, read the financial pages of a leading newspaper each day for a month, and then telephone a friendly stockbroker, and have a talk with him.

[1] See *Re Wakeman* [1945] Ch 177, [1945] 1 All ER 421; *Re Wellsted's Will Trusts* [1949] Ch 296, [1949] 1 All ER 577; Maudsley and Burn, *Land Law Cases and Materials* (3rd Edn) p. 197.

III. Duty to Distribute[2]

A beneficiary can compel a trustee to pay to him what he is entitled to under the trust. Usually this gives rise to no difficulties. But situations may arise where the trustees' duty is not clear; either because there is doubt as to the beneficiaries' entitlement, or because known beneficiaries cannot be found. In doubtful cases, a trustee may seek the directions of the court; and is of course safe in following them. There are various ways in which he may seek protection.

A. Release on Completion

Lewin on Trusts (16th Edn, 1964), p. 189

"In practice, trustees frequently require a release under seal, which throws on the beneficiary a heavy burden of proving fraud, concealment, mistake or undue influence[3]. But strictly a trustee (in contradistinction to an executor) cannot, in the absence of special circumstances, insist upon a release under seal[4]."

B. Advertisement for Claimants

TRUSTEE ACT 1925

27. Protection by means of advertisements.—(1) With a view to the conveyance to or distribution among the persons entitled to any real or personal property, the trustees of a settlement or of a disposition on trust for sale or personal representatives, may give notice by advertisement in the Gazette, and in a newspaper[5] circulating in the district in which the land is situated, and such other like notices, including notices elsewhere than in England and Wales, as would, in any special case, have been directed by a court of competent jurisdiction in an action for administration, of their intention to make such conveyance or distribution as aforesaid, and requiring any person interested to send to the trustees or personal representatives within the time, not being less than two months, fixed in the notice or, where more than one notice is given, in the last of the notices, particulars of his claim in respect of the property or any part thereof to which the notice relates.

(2) At the expiration of the time fixed by the notice the trustees or personal representatives may convey or distribute the property or any part thereof to which the notice relates, to or among the persons entitled thereto, having regard only to the claims, whether formal or not, of which the trustees or personal representatives then had notice and shall not, as respects the property so conveyed or distributed, be liable to any person of whose

[2] H & M, pp. 468–471; K & S, pp. 283–289; P & M, pp. 284–285; Pettit, pp. 328–330; Snell, pp. 260–262.

[3] *Fowler v Wyatt* (1857) 24 Beav 232.

[4] *Chadwick v Heatley* (1845) 2 Coll 137; *Re Wright's Trusts* (1857) 3 K & J 419; *Re Cater's Trusts (No. 2)* (1858) 25 Beav 366; *Re Foligno's Mortgage* (1863) 32 Beav 131. See also *King v Mullins* (1852) Drew 308 at 311.

[5] As amended by L.P. (A.) A. 1926, Schedule.

claim the trustees or personal representatives have not had notice at the time of conveyance or distribution; but nothing in this section—

(*a*) prejudices the right of any person to follow the property, or any property representing the same, into the hands of any person, other than a purchaser, who may have received it; or

(*b*) frees the trustees or personal representatives from any obligation to make searches or obtain official certificates of search similar to those which an intending purchaser would be advised to make or obtain.

(3) This section applies notwithstanding anything to the contrary in the will or other instrument, if any, creating the trust.

C. Setting Aside a Fund to Meet Claims in Respect of Rents and Covenants

TRUSTEE ACT 1925

26. Protection against liability in respect of rents and covenants. —(1) Where a personal representative or trustee liable as such for—

(*a*) any rent, covenant, or agreement reserved by or contained in any lease; or

(*b*) any rent, covenant or agreement payable under or contained in any grant made in consideration of a rentcharge; or

(*c*) any indemnity given in respect of any rent, covenant or agreement referred to in either of the foregoing paragraphs;

satisfies all liabilities under the lease or grant which may have accrued and been claimed[6], up to the date of the conveyance hereinafter mentioned, and, where necessary, sets apart a sufficient fund to answer any future claim that may be made in respect of any fixed and ascertained sum which the lessee or grantee agreed to lay out on the property demised or granted, although the period for laying out the same may not have arrived, then and in any such case the personal representative or trustee may convey the property demised or granted to a purchaser, legatee, devisee, or other person entitled to call for a conveyance thereof and thereafter—

(i) he may distribute the residuary real and personal estate of the deceased testator or intestate, or, as the case may be, the trust estate (other than the fund, if any, set apart as aforesaid) to or amongst the persons entitled thereto, without appropriating any part, or any further part, as the case may be, of the estate of the deceased or of the trust estate to meet any future liability under the said lease or grant;

(ii) notwithstanding such distribution, he shall not be personally liable in respect of any subsequent claim under the said lease or grant.

(2) This section operates without prejudice to the right of the lessor or grantor, or the persons deriving title under the lessor or grantor, to follow the assets of the deceased or the trust property into the hands of the persons amongst whom the same may have been respectively distributed, and applies notwithstanding anything to the contrary in the will or other instrument, if any, creating the trust.

(3) In this section "lease" includes an underlease and an agreement for a

[6] As amended by L.P. (A.) A. 1926, Schedule.

lease or underlease and any instrument giving any such indemnity as aforesaid or varying the liabilities under the lease; "grant" applies to a grant whether the rent is created by limitation, grant, reservation, or otherwise, and includes an agreement for a grant and any instrument giving any such indemnity as aforesaid or varying the liabilities under the grant; "lessee" and "grantee" include persons respectively deriving title under them.

D. Benjamin Order

In *Re Benjamin* ([1902] 1 Ch 723), Philip Benjamin was entitled, if he was living on June 25, 1893, the date of his father's death, to a share (about £30,000) in his father's estate. He had disappeared in September 1892, and searching enquiries failed to produce any news of him. JOYCE J said: "I think in this case that Philip David Benjamin must be presumed to be dead . . . The question is as to when he died. If he is to be presumed to be dead, I think the case of *Re Walker* ((1871) 7 Ch App 120) distinctly applies, and the onus of proof is on his administrator. He has failed to adduce any evidence to shew that P. D. Benjamin survived the testator. I myself consider it highly probable that he died on September 1, 1892, or at all events shortly after. I am clearly of opinion that the onus is on those claiming under him to prove that he survived the testator. In my opinion, therefore, the trustees are at liberty to distribute. I am anxious, however, not to do anything which would prevent his representative from making any claim if evidence of his death at any other time should be subsequently forthcoming. I shall not, therefore, declare that he is dead, but I will make an order in the following form:—

> In the absence of any evidence that the said P. D. Benjamin survived the testator, let the trustees of the testator's will be at liberty to divide the share of the testator's estate devised and bequeathed in favour of the said P. D. Benjamin, his wife and children, upon the footing that P. D. Benjamin was unmarried and did not survive the testator.[7]"

E. Personal Indemnity

Lewin on Trusts (16th Edn, 1964) p. 258

"Sometimes where there is only a shadow of a doubt as to the parties interested and the chance of an adverse claim being made is extremely remote, a trustee may be willing to distribute in reliance on an indemnity, but it should be realised that an indemnity (especially from an individual) is an unsatisfactory safeguard. For, when the danger arises, the person giving the indemnity may be insolvent or his assets may have been distributed. Sometimes an insurance company will issue an indemnity policy; in fixing the amount of the policy the impact of [capital transfer tax] and of any rise in the value of investments which may have to be replaced should be borne in mind."

[7] See RSC 1965 Ord. 85, r. 2 (2), p. 503, post; and Ord. 92, r. 5 (17); *Ministry of Health v Simpson* [1951] AC 251, [1950] 2 All ER 1137; *Re Lowe's Will Trusts* [1973] 1 WLR 882 at 887, [1973] 2 All ER 1136.

F. Payments by Personal Representatives to Minors

ADMINISTRATION OF ESTATES ACT 1925

42. Power to appoint trustees of infants' property.—(1) Where an infant is absolutely entitled under the will or on the intestacy of a person dying before or after the commencement of this Act (in this subsection called "the deceased") to a devise or legacy, or to the residue of the estate of the deceased, or any share therein, and such devise, legacy, residue or share is not under the will, if any, of the deceased, devised or bequeathed to trustees for the infant, the personal representatives of the deceased may appoint a trust corporation of two or more individuals not exceeding four (whether or not including the personal representatives or one or more of the personal representatives), to be the trustee or trustees of such devise, legacy, residue or share for the infant, and to be trustees of any land devised or any land being or forming part of such residue or share for the purposes of the Settled Land Act, 1925, and of the statutory provisions relating to the management of land during a minority, and may execute or do any assurance or thing requisite for vesting such devise, legacy, residue or share in the trustee or trustees so appointed.

On such appointment the personal representatives, as such, shall be discharged from all further liability in respect of such devise, legacy, residue, or share, and the same may be retained in its existing condition or state of investment, or may be converted into money, and such money may be invested in any authorised investment.

G. Application to the Court

ORDER 85

(RSC 1965)

ADMINISTRATION AND SIMILAR ACTIONS

Interpretation

1. In this Order "administration action" means an action for the administration under the direction of the Court of the estate of a deceased person or for the execution under the direction of the Court of a trust.

Determination of questions, etc., without administration

2.—(1) An action may be brought for the determination of any question or for any relief which could be determined or granted, as the case may be, in an administration action and a claim need not be made in the action for the administration or execution under the direction of the Court of the estate or trust in connection with which the question arises or the relief is sought.

(2) Without prejudice to the generality of paragraph (1), an action may be brought for the determination of any of the following questions:—

(*a*) any question arising in the administration of the estate of a deceased person or in the execution of a trust;

(*b*) any question as to the composition of any class of persons having a claim against the estate of a deceased person or a beneficial interest in the estate of such a person or in any property subject to a trust;

(*c*) any question as to the rights or interests of a person claiming to be a creditor of the estate of a deceased person or to be entitled under a will or on the intestacy of a deceased person or to be beneficially entitled under a trust.

(3) Without prejudice to the generality of paragraph (1), an action may be brought for any of the following reliefs:—

(*a*) an order requiring an executor, administrator or trustee to furnish and, if necessary, verify accounts;

(*b*) an order requiring the payment into court of money held by a person in his capacity as executor, administrator or trustee;

(*c*) an order directing a person to do or abstain from doing a particular act in his capacity as executor, administrator or trustee;

(*d*) an order approving any sale, purchase, compromise or other transaction by a person in his capacity as executor, administrator or trustee;

(*e*) an order directing any act to be done in the administration of the estate of a deceased person or in the execution of a trust which the Court could order to be done if the estate or trust were being administered or executed, as the case may be, under the direction of the Court.

Parties

3.—(1) All the executors or administrators of the estate or trustees of the trust, as the case may be, to which an administration action or such an action as is referred to in rule 2 relates must be parties to the action, and where the action is brought by executors, administrators or trustees, any of them who does not consent to being joined as a plaintiff must be made a defendant.

(2) Notwithstanding anything in Order 15, rule 4 (2), and without prejudice to the powers of the Court under that Order, all the persons having a beneficial interest in or claim against the estate or having a beneficial interest under the trust, as the case may be, to which such an action as is mentioned in paragraph (1) relates need not be parties to the action; but the plaintiff may make such of those persons, whether all or any one or more of them, parties as, having regard to the nature of the relief or remedy claimed in the action, he thinks fit.

(1966) 82 LQR 306 (R. E. M.)

"The facts in *Re Allen-Meyrick's Will Trusts* ([1966] 1 WLR 499, [1966] 1 All ER 740) were simple and elegant. A testatrix gave her residue to trustees in trust to apply the income thereof 'in their absolute discretion for the maintenance of my . . . husband', and subject to the exercise of this discretion, she gave the residue in trust for her two godchildren equally. The trustees had made certain payments for the benefit of the husband, who was bankrupt, but had been unable to agree whether any further income should be so applied. In these circumstances, the trustee sought to surrender their discretion to the court, and also sought to have it determined whether their discretion still existed in relation to past accumulations of income.

It is well settled that trustees confronted by a particular problem may surrender their discretion to the court, and so be relieved both of the agony of decision and the responsibility for the result. But it is another matter where it is sought to surrender discretion which is not merely present and confined but prospective and indefinite. The Court of Chancery had a long history of administrative jurisdiction; but it exercised this jurisdiction not on its own investigations but on facts duly put before it in evidence by those concerned. It is not surprising, therefore, that Buckley J. refused to accept the proffered general surrender of discretion. Whenever a specific problem arose upon specific facts, the aid of the court could be sought; but that was all. As regard past accumulations of income, the position was simple. The whole of the property, capital and income, belonged to the two godchildren except in so far as the trustees had effectually exercised their discretionary power to apply income to the husband. Trustees must, of course, be unanimous in exercising any powers vested in them, and so if within a reasonable time of receiving any income they had failed to exercise their discretion in favour of the husband, it ceased to be exercisable, and the godchildren became entitled to it. The principles are old, the facts new, and the result satisfactory".

H. Payment into Court

TRUSTEE ACT 1925

63. Payment into court by trustees.—(1) Trustees, or the majority of trustees, having in their hands or under their control money or securities belonging to a trust, may pay the same into court[8].

(2) The receipt or certificate of the proper officer shall be a sufficient discharge to trustees for the money or securities so paid into court.

(3) Where money or securities are vested in any persons as trustees, and the majority are desirous of paying the same into court, but the concurrence of the other or others cannot be obtained, the court may order the payment into court to be made by the majority without the concurrence of the other or others.

(4) Where any such money or securities are deposited with any banker, broker, or other depositary, the court may order payment or delivery of the money or securities to the majority of the trustees for the purpose of payment into court.

(5) Every transfer payment and delivery made in pursuance of any such order shall be valid and take effect as if the same had been made on the authority or by the act of all the persons entitled to the money and securities so transferred, paid, or delivered.

(1968) 84 LQR 65 (A. J. Hawkins)

"Payment into court, no matter how unjustified, was always effective, to give the trustees a good discharge. As Kindersley V-C said in *Re Lloyd's Trust*[9], 'The intention of the Trustee Act was for the present relief of trustees'.

[8] As amended by Administration of Justice Act 1965, s. 36 (4) and Sch. 3.

[9] (1854) 2 WR 371.

Relief might prove expensive, but it appears to have been effective to the extent that trustees were relieved of the burden of future administration. The sanction against unjustifiable payment into court was a disallowance of the costs incurred in paying in. Trustees were later condemned in the costs incurred in the payment out to the beneficiaries. In the early cases they were not entitled to costs of the payment in if their actions had been vexatious[10]. Later, they had to justify their actions by showing doubt as to the identity of the beneficiaries, the extent of their interest or their inability to give receipts[11]. 'The legislature did not intend that where the trust was clear, a trustee should pay the fund into court. A trustee cannot pay money into court merely to get rid of a trust he has undertaken to perform, and the Act would lead to greater oppression if it were otherwise.[12]' Furthermore the trustees' doubts should be bona fide. This appears to have meant such doubts as would assail and disturb a practical lawyer, rather than ruffle the academic conscience of eminent conveyancers[13]. What is the effect of payment in? Clearly, payment into court does operate as a discharge of trustees. In other words, by paying in the trustees retire from the trust[14]. They will, of course, still be liable for any breaches of trust in the past[15], and responsible for any money that should come into their hands in the future[16]. Apparently, they also remain trustees for the purposes of receiving notices relating to dealings with the trust funds[17]. Subject to these two matters, however, new trustees can be appointed, either by the persons nominated as appointors in the trust instrument[18], or by the Court.''[19]

IV. Duty to Act Impartially Between Life Tenant and Remainderman[20]

It is the duty of a trustee to act in the interests of all the beneficiaries. Where there are beneficiaries whose interests conflict, as in the case of life tenant and remainderman, the trustee, acting in the general interests of all, must act impartially between them.

Nowhere is this duty of greater significance than in the selection of investments. Even within the range of authorised investments, there are available

10 *Re Lane's Trust* (1854) 3 WR 134.
11 *Re Knight's Trusts* (1859) 27 Beav 45.
12 *Re Knight's Trusts* (1859) 27 Beav 45 at 49, per ROMILLY MR.
13 In *Re Knight's Trusts* (1859) 27 Beav 45, the fact that trustees acted on counsel's opinion was regretted but made no difference to their liability. In *Re Cull's Trusts* (1875) LR 20 Eq 561, the particular trustees were protected having taken counsel's opinion, but JESSEL MR added "the next set of trustees who come before me having so acted must pay costs".
14 *Re Williams' Settlement* (1858) 4 K & J 87.
15 *Barker v Peile* (1865) 2 Dr & Sm 340.
16 *Re Nettlefold's Trusts* (1888) 59 LT 315.
17 *Thompson v Tomkins* (1862) 2 Dr & Sm 8, and see also *Warburton v Hill* (1854) Kay 470.
18 *Re Bailey's Trust* (1854) 3 WR 31.
19 13 & 14 Vict. c. 60, ss. 32 and 33, replaced with significant changes by ss. 25 and 37 of the Trustee Act 1893. See now ss. 41 and 43 of the Trustee Act 1925.
20 H & M, pp. 472–484; K & S, pp. 260–283; P & M, pp. 312–326; Pettit, pp. 281–293; Snell, pp. 217–223. See also Lewin, p. 86.

fixed interest gilt-edged stocks giving a return of about 12 per cent., which will delight the life tenant; and a choice of "growth stocks" returning a mere 1 per cent., but with a prospect of substantial future capital growth, will be attractive to the remainderman. If we move outside the range of investments authorised by the general law, an even greater contrast can be seen. A copyright or an oil well may produce a handsome income, but for a limited time; while War Savings Certificates produce capital increase only and no income, and a new and developing business is likely to do the same.

(1943) 7 Conv (NS) 128 (S. J. Bailey)

"In ordinary circumstances, when property has been settled upon trust for A for life, and thereafter for B absolutely, the whole of the net income derived from the property until A dies is payable to him. Such is his right, neither more nor less. Though this income be abnormally high, nothing of it is held back for the benefit of B. Though it be abnormally low or non-existent, neither A nor his executors after him has any right to claim a compensation out of the capital value of the property or out of any enhanced income it may yield after he dies. So long as the trust comprises property which produces an abnormally low or high income, any incidental hardship to A or B must be borne. But if the trustees have the power to dispose of that particular property and re-invest in something which will produce a more fair and steady income, this inequitable state of affairs will cease if and when they choose to do so[1]. It is perhaps surprising that equity has not cast upon trustees, in every such case, a duty to convert the trust property as soon as practicable into something more likely to produce an equitable result. One might have expected further, perhaps, that in every such case equity would require the trustees to make some financial adjustment, as between the beneficiaries, to cover the intervening period during which the desired conversion is delayed. In fact, however, equity does not ordinarily intervene in these cases; but to this there are three celebrated exceptions. The three exceptions have much in common: they apply only where the trust is created by will, and only in so far as the property comprised in the trust is the residuary personal estate of the testator; and they are said to rest upon his presumed intention to deal evenly with the beneficiaries under the trust. This is no doubt the reason why they are often grouped together, and described as the rule in *Howe v Lord Dartmouth*[2]. In origin, however, they are three distinct rules: (i) the rule in *Gibson v Bott*[3], (ii) the rule in *Howe v Lord Dartmouth*; and (iii) the rule in *Re Chesterfield's*

1 The so-called equitable duty of trustees "to hold the scales evenly between the beneficiaries" does not ordinarily appear to compel them to realise and re-invest in such a case: see *Re Courtier* (1886) 34 ChD 136; *Re Searle* [1900] 2 Ch 829 at 834 ("if the estate produces nothing, the tenant for life can get nothing"), *per* KEKEWICH J. On the other hand, when trustees do exercise a power to invest, they must not allow themselves to be persuaded into an investment, prejudicial to one beneficiary, in order to benefit another of their beneficiaries: *Raby v Ridehalgh* (1855) 7 De GM & G 104.

2 (1802) 7 Ves 137. See, e.g., *Macdonald v Irvine* (1878), 8 ChD 101 at 112, per BAGGALLAY LJ.

3 (1802) 7 Ves 89.

Trusts[4]. Of these, rules (i) and (ii) operate chiefly to prevent a life tenant from obtaining an unjust advantage to the detriment of the remainderman[5], whilst rule (iii) operates in the reverse direction in order to prevent an injustice to the tenant for life."

A. The Rule in *Howe v Lord Dartmouth*[6]

i. DUTY TO CONVERT

A duty to convert may be imposed by statute[7], or by the trust instrument, or by the Rule in *Howe v Lord Dartmouth.*

Lewin on Trusts (16th Edn, 1964) p. 228

"The first branch of the Rule in *Howe v Lord Dartmouth* may be stated in outline as follows:

If a testator gives his residuary personal estate in trust for, or directly to, persons in succession without imposing a trust for sale and it comprises wasting assets or unauthorised investments then, unless the tenant for life can show that the testator meant him to enjoy the income of those assets or investments in specie, they must be sold and the proceeds invested in authorised securities."

ii. DUTY OF APPORTIONMENT PENDING CONVERSION

Lewin on Trusts (16th Edn, 1964) pp. 235–238

"The rule in *Howe v Lord Dartmouth* has a second branch which applies in the absence of a contrary intention where for any reason (be it a trust for sale expressed in the trust instrument or imposed by statute or implied by the first branch of the Rule) pure personal property which is held on trust for persons in succession ought to have been sold. When the second branch of the Rule applies then, as between tenant for life and remainderman, the settled property must be treated as if it had been sold and the proceeds reinvested in the proper investments; the life tenant is entitled to the fair equivalent of the income he would have received if that had been done, but no more. . . .

Calculation of the 'fair equivalent'

Where the second branch of the Rule applies the tenant for life is entitled before conversion to the fair equivalent of the income he would have

[4] (1883) 24 ChD 643. Note that the judgment of SIMONDS J in *Re Woodhouse* [1941] Ch 332, [1941] 2 All ER 265, which finally decided that this rule has no application to trusts of real estate, was based in part on the fact that the other two rules do not apply to real estate. And the learned Judge, throughout his judgment, treated the three rules as distinct from one another. "This is an equitable rule established by this Court in order to deal fairly in the administration of estates between persons having successive interests in a residuary estate. It is a rule of administration which, in my judgment, is to be regarded as complementary to other rules of administration established also to do justice as between persons entitled to successive interests, as, for example, the rule in *Howe v Earl of Dartmouth*": *Re Woodhouse* [1941] Ch at 334–335.

[5] It has recently been made clear, in *Re Fawcett* [1940] Ch 402, that these two rules may also operate to prevent injustice to the life tenant.

[6] (1802) 7 Ves 137. See (1943) 7 Conv (NS) 128, 191 (S. J. Bailey); (1952) 16 Conv (NS) 349 (L. A. Sheridan).

[7] A.E.A. 1925, s. 33.

enjoyed if conversion had taken place, that is, he is given interest on the value of the unconverted property.

In the days when the court always directed investment in consols the rate of interest was that which consols would have yielded[8], but when the range of authorised investments was extended[9] the rate of interest allowed was standardised at 4 per cent.[10], later reduced to 3 per cent.[11], but then increased again to 4 per cent.[12], at which rate it is generally assumed now to stand[13]. There seems to be no reported case in which the rate was reduced on account of the fall in interest rates generally after 1945 and if the 4 per cent. rate were to be changed it would be necessary to show that the yield of authorised investments when the trust was established was generally above or below 4 per cent.[14].

The interest is to be calculated on the value of the assets on the first anniversary of the testator's death[15] unless they are sold within that year, when the interest is calculated on the amount they fetched[16], or unless there is a power to postpone sale, when for want of any better date the assets are to be valued at the date of death[17].

Whenever the interest is calculated it runs from the testator's death to the date on which the asset is sold[18]."

In *Re Fawcett*[19] ([1940] Ch 402) a testatrix bequeathed her residuary estate, which contained unauthorised investments, upon trust to pay the income to her nieces and nephews in equal shares for their lives, and after their death to divide the capital money among their children on attaining the age of 21. In holding that the Rule in *Howe v Lord Dartmouth* applied, FARWELL J made an order as follows: "In answer to question 2 of the summons I will make a declaration that (*a*) in the case of unauthorized investments which were still retained unsold at the end of one year from the death of the testatrix the life tenants were and are entitled to interest at the rate of 4 per cent. per annum on the value of such investments taken at the end of such year but commencing from the date of the death and running on until the realization of such investments respectively; (*b*) in the case of unauthorized investments realized during the first year after the death of the testatrix the life tenants are entitled to interest at the rate aforesaid on the net proceeds of such realization respectively from the date of the death down to the respective

[8] *Howe v Earl of Dartmouth* (1802) 7 Ves 137.
[9] See *Re Fawcett* [1940] Ch 402 at 407, per FARWELL J.
[10] *Meyer v Simonsen* (1852) 5 De G & S 723.
[11] *Re Owen* [1912] 1 Ch 519.
[12] *Re Beech*, [1920] 1 Ch 40.
[13] *Re Fawcett*, [1940] Ch 402; *Re Parry* [1947] Ch 23.
[14] *Re Parry* [1947] Ch 23, especially at 46–47, per ROMER J.
[15] *Re Fawcett* [1940] Ch 402, especially at 407 and 409, para. (a).
[16] *Re Fawcett* [1940] Ch 402, especially at 409, para. (b).
[17] *Re Parry* [1947] Ch 23, [1946] 2 All ER 412, and cases there cited.
[18] *Re Fawcett* [1940] Ch 402; *Re Parry* [1947] Ch 23, [1946] 2 All ER 412. The rate of 4 per cent. is now so far out of line with the current return from gilt-edged investments that it is difficult to see how it could still be supported. Trustees may be well advised to take instructions from the court.
[19] For details of calculation and accounting, see Josling, *Apportionments for Executors and Trustees* (4th Edn, 1976) pp. 34–39.

dates of completions of such realizations; (*c*) the unauthorized investments for the time being unsold ought to be taken en bloc as one aggregate for the purposes of the rule in *Howe v Lord Dartmouth* ((1802) 7 Ves 137); (*d*) in applying that rule the Apportionment Act, 1870, ought not to be applied in the income accounts at the death of the testatrix or at the beginning or end of any accounting period with reference to the income of unauthorized investments; (*e*) any excess of income from unauthorized investments beyond the interest payable in respect of such investments to the life tenants ought to be invested in authorized investments as part of the capital with the other authorized investments, and accordingly the whole of the actual subsequent income of such invested excess income is payable as income; (*f*) the interest so payable in respect of unauthorized investments was and is payable out of moneys being income from unauthorized investments or, so far as such income is insufficient, being proceeds of realization of such investments, and any interest so payable for the time being in arrear is payable (but calculated as simple interest only) out of subsequent income from unauthorized investments which are for the time being retained and out of the proceeds of sale of such investments as and when realized, but neither any excess income from unauthorized investments, which at the end of any accounting period is available under head (*e*) for investment in authorized investments, nor any proceeds of realization of unauthorized investments not required at the date of realization to pay interest payable as aforesaid for the time being in arrear and accordingly available to be invested in authorized investments, were or are applicable towards payment of subsequently accruing interest as aforesaid in respect of unauthorized investments then still retained."

iii. EXCLUSION

The duty to convert or to apportion may be excluded by appropriate language in the will. The exclusion of the duty to convert necessarily excludes the duty to apportion. But the testator may desire the property to be converted, but may allow the life tenant the whole income pending conversion. There has been much litigation to determine these questions[20]. It is usual now to provide expressly for the exclusion of both duties.

Key & Elphinstone, *Precedents in Conveyancing* (15th Edn, 1953), Vol.2, p. 926

"CONVERSION AND INVESTMENT

1. UPON trust that my trustees shall sell, call in, collect and convert into money the said real and personal property at such time or times, and in such manner as they shall think fit (but as to reversionary property not until it falls into possession, unless it shall appear to my trustees that an earlier sale would be beneficial), with power to postpone the sale, calling in or conversion of the whole or any part or parts of the said property [including leaseholds or other property of a terminable hazardous or wasting nature] during such period as they shall think proper, and to retain the same or any part thereof in its actual form of investment, without being responsible for loss. And I direct that the income of such of the same premises as for the time being shall remain unsold shall as well during the first year after my

[20] H & M, p. 477; Pettit, pp. 283–285.

death as afterwards be applied as if the same were income arising from investments hereinafter directed to be made of the proceeds of sale thereof, and that no reversionary or other property not actually producing income shall be treated as producing income for the purposes of this my will[1]."

iv. THE RULE TODAY

Hanbury & Maudsley: *Modern Equity* (10th Edn, 1976), p. 479

"**Howe v Earl of Dartmouth Today**[2]. The rules relating to conversion and apportionment demonstrate basic principles of equity. But they should be understood in their proper perspective.

(a) *Exclusion of Duty to Apportion.* The duty to apportion is in practice nearly always excluded, both in respect of income from unauthorised securities and in respect of reversionary interests. The duty to convert, where it exists, thus appears in the context of a duty to change the investments.

(b) *Trustee Investments Act* 1961. Authorised securities now mean those investments which are authorised by the Trustee Investments Act 1961. It should be noted that wider-range securities and narrower-range requiring advice are only authorised when advice to retain them has been received. Presumably, therefore, 'if sale and reinvestment are recommended the rule [in *Howe v Earl of Dartmouth*] continues to apply until such sale[3].'

(c) *Paradoxical Effect of Current Investment Situation.* In the investment context of the present day, the rules of conversion and apportionment are in some way misplaced. The problem still exists of speculative and wasting securities. But the rule requires unauthorised investments, in the form of equities (other than those authorised by Trustee Investments Act 1961) to be sold in order to protect the capital for the benefit of the remainderman; and it deprives the life tenant of the high income which is supposedly earned by them. In fact, it is only by investment in equities that the value of the capital can be maintained; and for a decade now the average yield from fixed interest stocks has been higher than that from equities. The positions are therefore reversed. The life tenant now wants fixed interest investments in order to provide a high income; the remainderman wants unauthorised securities for the preservation of the real value of the capital. And it is the life tenant who will be pressing the trustees to convert urgently into gilt-edged securities; for they bring an income of three or four times the mere four per cent. allowed to the life tenant by the rule of apportionment."

B. Reversionary Interests

The problem previously discussed related to wasting and hazardous securities which may be expected to produce too high an income for the life tenant, and to leave unprotected the remainderman's interest in the capital. The converse problem is that of a reversionary interest; that is to say one which is not yet an interest in possession.

Assume that a fund of £500,000 is held on trust for A for life, remainder to B absolutely. A is entitled to the income, and B, on A's death, to

[1] Footnotes omitted.
[2] (1952) 16 Conv (NS) 349 (L.A. Sheridan).
[3] Nathan & Marshall, *Casebook on Trusts* (5th Edn, 1967), p. 406.

the capital. B dies before A, leaving his estate to Mrs. B for life with remainder to his children. The capital of B's testamentary trust is a valuable reversionary interest, its value depending, of course, on A's age and state of health, and also upon the total value of other transfers of capital made by A inter vivos or upon his death.

However that may be, the corpus of the testamentary trust is a valuable reversionary interest which is producing no income. It could of course be sold, and the proceeds of sale invested. But it is obvious, because of all the uncertainties involved, that it is difficult for the trustees to obtain a satisfactory price; usually it is uneconomical to sell a reversionary interest. If Mrs. B needs the income, something will have to be done, whether by selling, or by borrowing against the security of the fund, or by some other method.

Unless the reversionary interest is immediately sold and the proceeds reinvested the problem arises of apportioning the value of the reversionary interest. The solution is to take the value of the reversionary interest when it falls in (or when it is sold), and then calculate backwards to see what sum, if available at B's death, and if used to pay a reasonable income to Mrs. B until the date when the reversionary interest actually becomes available, would have produced the capital sum now available. That sum is notionally the capital of the fund. The children are entitled to that. Mrs. B, who has had no income in the meantime, is entitled to the balance.

In *Re Earl of Chesterfield's Trusts*[4], CHITTY J ordered the apportionment of a reversionary interest between life tenant and remainderman as follows: "Upon the petition &c, this Court is of opinion that the [reversionary] moneys are apportionable between principal and income by ascertaining the respective sums which, put out at £4 per cent. per annum on the [date of death of the testator] and accumulating at compound interest calculated at that rate with yearly rests, and deducting income tax, would, with the accumulations of interest, have produced, at the respective dates of receipt, the amounts actually received; and that the aggregate of the sums so ascertained ought to be treated as principal and be applied accordingly, and the residue should be treated as income."

The calculations are not as difficult as is sometimes supposed.

J. F. Josling: *Apportionments for Executors and Trustees* (4th Edn, 1976)[5] p. 39

"[A reversionary interest under the will of a testator dying on 1st January 1976] is allowed to remain for some time unrealised, and on realisation (or falling in) the sum of £15,000 is obtained. This sum is to be regarded as capital and income on that capital for the period of retention.

This item was realised on 2nd April, 1978, and the sum obtained therefore represents $2\frac{1}{4}$ years of £x accruing at 4 per cent. compound interest, less tax at 35 per cent.

[4] (1883) 24 ChD 643.

[5] See Chandler's *Trust Accounts* (6th Edn, 1936) pp. 117–118; Bailey, *Law of Wills* (7th Edn, 1973) pp. 131–134; P & M, pp. 315–317; Rowland's *Trust Accounts* (3rd Edn, 1964) pp. 95 et seq.

Invested on 2nd April, 1977, £100 at 4 per cent., less tax, would become £102·60. In order to discover the sum which would become £15,000 the formula is therefore:—

$$\frac{100}{102{\cdot}6} \times £15{,}000$$

This process is repeated for the previous year

$$\frac{100}{102{\cdot}6} \times \frac{100}{102{\cdot}6} \times £15{,}000$$

and in respect of the quarter from the date of death to 2nd April, 1976, the fraction is $\frac{100}{100{\cdot}65}$

The amount attributable to capital in respect of this interest is thus

$$\frac{100}{100{\cdot}65} \times \frac{100}{102{\cdot}6} \times \frac{100}{102{\cdot}6} \times £15{,}000 = £14{,}157{\cdot}37$$

and the balance amounting to £842·63 is apportionable to income.

These respective amounts should be credited to the capital account and to the income account under a heading to indicate the apportionment under this rule."

C. Leaseholds

The rule in *Howe v Lord Dartmouth* applied to leaseholds before 1926. Since 1925, however, leaseholds with sixty years or more unexpired are authorised trustee investments for settled land and for trustees of land held upon trust for sale.

It seems also that Law of Property Act 1925, s. 28 (2) (*infra*) excludes a duty to apportion the income of leaseholds. There may still be a duty to convert. In the absence of a duty to apportion, however, the duty to convert is of no significance in this context. As Pettit says (at p. 290): "The practical importance lies chiefly in whether the leasehold will be settled land . . . or land held on trust for sale."

In *Re Trollope's Will Trusts* ([1927] 1 Ch 596) TOMLIN J held that the rule in *Howe v Lord Dartmouth* applied after 1926 to unauthorised investments of residuary personalty which were retained under a power to postpone conversion. In discussing the application of the rule to leaseholds, he said (at p. 601): "The question is whether under the recent property statutes a change has been effected by the law in this respect. The material statutes are the Law of Property Act, 1925, and the Administration of Estates Act, 1925. The Law of Property Act, 1925, s. 28, sub-s. 2, contains a provision relating to trustees for sale of land in these terms: 'Subject to any direction to the contrary in the disposition on trust for sale or in the settlement of the proceeds of sale, the net rents and profits of the land until sale, after keeping down costs of repairs and insurance and other outgoings shall be paid or applied, except so far as any part thereof may be liable to be set aside as capital money under the Settled Land Act, 1925, in like manner as the income of investments representing the purchase money would be payable or applicable if a sale had been made and proceeds had been duly invested.'

The effect of that sub-section is that in regard to the property which is the subject-matter of the section, the rule in *Howe v Lord Dartmouth* no longer applies, because, subject to provision being made for outgoings, the income is to be applied as if it were income of proper investments of the proceeds of sale. Lawrence J in *Re Brooker* ([1926] WN 93) in fact held with regard to leaseholds which are included in the definition of 'land' in the Law of property Act 1925, s. 205, sub-s. 1 (ix), that 'the principle laid down in *Howe v Lord Dartmouth* hitherto applied by Courts of equity during the period of the postponement of the sale of leaseholds held on trust for sale, was no longer applicable to a case like the present.'

Therefore, so far as leaseholds held in trust for sale are concerned, the rule of *Howe v Lord Dartmouth* is gone."

In *Re Brooker* [1926] WN 93, the testator's estate, which included leasehold properties, was held upon an express trust for sale and conversion, with power to postpone. Each of his three daughters was tenant for life of one-fifth share of the estate. Since the testator's death in 1903, the trustees had paid to the three daughters interest at the rate of 3½ per cent. per annum on the probate value of the leasehold properties.

One question which arose in the administration of the estate was whether each daughter was entitled, as from January 1, 1926 to one-fifth of the net rents and profits of the leaseholds. LAWRENCE J held that they were.

QUESTIONS

1. Consider the various contexts (in addition to those here discussed) in which it is necessary to make a distinction between income and capital. For example:
   a) For the payment of income tax in respect of dividends earned partly before or partly after the death of the life tenant. Apportionment Act 1870, s. 2. Josling: *Apportionments for Executors and Trustees* (4th Edn, 1976), pp. 4–10.
   b) For the calculation of capital gains tax in respect of assets purchased prior to April 6, 1965. F.A. 1965, Sch. 6, paras. 23–27; Wheatcroft and Whiteman, *Capital Gains Tax* (2nd Edn, 1973) paras. 19–35 to 19–40; see also 11–21, 13–10, 14–16, 15–30.
   c) For the treatment of distributions by companies as capital distributions or as dividends: *Bouch v Sproule* (1887) 12 App Cas 385; (1975) 39 Conv (NS) 355 (W. H. Goodhart); *Re Sechiari* [1950] 1 All ER 417; *Re Kleinwort's Settlements* [1951] Ch 860, [1951] 2 All ER 328; *Re Rudd's Will Trusts* [1952] 1 All ER 254; (1953) 17 Conv (NS) 22 (A. J. Bland); *Re Malam* [1894] 3 Ch 578.
   d) For the allocation to income or capital the money used for the payment of debts: *Allhusen v Whittell* (1867) LR 4 Eq 295; Josling, op. cit., p. 26.
   e) For the allocation of the proceeds of sale of mortgaged property where the monies are insufficient to repay in full: *Re Atkinson,* [1904] 2 Ch. 160.

2. Observe that trustees may, by choosing among authorised investments and therefore consistently with the rule in *Howe v Lord Dartmouth,* produce an income of about 12 per cent. by investing in undated gilts (thereby favouring the life tenant); or an income of about 3 per cent. by choosing short-dated gilts and growth equities (thereby favouring the remainderman). Would not the rule of apportionment be more usefully applied if it provided a rule to deal with that problem, rather than assuming (wrongly at the present time) that investment in gilts preserves the capital?

v. Duty in Respect of Accounts and Audit[6]

A trustee must keep accounts of the trust and disclose them to the beneficiaries as requested[7]. Commonly, copies are given to the beneficiaries, but strictly a beneficiary is only entitled to a copy if he pays for it.

TRUSTEE ACT 1925

22. Reversionary interests, valuations, and audit.—(4) Trustees may, in their absolute discretion, from time to time, but not more than once in every three years unless the nature of the trust or any special dealings with the trust property make a more frequent exercise of the right reasonable, cause the accounts of the trust property to be examined or audited by an independent accountant, and shall, for that purpose, produce such vouchers and give such information to him as he may require; and the costs of such examination or audit, including the fee of the auditor, shall be paid out of the capital or income of the trust property, or partly in one way and partly in the other, as the trustees, in their absolute discretion, think fit, but, in default of any direction by the trustees to the contrary in any special case, costs attributable to capital shall be borne by capital and those attributable to income by income.

PUBLIC TRUSTEE ACT 1906

13. Investigation and audit of trust accounts[8].—(1) Subject to rules under this Act and unless the court otherwise orders, the condition and accounts of any trust shall, on an application being made and notice thereof given in the prescribed manner by any trustee or beneficiary, be investigated and audited by such solicitor or public accountant as may be agreed on by the applicant and the trustees or, in default of agreement, by the public trustee or some person appointed by him:

Provided that (except with the leave of the court) such an investigation or audit shall not be required within twelve months after any such previous investigation or audit, and that a trustee or beneficiary shall not be appointed under this section to make an investigation or audit.

[6] H & M, p. 484; K & S, pp. 325, 327–328; P & M, p. 278; Pettit, pp. 330–333; Snell, pp. 223–224.

[7] *Pearse v Green* (1819) 1 Jac & W 135 at 140, per PLUMER MR.

[8] See Public Trustee Rules 1912, rr. 31–37.

(2) The person making the investigation or audit (hereinafter called the auditor) shall have a right of access to the books, accounts, and vouchers of the trustees, and to any securities and documents of title held by them on account of the trust, and may require from them such information and explanation as may be necessary for the performance of his duties, and upon the completion of the investigation and audit shall forward to the applicant and to every trustee a copy of the accounts, together with a report thereon, and a certificate signed by him to the effect that the accounts exhibit a true view of the state of the affairs of the trust and that he has had the securities of the trust fund investments produced to and verified by him (or as the case may be) that such accounts are deficient in such respects as may be specified in such certificate.

(3) Every beneficiary under the trust shall, subject to rules under this Act, be entitled at all reasonable times to inspect and take copies of the accounts, report, and certificate, and, at his own expense, to be furnished with copies thereof or extracts therefrom.

JUDICIAL TRUSTEES ACT 1896

1. Power of court on application to appoint judicial trustee.[9]—(6): see p. 454, ante.

VI. Duty to Provide Information. Trust Documents[10]

A trustee must provide information to the beneficiaries concerning the state of the trust. For this purpose, it is convenient to keep a Minute Book and a Trust Diary, in which day to day events are recorded.

Documents connected with the trust are the property of the beneficiaries; and the beneficiaries are therefore entitled to them. However, we have seen that, where trustees exercise discretionary powers, they cannot be required to disclose their reasons; but where reasons are disclosed, they may be challenged, and, if unjustifiable, may be the subject of a suit by the beneficiaries[11]. A nice question thus arises: What are the rights of the beneficiaries where the reasons for the exercise by trustees of discretionary powers are contained in documents connected with the trust?

RE LONDONDERRY'S SETTLEMENT[12]

[1965] Ch 918, [1964] 3 All ER 855 (CA, Harman, Danckwerts and Salmon LJJ)

The trustees of a family settlement created by the Seventh Marquess of Londonderry decided, in accordance with the provisions of the settlement, to distribute the capital among the beneficiaries, and to bring the settlement to an end.

The defendant, a daughter of the settlor, was dissatisfied with the provision

[9] See Judicial Trustee Rules 1972, rr. 13–15.

[10] H & M, pp. 484–486; K & S, pp. 325–327; P & M, pp. 278–280; Pettit, pp. 330–333; Snell, pp. 223–224.

[11] See pp. 463, 466, ante.

[12] (1965) 81 LQR 192 (R.E.M.). See *Chaine-Nickson v Bank of Ireland* [1976] IR 393.

which the trustees decided to make for her and her children. She asked to see the minutes of the trustees' meetings, agendas and other documents prepared for their meetings, and the correspondence between the trustees, the settlor (then deceased), the trustees' solicitor, and other persons concerned with the administration of the trust. The trustees took the view that it was not in the interests of the family as a whole to disclose all these documents, and they supplied the complainant only with copies of the intended appointments of capital, and copies of the accounts of the trust. The question was whether she was entitled to inspect the other documents.

Held (reversing PLOWMAN J). The trustees were not under a duty to supply the documents or to disclose the reasons for their decisions.

HARMAN LJ: I have found this a difficult case. It raises what in my judgment is a novel question on which there is no authority exactly in point although several cases have been cited to us somewhere near it. The court is really required here to resolve two principles that come into conflict, or at least apparent conflict. The first is that, as the defendant beneficiary admits, trustees exercising a discretionary power are not bound to disclose to their beneficiaries the reasons actuating them in coming to a decision. This is a long-standing principle and rests largely I think on the view that nobody could be called upon to accept a trusteeship involving the exercise of a discretion unless, in the absence of bad faith, he were not liable to have his motives or his reasons called in question either by the beneficiaries or by the court. To this there is added a rider, namely, that if trustees do give reasons, their soundness can be considered by the court. Compare the observations of James LJ in *Re Gresham Life Assurance Society, Ex parte Penney* ((1872) 8 Ch App 446 at 449, 450) on the analogous position of directors.

It would seem on the face of it that there is no reason why this principle should be confined to decisions orally arrived at and should not extend to a case, like the present, where owing to the complexity of the trust and the large sums involved, the trustees, who act subject to the consent of another body called the appointors, have brought into existence various written documents, including, in particular, agenda for and minutes of their meetings from time to time held in order to consider distributions made of the fund and its income. It is here that the conflicting principle is said to emerge. All these documents, it is argued, came into existence for the purposes of the trust and are in the possession of the trustees as such and are, therefore, trust documents, the property of the beneficiaries, and as such open to them to inspect. . . .

The defendant relied on certain observations in *O'Rourke v Darbishire* ([1920] AC 581). The decision was that the plaintiff was not entitled to the production of what were called the "trust documents", and I find Lord Parmoor making this observation (at p. 619). "A cestui que trust, in an action against his trustees, is generally entitled to the production for inspection of all documents relating to the affairs of the trust. It is not material for the present purpose whether this right is to be regarded as a paramount proprietary right in the cestui que trust, or as a right to be enforced under the law of discovery." Lord Wrenbury says (at p. 626). "If the plaintiff is right in saying that he is a beneficiary, and if the documents are documents belonging to the executors as executors, he has a right to access to the documents which he desires to inspect upon what has been called in the judgments in this case a proprietary right. The beneficiary is entitled to see all the trust documents because they are trust documents and because he is a beneficiary. They are in a sense his own. Action or no action, he is entitled to access to them. This has nothing to do with discovery. The right to discovery is a right to see someone else's documents. A proprietary right is a right to access to documents which are your own. No question of professional privilege arises in such a case. Documents containing professional advice taken by the executors as trustees contain advice taken by trustees for their cestuis que trust, and the beneficiaries are entitled to see them because they are beneficiaries."

General observations of this sort give very little guidance, for first they beg the question what are trust documents, and secondly their lordships were not considering the point here that papers are asked for which bear on the question of the exercise of the trustees' discretion. In my judgment category (a) mentioned in the notice of appeal, viz., the minutes of the meetings of the trustees of the settlement; and part of (b), viz., agenda prepared for trustees' meetings, are, in the absence of an action impugning the trustees' good faith, documents which a beneficiary cannot claim the right to inspect. If the defendant is allowed to examine these, she will know at once the very matters which the trustees are not bound to disclose to her, namely, their motives and reasons. Trustees who wish to preserve their rights in this respect must either commit nothing to paper or destroy everything from meeting to meeting. Indeed, if the defendant be right, I doubt if the last course is open, for she must succeed, if at all, on the ground that the papers belong to her, and if so, the trustees have no right to destroy them.

I would hold that even if documents of this type ought properly to be described as trust documents, they are protected for the special reason which protects the trustees' deliberations on a discretionary matter from disclosure. If necessary, I hold that this principle overrides the ordinary rule. This is, in my judgment, no less in the true interest of the beneficiary than of the trustees. Again, if one of the trustees commits to paper his suggestions and circulates them among his co-trustees; or if inquiries are made in writing as to the circumstances of a member of the class; I decline to hold that such documents are trust documents the property of the beneficiaries. In my opinion such documents are not trust documents in the proper sense at all. On the other hand, if the solicitor advising the trustees commits to paper an aide-mémoire summarising the state of the fund or of the family and reminding the trustees of past distributions and future possibilities I think that must be a document which any beneficiary must be at liberty to inspect. It seems to me, therefore, that category (b) in the notice of appeal embraces documents on both sides of the line.

As to (c), which is: "Correspondence relating to the administration of the trust property or otherwise to the execution of the trusts of the said settlement and passing between (i) the individuals for the time being holding office as trustees of or appointors under the said settlement, (ii) the said trustees and appointors or any of them on the one hand and the solicitors to the trustees on the other hand; (iii) the said trustees and appointors or any of them on the one hand and the beneficiaries under the said settlement on the other hand"; I cannot think that communications passing between individual trustees and appointors are documents in which beneficiaries have a proprietary right. On the other hand, as to category (ii), in general the letters of the trustees' solicitors to the trustees do seem to me to be trust documents in which the beneficiaries have a property. As to category (iii), I do not think letters to or from an individual beneficiary ought to be open to inspection by another beneficiary. Thus I think the judge's order went too far, but it is very difficult to frame a declaration which will not cut down the rights of the beneficiaries too much. I would propose that we should discuss this matter after my brethren have given their opinions on the matter.

SALMON LJ: There is another possible approach to the present case. The category of trust documents has never been comprehensively defined. Nor could it be—certainly not by me. Trust documents do, however, have these characteristics in common: (1) they are documents in the possession of the trustees as trustees; (2) they contain information about the trust which the beneficiaries are entitled to know; (3) the beneficiaries have a proprietary interest in the documents and, accordingly, are entitled to see them. If any parts of a document contain information which the beneficiaries are not entitled to know, I doubt whether such parts can truly be said to be integral parts of a trust document. Accordingly, any part of a document that lacked the second characteristic to which I have referred would automatically be excluded from the document in its character as a trust document.

I agree with my Lords that the appeal should be allowed.

(1965) 81 LQR 196 (R.E.M.)

"It seems safe to say that the last of *Re Londonderry's Settlement* has not been heard. Perhaps the most obvious point which may arise is whether a beneficiary who is determined to discover all he can about the grounds upon which a discretion has been exercised may not achieve this by instituting litigation alleging that the trustees have exercised their discretion in some improper way, and then obtaining discovery of documents in those proceedings, as in *Talbot v Marshfield* (1865) 2 Drew & Sm 549. Will the courts permit the bonds of secrecy to be invaded by the simple process of commencing hostile litigation against the trustees? It is not easy to see how the courts can prevent this. True, questions of relevance may obviously arise; but on discovery the test of relevance is wide. The classical statement is that of Brett LJ: an applicant is entitled to discovery of any document 'which may fairly lead him to a train of inquiry' that may 'either directly or indirectly enable the party requiring the affidavit either to advance his own case or to damage the case of his adversary' (*Compagnie Financière et Commerciale du Pacifique v Peruvian Guano Co* (1882) 11 QBD 55 at 63). Indeed, the formal order of the court, . . . seems to recognise this possibility.

The other main point which plainly needs further exploration is the ambit of the term 'trust documents'. The negative proposition is now plain: not all documents held by trustees as such are 'trust documents'[13]. But even after a detailed examination of the judgments it is difficult to frame any positive proposition with any degree of confidence. Nor does the formal order of the court (see at p. 938) lessen the difficulty; indeed, it contributes its own quota of problems. The order states that without prejudice to any right of the defendant to discovery in any subsequent proceedings against the trustees, and subject to any order of the court in any particular circumstances, there are four categories of documents which the trustees are not bound to disclose to the defendant. The first of these categories is 'The agenda of the meetings of the trustees of the settlement'; the second and third categories consist of correspondence of the trustees *inter se* and with the beneficiaries; and the fourth category consists of minutes of the meetings of the trustees and other documents disclosing their deliberations as to the manner in which they should exercise their discretion or disclosing their reasons for any particular exercise of their discretion, or the materials therefor. It is thus only the minutes and the other documents in the fourth category which appear to be qualified by words relating to disclosure of the trustees' reasons for exercising their discretion in a particular way; the freedom from disclosure seems to apply to all agenda and correspondence, whether or not they would reveal any such reasons or the material on which they were based. Nor does the order make it plain how it applies to documents in the fourth category which not only disclose confidential matters but also deal with other points as well; the inclusion of any confidential matter seems to confer exemption upon the entire document, and not merely upon the confidential matter. The order did, however, declare that the trustees were bound to disclose to the defendant any written advice from their solicitors or counsel as to the manner in which the trustees were in law entitled to exercise their discretion.

Putting all the material together, it seems at present to be difficult to say more than that all documents held by trustees *qua* trustees are prima facie trust documents, but that there is a class of exceptions from this rule which is ill-defined but includes confidential documents which the beneficiaries ought not to see. For greater precision than that we must await further decisions by the courts. The Court of Appeal has taken a firm step in the right direction; but that is all."

[13] Per DANCKWERTS LJ at pp. 935–936.

15. Powers of Trustees[1]

I. General

Trustees have such powers as are given to them by statute or by the trust instrument. It is necessary therefore to read all the statutory provisions which give them their powers. Only the main provisions can be reproduced here.

II. Power of Sale[2]

TRUSTEE ACT 1925

12. Power of trustees for sale to sell by auction, &c.—(1) Where a trust for sale or a power of sale of property is vested in a trustee, he may sell or concur with any other person in selling all or any part of the property, either subject to prior charges or not, and either together or in lots, by public auction or by private contract, subject to any such conditions respecting title or evidence of title or other matter as the trustee thinks fit, with power to vary any contract for sale, and to buy in at any auction, or to rescind any contract for sale and to re-sell, without being answerable for any loss.

(2) A trust or power to sell or dispose of land includes a trust or power to sell or dispose of part thereof, whether the division is horizontal, vertical, or made in any other way.

(3) This section does not enable an express power to sell settled land to be exercised where the power is not vested in the tenant for life or statutory owner.

[1] H & M, pp. 487–511; K & S, pp. 236–241, 259, 290–305; P & M, pp. 239–245, 327–342; Pettit, pp. 320–327, 337–362; Snell, pp. 249–271.

[2] H & M, pp. 488–490; P & M, p. 259; Pettit, pp. 337–339; Snell, pp. 249–252.

16. Power to raise money by sale, mortgage, &c.—(1) Where trustees are authorised by the instrument, if any, creating the trust or by law to pay or apply capital money subject to the trust for any purpose or in any manner, they shall have and shall be deemed always to have had power to raise the money required by sale, conversion, calling in, or mortgage of all or any part of the trust property for the time being in possession[3].

(2) This section applies notwithstanding anything to the contrary contained in the instrument, if any, creating the trust, but does not apply to trustees of property held for charitable purposes, or to trustees of a settlement for the purposes of the Settled Land Act, 1925, not being also the statutory owners.

SETTLED LAND ACT 1925

38. Powers of sale and exchange[4]—A tenant for life—

(i) May sell the settled land, or any part thereof, or any easement, right or privilege of any kind over or in relation to the land; and

(ii) . . .[5]

(iii) May make an exchange of the settled land, or any part thereof, or of any easement, right, or privilege of any kind, whether or not newly created, over or in relation to the settled land, or any part thereof, for other land, or for any easement, right or privilege of any kind, whether or not newly created, over or in relation to other land, including an exchange in consideration of money paid for equality or exchange.

LAW OF PROPERTY ACT 1925

28. Powers of management, &c. conferred on trustees for sale.—(1) Trustees for sale shall, in relation to land or to manorial incidents and to the proceeds of sale, have all the powers of a tenant for life and the trustees of a settlement under the Settled Land Act, 1925, including in relation to the land the powers of management conferred by that Act during a minority and where by statute settled land is or becomes vested in the trustees of the settlement upon the statutory trusts, such trustees and their successors in office shall also have all the additional or larger powers (if any) conferred by the settlement on the tenant for life, statutory owner, or trustees of the settlement[6]: and (subject to any express trust to the contrary) all capital money arising under the said powers shall, unless paid or applied for any purpose authorised by the Settled Land Act, 1925, be applicable in the same manner as if the money represented proceeds of sale arising under the trust for sale.

All land acquired under this subsection shall be conveyed to the trustees on trust for sale.

[3] But this does not authorise trustees to raise money by charging existing investments in order to purchase others; *Re Suenson-Taylor's Settlement Trusts* [1974] 1 WLR 1280, [1974] 3 All ER 397.

[4] See also ss. 39, 40, 72.

[5] Para. (ii) was repealed by Statute Law (Repeals) Act 1969, s. 1, Schedule, Part III.

[6] As amended by L.P. (A.) A. 1926, Schedule.

The powers conferred by this subsection shall be exercised with such consents (if any) as would have been required on a sale under the trust for sale, and when exercised shall operate to overreach any equitable interests or powers which are by virtue of this Act or otherwise made to attach to the net proceeds of sale as if created by a trust affecting those proceeds.

SETTLED LAND ACT 1925

67. Sale and purchase of heirlooms under order of court.—(1) Where personal chattels are settled so as to devolve with settled land, or to devolve therewith as nearly as may be in accordance with the law or practice in force at the date of the settlement, or are settled together with land, or upon trusts declared by reference to the trusts affecting land, a tenant for life of the land may sell the chattels or any of them.

(2) The money arising by the sale shall be capital money arising under this Act, and shall be paid, invested, or applied and otherwise dealt with in like manner in all respects as by this Act directed with respect to other capital money arising under this Act, or may be invested in the purchase of other chattels of the same or any other nature, which, when purchased, shall be settled and held on the same trusts, and shall devolve in the same manner as the chattels sold.

(3) A sale or purchase of chattels under this section shall not be made without an order of the court.

In *Re Hope* ([1899] 2 Ch 679) the Court of Appeal refused to approve the sale by the tenant for life of the "Hope" diamond. His financial troubles, they said, had been brought about by his own extravagance. An account of the jewel and of its history is given on pp. 694, 695 of the report.

LAW OF PROPERTY ACT 1925

130. Creation of entailed interests in real and personal property.—(5) Where personal chattels are settled without reference to settled land on trusts creating entailed interests therein, the trustees, with the consent of the usufructuary for the time being if of full age, may sell the chattels or any of them, and the net proceeds of any such sale shall be held in trust for and shall go to the same persons successively, in the same manner and for the same interests, as the chattels sold would have been held and gone if they had not been sold, and the income of investments representing such proceeds of sale shall be applied accordingly.

TRUSTEE ACT 1925

57. Power of court to authorise dealings with trust property—(1) Where in the management or administration of any property vested in trustees, any sale, lease, mortgage, surrender, release, or other disposition, or any purchase, investment, acquisition, expenditure, or other transaction, is in the opinion of the court expedient, but the same cannot be effected by reason of the absence of any power for that purpose vested in the trustees by the trust instrument, if any, or by law, the court may by order confer upon the trustees, either generally or in any particular instance, the necessary power for the purpose, on such terms, and subject to such provisions and conditions, if any, as the court may think fit and may direct in what manner any money authorised to be expended, and the costs of any transaction, are to be paid or borne as between capital and income.

(2) The court may, from time to time, rescind or vary any order made under this section, or may make any new or further order.

(3) An application to the court under this section may be made by the trustees, or by any of them, or by any person beneficially interested under the trust.

(4) This section does not apply to trustees of a settlement for the purposes of the Settled Land Act, 1925.

In *Re Hope's Will Trusts* ([1929] 2 Ch 136) the Court approved under s. 57 (1) the sale of family portraits which were held upon trusts which should, as nearly as the rules of law and equity would permit, correspond with the limitations of real estate in tail. EVE J said (at p. 140): "Having come to the clear conclusion that the sale is one which will be beneficial to all parties interested, and indeed is almost unavoidable, I find no difficulty in authorizing the trustees to carry it out under s. 57."

III. Power to Give Receipts[7]

TRUSTEE ACT 1925

14. Power of trustees to give receipts.—(1) The receipt in writing of a trustee for any money, securities, or other personal property or effects payable, transferable, or deliverable to him under any trust or power shall be a sufficient discharge to the person paying, transferring, or delivering the same and shall effectually exonerate him from seeing to the application or being answerable for any loss or misapplication thereof.

(2) This section does not, except where the trustee is a trust corporation, enable a sole trustee to give a valid receipt for—

(*a*) the proceeds of sale or other capital money arising under a . . . trust for sale of land[8];

(*b*) capital money arising under the Settled Land Act, 1925.

(3) This section applies notwithstanding anything to the contrary in the instrument, if any, creating the trust.

[7] H & M, p. 490; K & S, p. 245; P & M, pp. 220, 231; Pettit, pp. 339–340; Snell, p. 252.
[8] As amended by L.P. (A.) A. 1926, Schedule.

IV. Power to Compound Liabilities and to Settle Claims[9]

TRUSTEE ACT 1925

15. Power to compound liabilities.—A personal representative, or two or more trustees acting together, or, subject to the restrictions imposed in regard to receipts by a sole trustee not being a trust corporation, a sole acting trustee where by the instrument, if any, creating the trust, or by statute, a sole trustee is authorised to execute the trusts and powers reposed in him, may if and as he or they think fit—

(*a*) accept any property, real or personal, before the time at which it is made transferable or payable; or

(*b*) sever and apportion any blended trust funds or property; or

(*c*) pay or allow any debt or claim on any evidence that he or they think sufficient; or

(*d*) accept any composition or any security, real or personal, for any debt or for any property, real or personal, claimed; or

(*e*) allow any time of payment of any debt; or

(*f*) compromise, compound, abandon, submit to arbitration, or otherwise settle any debt, account, claim, or thing whatever relating to the testator's or intestate's estate or to the trust;

and for any of those purposes may enter into, give, execute, and do such agreements, instruments of composition or arrangement, releases, and other things as to him or them seem expedient, without being responsible for any loss occasioned by any act or thing so done by him or them in good faith[10].

V. Power to Insure[11]

TRUSTEE ACT 1925

19. Power to insure.—(1) A trustee may insure against loss or damage by fire any building or other insurable property to any amount, including the amount of any insurance already on foot, not exceeding three fourth parts of the full value of the building or property, and pay the premiums for such insurance out of the income thereof or out of the income of any other property subject to the same trusts without obtaining the consent of any person who may be entitled wholly or partly to such income.

(2) This section does not apply to any building or property which a trustee is bound forthwith to convey absolutely to any beneficary upon being requested to do so.

[9] H & M, p. 491; K & S, p. 245; P & M, p. 282; Pettit, pp. 282–283; Snell, pp. 258–259.

[10] *Re Greenwood* (1911) 105 LT 509 (inaction by a trustee provides no defence). There was no such statutory power before the Conveyancing Act 1881 came into effect. It was not therefore available to the trustees in *Re Brogden* (1888) 38 ChD 546, p. 473, ante, where the incidents occurred before that time.

[11] H & M, pp. 490–491; K & S, pp. 258–259; P & M, p. 282; Pettit, pp. 340–341; Snell, pp. 253–254.

20. Application of insurance money where policy kept up under any trust, power or obligation.—(1) Money receivable by trustees or any beneficiary under a policy of insurance against the loss or damage of any property subject to a trust or to a settlement within the meaning of the Settled Land Act, 1925, whether by fire or otherwise, shall, where the policy has been kept up under any trust in that behalf or under any power statutory or otherwise, or in performance of any covenant or of any obligation statutory or otherwise, or by a tenant for life impeachable for waste, be capital money for the purposes of the trust or settlement, as the case may be.

(3) Any such money—

(*a*) if it was receivable in respect of settled land within the meaning of the Settled Land Act, 1925, or any building or works thereon, shall be deemed to be capital money arising under that Act from the settled land, and shall be invested or applied by the trustees, or, if in court, under the direction of the court, accordingly;

(*b*) if it was receivable in respect of personal chattels settled as heirlooms within the meaning of the Settled Land Act, 1925, shall be deemed to be capital money arising under that Act, and shall be applicable by the trustees, or, if in court, under the direction of the court, in like manner as provided by that Act with respect to money arising by a sale of chattels settled as heirlooms as aforesaid;

(*c*) if it was receivable in respect of property held upon trust for sale, shall be held upon the trusts and subject to the powers and provisions applicable to money arising by a sale under such trust;

(*d*) in any other case, shall be held upon trusts corresponding as nearly as may be with the trusts affecting the property in respect of which it was payable.

(4) Such money, or any part thereof, may also be applied by the trustees, or, if in court, under the direction of the court, in rebuilding, reinstating, replacing, or repairing the property lost or damaged, but any such application by the trustees shall be subject to the consent of any person whose consent is required by the instrument, if any, creating the trust to the investment of money subject to the trust, and, in the case of money which is deemed to be capital money arising under the Settled Land Act, 1925, be subject to the provisions of that Act with respect to the application of capital money by the trustees of the settlement.

VI. Power in Connection with Reversionary Interests[12]

TRUSTEE ACT 1925

22. Reversionary interests, valuations and audit.—(1) Where trust property includes any share or interest in property not vested in the trustees, or the proceeds of the sale of any such property, or any other thing in action, the trustees on the same falling into possession, or becoming payable or transferable may—

[12] H & M, p. 491; K & S, pp. 242–243; Pettit, pp. 342–343; Snell, pp. 259–260.

(*a*) agree or ascertain the amount or value thereof or any part thereof in such manner as they may think fit;
(*b*) accept in or towards satisfaction thereof, at the market or current value, or upon any valuation or estimate of value which they may think fit, any authorised investments;
(*c*) allow any deductions for duties, costs, charges and expenses which they may think proper or reasonable;
(*d*) execute any release in respect of the premises so as effectually to discharge all accountable parties from all liability in respect of any matters coming within the scope of such release;

without being responsible in any such case for any loss occasioned by any act or thing so done by them in good faith.

(2) The trustees shall not be under any obligation and shall not be chargeable with any breach of trust by reason of any omission—

(*a*) to place any distringas notice or apply for any stop or other like order upon any securities or other property out of or on which such share or interest or other thing in action as aforesaid is derived, payable or charged; or
(*b*) to take any proceedings on account of any act, default, or neglect on the part of the persons in whom such securities or other property or any of them or any part thereof are for the time being, or had at any time been, vested;

unless and until required in writing so to do by some person, or the guardian of some person, beneficially interested under the trust, and unless also due provision is made to their satisfaction for payment of the costs of any proceedings required to be taken:

Provided that nothing in this subsection shall relieve the trustees of the obligation to get in and obtain payment or transfer of such share or interest or other thing in action on the same falling into possession.

(3) Trustees may, for the purpose of giving effect to the trust, or any of the provisions of the instrument, if any, creating the trust or of any statute, from time to time (by duly qualified agents) ascertain and fix the value of any trust property in such manner as they think proper, and any valuation so made in good faith shall be binding upon all persons interested under the trust.

VII. Power to Delegate[13]

Originally a trustee was expected, in theory, to perform all his duties personally. *Delegatus non potest delegare*. Whether or not this was ever a practical proposition, it early became impracticable because of the increasing complications of business life.

By 1925, it could be said that a trustee could delegate certain functions; not, of course, his discretionary powers. He had to show that the appointment of some person to perform them was reasonably necessary in the

[13] H & M, pp. 492–499; K & S, pp. 236–241; P & M, pp. 239–245; Pettit, pp. 320–327; Snell, pp. 254–258; (1931) 47 LQR 330 (H.P.), 463 (W.S.H.); (1959) 22 MLR 381 (G. H. Jones).

circumstances, or was in accordance with ordinary business practice[14]. The trustee must exercise proper care in the selection of the agent, must employ him in his proper field, and must exercise general supervision[15]. Further, an exculpatory clause, limiting the trustee's liability to wilful default, was strictly construed; it was said in 1889 that such a clause merely had the effect of changing the onus of proof and of placing it on "those who seek to charge a . . . trustee with a loss arising from the default of an agent, when the propriety of employing the agent has been established"[16].

It is clear that the power of a trustee to delegate is widened by the Trustee Act 1925. The effect of ss. 23 and 30 has been the subject of differences of opinion, among which the reader must judge[17]. Sir William Holdsworth[18] said that s. 23 required no more of a trustee than subjective good faith in selecting an agent; that *Re Vickery*[19] was correctly decided, but "it shows that the Legislature has gone too far in whittling away the liabilities of trustees, with the result that, in some respects, the *cestui que trust* is insufficiently protected". Parker and Mellows "have no doubt that the decision in *Re Vickery* was technically incorrect on the legal principles previously established. They also believe that the result of the case is desirable . . . Surely Maugham J, while admittedly changing the law, introduced a measure of equity where little existed before. A trustee is still plainly liable if he is consciously negligent or reckless: why should he be liable for more?"[20] Gareth Jones took the view that although *Re Vickery* might, in the result, be correctly decided, the reasoning is fallacious, and that the 1925 legislation, properly understood, while widening the permitted scope for delegation, retains the old principles of liability[21].

TRUSTEE ACT 1925

23. Power to employ agents.—(1) Trustees or personal representatives may, instead of acting personally, employ and pay an agent, whether a solicitor, banker, stockbroker, or other person, to transact any business or do any act required to be transacted or done in the execution of the trust, or the administration of the testator's or intestate's estate, including the receipt and payment of money, and shall be entitled to be allowed and paid all charges and expenses so incurred, and shall not be responsible for the default of any such agent if employed in good faith.

(2) Trustees or personal representatives may appoint any person to act as their agent or attorney for the purpose of selling, converting, collecting, getting in, and executing and perfecting insurances of, or managing or cultivating, or otherwise administering any property, real or personal, moveable or immoveable, subject to the trust or forming part of the testator's or intestate's estate, in any place outside the United Kingdom or executing or exercising any discretion or trust or power vested in them in relation

14 *Re Parsons, Ex parte Belchier* (1754) Amb 218; *Speight v Gaunt* (1883) 9 App Cas 1.
15 *Speight v Gaunt*, supra; *Learoyd v Whiteley* (1887) 12 App Cas 727; *Fry v Tapson* (1884) 28 ChD 268.
16 *Re Brier* (1884) 26 ChD 238 at 243 per Lord Selborne.
17 See also T.A. 1925, ss. 8, 21, 22 and 25 (as amended by Powers of Attorney Act 1971).
18 (1931) 47 LQR 463.
19 [1931] 1 Ch 572; p. 531, post.
20 P & M, pp. 242–243.
21 (1959) 22 MLR 381, p. 535, post.

to any such property, with such ancillary powers, and with and subject to such provisions and restrictions as they may think fit, including a power to appoint substitutes, and shall not, by reason only of their having made such appointment, be responsible for any loss arising thereby.

(3) Without prejudice to such general power of appointing agents as aforesaid—

(*a*) A trustee may appoint a solicitor to be his agent to receive and give a discharge for any money or valuable consideration or property receivable by the trustee under the trust, by permitting the solicitor to have the custody of, and to produce, a deed having in the body thereof or endorsed thereon a receipt for such money or valuable consideration or property, the deed being executed, or the endorsed receipt being signed, by the person entitled to give a receipt for that consideration;

(*b*) A trustee shall not be chargeable with breach of trust by reason only of his having made or concurred in making any such appointment; and the production of any such deed by the solicitor shall have the same statutory validity and effect as if the person appointing the solicitor had not been a trustee;

(*c*) A trustee may appoint a banker or solicitor to be his agent to receive and give a discharge for any money payable to the trustee under or by virtue of a policy of insurance, by permitting the banker or solicitor to have the custody of and to produce the policy of insurance with a receipt signed by the trustee, and a trustee shall not be chargeable with a breach of trust by reason only of his having made or concurred in making any such appointment:

Provided that nothing in this subsection shall exempt a trustee from any liability which he would have incurred if this Act and any enactment replaced by this Act had not been passed, in case he permits any such money, valuable consideration, or property to remain in the hands or under the control of the banker or solicitor for a period longer than is reasonably necessary to enable the banker or solicitor, as the case may be, to pay or transfer the same to the trustee.

This subsection applies whether the money or valuable consideration or property was or is received before or after the commencement of this Act.

25. Power to delegate trusts during absence abroad.[1]—(1) Notwithstanding any rule of law or equity to the contrary, a trustee may, by power of attorney, delegate for a period not exceeding twelve months the execution or exercise of all or any of the trusts, powers and discretions vested in him as trustee either alone or jointly with any other person or persons.

(2) The persons who may be donees of a power of attorney under this section include a trust corporation but not (unless a trust corporation) the only other co-trustee of the donor of the power.

[1] As amended by Powers of Attorney Act 1971, s. 9, which, by sub-s. (4), "applies whenever the trusts, powers or discretions in question arose but does not invalidate anything done by virtue of the said section 25 as in force at the commencement of this Act." The exercise of the power no longer depends on absence abroad; the marginal note was not amended and is therefore inaccurate.

(3) An instrument creating a power of attorney under this section shall be attested by at least one witness.

(4) Before or within seven days after giving a power of attorney under this section the donor shall give written notice thereof (specifying the date on which the power comes into operation and its duration, the donee of the power, the reason why the power is given and, where some only are delegated, the trusts, powers and discretions delegated) to—

(*a*) each person (other than himself), if any, who under any instrument creating the trust power (whether alone or jointly) to appoint a new trustee; and

(*b*) each of the other trustees, if any;

but failure to comply with this subsection shall not, in favour of a person dealing with the donee of the power, invalidate any act done or instrument executed by the donee.

(5) The donor of a power of attorney given under this section shall be liable for the acts or defaults of the donee in the same manner as if they were the acts or defaults of the donor.

(6) For the purpose of executing or exercising the trusts or powers delegated to him, the donee may exercise any of the powers conferred on the donor as trustee by statute or by the instrument creating the trust, including power, for the purpose of the transfer of any inscribed stock, himself to delegate to an attorney power to transfer but not including the power of delegation conferred by this section.

(7) The fact that it appears from any power of attorney given under this section, or from any evidence required for the purposes of any such power of attorney or otherwise, that in dealing with any stock the donee of the power is acting in the execution of a trust shall not be deemed for any purpose to affect any person in whose books the stock is inscribed or registered with any notice of the trust.

(8) This section applies to a personal representative, tenant for life and statutory owner as it applies to a trustee except that subsection (4) shall apply as if it required the notice there mentioned to be given—

(*a*) in the case of a personal representative, to each of the other personal representatives, if any, except any executor who has renounced probate;

(*b*) in the case of a tenant for life, to the trustees of the settlement and to each person, if any, who together with the person giving the notice constitutes the tenant for life;

(*c*) in the case of a statutory owner, to each of the persons, if any, who together with the person giving the notice constitute the statutory owner and, in the case of a statutory owner by virtue of section 23 (1) (*a*) of the Settled Land Act 1925, to the trustees of the settlement.

30. Implied indemnity of trustees.—(1) A trustee shall be chargeable only for money and securities actually received by him notwithstanding his signing any receipt for the sake of conformity, and shall be answerable and accountable only for his own acts, receipts, neglects, or defaults, and not for those of any other trustee, nor for any banker, broker, or other person with whom any trust money or securities may be deposited, nor for the insufficiency or deficiency of any securities, nor for any other loss, unless the same happens through his own wilful default.

RE VICKERY
[1931] 1 Ch 572 (ChD, MAUGHAM J)

The defendant, Mr. Stephens, was a missionary, ignorant of business affairs. He was the sole executor of Mrs. Vickery who died in December, 1926, leaving an estate worth about £300. Stephens employed a solicitor named Jennens, who, unknown to him, had at one time been suspended from practice.

The plaintiffs, sons of Mrs. Vickery, objected to the appointment, pressed the defendant to expedite the administration of the estate, and in September, 1927 told the defendant of the past improprieties of Jennens, and asked the defendant to instruct a different solicitor. Jennens repeatedly assured the defendant that the matter would be quickly completed. Another solicitor was instructed in December, 1927. Proceedings were taken against Jennens, who absconded without payment.

The plaintiffs asked for a declaration that the defendant was guilty of a breach of trust in permitting sums of £214 14s. 5d. in the Post Office Savings Bank and £62 4s. 0d. in Savings Certificates to be received and retained by Jennens.

Held. The defendant was not liable.

MAUGHAM J: The question that arises is whether in the circumstances, and in view of my findings as to the facts, the defendant is liable to make good these sums with interest by reason of his negligence either in employing Jennens to receive the sums, or in permitting those sums to remain in his hands, in the circumstances of the case, for a longer period than was necessary.

In considering this question the Court has to bear in mind in particular two sections of the Trustee Act, 1925. Sect. 23, sub-s. 1, is as follows: [His Lordship read the sub-section, and continued:] This sub-section is new and, in my opinion, authorized the defendant in signing the authorities to Jennens & Jennens to collect the two sums in question; for I do not think it can be doubted that the defendant acted in good faith in employing Jennens for the purpose. It will be observed that the sub-section has no proviso or qualification to it such as we find in relation to s. 23, sub-s. 3. It is hardly too much to say that it revolutionizes the position of a trustee or an executor so far as regards the employment of agents. He is no longer required to do any actual work himself, but he may employ a solicitor or other agent to do it, whether there is any real necessity for the employment or not. No doubt he should use his discretion in selecting an agent, and should employ him only to do acts within the scope of the usual business of the agent; but, as will be seen, a question arises whether even in these respects he is personally liable for a loss due to the employment of the agent unless he has been guilty of wilful default.

Sect. 23, sub-s. 3, is in the following terms: [His Lordship read the sub-section and continued:] This sub-section is a reproduction with amendments of s. 17 of the Trustee Act, 1893, which replaced s. 2 of the Trustee

Act, 1888. It will be observed that para. (*a*) of the sub-section relates to the production of a deed having endorsed thereon a receipt for money or other property, and that para. (*c*) refers to the receipt of money payable to the trustee under a policy of insurance. In these cases, no doubt, there is no reason why the banker or the solicitor should do anything more than receive the money and pay the same to the trustee or as he shall direct. The proviso must, I think, be limited to these two cases; and, of course, it is not intended to preclude a trustee from keeping trust funds at his bank pending investment or other proper use of them; and it has nothing to do, in my opinion, with the case I have to decide, in which the powers given by paras. (*a*) and (*c*) were not utilized by the defendant. There was no doubt a good reason for not making the proviso extend to sub-s. 1 of s. 23, since in many cases where, for example, a banker or other agent is employed by a trustee to receive money, the money cannot at once be conveniently paid to the trustee, but has to be employed by the banker or other agent in a number of ways.

I have now to consider s. 30, sub-s. 1, of the Trustee Act, 1925, a section which replaces s. 24 of the Trustee Act, 1893, which in its turn re-enacted Lord Cranworth's Act, s. 31. It is in the following terms: [His Lordship read the sub-section, and continued:] Reliance has been placed on the words concluding the sub-section "nor for any other loss, unless the same happens through his own wilful default." To avoid misconception I wish to say that, having regard to the numerous decisions since the enactment of Lord Cranworth's Act in relation to the liability of trustees for innocent breaches of trust, it is impossible now to hold that the words "for any other loss" are quite general, with the result that no trustee is ever liable for breach of trust unless the breach is occasioned by his own wilful default. In my opinion the words are confined to losses for which it is sought to make the trustee liable occasioned by his signing receipts for the sake of conformity or by reason of the wrongful acts or defaults of another trustee or of an agent with whom trust money or securities have been deposited, or for the insufficiency or deficiency of securities or some other analogous loss. It may be noted that if the phrase is not so limited it is difficult to see how there could have been any need for s. 3 of the Judicial Trustee Act, 1896, now re-enacted as s. 61 of the Trustee Act, 1925, or for s. 29 of that Act; nor would it be possible to explain the numerous cases before 1896 where trustees were made liable for honest mistakes either of construction or fact: see, for example, *Learoyd v Whiteley* ((1887) 12 App Cas 727), *National Trustees Co of Australasia v General Finance Co of Australasia* ([1905] AC 373), and cases there cited.

On the other hand, since s. 30, sub-s. 1, expressly refers to the defaults of bankers, brokers, or other persons with whom any trust money or other securities may be deposited, I am unable—dealing here with the more limited case—to escape the conclusion that the trustee cannot be made liable for the default of such a person unless the loss happens through the "wilful default" of the trustee. Before considering the meaning of the words "wilful default" in this connection, I would observe that in the case of *Re Brier* ((1884) 26 ChD 238) the Court of Appeal, consisting of Lord Selborne LC, and Cotton and Fry LJJ, gave effect to Lord Cranworth's Act, s. 31, and held the trustees and executors not liable inasmuch as it had not been established that the loss occasioned by the agent's insolvency (in a case where, as the law then required, it was shown that the employment of the agent was a proper one) was due to the wilful default of the trustees and executors.

Now the meaning of the phrase "wilful default" has been expounded by the Court of Appeal in the case of *Re Trusts of Leeds City Brewery, Ltd's Deed* ([1925] Ch 532n), and in the case of *Re City Equitable Fire Insurance Co* ([1925] Ch 407). It should be noted that in both those cases the indemnity, given to the trustees in the first case and to the directors and officers of the company in the second case, was worded in a general form so that it could not be contended that they were liable for any matter or thing done or omitted unless it could be shown that the loss so occasioned arose from their own wilful default. This, as I have said, is not true of an ordinary executor or trustee; but the exposition of the phrase "wilful default" is not the less valuable. The Court of Appeal held, following in the case of *Re City Equitable Fire Insurance Co.* the decision of Romer J, that a person is not guilty of wilful neglect or default unless he is conscious that, in doing the act which is complained of or in omitting to do the act which it is said he ought to have done, he is committing a breach of his duty, or is recklessly careless whether it is a breach of his duty or not. I accept with respect what Warrington LJ said ([1925] Ch at 524)—namely, that in the case of trustees there are definite and precise rules of law as to what a trustee may or may not do in the execution of his trust, and that a trustee in general is not excused in relation to a loss occasioned by a breach of trust merely because he honestly believed that he was justified in doing the act in question. But for the reasons which I have given I think that, where an executor employs a solicitor or other agent to receive money belonging to the estate in reliance on s. 23, sub-s. 1, of the Trustee Act, 1925, he will not be liable for a loss of the money occasioned by misconduct of the agent unless the loss happens through the wilful default of the executor, using those words as implying, as the Court of Appeal have decided, either a consciousness of negligence or breach of duty, or a recklessness in the performance of a duty.

Returning to the facts of the present case, it should be noted that, having taken the step of employing a solicitor not merely to obtain probate and to wind up the estate, but also to collect the War Bonds, the sums in the Post Office Savings Bank, and the sums in Savings Certificates, the position was different from that of a trustee who has simply employed a solicitor or other agent to collect money; for the only practical way of compelling the solicitor to account in the circumstances under consideration was to require him by the usual process to deliver a bill of costs and cash account. This procedure, I may observe, is not a very effective one in the case of a fraudulent solicitor, since it lends itself in dishonest hands, as it did in the present case, to serious delay.

It is essential in this case to guard oneself against judging the conduct of the defendant in the light of subsequent events. To have employed a new solicitor as soon as the defendant became aware that H. H. Jennens was a person with a tarnished reputation for honesty would certainly have meant further costs. It might have proved quite unnecessary even on the supposition that Jennens was a rogue. Even a man of the world might have thought that the sum involved—the sum of 300*l*. or thereabouts—was far too small to make it probable that the solicitor would be likely —unless, indeed, in the case of stern necessity—for such a sum to expose himself to the orders of the Court and to the action of the Law Society. Nor must it be forgotten that upon the facts as I find them it was not till the month of September, 1927, that the defendant had any real reason for suspecting that Jennens was unworthy of confidence; and it seems that after that date he kept on pressing for an immediate settlement and kept on being assured that a settlement would immediately take place. On the whole I have come to the conclusion that the defendant was on any view of the facts guilty only of an error of judgment, and this, in the case of a loss occasioned by the defalcations of a solicitor, does not amount to wilful default on the part of the executor. The action accordingly in my judgment fails and must be dismissed.

In *Re Lucking's Will Trusts* ([1968] 1 WLR 866, [1967] 3 All ER 726) the trust fund consisted of a majority holding in Stephen Lucking, Ltd. Philip Charles Lucking, a shareholder and also a beneficiary, was sole trustee.

Peter Dewar, an old friend of Lucking, was appointed managing director of the company. Considerable sums of money were applied by Dewar for his own purposes, the money being drawn by cheques which Lucking signed in blank and Dewar counter-signed. Some £15,000 was irrecoverable in Dewar's subsequent bankruptcy.

Lucking was held liable for the breach of trust. On the question of the application of Trustee Act 1925, ss. 23 (1) and 30 (1), Cross J said (at p. 874): "In support of the proposition that a trustee who is carrying on an unincorporated business is only liable for negligence in his supervision of a manager employed by him if the negligence amounts to 'wilful default', counsel relied on the decision of Maugham J in *Re Vickery* ([1931] 1 Ch 572). In that case an executor employed a solicitor to obtain payment of sums of money due to the estate and furnished him with documents for the purpose. The solicitor made away with the money and it was said that having regard to what the executor had learnt of the reputation of the solicitor in question he ought to have cancelled the authority given him before the money got into his hands. Maugham J held that section 23 of the Trustee Act 1925 empowered the executor to employ the solicitor for the purpose in question in the first instance and that as section 30 of the Act provides, inter alia, that a trustee shall not be liable for the defaults of any person with whom any trust money or securities may be distributed unless the resulting loss happens through his own wilful default. The executor in the case before him would only be liable if he was guilty of wilful default. I see no reason whatever to think that Maugham J would have considered that a person employed by a trustee to manage a business owned by the trust was a person with whom trust money or securities were deposited within the meaning of section 30. In support of the proposition that directors are only liable for 'wilful default' counsel referred to the *City Equitable* case ([1925] Ch 407), but there one of the company's articles provided that directors should only be liable for 'wilful default'. Romer J made it clear in his judgment that but for that article he would have held some of the directors liable in some matters for negligence falling short of 'wilful default'. In my view, 'wilful default' does not enter into the picture in this case at all. The conduct of the defendant trustees is, I think, to be judged by the standard applied in *Speight v Gaunt* ((1883) 9 App Cas 1), namely, that a trustee is only bound to conduct the business of the trust in such a way as an ordinary prudent man would conduct a business of his own."

(1959) 22 MLR 388 (Gareth H. Jones)

"Re Vickery—a criticism

It is the present writer's submission that, although in the result *Re Vickery* might be correctly decided, the reasons given by Maugham J for the decision cannot be supported, and that it is consequently not safe or desirable for a trustee to rely on this decision as authority for the proposition that, 'I am safe if I act honestly but foolishly in appointing my agents.'[2] His Lordship's interpretation of section 23 (1) must inevitably lead to a conflict between that section and the remaining delegation sections of the Act. Indeed, some of the sections would seem to be otiose if Maugham J is correct.

(i) The interpretation of Maugham J of section 23 (1) has rendered section 23 (3) of the Trustee Act 'meaningless and unnecessary.'[3] This subsection allows a banker or solicitor to give a discharge for any monies which have been paid to them, and allows the trustee to give to such agents custody of a deed or receipt signed by the trustee. The trustee is made liable if the trust monies are permitted to remain in the hands of the banker or solicitor for a 'period longer than is reasonably necessary to enable the banker or solicitor, as the case may be, to pay or transfer the same to the trustee[4]'. The learned judge held that section 23 (3) was irrelevant in *Re Vickery* since the trustee had not purported to act thereunder. Foolish indeed will be the trustee who will so act; if the banker or solicitor is appointed 'in good faith' within section 23 (1), then the trustee is protected even if the agent subsequently defaults. Harmony between the two subsections cannot be achieved by limiting section 23 (1) to agents other than bankers or solicitors, for the section is quite general in terms. The most obvious reconciliation of section 23 (1) and section 23 (3) is, of course, to construe the words ' in good faith' in section 23 (1) so that they limit only the *act* of employment. In fact, the trustee will not be liable for his agent's defaults by reason only of an appoinment, which was not legally or morally necessary,

[2] Lewin (15th Edn) p. 185, and Underhill (10th Edn) p. 351, accept cautiously the decision. Hanbury (7th Edn) pp. 228–229) also accepts the case but subject to important limitations, namely, that a trustee advancing money on a mortgage should not employ the solicitor or valuer of the mortgagor, that a trustee must pay an agent only reasonable remuneration and that the *ejusdem generis* rule of interpretation will be applied to the words "or other person" within s. 23 (1). Keeton, in the latest edition of his *Law of Trusts* (8th Edn) p. 257, is of opinion that the reasoning of MAUGHAM J is erroneous.

[3] (1931) 47 LQR 330 (H. Potter).

[4] The learned judge's reasons for the absence of this proviso in s. 23 (1) are, with respect, unconvincing: "in many cases where, for example, a banker or other agent is employed by a trustee to receive money, the money cannot at once be conveniently paid to the trustee, but has to be employed by the banker or other agent in a number of ways" (at p. 581).

provided the appointment was in good faith[5]. Such an interpretation, which gives meaning to the words 'without prejudice to such general power of appointing agents as aforesaid,' which introduce and limit section 23 (3), was not acceptable to the learned judge[6].

(ii) If *Re Vickery* is correct it is difficult to see what is the precise scope of sections 23 (2) and 25. Both sections deal with situations where either the trustee or the trust property is outside the United Kingdom. It will be remembered that Eve J in *Green v Whitehead*[7] had considered section 23 (2) to be of much wider application than section 23 (1) and, certainly, there is a significant difference of wording. Whereas section 23 (1) speaks of the employment of an agent 'to transact any business' in the execution of the trust, section 23 (2) enables the trustee to delegate in addition his 'discretion'; similarly, section 25 permits a trustee to delegate his 'discretions.' It is clear that section 23 (1) is limited to ministerial acts but it is difficult to see what extra powers are delegable under sections 23 (2) and 25. It is submitted that under neither section can the trustee rid himself of his trusteeship. The draftsman, in all probability, envisaged that under sections 23 (2) and 25 the trustee would be able to delegate certain particular discretions, such as the discretion to choose between various tenders, or the discretion to pay agents a reasonable sum in remuneration, or even the discretion to appoint an agent. Only if a trustee desires his agent to have such discretion should he purport to act under these sections, otherwise, the trustee should act under section 23 (1). The reason for this is a simple one—*Speight v Gaunt*[8]. Section 25 enacts specifically that the trustee shall be liable for the acts or defaults of his agent[9] and while it is true that section 23 (2) does not contain such a provision, it is significant that this subsection does say that the trustee shall not be liable for any loss by reason only of making the *appointment*. Consequently, even under section 23 (2) it is most probable that the norm of the reasonable man of business will determine the liability of the trustee for the acts or defaults of his agent once appointed. Thus, the wise trustee, if *Re Vickery* represents the law, will act in all cases under section 23 (1) and be protected by the umbrella of an honest appointment—even though the trustee will be out of the United Kingdom for more than a month and even though the trust property is outside the United Kingdom.

(iii) His Lordship in *Re Vickery* did not directly address his mind to the problem of reconciling section 30 (1) of the Trustee Act, 1925 with section 23 (1)[10]. Maugham J limited section 30 (1) to 'bankers and brokers' and the words 'any other loss'[11] to cases where the loss had arisen through the signing of receipts for the sake of conformity, or where the wrongful acts of

[5] Cf. the words of s. 23 (2), which concludes that trustees "shall not, by reason only of their having made such appointment, be responsible for any loss arising thereby."

[6] For he had held that s. 23 (1) protected a trustee even for his agent's defaults after appointment.

[7] [1930] 1 Ch 38.

[8] (1883) 9 App Cas 1.

[9] Section 25 (2).

[10] Semble, MAUGHAM J was of opinion that if the trustee was guilty of wilful default then he would have been liable. But he did not discuss the effect of this view on s. 23 (1).

[11] Section 30 (1) states that the trustee shall not be responsible for "... the insufficiency or deficiency of any securities, nor for *any other loss*, unless the same happens through his own wilful default." (Italics supplied).

another trustee or the agent with whom the trust money had been deposited had resulted in the loss, or where the loss is due to the deficiency or insufficiency of securities or other analogous loss[12]. This limitation does not solve, unfortunately, the conundrum of how a trustee can be free of liability if he appoints in good faith and yet later be liable for the acts or defaults of these particular agents if he, the trustee, has been guilty of a wilful default. Further, the learned judge's definition of 'wilful default' as a conscious or reckless breach of duty on the part of the trustee cannot be supported; the words should have been construed, in their pre-1926 sense, so as to include want of reasonable care. His Lordship purported to follow the judgment of Romer J in the *Re City Equitable* case. In that decision, Romer J was called upon, *inter alia,* to construe a set of articles of association, and in particular, a clause which was in terms similar to the indemnity clause (s. 24) of the Trustee Act, 1893. It was inevitable, therefore, that counsel should rely[13] on the *Re Brier*[14] line of cases, which had impliedly interpreted 'wilful default' to include lack of reasonable care, as well as a conscious act of commission or recklessness on the part of the trustee. Romer J rejected this argument. He pointed out that these cases did not involve a consideration of these precise words and that, in the *Re Brier* line of cases, the court was concerned with the 'law as to the employment of agents by trustees.'[15] Directors and auditors were not trustees in the strict sense of the word and there is little resemblance between their duties and the 'duties of a trustee of a will or a marriage settlement.' His Lordship preferred to follow a number of company law decisions, which were authority for a *Derry v Peek*[16] definition of 'wilful default.'

> 'An act, or an omission to do an act, is wilful where the person of whom we are speaking knows what he is doing and intends to do what he is doing. But if that act or omission amounts to a breach of his duty, and therefore to negligence, is the person guilty of wilful negligence? In my opinion that question must be answered in the negative unless he knows that he is committing, and intends to commit, a breach of this duty, or is recklessly careless in the sense of not caring whether his act or omission is or is not a breach of duty.'[17]

This definition was later accepted by Astbury J in *Re Munton*[18], a decision which was concerned with the liability of a trustee for the acts or defaults of his agent. The learned judge held that a retiring trustee was not guilty of a breach of trust in executing a power of attorney authorising a broker to sell stock and receive the purchase price, the broker having, without authority, handed over the proceeds of sale to a co-trustee who had misappropriated them. The reasoning of the learned judge is, with respect, a little difficult to follow. The following passage is significant:

> 'The indemnity clauses, containing the exception of wilful default,

[12] At p. 582.
[13] *Re City Equitable* [1925] Ch 407 at 424.
[14] (1884) 26 ChD 238.
[15] At p. 439. MAUGHAM J in *Re Vickery* recognised this distinction but found the exposition of ROMER J of "wilful default" none the less valuable (at p. 583).
[16] (1889) 14 App Cas 337.
[17] At p. 434.
[18] [1927] 1 Ch 262.

> in the Trustee Acts, may or may not have added anything to the previous law, but in *Re City Equitable Fire Insurance Co Ltd* the whole question of wilful default as regards a fiduciary agent is dealt with at great length. Warrington LJ says: "Romer J was quite right in arriving at the conclusion that a person is not guilty of 'wilful neglect or default' unless he is conscious that in doing the act which is complained of, or in omitting to do the act which it is said he ought to have done, he is committing a breach of his duty, and also, as he said, recklessly careless whether it is a breach of the duty or not. . . ."
>
> The plaintiff's counsel say that the *City Equitable* case has made no change in the law as regards an ordinary trustee's liability. I do not propose to discuss that. I have read the passage representing the general result of the decision and it seems to me to apply to the present case'.[19]

The question was not raised in the Court of Appeal and their Lordships did not comment on these observations of Astbury J.

It is submitted, with respect, that the translation of the definition of 'wilful default' in *Re City Equitable* to section 30 (1) of the Trustee Act, 1925, was completely unjustified. Romer J was construing a particular set of articles of association and the decision on the facts of *Re City Equitable* was to have no application to the case of trustees, *stricto sensu*. This, indeed, was the view of Warrington LJ, in the Court of Appeal, in that case, and his approval of Romer J's definition, quoted by Astbury J in the above passage, was a strictly limited approval. The following extract from the learned Lord Justice's judgment is relevant[20].

> 'With all respect to counsel who cited those trustee cases to us, I think there is great danger of being misled if we attempt to apply decisions as to the duties of trustees to a case as to the conduct of persons in the position of auditors in this case. In the case of trustees there are certain definite and precise rules of law as to what a trustee may or may not do in the execution of his trust, and it is no answer for a trustee to say, if, for example, he invests the trust property in his hands in a security which the law regards as an unauthorised security: 'I honestly believed that I was justified in doing that.' No honest belief will justify him in committing that which is a breach of such a rule of law, and therefore the question which we have to determine in expressing a view on the construction of such words in a contract like the present is not solved by seeing how the question has been determined in a case relating to the duties of a trustee.'

In effect, neither Romer J nor the Court of Appeal in *Re City Equitable* intended to derogate from the pre-1926 decisions, which, impliedly if not expressly, interpreted the words 'wilful default', within section 24 of the 1893 Act, so as to include lack of reasonable care. Section 30 (1) is a mere re-enactment of section 24 of the Trustee Act, 1893, and like that section should, it is submitted, render the trustee liable if he failed to act with reasonable care.

[19] At p. 274.

[20] *Re City Equitable Fire Insurance Co Ltd* [1925] Ch 407 at 523–524.

The delegation sections—a suggested interpretation

It must be remembered in construing the Trustee Act, 1925, that primarily it 'is a Consolidation Act' and that it is 'therefore extremely unlikely, to say the least of it, that it effected any substantial change in the pre-existing law.'[1] If a literal interpretation of the delegation sections leads to conflict between these sections, then the sections should be narrowly construed in accordance with the pre-1926 law, and, in particular, the principles laid down in *Speight v Gaunt*.

For reasons just set out, it is suggested that section 30 (1) should be regarded as a re-enactment of section 24 of the 1893 Act and interpreted accordingly. Sections 23 (2) and 25 present no great difficulty. They were enacted to meet the case of the trustee being absent from the United Kingdom or where the trust property was abroad, and for these special reasons the trustee is permitted to delegate his discretions. Sections 23 (2) and 25 do not, however, allow the trustee to rid himself of his trusteeship; he should still exercise, as far as is reasonably possible, an anxious surveillance over the trust interests, and his liability for his agent's defaults should be judged by the norm of the reasonable business man, the same standard as is imposed on bankers and solicitors by the proviso to section 23 (3). But what of section 23 (1)? If the *Re Vickery* interpretation is unacceptable, what is the scope of section 23 (1)? The words of the section are sweeping and it is probable that the section does at least remove the limitation imposed on the trustee's power to delegate by the decision in *Ex p. Belchier*[2]—a trustee can now delegate even though there is no legal or moral necessity so to do. In our submission the subsection does no more. A trustee should not, by means of an honest appointment, be able to ignore with complacency the activities of his agent; his liability for that agent's acts or defaults should still be determined by the rule in *Speight v Gaunt* and the norm of the reasonable man of business. Such an interpretation would afford meaning to section 23 (1) and would reconcile the section with the remaining delegation sections of the Trustee Act, 1925, and, in particular, section 30 (1).

It must be admitted, however, that section 23 (1) is open to an alternative construction, namely, that the words 'in good faith' qualify not only the *act* of employment but the defaults of the agent once appointed. The section, in fact, concludes with the words, that the trustee 'shall not be responsible for the default of any such agent if employed in good faith.' If this interpretation is given to the section, then section 23 (1) can be reconciled with the other delegation sections only by interpreting "in good faith" restrictively, so as to mean in good faith and without negligence. Eve J in *Re Greenwood*[3] was required to consider section 21 (2) of the Trustee Act, 1893, and adopted a similar construction. This section, which was concerned with the composition of debts, laid down that the trustee was not responsible 'for any loss occasioned by any act or thing so done by him or them in good faith.' His Lordship commented upon these words as follows[4]:

[1] ROMER J in *Re Turner's Will Trusts* [1937] Ch 15 at 24.
[2] (1754) Amb 218. It is suggested that the *Belchier* principle does not limit ss. 23 (2) and 25.
[3] (1911) 105 LT 509.
[4] At p. 514.

'The question whether that section applies turns mainly on the proper meaning to be attributed to the concluding words of the subsection I have read. They seem to involve the doing of some act, or at least the exercise of some active discretion on the part of the trustee, not the mere passive attitude of leaving matters alone. Inaction . . . cannot be the same thing as "an act or thing done in good faith. . . ." In determining, therefore, whether the conduct of the trustees has or has not been *bona fide* in any particular case, the court is bound to have regard to all the circumstances, and if these lead to the conclusion that the loss has arisen from the neglect or carelessness or supineness of the trustee, and not from a mistaken but *bona fide* exercise by him of the statutory powers vested in him, then, in my opinion, the case is outside the subsection altogether, and in respect of which no relief is thereby afforded to the trustee.'

The Court of Appeal has recently adopted a similar approach in a decision, involving consideration of section 72 of the National Health Service Act, 1946[5]. Such an interpretation is not as radical, therefore, as it may seem at first.

In conclusion, it is to be noted that section 23 (1) speaks simply of the liability of the trustee for the acts of his *agent*, and the section concludes that the trustee shall 'not be responsible for the default of any such agent if employed in good faith? The section does not deal with responsibility, which the *trustee* himself assumed when he undertook the trust. Thus, in *Re Vickery* Maugham J was concerned with liability of the trustee for the act of the solicitor, and not with the question whether the trustee was in breach of his own *primary* duty as trustee to supervise the trust, and, in particular, his agents. What norm is to determine if the trustee has properly supervised the acts of his agents? The reasonable business man of *Speight v Gaunt*? If this be the standard, and it is suggested that it is, then the decision in *Re Vickery* is effectively circumscribed. The judgment of the trustee must be constantly exercised. To exercise this judgment, as a reasonable trustee should, will demand that the trustee appoints an agent to do work which he is qualified to do, to appoint a solicitor as a solicitor, a broker as a broker[6], and, after the appointment of such agents, to supervise their acts. A trustee cannot give an agent a carte blanche. This 'primary' liability of the trustee is independent of his vicarious liability for the acts or defaults of his agent, and it is with this latter head of liability that section 23 (1) is concerned[7]. It is suggested, therefore, that it is open for the courts to hold that the trustee has a primary duty, imposed on him by equity, to supervise at all times the trust and the trust funds; and it is further submitted that the norm of the reasonable man of business will determine whether in fact he has discharged that duty."

[5] In *Bullard v Croydon Hospital Group Management Committee* [1953] 1 QB 511, [1953] 1 All ER 596.

[6] But see MAUGHAM J in *Re Vickery*, at p. 581.

[7] Cf. the words of s. 30 (1), which gives the trustee an indemnity, unless "the same happens through his own wilful default". The master and servant cases in tort are, of course, an obvious parallel: see *Gold v Essex County Council* [1942] 2 KB 293, [1942] 2 All ER 237; *Carmarthenshire County Council v Lewis* [1955] AC 549, [1955] 1 All ER 565; *Staveley Iron and Chemical Co Ltd v Jones* [1956] AC 627, [1956] 1 All ER 403. The analogy is only a limited one.

VIII. Power of Maintenance[8]

The statutory power of Maintenance gives to trustees a power to apply income for the benefit of beneficiaries who are minors, or who are not yet entitled to the income. Minors and persons contingently entitled would otherwise be unable to benefit from the income. The policy is to allow the gift to "carry the intermediate income" unless the income is otherwise disposed of, or there are good reasons to the contrary. Thus, the trustees may apply the income for the maintenance education and benefit of minor beneficiaries; and are required to pay the income to adult persons who are contingently entitled to the capital on the happening of some future event.

The statutory power of Advancement relates to the payment of capital for special purposes. Those purposes related, and until recent times were limited, to specific occasions in the establishment in life of a beneficiary[9]. In modern cases however, a wide construction is given to the phrase "advancement or benefit", and this was used to permit blocks of capital to be paid to contingent remaindermen in order to avoid estate duty liability in respect of that property on the death of a life tenant. The fiscal advantages are less significant under capital transfer tax, because tax is chargeable (at the lower rate) on the termination of the life tenant's interest[10]. Where, however, the property is held on trust for a minor contingently on obtaining an age not in excess of 25, and there is no prior interest in possession, there is no charge to tax upon the minor's attainment of majority, nor upon payments of capital being made to him[11].

A. The Statutory Power

TRUSTEE ACT 1925

31. Power to apply income for maintenance and to accumulate surplus income during a minority.—(1) Where any property is held by trustees in trust for any person for any interest whatsoever, whether vested or contingent, then, subject to any prior interests or charges affecting that property—

(i) during the infancy of any such person, if his interest so long continues, the trustees may, at their sole discretion, pay to his parent or guardian, if any, or otherwise apply for or towards his maintenance, education, or benefit, the whole or such part, if any, of the income of that property as may, in all the circumstances, be reasonable, whether or not there is—

(*a*) any other fund applicable to the same purpose; or

(*b*) any person bound by law to provide for his maintenance or education; and

(ii) if such person on attaining the age of eighteen years has not a vested interest in such income, the trustees shall thenceforth pay the income of that property and of any accretion thereto under

[8] H & M, pp. 499–504; K & S, pp. 290–297; P & M, pp. 327–334; Pettit, pp. 343–349; Snell, pp. 262–267. See generally (1953) 17 Conv (NS) 273 (B. S. Ker).

[9] See *Pilkington v IRC* [1964] AC 612, [1962] 3 All ER 622, p. 549, post.

[10] F.A. 1965, Sch. 5, para. 4 (2), p. 157, ante.

[11] Ibid., Sch. 5, para. 15 (2). Other qualifications are introduced by F.A. 1976, s. 106. See p. 169, ante.

subsection (2) of this section to him, until he either attains a vested interest therein or dies, or until failure of his interest:

Provided that, in deciding whether the whole or any part of the income of the property is during a minority to be paid or applied for the purposes aforesaid, the trustees shall have regard to the age of the infant and his requirements and generally to the circumstances of the case, and in particular to what other income, if any, is applicable for the same purposes; and where trustees have notice that the income of more than one fund is applicable for those purposes, then, so far as practicable, unless the entire income of the funds is paid or applied as aforesaid or the court otherwise directs, a proportionate part only of the income of each fund shall be so paid or applied.

(2) During the infancy of any such person, if his interest so long continues, the trustees shall accumulate all the residue of that income in the way of compound interest by investing the same and the resulting income thereof from time to time in authorised investments, and shall hold those accumulations as follows:—

(i) If any such person—

(*a*) attains the age of eighteen[12] years, or marries under that age, and his interest in such income during his infancy or until his marriage is a vested interest; or

(*b*) on attaining the age of eighteen[12] years or on marriage under that age becomes entitled to the property from which such income arose in fee simple, absolute or determinable[13], or absolutely, or for an entailed interest;

the trustees shall hold the accumulations in trust for such person absolutely, but without prejudice to any provision with respect thereto contained in any settlement by him made under any statutory powers during his infancy, and so that the receipt of such person after marriage, and though still an infant, shall be a good discharge; and

(ii) In any other case the trustees shall, notwithstanding that such person had a vested interest in such income, hold the accumulations as an accretion to the capital of the property from which such accumulations arose, and as one fund with such capital for all purposes, and so that, if such property is settled land, such accumulations shall be held upon the same trusts as if the same were capital money arising therefrom;

but the trustees may, at any time during the infancy of such person if his interest so long continues, apply those accumulations, or any part thereof, as if they were income arising in the then current year.

(3) This section applies in the case of a contingent interest only if the limitation or trust carries the intermediate income of the property, but it applies to a future or contingent legacy by the parent of, or a person standing in loco parentis to, the legatee, if and for such period as, under

[12] As amended by Family Law Reform Act 1969. The age, however, remains 21 in the case of instruments made (not only those coming into effect) on or after January 1, 1970. A will made before that date is not to be treated as made on or after that date by reason only that the will is confirmed by a codicil executed on or after that date. S. 1 and Sch. 3, para. 1.

[13] *Re Sharp's Settlement Trusts* [1973] Ch 331, [1972] 3 All ER 151; (1974) 34 Conv (NS) 436 (D. J. Hayton).

the general law, the legacy carries interest for the maintenance of the legatee, and in any such case as last aforesaid the rate of interest shall (if the income available is sufficient, and subject to any rules of court to the contrary) be five pounds per centum per annum.

(4) This section applies to a vested annuity in like manner as if the annuity were the income of property held by trustees in trust to pay the income thereof to the annuitant for the same period for which the annuity is payable, save that in any case accumulations made during the infancy of the annuitant shall be held in trust for the annuitant or his personal representatives absolutely.

(5) This section does not apply where the instrument, if any, under which the interest arises came into operation before the commencement of this Act.

B. Contrary Intention

TRUSTEE ACT 1925

69. Application of Act.—(2) The powers conferred by this Act on trustees are in addition to the powers conferred by the instrument, if any, creating the trust, but those powers, unless otherwise stated, apply if and so far only as a contrary intention is not expressed in the instrument, if any, creating the trust, and have effect subject to the terms of that instrument.

In *Re Turner's Will Trust* ([1937] Ch 15, [1936] 2 All ER 1435) Robert Turner, the testator, gave a share of his residuary estate in trust for such of the children of his late son Charles as should attain the age of 28 years. The will contained an express power of maintenance and a power to pay the income to such of them as shall have attained the age of 21 years, and instructed the trustees to accumulate the surplus.

Two of the testator's grandchildren had attained the age of 28 years at the testator's death. The third grandchild, Geoffrey, was then aged 21, and died three years later. His share of the income had all been accumulated. The question was whether he had been entitled to such income under Trustee Act 1925, s. 31. If so, the fund would pass on his death for estate duty purposes. The Court of Appeal, reversing BENNETT J, held that Geoffrey had not been entitled to the income. The imperative terms of s. 31 must be read subject to s. 69 (2), so that the contrary intention prevailed. ROMER LJ said (at pp. 27-28): "The fact that s. 31 contains provisions that are directory is immaterial. Powers of maintenance, in the comprehensive meaning of that term, usually do. Nothing is more common, for instance, than a direction to trustees to accumulate during the minority income not applied in maintenance. Such a direction is merely ancillary to the power of maintenance strictly so called, and may well be regarded as a part of the power of maintenance in its comprehensive sense. Such a direction is indeed contained in sub-s. 2 of s. 31 of the Trustee Act, 1925, and is an essential part of the statutory power of maintenance conferred upon trustees by the section. In the same way the direction contained in cl. (ii) of sub-s. 1 can be regarded as being merely an essential part of the new statutory power. This statutory power of maintenance, that is to say, the totality of the provisions to be found in s. 31 of the Act, is, in our opinion, one of the 'powers conferred by this Act' within the meaning of s. 69, sub-s. 2, and therefore only applies if and so far as a contrary intention is not expressed in the instrument creating the trust and has effect subject to the terms of that instrument. For these reasons we are of opinion that the accumulations of the income of the presumptive share of Geoffrey Heap Turner made by the trustees did not form part of his estate, but accrued by way of addition to the shares of the defendants Robert Heap Turner and Doris Heap Lyons in the residuary estate of the testator."

C. Intermediate Income[14]

(1953) 17 Conv (NS) pp. 275–276 (B. S. Ker)

"The question now arises as to when a 'limitation or trust' carries the intermediate income of the property. The rules are as follows:

1. A contingent gift by will of *residuary* personalty carries with it all the income it earns from the testator's death, for the simple reason that there is no one besides the residuary legatee to whom it could go. North J said in *Re Adams* [1893] 1 Ch 329, at 334, 'Here no child has [a vested interest in the residue]. How does the matter stand as to the income? It is said that they take an interest in that also. I think it is fallacious to say that they take an interest in the income, *qua* income of the capital they take an interest in. *But it is undisposed-of income, and as such becomes part of the residue*; but, being part of the residue, the income belongs contingently to the children, in the same way as the capital belongs contingently to them.' If this income is accumulated until the contingency vesting the money in the beneficiaries happens the rules in sections 164–166 of the Law of Property Act, 1925, must be observed. (See *Bective v Hodgson* (1864) 10 HL Cas 656.)

2. The rule as to contingent *specific* gifts of personalty and contingent specific or residuary gifts of realty is contained in section 175 of the Law of Property Act, 1925: 'A contingent or future specific devise or bequest of property, whether real or personal, and a contingent residuary devise of freehold land, and a specific or residuary devise of freehold land to trustees upon trust for persons whose interests are contingent or executory shall, subject to the statutory provisions relating to accumulations, carry the intermediate income of that property from the death of the testator, except so far as such income, or any part thereof, may be otherwise expressly disposed of.' This section applies only to *wills* coming into operation after 1925, but it has been held in *Re Raine* [1929] 1 Ch 716, not to apply to a pecuniary legacy. Further, it draws a distinction between 'land' and 'freehold' land. This is because leaseholds rank as personal property and therefore the ordinary rules (*supra* and *infra*) as to the income of contingent gifts of personalty apply: see *Guthrie v Walrond* (1883) 22 ChD 573, and *Re Woodin* [1895] 2 Ch 309, per Lindley LJ and Kay LJ.

Pecuniary Legacies

3. In view of the decision on *Re Raine* (*supra*) the rules of the general law

[14] For a tabular presentation, see (1976) 95 Law Notes 110 (M. J. Wells).

as to when contingent pecuniary legacies bear interest require examination. The broad rule is that no interest is payable on a contingent pecuniary legacy from the testator's death while the gift is in suspense (see *per* Kay LJ, in *Re George* (1877) 5 ChD 837). There are, however, the following exceptions in which the legacy, subject to any contrary intention in the will, carries interest from the testator's death . . .

Summarising, then: the three cases in which, apart from statute, contingent legacies carry interest from the date of death are—

(*a*) where the testator was the father of, or *in loco parentis* to, the legatee,

(*b*) where, without being either of the foregoing, the testator shows an intention to maintain (*Re Churchill*[15]), or

(*c*) where the testator has segregated the legacy for the legatee (*Re Medlock*[16]).

It will be noticed that section 31 (3) of the Trustee Act, 1925, expressly mentions the rule in (*a*) only—the golden rule. Does it impliedly exclude the rules in (*b*) and (*c*), or does it merely single out that in (*a*) for the purpose of fixing interest at 5 per cent. per annum? If it excludes (*b*) and (*c*) then section 31 will not apply at all to cases of the *Re Churchill* and *Re Medlock* kinds and this would need to be borne in mind when considering, in particular, subsection (1) (ii) and (2). The arguments both ways have already been set out (p. 275, *ante*). It is submitted that the correct view is that subsection (3) does embrace the *Re Churchill* and *Re Medlock* types of case and that the specific mention of the rule in (*a*) above is only for the purpose of establishing a suitable rate of interest. The learned author of Williams on Wills (p. 803) seems to take this view.

Before leaving subsection (3) it may be worth noticing that while the rule —(*a*) above—of the general law is that the donor of the legacy must be the *father* of the legatee, the statute, in adopting the rule has used the word 'parent' instead of father. At common law, of course, it is the father's duty to maintain his child—not the mother's unless she has deliberately taken upon herself a father's duty. Section 31 (3) may thus have enlarged the law here to cover a legacy by a mother not *in loco parentis*. However, the term 'parent' would probably be held to mean 'parent responsible in law for the children's maintenance' and thus refer only to the legatee's father, unless the mother had assumed the duty of maintenance."

In *Re McGeorge* ([1963] Ch 544, [1963] 1 All ER 519)[17] the testator devised land to his daughter and provided that the devise "shall not take effect until after the death of my . . . wife should she survive me". If the daughter should die before the wife, leaving issue, the issue, on attaining the age of 21, were to take by substitution the devise to the daughter. Cross J held that the devise to the daughter carried the intermediate income; that the income must be accumulated, to be paid to whoever became entitled to it—that is, the daughter or her issue, depending on whether the daughter survived the widow. Cross J said (at p. 550): "The

[15] [1909] 2 Ch 431.
[16] (1886) 55 LJ Ch 738.
[17] (1963) 79 LQR 184 (P.V.B.).

devise . . . is, it is said, a future specific devise within the meaning of the section [L.P.A. 1925, s. 175]; the testator has not made any express disposition of the income accruing from it between his death and the death of his widow, therefore that income is carried by the gift. At first sight it is hard to see how Parliament could have enacted a section which produces such a result. If a testator gives property to A after the death of B, then whether or not he disposes of the income accruing during B's life he is at all events showing clearly that A is not to have it. Yet if the future gift to A is absolute and the intermediate income is carried with it by force of this section, A can claim to have the property transferred to him at once, since no one else can be interested in it. The section, that is to say, will have converted a gift in remainder into a gift in possession in defiance of the testator's wishes. The explanation for the section taking the form it does is, I think, probably as follows. It has long been established that a gift of residuary personalty to a legatee in being on a contingency or to an unborn person at birth, carries the intermediate income so far as the law will allow it to be accumulated, but that rule had been held for reasons depending on the old land law not to apply to gifts of real property, and it was apparently never applied to specific dispositions of personalty. Section 175 of the Law of Property Act was plainly intended to extend the rule to residuary devises and to specific gifts whether of realty or of personalty. It is now, however, established at all events in courts of first instance that the old rule does not apply to residuary bequests whether vested or contingent which are expressly deferred to a future date which must come sooner or later. (See *Re Oliver* ([1947] 2 All ER 162), *Re Gillett's Will Trusts* ([1950] Ch 102, [1949] 2 All ER 893), and *Re Geering* ([1964] Ch 136, [1962] 3 All ER 1043). There is a good reason for this distinction. If a testator gives property to X contingently on his attaining the age of 30 it is reasonable to assume, in the absence of a direction to the contrary, that he would wish X if he attains 30 to have the income produced by the property between his death and the happening of the contingency. If, on the other hand, he gives property to X for any sort of interest after the death of A, it is reasonable to assume that he does not wish X to have the income accruing during A's lifetime unless he directs that he is to have it. But this distinction between an immediate gift on a contingency and a gift which is expressly deferred was not drawn until after the Law of Property Act, 1925, was passed. There were statements in textbooks and even in judgments to the effect that the rule applied to deferred as well as to contingent gifts of residuary personalty. (See Jarman, 7th Edn (1930) p. 1006).

The legislature, when it extended this rule to residuary devises and specific gifts, must, I think, have adopted this erroneous view of the law. I would have liked, if I could, to construe the reference to 'future specific devises' and 'executory interest' in the section in such a way as to make it consistent with the recent cases on the scope of the old rule applicable to residuary bequests. But to do that would be to rectify the Act, not to construe it, and I see no escape from the conclusion that whereas before 1926 a specific gift or a residuary devise which was not vested in possession did not prima facie carry intermediate income at all, now such a gift may carry intermediate income in circumstances in which a residuary bequest would not carry it.

It was argued in this case that the fact that the will contained a residuary gift constituted an express disposition of the income of the land in question which prevented the section from applying. I am afraid that I cannot accept this submission. I have little doubt that the testator expected the income of the land to form part of the income of residue during his widow's lifetime, but he has made no express disposition of it. I agree with what was said in this connection by Eve J in *Re Raine* ([1929] 1 Ch 716 at 719).

As the devise is not vested indefeasibly in the daughter but is subject to defeasance during the mother's lifetime the intermediate income which the gift carries by virtue of section 175 ought prima facie to be accumulated to see who eventually becomes entitled to it. It was, however, submitted by counsel for the daughter that she could claim payment of it under section 31 (1) of the Trustee Act, 1925. So far as material, that subsection provides that where any property is held by trustees in trust for any person for any interest whatsoever, whether vested or contingent, then, subject to any prior interests or charges affecting that property, if such person on attaining the age of 21 years has not a vested interest in such income, the trustees shall thenceforth pay the income of that property and of any accretion of such income made during his infancy to him until he either attains a vested interest therein or dies or until failure of his interest. There are, as I see it, two answers to the daughter's claim. The first—and narrower—answer is that her interest in the income of the devised land is in a vested interest. It is a future interest liable to be divested but it is not contingent. Therefore, section 31 (1) (ii) does not apply to it. The second—and wider— answer is that the whole framework of section 31 shows that it is inapplicable to a future gift of this sort and that a will containing such a gift expresses a contrary intention within section 69 (2) which prevents the section from applying. By deferring the enjoyment of the devise until after the widow's death the testator has expressed the intention that the daughter shall not have the immediate income. It is true that as he has not expressly disposed of it in any other way, section 175 of the Law of Property Act, 1925, defeats that intention to the extent of making the future devise carry the income so that the daughter will get it eventually if she survives her mother or dies before her leaving no children to take by substitution. But even if the words of section 31 fitted the case, there would be no warrant for defeating the testator's intention still further by reading it into the will and thus giving the daughter an interest in possession in the income during her mother's lifetime. In the result, in my judgment the income of the fund must be accumulated for 21 years if the widow so long lives."

D. Tax Considerations

i. CHILD OF THE SETTLOR

Where income is paid to or for the maintenance or benefit of a minor and unmarried child of the *settlor*, that income is treated for tax purposes as the income of the settlor[18].

[18] I.C.T.A. 1970, ss. 437–444, p. 147, ante.

There are further provisions by which any sum paid to a child of the *settlor*, whether from capital or income, is treated as income for the purpose of aggregation up to an amount equal to the total undistributed income of the settlement up to that date[19].

ii. OTHER MINORS

From 1969 until 1972, all the income of a minor unmarried child not regularly working was aggregated with the income of the parent. These provisions were repealed by the Finance Act 1970, but the Labour Government, elected in 1974, has promised their return.

iii. CAPITAL TRANSFER TAX

Accumulation and Maintenance settlements[20] have been given, as has been seen, a privileged position under the capital transfer tax legislation. Although there is no interest in possession during the minority of the beneficiaries, the settlement is not subjected to the 10-year periodic charge to tax; nor is a capital distribution treated as being made when a minor attains majority, or when payments of capital are made to him[1]. For capital transfer tax purposes, the property is treated, in effect, as if it was beneficially owned by the minor. Tax will be payable of course if, having attained a vested interest, and received the property, he gives it away.

IX. Power of Advancement[2]

A. The Statutory Power

TRUSTEE ACT 1925

32. Power of advancement.—(1) Trustees may at any time or times pay or apply any capital money subject to a trust, for the advancement or benefit, in such manner as they may, in their absolute discretion, think fit, of any person entitled to the capital of the trust property or of any share thereof, whether absolutely or contingently on his attaining any specified age or on the occurrence of any other event, or subject to a gift over on his death under any specified age or on the occurrence of any other event, and whether in possession or in remainder or reversion, and such payment or application may be made notwithstanding that the interest of such person is liable to be defeated by the exercise of a power of appointment or revocation, or to be diminished by the increase of the class to which he belongs:

Provided that—

(*a*) the money so paid or applied for the advancement or benefit of any person shall not exceed altogether in amount one-half of the

[19] Ibid., s. 438 (2), (3).
[20] Defined in F.A. 1975, Sch. 5, para. 15 (1), as amended by the F.A. 1976, s. 106, p. 169, ante.
[1] Ibid., Sch. 5, para. 15 (2).
[2] H & M, pp. 504–511; K & S, pp. 297–303; P & M, pp. 334–341; Pettit, pp. 349–352; Snell, pp. 267–271; (1958) 22 Conv (NS) 413; (1959) 23 Conv (NS) 27, 423 (D. W. M. Waters).

presumptive or vested share or interest of that person in the trust property; and

(*b*) if that person is or becomes absolutely and indefeasibly entitled to a share in the trust property the money so paid or applied shall be brought into account as part of such share; and

(*c*) no such payment or application shall be made so as to prejudice any person entitled to any prior life or other interest, whether vested or contingent, in the money paid or applied unless such person is in existence and of full age and consents in writing to such payment or application.

(2) This section applies only where the trust property consists of money or securities or of property held upon trust for sale calling in and conversion, and such money or securities, or the proceeds of such sale calling in and conversion are not by statute or in equity considered as land, or applicable as capital money for the purposes of the Settled Land Act, 1925.

(3) This section does not apply to trusts constituted or created before the commencement of this Act.

B. Advancement or Benefit

PILKINGTON v INLAND REVENUE COMMISSIONERS[3]
[1964] AC 612, [1962] 3 All ER 622 (HL, Lord Reid, Viscount Radcliffe, Lords Jenkins, Hodson and Devlin)

William Norman Pilkington, by his will dated December 14, 1934, gave the income of his residuary estate upon trusts for his nephews and nieces (the beneficiaries) in equal shares. Each share was settled on protective trusts, and the will provided that the consent of a beneficiary to the exercise by the trustees of their statutory power of advancement should not cause a forfeiture. The capital was to be held upon trust for the children of each beneficiary in such shares as the beneficiary should appoint, and in default of appointment in equal shares.

Richard Godfrey Pilkington was one of the beneficiaries. He was married and had three children, one of whom was Penelope, a child two years old and born after the death of the testator. The trustees decided, with Richard's consent, to advance one half of Penelope's expectant share in the trust, and to pay it to the trustees of a new trust which was being set up for Penelope's benefit. The main object of the trustees was to save the estate duty which would be payable upon that part of the fund in the event of Richard's death. The new trusts were that until Penelope attained the age of 21 the income should be applied for her maintenance, education and benefit, and the surplus accumulated; and that on her attaining the age of 21 the income should be paid to her; and that the capital should be paid to her on attaining the age of 30.

[3] (1963) 27 Conv (NS) 65 (F. R. Crane); *Re Wills' Will Trusts* [1959] Ch 1, [1958] 2 All ER 472 (advancement upon new trusts); *Re Clore's Settlement Trusts* [1966] 1 WLR 955, [1966] 2 All ER 272 (payment to charity held to be for the benefit of rich minor who felt himself under moral obligation to make the gift); *Re Pauling's Settlement Trusts* [1964] Ch 303, [1963] 3 All ER 1 (advancement nominally to children was really made to benefit parents); p. 556, post.

The question was whether the trustees could properly so exercise the power of advancement.

Held. (i) Such an exercise was within the statutory power as being for Penelope's benefit, although her interest under the trust would vest later than under the will; (ii) But the particular exercise was void for perpetuity[4].

VISCOUNT RADCLIFFE: The word "advancement" itself meant in this context the establishment in life of the beneficiary who was the object of the power or at any rate some step that would contribute to the furtherance of his establishment. Thus it was found in such phrases as "preferment or advancement" (*Lowther v Bentinck* (1874) LR 19 Eq 166), "business, profession, or employment or . . . advancement or preferment in the world" (*Roper-Curzon v Roper-Curzon* (1871) LR 11 Eq 452) and "placing out or advancement in life" (*Re Breeds' Will* (1875) 1 ChD 226). Typical instances of expenditure for such purposes under the social conditions of the nineteenth century were an apprenticeship or the purchase of a commission in the army or of an interest in business. In the case of a girl there could be advancement on marriage (*Lloyd v Cocker* (1860) 27 Beav 645). Advancement had, however, to some extent a limited range of meaning, since it was thought to convey the idea of some step in life of permanent significance, and accordingly, to prevent uncertainties about the permitted range of objects for which moneys could be raised and made available, such words as "or otherwise for his or her benefit" were often added to the word "advancement". It was always recognised that these added words were "large words" (see Jessel MR in *Re Breeds' Will* (1875) 1 ChD 226 at 228) and indeed in another case (*Lowther v Bentinck* (1874) LR 19 Eq 166 at 169) the same judge spoke of preferment and advancement as being "both large words" but of "benefit" as being the "largest of all". So, too, Kay J in *Re Brittlebank* ((1881) 30 WR 99 at 100). Recent judges have spoken in the same terms—see Farwell J in *Re Halsted's Will Trusts* ([1937] 2 All ER 570 at 571) and Danckwerts J in *Re Moxon's Will Trusts* ([1958] 1 WLR 165 at 168, [1958] 1 All ER 386). This wide construction of the range of the power, which evidently did not stand upon niceties of distinction provided that the proposed application could fairly be regarded as for the benefit of the beneficiary who was the object of the power, must have been carried into the statutory power created by section 32, since it adopts without qualification the accustomed wording "for the advancement or benefit in such manner as they may in their absolute discretion think fit".

So much for "advancement," which I now use for brevity to cover the combined phrase "advancement or benefit." It means any use of the money which will improve the material situation of the beneficiary. It is important, however, not to confuse the idea of "advancement" with the idea of advancing the money out of the beneficiary's expectant interest. The two things have only a casual connection with each other. The one refers to the operation of finding money by way of anticipation of an interest not yet absolutely vested in possession or, if so vested, belonging to an infant: the other refers to the status of the beneficiary and the improvement of

[4] *Re Abraham's Will Trusts* [1969] 1 Ch 463, [1967] 2 All ER 1175; *Re Hastings-Bass* [1975] Ch 25, [1974] 2 All ER 193.

his situation. The power to carry out the operation of anticipating an interest is not conferred by the word "advancement" but by those other words of the section which expressly authorise the payment or application of capital money for the benefit of a person entitled "whether absolutely or contingently on his attaining any specified age or on the occurrence of any other event, or subject to a gift over on his death under any specified age or on the occurrence of any other event, and whether in possession or in remainder or reversion," etc.

I think, with all respect to the commissioners, a good deal of their argument is infected with some of this confusion. To say, for instance, that there cannot be a valid exercise of a power of advancement that results in a deferment of the vesting of the beneficiary's absolute title (Miss Penelope, it will be remembered, is to take at 30 under the proposed settlement instead of at 21 under the will) is in my opinion to play upon words. The element of anticipation consists in the raising of money for her now before she has any right to receive anything under the existing trusts: the advancement consists in the application of that money to form a trust fund, the provisions of which are thought to be for her benefit. I have not forgotten, of course, the references to powers of advancement which are found in such cases as *Re Joicey* ([1915] 2 Ch 115), *Re May's Settlement* ([1926] Ch 136) and *Re Mewburn's Settlement* ([1934] Ch 112), to which our attention was called, or the answer supplied by Cotton LJ in *Re Aldridge*[5] to his own question "What is advancement?"; but I think that it will be apparent from what I have already said that the description that he gives (it cannot be a definition) is confined entirely to the aspect of anticipation or acceleration which renders the money available and not to any description or limitation of the purposes for which it can then be applied.

I have not been able to find in the words of section 32, to which I have now referred, anything which in terms or by implication restricts the width of the manner or purpose of advancement. It is true that, if this settlement is made, Miss Penelope's children, who are not objects of the power, are given a possible interest in the event of her dying under 30 leaving surviving issue. But if the disposition itself, by which I mean the whole provision made, is for her benefit, it is no objection to the exercise of the power that other persons benefit incidentally as a result of the exercise. Thus a man's creditors may in certain cases get the most immediate advantage from an advancement made for the purpose of paying them off, as in *Lowther v Bentinck* ((1874) LR 19 Eq 166), and a power to raise money for the advancement of a wife may cover a payment made direct to her husband in order to set him up in business (*Re Kershaw's Trusts* (1868) LR 6 Eq 322). The exercise will not be bad therefore on this ground.

Nor in my opinion will it be bad merely because the moneys are to be tied up in the proposed settlement. If it could be said that the payment or application permitted by section 32 cannot take the form of a settlement

[5] (1886) 55 LT 554 at 556, "It is a payment to persons who are presumably entitled to, or have a vested or contingent interest in, an estate or a legacy, before the time fixed by the will for their obtaining the absolute interest in a portion or the whole of that to which they would be entitled."

in any form but must somehow pass direct into or through the hands of the object of the power, I could appreciate the principle upon which the commissioners' objection was founded. But can that principle be asserted? Anyone can see, I think, that there can be circumstances in which, while it is very desirable that some money should be raised at once for the benefit of an owner of an expectant or contingent interest, it would be very undesirable that the money should not be secured to him under some arrangement that will prevent him having the absolute disposition of it. I find it very difficult to think that there is something at the back of section 32 which makes an advancement impossible. Certainly neither Danckwerts J nor the members of the Court of Appeal in this case took that view. Both Lord Evershed MR and Upjohn LJ ([1961] Ch 466 at 481, 486) explicitly accept the possibility of a settlement being made in exercise of a power of advancement. Farwell J authorised one in *Re Halsted's Will Trusts* ([1937] 2 All ER 570 at 572), a case in which the trustees had left their discretion to the court. The trustees should raise the money and "have" it "settled," he said. So too, Harman J in *Re Ropner's Settlement Trusts* ([1956] 1 WLR 902 at 906) authorised the settlement of an advance provided for an infant, saying that the child could not "consent or request the trustees to make the advance, but the transfer of a part of his contingent share to the trustees of the settlement for him must advance his interest and thus be for his benefit . . ." All this must be wrong in principle if a power of advancement cannot cover an application of the moneys by way of settlement.

The truth is, I think, that the propriety of requiring a settlement of moneys found for advancement was recognised as long ago as 1871 in *Roper-Curzon v Roper-Curzon* ((1871) LR 11 Eq 452) and, so far as I know, it has not been impugned since. Lord Romilly M.R.'s decision passed into the text-books and it must have formed the basis of a good deal of subsequent practice. True enough, as counsel for the commissioners has reminded us, the beneficiary in that case was an adult who was offering to execute the post-nuptial settlement required: but I find it impossible to read Lord Romilly's words as amounting to anything less than a decision that he would permit an advancement under the power only on the terms that the money was to be secured by settlement. That was what the case was about. If, then, it is a proper exercise of a power of advancement for trustees to stipulate that the money shall be settled, I cannot see any difference between having it settled that way and having it settled by themselves paying it to trustees of a settlement which is in the desired form.

It is not as if anyone were contending for a principle that a power of advancement cannot be exercised "over the head" of a beneficiary, that is, unless he actually asks for the money to be raised and consents to its application. From some points of view that might be a satisfactory limitation, and no doubt it is the way in which an advancement takes place in the great majority of cases. But, if application and consent were necessary requisites of advancement, that would cut out the possibility of making any advancement for the benefit of a person under age, at any rate without the institution of court proceedings and formal representation of the infant: and it would mean, moreover, that the trustees of an adult could not in any circumstances insist on raising money to pay his debts, however much the operation might be to his benefit, unless he agreed to that course. Counsel for the commissioners did not contend before us that the power of advancement was inherently limited in this way: and I do not think that such a limitation would accord with the general understanding. Indeed its "paternal" nature is well shown by the fact that it is often treated as being peculiarly for the assistance of an infant.

The commissioners' objections seem to be concentrated upon such propositions as that the proposed transaction is "nothing less than a resettlement" and that a power of advancement cannot be used so as to alter or vary the trusts created by the settlement from which it is derived. Such a transaction, they say, amounts to using the power of advancement as a way of appointing or declaring new trusts different from those of the settlement. The reason why I do not find that these propositions have any compulsive effect upon my mind is that they seem to me merely vivid ways of describing the substantial effect of that which is proposed to be done and they do not in themselves amount to convincing arguments against doing it. Of course, whenever money is raised for advancement on terms that it is to be settled on the beneficiary, the money only passes from one settlement to be caught up in the other. It is therefore the same thing as a resettlement. But, unless one is to say that such moneys can never be applied by way of settlement, an argument which, as I have shown, has few supporters and is contrary to authority, it merely describes the inevitable effect of such an advancement to say that it is nothing less than a resettlement. Similarly, if it is part of the trusts and powers created by one settlement that the trustees of it should have power to raise money and make it available for a beneficiary upon new trusts approved by them, then they are in substance given power to free the money from one trust and to subject it to another. So be it: but, unless they cannot require a settlement of it at all, the transaction they carry out is the same thing in effect as an appointment of new trusts.

In the same way I am unconvinced by the argument that the trustees would be improperly delegating their trust by allowing the money raised to pass over to new trustees under a settlement conferring new powers on the latter. In fact I think that the whole issue of delegation is here beside the mark. The law is not that trustees cannot delegate: it is that trustees cannot delegate unless they have authority to do so. If the power of advancement which they possess is so read as to allow them to raise money for the purpose of having it settled, then they do have the necessary authority to let the money pass out of the old settlement into the new trusts. No question of delegation of their powers or trusts arises. If, on the other hand, their power of advancement is read so as to exclude settled advances, cadit quaestio.

I ought to note for the record (1) that the transaction envisaged does not actually involve the raising of money, since the trustees propose to appropriate a block of shares in the family's private limited company as the trust investment, and (2) there will not be any actual transfer, since the trustees of the proposed settlement and the will trustees are the same persons. As I have already said, I do not attach any importance to these factors nor, I think, do the commissioners. To transfer or appropriate outright is only to do by short cut what could be done in a more roundabout way by selling the shares to a consenting party, paying the money over to the new settlement with appropriate instructions and arranging for it to be used in buying back the shares as the trust investment. It cannot make any difference to follow the course taken in *Re Collard's Will Trusts* ([1961] Ch 293, [1961] 1 All ER 821) and deal with the property direct. On the other point, so long as there are separate trusts, the property effectually passes out of the old settlement into the new one, and it is of no relevance that, at any rate for the time being, the persons administering the new trust are the same individuals.

I have not yet referred to the ground which was taken by the Court of Appeal as their reason for saying that the proposed settlement was not permissible. To put it shortly, they held that the statutory power of advancement could not be exercised unless the benefit to be conferred was "personal to the person concerned, in the sense of being related to his or her own real or personal needs" ([1961] Ch 466 at 481). Or, to use other words of the learned Master of the Rolls ([1961] Ch at 484), the exercise of the power "must be an exercise done to meet the circumstances as they present themselves in regard to a person within the scope of the section, whose circumstances call for that to be done which the trustees think fit to do." Upjohn LJ ([1961] Ch at 487) expressed himself in virtually the same terms.

My Lords, I differ with reluctance from the views of judges so learned and experienced in matters of this sort: but I do not find it possible to import such restrictions into the words of the statutory power which itself does not contain them. First, the suggested qualification, that the considerations or circumstances must be "personal" to the beneficiary, seems to me uncontrollably vague as a guide to general administration. What distinguishes a personal need from any other need to which the trustees in their discretion think it right to attend in the beneficiary's interest? And, if the advantage of preserving the funds of a beneficiary from the incidence of death duty is not an advantage personal to that beneficiary, I do not see what is. Death duty is a present risk that attaches to the settled property in which Miss Penelope has her expectant interest, and even accepting the validity of the supposed limitation, I would not have supposed that there was anything either impersonal or unduly remote in the advantage to be conferred upon her of some exemption from that risk. I do not think, therefore, that I can support the interpretation of the power of advancement that has commended itself to the Court of Appeal, and, with great respect, I think that the judgments really amount to little more than a decision that in the opinion of the members of that court this was not a case in which there was any occasion to exercise the power. That would be a proper answer from a court to which trustees had referred their discretion with a request for its directions; but it does not really solve any question where, as here, they retain their discretion and merely ask whether it is impossible for them to exercise it.

To conclude, therefore, on this issue, I am of opinion that there is no maintainable reason for introducing into the statutory power of advancement a qualification that would exclude the exercise in the case now before us. It would not be candid to omit to say that, though I think that that is what the law requires, I am uneasy at some of the possible applications of this liberty, when advancements are made for the purposes of settlement or on terms that there is to be a settlement. It is quite true, as the commissioners have pointed out, that you might have really extravagant cases of resettlements being forced on beneficiaries in the name of advancement, even a few months before an absolute vesting in possession would have destroyed the power. I have tried to give due weight to such possibilities, but when all is said I do not think that they ought to compel us to introduce a limitation of which no one, with all respect, can produce a satisfactory definition. First, I do not believe that it is wise to try to cut down an admittedly wide and discretionary power, enacted for general use, through fear of its being abused in certain hypothetical instances. And moreover, as regards this fear, I think that it must be remembered that we are speaking of a power intended to be in the hands of trustees chosen by a settlor because of his confidence in their discretion and good sense and subject to the external check that no exercise can take place without the consent of a prior life-tenant; and that there does remain at all times a residual power in the court to restrain or correct any purported exercise that can be shown to be merely wanton or capricious and not to be attributable to a genuine discretion. I think, therefore, that, although extravagant possibilities exist, they may be more menacing in argument than in real life.

The other issue on which this case depends, that relating to the application of the rule against perpetuities, does not seem to me to present much difficulty. It is not in dispute that, if the limitations of the proposed settlement are to be treated as if they had been made by the testator's will and as coming into operation at the date of his death, there are trusts in it which would be void ab initio as violating the perpetuity rule. They postpone final vesting by too long a date. It is also a familiar rule of law in this field that, whereas appointments made under a general power of appointment conferred by will or deed are held as taking effect from the date of the exercise of the power, trusts declared by a special power of appointment, the distinguishing feature of which is that it can allocate property among a limited class of persons only, are treated as coming into operation at the date of the instrument that creates the power. The question therefore resolves itself into asking whether the exercise of a power of advancement which takes the form of a settlement should be looked upon as more closely analogous to a general or to a special power of appointment.

On this issue I am in full agreement with the views of Upjohn LJ in the Court of Appeal ([1961] Ch 466 at 488 et seq.). Indeed, much of the reasoning that has led me to my conclusion on the first issue that I have been considering leads me to think that for this purpose there is an effective analogy between powers of advancement and special powers of appointment. When one asks what person can be regarded as the settlor of Miss Penelope's proposed settlement, I do not see how it is possible to say that she is herself or that the trustees are. She is the passive recipient of the benefit extracted for her from the original trusts; the trustees are merely exercising a fiduciary power in arranging for the desired limitations. It is not their property that constitutes the funds of Miss Penelope's settlement; it is the property subjected to trusts by the will of the testator and passed over into the new settlement through the instrumentality of a power which by statute is made appendant to those trusts. I do not think, therefore, that it is important to this issue that money raised under a power of advancement passes entirely out of the reach of the existing trusts and makes, as it were, a new start under fresh limitations, the kind of thing that happened under the old form of family resettlement when the tenant in tail in remainder barred the entail with the consent of the protector of the settlement. I think that the important point for the purpose of the rule against perpetuities is that the new settlement is only effected by the operation of a fiduciary power which itself "belongs" to the old settlement.

In the conclusion, therefore, there are legal objections to the proposed settlement which the trustees have placed before the court. Again I agree with Upjohn LJ that these objections go to the root of what is proposed and I do not think that it would be satisfactory that the court should try to frame a qualified answer to the question that they have propounded, which would express the general view that the power to advance by way of a settlement of this sort does exist and the special view that the power to make this particular settlement does not. Nor, I think, is such a course desired either by the appellants or the trustees. They will, I hope, know where they stand for the future, and so will the commissioners, and that is enough.

C. Application of the Money

In *Re Pauling's Settlement Trusts* ([1964] Ch 303, [1963] 3 All ER 1)[6] one question was whether trustees, in making an advancement, were under an obligation to ensure that the money advanced was in fact applied for the purposes for which it was advanced. The Court of Appeal, per WILLMER LJ said (at p. 334): "Furthermore, it is clear that the power under the first limb [of the express power of appointment, giving the trustees power to advance up to one half of a child's expectant, presumptive or vested share and to pay the same to him for his absolute use or for his advancement or otherwise for his benefit in such manner as the trustees should think fit] may be exercised, if the circumstances warrant it, either by making an out-and-out payment to the person to be advanced, or for a particular purpose specified by the trustees. Thus in argument an example was given that when George [one of the beneficiaries] was called to the Bar the trustees might have quite properly advanced to him a sum of capital quite generally for his living expenses to support him while starting to practice, provided they thought that this was a reasonable thing to do, and that he was a type of person who could reasonably be trusted to make proper use of the money. On the other hand, if the trustees make the advance for a particular purpose which they state, they can quite properly pay it over to the advancee if they reasonably think they can trust him or her to carry out the prescribed purpose. What they cannot do is

[6] See p. 630, post.

to prescribe a particular purpose, and then raise and pay the money over to the advancee leaving him or her entirely free, legally and morally, to apply it for that purpose or to spend it in any way he or she chooses, without any responsibility on the trustees even to inquire as to its application."

16. Variation of Trusts[1]

I. Introduction

A trustee must administer the trust in accordance with its terms; otherwise he commits a breach of trust. Sometimes, however, the observance of the terms is harmful to the beneficiaries. This has been seen in the context of the limited investment powers available to trustees before 1961[2]. It appears in many other contexts; and most especially in that of tax planning. In short, the old-fashioned settlement containing a successsion of limited interests can be disadvantageous in terms of the liability to taxation on death. How can such a settlement, once established, be changed?

There is no difficulty if all the beneficiaries are of full age, under no disability, and all agree[3]. They can terminate the trust and share out; or agree to re-settle upon other trusts. But it is usual in a family settlement that there should be some beneficiaries of later generations who are minor or unborn, and who could not therefore join in a termination or reconstruction of the settlement. Could the court approve a reconstruction on behalf of minors or unborn beneficiaries when it was for their benefit? The House of Lords decided that it could not[4]. As Lord MORTON OF HENRYTON said in *Chapman v Chapman*[5]: ". . . if the court had power to approve, and did approve schemes such as the present scheme, the way would be open for a most undignified game of chess between the Chancery Division and the legislature". If, of course, there was a dispute between the beneficiaries, which the beneficiaries were prepared to compromise, the

[1] H & M, pp. 528–542; K & S, pp. 347–372; P & M, pp. 350–366; Pettit, pp. 294–302; Snell, pp. 228–235; Harris, *Variation of Trusts* (1975).
[2] See p. 479, ante.
[3] *Saunders v Vautier* (1841) 4 Beav 115; Cr & Ph 240; H & M, p. 528; *Re Chardon* [1928] Ch 464; *Re Smith* [1928] 1 Ch 915, p. 27, ante.
[4] *Chapman v Chapman* [1954] AC 429, [1954] 1 All ER 798.
[5] At p. 468.

Court could sanction the compromise[6]. It must be a real dispute; but it is hardly necessary to add that greater ingenuity was needed to find a dispute in some cases than was necessary to find a tax-saving compromise.

Various statutory provisions relate to variation of trusts, and these will be mentioned[7]. The court also has inherent power to authorise certain acts by trustees which are beyond their powers. The inherent jurisdiction is narrow and is generally restricted to emergency and salvage operations[8]. Towering above them however in significance is the Variation of Trusts Act 1958, under which most variations are now effected.

II. Trustee Act 1925, s. 57

TRUSTEE ACT 1925

57. Power of court to authorise dealings with trust property: see p. 523 ante.

Pettit: *Equity and the Law of Trusts* (3rd Edn, 1974) pp. 299–300

"Of primary importance is the interpretation of the words 'management' and 'administration', which are largely, though very possibly not entirely, synonymous. The subject-matter of both words in section 57 is trust property which is vested in trustees, and 'trust property' cannot by any legitimate stretch of the language include the equitable interests which a settlor has created in that property. The application of both words is confined to the managerial supervision and control of trust property on behalf of beneficiaries, and the section accordingly does not permit the remoulding of the beneficial interests. The object of section 57, it was said[9], is

> 'to secure that trust property should be managed as advantageously as possible in the interests of the beneficiaries, and, with that object in view, to authorise specific dealings with the property which the court might have felt itself unable to sanction under the inherent jurisdiction, either because no actual "emergency" had arisen or because of inability to show that the position which called for intervention was one which the creator of the trust could not reasonably have foreseen, but it was no part of the legislative aim to disturb the rule that the court will not re-write a trust or to add to such exceptions to that rule as had already found their way into the inherent jurisdiction'.

Later in the judgment the majority adopted the statement of Farwell J in *Re Mair*[10], that 'if and when the court sanctions an arrangement or transaction under section 57, it must be taken to have done it as though the power which is being put into operation had been inserted in the trust instrument

6 See *Allen v Distillers Co (Biochemicals) Ltd* [1974] QB 384, [1974] 2 All ER 365; *Re Barbour's Settlement* [1974] 1 WLR 1198, [1974] 1 All ER 1188.

7 See pp. 559–564, post; (1954) 17 MLR 420 (O. R. Marshall).

8 *Re New* [1901] 2 Ch 534; *Re Tollemache* [1903] 1 Ch 955.

9 Per EVERSHED MR and ROMER LJ, in *Re Downshire Settled Estates* [1953] Ch 218 at 248, 264 and 265, [1953] 1 All ER 103 at 119, and see also pp. 129 and 132. And see *Municipal and General Securities Co Ltd v Lloyds Bank Ltd* [1950] Ch 212, [1949] 2 All ER 937.

10 [1935] Ch 562 at 565.

as an overriding power'. Perhaps Farwell J put it even more clearly later in his judgment where he said[11] 'the effect of the court permitting the exercise by trustees of some power which is not in the trust document itself, and, therefore, something which the trustees could not do except by the direction of the court, is the same as though that power had been inserted as an overriding power in the trust document'.

Applications under section 57 are almost invariably heard and disposed of in chambers and accordingly not reported. There are, however, a few reported cases which show that in the exercise of its jurisdiction under this section the court has authorised the sale of settled chattels[12], a partition of land[13] and a sale of land where the necessary consent could not be obtained[14]. It has authorised two residuary estates left on identical charitable trusts to be blended into one fund[15]. It has, apparently commonly, authorised capital money to be expended on paying off the tenant for life's debts, on having its replacement secured by a policy of insurance so that the beneficial interests remain unaltered[16], but although it has in exceptional circumstances sanctioned a similar expenditure of capital to purchase the life tenant's interest[17], it is doubtful whether it would do so in an ordinary case, as it would come 'at least very near to altering the beneficial interests of the tenant for life'[18]. The court has also authorised the sale of a reversionary interest which under the trust instrument was not to be sold until it should fall into possession."[19]

III. Settled Land Act 1925, s. 64

SETTLED LAND ACT 1925

64. General power for the tenant for life to effect any transaction under an order of the court.—(1) Any transaction affecting or concerning the settled land, or any part thereof, or any other land (not being a transaction otherwise authorised by this Act, or by the settlement) which in the opinion of the court would be for the benefit of the settled land, or any part thereof, or the persons interested under the settlement, may, under an order of the court, be effected by a tenant for life, if it is one which could have been validly effected by an absolute owner.

(2) In this section "transaction" includes any sale, exchange, assurance,

[11] Supra, at 566.
[12] *Re Hope's Will Trust* [1929] 2 Ch 136.
[13] *Re Thomas* [1930] 1 Ch 194.
[14] *Re Beale's Settlement Trusts* [1932] 2 Ch 15.
[15] *Re Harvey* [1941] 3 All ER 284. The contrary decision in *Re Royal Society's Charitable Trusts* [1956] Ch 87, [1955] 3 All ER 14, where *Re Harvey* does not appear to have been cited, would seem to be wrong in the light of *Re Shipwrecked Fishermen and Mariners' Royal Benevolent Society Charity* [1959] Ch 220, [1958] 3 All ER 465.
[16] *Re Salting* [1932] 2 Ch 57; *Re Mair* [1935] Ch 562. These cases must be read in the light of the observations of the majority of the Court of Appeal in *Re Downshire Settled Estates* [1953] Ch 218 at 249–251, [1953] 1 All ER 103 at 119–121; and see *Re Forster's Settlement* [1954] 3 All ER 714.
[17] *Re Forster's Settlement*, supra.
[18] *Re Forster's Settlement*, supra, per HARMAN J at 720.
[19] *Re Cockerell's Settlement Trusts* [1956] Ch 372, [1956] 2 All ER 172.

grant, lease, surrender, reconveyance, release, reservation, or other disposition, and any purchase or other acquisition, and any covenant, contract, or option, and any application of capital money and any compromise or other dealing, or arrangement; and "effected" has the meaning appropriate to the particular transaction; and the references to land include references to restrictions and burdens affecting land[20].

Harris: *Variation of Trusts* (1975), p. 19[1]

"The jurisdiction was extended by section 1 of the Settled Land and Trustee Acts (Courts' General Powers) Act 1943 (as amended by section 9 of the Emergency Laws (Miscellaneous Provisions) Act 1953); which empowers the court to authorise any expense of an action taken or proposed in or for the management of settled land to be treated as a capital outgoing, if the expenditure cannot otherwise be met and the action is for the benefit of those interested under the settlement.

The jurisdiction conferred by section 64 of the Settled Land Act enables the court to add to the powers conferred upon a tenant for life of settled land by the Act and by the settlement. As section 28 (1) of the Law of Property Act 1925 confers upon the trustees of land held upon trust for sale all the powers which the Settled Land Act confers upon a tenant for life of settled land, it has been held that the jurisdiction conferred by section 64 extends to land held on trust for sale: (*Re Simmons* [1956] Ch 125, [1955] 3 All ER 818).

For a transaction to come within the jurisdiction, it must affect land. Acts performed in the management or administration of trusts of other kinds of property will normally come within the jurisdiction of section 57 of the Trustee Act. However, because of the wording of subsection 4 of section 57, neither section will apply '. . . in the case of a settlement the trustees of which are trustees for the purposes of the Settled Land Act, but which no longer comprises any unsold land': (*Re Downshire's Settled Estates* [1953] Ch 218 at 254 per Evershed MR). The Law Reform Committee recommended that section 64 should be amended to plug this gap: (1957 Cmnd. 310, para. 25). This recommendation has not been put into effect; and, in view of the breadth of the jurisdiction conferred by the V.T.A., the practical consequences of doing so would be small.

The major difference between section 64 of the Settled Land Act and section 57 of the Trustee Act, which was brought to light in *Downshire*, is that the former section enables the court to authorise alterations in the beneficial interests under a settlement as well as alterations in its administrative provisions.

In *Downshire*, the court was asked to approve an arrangement under which the tenant for life of settled land would surrender a protected life interest, and provision would be made by means of insurance for any possible future beneficiaries under the protective trusts which would have arisen

20 As amended by Settled Land and Trustee Acts (Courts' General Powers) Act 1943, s. 2, and Statute Law (Repeals) Act 1969, Schedule, Part III.

1 See Maudsley and Burn, *Land Law Cases and Materials*, pp. 194–196, for further cases in which s. 64 has been applied.

upon a forfeiture of the protected life interest. The corpus of the settlement comprised land worth £400,000 and capital money worth £700,000. Roxburgh J, at first instance, held that the word 'transaction' was limited to acts of administration: (*Re D's Settled Estates* [1952] 2 All ER 603 at 606). But the Court of Appeal took the view that it was a '. . . word of the widest import as is emphasised, in our judgment, by the terms of the second subsection which make the meaning of the word comprehend (*inter alia*) any application of capital money and any compromise or other dealing or arrangement': ([1953] Ch 218 at 252, per Evershed MR).

The result was, so the court held, that section 64 enabled the court to authorise the tenant for life to make an arrangement with the trustees and with other adult beneficiaries under the settlement which completely remodelled the beneficial interests under the settlement. The court could do this, provided only that the 'transaction' benefited the settled land or any part thereof '. . . or the persons interested under the settlement. . . .'

Thus, in the case of settlements whose trust corpus includes settled land, there was already before 1958 a wide jurisdiction to approve tax-avoiding rearrangements of the beneficial interests. The jurisdiction might be applicable today in circumstances in which the V.T.A. jurisdiction is not."

IV. Trustee Act 1925, s. 53[2]

TRUSTEE ACT 1925

53. Vesting orders in relation to infant's beneficial interests.— Where an infant is beneficially entitled to any property the court may, with a view to the application of the capital or income thereof for the maintenance, education, or benefit of the infant, make an order—

(*a*) appointing a person to convey such property; or

(*b*) in the case of stock, or a thing in action, vesting in any person the right to transfer or call for a transfer of such stock, or to receive the dividends or income thereof, or to sue for and recover such thing in action, upon such terms as the court may think fit.

Pettit: *Equity and the Law of Trusts* (3rd Edn, 1974) p. 298

"Under this section it was held in *Re Gower's Settlement*[3] that where there was an infant tenant in tail in remainder of Blackacre with divers remainders over, the court could effectually authorise a mortgage of Blackacre (subject to the interests having priority over the infant's tenancy in tail) framed so as to vest in the mortgagee a security which would be as effective a bar against the infant's issue taking under the entail and the subsequent remaindermen as if the infant were of full age and had executed the conveyance in accordance with the Fines and Recoveries Act 1833.

It was expressly assumed in *Re Gower's Settlement*[4] that the requirement of the section that the mortgage should be made 'with a view to the application of the capital or income thereof for the maintenance, education or benefit of the infant' was satisfied. It was held that there was no such

[2] See (1957) 21 Conv (NS) 448 (O. R. Marshall).
[3] [1934] Ch 365; *Re Lansdowne's Will Trusts* [1967] Ch 603, [1967] 1 All ER 888.
[4] Supra.

'application' in *Re Heyworth's Settlements*[5] where it was proposed to put an end to the trusts created by the settlement by selling the infant's contingent reversionary interest to the life tenant for an outright cash payment. This decision was distinguished in *Re Meux's Will Trusts*[6] where the proceeds of sale were to be settled. It was held that the sale and settlement of the proceeds of sale were to be regarded as a single transaction, which did constitute an 'application' for the purposes of the section[7]. And in *Re Bristol's Settled Estates*[8] a person was appointed to execute a disentailing assurance to bar the infant's entail with a view to a settlement to be made with the assistance of the court under the Variation of Trusts Act 1958."

v. Matrimonial Causes Act 1973, s. 24

MATRIMONIAL CAUSES ACT 1973

24. Property adjustment orders in connection with divorce proceedings, etc.[9]—(1) On granting a decree of divorce, a decree of nullity of marriage or a decree of judicial separation or at any time thereafter (whether, in the case of a decree of divorce or of nullity of marriage, before or after the decree is made absolute), the court may make any one or more of the following orders that is to say—

(*a*) an order that a party to the marriage shall transfer to the other party, to any child of the family or to such person as may be specified in the order for the benefit of such a child such property as may be so specified, being property to which the first-mentioned party is entitled either in possession or reversion;

(*b*) an order that a settlement[10] of such property as may be so specified, being property to which a party to the marriage is so entitled, be made to the satisfaction of the court for the benefit of the other party to the marriage and of the children of the family or either or any of them;

(*c*) an order varying for the benefit of the parties to the marriage and of the children of the family or either or any of them any ante-nuptial or post-nuptial settlement[10] (including such a settlement made by will or codicil) made on the parties to the marriage;

(*d*) an order extinguishing or reducing the interest of either of the parties to the marriage under any such settlement[10];

[5] [1956] Ch 364, [1956] 2 All ER 21.

[6] [1958] Ch 154, [1957] 2 All ER 630; *Re Lansdowne's Will Trusts*, supra.

[7] Cf. *Re Ropner's Settlement Trusts*, [1956] 1 WLR 902, [1956] 3 All ER 332–a decision on similar words in T.A. 1925, s. 32.

[8] [1964] 3 All ER 939.

[9] For the factors to be taken into account in making an order under this section, see s. 25. Orders made under s. 24 (1) may be varied or discharged by the Court (s. 31). See also Bromley, *Family Law* (5th Edn) pp. 537–543, 558–560; Cretney, *Principles of Family Law* (2nd Edn) pp. 170–172, 210–213. Cf. the power to vary ante– and post–nuptial settlements under Inheritance (Provision for Family and Dependants) Act 1975, s. 2 (1) (*f*).

[10] A wide meaning has been given to the word "settlement". It includes any provision (other than an absolute gift) made for the benefit of the parties to the marriage. See *Ulrich v Ulrich* [1968] 1 WLR 180, [1968] 1 All ER 67 (purchase of house intended to be matrimonial home held to be settlement).

subject, however, in the case of an order under paragraph (*a*) above, to the restrictions imposed by section 29 (1) and (3) below on the making of orders for a transfer of property in favour of children who have attained the age of eighteen.

VI. Mental Health Act 1959, s. 103

Section 103 gives to the Court of Protection wide powers of making settlements of the property of mental patients; as to variation:

103. Powers of the judge as to patient's property and affairs.—(4) Where under this section a settlement has been made of any property of a patient, and the Lord Chancellor or a nominated judge is satisfied, at any time before the death of the patient, that any material fact was not disclosed when the settlement was made, or that there has been any substantial change in circumstances, he may by order vary the settlement in such manner as he thinks fit, and give any consequential directions[11].

VII. Variation of Trusts Act 1958[12]

A. Section 1

1. Jurisdiction of courts to vary trusts.—(1) Where property, whether real or personal, is held on trusts arising, whether before or after the passing of this Act, under any will, settlement or other disposition, the court may if it thinks fit by order approve on behalf of—

(*a*) any person having, directly or indirectly, an interest, whether vested or contingent, under the trusts who by reason of infancy or other incapacity is incapable of assenting, or

(*b*) any person (whether ascertained or not) who may become entitled, directly or indirectly, to an interest under the trusts as being at a future date or on the happening of a future event a person of any specified description or a member of any specified class of persons, so however that this paragraph shall not include any person who would be of that description, or a member of that class, as the case may be, if the said date had fallen or the said event had happened at the date of the application to the court, or

(*c*) any person unborn, or

(*d*) any person in respect of any discretionary interest of his under protective trusts where the interest of the principal beneficiary has not failed or determined,

[11] *Re C.W.H.T.* [1977] 3 WLR 880, [1978] 1 All ER 210.

[12] H & M, pp. 534–542; K & S, pp. 355–366; P & M, pp. 355–366; Pettit, pp. 301–307; Snell, pp. 231–235; Harris, *Variation of Trusts* (1957) chap. 3 et seq. The Act was based on the recommendation of Law Reform Committee Sixth Report (Court's Power to Sanction Variation of Trusts) (1957) Cmnd. 310. See generally (1958) 22 Conv (NS) 373 (M. J. Mowbray); (1963) 27 Conv (NS) 6 (D. M. Evans); (1965) 43 Can BR 181 (A. J. Maclean); (1969) 33 Conv (NS) 113, 183 (J. W. Harris).

any arrangement (by whomsoever proposed, and whether or not there is any other person beneficially interested who is capable of assenting thereto) varying or revoking all or any of the trusts, or enlarging the powers of the trustees of managing or administering any of the property subject to the trusts:

Provided that except by virtue of paragraph (*d*) of this subsection the court shall not approve an arrangement on behalf of any person unless the carrying out thereof would be for the benefit of that person.

(2) In the foregoing subsection "protective trusts" means the trusts specified in paragraphs (i) and (ii) of subsection (1) of section thirty-three of the Trustee Act, 1925, or any like trusts, "the principal beneficiary" has the same meaning as in the said subsection (1) and "discretionary interest" means an interest arising under the trust specified in paragraph (ii) of the said subsection (1) or any like trust.

(3) The jurisdiction conferred by subsection (1) of this section shall be exercisable by the High Court, except that the question whether the carrying out of any arrangement would be for the benefit of a person falling within paragraph (*a*) of the said subsection (1) shall be determined by order of the authority having jurisdiction under Part VIII of the Mental Health Act, 1959, if that person is a patient within the meaning of the said Part VIII[13].

(6) Nothing in this section shall be taken to limit the powers conferred by section sixty-four of the Settled Land Act 1925[14], section fifty-seven of the Trustee Act, 1925[15], or the powers of the authority having jurisdiction under Part VIII of the Mental Health Act, 1959[16].

B. Persons on Whose Behalf Approval May be Given

In *Re Suffert's Settlement* ([1961] Ch 1, [1960] 3 All ER 561) the income of a family trust fund was held on protective trusts for Miss Suffert, a spinster aged 61, and after her death, upon trusts, as to capital and income, in favour of her issue; and in default of such issue, and subject to a general testamentary power of appointment, in trust for those persons who would be her statutory next-of-kin if she died a spinster.

Miss Suffert sought a variation of the settlement under which a fund of £500 would be held on trusts in favour of persons interested in the original trust, and the remainder of the fund, amounting to some £8,300, should be held on trust for herself absolutely.

At the date of the application to the court, her nearest relatives were three adult first cousins. One of them was made a party and consented to the variation. The other two were not made parties. The court was asked to approve on behalf of those two, and on behalf of unborn and unascertained persons who might become interested. BUCKLEY J held that he could approve the variation on behalf of the unborn and unascertained persons;

[13] As amended by County Courts Act 1959, s. 204, Sch. 3, and Mental Health Act 1959, s. 149, Sch. 7.

[14] See p. 560, ante.

[15] See p. 559, ante.

[16] As amended by Mental Health Act 1959, s. 149, Sch. 7.

but not on behalf of the two cousins. They were within the exception contained in para. (*b*) of s. 1 (1) of the Act. The two cousins should themselves decide whether to consent or refuse.

In *Re Moncrieff's Settlement Trusts* ([1962] 1 WLR 134, [1962] 3 All ER 838n) approval was requested on behalf of the statutory next-of-kin of Mrs. Joan Parkin. Her next-of-kin at the date of the application was an infant adopted son, Alan James Parkin, the first respondent. If she survived him, her next-of-kin would be the four infant grandchildren of her maternal aunt. They were made respondents to the summons, as were the trustees.

BUCKLEY J approved the arrangement. He could do so on behalf of the first respondent under para. (*a*) of s. 1 (1) on the grounds of infancy, and in respect of the four infant grandchildren under para. (*b*). It was not necessary therefore that the infant grandchildren should be made parties. BUCKLEY J said (at p. 1346): "Section 1 (1) (*b*) of the Variation of Trusts Act, 1958, enables me to approve the arrangement on behalf of 'any person (whether ascertained or not) who may become entitled, directly or indirectly, to an interest under the trusts as being at a future date or on the happening of a future event a person of any specified description or a member of any specified class of persons. . . .' The first respondent would fall within that description, but the section goes on: 'so however that this paragraph shall not include any person who would be of that description, or a member of that class, as the case may be, if the said date had fallen or the said event had happened at the date of the application to the court. . . .' The first respondent is excluded, therefore, from the persons on whose behalf I can sanction the arrangement under section 1 (1) (*b*), but none of the other persons who might become entitled to participate in the estate of the settlor were she to survive the first respondent and then die intestate is excluded because none of them would be within the class of next-of-kin if she died today. Therefore, I am in a position to approve the arrangement on behalf of all persons whether ascertained or not who might become interested in the settlor's estate at a future date with the exception of the first respondent.

At the time the summons was drafted, the effect of that was not appreciated and certain persons were joined who would, in certain events, be the persons who would be the settlor's next-of-kin. In my view, it was unnecessary for those persons to be joined. Their interests can be looked after by the trustees, and they are persons who may never fall within the class of beneficiaries because they may predecease the settlor or the first respondent may survive the settlor. The summons could have been framed with the settlor as applicant and the first respondent and the trustees as respondents. I am not criticising counsel for the way in which the summons was framed because at the time it was settled it was not realised that it was not necessary to join all possible future next-of-kin."

[His Lordship then considered the scheme and approved it on behalf of the infant respondents and all other persons who might thereafter become entitled to an interest in the trust fund.]

In *Re Christie-Miller's Marriage Settlement* ([1961] 1 WLR 462, [1961] 1 All ER 855) the question was whether persons who were possible objects of a power of appointment should be made parties to an application. The appointor was a party, and counsel agreed that the order should recite that he released the power. WILBERFORCE J held that it was not necessary to join as parties the possible objects of the power. Their possibility of ever becoming interested had been extinguished by the release.

PRACTICE DIRECTION
(VARIATION OF TRUSTS: COUNSEL'S OPINION)

[No. 2 of 1976]

[1976] 1 WLR 884, [1976] 3 All ER 160

1. Where any infants or unborn beneficiaries will be affected by an arrangement under the Variation of Trusts Act 1958, evidence must normally be before the court which shows that their guardians ad litem or the trustees support the arrangement as being in the interests of the infants or unborn beneficiaries, and exhibits a case to counsel and counsel's written opinion to this effect. In nearly every case such a written opinion is helpful, and in complicated cases it is usually essential to the understanding of the guardian ad litem and the trustees, and to the consideration by the court of the merits and the fiscal consequences of the arrangement.

2. Where the interests of two or more infants, or two or more of the infants and unborn beneficiaries, are similar, a single written case to counsel and opinion will suffice; and no case to counsel or written opinion is required in respect of those who fall within the proviso to section 1 (1) of the Act (discretionary interests under protective trusts). Further, in proper cases the requirement of a case to counsel and a written opinion may at any stage be dispensed with by the master or the judge.

3. The effect of this practice direction is to extend to variations of trusts the long-established practice in the Chancery Division of requiring a case to counsel and counsel's opinion when proceedings in which an infant is interested are compromised: see *The Supreme Court Practice* (1976), vol 2, para 2073.

By the direction of the Vice-Chancellor.

R. E. BALL,
Chief Master.

July 27, 1976.

C. How a Variation Takes Effect

i. THE EFFECT OF APPROVAL OF THE COURT

RE HOLT'S SETTLEMENT[17]

[1969] 1 Ch 100, [1968] 1 All ER 470 (ChD, MEGARRY J)

In 1959 the settlor settled £15,000 on trust for his daughter Mrs. Wilson for

[17] (1968) 84 LQR 162 (P.V.B.).

life, and after her death on trust for such of her children as should attain the age of 21.

The fund was invested in a private company, and it increased in value to some £320,000. Mrs. Wilson wished to surrender her life interest in one half of the fund in favour of her children, and to vary the trusts in such a way that the children would become entitled at the age of 30; and that one half of the income of each child's share should be accumulated until the child attained the age of 25, or until the earlier expiration of 21 years from the date of the court's order.

In the application to MEGARRY J for approval, various questions arose: (i) whether, on a variation after 1964, the periods of perpetuity permitted by the Perpetuities and Accumulations Act 1964 could be utilised; (ii) whether the application was properly a variation of existing trusts or whether it was a revocation and resettlement; (iii) whether a variation under the Variation of Trusts Act 1958 took effect upon the court's order alone or upon some other basis.

Held. The application was approved. It took effect by virtue of the order of the court, and the new periods of perpetuity could be included.

MEGARRY J: Two main questions have been debated before me. I propose to consider these now, and to deal separately with certain details of the proposed arrangement. These questions are: first, does an order under the Act of 1958 ipso facto vary the terms of the trust without the execution of the arrangement or any other document by or on behalf of any beneficiary, apart from those on whose behalf section 1 (1) of the Act empowers the court to approve the arrangement? Secondly, if after the commencement of the Perpetuities and Accumulations Act, 1964, a variation is made in trusts constituted before the commencement of that Act, can that variation take advantage of the changes in the rules against perpetuities and accumulations which that Act has made?

Under the first head, the basic issue is whether an order under the Act of 1958 by itself varies the terms of the trust. Put rather differently, the question is whether the Act does no more than empower the court to supply on behalf of the infants, unborn persons and others mentioned in section 1 (1) that binding approval which they cannot give, leaving the other beneficiaries to provide their own approvals in some other document which will bind them. In the present case the arrangement was drafted on the assumption that the order of the court will ipso facto vary the terms of the trusts; for the "operative date" is defined as being the date of the order approving this arrangement, and the perpetuity period and the accumulation period (which are made use of in the terms of the trusts) each commences on the operative date.

The only authority directly on the point which has been cited to me is the decision in *Re Hambleden's Will Trusts* ([1960] 1 WLR 82, [1960] 1 All ER 353). I do not think I need read the provisions of the trusts in that case. It was a summons under the Act of 1958, and the judgment of Wynn-Parry J as reported is very short. The report does, however, include certain interlocutory observations. Wynn-Parry J made it clear that his view was that the order of the court ipso facto varied the trusts. He had had cited to him the decision of Vaisey J in *Re Joseph's Will Trusts* ([1959] 1 WLR 1019,

[1959] 3 All ER 474) where that learned judge had inserted words in the order of the court which authorised and directed the trustees to carry the arrangement into effect. Wynn-Parry J said:

> "I do not agree with that decision. I take the view that I have no jurisdiction to make an order including words directing the trustees to carry the arrangement into effect, and those words should be deleted from the draft minutes. Nothing is required except the approval of the court to the arrangement. If that approval is given the trusts are ipso facto altered, and the trustees are bound thereafter to give effect to the arrangement."

Later in the course of the argument he said ([1960] 1 WLR 82 at 85): "If I approve an arrangement, I alter the trusts. Res ipsa loquitur." Again, a little later, he said (at p. 85): "If I approve an arrangement, I vary the trusts." His judgment (at p. 86) I will recite in its entirety:

> "Very well. I hold that the effect of my approval is effective for all purposes to vary the trusts. Thereafter, the trusts are the trusts as varied. I approve the minutes of order, with the slight alterations which have been referred to, and the arrangement in the schedule."

If that were a decision of the Court of Appeal I could venerate and obey, even without fully comprehending. But the decision is at first instance, and so is of persuasive and not binding authority. It is my misfortune not to be persuaded by such assertions, even though fourfold, when made without explanation. . . .

Where the arrangement is put into effect there is a disposition of an equitable interest, so that unless there is some document signed by the adult beneficiaries, or by some agent authorised by them in writing, the requirements of section 53 (1) (*c*) [of the Law of Property Act 1925] are not satisfied. This contention is supported by a reference to the decision by the House of Lords in *Grey v IRC* ([1960] AC 1, [1959] 3 All ER 603)[18] that an oral direction by a beneficiary to his trustees to hold property on certain trusts is a disposition, and that "disposition" must be given its ordinary wide meaning. It is further said that as there is here a transaction under which a moiety of a life interest will pass from Mrs. Wilson to her children, this is a fortiori a "disposition". I may add that there is the minor point that the common form of order under the Act does not normally recite that all the adults have consented to the transaction, though where the insertion of such a recital is required by the parties, the registrars insert it.

Let me say at once that there would seem to be no great difficulty in averting the consequences of this argument for the future. The adults could either execute the arrangement or, perhaps more conveniently, give written authority to their solicitors or counsel to execute it on their behalf. The latter course would usually be the more convenient, because not infrequently changes (often minor) have to be made to the arrangement put before the court. It is, however, a fact that many thousands of orders must have been made in the past on the footing of *Re Hambleden's Will Trusts* ([1969] 1 WLR 82, [1960] 1 All ER 353). If the argument is right,

[18] See p. 33, ante.

there is the very real difficulty that those orders will, perhaps in most cases, perhaps only in some, have effected no variation of the trusts. This is a consideration which is particularly awkward in that a question of jurisdiction is involved; for if the court has no jurisdiction to make an order which itself varies the trusts, and orders have been made on the footing that the orders do ipso facto vary the trusts, then it seems at least arguable that such orders were made without jurisdiction. It has also been pointed out that the Inland Revenue has for some while acted upon the decision, and that orders of the court have been stamped on the footing that they ipso facto vary the terms of the trusts. Yet again, it is plain that present practice is convenient. It avoids the burden which usually, perhaps, would not be very great, but in individual cases might be substantial, of getting the necessary signatures of the adults either to the document itself or to written authorities. I bear all those considerations in mind; nevertheless, it seems to me that there is very considerable force in the argument that has been advanced. The decision in *Re Hambleden's Will Trusts* provides authority to the contrary but no explanation of the grounds for the decision. Accordingly, a substantial part of the argument in this case has been directed to the discovery of some basis upon which the convenient practice of *Re Hambleden's Will Trusts* can be rested.

In attempting to summarise Mr. Godfrey's argument for the settlor, I am sure I shall fail to do it justice. As I understood it, he submitted that the decision in *Re Hambleden's Will Trusts* was quite wrong but that in effect this did not matter. All that the court has to do, he said, is to approve the arrangement (i.e., the proposal made), and there was no question of the court approving anything which in law amounted to a disposition. The arrangement was not a disposition but merely a bargain or proposal, which was not within the ambit of section 53 (1) (*c*) of the Law of Property Act, 1925. The court, he urged, was not concerned to see that the adults consented and certainly not that they executed any disposition. There might thus be no disposition at all; but the persons specified by section 1 (1) of the Act of 1958 would be bound by the order of the court approving the arrangement, and the other beneficiaries could not in practice go back on what their counsel had assented to, at any rate so far as it had been acted upon. The result would be that, although there would be no new equitable interests actually created under the arrangement, all the beneficiaries would by a species of estoppel be treated as if they had those interests. I hope that Mr. Godfrey will forgive me if I say that I find this argument somewhat unattractive[19]. In particular, I find it very hard to believe that Parliament intended the court to approve on behalf of infants arrangements which depended for their efficacy upon the uncertainties of estoppel. I bear in mind, too, the wide meaning which *Grey v IRC* ([1960] AC 1, [1959] 3 All ER 603) gave to the word "disposition" in section 53 (1) (*c*).

Mr. Brookes, for the trustees, boldy asserted that, when correctly read, the Act of 1958 indirectly did what *Re Hambleden's Will Trusts* said it did. He went back to the words of section 1 (1), and emphasised that the power of the court was a power exercisable "by order" and that that power was a power

[19] See *Spens v IRC* [1970] 1 WLR 1173 at 1183–1185, [1970] 3 All ER 295.

to approve an arrangement "varying or revoking" all or any of the trusts. In emphasising those phrases, he said that the right way to read the section was to say that the power of the court was merely a power to make an order approving an arrangement which in fact varied or revoked the trusts, and not an arrangement which failed to do any such thing. When the adults by their counsel assented to the arrangement, and the court on behalf of the infants by order approved the arrangement, then there was an arrangement which varied or revoked the trusts. So the order of the court both conferred jurisdiction and exercised it. His escape from section 53 (1) (*c*) had a similar dexterity about it: by conferring an express power on the court to do something by order, Parliament in the Act of 1958 had provided by necessary implication an exception from section 53 (1) (*c*). He buttressed his contention by a reference to *Re Joseph's Will Trusts* ([1959] 1 WLR 1019, [1959] 3 All ER 474). Vaisey J there accepted that the order which he made, directing the trustees to carry the order of the court into effect, was neither contemplated by the Act nor expressly authorised by it. Rather than read into the Act words that are not there, said Mr. Brookes, one should construe the Act as authorising an order which is efficacious to achieve its avowed object. He pointed to the long title of the Act which reads: "An Act to extend the jurisdiction of courts of law to vary trusts in the interests of beneficiaries and sanction dealings with trust property."

I hope that Mr. Brookes, too, will pardon me if I say that I did not find his argument compelling. Indeed, at times I think it tended to circularity. But I find it tempting; and I yield. It is not a construction which I think the most natural. But it is not an impossible construction; it accords with the long title; it accords with the practice which has been relied upon for many years in some thousands of cases; and it accords with considerations of convenience. The point is technical, and I do not think that I am doing more than straining a little at the wording in the interests of legislative efficacy.

However that is not all. Mr. Millett, for Mrs. Wilson, the tenant for life, provided another means of escape from section 53 (1) (*c*) in his helpful reply. Where, as here, the arrangement consists of an agreement made for valuable consideration, and that agreement is specifically enforceable, then the beneficial interests pass to the respective purchasers on the making of the agreement. Those interests pass by virtue of the species of constructive trust made familiar by contracts for the sale of land, whereunder the vendor becomes a constructive trustee for the purchaser as soon as the contract is made, albeit the constructive trust has special features about it. Section 53 (2), he continued, provides that "This section does not affect the creation or operation of resulting, implied or constructive trusts." Accordingly, because the trust was constructive, section 53 (1) (*c*) was excluded. He supported this contention by the House of Lords decision in *Oughtred v IRC* ([1960] AC 206, [1959] 3 All ER 623). He relied in particular upon passages in the speeches ([1960] AC at 227, 231) of Lord Radcliffe and Lord Cohen, albeit that they were dissenting on the main point for decision. He pointed out that although Lord Jenkins (with whom Lord Keith concurred) had not decided the point, he had assumed for the purposes of his speech that it was correct (at p. 239), and that the rejection of the contention by Lord Denning (at

p. 233) was in a very brief passage. Mr. Millett accepts that if there were to be some subsequent deed of family arrangement which would carry out the bargain, then this deed might well be caught by section 53 (1) (*c*); but that, he said, cannot affect the "arrangement", and the parties might well be willing to let matters rest on that. It seems to me that there is considerable force in this argument in cases where the agreement is specifically enforceable, and in its essentials I accept it. At all events it supports the conclusion that in such cases the practice established by *Re Hambleden's Will Trusts* ([1960] 1 WLR 82, [1960] 1 All ER 353) is right. For this and the other reasons that I have given, though with some hesitation, I accordingly hold this to be the case.

Finally, before turning to the second main point, I should mention that in this case the arrangement carries out its purpose by revoking all the existing trusts and establishing a new set of trusts. That being so, it is said that some difficulty arises on the wording of section 1 (1) of the Act of 1958. This merely empowers the court to approve an arrangement "varying or revoking all or any of the trusts", and so, it is said, the court cannot approve an arrangement which, instead of merely "revoking" or merely "varying", proceeds to revoke and then to set up new trusts, thereby producing an effect equivalent to the process of settlement and resettlement. The section, it is argued, says nothing of establishing new trusts for old. As a matter of principle, however, I do not really think that there is anything in this point, at all events in this case. Here the new trusts are in many respects similar to the old. In my judgment, the old trusts may fairly be said to have been varied by the arrangement whether the variation is effected directly, by leaving some of the old words standing and altering others, or indirectly, by revoking all the old words and then setting up new trusts partly, though not wholly, in the likeness of the old. One must not confuse machinery with substance; and it is the substance that matters. Comparing the position before and after the arrangement takes effect, I am satisfied that the result is a variation of the old trusts, even though effected by the machinery of revocation and resettlement.

[His Lordship considered *Re T.'s Settlement Trusts* [1964] Ch 158, [1963] 3 All ER 759, and continued:] A line may, perhaps, one day emerge from a sufficiently ample series of reported decisions; but for the present all that is necessary for me to say is whether the particular case before me is on the right side or the wrong side of any reasonable line that could be drawn. In this case I am satisfied that the arrangement proposed falls on the side of the line which bears the device "variation".

I can now turn to the second main point, namely, that under the Perpetuities and Accumulations Act, 1964. The settlement in this case was made prior to the commencement of that Act, and any variation will be made after that commencement. Section 15 (5) provides that "The foregoing sections of this Act shall apply . . .' (and there is then an exception with which I am not concerned) ". . . only in relation to instruments taking effect after the commencement of this Act. . . ." There follows a reference to instruments made in the exercise of a special power of appointment. The Act received the Royal Assent on July 16, 1964, so that this is the date of its commencement.

The kind of question that arises is this. Suppose an instrument taking effect in 1959, as the original trusts did in this case, and a variation made under the Act of 1958 which merely alters a few words: will such a variation allow the Act of 1964 to apply to the trusts in their revised form? Again, suppose that, as here, there is a revocation of the old trusts and a declaration of new trusts, so that in form there is a new start, although in substance merely a variation: does this alter the position? Could something be done by the second method which cannot be done by a method which in form as well as in substance is a mere variation? Is it possible to have a variation under the Act of 1958 once every generation, and then with each variation start afresh with a relaxed perpetuity rule and a new accumulation period bounteously provided by the Act of 1964?

Mr. Millett boldly answered "Yes" to this last question, and harked back to those spacious days when strict settlements of land were common, and once a generation there was a process of settlement and resettlement, with all the old entails securely barred and new entails established. He pointed out that on each resettlement the settlors in effect changed, and that often there would be a similar result on a variation under the Act of 1958. When the settlement was first made the original settlor was the settlor; but when the first variation came to be made, then if there was any alteration in the beneficial interests (as distinct from the mere conferring of additional administrative powers quoad those beneficial interests) the beneficiaries concerned would be the settlors, transferring their interests to be held on new trusts. Thus in effect there would be a new start each time. Mr. Millett drew my attention to the decision of Plowman J in *Re Lloyd's Settlement* ([1967] 2 WLR 1078, [1967] 2 All ER 314), where, he said, this in effect was done. In that case a settlement inter vivos was made on March 21, 1958 (March 21, 1959, in the headnote and March 31, 1958, in the statement of facts seem to be erroneous). The settlement directed an accumulation, and in the result the only appropriate accumulation period was that of the settlor's life. The effect was to expose the trust property to estate duty risks in respect of an interest which would pass on the settlor's death, and accordingly in 1966 a variation of the trusts was sought under the Act of 1958. By then the Act of 1964 had come into effect. Under the trusts as varied by the arrangement, accumulation was directed for a period of 21 years from the date of the settlement; and this period is one which was made available for the first time by the Act of 1964. Accordingly, under the Act of 1958 a settlement made prior to the Act of 1964 was varied after that Act in a way which took advantage of the provisions of that Act. The case is shortly reported, setting out the facts at some length, the cases cited in the argument, and the order made; but unfortunately there is no statement of the reasons of the learned judge. Nevertheless it seems to me that the variation in fact there made supports Mr. Millett's contention.

Mr. Millett also referred me to Lewin on Trusts, 16th Edn (1964), at p. 741, where an argument which is in accord with Mr. Millett's submission is advanced by the learned editor (the passage cannot have been the work of the late Mr. Lewin). I would only observe that there appears on page 742 to have been a slip in the statement of *Pilkington v IRC*,

([1964] AC 612, [1962] 3 All ER 622), for the reference in the text should, it seems, be to a power of advancement rather than to a power of appointment, and the citation of the case is also erroneous. For myself, I find any analogy with powers of appointment and powers of advancement unsatisfactory. The mischief attacked by the rule against perpetuities in the case of powers of appointment, and now, since *Pilkington v IRC*, in the case of powers of advancement as well, is that the property is tied up ab initio. The power is conferred by the settlement, and that person exercising the power can do so only within pre-ordained limits. The power indeed "belongs" to the old settlement, if I may respectfully adopt the language of Lord Radcliffe in the *Pilkington* case ([1964] AC 612 at 642). Under the Act of 1958, there are no such limits. The property, as it seems to me, is freely disposable. Under an arrangement approved by the court the trusts may be brought wholly to an end. On the other hand, they may be varied; and there is no limit, other than the discretion of the court and the agreement of the parties, to the variation which may be made. Any variation owes its authority not to anything in the initial settlement but to the statute and the consent of the adults coming, as it were, ab extra. This certainly seems to be so in any case not within the Act where a variation or resettlement is made under the doctrine of *Saunders v Vautier* ((1841) 4 Beav 115) by all the adults joining together; and I cannot see any real difference in principle in a case where the court exercises its jurisdiction on behalf of the infants under the Act of 1958. It seems to me that the arrangement, coupled with the order of the court, constitute an "instrument", or, since the singular includes the plural, "instruments", which take effect after July 15, 1964. Whether the documents are regarded as separate instruments or as together constituting one composite instrument, the effect is produced by the complex of documents; and what takes effect after July 15, 1964, is the result of this complex of documents. In my judgment, therefore, it is permissible to insert provisions deriving their validity from the Act of 1964 into an arrangement approved under the Act of 1958.

That, I think, suffices to dispose of the two substantial points; and I should perhaps say that I have been astute to do so without resort to the Fourth ([1956] Cmnd. 18) and Sixth ([1957] Cmnd. 310) Reports of the Law Reform Committee or the discussions which led to those reports, despite their relationship to the Acts of 1964 and 1958 respectively. I propose now to consider the merits of the arrangement put forward.

I can deal with the merits of this application quite shortly.

[His Lordship approved the arrangement as being for the benefit of each of the beneficiaries categorised by s. 1 (1) of the Act.]

In *Inland Revenue Commissioners v Holmden* ([1968] AC 685, [1968] 1 All ER 148) Lord Reid said (at p. 701): "Each beneficiary is bound because he has consented to the variation. If he was not of full age when the arrangement was made he is bound because the court was authorised by the Act to approve it on his behalf and did so by making an order . . . So the arrangement must be regarded as an arrangement made by the beneficiaries themselves. The court merely acted on behalf of or as representing those beneficiaries who were not in a position to give their own consent and approval." And Lord HODSON (at p. 705): "In my opinion, the effect of the arrangement varying the settlement was, as Harman LJ pointed out, to re-write the settlement from the date of the order in the terms proposed and approved by the court."

ii. VARIATION OR RE-SETTLEMENT

In *Re Ball's Settlement Trusts*[20] ([1968] 1 WLR 899, [1968] 2 All ER 438) MEGARRY J, approving an arrangement "revoking the trusts of the . . . settlement and resettling the subject-matter of the . . . settlement", said (at p. 903): "What section 1 (1) of the Act authorises the court to approve is

> 'any arrangement . . . varying or revoking all or any of the trusts, or enlarging the powers of the trustees of managing or administering any of the property subject to the trusts.'

The word 'resettling' or its equivalent nowhere appears. Accordingly, while there is plainly jurisdiction to approve the arrangement in so far as it revokes the trusts, in my view there is equally plainly no jurisdiction to approve the arrangement as regards 'resettling' the property, at any rate eo nomine. In this connection, I bear in mind the words of Wilberforce J in *Re T.'s Settlement Trusts* ([1964] Ch 158, [1963] 3 All ER 759). He there said ([1964] Ch at 162):

> 'I have no desire to cut down the very useful jurisdiction which this Act has conferred upon the court. But I am satisfied that the proposal as originally made to me falls outside it. Though presented as "a variation" it is in truth a complete new resettlement. The former trust funds were to be got in from the former trustees and held upon wholly new trusts such as might be made by an absolute owner of the funds. I do not think that the court can approve this.'

It seems to me that the originating summons correctly describes what is sought to be done in this case, and as so described there is clearly no jurisdiction for the court to approve the arrangement. But it does not follow that merely because an arrangement can correctly be described as effecting a revocation and resettlement, it cannot also be correctly described as effecting a variation of the trusts. The question then is whether the arrangement in this case can be so described. In the course of argument I indicated that it seemed desirable for the summons to be amended by substituting the words 'varying' for the word 'revoking' and deleting the reference to 'resettling', and that I would give leave for this amendment to be made. On the summons as so amended the question is thus whether the arrangement can fairly be said to be covered by the word 'varying' so that the court has power to approve it.

There was some discussion of the ambit of this word in *Re Holt's Settlement* ([1969] 1 Ch 100, [1968] 1 All ER 470). It was there held that if in substance the new trusts were recognisable as the former trusts, though with variations, the change was comprehended within the word 'varying', even if it had

[20] (1968) 84 LQR 459 (P.V.B.); *Allen v Distillers Co (Biochemicals) Ltd* [1974] QB 384, [1974] 2 All ER 365; (1974) ASCL 524 (J. Hackney).

been achieved by a process of revocation and new declaration. In that case, the new trusts were plainly recognisable as the old trusts with variations. In the present case, the new trusts are very different from the old. The settlor's life interest vanishes; so does the power of appointment, though that will now be released. In place of the provision in default of appointment for absolute interests for the two sons if they survive the settlor, and if not, for their issue stirpitally, there is now a life interest for each son, and vested absolute interests for the children of the sons born before October 1, 1977. There is a clean sweep of the somewhat exiguous administrative provisions and an equally exiguous new set in their place. The arrangement also makes altogether new provisions for insurance policies, both those which provide for death duties and are to be added to the trust fund and those which provide for the excluded persons and are to be held on separate trusts; but these portions of the arrangement, I should say, are not made part of the settlement as revised, but are to operate independently and outside its terms. All that remains of the old trusts are what I may call the general drift or purport, namely, that a moiety of the trust fund is to be held on certain trusts for each son and certain of his issue. Is the word 'varying' wide enough to embrace so categorical a change?

[His Lordship referred to *Re Dyer* [1935] VLR 273, and continued:] If an arrangement changes the whole substratum of the trust, then it may well be that it cannot be regarded merely as varying that trust. But if an arrangement, while leaving the substratum, effectuates the purpose of the original trust by other means, it may still be possible to regard that arrangement as merely varying the original trusts, even though the means employed are wholly different and even though the form is completely changed.

I am, of course, well aware that this view carries me a good deal farther than I went in *Re Holt's Settlement* ([1969] 1 Ch 100, [1968] 1 All ER 470). I have felt some hesitation in the matter, but on the whole I consider that this is a proper step to take. The jurisdiction of the Act is beneficial and, in my judgment, the court should construe it widely and not be astute to confine its beneficent operation. I must remember that in essence the court is merely contributing on behalf of infants and unborn and unascertained persons the binding assents to the arrangement which they, unlike an adult beneficiary, cannot give. So far as is proper, the power of the court to give that assent should be assimilated to the wide powers which the ascertained adults have.

In this case, it seems to me that the substratum of the original trusts remains. True, the settlor's life interest disappears; but the remaining trusts are still in essence trusts of half of the fund for each of the two named sons and their families, with defined interests for the sons and their children in place of the former provisions for a power of appointment among the sons and their children and grandchildren and for the sons to take absolutely in default of appointment. In the events which are likely to occur, the differences between the old provision and the new may, I think, fairly be said to lie in detail rather than in substance. Accordingly, in my judgment, the arrangement here proposed, with the various revisions to it made in the course of argument, can properly be described as varying the trusts of the settlement. Subject to the summons being duly amended, I therefore approve the revised arrangement."

D. Fraud on a Power

Parker and Mellows: *Modern Law of Trusts* (3rd Edn) pp. 362–363

"It is a statement of the obvious that if a variation is fraudulent or contrary to public policy it will not be sanctioned. A case of some interest on this point is *Re Robertson's Will Trusts*[21], where the applicant had exercised a special power of appointment in favour of his children as a preliminary to the proposed arrangement. His purpose and intention in making the appointment was to benefit his children and not himself. Later he was advised that his financial position would in fact be improved if the appointment were made and the scheme approved. But Russell J held that to suppose his original purpose and intention had been changed or added to was unjustified. It followed that there was no fraud on the power, though, if there had been, the court would not have been able to approve the scheme.

However, subsequent case-law appears to indicate a certain conflict as to the precise principles to be applied. In *Re Wallace's Settlement*[1] Megarry J said that the fact that protected life tenants had executed appointments in favour of their children in itself raised a case for inquiry because the life tenants benefited by the arrangement; but on the evidence he was satisfied that there was no fraud on the power because the benefit to the life tenants was not substantial and they had intended to make the appointment before the arrangement was approved. However, in *Re Brook's Settlement*[2] Stamp J adopted a rather different approach. He held that the exercise of a special power of appointment amounted to a fraud on the power and he was unable to approve the variation. Here one of the purposes of the appointment (by a protected life tenant in favour of his children from which he would also benefit from a division of the capital) was to enable the life tenant to obtain what he could not otherwise get, namely capital rather than income. This was enough to invalidate the appointment.

The important feature of *Re Brook* is that the judge emphasised that the question is whether the *purpose* of the appointment amounted to a fraud, not, as was apparently suggested in *Re Wallace,* the *effect* of the appointment on the financial position of the appointor. It is thought that *Re Brook* applies the correct principle.

Release. The difficulties that may thus arise as a result of a fraud on the power, however inadvertent, may in some circumstances be avoided by releasing the power. For no question of a fraud on a power can arise on a mere release. And it has been held that, provided that the power in question can be released[3], the court will approve an arrangement varying a settlement even though the objects of the power are ignored[4]. There appears to be

[21] [1960] 1 WLR 1050, [1960] 3 All ER 146.
[1] [1968] 1 WLR 711, [1968] 2 All ER 209.
[2] [1968] 1 WLR 1661, [1968] 3 All ER 416.
[3] See *Re Wills' Trust Deeds* [1964] Ch 219, [1963] 1 All ER 390; (1968) 84 LQR 64 (A. J. Hawkins).
[4] *Re Christie-Miller's Marriage Settlement* [1961] 1 WLR 462, [1961] 1 All ER 855; *Re Courtauld's Settlement* [1965] 1 WLR 1385, [1965] 2 All ER 544; *Re Ball's Settlement* [1968] 1 WLR 899, [1968] 2 All ER 438.

some doubt whether the release should be effected by deed, or whether it can be inferred from the facts. The latter would seem sufficient[5].

Even if the power cannot be released (e.g. if it was given to the donee *qua* trustee) it still seems possible to apply to the court for an arrangement extinguishing the power because this amounts to varying or revoking a trust within section 1 of the 1958 Act. But because the power is not of itself releasable the court is likely to impose conditions on the release. Thus Stamp J in *Re Drewe's Settlement*[6], in approving an arrangement, insisted that it could only be effected by deed and with the consent of the trustees.''

E. Principles Applicable to the Exercise of the Discretion

i. OBSERVING THE SETTLOR'S INTENTION

RE STEED'S WILL TRUSTS[7]

[1960] Ch 407; [1960] 1 All ER 487 (CA, Lord EVERSHED MR, WILLMER and UPJOHN LJJ)

The testator gave property which included Loft Farm to trustees "upon protective trusts as defined by section 33 of the Trustee Act, 1925" for his housekeeper Gladys Sandford for her life, and after her death for such persons as she may by deed or will appoint; and in default of appointment upon trust for her next of kin.

The will declared (clause 9) that it was the testator's "wish that she shall have the use and enjoyment of the capital value thereof if she needs it during her life. And . . . that if and when such property shall be sold my trustees may apply capital moneys from such sale to or for her benefit . . . provided that they shall consider the necessity for retaining sufficient capital to prevent her from being without adequate means at any time during her life . . ."

Gladys exercised the power of appointment in her own favour.

The farm was let to Gladys's brother. There was some doubt whether he paid any rent, or was able to do so. The trustees decided that the farm should be sold, and they received a good offer. Gladys asked the court to restrain the sale, and brought a summons under the Variation of Trusts Act 1958, asking the court to approve an arrangement under which the trustee should hold the property on trust for herself absolutely.

Held. The court refused its approval.

LORD EVERSHED MR: This is in more ways than one, including matters of procedure, a somewhat unusual case, as Mr. Newsom observed. It is also in many respects an unhappy case, and I cannot refrain from expressing my own sympathy for the plaintiff on the one side, and for the three defendant trustees on the other.

I propose in this judgment to forbear from entering, except where absolutely necessary, into matters of fact which might only serve to rub salt into existing wounds. Suffice it to say that the plaintiff was one who served

[5] In *Re Ball* MEGARRY J insisted on a formal release, but in *Re Christie-Miller* and *Re Courtauld* an inferred release was regarded as sufficient: see note 4, supra.
[6] [1966] 1 WLR 1518, [1966] 2 All ER 844.
[7] See also *Re Michelham's Will Trusts* [1964] Ch 550, [1963] 2 All ER 188.

loyally and most skilfully for a long period of time the testator and the testator's wife. In consideration for those services the testator included in his will provisions for her benefit . . .

It is, I think, quite plain on the evidence that the testator, while anxious to show his gratitude to the plaintiff, was no less anxious she should be well provided for and not exposed to the temptation, which he thought was real, of being, to use a common phrase, sponged upon by one of her brothers. I fully realise that the plaintiff's natural affection for that brother is not a matter which one can in any sense condemn. Blood is, after all, thicker than water, and the happiness of the plaintiff, according to her own view at any rate, is very much linked up with the association with that brother and the brother's daughter and wife.

[His Lordship decided that the court ought not to interfere with the exercise by the trustees of their discretion; and continued]: I now come to what has caused me greater difficulty, namely, the effect of the Variation of Trusts Act, 1958 . . .

In the present case, the proposed variation (that is, the "arrangement") which the plaintiff puts forward may be most briefly and accurately stated as involving this: in clause 9 of the will the words: "upon protective trusts as defined by section 33 of the Trustee Act, 1925", should be omitted, and similarly in the next clause the words "protective" should be omitted. If those words were omitted, the result would be that the plaintiff would become absolutely entitled to the property, because she would then be the life tenant, having appointed by irrevocable deed to herself the reversion; and that is what she seeks.

The trustees have taken the view that it is not an arrangement which, having regard to their conception of their duties and the wishes of their testator, they should approve. For my part, I do not think that approval on behalf of the trustees is the court's function in this case, though the court in exercising its general discretion will certainly pay regard to what the trustees say and the grounds for their saying it. Nor can I see, if this was the judge's view, that the court is called upon by the language of this section to approve the arrangement or proposal on behalf of the proposer; that is to say, whether they think she was wise or unwise to put her idea forward.

The duty of the court, as I read the section on the facts of this case, is that they must approve it on behalf of the only person or persons who might have an interest under the discretionary trusts and whose presence under the trusts now prevents the plaintiff saying that she can put an end to the settlement.

Having regard to the plaintiff's age, no doubt it is true to say that she will not and cannot now have children, but she might marry, and marry more than once. She says, with some reason, that having lived for 53 years unmarried she does not feel in the least likely to marry now. That may well be right, though many have said that before and subsequent events have proved them wrong. That, however, is neither here nor there. There does exist a discretionary trust, and a future husband of the plantiff's is a person interested under those trusts, on whose behalf the court must now approve the proposal.

Having regard to what has happened between the plaintiff and her brother, it is possible that, strictly speaking, there has been a forfeiture, and if so, the future husband or husbands would be within paragraph (*b*) of the subsection, but if not, he would be within paragraph (*d*). Again, I think that does not, for present purposes, matter.

I repeat that the duty of the court is now to consider whether in the exercise of its discretion, which is framed in the widest possible language, it should approve the arrangement on behalf of what has been described in argument as the spectral spouse of the plaintiff. In doing that, what must the court consider? Not, I conceive, merely the material benefit or detriment of such spouse. Certainly not if he is to be regarded as being a person, under paragraph (*d*), though if he is to be regarded as falling under paragraph (*b*) it is expressly enjoined that the court shall not approve the arrangement unless it is for his benefit.

As I have said, I do not so read this Act as to mean that the court's duty in the exercise of this very wide and, indeed, revolutionary discretion is confined to saying: "Would it really much harm this spectral spouse if we approve the proposal?" Bearing in mind, of course, the admitted possibility that the spouse might cease to be spectral and become a reality, I think what the court is bound to do is to see whether, looked at on behalf of the person indicated, it approves the arrangement. It is the arrangement which has to be approved, not just the limited interest of the person on whose behalf the court's duty is to consider it.

If that is right, it then follows that the court must regard the proposal as a whole, and so regarding it, then ask itself whether in the exercise of its jurisdiction it should approve that proposal on behalf of the person who cannot give a consent, because he is not in a position to do so. If that is a right premise, then it follows that the court is bound to look at the scheme as a whole, and when it does so, to consider, as surely it must, what really was the intention of the benefactor. That such is a proper approach is at least supported by the provisions of RSC Ord. 55, r. 14A (3A)[8], which provides that in the case of an application under this Act, where there is a living settlor the living settlor is to be a party before the court. That rule seems to me to reinforce what I conceive to underly this provision, namely, that the court must, albeit that it is performing its duty on behalf of some person who cannot consent on his or her own part, regard the proposal in the light of the purpose of the trust as shown by the evidence of the will or settlement itself, and of any other relevant evidence available.

Having so formulated the duty, I have, for my part, come to the conclusion that it would not be right for the court in the exercise of its discretion to approve this variation or arrangement. I am not uninfluenced in coming to that conclusion by any means by the circumstance that the judge obviously did not think it was a proposal which should be approved, though it is quite true that for reasons which I have indicated it may be said he was looking at it and basing his jurisdiction upon an interpretation of the section which I have not been altogether able to share, namely, it

[8] Now Ord. 93, r. 6 (2).

was his duty to approve it on behalf of the proposer, the plaintiff, and also that the scheme must be regarded as intended to be in some sense inter partes and, therefore, that he had to approve it on behalf of the trustees.

Disagreeing, if that is a fair view of his judgment, with that premise, nevertheless it is quite clear, I think, that the judge was by no means unsympathetic to the feelings and views of the plaintiff, but, on the other hand, was no less clear in his mind that the arrangement was one which so cut at the root of the testator's wishes and intentions that it was not one which the court should approve.

After all, if the court is asked to approve this proposal on behalf of a spectral spouse (if I may revert to that phrase), it must ask, I take it, why is the spectral spouse there at all under the trust? If one asks that question, nearly everything else, as it seems to me, follows. There is no doubt why the spectral spouse is there. It was part of the testator's scheme, made as I think manifest by the language which I have read from the clauses in the will, that it was the intention and the desire of the testator that this trust should be available for the plaintiff so that she would have proper provision made for her throughout her life, and would not be exposed to the risk that she might, if she had been handed the money, part with it in favour of another individual about whom the testator felt apprehension, which apprehension is plainly shared by the trustees.

For those reasons, therefore, I also conclude adversely to the plaintiff that we should not exercise jurisdiction under the Act of 1958 to approve the arrangement which has been put forward, and which I have tried to define. That is the end of the case. I only repeat the sympathy I have felt in a distressing matter of this kind, both with the plaintiff and with the trustees, whose difficulties in discharging their duty are obvious. I should like to express the hope that perhaps time, the healer, will do much to put an end to these troubles.

ii. BENEFIT: FISCAL, SOCIAL AND MORAL

RE WESTON'S SETTLEMENTS[9]

[1969] 1 Ch 223, [1968] 3 All ER 338 (CA, Lord DENNING MR, HARMAN and DANCKWERTS LJJ)

In 1964 Mr. Stanley Weston made two settlements, one in consideration of the marriage of his elder son Robert, who was born in 1942, and the other a voluntary settlement in favour of his younger son Alan, born in 1949. Under each settlement, the son in question received a life interest with a general power of appointment over part of the fund and subject thereto on trust for such of his childeren as he shall appoint and in default of appointment on trust for his children absolutely. The investments of both settlements were in the Stanley Weston Group Ltd.

These settlements were subject to fiscal disadvantages, namely to capital gains tax on disposal (introduced by the Finance Act 1965) and to estate duty upon the deaths of each of the sons. These problems were explained by STAMP J in the lower court ([1969] 1 Ch 231–232).

[9] (1969) 85 LQR 15 (P.V.B.); (1968) 32 Conv (NS) 431 (F. R. Crane); (1976) 40 Conv (NS) 295 (T. G. Watkins).

The settlor and the two sons (and the family of the elder son) moved their homes to Jersey, and claimed to be resident and domiciled there. The settlor asked the court to appoint (under Trustee Act 1925, s. 41[10]) two persons of good repute, resident in Jersey, in the place of the existing English trustees; and asked the court to approve an arrangement under the Variation of Trusts Act 1958 which inserted in the trusts a power in the new trustees to discharge the property from the trusts of the English settlements and to subject it to identical trusts of a Jersey settlement.

Held (affirming STAMP J). The court refused.

LORD DENNING MR: If the court gives its approval to the proposed scheme, the result will be that the new trustees will be able to sell the shares in the Stanley Weston Group and buy other shares, without being accountable for capital gains. There will be also considerable savings of estate duty on the deaths of the two sons Robert and Alan. In short, there will be a tremendous tax advantage to the sons and grandchildren of Mr. Stanley Weston. The question is whether the court ought to sanction the scheme.

There is one reported case in which a scheme on these lines was approved. It was *Re Seale's Marriage Settlement* ([1961] Ch 574, [1961] 3 All ER 136). In that case husband and wife married in 1931. They were both domiciled and resident in England: and a marriage settlement was made in an English trust in the ordinary form. They had three children who appear to have been born in England. But when the children were quite small the family emigrated to Canada. The children were brought up as Canadians and were likely to continue to live in Canada. The husband and wife intended to continue to live there. It was obviously advantageous for the settlement to be turned from an English settlement into a Canadian settlement—quite irrespective of tax advantages—and Buckley J made orders enabling Canadian trustees to be appointed and a Canadian settlement to be drawn up substantially in the same terms as the English settlement.

Those advising Mr. Weston ask the court to approve a similar scheme here. The judge refused. He said that this was a "cheap exercise in tax avoidance" which he ought not to sanction: but he hoped that the case would be taken to the Court of Appeal so as to have the views of this court.

Before the Variation of Trusts Act, 1958, there was much discussion as to the power of the court to sanction the variation of trusts. If the beneficiaries were all sui juris, they could agree between themselves to revoke or vary the trusts. If there were infant beneficiaries or unborn persons, it needed the consent of the court. But the jurisdiction of the court so to consent was very limited. The court could not sanction it except in case of a compromise of disputed rights: see *Chapman v Chapman* ([1954] AC 429, [1954] 1 All ER 798). By the Variation of Trusts Act, 1958, this limitation was removed. The court has power to approve a variation or revocation of the trust, if it thinks fit, on behalf of infants or unborn persons. The statute gives no guide as to the way in which this discretion should be exercised. It says: "The court may *if it thinks fit* by order approve . . .". Likewise

[10] See p. 441, ante.

with the appointment of new trustees, the Trustee Act, 1925, gives no guide. It simply says the court may appoint new trustees "whenever it is expedient". There being no guidance in the statutes, it remains for the court to do the best it can.

Two propositions are clear: (i) In exercising its discretion, the function of the court is to protect those who cannot protect themselves. It must do what is truly for their benefit. (ii) It can give its consent to a scheme to avoid death duties or other taxes. Nearly every variation that has come before the court has tax avoidance for its principal object: and no one has ever suggested that this is undesirable or contrary to public policy.

But I think it necessary to add this third proposition: (iii) The court should not consider merely the financial benefit[11] to the infants or unborn children, but also their educational and social benefit. There are many things in life more worth while than money. One of these things is to be brought up in this our England, which is still "the envy of less happier lands". I do not believe it is for the benefit of children to be uprooted from England and transported to another country simply to avoid tax. It was very different with the children of the Seale family, which Buckley J considered. That family had emigrated to Canada many years before, with no thought of tax avoidance, and had brought up the children there as Canadians. It was very proper that the trust should be transferred to Canada. But here the family had only been in Jersey three months when they presented this scheme to the court. The inference is irresistible: the underlying purpose was to go there in order to avoid tax. I do not think that this will be all to the good for the children. I should imagine that, even if they had stayed in this country, they would have had a very considerable fortune at their disposal, even after paying tax. The only thing that Jersey can do for them is to give them an even greater fortune. Many a child has been ruined by being given too much[12]. The avoidance of tax may be lawful, but it is not yet a virtue. The Court of Chancery should not encourage or support it—it should not give its approval to it—if by so doing it would imperil the true welfare of the children, already born or yet to be born.

There is one thing more. I cannot help wondering how long these young people will stay in Jersey. It may be to their financial interest at present to make their home there permanently. But will they remain there once the capital gains are safely in hand, clear of tax? They may well change their minds and come back to enjoy their untaxed gains. Is such a prospect really for the benefit of the children? Are they to be wanderers over the face of the earth, moving from this country to that, according to where they can best avoid tax? I cannot believe that to be right. Children are like trees: they grow stronger with firm roots.

The long and short of it is, as the judge said, that the exodus of this family to Jersey is done to avoid British taxation. Having made great wealth

[11] "The word 'benefit' is, I think, plainly not confined to financial benefit, but may extend to moral or social benefit." *Re Holt's Settlement* [1969] Ch 100 at 121, per MEGARRY J. See also *Re T.'s Settlement Trusts* [1964] Ch 158, [1963] 3 All ER 759; *Re CL* [1969] Ch 587, [1968] 1 All ER 1104; *Re Remnant's Settlement Trusts* [1970] Ch 560, [1970] 2 All ER 554.

[12] Each settlement was worth some £400,000.

here, they want to quit without paying the taxes and duties which are imposed on those who stay. So be it. If it really be for the benefit of the children, let it be done. Let them go, taking their money with them. But, if it be not truly for their benefit, the court should not countenance it. It should not give the scheme its blessing. The judge refused his approval. So would I. I would dismiss this appeal[13].

HARMAN LJ: This is an essay in tax avoidance naked and unashamed, and none the worse for that, says the applicant. Indeed the judge agreed that this court is not the watch-dog of the Inland Revenue, and it is well known that much and perhaps the main use which has been made of the Act has been to produce schemes of variation of English trusts which will have the effect of reducing liabilities either on the capital of the trusts or the income of the beneficiaries. . . .

Now, the linchpin of the scheme is not to be carried out under the Variation of Trusts Act at all. It is essential that the court should exercise its powers under the Trustee Act, 1925, either by appointing new trustees out of the jurisdiction or giving leave to the existing trustees to make the appointment. It is not suggested that the present trustees are unsuitable or that any difficulty has arisen in the administration of the trusts. The scheme is entirely conditioned by the wish to avoid the incidence of capital gains tax. For this purpose it is essential that the affairs of the trust should be administered from outside the United Kingdom and that this should be done by appointing two persons so resident as trustees. It is proposed that these trustees should then be empowered while still trustees of the English settlements to revoke the whole of the trusts of those instruments and to transfer the assets to themselves as trustees of the two settlements framed, it is said, so as to conform with the Jersey law.

Now, this law has never had any experience of trusts and so far as appears, the courts of Jersey have never made an order executing the trusts of a settlement. There is not, it appears, any Trustee Act in Jersey at all, and the effect of this last transaction must, so far as I can see, have nothing to recommend it from a trust point of view.

In the circumstances the judge was entitled to consider whether the court "should think fit" to accede to the scheme. The judge professed himself unsatisfied, and I think he was entitled to take that view. It is true that he expressed some dislike of tax avoidance of this sort, and in that he may have been mistaken, but he was in my opinion well justified in not being satisfied that a transfer of the whole trust to Jersey is expedient. The two young men who alone may be considered cannot be said to have proved that they truly intend to make Jersey their home. Indeed the younger of them has expressed no views on the subject at all. It seems to me most unlikely that two wealthy young men of this sort will be content at the threshold of their lives to settle down in the island and will not within a short time seek wider opportunities for their talents and wealth than that island affords. It follows,

[13] Cf. *Re Windeatt's Will Trusts* [1969] 1 WLR 692, [1969] 2 All ER 324, p. 445, ante (variation approved by PENNYCUICK J where the "family had been in Jersey for 19 years and had made a genuine and permanent home there. The children were born there".); *Re Whitehead's Will Trusts* [1971] 1 WLR 833, [1971] 2 All ER 1334, p. 437, ante (appointment of trustees resident overseas approved by the court where beneficiaries were resident and domiciled in Jersey).

as it seems to me, that on the facts of this case no case has been made out for the removal of the trusts to Jersey rather than any other part of the world. These are English settlements and they should I think remain so unless some good reason connected with the trusts themselves can be put forward. I am of opinion, therefore, that the judge was entitled in the exercise of his discretion to say that to use the powers of the Trustee Act in this way was not justified and I would dismiss the appeal.

iii. FAMILY HARMONY

In *Re Remnant's Settlement Trusts* ([1970] Ch 560 [1970] 2 All ER 554) a trust fund in favour of the children of two sisters Mrs. Hooper ("Dawn") and Mrs. Crosthwaite ("Merrial") was subject to forfeiture in respect of any of their children who practised Roman Catholicism or was married to a Roman Catholic, with an accruer provision in favour of the children of the other. The children of Dawn were Protestant, those of Merrial were Roman Catholic. PENNYCUICK J was asked to approve an arrangement which deleted the forfeiture provision and accelerated the interest of the children of each sister in a sum of £10,000, part of the trust fund.

The deletion of the forfeiture clause was clearly not for the financial benefit of Dawn's children; for they stood a very good chance of benefiting from it under the accruer provision. Nevertheless, PENNYCUICK J approved the arrangement. He said (at p. 566): "The three considerations set out by Mrs. Crosthwaite, and elaborated by counsel, are these: first, that the forfeiture provisions represent a deterrent to each of the Hooper children from adopting the Roman Catholic faith should she be minded to do so; secondly, that they operate as a deterrent to each of the Hooper children in the selection of a husband when the time comes; and thirdly, that the forfeiture provisions represent a source of possible family dissension. I am not sure that there is very much weight in the first of those considerations because there is no reason to suppose that any of these children has any particular concern with the Roman Catholic faith. On the other hand, I do think there is very real weight in the second and in the third considerations. Obviously a forfeiture provision of this kind might well cause very serious dissension between the families of the two sisters. On the best consideration I can give it I think that the deletion of the forfeiture provisions on the terms contained in the arrangement, including the provision for acceleration in £10,000, should be regarded as for the benefit of the three Hooper children.

I have not found this an easy point, but I think I am entitled to take a broad view of what is meant by 'benefit', and so taking it, I think this arrangement can fairly be said to be for their benefit . . .

I conclude then that the carrying out of this arrangement will be for the benefit of all the persons born and unborn on whose behalf I am concerned to approve the arrangement.

It remains to consider whether the arrangement is a fair and proper one. As far as I can see, there is no reason for saying otherwise, except that the arrangement defeats this testator's intention. That is a serious but by no means conclusive consideration. I have reached the clear conclusion that these forfeiture provisions are undesirable in themselves in the circumstances of this case and that an arrangement involving their deletion is a fair and proper one. I propose accordingly to approve the arrangement with one or two modifications which are not material to this judgment.

I would only like to add this word of caution. The effect of any particular forfeiture provision must depend on the nature of the provision itself and upon the circumstances in which it is likely to operate. A forfeiture provision is by no means always intrinsically undesirable. Again, you may have the position that a forfeiture provision benefits exclusively one or the other party concerned, and in that case it might be very difficult to say that the deletion of the provision was for the benefit of that party, unless there was the fullest financial compensation. However, I am not concerned to go futher into those matters. It is sufficient for me to say that on the facts of this particular case the deletion of the forfeiture provisions, upon the terms of the arrangement, is for the benefit of everyone concerned and that the arrangement is a fair and proper one."

(1971) 34 MLR 98 (R. B. M. Cotterrell)

"Even more difficult problems arise in cases such as *Re Remnant* and *Re Weston* where it becomes necessary to weigh the relative importance of countervailing financial and non-financial considerations. Thus the court may find itself forced to evaluate such considerations as the benefit to an English child in being brought up in England[14], or the benefit to a mental patient in releasing a trust interest which she would probably have wished to release if sane[15]. In such circumstances it is hard to avoid the conclusion that benefit and the measure of it is simply what the court says it is.

Since each case in this area of the law must be largely a matter of decision on the facts, comparison of the reported cases is difficult. Nevertheless they offer some guidance in an area where there is little else to guide the court and it is unfortunate that no cases other than *Re Weston* were discussed in *Re Remnant*. In the case of *Re Tinker's Settlement*[16], Russell J refused to approve a variation on behalf of unborn children under which they would lose a contingent interest under the trust on the ground that the variation would not be for their benefit even though it might prevent dissatisfaction and conflict in the family. While the remarks in *Re Tinker's Settlement*[17] which suggest that financial benefit must be present to satisfy the requirement of 'benefit' now seem unacceptable, the actual decision in the case has not been challenged and was approved by Cross J in *Re C.L*[18]. The position in *Re Tinker* was strikingly similar to that in *Re Remnant* and, while grounds of distinction could have been found, it would have been more satisfactory to have some consideration of the relevant pre-*Weston* cases. In view of the awesome width of the court's

[14] *Re Weston* [1969] 1 Ch 223, [1968] 3 All ER 338, p. 581, ante.

[15] *Re C.L.* [1969] 1 Ch 587, [1968] 1 All ER 1104.

[16] [1960] 1 WLR 1011, [1960] 3 All ER 85. The part of the proposed variation which conferred a purely financial benefit on the unborn children was approved.

[17] The case was not cited in *Re Weston* or *Re Remnant* but see per Cross J in *Re C.L.* (supra), at p. 599.

[18] [1969] 1 Ch 587, [1968] 1 All ER 1104.

present discretion, it will be regrettable if judges underestimate the importance of precedent, wisely used, as an aid to uniformity of treatment and coherence in trust variation law. Where such a heavy burden of decision is placed on the court these qualities seem particularly important and desirable."

iv. TAKING A CHANCE

The question arises whether the court should approve on behalf of a beneficiary who will in almost every conceivable set of circumstances be benefited, but might be prejudiced in one possible foreseeable situation. To what extent should the court take the chance of his receiving a benefit?

In *Re Holt's Settlement* ([1969] 1 Ch 100, [1968] 1 All ER 470)[19] MEGARRY J said (at p. 121): "The point that at one stage troubled me concerns the unborn issue. Mr. Brookes, as in duty bound, put before me a contention that it was possible to conceive of an unborn infant who would be so circumstanced that a proposed rearrangement would be entirely to his disadvantage. He postulated the case of a child born to Mrs. Wilson next year, and of Mrs. Wilson dying in childbirth, or shortly after the child's birth. In such a case, he said, the benefit of the acceleration of interest resulting from Mrs. Wilson surrendering the moiety of her life interest would be minimal, and there would be no saving of estate duty. All that would happen in regard to such an infant would be that the vesting of his interest would be postponed from age 21 to age 30; and the only possible advantage in that would be the non-financial moral or social advantage to which I have just referred. In support of this contention he referred me to the decision of Stamp J in *Re Cohen's Settlement Trusts* ([1965] 1 WLR 1229, [1965] 3 All ER 139). There, the scheme originally proposed was not approved by the court because there was a possibility of there being a beneficiary who would get no advantage whatsoever from the proposed arrangement; it would merely be to his detriment.

Mr. Millett, however, points out that there is an essential distinction between that case and this; for there, whatever the surrounding circumstances, the unborn person contemplated could not benefit from the arrangement. In the present case, he says, all that Mr. Brookes has done is to put forward the case of an infant who might be born next year; and it would be a result of the surrounding circumstances, and not of the time of birth or the characteristics of the infant, that that infant might derive no benefit from the arrangement proposed. Mr. Millett referred me to *Re Cohen's Will Trusts* ([1959] 1 WLR 865, [1959] 3 All ER 523)[20] where Danckwerts J held that in exercising the jurisdiction under the Act of 1958 the court must, on behalf of those persons for whom it was approving the arrangement, take the sort of risk which an adult would be prepared to take. Accordingly, says Mr. Millett, Mr. Brookes' special infant to be born next year was in the position that although there was the chance that its mother would die immediately afterwards, there was also the alternative chance that its mother would survive its birth for a

[19] For the facts see p. 567, ante. See also *Re Robinson's Settlement Trusts* [1976] 1 WLR 806, [1976] 3 All ER 61, p. 589, post.

[20] See (1960) 76 LQR 22 (R.E.M.).

substantial period of time. In the latter event, which was the more probable, the advantages of the arrangement would accrue to the infant. In short, he distinguishes the decision of Stamp J in *Re Cohen's Settlement Trusts* ([1965] 1 WLR 1229, [1965] 3 All ER 139) on the footing that that was the case of an unborn person whose prospects were hopeless, whatever the events, whereas in the present case the hypothetical unborn person has the normal prospects of events occurring which will either improve or not improve his position. Such an unborn person falls, he says, into the category of unborn persons on whose behalf the court should be prepared to take a risk if the arrangement appears on the whole to be for their benefit.

It seems to me that this is a proper distinction to make, and I accept it. Accordingly, I hold that the arrangement is for the benefit of the classes of persons specified in section 1 (1) of the Act, and I approve it."

F. Capital Transfer Tax

Estate duty was charged on the passing of property on a death, and on gifts made within seven years of death. There was thus no liability where the donor disposed of his property more than seven years before he died; or, in the case of a trust, where the life tenant's interest terminated more than seven years before his death. With a large fund, therefore, enormous savings were made by splitting up the fund in good time, and there was little difficulty in showing that the variation was for the benefit of the persons on whose behalf the court was asked to approve.

For example: A fund of £1,010,000 is held on trust for A for life and after A's death on trust for B absolutely. If nothing is done, A will receive the income from the fund. On the annual return of 6% gross, his income would be £60,600 per annum, before tax. Even if he has no other income, his income after tax would be (depending on his personal allowances) about £8,000. B, the remainderman, will receive the capital on A's death. This would be £317,750, after estate duty. If the fund were shared out and A took £500,000 and B took £510,000 it is obvious that they will both benefit. The risk of A's death within seven years, attracting estate duty liability, could be covered by insurance.

The introduction of capital transfer tax will dramatically reduce the occasions on which the necessary benefit can be shown. On a division of a trust on the lines of the previous example, capital transfer tax would be payable upon the share of the fund taken by B, because A's life interest in that part of the fund would terminate. Thus, if nothing is done to terminate the trust, B, under the capital transfer tax scales would receive £420,250. If the division were made as above, he would receive £286,125. He would thus receive £134,125 less; but he would receive it immediately. Whether this is a benefit or not would depend on how long A will in fact live.

The question whether a lesser sum now rather than a larger sum later is a sufficient benefit was before Templeman J in *Re Robinson's Settlement Trusts* [1976] 1 WLR 806, [1976] 3 All ER 61. It will be seen that there was some doubt whether capital transfer tax would be payable on the part of the fund in which the protected life interest was terminated. This was because of erroneous drafting of Finance Act 1975, Sch. 5, para. 18 (2) (a).

This has been amended in the Finance Act 1976, Sch. 14, para. 19. Capital transfer tax would now be chargeable on those facts.

RE ROBINSON'S SETTLEMENT TRUSTS

[1976] 1 WLR 806, [1976] 3 All ER 61 (ChD, TEMPLEMAN J)[1]

The plaintiff, aged 55, was a protected life tenant of a family trust of the value of some £368,000. Subject to a power of appointment, her children were entitled on her death. They were David and Margaret, both over 21, and Nicola, aged 17.

The plan was to divide the fund; the plaintiff taking 52% (which was her actuarial share), and the children dividing the balance in equal shares. On the assumption that capital transfer tax was payable on the children's shares, each child's share would be £11,000–14,000 less than it would be if the plaintiff died immediately with no variation being made. The elder children consented. The question was whether the variation was for the benefit of Nicola.

Held. Variation approved upon an insurance policy being obtained to cover the shortfall, and paid for out of the income of Nicola's share.

TEMPLEMAN J: This is an application under the Variation of Trusts Act 1958 which involves the division of a trust fund between life tenant and remaindermen. One of the remaindermen is an infant of about 17.

Under what might be termed the old fashioned calculations for estate duty, such a division was comparatively simple. The rates of estate duty were such that the amount which a remainderman stood to inherit if nothing was done was usually very small. In most schemes it was possible to make a division whereby the remainderman took more in any event than he would otherwise take on the death of the life tenant.

Into that simple form of division complications were introduced by the abolition of estate duty and its replacement by capital transfer tax. Evidence in these proceedings demonstrates that the old calculations simply do not fit the new tax. For example, whereas in the old days a tax was payable on death and so all one had to do was to find out what would be left on death after deduction of estate duty, now capital transfer tax is payable on the coming into operation of the division effected by the arrangement.

For that and for other reasons it is very difficult to provide for every possible contingency. The impact of the tax has also this quirk, that the actuarial value of the interest of the life tenant is much reduced. In the present instance, figures have been produced which show, for example, that if nothing is done and capital transfer tax is paid on the death of the life tenant, the plaintiff, then the share of the infant remainderman, the third defendant, will be somewhere between £58,000 and £60,000, if no alterations in the law are made in the meantime. Under the proposed arrangement, produced as a result of the independent advice of actuaries, the share which the third defendant gets is of a gross value of £58,000, and if capital transfer tax is payable—as to which there is a doubt in the present instance—the tax will reduce the share by something like £11,000 or

[1] (1976) 40 Conv (NS) 370 (F. R. Crane).

£14,000. This entails a serious possibility of a loss accruing to the third defendant. I was much pressed by all counsel, including counsel for the third defendant, with the observations of Stamp J and Danckwerts J in *Re Cohen's Settlement Trusts* [1965] 1 WLR 1229, [1965] 3 All ER 139 and in *Re Cohen's Will Trusts* [1959] 1 WLR 865, [1959] 3 All ER 523 respectively, to the effect that a reasonable view of a bargain must be taken. It is not necessary to insist that in all possible circumstances the infant is bound to benefit. It is said that capital transfer tax may not be payable and if it is then even taking into account the possible shortfall of £14,000, there will be acceleration of the income of the share which the third defendant is to take, and her mother, the plaintiff, is only about 55 years old, and so, in the normal course of events, acceleration will catch up with the shortfall.

Acceleration of income, at present rates of taxation on income, will take a good deal of catching up to compensate for a shortfall of £14,000. I cannot assume that the plaintiff will live long enough to procure that the arrangement viewed as a whole will benefit the third defendant. I must be satisfied that the arrangement is beneficial.

I expressed doubts and sent the parties away to consider insurance. In the old days of estate duty insurance could be effected by the life tenant to make good any shortfall so far as the reversion was concerned. Capital transfer tax introduces a new complication in that an insurance policy effected and kept up by the plaintiff may itself be liable to capital transfer tax with disastrous consequences. Although it is slightly anomalous, if the third defendant is to be protected against the possibility of shortfall, that protection can only be, to some extent, at the expense of the third defendant in that a policy must be kept up out of income.

I am quite satisfied that it would not be sensible to leave matters entirely as they are. There are other people interested besides the third defendant, and to preserve the present trusts with present, and future, rates of income and capital taxation does not seem sensible. I am satisfied that the plaintiff will only receive under the arrangement a reasonable and fair proportion having regard to the value of her life interest in her present situation.

In these circumstances I think I can accept the arrangement, provided that the third defendant's income is to a certain extent made available for insurance in order to protect the third defendant's own share against loss caused by the premature death of the plaintiff. A quotation has been obtained, and it would appear that to insure a shortfall of £14,000 would cost about £800 a year. Having regard to the amount of the income that seems to me to be weighing too much on the future and not enough on the present. A policy for £8,000, which with profits will yield something over £11,000 in 10 years and more thereafter, will only cost about £400 a year. That will still leave a substantial income for the third defendant to receive straight away.

It seems to me if insurance of £8,000 with profits is effected, I can, relying on the observations of Stamp J in *Re Cohen's Settlement Trusts* [1965] 1 WLR 1229, [1965] 3 All ER 139 and Danckwerts J in *Re Cohen's Will Trusts* [1959] 1 WLR 865, [1959] 3 All ER 523, approve this arrangement, although I still think it is a borderline case. Great powers of advocacy were used to persuade me that capital transfer tax has made such a change that the possible result of a death must be disregarded, the actuarial division accepted and a risk taken. I do not take that view. I start with the principle that all these schemes should, if possible, prove that an infant is not going to be materially worse off. There are difficulties with capital transfer tax, and borderline cases, and one may then have to take a broad view, but not a galloping, gambling view.

In my judgment, taking a reasonably prudent view, insurance of £8,000 in the present instance will be sufficient, and I am prepared to sanction the arrangement thus amended.

QUESTIONS

1. Which of the theories concerning the operation of the Variation of Trusts Act 1958 do you think is convincing? Should evidence in writing be required to effect a change in the beneficial interests of assenting adults? *Grey v IRC* [1960] AC 1, [1959] 3 All ER 603, p. 33, ante; *Oughtred v IRC* [1960] AC 206; [1959] 3 All ER 623; *Re Holt's Settlement* [1969] 1 Ch 100, [1968] 1 All ER 470, p. 567, ante.
2. Do you think that the Variation of Trusts Act 1958 provides too generous fiscal advantages for those lucky enough to have interests under settlements? Do you think it right that minors should suffer from the disadvantage that they are unable to make fiscally advantageous changes in their interests under settlements when adults in their situation could do so freely? How will the practice be affected by the introduction of capital transfer tax?
   L.R.C. Seventh Report, Cmnd. 310; (1965) 43 Can BR 181 (A.J.Maclean).
3. Observe the differences in the meaning given to the word "benefit" in
   a) Variation of Trusts Act 1958; (1969) 33 Conv (NS) pp. 122–131.
   b) Trustee Act 1925, s. 31 (1) (power to apply income for maintenance education or benefit), p. 541, ante.
   c) Trustee Act 1925, s. 32 (1) (power to apply capital of a settlement for the advancement or benefit of beneficiaries), p. 548, ante.

17. Fiduciary Position of Trustees[1]

I. General

The principle of Equity is that a trustee must not benefit from his position as trustee. He must not put himself in a position in which his duty to the trust may conflict with his personal interest. This, as will be seen, is manifested in various ways. A trustee must not trade in the trust estate, nor take profits or commissions. The rules have been laid down in the strongest terms; but the cases will show how difficult are the borderlines of its application. On the other hand, he has always been entitled to reimbursement of out-of-pocket expenses properly incurred[2]. And there is no objection to a provision in the trust instrument that trustees shall be remunerated. Indeed the complications of the administration of trusts at the present day necessitate the appointment of professionals.

II. Payments to a Trustee[3]

A. Reimbursement of Expenses

TRUSTEE ACT 1925

30. Implied indemnity of trustees.—(2) A trustee may reimburse himself or pay or discharge out of the trust premises all expenses incurred in or about the execution of the trusts or powers[4].

In *Hardoon v Belilios* ([1901] AC 118) the plaintiff was employed by a firm of share brokers. In order to assist a syndicate speculating in shares, fifty £10 shares in the Bank of China, Japan and the Straits Ltd. were placed in his name. The defendant was the absolute beneficial owner of the shares.

[1] H & M, pp. 512–527; K & S, pp. 306–325; P & M, pp. 257–270, 283–284; Pettit, pp. 307–320, 353–357; Snell, pp. 235–248.
[2] T.A. 1925, s. 30 (2), infra; *Stott v Milne* (1884) 25 ChD 710; *Re Chapman* (1895) 72 LT 66 (expenses unreasonable).
[3] H & M, pp. 512–514; K & S, pp. 317–325; P & M, pp. 257–262, 283–284; Pettit, pp. 307–310, 353–357; Snell, pp. 243–248.
[4] *Stott v Milne* (1884) 25 ChD 710; *Re Chapman* (1895) 72 LT 66.

On the liquidation of the Bank, the liquidator made calls upon the plaintiff for over £400. The Privy Council held that the defendant was personally liable to reimburse him. Lord LINDLEY said (at p. 124): "... . where the only cestui que trust is a person sui juris, the right of the trustee to indemnity by him against liabilities incurred by the trustee by his retention of the trust property has never been limited to the trust property; it extends further, and imposes upon the cestui que trust a personal obligation enforceable in equity to indemnify his trustee. This is no new principle, but is as old as trusts themselves."

B. Remuneration[6]

A professional trustee will always insist upon provision being made for the payment of proper fees for his work.

Encyclopaedia of Forms and Precedents (4th Edn) vol. 20, p. 635

"Power to professional trustee to charge

Any trustee for the time being hereof (other than any wife of the settlor) being a solicitor or other person engaged in any profession or business shall be entitled to charge and be paid all usual professional or other charges for business done by him or his firm in relation to the trusts hereof and also his reasonable charges in addition to the trusts hereof and also his reasonable charges in addition to disbursements for all other work and business done and all time spent by him or his firm in connection with matters arising in the premises including matters which might or should have been attended to in person by a trustee not being a solicitor or other person so engaged but which such a trustee might reasonably require to be done by a solicitor or other person so engaged."

C. Authorisation by the Court in Special Cases

The court may in appropriate cases authorise remuneration in favour of trustees or other persons acting in a fiduciary capacity.

In *Brown v Litton* ((1711) 1 PWms 140) the plaintiff's testator was captain of a ship, and had $800 with him on a voyage. He died. The defendant, the mate, became captain, took the dollars and traded successfully with them. On his return to England, the question was whether the defendant's obligation was to return the money with interest, or whether he was liable to account for the profits. Lord Keeper HARCOURT held that he must account for the profits; but that he should be given a proper reward for his work.

In *Re Jarvis* ([1958] 1 WLR 815, [1958] 2 All ER 336) two sisters, Rosetta and Sheila, became entitled to half shares in their deceased father's shop.

[6] See also Public Trustee Act 1906, ss. 4, 9, pp. 456, 458, ante; Public Trustee (Fees) Act 1957; Administration of Justice Act 1925, s. 2; Judicial Trustee Act 1896, s. 1, p. 453, ante (under which a corporation appointed to act as custodian trustee, the Public Trustee and a judicial trustee are authorised to charge fees); (1952) 16 Conv (NS) 13 (G. Boughen Graham).

The shop was largely destroyed by enemy bombing in 1940. Sheila had it repaired and built up the business. UPJOHN J held that Sheila was accountable as constructive trustee as to half for Rosetta "subject to all just allowances for her time, energy and skill, for the assets she has contributed and the debts of the testator which she has paid."

In *Re Masters* ([1953] 1 WLR 81, [1953] 1 All ER 19) on the death of Leslie Ninian Masters, a grant of administration was made to Coutts and Co., a trust corporation, and to the widow. No provision was made for remuneration. The estate was worth £95,000 gross. DANCKWERTS J held that Trustee Act 1925, s. 42 (which permits the court to authorise remuneration for a corporation appointed by it as trustee) applied to this case. The court also had inherent jurisdiction to authorise remuneration.

In *Boardman v Phipps* ([1967] 2 AC 46, [1966] 3 All ER 721, p. 600, post) the defendant, Boardman, acted as solicitor to the Phipps family trust. Most of the funds were invested in a family firm, which was badly managed and unprofitable. Acting in good faith throughout, Boardman purchased shares which enabled him to take control of the company. He made it highly profitable, and brought about a great increase in the value of the shares owned by the Phipps trust and those which he owned himself. The House of Lords held that he was accountable to the Phipps trust for the profits he had made, on the ground that the opportunity to make them arose from his fiduciary position; but that he was entitled to payment on a liberal scale in respect of his work and skill[7].

III. Purchase of Trust Property[8]

HOLDER v HOLDER

[1968] Ch 353, [1968] 1 All ER 665 (CA, HARMAN, DANCKWERTS and SACHS LJJ)

The testator was the owner of two farms in Gloucestershire. His third son Victor, the defendant, was tenant with one Denley of part of one farm; and, as his father became advanced in years, Victor undertook responsibility for the farming of the remainder of the land, making annual payments to his father.

The testator died in 1959, having appointed his widow, a daughter and Victor his executors, and provided by his will that the estate should be divided equally between the widow and all the children. The executors took the preliminary steps towards the administration of the estate, which Victor later conceded were sufficient to prevent him from renouncing, as he attempted to do.

[7] See also *Re Barbour's Settlement* [1974] 1 WLR 1198, [1974] 1 All ER 1188; cf. *Re Codd's Will Trusts* [1975] 1 WLR 1139, [1975] 2 All ER 1051.

[8] H & M, pp. 514–515; K & S, pp. 308–317; P & M, pp. 267–270; Pettit, pp. 316–320; Snell, pp. 239–241; (1936) 49 HLR 521 (A. W. Scott); (1955) 8 CLP 91 (O. R. Marshall); Goff & Jones, *The Law of Restitution* (1966) chap. 35; (1968) 84 LQR 472 (G. H. Jones).

The farms were valued on the basis that Victor was tenant with Denley of part of one farm as previously stated, and also tenant of the remainder of the land. The eldest son Frank, the plaintiff, disputed this.

Victor purported to renounce the executorship, and subsequently purchased the farms at a fair price at an auction. The plaintiff received a cheque in respect of his share of the proceeds of sale. He later changed his solicitors and the new solicitor took, for the first time, the point that Victor, having begun to administer the estate, could not renounce, and could not therefore be a purchaser.

Held (reversing CROSS J). (i) In the special circumstances of the case, Victor, although an executor, was not precluded from purchasing; (ii) Frank had, by receiving his share of the purchase money, precluded himself from relief.

HARMAN LJ: The cross-appeal raises far more difficult questions and they are broadly three. First, whether the actions of Victor before probate made his renunciation ineffective. Secondly, whether on that footing he was disentitled from bidding at the sale. Thirdly, whether the plaintiff is disentitled from taking this point because of his acquiescence.

It was admitted at the bar in the court below that the acts of Victor were enough to constitute intermeddling with the estate and that his renunciation was ineffective. On this footing he remained a personal representative, even after probate had been granted to his co-executors, and could have been obliged by a creditor or a beneficiary to re-assume the duties of an executor. The judge decided in favour of the plaintiff on this point because Victor at the time of the sale was himself still in a fiduciary position and like any other trustee could not purchase the trust property. I feel the force of this argument, but doubt its validity in the very special circumstances of this case. The reason for the rule is that a man may not be both vendor and purchaser; but Victor was never in that position here. He took no part in instructing the valuer who fixed the reserves or in the preparations for the auction. Everyone in the family knew that he was not a seller but a buyer. In this case Victor never assumed the duties of an executor. It is true that he concurred in signing a few cheques for trivial sums and endorsing a few insurance policies, but he never, so far as appears, interfered in any way with the administration of the estate. It is true he managed the farms, but he did that as tenant and not as executor. He acquired no special knowledge as executor. What he knew he knew as tenant of the farms.

Another reason lying behind the rule is that there must never be a conflict of duty and interest, but in fact there was none here in the case of Victor, who made no secret throughout that he intended to buy. There is of course ample authority that a trustee cannot purchase. The leading cases are decisions of Lord Eldon—*Ex parte Lacey* ((1802) 6 Ves 625) and *Ex parte James* ((1803) 8 Ves 337 at 344). In the former case the Lord Chancellor expressed himself thus (at p. 626):

> "The rule I take to be this; not, that a trustee cannot buy from his cestuy que trust, but, that he shall not buy from himself. If a trustee will so deal with his cestuy que trust, that the amount of the transaction

shakes off the obligation, that attaches upon him as trustee, then he may buy. If that case[9] is rightly understood, it cannot lead to much mistake. The true interpretation of what is there reported does not break in upon the law as to trustees. The rule is this. A trustee, who is entrusted to sell and manage for others, undertakes in the same moment, in which he becomes a trustee, not to manage for the benefit and advantage of himself."

In *Ex parte James* the same Lord Chancellor said (at p. 344):

"This doctrine as to purchases by trustees, assignees, and persons having a confidential character, stands much more upon general principle than upon the circumstances of any individual case. It rests upon this; that the purchase is not permitted in any case, however honest the circumstances; the general interests of justice requiring it to be destroyed in every instance."

These are no doubt strong words, but it is to be observed that Lord Eldon was dealing with cases where the purchaser was at the time of sale acting for the vendors. In this case Victor was not so acting: his interference with the administration of the estate was of a minimal character and the last cheque he signed was in August before he executed the deed of renunciation. He took no part in the instructions for probate, nor in the valuations or fixing of the reserves. Everyone concerned knew of the renunciation and of the reason for it, namely, that he wished to be a purchaser. Equally, everyone, including the three firms of solicitors engaged, assumed that the renunciation was effective and entitled Victor to bid. I feel great doubt whether the admission made at the bar was correct, as did the judge, but assuming it was right, the acts were only technically acts of intermeddling and I find no case where the circumstances are parallel. Of course, I feel the force of the judge's reasoning that if Victor remained an executor he is within the rule, but in a case where the reasons behind the rule do not exist I do not feel bound to apply it. My reasons are that the beneficiaries never looked to Victor to protect their interests. They all knew he was in the market as purchaser; that the price paid was a good one and probably higher than anyone not a sitting tenant would give. Further, the first two defendants alone acted as executors and sellers: they alone could convey: they were not influenced by Victor in connection with the sales.

I hold, therefore, that the rule does not apply in order to disentitle Victor to bid at the auction, as he did. If I be wrong on this point and the rule applies so as to disentitle Victor to purchase, there arises a further defence, namely, that of acquiescence . . .

On the whole I am of opinion that in the circumstances of this case it would not be right to allow the plaintiff to assert his right (assuming he has one) because with full knowledge of the facts he affirmed the sale. He has had £2,000 as a result. He has caused [Victor] to embark on liabilities which he cannot recoup. There can in fact be no restitutio in integrum, which is a necessary element in rescission . . .

DANCKWERTS LJ: . . . The principle that a trustee cannot purchase part

[9] *Whichcote v Lawrence* (1798) 3 Ves Junr 740 at 749.

of the trust estate goes back to the statement of it by Lord Eldon in 1802 in *Ex parte Lacey* (1802) 6 Ves 625 . . .

It is said that it makes no difference, even though the sale may be fair and honest and may be made at a public auction: see Snell's Equity, [26th Edn, 1966] p. 260. But the court may sanction such a purchase, and if the court can do that (see Snell's Equity, p. 219), there can be no more than a practice that the court should not allow a trustee to bid. In my view it is a matter for the discretion of the judge.

IV. Incidental Profits[10]

A. Directors' Fees

RE MACADAM[11]
[1946] Ch 73, [1945] 2 All ER 664 (ChD, COHEN J)

The articles of a company provided that the trustees of the testator's will may "so long as they shall hold shares in the company as such trustees, appoint two persons . . . to be directors of the company." The trustees appointed themselves.

The question was whether the trustees could retain, as their own, the directors' fees.

Held. They were accountable.

COHEN J: The question has been raised whether the plaintiffs are entitled to retain the directors' fees received by them from the company or whether they are accountable to the trust estate for the sums received by them as remuneration in respect of the office of director. I desire to say at once that nobody suggested any impropriety on their part in regard to this remuneration. The question was asked purely as one of law whether, having regard to all the provisions of the material documents, on general principles of law, they are accountable or not. My attention was called to a number of cases bearing on this matter, but I think that Mr. Gray and Mr. Timins were right in saying that they are all applications of the same general principle, though the consequence of applying that principle has resulted in some cases in the person concerned being allowed to retain the remuneration, and in others in his being held accountable. The principle, I think, is well stated in a passage from the speech of Lord Herschell in *Bray v Ford* ([1896] AC 44 at 51) which was cited by Russell J in *Williams v Barton* ([1927] 2 Ch 9 at 11). The citation is as follows: "It is an inflexible rule of a court of equity that a person in a fiduciary position . . . is not, unless otherwise expressly provided, entitled to make a profit; he is not allowed to put himself in a position where his interest and duty conflict."

10 H & M, pp. 515–527; K & S, pp. 306–308; P & M, pp. 152–154, 262–267; Pettit, pp. 310–314; Snell, pp. 238–239, 241–243; (1968) 84 LQR 472 (G. H. Jones). See generally [1967] CLJ 83 (L. S. Sealy).

11 *Re Gee* [1948] Ch 284, [1948] 1 All ER 498 (trustees appointed independently of the voters of the trust shares); *Re Francis* (1905) 74 LJ Ch 198; *Re Lewis* (1910) 103 LT 495 (independent appointment); *Re Llewellin's Will Trusts* [1949] Ch 225, [1949] 1 All ER 487 (appointment authorised by trust instrument).

The first of the cases to which my attention was called was *Re Francis* (1905) 92 LT 77. [His Lordship referred also to *Re Dover Coalfield Extension Ltd* [1907] 2 Ch 76, [1908] 1 Ch 65, and to *Re Lewis* (1910) 103 LT 495, of which case he said:] It seems to me that the distinction between that case and this is that there he secured the appointment as salesman not by virtue of the exercise of any discretion in him as trustee, but by virtue of a bargain with his co-partners; whereas in the present case the plaintiffs got their appointment, by the exercise of a power which is vested in them—not, it is true, by the testator's will, but by the articles of the company approved by the court, but none the less vested in them as trustees.

The last, and perhaps the nearest, case to the present—although it is a much stronger case than the one I have to decide—is *Williams v Barton* ([1927] 2 Ch 9) decided by Russell J from which I have already cited a short passage. In that case the headnote says: "The defendant, one of two trustees of a will, was employed as a clerk by a firm of stockbrokers on the terms that his salary should consist of half the commission earned by the firm on business introduced by him. At the recommendation of the defendant, the firm was employed to value his testator's securities. The firm's charges were paid out of the testator's estate and, in accordance with their contract with the defendant, they paid to him half the fees so earned. The defendant took no part in making the valuations or in fixing the fees to be charged. In an action by his co-trustee claiming that the defendant was bound to treat the fees so paid to him as part of the testator's estate:—*Held,* that it was the defendant's duty as a trustee to give the estate the benefit of his unfettered advice in choosing stockbrokers to act for the estate, but, as the recipient of half the fees earned by the firm on business introduced by him, it was to his interest to choose his firm to act. The services rendered to the firm by the defendant remained unchanged but his remuneration for them was increased, and increased by virtue of his trusteeship. That increase was a profit which the defendant would not have made but for his position as trustee and he was therefore bound to treat it as part of the estate of his testator." After citing the passage which I have read from the speech of Lord Herschell in *Bray v Ford* ([1896] AC 44), Russell J continued—and I think his remarks apply to this case too—"The point is not an easy one and there is little, if any, authority to assist in its determination . . . it seems to me evident that the case falls within the mischief which is sought to be prevented by the rule. The case is clearly one where his duty as trustee and his interest in an increased remuneration are in direct conflict. As a trustee it is his duty to give the estate the benefit of his unfettered advice in choosing the stockbrokers to act for the estate; as the recipient of half the fees to be earned by George Burnand & Co. on work introduced by him his obvious interest is to choose or recommend them for the job." Pausing there, it seems to me that, with a certain substitution, that last sentence applies to this case. As trustees it is the duty of the plaintiffs to give the estate the benefit of their unfettered advice in choosing the persons to act as directors of the company, as, if appointed, they will receive such remuneration as may be voted to them; as recipients of the remuneration of directors their obvious interest is to choose themselves for the job. Then the learned judge goes on: "In the event that has happened they have been chosen, and chosen because the defendant was a trustee, with the result that half of what the estate pays must necessarily pass through them to the defendant as part of his remuneration for other services rendered, but as an addition to the remuneration which he would otherwise have received for those self-same services. The services rendered remain unchanged but the remuneration for them has been increased. He has increased his remuneration by virtue of his trusteeship. In my opinion this increase of remuneration is a profit made by the defendant out of and by reason of his trusteeship, which he would not have made but for his position as trustee." Then he goes on to deal with *Re Dover Coalfield Extension Ltd* ([1907] 2 Ch 76), and says: "But that case seems to me very different. At the request of the Dover company Mr. Cousins had entered into a contract with the Kent company to serve them as a director, the Kent company paying him remuneration for his services. The necessary qualification shares were provided by the Dover company and in respect of those shares he became a trustee for the Dover company. He had not, however, used his position as a trustee for the purpose of acquiring his directorship. He had, in fact, been appointed a director before he became a trustee of the shares. The profit which he gained was not procured by him by the use of his position as trustee but was a profit earned by reason of work which he did for the Kent company and which would not have been earned by him had he not been willing to do the work for which it was the remuneration. It was not (as in the present case) a profit acquired solely by reason of his use of his position as trustee and a profit in respect of which no extra services were rendered."

That case is, as Mr. Christie rightly says, much stronger than the present case, because, first, the profit in a sense came directly out of the estate, and, secondly, because it was a profit earned in a sense without any work done by him. I think that the root of the matter really is: Did he acquire the position in respect of which he drew the remuneration by virtue of his position as trustee? In the present case there can be no doubt that the only way in which the plaintiffs became directors was by exercise of the powers vested in the trustees of the will under art. 68 of the articles of association of the company. The principle is one which has always been regarded as of the greatest importance in these courts, and I do not think I ought to do anything to weaken it. As I have said, although the remuneration was remuneration for services as director of the company, the opportunity to receive that remuneration was gained as a result of the exercise of a discretion vested in the trustees, and they had put themselves in a position where their interest and duty conflicted. In those circumstances, I do not think this court can allow them to make a profit out of doing so, and I do not think the liability to account for a profit can be confined to cases where the profit is derived directly from the trust estate. I leave over the matter of the exact wording of the order, because I do not want to do anything to prejudice the question whether, in the circumstances, I ought not to allow the plaintiffs to retain the whole or a part of the remuneration. If I can be satisfied (and that is the point I have not considered) that they were the best persons to be directors, I do not think it would be right for me to expect them to do the extra work for nothing.

B. Profits by Fiduciaries

BOARDMAN v PHIPPS[12]

[1967] 2 AC 46, [1966] 3 All ER 721 (HL, Viscount DILHORNE, Lords COHEN, HODSON, GUEST and UPJOHN)

Charles William Phipps left his residuary estate, which included 8,000 shares (approximately 27 per cent.) in Lester and Harris Ltd., upon trust for his widow for life and after her death for his four children. The trustees in 1955 were his widow (the life tenant), Mrs. Noble (his daughter) and William Fox (a professional trustee and an accountant).

John Phipps, the plaintiff and respondent, was a son of the testator, and one of the beneficiaries. The defendants, now the appellants, were his brother Tom, also a beneficiary, and Thomas Gray Boardman, who acted as solicitor to the trust, and to the Phipps family.

In 1956, the appellants were dissatisfied with the way in which the business of Lester and Harris Ltd. was conducted. They made enquiries and took various steps, recorded in more detail below, which culminated in the purchase by the appellants of all the shares in the company other than those owned by the trust. They then effected sales of the company's premises in Australia and in Coventry, and distributed the proceeds of sale as capital profits; and reorganised the part of the business which remained. The transactions were highly profitable both for the trust and for the appellants.

The steps by which this was effected were grouped by the court into three phases. In Phase I, lasting from December 1955 to April 1957 the appellants, acting on behalf of the trustees, obtained valuable information about the company. They made an unsuccessful bid in their own names for the remainder of the shares of the company at £3 per share. Fox and Mrs. Noble were informed, and approved. Mrs. Phipps, the testator's widow, aged and in failing health, was not consulted.

In Phase 2, April 1957 to August 1958, Boardman, again acting on behalf of the trustees, was attempting to reach a solution by effecting a sharing of the assets between the Harris family, and the directors and the Phipps family. The plan failed, but, again during this phase, Boardman obtained further information about the company and the potential value of its shares.

In Phase 3, from 1958 to 1961, an agreement was reached in March 1959 under which Boardman and Tom Phipps should buy the directors' holdings for £4 10s. per share and would make a bid for the remainder of the shares on the same terms. The life tenant had died in 1958. Boardman wrote to the remaindermen, including the respondent, asking their approval to his taking a personal interest in the negotiation. Throughout the negotiations, Boardman acted with unquestioned bona fides, and thought that he had the approval of the trustees while the trust lasted, and of the remaindermen

[12] (1967) 31 Conv (NS) 63 (F. R. Crane); (1968) 84 LQR 472 (G. H. Jones); p. 609, post; *New Zealand Netherlands Society Oranje Inc. v Kuys* [1973] 1 WLR 1126, [1973] 2 All ER 1222; (1973) 37 Conv (NS) 362 (F. R. Crane); (1975) CLP 39 (J. D. Stephens); *English v Dedham Vale Properties Ltd* [1978]1 WLR 93, [1978] 1 All ER 382 (duty to account imposed upon "self-appointed agent", where purchaser, without disclosure to vendor, applied for planning permission in vendor's name prior to contract and obtained it prior to completion).

after the life tenant's death. This was not so; he never obtained the approval of old Mrs. Phipps; and WILBERFORCE J, found that the respondents had not been given complete information.

The agreements were carried out, and the profits distributed. The respondent then called upon the appellants to account for their profits on the ground that they held the shares as constructive trustees for the Phipps family.

Held (Viscount DILHORNE and Lord UPJOHN dissenting; and affirming WILBERFORCE J [1964] 1 WLR 993, [1964] 2 All ER 187, and the Court of Appeal [1965] Ch 992, [1965] 1 All ER 849): (i) The appellants, being persons who were enabled to make a profit by reason of a fiduciary relation, were liable to account for it; but (ii) having acted bona fide throughout, were entitled to payment on a liberal scale for their work and skill.

LORD COHEN: In the case before your Lordships it seems to me clear that the appellants throughout were obtaining information from the company for the purpose stated by Wilberforce J but it does not necessarily follow that the appellants were thereby debarred from acquiring shares in the company for themselves. They were bound to give the information to the trustees but they could not exclude it from their own minds. As Wilberforce J said ([1964] 1 WLR 993 at 1011), the mere use of any knowledge or opportunity which comes to the trustee or agent in the course of his trusteeship or agency does not necessarily make him liable to account. In the present case had the company been a public company and had the appellants bought the shares on the market, they would not, I think, have been accountable. But the company is a private company and not only the information but the opportunity to purchase these shares came to them through the introduction which Mr. Fox gave them to the board of the company and in the second phase when the discussions related to the proposed split-up of the company's undertaking it was solely on behalf of the trustees that Mr. Boardman was purporting to negotiate with the board of the company. The question is this: when in the third phase the negotiations turned to the purchase of the shares at £4 10s. a share, were the appellants debarred by their fiduciary position from purchasing on their own behalf the 21,986 shares in the company without the informed consent of the trustees and the beneficiaries?

Wilberforce J and, in the Court of Appeal, both Lord Denning MR and Pearson LJ based their decision in favour of the respondent on the decision of your Lordships' House in *Regal (Hastings) Ltd v Gulliver* ([1967] 2 AC 46 at 134). I turn, therefore, to consider that case. Mr. Walton relied upon a number of passages in the judgments of the learned Lords who heard the appeal: in particular on (1) a passage in the speech of Lord Russell of Killowen where he says (at pp. 134, 144G–145A):

> "The rule of equity which insists on those, who by use of a fiduciary position make a profit, being liable to account for that profit, in no way depends on fraud, or absence of bona fides; or upon such questions or considerations as whether the profit would or should otherwise have gone to the plaintiff, or whether the profiteer was under a duty to obtain the source of the profit for the plaintiff, or whether he took a risk or acted as he did for the benefit of the plaintiff, or whether the plaintiff has in fact been damaged or benefited by his action. The

liability arises from the mere fact of a profit having, in the stated circumstances, been made."

(2) a passage in the speech of Lord Wright, where he says (at pp. 134, 154B-C):

> "That question can be briefly stated to be whether an agent, a director, a trustee or other person in an analogous fiduciary position, when a demand is made upon him by the person to whom he stands in the fiduciary relationship to account for profits acquired by him by reason of his fiduciary position, and by reason of the opportunity and the knowledge, or either, resulting from it, is entitled to defeat the claim upon any ground save that he made profits with the knowledge and assent of the other person. The most usual and typical case of this nature is that of principal and agent. The rule in such cases is compendiously expressed to be that an agent must account for net profits secretly (that is, without the knowledge of his principal) acquired by him in the course of his agency. The authorities show how manifold and various are the applications of the rule. It does not depend on fraud or corruption."

These paragraphs undoubtedly help the respondent but they must be considered in relation to the facts of that case. In that case the profit arose through the application by four of the directors of Regal for shares in a subsidiary company which it had been the original intention of the board should be subscribed for by Regal. Regal had not the requisite money available but there was no question of it being ultra vires Regal to subscribe for the shares. In the circumstances Lord Russell of Killowen said ([1967] 2 AC 134 at 146G–147A):

> "I have no hesitation in coming to the conclusion, upon the facts of this case, that these shares, when acquired by the directors, were acquired by reason, and only by reason of the fact that they were directors of Regal, and in the course of their execution of that office."

He goes on to consider whether the four directors were in a fiduciary relationship to Regal and concludes that they were. Accordingly, they were held accountable. Mr. Bagnall argued that the present case is distinguishable. He puts his argument thus. The question you ask is whether the information could have been used by the principal for the purpose for which it was used by his agents? If the answer to that question is no, the information was not used in the course of their duty as agents. In the present case the information could never have been used by the trustees for the purpose of purchasing shares in the company; therefore purchase of shares was outside the scope of the appellant's agency and they are not accountable.

This is an attractive argument, but it does not seem to me to give due weight to the fact that the appellants obtained both the information which satisfied them that the purchase of the shares would be a good investment and the opportunity of acquiring them as a result of acting for certain purposes on behalf of the trustees. Information is, of course, not property in the strict sense of that word and, as I have already stated, it does not necessarily follow that because an agent acquired information and opportunity while acting in a fiduciary capacity he is accountable to his principals for any profit that comes his way as the result of the use he makes of that information and opportunity. His liability to account must depend on the facts of the case. In the present case much of the information came the appellants' way when Mr. Boardman was acting on behalf of the trustees on the instructions of Mr. Fox and the opportunity of bidding for the shares came because he purported for all purposes except for making the bid to be acting on behalf of the owners of the 8,000 shares in the company. In these circumstances it seems to me that the principle of the *Regal* case ([1967] 2 AC 134) applies and that the courts below came to the right conclusion.

That is enough to dispose of the case but I would add that an agent is, in my opinion, liable to account for profits he makes out of trust property if there is a possibility of conflict between his interest and his duty to his principal. Mr. Boardman and Tom Phipps were not general agents of the trustees but they were their agents for certain limited purposes. The information they had obtained and the opportunity to purchase the 21,986 shares afforded them by their relations with the directors of the company—an opportunity they got as the result of their introduction to the directors by Mr. Fox—were not property in the strict sense but that information and that opportunity they owed to their representing themselves as agents for the holders of the 8,000 shares held by the trustees. In these circumstances they could not, I think, use that information and that opportunity to purchase the shares for themselves if there was any possibility that the trustees might wish to acquire them for the trust. Mr. Boardman was the solicitor whom the trustees were in the habit of consulting if they wanted legal advice. Granted that he would not be bound to advise on any point unless he is consulted, he would still be the person they would consult if they wanted advice. He would clearly have advised them that they had no power to invest in shares of the company without the sanction of the court. In the first phase he would also have had to advise on the evidence then available that the court would be unlikely to give such sanction: but the appellants learnt much more during the second phase. It may well be that even in the third phase the answer of the court would have been the same but, in my opinion, Mr. Boardman would not have been able to give unprejudiced advice if he had been consulted by the trustees and was at the same time negotiating for the purchase of the shares on behalf of himself and Tom Phipps. In other words, there was, in my opinion, at the crucial date (March, 1959), a possibility of a conflict between his interest and his duty.

In making these observations I have referred to the fact that Mr. Boardman was the solicitor to the trust. Tom Phipps was only a beneficiary and was not as such debarred from bidding for the shares, but no attempt was made in the courts below to differentiate between them. Had such an attempt been made it would very likely have failed as Tom Phipps left the negotiations largely to Mr. Boardman and it might well be held that if Mr. Boardman was disqualified from bidding Tom Phipps could not be in a better position. Be that as it may, Mr. Bagnall rightly did not seek at this stage to distinguish between the two. He did, it is true, say that Tom Phipps as a beneficiary would be entitled to any information the trustees obtained. This may be so, but nonetheless I find myself unable to distinguish between the two appellants. They were, I think, in March, 1959, in a fiduciary position vis-à-vis the trust. That fiduciary position was of such a nature that (as the trust fund was distributable) the appellants could not purchase the shares on their own behalf without the informed consent of the beneficiaries: it is now admitted that they did not obtain that consent. They are therefore, in my opinion, accountable to the respondent for his share of the net profits they derived from the transaction.

I desire to repeat that the integrity of the appellants is not in doubt. They acted with complete honesty throughout and the respondent is a fortunate man in that the rigour of equity enables him to participate in the profits which have accrued as the result of the action taken by the appellants in March, 1959, in purchasing the shares at their own risk. As the last paragraph of his judgment clearly shows, the trial judge evidently shared this view. He directed an inquiry as to what sum is proper to be allowed to the appellants or either of them in respect of his work and skill in obtaining the said shares and the profits in respect thereof. The trial judge concluded by expressing the opinion that payment should be on a liberal scale. With that observation I respectfully agree.

In the result I agree in substance with the judgments of Wilberforce J and of Lord Denning MR and Pearson LJ in the Court of Appeal, and I would dismiss the appeal.

Lord Upjohn (dissenting): It is of cardinal importance, and, in my view fundamental to the decision of this case, to appreciate that at this stage there was no question whatever of the trustees contemplating the possibility of a purchase of further shares in the company. Mr. Fox (whose evidence was accepted by the judge) made it abundantly plain that he would not consider any such proposition. The reasons for this attitude are worth setting out in full: (*a*) The acquisition of further shares in the company would have been a breach of trust, for they were not shares authorised by the investment clause in the will; (*b*) although not developed in evidence it must have been obvious to those concerned that no court would sanction the purchase of further shares in a small company which the trustees considered to be badly managed. It would have been throwing good money after bad. It would also have been necessary to bring in proposals for installing a new management. Mr. Fox was a busy practising chartered accountant who obviously would not have considered it; no one from start to finish ever suggested that Tom, who was running the family concern of Phipps & Son Ltd., would be willing to undertake this arduous task on behalf of the trustees; (*c*) the trustees had no money available for the purchase of further shares. . . .

In these circumstances the respondent rather surprisingly seeks to hold the appellants accountable to him for his 5/18ths share of the 21,986 shares so purchased, on the footing that the appellants are constructive trustees of these shares for and on behalf of the trust. So I turn to the relevant law upon which this claim is based, but start by stating what is not in dispute, that the conduct of the appellants and each of them has never been anything except utterly honest and above board in every way. If they or either of them are accountable it is because of the operation of some harsh doctrine of equity upon consciences completely innocent in every way.

Rules of equity have to be applied to such a great diversity of circumstances that they can be stated only in the most general terms and applied with particular attention to the exact circumstances of each case. The relevant rule for the decision of this case is the fundamental rule of equity that a person in a fiduciary capacity must not make a profit out of his trust which is part of the wider rule that a trustee must not place himself in a position where his duty and his interest may conflict. I believe the rule is best stated in *Bray v Ford* ([1896] AC 44 at 51) by Lord Herschell, who plainly recognised its limitations:

> "It is an inflexible rule of a Court of Equity that a person in a fiduciary position, such as the respondent's, is not, unless otherwise expressly provided, entitled to make a profit; he is not allowed to put himself in a position where his interest and duty conflict. It does not appear to me that this rule is, as has been said, founded upon principles of morality. I regard it rather as based on the consideration that, human nature being what it is, there is danger, in such circumstances, of the person holding a fiduciary position being swayed by interest rather than by duty, and thus prejudicing those whom he was bound to protect. It has, therefore, been deemed expedient to lay down this positive rule. But I am satisfied that it might be departed from in many cases, without any breach of morality, without any wrong being inflicted, and without any consciousness of wrong-doing. Indeed, it is obvious that it might sometimes be to the advantage of the beneficiaries that their trustee should act for them professionally rather than a stranger, even though the trustee were paid for his services."

[His Lordship referred to *Aberdeen Railway v Blaikie* (1854) 1 Macq 461, *Regal (Hastings) Ltd v Gulliver* [1967] 2 AC 134, [1942] 1 All ER 378; *Keech v Sandford* (1726) Sel Cas Ch 61, and continued:] Secondly, as to the position of Mr. Boardman himself. There is no doubt that from time to time he acted as solicitor to the trust and to the family and he was therefore throughout in a fiduciary capacity at least to the trustees. Whether he was ever in a fiduciary capacity to the respondent was not debated before your Lordships and I do not think it matters. I think, again, that some of the trouble that has arisen in this case, it being assumed rightly that throughout he was in such a capacity, is that it has been assumed that it has necessarily followed that any profit made by him renders him accountable to the trustees. This is not so. A solicitor who acts for a client from time to time is no doubt rightly described throughout as being in a fiduciary capacity to him but that means fundamentally no more than this, that if he has dealings with his client, e.g., accepts a present from him or buys property from him, there is a presumption of undue influence and the onus is on the solicitor to justify the present or purchase (see, for example, *McMaster v Byrne* [1952] 1 All ER 1362 at 1368). That principle has no relevance to the present case. There is no such thing as an office of being solicitor to a trust (*Saffron Walden Second Benefit Building Society v Rayner* (1880) 14 ChD 406 at 409, *per* James LJ). Though these remarks of James LJ were admittedly obiter they represent the law. It is perfectly clear that a solicitor can if he so desires act against his clients in any matter in which he has not been retained by them provided, of course, that in acting for them generally he has not learnt information or placed himself in a position which would make it improper for him to act against them. This is an obvious application of the rule that he must not place himself in a position where his duty and his interest conflict. So in general a solicitor can deal in shares in a company in which the client is a shareholder, subject always to the general rule that the solicitor must never place himself in a position where his interest and his duty conflict; and in this connection it may be pointed out that the interest and duty may refer (and frequently do) to a conflict of interest and duty on behalf of different clients and have nothing to do with any conflict between the personal interest and duty of the solicitor, beyond his interest in earning his fees.

[His Lordship then referred to Wilberforce J and the Court of Appeal, and continued:] Before applying these principles to the facts, however, I shall refer to the judgment of Russell LJ, which proceeded on a rather different basis. He said ([1965] Ch 992 at 1031):

> "The substantial trust shareholding was an asset of which one aspect was its potential use as a means of acquiring knowledge of the company's affairs, or of negotiating allocations of the company's assets, or of inducing other shareholders to part with their shares. That aspect was part of the trust assets".

My Lords, I regard that proposition as untenable.

In general, information is not property at all. It is normally open to all who have eyes to read and ears to hear. The true test is to determine in what circumstances the information has been acquired. If it has been acquired in such circumstances that it would be a breach of confidence to disclose it to another then courts of equity will restrain the recipient from communicating it to another. In such cases such confidential information is often and for many years has been described as the property of the donor, the books of authority are full of such references; knowledge of secret processes, "know-how", confidential information as to the prospects of a company or of someone's intention or the expected results of some horse race based on stable or other confidential information. But in the end the real truth is that it is not property in any normal sense but equity will restrain its transmission to another if in breach of some confidential relationship.

With all respect to the views of Russell LJ, I protest at the idea that information acquired by trustees in the course of their duties as such is necessarily part of the assets of the trust which cannot be used by the trustees except for benefit of the trust. Russell LJ referred ([1965] Ch 992 at 1031) to the fact that two out of three of the trustees could have no authority to turn over this aspect of trust property to the appellants except for the benefit of the trust; this I do not understand, for if such information is trust property not all the trustees acting together could do it for they cannot give away trust property.

We heard much argument upon the impact of the fact that the testator's widow was at all material times incapable of acting in the trust owing to disability. Of course trustees must act all of them and unanimously in matters affecting trust affairs, but in this case they never performed any relevant act on behalf of the trust at all; I quoted Mr Fox's answer earlier for this reason. At no time after going to the meeting in December, 1956, did Mr Boardman or Tom rely on any express or implied authority or consent of the trustees in relation to trust property. They understood rightly that there was no question of the trustees acquiring any further trust property by purchasing further shares in the company, and it was only in the purchase of other shares that they were interested.

There is, in my view, and I know of no authority to the contrary, no general rule that information learnt by a trustee during the course of his duties is property of the trust and cannot be used by him. If that were to be the rule it would put the Public Trustee and other corporate trustees out of business and make it difficult for private trustees to be trustees of more than one trust. This would be the greatest possible pity for corporate trustees and others may have much information which they may initially acquire in connection with some particular trust but without prejudice to that trust can make it readily available to other trusts to the great advantage of those other trusts.

The real rule is, in my view, that knowledge learnt by a trustee in the course of his duties as such is not in the least property of the trust and in general may be used by him for his own benefit or for the benefit of other trusts unless it is confidential information which is given to him (1) in circumstances which, regardless of his position as a trustee, would make it a breach of confidence for him to communicate to anyone for it has been given to him expressly or impliedly as confidential, or (2) in a fiduciary capacity, and its use would place him in a position where his duty and his interest might possibly conflict. Let me give one or two simple examples. A, as trustee of two settlements X and Y holding shares in the same small company, learns facts as trustee of X about the company which are encouraging. In the absence of special circumstances (such, for example, that X wants to buy more shares) I can see nothing whatever which would make it improper for him to tell his co-trustees of Y who feel inclined to sell that he has information that this would be a bad thing to do. Another example: A as trustee of X learns facts that make him and his co-trustees want to sell. Clearly he could not communicate this knowledge to his co-trustees of Y until at all events the holdings of X have been sold for there would be a plain conflict, reflected in the prices that might or might possibly be obtained. . . .

As a result of the information they acquired, admittedly by reason of the trust holding, they found it worth while to offer a good deal more for the shares than in [the period January—April 1957]. I cannot see that in offering to purchase non-trust shares at a higher price they were in breach of any fiduciary relationship in using the information they had acquired for this purpose . . .

I have dealt with the problems that arise in this case at considerable length but it could, in my opinion, be dealt with quite shortly.

In *Barnes v Addy* ((1874) 9 Ch App 244 at 251) Lord Selborne LC said:

"It is equally important to maintain the doctrine of trusts which is established in this court, and not to strain it by unreasonable construction beyond its due and proper limits. There would be no better mode of undermining the sound doctrines of equity than to make unreasonable and inequitable applications of them."

That, in my judgment, is applicable to this case.

The trustees were not willing to buy more shares in the company. The active trustees were very willing that the appellants should do so themselves for the benefit of their large minority holding. The trustees, so to speak, lent their name to the appellants in the course of prolonged and difficult negotiations and, of course, the appellants thereby learnt much which would have otherwise been denied to them. The negotiations were in the end brilliantly successful.

And how successful Tom was in his reorganisation of the company is apparent to all. They ought to be very grateful.

In the long run the appellants have bought for themselves at entirely their own risk with their own money shares which the trustees never contemplated buying and they did so in circumstances fully known and approved of by the trustees.

To extend the doctrines of equity to make the appellants accountable in such circumstances is, in my judgment, to make unreasonable and unequitable applications of such doctrines.

I would allow the appeal and dismiss the action.

In *Industrial Development Consultants Ltd v Cooley* ([1972] 1 WLR 443, [1972] 2 All ER 162)[13] the defendant was a director and general manager of the plaintiffs, a company which provided consultancy services for industrial development.

Cooley tried to interest the Eastern Gas Board in a project, but he was unable to do so because the Board, as a matter of policy, would not employ development companies. When it became clear to Cooley that he could obtain the contract for himself, he obtained a release from the plaintiffs by a false representation of illness. He made a profit from the contract, and was held liable to account to the plaintiffs.

In *Reading v A-G* ([1951] AC 507, [1951] 1 All ER 617)[14] Sergeant Reading had, when stationed in Cairo, been asked to ride across the city in civilian lorries carrying contraband goods. His presence would enable the lorries to pass Egyptian check posts without difficulty. For this service, he received large sums of money.

The British military authorities seized some £20,000 in cash in Reading's flat. He was tried by court-martial and convicted. He later petitioned to

13 (1973) 89 LQR 187 (A. Yoran); (1972) CLJ 222 (J. G. Collier); (1972) 35 MLR 655 (M. Rajak); *Canadian Aero Service Ltd v Malley* (1973) 40 DLR (3d) 371; (1974) 37 MLR 464 (D. D. Prentice).

14 *A-G v Goddard* (1929) 98 LJKB 743 (bribes to policeman on duty); *Brown v IRC* [1965] AC 244, [1964] 3 All ER 119 (solicitor liable to clients for interest earned by money in clients' current account); (1968) 84 LQR 472 (G. H. Jones); Goff and Jones, *The Law of Restitution*, p. 458.

recover the money, arguing that, although it had been obtained illegally, the authorities had no right to take it from him.

He failed; one of the grounds being that, as a non-commissioned officer, he was in a fiduciary relation to the Crown, and under a duty to account for any profit he made.

(1968) 84 LQR 472 at p. 483 (G. H. Jones)[15]

"Lord Hodson and Lord Guest were of the opinion that confidential information could properly be regarded as 'the property of the trust,' and for this reason alone Phipps and Boardman must account for the fruit of that property[16]. Lord Hodson went on to say that because the appellants had acted as agents and had 'obtained knowledge by reason of their fiduciary position . . . they cannot escape liability by saying that they were acting for themselves and not as agents of the trustees.'[17] And Lord Guest based his final conclusion on the ground that 'Boardman and Tom Phipps . . . [had] placed themselves in a special position which was of a fiduciary character in relation to the negotiations with the directors. . . . Out of such special position and in the course of such negotiations they obtained the opportunity to make a profit out of the shares and knowledge that the profit was there to be made.'[18] . . .

To say that the fiduciaries' profit was made solely through the use of property (the information) received *qua* fiduciaries, when the trust could not have utilised it and when the negotiations would have failed but for Boardman's business acumen and Boardman and Phipps' financial intervention, offends legal as well as common sense[19]. To categorise confidential information as 'property' or 'equitable property' cannot solve the essential questions whether Boardman and Phipps were unjustly enriched, and whether policy demands that they should disgorge their enrichment even though they were not unjustly enriched[20].

[15] See also *Seager v Copydex Ltd* [1967] 1 WLR 923, [1967] 2 All ER 415; (1970) 86 LQR 463 (G. H. Jones).

[16] In *Phipps v Boardman* the plaintiff in his writ had claimed that Boardman and Tom Phipps held 5/18ths of the shareholding as constructive trustees for the plaintiff (5/18ths being the extent of the plaintiff's beneficial interest in the trust fund); an account of profits made by Boardman and Phipps from the holdings; and an order that they should transfer the shares held as constructive trustees to the plaintiff, and pay him 5/18ths of the profit: see [1965] Ch 992 at 1006.

At first instance ([1964] 1 WLR 993 at 1018), WILBERFORCE J had declared that the defendants were accountable and directed an account and an inquiry as to the allowances to which they were entitled. The order went on to say that "further consideration [would be given] of order to transfer the shares held by the defendants and payment of any profit found on the taking of the account adjourned".

[17] [1967] 2 AC 46 at 111.

[18] At p. 118.

[19] In the Court of Appeal, Lord DENNING MR suggested that the appellants should have told the trustees that the shares were a good buy, that they ought to purchase them and that they should apply to the court for power to do so: see [1965] Ch 992 at 1020. No other judge in the Court of Appeal or House of Lords took up this point. Lord UPJOHN considered that it was a "difficult point," but was able to avoid it by saying that it was neither pleaded nor relied upon in argument: see [1967] 2 AC 46 at 131. In any event, is it realistic to assume that parties would contemplate an application to the court during the course of confidential and protracted negotiations?

[20] See Goff and Jones, *The Law of Restitution* pp. 38–40; and cf. Austin W. Scott, "Constructive Trusts" (1955) 71 LQR 39.

The main ground of the decision was that there was a conflict between Boardman and Phipps' self-interest and their fiduciary duty; they had made a profit out of their special position of trust. It is difficult to accept, however, that any reasonable person could conclude on these facts that there was any real (as distinct from a hypothetical) conflict of interest. In our view the reasoning of the dissenting law lords is convincing. Lord Upjohn's realistic, commonsense approach is that of Justice Clark in the *Becker* case[21]. Both judges refused to apply blindly a rule of equity. In neither *Becker's* case nor *Phipps v Boardman* had the profit been made at the expense of the fiduciary's principal. In both cases the fiduciary's actions had benefited the principal: the purchase of the debentures in the *Becker* case encouraged public confidence in a company which was in a parlous financial position; in *Phipps v Boardman* the long negotiations conducted with considerable skill by Boardman, and the purchase of the outstanding shares by Boardman and Tom Phipps, had resulted in great financial benefit to the trust. Neither the *Becker* directors nor Boardman was a Sergeant Reading. They had not unjustly enriched themselves at their principal's expense.

Conclusion

'Rules of equity have to be applied to such a great diversity of circumstances that they can be stated only in the most general terms and applied with particular attention to the exact circumstances of each case[1].' The rule that a fiduciary must not profit from his trust is used to recover the fiduciary's unjust enrichment *and* to ensure that the conduct of all fiduciaries is maintained 'at a level higher than that trodden by the crowd.'[2]

In many cases these objects do not conflict. The dishonest fiduciary who is punished as a warning to others has been unjustly enriched. It is irrelevant that his gain has not been made at his principal's expense, in the sense that something has been taken 'from [the] plaintiff and added to the treasury of [the] defendant.'[3] For he has abused his position of trust, and 'in equity and good conscience [he] should not be permitted to retain that by which [he] has been enriched.'[3] In other cases, however, the fiduciary's enrichment has not been unjustly gained. There is then a variance between the two objects which underlie equity's inflexible rule. Some but not all courts and judges have been aware of this clash of principle. A conscious appreciation and consideration of the qualifications of the large generalisation of unjust enrichment[4]—the inherent fairness of the transaction, the fiduciary's honesty and concern to protect his principal's interests, and the fact that the principal has suffered no real loss (the 'complex equation' of loss and gain)—has helped them to decide that there was, on the particular facts,no real sensible possibility of conflict between duty and self-interest.

The boundaries between just and unjust enrichment do not inevitably compose the limits of equity's 'inflexible rule.' There may be cases where

21 *Manufacturers Trust Co v Becker* 338 US 304, 70 S. Ct 127 (1949).

1 *Boardman v Phipps* [1967] 2 AC 46 at 123, per Lord Upjohn.

2 *Meinhard v Salmon*, 249 NY 456 at 464, 164 NE 545 at 546, per Chief Judge Cardozo (1928).

3 *Federal Sugar Refining Co v U.S. Sugar Equalization Board Inc* 268 F 575 at 582, per Judge Mayer (1920).

4 *Fibrosa Spolka Akcyjna v Fairbairn Lawson Combe Barbour Ltd* [1943] AC 32 at 62–63, per Lord Wright.

it is absolutely necessary to punish the fiduciary whose enrichment cannot be said to be unjustly gained. That wise public policy which desires to remove all temptation and to extinguish all possibility of profit may insist that a fiduciary whose integrity is beyond doubt and who has materially benefited his principal should be deprived of profit. But this decision should be taken only after due and careful regard has been paid to the relevant policy considerations, to the nature of the responsibilities which the particular fiduciary owes his principal and to the question whether it is necessary to make an example of the innocent and conscientious that others may learn from their fate.

Finally, there is the question of the extent and degree of the fiduciary's liability. In our view the principal should be allowed a proprietary claim only if the court considers it appropriate that he should be granted the additional benefits which naturally flow from such a grant. The honest fiduciary who is deemed to have breached his duty of loyalty but who has not been unjustly enriched and whose principal has suffered no loss should only be liable to account for his profits. On the other hand a fiduciary who is dishonest or who has otherwise manifestly disregarded his principal's interest should be held to be a constructive trustee of the benefits obtained at his principal's expense. If, as a matter of policy, the court imposes on him a further and penal liability for profits made by third parties, his liability should only be a personal one, to account to his principal for those profits."

C. Insider Dealing[5]

Department of Trade. The Conduct of Company Directors, paras. 22–23, 25–26 (1977 Cmnd. 7037)

"22. Insider dealing is understood broadly to cover situations where a person buys or sells securities when he, but not the other party to the transaction, is in possession of confidential information which affects the value to be placed on those securities. Furthermore the confidential information in question will generally be in his possession because of some connection which he has with the company whose securities are to be dealt in (e.g. he may be a director, employee or professional adviser of that company) or because someone in such a position has provided him, directly or indirectly, with the information. Public confidence in directors and others closely associated with companies requires that such people should not use inside information to further their own interests. Furthermore, if they were to do so, they would frequently be in breach of their obligations to the companies, and could be held to be taking an unfair advantage of the people with whom they were dealing.

23. There are at present in this country no legal sanctions aimed specifically at discouraging insider dealing although, for example, both the 1967 and the 1976 Companies Acts contain provisions requiring disclosure of dealings by directors and substantial shareholders. In addition,

[5] H & M, pp. 519–521; Gower, *Modern Company Law* (3rd Edn, 1969), pp. 555–556; (1970) 86 MLR 463 (G. Jones); (1977) 40 MLR 471 (B. A. K. Rider). The Government's intention to legislate on insider dealing and the private interests of directors was reaffirmed on July 28, 1977. See (1977) 127 NLJ 784.

the Stock Exchange regulations and the City Code on Take-overs and Mergers contain provisions against insider dealing and the Stock Exchange has recently announced details of 'a model code' which it intends to introduce as part of its Listing Agreement; this lays down principles to be observed by directors and employees wishing to deal in their company's securities. The Government has looked carefully at the issues involved and has paid attention both to what is done in other countries and to the views expressed by various organisations in this country. The question of what should be done about insider dealing has attracted considerable debate here and overseas and this has served to clarify the issues and to identify the conflicting considerations which have to be balanced. That insider dealing is wrong is widely accepted and the Government has concluded that this should be underlined by statutory provisions which would make insider dealing in certain circumstances a criminal offence. It will not be possible to produce a perfect answer to the problem which will enable the immediate identification and conviction of every wrongdoer but the Government intends to establish as soon as possible that insider dealing is an offence and to create penalties which will be sufficient in most cases to deter those who are tempted to use inside information for their own personal gain. If the provisions proposed prove insufficient in the light of experience, the Government will not hesitate to modify and refine them.

25. The Government's principal proposal is that it shall be a criminal offence for an insider to deal on the market in quoted securities in certain circumstances where he has inside information. We intend, however, that this offence should not be one of absolute liability. The prosecution will need to show that the insider knew or had reasonable grounds to believe that the information was not generally known and was price sensitive and that he dealt nevertheless. Also, it will be possible for a person to offer as a defence that his purpose in dealing was not to make a profit or avoid a loss by the use of his inside information.

26. In making these proposals the Government has recognised that the creation of insider dealing as an offence must not be such as to inhibit dealings which are not under criticism. It has particularly in mind that the directors and employees of a company will not infrequently hold shares in the company for which they work. By the very nature of their employment they will usually be in possession of confidential information and they could be inhibited from dealing perfectly innocently unless their special position was recognised. The difficulty is a real one, but the Government believes that the defence set out in the preceding paragraph will afford a suitable measure of protection in relation to innocent dealings by directors and employees."

D. Services to Charities

Annual Report of the Charity Commissioners for England and Wales for the year 1970, paras. 92–93

"*Trustees supplying goods or services to a charity*

92. We considered during the year an interesting and specialised point relating to the fiduciary nature of trusteeship. It is a well established rule of

law that, unless specifically authorised in the trust instrument, a charity trustee shall not derive any personal profit from his trust or be placed in a position where his duty as a trustee conflicts with his interests as a private individual. It has been our practice for a long time to include in our schemes a clause providing that no trustee shall take or hold any interest in property belonging to the charity otherwise than as a trustee and that no trustee shall receive remuneration or be interested in the supply of goods or services at the cost of the charity. Representations were, however, made to us objecting to such a strict provision and claiming that charities often suffer as a result, since persons who are in a position to supply a charity with goods or services are frequently also suitable persons to be trustees and in small villages, in particular, might be the only persons suitable for appointment. Such persons are often willing to supply goods and services at reduced or cost price to the benefit of the charity, and in country districts they may be the only persons living locally who can supply such work or goods, but because of the restrictions imposed by the scheme they are faced with the choice of accepting trusteeship and dissociating themselves from supplying work or goods to the charity, or of declining trusteeship.

93. We came to the conclusion that while our common-form clause would still be appropriate in a large proportion of cases, and would continue to be used, it was too restrictive in the circumstances indicated above. We therefore adopted an alternative form of clause which, while providing reasonable safeguards, will permit the appointment of suitable persons as trustees without preventing them from supplying work or goods to a charity. The new clause will provide that a trustee shall absent himself from any meeting of the trustees at which they are discussing any transaction in which he is interested in the supply of services, work or goods at the cost of the charity and, further, that the other trustees must be satisfied that any transaction arising out of their deliberations is advantageous to the charity."

QUESTIONS

1. In determining the borderline of a fiduciary liability, how relevant is it that:
    a) the plaintiff suffered no loss;
    b) the plaintiff benefited in addition to the fiduciary;
    c) the fiduciary was bona fide;
    d) the profit came through a decision of a third party (the Gas Board in *Industrial Development Consultants Ltd v Cooley* [1972] 1 WLR 443, [1972] 1 All ER 162, p. 608, ante.
    e) the fiduciary is a trustee, solicitor, director;
    f) the defendant is a friend of the fiduciary (the tippee)?
2. The directors of a corporation purchased debentures at a discount, at prices varying from 3% to 14% of their face value. At the time of the purchase, the corporation was a going concern, but the market value of its property was insufficient to pay its outstanding debts. The purchase was made without failure to disclose any material facts to the sellers. On the liquidation of the corporation the directors stood to make a profit if their

claims as debenture holders were allowed. The trustee for the debenture holders objected on the ground that the directors could not make a profit from the purchase of claims against an insolvent corporation.

What result? *Manufacturers Trust Co v Becker* 338 US 304, 70 Sup Ct 127 (1949); (1968) 84 LQR at pp. 479 et seq. See also [1967] 2 AC at 90, where Viscount DILHORNE quoted LINDLEY LJ in *Aas v Benham* [1891] 2 Ch 244 at 255–256: "to hold that a partner can never derive any personal benefit from information which he obtains from a partner would be manifestly absurd." H & M, p. 523.

3. If you had been the fifth Lord of Appeal in *Boardman v Phipps,* what would you have said?
4. Was *Boardman v Phipps* a case concerning constructive trusts, or personal accountability? H & M, p. 527; (1968) 84 LQR 502.

18. Breach of Trust[1]

I. Personal Liability to the Beneficiaries[2]

A trustee is personally liable to compensate the beneficiaries for the loss which a breach of trust causes to the trust property.

The liability is joint and several. It is personal, not vicarious. A trustee is not vicariously liable for the acts of his co-trustees. But, and this is of great significance, trustees are required to act jointly. One trustee cannot escape liability by leaving his co-trustees to do all the work; indeed, as was said in *Bahin v Hughes* ((1886) 31 ChD 390 at 396, per COTTON LJ)[3]: "... it would be laying down a wrong rule to hold that where one trustee acts honestly, though erroneously, the other trustee is to be held entitled to indemnity who by doing nothing neglects his duty more than the acting trustee".

A trustee's liability may be reduced by a provision in the trust instrument; and, as has been seen, it is limited by statute[4]. It is common also for professional trustees to protect themselves by insurance.

A. Measure of Liability[5]

i. UNAUTHORISED INVESTMENT

In *Knott v Cottee* ((1852) 16 Beav 77) the testator, who died in 1844,

[1] H & M, pp. 543–576; K & S, pp. 373–412; P & M, pp. 384–413; Pettit, pp. 363–382; Snell, pp. 272–292. For criminal liability, see Theft Act 1968, Debtors' Act 1869, s. 4; (1975) 39 Conv (NS) 29 (R. Brazier).

[2] H & M, pp. 543–560; K & S, pp. 373–383; P & M, pp. 384–403; Pettit, pp. 363–382; Snell, pp. 272–284.

[3] See p. 620, post.

[4] T.A. 1925, s. 30, p. 530, ante; *Re Brier* (1884) 26 ChD 238.

[5] H & M, pp. 545–549; K & S, pp. 373–375; P & M, pp. 387–392; Pettit, pp. 364–368; Snell, pp. 276–278.

bequeathed his personal estate to trustees upon trust to invest in "the public or Government Stocks or Funds of Great Britain, or upon real security in England or Wales".

The executor invested in foreign stocks and in Exchequer bills. In a suit by the beneficiaries, he was required to deposit the Exchequer bills in court, and on November 18, 1846 they were sold, under an order of the court, at a loss. The court made a decree in 1848 declaring the investments to be unauthorised. By that time, the price of the bills had risen; if they had been sold then, there would have been a profit.

The question was whether the executor should be charged with the original sum due for investment plus 5 per cent., or with the sum which would have been produced if invested in Consols; and whether he should be credited with the proceeds of the Exchequer bills as sold in 1846, or with their (increased) value in 1848 when they were declared to be unauthorised. ROMILLY MR held that the executors should be charged with the amount improperly invested, and credited with the proceeds actually received on their sale. He said (at p. 81): "As to the mode of charging the executor in respect of the Exchequer bills, I treat the laying out in Exchequer bills in this way: The persons interested were entitled to ear-mark them, as being bought with the testator's assets, in the same manner as if the executor had bought a house with the trust funds; and though they do not recognize the investment, they had a right to make it available for what was due; and though part of the property of the executor, it was specifically applicable to the payment. When the Exchequer bills were sold and produced £3,955, the Court must consider the produce as a sum of money refunded by the executor to the testator's estate on that day; and on taking the account, the Master must give credit for this amount as on the day on which the Exchequer bills were sold."

ii. IMPROPER RETENTION OF UNAUTHORISED INVESTMENTS[6]

In *Fry v Fry* ((1859) 27 Beav 144) a testator, who died in 1834, provided by his will that the Langford Inn should be sold "as soon as convenient after his decease . . . either by auction or private sale, and for the most money that could be reasonably obtained for the same".

The trustees had difficulty in selling. In 1836 they advertised and offered to sell for £1,000. They refused an offer of £900. In 1843 the Bristol and Exeter Railway was opened, and deprived the Inn of most of its coaching traffic. It was again advertised in 1854, but no offer was received. It remained unsold.

ROMILLY MR held the trustees liable in consequence of their negligence for so many years in not selling the property. The estates of the trustees (who had died) would be liable for the difference between the amount eventually received and £900.

iii. IMPROPER SALE OF AUTHORISED INVESTMENTS

In *Re Massingberd's Settlement* ((1890) 63 LT 296)[7] the trustees of a settlement had power to invest in Government or real securities. In 1875 they sold

[6] T.A. 1925, s. 4; Trustee Investments Act 1961, ss. 3 (4), 6 (2), pp. 486, 488 ante.

[7] *Phillipson v Gatty* (1848) 7 Hare 516.

Consols and reinvested in certain unauthorised mortgages. The mortgages were called in and the whole of the money invested was recovered.

Proceedings began in 1887, at which time Consols stood higher than they had done in 1875. The trustees argued that their obligation was only to produce the capital sum; but the Court of Appeal held that they must produce the stock sold or its present money equivalent.

iv. A PROFIT IN ONE TRANSACTION CANNOT BE SET OFF AGAINST A LOSS IN ANOTHER

DIMES v SCOTT
((1828) 4 Russ 195 (LC, Lord LYNDHURST))

By his will the testator, who died in 1802, left his estate upon trust for his widow for her life, and after her death upon trust for the plaintiff. The estate included an investment in an East India Company 10 per cent. loan whose retention was not authorised by the will.

Instead of selling this unauthorised investment within a year of the testator's death, the trustees retained it, and paid the whole income to the widow.

In 1813 the loan was repaid, and the proceeds were invested in 3 per cent. Consols. The price of Consols was lower than it was a year from the testator's death, and the trustees were able to purchase more Consols than they would have been able to purchase if they had made the switch a year from the testator's death.

The question was whether the trustees had committed a breach of trust by paying the whole income to the widow; and, if they had, whether they could set off, against that liability, the extra Consols which the delay had enabled them to purchase.

Held. The payments to the tenant for life were excessive; and the trustees could claim no credit in respect of the extra Consols.

LORD LYNDHURST: This testator left his property to trustees, who were directed to convert it into money, and to invest the proceeds in government or real securities; and he gave the interest of the money so to be invested to his widow for life, with remainder to the lady who is one of the present Plaintiffs. Part of his property consisted of a sum which he had subscribed to what is called the decennial loan. The trustees did not convert his share of this loan into money; but, suffering it to remain as they found it, paid the interest, which was £10 per cent., to the tenant for life. Was that a proper performance of their duty?

The directions of the will were most distinct; and, according to the case of *Howe v Lord Dartmouth* ((1802) 7 Ves 137), and the principles of this Court, it was the duty of the trustees to have sold the property within the usual period after the testator's death. If they neglected to sell it, still, so far as regarded the tenant for life, the property was to be considered as if it had been duly converted. Had the conversion taken place, and the proceeds been invested in that which is considered in this Court as the fit and proper security, namely, £3 per cent., stock, the tenant for life would not have been entitled to more than the interest which would have resulted from such stock. The executor is therefore chargeable with the difference between the interest which the fund, if so converted, would have yielded, and the £10 per cent. which was actually produced by the fund, and was paid over by him to the tenant for life.

It is said, that, if the subscription to the decennial loan had been sold, and the produce invested in stock at the end of a year from the testator's death, the sale would have been much less advantageous to the estate than the course which has been actually followed; and that, if the executor is to be charged for not having made the conversion at the proper time, he ought on the other hand, to have the benefit of the advantage which has accrued from his course of conduct. The answer is this: With respect to the principal sum, at whatever period the subscription to the decennial loan was sold, the estate must have the whole amount of the stock that was bought; and if it was sold at a later period than the rules of the Court require, the executor is not entitled to any accidental advantage thence arising. As to the payments to the tenant for life, the executors are entitled to have credit only for sums I have adverted to, namely, the dividends on so much £3 per cent. stock as would have been purchased with the proceeds of the subscription to the decennial loan, if the conversion had taken place at the proper time. On the other hand, he is chargeable with the whole of the difference between the amount of those dividends and the amount of the sums which have been received in respect of interest on the money which was continued in the decennial loan. I think, therefore, that the judgment of the *Master of the Rolls* [Lord Gifford] must be affirmed.

Hanbury & Maudsley: *Modern Equity,* 10th Edn (1976), p. 548.

"The rule is harsh though logical. It has not been applied where the court finds that the gain and loss were part of the same transaction. If that were not so, the liability of trustees purchasing unauthorised securities would automatically be calculated by a reference to the highest price reached by the unauthorised investment while the trustees held it. There is often difficulty in determining whether the question should or should not be regarded as a single transaction.

In *Fletcher v Green*[8] trust money was lent on mortgage to a firm of which one trustee was a partner. The trustees reclaimed the money; the security was sold at a loss and the proceeds paid into court and invested in Consols. The question was whether the trustees' accounts should credit them with the amount of the proceeds of sale or with the value of the Consols, which had risen in price. They were held entitled to take advantage of the rise. No reasons were given. The case is usually explained on the ground that the whole matter was treated as one transaction. If that is so, they should logically have been at risk in relation to a possible fall in the price of Consols; the trustees can hardly be allowed to take advantage of a rise but not the burden of a fall; but it would be hard on the trustees if they have to run the risk of loss on an investment made by the court."

[8] (1864) 33 Beav 426.

V. INTEREST

A fiduciary may be liable, not only to replace trust capital which has been misapplied, but also to pay interest on that sum from the date of misapplication. In some cases interest is compounded. The nineteenth century cases laid down 4 per cent. as the normal rate of interest, with 5 per cent. in cases of fraud, actual misconduct and the like. Those figures are a long way below current interest rates, and a rate of 1 per cent. over the minimum lending rate[9] was charged in *Wallersteiner v Moir (No 2)* ((1975) QB 373, [1975] 1 All ER 849), where the defendant, a company director and international financier, was shown to have improperly used company funds for his own benefit. SCARMAN LJ said (at p. 406): "I agree that we have power under the equitable jurisdiction of the court to include interest in the judgment entered against Dr. Wallersteiner. This judgment we have already said is to be for £234,773 and interest, but at the time we had not heard argument as to the propriety of including interest. The principle on which equitable interest is awarded was stated by Lord Hatherley LC in *Burdick v Garrick* (1870) 5 Ch App 233 at 241, and has been frequently applied to situations in which there was a fiduciary relationship at the time when the money was appropriated. In *Atwool v Merryweather* (1867) LR 5 Eq 464n, interest was awarded to a company upon money recovered for it in a minority shareholder's action.

There is, therefore, ample authority to support the claim made by Mr. Moir on behalf of the companies to interest from the date on which the companies made their loan to I.F.T.—a loan which in default of defence this court has accepted was instigated by Dr. Wallersteiner in breach of his duty as a director.

The question whether the interest to be awarded should be simple or compound depends upon evidence as to what the accounting party has, or is to be presumed to have done with the money. As Lord Hatherley LC said in *Burdick v Garrick* (1890) 5 Ch App 233 at 241:

> 'the court does not proceed against an accounting party by way of punishing him for making use of the plaintiff's money by directing rests, or payment of compound interest, but proceeds upon this principle, either that he has made, or has put himself into such a position as that he is to be presumed to have made, 5 per cent., or compound interest, as the case may be.'

Dr. Wallersteiner was at all material times engaged in the business of finance. Through a complex structure of companies he conducted financial operations with a view to profit. The quarter million pounds assistance which he obtained from the two companies in order to finance the acquisition of the shares meant that he was in a position to employ the money or its capital equivalent in those operations. Though the truth is unlikely ever to be fully known, shrouded as it is by the elaborate corporate structure within which Dr. Wallersteiner chose to operate, one may safely presume that the use of the money (or the capital it enabled him to acquire) was worth to him the equivalent of compound interest at commercial rates with yearly rests, if not more. I, therefore, agree that he should be ordered

[9] 6½ per cent. in April 1976. It was as high as 15 per cent. in October 1976.

to pay compound interest at the rates, and with the rests, proposed by Lord Denning MR and Buckley LJ. This being a case for equitable interest, no question arises as to interest under section 3 of the Law Reform (Miscellaneous Provisions) Act 1934; I therefore express no opinion as to the true construction of subsection (1) of that section."

B. Liability Inter Se[10]

i. CONTRIBUTION

BAHIN v HUGHES

(1886) 31 ChD 390 (CA, COTTON, BOWEN and FRY LJJ)

The testator gave a legacy of £2,000 to his three daughters, Miss Hughes, Mrs. Edwards and Mrs. Burden, upon trust to pay the income to Mrs. Bahin, the plaintiff, for her life, and after her death to her children.

Miss Hughes managed the whole business of the trust. The money was placed in the name of Miss Hughes and Mrs. Burden's husband, and they effected an unauthorised investment in leasehold house property. Mrs. Edwards was informed by letter.

When the security proved insufficient, Mrs. Bahin and her children sought to hold all the trustees liable. Mrs. Edwards having died, her husband served a notice on Miss Hughes, claiming an indemnity from her.

Held. The trustees were jointly and severally liable. Mr. Edwards was not entitled to an indemnity.

FRY LJ: It appears to me that on the first point arising in this appeal there is no case at all. It appears that in a certain trust the wife of the Defendant Mr. *Edwards* was one of the trustees, and that he has been rendered liable for breaches of trust committed by her, which liability he repudiates by alleging that a husband is not responsible for all, but only for some, of the breaches of trust which a wife may commit. I rather understand that he draws a distinction between active and passive breaches of trust, but it was admitted by Mr. *Smith* that there is no authority for such distinction, and I can see no principle in law for such a distinction. The law of *England*, which has long existed, is that the husband is responsible for the breaches of trust of his wife. Upon the second point I also agree with my Brother Lord Justice *Cotton*. This part of the appeal is based upon some notion that one trustee is liable to indemnify his co-trustee against loss or injury from his acts, but I cannot think that such liability exists, for if it did exist the books would be full of authorities bearing upon the point, and the Courts would be crowded with litigation on the subject. It is well known that the authorities are extremely few, and the authorities which do exist do not favour the Appellant's contention. It has been pointed out by Lord Justice *Cotton* that in each of the two cases cited[11] the trustee who was held to be secondarily liable, and who had a right of indemnity, had been misled by his co-trustee, who was the solicitor to the trust, and had been proved to have been guilty of negligence in his duty as such solicitor. In my judgment the

[10] H & M, pp. 549–550; K & S, pp. 380–382; P & M, pp. 392–394; Pettit, pp. 368–370; Snell, pp. 283–284.

[11] *Lockhart v Reilly* (1856) 25 LJ Ch 697; *Thompson v Finch* (1856) 8 DeG M & G 560.

Courts ought to be very jealous of raising any such implied liability as is insisted on, because if such existed it would act as an opiate upon the consciences of the trustees; so that instead of the *cestui que trust* having the benefit of several acting trustees, each trustee would be looking to the other or others for a right of indemnity, and so neglect the performance of his duties. Such a doctrine would be against the policy of the Court in relation to trusts.

In the present case, in my judgment, the loss which has happened is the result of the combination of the action of Miss *Hughes* with the inaction of Mr. *Edwards*. If Miss *Hughes* has made a mistake, it was through simple ignorance and want of knowledge, and if on the other hand Mr. *Edwards* had used all the diligence which he ought to have done, I doubt whether any loss would have been incurred. The money might have been recovered before the property went down in value. I think therefore that it is not possible for Mr. *Edwards* to obtain any relief, and I concur with my Brethren that this appeal must be dismissed with costs.

ii. INDEMNITY

In *Re Partington* ((1887) 57 LT 654) the trustees of a fund were Mr. Allen, a solicitor, and Mrs. Partington, the widow of the testator. A breach of trust was committed. Mr. Allen undertook the whole administration of the trust. STIRLING J held that he had not communicated sufficiently to Mrs. Partington concerning the affairs of the trust to enable her to exercise a judgment upon the unauthorised investment. "The trustee, Mrs. Partington, appears to me to have been misled by her co-trustee by reason of his not giving her full information as to the nature of the investments which he was asking her to advance the money upon, and I think he has been guilty of negligence also in his duty as a solicitor." Mrs. Partington was entitled to an indemnity.

In *Head v Gould* ([1898] 2 Ch 250) an attempt to obtain an indemnity against a solicitor trustee failed. KEKEWICH J said (at p. 265): "True it is that the defendant Gould is a solicitor, and that he was appointed trustee for that very reason. True no doubt, also, that the legal business was managed by him, and I do not propose to absolve him from any responsibility attaching to him on that ground; but I do not myself think that BYRNE J[12], or any other judge ever intended to hold that a man is bound to indemnify his co-trustee against loss merely because he was a solicitor, when that co-trustee was an active participator in the breach of trust complained of, and is not proved to have participated merely in consequence of the advice and control of the solicitor . . ."

In *Chillingworth v Chambers* ([1896] 1 Ch 685) the plaintiff and defendant were trustees of a testamentary trust. The plaintiff, Chillingworth, was married to one of the beneficiaries, and, on her death, became himself a beneficiary.

[12] In *Re Turner* [1897] 1 Ch 536.

The trustees made an unauthorised investment in mortgages of leasehold property, some being made before Mrs. Chillingworth's death, and some after. The mortgages proved insufficient. The deficiency of £1,580 was made good out of Mr. Chillingworth's interest.

He brought this action claiming contribution from Chambers, and failed. KAY LJ said (at p. 707); "On the whole, I think that the weight of authority is in favour of holding that a trustee who, being also cestui que trust, has received, as between himself and his co-trustee, an exclusive benefit by the breach of trust, must indemnify his co-trustee to the extent of his interest in the trust fund, and not merely to the extent of the benefit which he has received. I think that the plaintiff must be treated as having received such an exclusive benefit."

C. Protection of Trustees[13]

i. RELIEF BY THE COURT[14]

TRUSTEE ACT 1925

61. Power to relieve trustee from personal liability.—If it appears to the court that a trustee, whether appointed by the court or otherwise, is or may be personally liable for any breach of trust, whether the transaction alleged to be a breach of trust occurred before or after the commencement of this Act, but has acted honestly and reasonably, and ought fairly to be excused for the breach of trust and for omitting to obtain the directions of the court in the matter in which he committed such breach, then the court may relieve him either wholly or partly from personal liability for the same.

It is not possible to lay down with precision the occasions on which the section will be applied. The question has usually arisen in connection with the making of unauthorised investments, and the payment of money to the wrong beneficiaries.

Where a trustee is in doubt, he should always take legal advice. Having done so, an amateur trustee will nearly always be covered; but relief is not automatic. A solicitor should likewise take counsel's opinion. Professional trustees are within the section, but the court is less willing to apply its provisions in their favour[15].

The best general explanation of the section—or rather its predecessor, Judicial Trustees Act 1896, s. 3—is found in *Perrins v Bellamy* ([1898] 2 Ch 521), per KEKEWICH J and in *Re Stuart* ([1897] 2 Ch 583) per STIRLING J. In each case trustees were guilty of a breach of trust. In the former they were excused; but not in the latter.

[13] H & M, pp. 551–561; K & S, pp. 402–412; P & M, pp. 394–403; Pettit, pp. 370–381; Snell, pp. 278–283.

[14] H & M, pp. 554–557; K & S, pp. 402–405; P & M, pp. 398–400; Pettit, pp. 373–381; Snell, pp. 278–279. See generally (1955) 19 Conv (NS) 420 (L. A. Sheridan).

[15] *National Trustees Co of Australasia Ltd v General Finance Co of Australasia Ltd* [1905] AC 373; *Re Pauling's Settlement Trusts* [1964] Ch 303, [1963] 3 All ER 1, p. 630, post; *Re Rosenthal* [1972] 1 WLR 1273, [1972] 3 All ER 552.

KEKEWICH J (at p. 527): "Broadly speaking, these trustees have committed a breach of trust, and they are responsible for it. But then the statute comes in, and the very foundation for the application of the statute is that the trustee whose conduct is in question 'is or may be personally liable for any breach of trust'. I am bound to look at the rest of the section by the light of those words, and with the view that, in cases falling within the section, the breach of trust is not of itself to render the trustee personally liable. Leaving out the intervening words, which merely make the section retrospective, I find when in general the trustee is to be relieved from personal liability. He is not to be held personally liable if he 'has acted honestly and reasonably, and ought fairly to be excused for the breach of trust'. In this case, as in the large majority of cases of breach of trust which come before the Court, the word 'honestly' may be left out of consideration. Cases do unfortunately occur from time to time in which trustees, and even solicitors in whom confidence has been reposed, run away with the money of their cestuis que trust, and where such flagrant dishonesty occurs breach of trust becomes a minor consideration. In the present case there is no imputation or ground for imputation of any dishonesty whatever. The Legislature has made the absence of all dishonesty a condition precedent to the relief of the trustee from liability. But that is not the grit of the section. The grit is in the words 'reasonably, and ought fairly to be excused for the breach of trust'. How much the latter words add to the force of the word 'reasonably' I am not at present prepared to say. I suppose, however, that in the view of the Legislature there might be cases in which a trustee, though he had acted reasonably, ought not fairly to be excused for the breach of trust. Indeed, I am not sure that some of the evidence adduced in this case was not addressed to a view of that kind, as, for instance, the evidence by which it was attempted to shew that these trustees, though they acted reasonably in selling the property, ought not fairly to be excused because the plaintiff Mrs. Perrins objected to their selling, and her objection was brought to their notice. In the section the copulative 'and' is used, and it may well be argued that in order to bring a case within the section it must be shewn not merely that the trustee has acted 'reasonably', but also that he ought 'fairly' to be excused for the breach of trust. I venture, however, to think that, in general and in the absence of special circumstances, a trustee who has acted 'reasonably' ought to be relieved, and that it is not incumbent on the Court to consider whether he ought 'fairly' to be excused, unless there is evidence of a special character shewing that the provisions of the section ought not to be applied in his favour. I need not pursue that subject further, because in the present case I find no ground whatever for saying that these trustees, if they acted reasonably, ought not to be excused. The question, and the only question, is whether they acted reasonably. In saying that, I am not unmindful of the words of the section which follow, and which require that it should be shewn that the trustee ought 'fairly' to be excused, not only 'for the breach of trust', but also 'for omitting to obtain the directions of the Court in the matter in which he committed such breach of trust'. I find it difficult to follow that. I do not see how the trustee can be excused for the breach of trust without being also excused for the omission referred to, or how he can be excused for the omission without also being excused for the breach of trust. If I am at liberty to guess, I should suppose that these words were added by way of amendment, and crept into the statute without due regard being had to the meaning of the context. The fact that a trustee has omitted to obtain the directions of the Court has never been held to be a ground for holding him personally liable, though it may be a reason guiding the Court in the matter of costs, or in deciding whether he has acted reasonably or otherwise, and especially so in these days when questions of difficulty, even as regards the legal estate, can be decided economically and expeditiously on originating summons. But if the Court comes to the conclusion that a trustee has acted reasonably, I cannot see how it can usefully proceed to consider, as an independent matter, the question whether he has or has not omitted to obtain the directions of the Court."

STIRLING J (at p. 590): "The effect of s. 3 of the Judicial Trustees Act, 1896, appears to me to be this. The law as it stood at the passing of the Act is not altered, but a jurisdiction is given to the Court under special circumstances, the Court being satisfied as to the several matters mentioned in the section, to relieve the trustee of the consequences of a breach of trust as regards his personal liability. But the Court must first be satisfied that the trustee has acted honestly and reasonably. As to the honesty of the trustee in this case there is no question; but that is not the only condition to be satisfied, and the question arises whether the other conditions are satisfied. I quite agree that this section applies to a trustee making an improper investment of the trust funds as well as to any other breach of trust. This matter has been considered by Byrne J in *Re Turner* ([1897] 1 Ch at 542), where he says this: 'I think that the section relied on is meant to be acted upon freely and fairly in the exercise of judicial discretion, but think that the Court ought to be satisfied, before exercising the very large powers conferred upon it, by sufficient evidence, that the trustee acted reasonably. I do not think that I have sufficient evidence in this case that he so acted; in fact, it does not appear from the letters that Mr. Turner acted in respect of this mortgage as he would probably have acted had it been a transaction of his own. I think that if he was—and he well may have been—a businesslike man, he would not, before lending his money, have been satisfied without some further inquiry as to the means of the mortgagor and as to the nature and value of the property upon which he was about to advance his money.' That has since been approved by the Court of Appeal; and I willingly adopt what is there laid down as a guide to me in this matter. In my opinion the burden lies on the trustee who asks the Court to exercise the jurisdiction conferred by this section to shew that he has acted reasonably; and, certainly, it is fair in dealing with such a question to consider whether Mr. Box would have acted with reference to these investments as he did if he had been lending money of his own".

ii. IMPOUNDING A BENEFICIARY'S INTEREST[16]

TRUSTEE ACT 1925

62. Power to make beneficiary indemnify for breach of trust.—(1) Where a trustee commits a breach of trust at the instigation or request or with the consent in writing of a beneficiary, the court may, if it thinks fit, make such order as to the court seems just, for impounding all or any part of the interest of the beneficiary in the trust estate by way of indemnity to the trustee or persons claiming through him[17].

(2) This section applies to breaches of trust committed as well before as after the commencement of this Act.

In *Re Somerset* ([1894] 1 Ch 231) the trustees of a marriage settlement lent an excessive sum upon mortgage. They lent the money at the instigation, request and consent in writing of the tenant for life, Vere Somerset. When the security proved to be inadequate, Vere Somerset and his infant children sued the trustees for breach of trust. Liability to the children was admitted, but the defendant trustees claimed, *inter alia*, that they were entitled to impound the life interest of Vere Somerset for the purposes of meeting the claim.

The Court of Appeal refused. Vere Somerset, though approving the investment, had not intended to be a party to a breach of trust, and in effect left the trustees to determine whether the investment was a proper one for the sum advanced. LINDLEY MR said (at p. 265): "Did the trustees commit the breach of trust for which they have been made liable at the instigation or request, or with the consent in writing of the Appellant? The section is intended to protect trustees, and ought to be construed so as to carry out that intention. But the section ought not, in my opinion, to be construed as if the word 'investment' had been inserted instead of 'breach of trust'. An enactment to that effect would produce great injustice in many cases. In order to bring a case within this section the *cestui que trust* must instigate, or request, or consent in writing to some act or omission which is itself a breach of trust, and not to some act or omission which only becomes a breach of trust by reason of want of care on the part of the trustees. If a *cestui que trust* instigates, requests, or consents in writing to an investment not in terms authorized by the power of investment, he clearly falls within the section; and in such a case his ignorance or forgetfulness of the terms of the power would not, I think, protect him—at all events, not unless he could give some good reason why it should, *e.g.*, that it was caused by the trustee. But if all that a *cestui que trust* does is to instigate, request, or consent in writing to an investment which is authorized by the terms of the power, the case is, I think, very different. He has a right to expect that the trustees will act with proper care in making the investment, and if they do not they cannot throw the consequences

[16] H & M, pp. 554–555; K & S, pp. 405–406; P & M, pp. 402–403; Pettit, pp. 373–375; Snell, pp. 272–278.

[17] As amended by Married Women (Restraint upon Anticipation) Act 1949, s. 1 (4) and Sch. 2.

on him unless they can shew that he instigated, requested, or consented in writing to their non-performance of their duty in this respect.

This is, in my opinion, the true construction of this section."

In *Re Pauling's Settlement Trusts (No. 2)* ([1963] Ch 576, [1963] 1 All ER 857) Coutts and Co., the trustees of a family trust, were held liable for breach of trust in respect of a number of advances of capital to the children of the life tenant, Mrs. Younghusband. At first instance, WILBERFORCE J made his order without prejudice to any right which the defendant bank might have to impound the interests of any beneficiary during the lives of the wife and any surviving husband of hers. The bank claimed to be entitled to impound the life interest of Mrs. Younghusband. The plaintiffs sought the appointment of two new trustees in the place of the bank, who opposed this on the ground that such an appointment might negate their right to impound.

WILBERFORCE J appointed new trustees, holding that such an appointment would not imperil the defendants' right to impound. After dealing with a number of other matters, he said (at p. 583): "Next I come to a separate series of objections which raise some difficult questions of law. The defendants, as I have already mentioned, have a claim to impound the life interest of Mrs. Younghusband now vested in the Guardian Assurance Co. Ltd. in order to recoup themselves against any money which they may be ordered to repay. What is said by the defendants is that that right to impound would be prejudiced if new trustees were appointed now and the trust fund handed over to them. That involves a consideration as to what is the nature of the right to impound which exists in favour of a trustee who has committed a breach of trust at the instigation of a beneficiary. I have to consider both the ordinary right which exists in equity apart from statute and also the further statutory right which has been conferred by section 62 of the Trustee Act, 1925, both of which are invoked by the defendants as plaintiffs in the Chancery action now pending. It seems to me that it is not possible to maintain, as is the defendants' contention here, that a trustee, having committed a breach of trust, is entitled to remain as a trustee until it has exercised its right to impound the income of the beneficiary in order to recoup itself. That seems to me an impossible proposition. It is quite true that, in the reported authorities, there is no case where the right to impound has been exercised by a former trustee as distinct from an existing trustee, but it seems to me in principle that it is impossible to contend that the right to impound is limited to the case where the trustee seeking the right is an actual trustee. The nature of the right to impound seems to me to turn on two things: first, that the money paid back to capital is in its origin the money of the trustee, and that when it comes to considering who should get the income of it, the trustee who has provided the money has a better right to it than the tenant for life who has instigated the breach of trust. The alternative way of putting the matter is that the trustee in breach of trust is in some way subrogated to the rights of the beneficiary. He stands in his position in order that he may be indemnified.

That seems to me the way in which it was put by the Lords Justices in *Raby v Ridehalgh* ((1855) 7 DeGM & G 104). It does not seem to me that there is any support in authority or in principle for saying that the right depends upon the actual possession of the trust fund, and it appears to me that the analogy which has been sought to be drawn with the executor's right to retain is a false one and does not apply to this case. So much for the equitable right to impound as opposed to the statutory right.

As regards the statutory right, that depends on the language of section 62 of the Trustee Act, 1925, and at first sight it might look as if that right only exists in favour of a person who is actually a trustee. But, on consideration, that seems to me to be a misconstruction of the section. In the first place, the same objection against limiting the right in that way applies to the statutory jurisdiction. It seems to me an absurdity that it is required as a condition of exercising the right to obtain an impounding order, that the trustee who, ex hypothesi, is in breach of trust, must remain the trustee in order to acquire a right of indemnity. Further, it seems to me on the authorities, and, indeed, on the very terms of the section, that the section is giving an additional right, among other things, to deal with the case of a married woman beneficiary; that the statutory right is extending the equitable right and not limiting it, and that it is not right to read the section so as to apply only to a person who was formerly a trustee. The section begins with the words: 'Where a trustee commits a breach of trust', thereby indicating that at the time the breach of trust is committed the person in question must be a trustee. Then further down in the section there is a reference to a trustee and that appears to me to be merely a reference back to the same person as the person who committed the breach of trust and not as an indication that the person in question must be a trustee at the date of the order. I would add to that, that here the writ which has been issued in the Chancery Division was issued at a time when the defendants were trustees, and, therefore, at the date of the writ the requirement of being a trustee was fulfilled. So that, although I entirely appreciate that the defendants may be anxious not to lose their right to impound the income of the tenant for life, that right could not, in my view, be prejudiced by appointing new trustees at this stage."

iii. LIMITATION ACT 1939[18]

19. Limitation of actions in respect of trust property.—(1) No period of limitation prescribed by this Act shall apply to an action by a beneficiary under a trust, being an action—

(*a*) in respect of any fraud or fraudulent breach of trust to which the trustee was a party or privy[19], or

(*b*) to recover from the trustee trust property or the proceeds thereof

[18] H & M, pp. 557–561; K & S, pp. 405–412; P & M, pp. 394–397; Pettit, pp. 375–379; Snell, pp. 279–282. See Preston and Newsom, *Limitation of Actions* (3rd Edn, 1953) chap. 5; Franks, *Limitation of Actions* (1959), pp. 62–80; *Tito v Waddell (No. 2)* [1977] 2 WLR 496 at 622–629; Law Reform Committee 21st Report (Final Report on Limitation of Actions) (1977) Cmnd. 6923, pp. 53–54.

[19] *North American Land and Timber Co Ltd v Watkins* [1904] 1 Ch 242, [1904] 2 Ch 233; *Thorne v Heard* [1894] 1 Ch 599; on appeal [1895] AC 495.

in the possession of the trustee, or previously received by the trustee and converted to his use[20].

(2) Subject as aforesaid, an action by a beneficiary to recover trust property or in respect of any breach of trust, not being an action for which a period of limitation is prescribed by any other provision of this Act, shall not be brought after the expiration of six years from the date on which the right of action accrued:

Provided that the right of action shall not be deemed to have accrued to any beneficiary entitled to a future interest in the trust property, until the interest fell into possession[1].

(3) No beneficiary as against whom there would be a good defence under this Act shall derive any greater or other benefit from a judgment or order obtained by any other beneficiary than he could have obtained if he had brought the action and this Act had been pleaded in defence.

20. Limitation of actions claiming personal estate of a deceased person. —Subject to the provisions of subsection (1) of the last foregoing section, no action in respect of any claim to the personal estate of a deceased person or to any share or interest in such estate, whether under a will or on intestacy, shall be brought after the expiration of twelve years from the date when the right to receive the share or interest accrued, and no action to recover arrears of interest in respect of any legacy, or damages in respect of such arrears, shall be brought after the expiration of six years from the date on which the interest became due.

For the definition of trustee, see Limitation Act 1939, s. 31 (1); T.A. 1925, s. 68 (17). It includes personal representatives, certain fiduciary agents (*Burdick v Garrick* (1870) 5 Ch App 233), company directors (*Re Lands Allotment Co* [1894] 1 Ch 616), a mortgagee in respect of the proceeds of sale (*Thorne v Heard* [1895] AC 495), but not a trustee in bankruptcy (*Re Cornish* [1896] 1 QB 99), nor the liquidator of a company in voluntary liquidation (*Re Windsor Steam Coal Co (1901) Ltd* [1928] Ch 609; on appeal [1929] 1 Ch 151).

LIMITATION ACT 1939

22. Extension of limitation period in case of disability.—(1) If on the date when any right of action accrued for which a period of limitation is prescribed by this Act, the person to whom it accrued was under a disability, the action may be brought at any time before the expiration of six years from the date when the person ceased to be under a disability or died, whichever event first occurred, notwithstanding that the period of limitation has expired[2]:

[20] *Re Sharp* [1906] 1 Ch 793; *Re Howlett* [1949] Ch 767, [1949] 2 All ER 490; *Wassell v Leggatt* [1896] 1 Ch 554; *Re Eyre-Williams* [1923] 2 Ch 533; *Re Clark* (1920) 150 LT Jo 94.

[1] *Re Somerset* [1894] 1 Ch 231; *Re Pauling's Settlement Trusts* [1964] Ch 303, [1963] 3 All ER 1, p. 630, post.

[2] As amended by Law Reform (Limitation of Actions, &c) Act 1954, Schedule.

Provided that—

(*a*) this section shall not affect any case where the right of action first accrued to some person (not under a disability) through whom the person under a disability claims;

(*b*) when a right of action which has accrued to a person under a disability accrues, on the death of that person while still under a disability, to another person under a disability, no further extension of time shall be allowed by reason of the disability of the second person;

(*c*) no action to recover land or money charged on land shall be brought by virtue of this section by any person after the expiration of thirty years from the date on which the right of action accrued to that person or some person through whom he claims;

(*e*) this section shall not apply to any action to recover a penalty or forfeiture, or sum by way thereof, by virtue of any enactment, except where the action is brought by an aggrieved party.

26. Postponement of limitation period in case of fraud or mistake.—Where, in the case of any action for which a period of limitation is prescribed by this Act, either—

(*a*) the action is based upon the fraud of the defendant or his agent or of any person through whom he claims or his agent, or

(*b*) the right of action is concealed by the fraud of any such person as aforesaid[3], or

(*c*) the action is for relief from the consequences of a mistake,

the period of limitation shall not begin to run until the plaintiff has discovered the fraud or the mistake, as the case may be, or could with reasonable diligence have discovered it:

Provided that nothing in this section shall enable any action to be brought to recover, or enforce any charge against, or set aside any transaction affecting, any property which—

(i) in the case of fraud, has been purchased for valuable consideration by a person who was not a party to the fraud and did not at the time of the purchase know or have reason to believe that any fraud had been committed, or

(ii) in the case of mistake, has been purchased for valuable consideration, subsequently to the transaction in which the mistake was made, by a person who did not know or have reason to believe that the mistake had been made.

29. Acquiescence.—Nothing in this Act shall affect any equitable jurisdiction to refuse relief on the ground of acquiescence or otherwise.

An assignee, with notice, from a trustee is in the same position as the trustee was. In *Eddis v Chichester Constable* ([1969] 2 Ch 345, [1969] 2 All ER 912)[4] a tenant for life of a painting attributed to Caravaggio sold

[3] *Beaman v ARTS* [1949] 1 KB 550, [1949] 1 All ER 465 (the fraud need not be such as to give rise to an independent cause of action); *Phillips-Higgins v Harper* [1954] 1 QB 411, [1954] 2 All ER 51n (concealment by mistake).

[4] *Re Dixon* [1900] 2 Ch 561; *Re Eyre-Williams* [1923] 2 Ch 533; *G. L. Baker Ltd v Medway Building and Supplies Ltd* [1958] 1 WLR 1216, [1958] 3 All ER 540.

it in 1951, through the agency of one Mrs. Blois, to an art consortium who resold it in 1952 to the William Rockhill Nelson Gallery of Art, Kansas City, Missouri, U.S.A. In 1963 the tenant for life died and the trustees for the first time became aware of the absence of the painting. In 1966 they sued the representative of the tenant for life for breach of trust and the art consortium for conversion. The Limitation Act 1939 was pleaded.

The main question was whether, assuming that the trustees' right of action was concealed by the fraud of the tenant for life, s. 26 prevented time from running against the trustees in favour of the art consortium. The Court of Appeal, affirming GOFF J, held that time did not run against the trustees until the fraud was discovered.

iv. SUMMARY

The various forms of protection of trustees were before the Court of Appeal in *Re Pauling's Settlement Trusts* ([1964] Ch 303, [1963] 3 All ER 1). Commander and Mrs. Younghusband were married in 1919; their marriage settlement contained in clause 11 a power of advancement for the trustees, Coutts & Co., to raise, with the written consent of Mrs. Younghusband, any part not exceeding one half of the expectant or presumptive or vested share of any child of the wife and to pay to him for his own absolute use, or advancement or benefit in such manner as the trustees should think fit. Between 1948 and 1954 the trustees made a number of advancements to the children (Francis, George, Ann and Anthony) who, on some though not every occasion, received independent legal advice as to their rights under the settlement. The mother's consent was obtained in every case.

In 1954, as a result of a scheme of George's for avoiding estate duty on his mother's death, the children first became aware that the advancements might have been in breach of trust. In 1958 they brought an action against the trustees claiming £29,160, on the ground that this sum had been improperly paid out by way of advancement to beneficiaries who were presumed to be subject to undue influence and who were not emancipated from parental control.

WILLMER LJ said (at p. 338): "The bank also rely for relief from the consequences of any breach of trust upon section 61 of the Trustee Act, 1925. At this stage all we propose to say is that it would be a misconstruction of the section to say it does not apply to professional trustees, but, as was pointed out in the Judicial Committee of the Privy Council in *National Trustees Company of Australasia Ltd v General Finance Company of Australasia Ltd* ([1905] AC 373 at 381) '. . . without saying that the remedial provisions of the section should never be applied to a trustee in the position of the appellants, their Lordships think it is a circumstance to be taken into account . . .' Where a banker undertakes to act as a paid trustee of a settlement created by a customer, and so deliberately places itself in a position where its duty as trustee conflicts with its interest as a banker, we think that the court should be very slow to relieve such a trustee under the provisions of the section.

We propose to deal with the bank's plea of the Limitation Act 1939 and the pleas of laches, acquiescence and delay when we have considered the detailed transactions. It only remains to state that the question of law on which this case was reported in the court below, *Re Pauling's Settlement Trusts* ([1962] 1 WLR 86, [1961] 3 All ER 713), has not been argued before us, and many of the cases there cited have not been cited to us. Mr. Bagnall, however, accepts as accurate the proposition that 'The result of these authorities appears to me [Wilberforce J] to be that the court has to consider all the circumstances in which the concurrence of the cestui que trust was given with a view to seeing whether it is fair and equitable that, having given his concurrence, he should afterwards turn round and sue the trustees: that, subject to this, it is not necessary that he should know that what he is concurring in is a breach of trust, provided that he fully understands what he is concurring in, and that it is not necessary that he should himself have directly benefited by the breach of trust ([1962] 1 WLR 86 at 108)'. We express no opinion on it.

[His Lordship then dealt with the impugned transactions *seriatim*. UPJOHN LJ continued the reading of the judgment of the court, and, on the question of undue influence, said (at p. 347):] At the time of this advance the son George was twenty-three years old. He had done his military service, and was up at Cambridge. The judge thought him an exceptionally able young man, well acquainted with his rights, and able to take care of himself. He had no separate advice about this £2,000 advance, but he had been advised about the Hodson loan transaction, and in the course of receiving the explanations then offered he must have realised what the power was which the trustees were purporting to exercise. Indeed, the fatal opinion of counsel advising on the possibility of using clause 11 to purchase a house in the Isle of Man was, on the evidence, familiar not only to George, but to Ann. The judge held that he was emancipated from parental control, and well enough acquainted with his position to make his consent to this advance binding upon him, and this court cannot reverse that finding, depending, as it does, so much upon the demeanour of the witness.

The case of the other son, Francis, is quite different. He was at this time 28 years old, and was apparently living for the most part with his grandmother, so that he was removed from immediate parental control. On the other hand, we now know that he was a schizophrenic. This diagnosis had been made in 1940 when he found one day of life in the Royal Air Force altogether too much for him, and was repeated by a doctor who saw him in 1951. He was not called by either side, it being agreed that his memory was not at all to be trusted. Consent to this, as to other transactions in which he was involved, was written out and sent to him by his father. There is no letter from him anywhere in the correspondence. No representative of the bank ever saw him. He was obviously left purposely in the background. On the other hand, he was capable of teaching in a boys school, which he did for two years towards the end of the war, and was accepted for entry to Edinburgh University after the war, where also he continued for two years as a student. Further, when he went with his brother to be advised over the Hodson loan, the partner in Farrer & Co. who saw him thought him capable of understanding the transaction. Moreover, it has never been alleged that he was at any material time incapacitated from contracting or conducting business affairs by reason of his mental health, though we cannot think that if the bank had known of his history of ill-health they would have acted on the consents he returned signed to his father. But the bank did not know the facts. We have considered anxiously whether, before making an advance, they should have made some inquiry into his circumstances. It is alleged in the particulars of the statement of claim (paragraph 10) that the law presumes undue influence to exist between a person suffering from mental ill-health and the person with whom he resides; but in the end Mr. Bagnall rightly abandoned this plea, for there is no such presumption though actual undue influence may not be difficult to prove. The presumption exists only as to the medical adviser. On the whole, we do not feel able to say that the presumption of undue influence must be held to exist between Francis and his parents having regard to his age and his absence from home, and we conclude that the bank were not bound to make inquiries as to his state of mind or fitness as an object of the power they were affecting to exercise. Accordingly, though this was the plainest breach of trust, we agree with the judge that the bank have a good defence, for they obtained consents from the two children concerned, and they were emancipated . . .

The bank pleads the Limitation Act 1939, and as to this we wholly agree with what the judge said and need not repeat it. So, too, as to the defence of laches[5]. As to acquiescence, we think that this must be looked at rather broadly. We were, of course, pressed with the leading case of *Allcard v Skinner* ((1887) 36 ChD 145), but in that case the plaintiff had her rights fully explained to her by a brother, who was a barrister, and by her solicitor, and yet she took no steps until five or six years later. Even that gave rise to a difference of opinion in a very strong Court of Appeal. In this case it would be wrong, we feel, to place any disability upon the beneficiaries because it so happened that George was a member of the bar, and had been in well-known chambers. He had not been in Chancery chambers where it may be said that these things are better understood; but the real truth of the matter is that a party cannot be held to have acquiesced unless he knew, or ought to have known, what his rights were. On the facts of this case we cannot criticise any of the plaintiffs for failing to appreciate their rights until another junior counsel, whom they consulted on a far-fetched and futile scheme of George's for avoiding estate duty on his mother's death, advised that the advances might be improper. That was in 1954, and thereupon the family, headed, of course, by George, took immediate steps to explore this matter. This is a most complicated action, and many matters had to be explored before an action for breach of trust could properly be mounted. The writ was issued in 1958, and we do not think it right to hold that the plaintiffs

[5] [1962] 1 WLR 86 at 115, per WILBERFORCE J: "I must now deal with certain special defences. (1) The Limitation Act 1939. The relevant provision is section 19 (2), and the whole question is whether the plaintiffs' rights are preserved by the proviso. In my judgment, they are. Undoubtedly they had 'a future interest' and, in my judgment, that interest did not fall into possession when the trustees by an (ex hypothesi) invalid advance raised a sum of money out of the capital. Mrs. Younghusband's consent to the advance was not, in my view, equivalent to a release of her life interest, and the only way (without a release) in which a capital sum could fall into possession would be by means of a valid advance. This defence, in my judgment fails.

(2) Laches. There being an express statutory provision, providing a period of limitation for the plaintiffs' claims, there is no room for the equitable doctrine of laches."

were debarred by acquiescence from bringing an action which otherwise, to the extent we have indicated, is justified.

We have already dealt with the impact of section 61 in general and in detail as we have gone through the various impugned transactions, and on that we need say nothing further."

The Court of Appeal differed on the application of s. 61 to one of the advances. WILBERFORCE J described it (at p. 310): "On September 13, 1948, the bank, as trustees, had also advanced to Francis and George a sum of £2,600 (Advance No. 5) which was applied in discharging a loan, which the bank, as trustee of a settlement of another customer of the bank, a Mrs. Hodson, had made to their mother and which had been charged as a mortgage on their mother's life interest under her uncle's will. This loan (known as the Hodson loan) was also secured by four life insurance policies on the mother's life of a total nominal value of £3,000, whose surrender value was then about £650. On this transaction the sons did have separate advice. Charles Russell & Co. advised that it would be a proper exercise of the power of advancement provided that Francis and George received an adequate quid pro quo in the shape of the assignment to them of the four policies, coupled with covenants by the mother to maintain the premiums and to pay interest on the money advanced. However, the assignment of the life policies, as executed, contained no such covenants by the mother. Burrell of Farrer & Co. approved the draft assignment on behalf of the sons without ever consulting them. The sons retained the life policies till 1953 when they gave them back to their mother, on joining with their mother in executing a mortgage dated March 18, 1953, by the mother to the bank of her life interest under her uncle's will for the sum of £2,000. Apparently this was for the purpose of enabling the commander to raise further sums by charging them again."

The Court of Appeal held that the payment of the £2,000 was a clear breach of trust. UPJOHN LJ, with whom HARMAN LJ concurred, said (at p. 358): "In my judgment, therefore, the only question that arises is whether the bank should be relieved from the consequences of their breach of trust under section 61 of the Trustee Act, 1925, to any, and if so, what extent. This, I think, is a very difficult question. The judgment of the court has already pointed out that the bank were personally innocent, but they were ill-advised by their own solicitors; but the bank must accept responsibility for such negligence, and section 61 cannot possibly be invoked to relieve them from its consequences without more. The circumstance that seems to me to make the application of the section possible is that the bank received the letter quoted in the judgment of the court written by Burrell on behalf of Francis and George saying that the matter was in a satisfactory state. Thereafter it would have been quite unreasonable for the bank to take any further step to assure themselves that the transaction had been properly carried out, and they were lulled into a false sense of security. Section 61 is purely discretionary, and its application necessarily depends on the particular facts of each case. I think, in the circumstances of this case, that I am prepared to hold that the bank acted honestly (that is not in dispute) and reasonably and ought fairly to be excused to the extent of the surrender value of the policies transferred to the boys at the date of the transaction, about £650, but no doubt the exact figure can be ascertained. I do not see how the bank can properly be relieved to any greater extent. The fact that the mother paid the premiums for a few years, so enhancing the value of the policies, is (so far as the bank is concerned) as irrelevant as the fact that, as was to be expected, in due course the boys gave the policies back to their mother, and so, of course, to the commander, thereby losing all benefit from them."

II. Proprietary Remedies[6]

A proprietary remedy is one in which the plaintiff can claim that property in the hands of the defendant is to be treated as that of the plaintiff. It is not the same as a "real" remedy, which entitles the plaintiff to specific recovery. A proprietary remedy entitles the plaintiff to treat any property —usually, of course, money—in the hands of the defendant as being the plaintiff's to the extent that he can claim repayment in full regardless of the defendant's insolvency.

A. Tracing at Common Law

If A lends his car to B and B becomes insolvent, then, with a few exceptions[7], A's car does not go into B's bankruptcy. A steps in and claims it ahead of B's creditors. If B's trustee in bankruptcy refuses to return it, A has an action in detinue and conversion; and, whether or not A succeeds in obtaining an order for specific recovery under the Common Law Procedure Act 1852, A will at least obtain judgment for the full value of the car. However, if A had lent B £500, A's claim for repayment would be reduced to a personal claim and he would have to compete in the bankruptcy with the other creditors.

Sometimes, and within very narrow limits, there is a proprietary remedy at common law. What should be A's right if he lent the car to B, and B wrongfully sold it to C for £500 and then went bankrupt, still holding the £500? Can A claim that the £500 is his, just as the car was? Or does it now turn into a money claim and abate with the other creditors? Or if a factor has received notes payable to A, and the notes have not been paid at the time of the factor's bankruptcy, should A be entitled to claim the money or merely a dividend in the factor's bankruptcy? In *Scott v Surman*[8] WILLES LCJ said: "The assignees [in bankruptcy] having received this money which belongs to the plaintiffs and ought not to be applied

[6] H & M, pp. 561–576; K & S, pp. 386–401; P & M, pp. 403–411; Pettit, pp. 460–470; Snell, pp. 284–292. Goff and Jones, *Law of Restitution* (1966) chap. 2; (1959) 75 LQR 234 (R. H. Maudsley); (1971) 34 MLR 12 (F. O. B. Babafemi); (1975) 28 CLP 64 (A. J. Oakley); (1976) 40 Conv (NS) 277 (R. A. Pearce). For a penetrating analysis of tracing rules in the trust context and of their application in the sphere of commerce, see (1976) 92 LQR 360, 528; (1977) 93 LQR 487 (R. M. Goode); *Aluminium Industrie Vaassen BV v Ramalpa Aluminium Ltd* [1976] 1 WLR 676; [1976] 2 All ER 552.

[7] E.g. Bankruptcy Act 1914, s. 5 (reputed ownership).

[8] (1742) Willes 400 at 405.

to pay the bankrupt's debts, and they ought to have paid it to the plaintiffs, and not having done so, this action will lie against them for so much money had and received to the use of the plaintiffs." That is an example of the common law action for money had and received being used as a proprietary remedy, and entitling the plaintiff to claim the full amount due from the assignee in bankruptcy.

Little is heard of this doctrine in real life. The leading case is *Taylor v Plumer*[9]. Sir Thomas Plumer had given money to Walsh, a stockbroker, for investment. Walsh improperly purchased American investments and bullion and hurried to Falmouth to take a packet for Lisbon and so to North America. He was apprehended while waiting for the packet to put to sea, and the investments and bullion were seized. His assignees in bankruptcy claimed in this action to recover them from Sir Thomas. They failed. In other words Sir Thomas had a right to claim against Walsh the full value of the property into which money given to Walsh had been converted, and not merely a dividend in the bankruptcy. The limits of such a claim were laid down by Lord ELLENBOROUGH[10]. "It makes no difference in reason or law into what other form, different from the original, the change may have been made, whether it be into that of promissory notes for the security of the money which was produced by the sale of the goods of the principal, as in *Scott v Surman* ((1742) Willes 400), or into other merchandize, as in *Whitecomb v Jacob* ((1710) 1 Salk 160), for the product of or substitute for the original thing still follows the nature of the thing itself, as long as it can be ascertained to be such, and the right only ceases when the means of ascertainment fail, which is the case when the subject is turned into money, and mixed and confounded in a general mass of the same description. The difficulty which arises in such a case is a difficulty of fact and not of law, and the dictum that money has no ear-mark must be understood in the same way; i.e., as predicated only of an undivided and undistinguishable mass of current money. But money in a bag, or otherwise kept apart from other money, guineas, or other coin marked (if the fact were so) for the purpose of being distinguished, are so far ear-marked as to fall within the rule on this subject, which applies to every other description of personal property whilst it remains, (as the property in question did), in the hands of the factor, or his general legal representatives. That trust property in the possession of a factor empowered to dispose of it for his principal does not pass to his assignees under the stat. *Jac.* 1, upon his becoming a bankrupt, was established in the case of *L'Apostre v Le Plaistrier* ((1708) 2 Eq Abr 133 (n)), first tried before Lord *Holt* at Nisi Prius in 1708, and afterwards so adjudged upon a case made for the opinion of the Court of King's Bench. The same point was held by Lord *Cowper* in *Copeman v Gallant* ((1716) 1 P Wms 318 at 320). And in *Whitecomb v Jacob*, in Chancery (1710) Trin. 9 Ann. (1 Salk 160), the doctrine was carried further, and to an extent which fully comprehends the present case. There, a factor entrusted with the disposal of merchandize for his principal, sold it, received the money, and, instead of paying the money to his principal, vested the produce in other goods, and died indebted in debts of a higher nature. There it was held that those goods

[9] (1815) 3 M & S 562.
[10] At p. 575.

should be taken as the merchant's estate, and not the factor's; and though that was not the case of a factor becoming a *bankrupt*, yet it makes no difference whether the person claiming to represent the factor was his executor or administrator, or his *assignee*; except only as far as the case might be affected by the stat. *Jac.* 1, and which it cannot be, if the factor bankrupt had the order and disposition of the property entrusted to him in the character of factor only, and not as owner: for that point the above-cited cases of *L'Apostre v Le Plaistrier* and *Copeman v Gallant*, are authorities."[11]

In real life, of course, transfers of money are usually made by way of payment through bank accounts, and the money so paid has become mixed with other money of the payee. That situation is beyond the limit of the common law proprietary remedy.

B. Tracing in Equity

i. UNMIXED FUNDS

Where property is taken by a person in a fiduciary relation to the plaintiff, the plaintiff may claim that property from the fiduciary, or, if it has been sold, may claim the proceeds of sale; or may follow the property into the hands of a third party, until it comes into the hands of a bona fide purchaser for value[12].

ii. MIXED FUNDS

In *Banque Belge pour l'Etranger v Hambrouck* ([1921] 1 KB 321) ATKIN LJ said (at p. 335): "The question always was, Had the means of ascertainment failed? But if in 1815 the common law halted outside the bankers' door, by 1879 equity had had the courage to lift the latch, walk in and examine the books: *Re Hallett's Estate* ((1880) 13 ChD 696). I see no reason why the means of ascertainment should not now be available both for common law and equity proceedings."

RE HALLETT'S ESTATE

(1880) 13 ChD 696 (CA, Sir George JESSEL MR, BAGGALLAY and THESIGER LJJ.)

Henry Hughes Hallett was a solicitor. He was trustee of his own marriage settlement, and had paid some moneys from that trust into his own bank account.

He was solicitor to Mrs. Cotterill, and had been entrusted by her with money for investment. Part of this money was also paid into Hallett's bank account.

Hallett made various payments from, and into, the account, and also incurred further debts. At the date of his death, the account held sufficient funds to meet the claims of the trustees of the marriage settlement and of Mrs. Cotterill, but not the personal debts as well.

[11] See also *Banque Belge pour l'Etranger v Hambrouck*, [1921] 1 KB 321.
[12] *Thorndike v Hunt* (1859), 3 De G & J 563; *Taylor v Blakelock* (18861), 32 ChD 560; *Thomson v Clydesdale Bank* [1893] AC 282; *Coleman v Bucks and Oxon Union Bank* [1897] 2 Ch 243.

In an action for the administration of Hallett's estate, the main question was whether the trust and Mrs. Cotterill could claim in priority to the creditors.

Held. (i) Both the trust and Mrs. Cotterill were entitled to a charge upon the moneys in the bank account in priority to the general creditors; (ii) (THESIGER, LJ, dissenting) the various payments by Hallett out of the account must be treated as payments of his own money and not that of the trust or Mrs. Cotterill.

JESSEL MR: There is no doubt, therefore, that Mr. *Hallett* stood in a fiduciary position towards Mrs. *Cotterill*. Mr. *Hallett*, before his death, I regret to say, improperly sold the bonds and put the money to his general account at his bankers. It is not disputed that the money remained at his bankers mixed with his own money at the time of his death; that is, he had not drawn out that money from his bankers. In that position of matters Mrs. *Cotterill* claimed to be entitled to receive the proceeds, or the amount of the proceeds, of the bonds out of the money in the hands of Mr. *Hallett's* bankers at the time of his death, and that claim was allowed by the learned Judge of the Court below, and I think was properly so allowed. Indeed, as I understand the doctrines of Equity, it would have been too clear a case for argument, except for another decision of that learned Judge himself, *Ex parte Dale & Co* ((1879) 11 ChD 772). The modern doctrine of Equity as regards property disposed of by persons in a fiduciary position is a very clear and well-established doctrine. You can, if the sale was rightful, take the proceeds of the sale, if you can identify them. If the sale was wrongful, you can still take the proceeds of the sale, in a sense adopting the sale for the purpose of taking the proceeds, if you can identify them. There is no distinction, therefore, between a rightful and a wrongful disposition of the property, so far as regards the right of the beneficial owner to follow the proceeds. But it very often happens that you cannot identify the proceeds. The proceeds may have been invested together with money belonging to the person in a fiduciary position, in a purchase. He may have bought land with it, for instance, or he may have bought chattels with it. Now, what is the position of the beneficial owner as regards such purchases? I will, first of all, take his position when the purchase is clearly made with what I will call, for shortness, the trust money, although it is not confined, as I will shew presently, to express trusts. In that case, according to the now well-established doctrine of Equity, the beneficial owner has a right to elect either to take the property purchased, or to hold it as a security for the amount of the trust money laid out in the purchase; or, as we generally express it, he is entitled at his election either to take the property, or to have a charge on the property for the amount of the trust money. But in the second case, where a trustee has mixed the money with his own, there is the distinction, that the *cestui que trust*, or beneficial owner, can no longer elect to take the property, because it is no longer bought with the trust-money simply and purely, but with a mixed fund. He is, however, still entitled to a charge on the property purchased, for the amount of the trust-money laid out in the purchase; and that charge is quite independent of the fact of the amount laid out by the trustee. The moment you get a substantial portion of it furnished by the trustee, using the word "trustee" in the sense I have mentioned, as including all persons in a fiduciary relation, the right to the charge follows. That is the modern doctrine of Equity. Has it ever been suggested, until very recently, that there is any distinction between an express trustee, or an agent, or a bailee, or a collector of rents, or anybody else in a fiduciary position? I have never heard, until quite recently, such a distinction suggested. It cannot, as far as I am aware (and since this Court sat last to hear this case, I have taken the trouble to look for authority), be found in any reported case even suggested, except in the recent decision of Mr. Justice *Fry*, to which I shall draw attention presently. It can have no foundation in principle, because the beneficial ownership is the same, wherever the legal ownership may be. If you have goods bargained and sold to a man upon trust to sell and hand over the net proceeds to another, that other is the beneficial owner; but if instead of being bargained and sold, so as to vest the legal ownership in the trustee, they are deposited with him to sell as agent, so that the legal ownership remains in the beneficial owner, can it be supposed, in a Court of Equity, that the rights of the beneficial owner are different, he being entire beneficial owner in both cases? I say on principle it is impossible to imagine there can be any difference. In practice we know there is no difference, because the moment you get into a Court of Equity, where a principal can sue an agent as well as a *cestui que trust* can sue a trustee, no such distinction was ever suggested, as far as I am aware. Therefore, the moment you establish the fiduciary relation, the modern rules of Equity, as regards following trust money, apply. I intentionally say modern rules, because it must not be forgotten that the rules of Courts of Equity are not, like the rules of the Common Law, supposed to have been established from time immemorial. It is perfectly well known that they have been established from time to time—altered, improved, and refined from time to time. In many cases we know the names of the Chancellors who invented them. No doubt they were invented for the purpose of securing the better administration of justice, but still they were invented. Take such things as these: the separate use of a married woman, the restraint on alienation, the modern rule against perpetuities, and the rules of equitable waste. We can name the Chancellors who first invented them, and state the date when they were first introduced into Equity jurisprudence; and, therefore, in cases of this kind, the older precedents in Equity are of very little value. The doctrines are progressive, refined, and improved; and if we want to know what the rules of Equity are, we must look, of course, rather to the more modern than the more ancient cases.

Now that being the established doctrine of Equity on this point, I will take the case of the pure bailee. If the bailee sells the goods bailed, the bailor can in Equity follow the proceeds, and can follow the proceeds wherever they can be distinguished, either being actually kept separate, or being mixed up with other moneys. I have only to advert to one other point, and that is this—supposing, instead of being invested in the purchase of land or goods, the moneys were simply mixed with other moneys of the trustee, using the term again in its full sense as including every person in a fiduciary relation, does it make any difference according to the modern doctrine of Equity? I say none. It would be very remarkable if it were to do so. Supposing the trust money was 1,000 sovereigns, and the trustee put them into a bag, and by mistake, or accident, or otherwise, dropped a sovereign of his own into the bag. Could anybody suppose that a Judge in Equity would find any difficulty in saying that the *cestui que trust* had a right to take 1,000 sovereigns out of that bag? I do not like to call it a charge of 1,000 sovereigns on the 1,001 sovereigns, but that is the effect of it. I have no doubt of it. It would make no difference if, instead of one sovereign, it was another 1,000 sovereigns. . . .

[His Lordship referred to various authorities, including *Taylor v Plumer* ((1815) 3 M & S 562) from which he quoted Lord ELLENBOROUGH:] "and the right only ceases when the means of ascertainment fail". That is correct. Now there comes a point which is not correct, but which I am afraid only ceases to be correct because Lord *Ellenborough's* knowledge of the rules of Equity was not quite commensurate with his knowledge of the rules of Common Law, "which is the case when the subject is turned into money, and mixed and confounded in a general mass of the same description". He was not aware of the rule of Equity which gave you a charge—that if you lent £1,000 of your own and £1,000 trust money on a bond for £2,000, or on a mortgage for £2,000, or on a promissory note for £2,000, Equity could follow it, and create a charge; but he gives that, not as law—the law is that it only fails when the means of ascertainment fail—he gives it as a case in which the means of ascertainment fail, not being aware of this refinement of Equity by which the means of ascertainment still remain. With the exception of that one fact, which is rather a fact than a statement of law, the rest of the judgment is in my opinion admirable. It goes on: "The difficulty which arises in such a case is a difficulty of fact, and not of law, and the *dictum* that money has no ear-mark must be understood in the same way, *i.e.*, as predicated only of an undivided and undistinguishable mass of current money." There, again, as I say, he did not know that Equity would have followed the money, even if put into a bag or into an undistinguishable mass, by taking out the same quantity . . .

I think after those authorities it must now be considered settled that there is no distinction, and never was a distinction, between a person occupying one fiduciary position or another fiduciary position as to the right of the beneficial owner to follow the trust fund, and that those cases which have been cited at Law so far from establishing a distinction, establish the contrary; and that the mere error of supposing that Equity could not follow or distinguish money in the cases supposed, if error it was, and perhaps it was not so originally (I am not sure that the doctrine of equity had got so far at the first start, but it was certainly an error at a later period), is attributable really to the fact that the Judges who followed the earlier cases were not aware of what I may call the gradual refinement of the doctrine of equity. Therefore, looking at the authorities to find out the principle, you do not find out any such distinction established as that suggested by Mr. Justice *Fry*, or anything of the kind even mentioned in them; and I do not know of anything more mischievous than for a Judge to say, "The cases before me establish no principle, but they quite establish something else which I will now enunciate, and therefore hold myself bound by those cases to establish another principle which was never suggested or thought of by the Judges who decided the original cases." It is only out of my great respect and esteem for the learned Judge from whom this appeal comes that I have thought it right to go so fully into the cases to shew that there is no foundation whatever for the suggested distinction, and therefore his decision in this case rests on no trivial or slight distinction between this case and the case of *Ex parte Dale & Co* ((1879) 11 ChD 772), but is grounded on the well-ascertained doctrines of equity.

[On the question whether the Rule in *Clayton's* case (1816) 1 Mer 572 applied as between the claims of the beneficiaries and Hallett's estate[13], his Lordship continued:] I will first of all consider the case on principle, and then I will consider how far we are bound by authority to come to a decision opposed to principle. It may well be, and sometimes does so happen, that we are bound to come to a decision opposed to principle. Now, first upon principle, nothing can be better settled, either in our own law, or, I suppose, the law of all civilised countries, than this, that where a man does an act which may be rightfully performed, he cannot say that that act was intentionally and in fact done wrongly. A man who has a right of entry cannot say he committed a trespass in entering. A man who sells the goods of another as agent for the owner cannot prevent the owner adopting the sale, and deny that he acted as agent for the owner. It runs throughout our law, and we are familiar with numerous instances in the law of real property. A man who grants a lease believing he has sufficient estate to grant it, although it turns out that he has not, but has a power which enables him to grant it, is not allowed to say he did not grant it under the power. Wherever it can be done rightfully, he is not allowed to say, against the person entitled to the property or the right, that he has done it wrongfully. That is the universal law.

When we come to apply that principle to the case of a trustee who has blended trust moneys with his own, it seems to me perfectly plain that he cannot be heard to say that he took away the trust money when he had a right to take away his own money. The simplest case put is the mingling of trust moneys in a bag with money of the trustee's own. Suppose he has a hundred sovereigns in a bag, and he adds to them another hundred sovereigns of his own, so that they are commingled in such a way that they cannot be distinguished, and the next day he draws out for his own purposes £100, is it tolerable for anybody to allege that what he drew out was the first £100, the trust money, and that he misappropriated it, and left his own £100 in the bag? It is obvious he must have taken away that which he had a right to take away, his own £100. What difference does it make if, instead of being in a bag, he deposits it with his banker, and then pays in other money of his own, and draws out some money for his own purposes? Could he say that he had actually drawn out anything but his own

[13] As there were sufficient moneys to satisfy both those prior claims, no question of competition between the marriage settlement trustees and Mrs. Cotterill arose. FRY J had held, below, that as between two *cestuis que trust* whose money had been paid by a trustee into his own account, the rule in *Clayton*'s case applied. See *Re Diplock* [1948] Ch 465 at 554.

money? His money was there, and he had a right to draw it out, and why should the natural act of simply drawing out the money be attributed to anything except to his ownership of money which was at the bankers.

It is said, no doubt, that according to the modern theory of banking, the deposit banker is a debtor for the money. So he is, and not a trustee in the strict sense of the word. At the same time one must recollect that the position of a deposit banker is different from that of an ordinary debtor. Still he is for some purposes a debtor, and it is said if a debt of this kind is paid by a banker, although the total balance is the amount owing by the banker, yet considering the repayments and the sums paid in by the depositor, you attribute the first sum drawn out to the first sum paid in. That was a rule first established by Sir *William Grant* in *Clayton's Case* ((1816) 1 Mer 572), a very convenient rule, and I have nothing to say against it unless there is evidence either of agreement to the contrary or of circumstances from which a contrary intention must be presumed, and then of course that which is a mere presumption of law gives way to those other considerations. Therefore, it does appear to me there is nothing in the world laid down by Sir *William Grant* in *Clayton's Case*, or in the numerous cases which follow it, which in the slightest degree affects the principle, which I consider to be clearly established.

[His Lordship then held that he was not bound by *Pennell v Deffell* (1853) 4 De GM & G 372, and concluded:] Therefore in my opinion, the appeal must be allowed[14].

In *Roscoe v Winder* ([1915] 1 Ch 62) an agreement for the sale of the goodwill of a business provided that the purchaser, one Wigham, should collect certain of the book debts and pay that money over to the vendor. Wigham collected the debts and paid part of the money, £455 18s. 11d., into his private account. A few days later the balance in the account was reduced to £25 18s. At the date of Wigham's death, the balance had risen to £358 5s., 5d.

The question was the extent to which the plaintiffs could claim a charge under the rules in *Hallett's* case. SARGANT J held that Wigham had held the money as trustee; but that the charge was limited to £25 18s., the lowest intermediate balance subsequent to the appropriation. He said (at p. 67): "But there is a further circumstance in the present case which seems to me to be conclusive in favour of the defendant as regards the greater part of the balance of 358*l*. 5*s*. 5*d*. It appears that after the payment in by the debtor of a portion of the book debts which he had received the balance at the bank on May 19, 1913, was reduced by his drawings to a sum of 25*l*.18*s*. only on May 21. So that, although the ultimate balance at the debtor's death was about 358*l*., there had been an intermediate balance of only 25*l*. 18*s*. The result of that seems to me to be that the trust moneys cannot possibly be traced into this common fund, which was standing to the debtor's credit at his death, to an extent of more than 25*l*. 18*s*., because, although prima facie under the second rule in *Re Hallett's Estate* ((1880) 13 ChD 696) any drawings

[14] See also *Re Oatway* [1903] 2 Ch 356, explained in *Re Tilley's Will Trusts* [1967] Ch 1179, [1967] 2 All ER 303, p. 648, post.

out by the debtor ought to be attributed to the private moneys which he had at the bank and not to the trust moneys, yet, when the drawings out had reached such an amount that the whole of his private money part had been exhausted, it necessarily followed that the rest of the drawings must have been against trust moneys. There being on May 21, 1913, only 25*l*. 18*s*., in all, standing to the credit of the debtor's account, it is quite clear that on that day he must have denuded his account of all the trust moneys there—the whole 455*l*. 18*s*. 11*d*.—except to the extent of 25*l*. 18*s*.

Practically, what Mr. Martelli and Mr. Hansell have been asking me to do—although I think Mr. Hansell in particular rather disguised the claim by the phraseology he used—is to say that the debtor, by paying further moneys after May 21 into this common account, was impressing upon those further moneys so paid in the like trust or obligation, or charge of the nature of a trust, which had formerly been impressed upon the previous balances to the credit of that account. No doubt, Mr. Hansell did say 'No. I am only asking you to treat the account as a whole, and to consider the balance from time to time standing to the credit of that account as subject to one continual charge or trust.' But I think that really is using words which are not appropriate to the facts. You must, for the purpose of tracing, which was the process adopted in *Re Hallett's Estate*, put your finger on some definite fund which either remains in its original state or can be found in another shape. That is tracing, and tracing, by the very facts of this case, seems to be absolutely excluded except as to the 25*l*. 18*s*.

Then, apart from tracing, it seems to me possible to establish this claim against the ultimate balance of 358*l*. 5*s*. 5*d*. only by saying that something was done, with regard to the additional moneys which are needed to make up that balance, by the person to whom those moneys belonged, the debtor, to substitute those moneys for the purpose of, or to impose upon those moneys a trust equivalent to, the trust which rested on the previous balance. Of course, if there was anything like a separate trust account, the payment of the further moneys into that account would, in itself, have been quite a sufficient indication of the intention of the debtor to substitute those additional moneys for the original trust moneys, and accordingly to impose, by way of substitution, the old trusts upon those additional moneys. But, in a case where the account into which the moneys are paid is the general trading account of the debtor on which he has been accustomed to draw both in the ordinary course and in breach of trust when there were trust funds standing to the credit of that account which were convenient for that purpose, I think it is impossible to attribute to him that by the mere payment into the account of further moneys, which to a large extent he subsequently used for purposes of his own, he intended to clothe those moneys with a trust in favour of the plaintiffs.

Certainly, after having heard *Re Hallett's Estate* ((1880) 13 ChD 696) stated over and over again, I should have thought that the general view of that decision was that it only applied to such an amount of the balance ultimately standing to the credit of the trustee as did not exceed the lowest balance of the account during the intervening period."

RE DIPLOCK

[1948] Ch 465, [1948] 2 All ER 318 (CA, Lord GREENE MR, WROTTESLEY and EVERSHED LJJ)

By his will, Caleb Diplock directed his executors to apply his residuary estate "for such charitable institutions or other charitable or benevolent object or objects in England" as they should "in their . . . absolute discretion select".

It was assumed that the will created a valid charitable trust; and the executors distributed some £203,000 among 139 different charities before its validity was challenged by the next of kin. The House of Lords held the bequest void in *Chichester Diocesan Fund and Board of Finance (Inc) v Simpson* ([1944] AC 341, [1944] 2 All ER 60, p. 366, ante).

The next of kin of the testator, having exhausted their remedy against the executors, made claims to recover the money from the charities. These claims against the different charities varied in details; but on principle,

Held. The next of kin could succeed; both in respect of (i) a claim *in personam*. An unpaid or under-paid legatee was entitled to a personal claim in equity against an overpaid or wrongly paid legatee. This aspect of the case was later affirmed on appeal to the House of Lords in *Ministry of Health v Simpson* ([1951] AC 251, [1950] 2 All ER 1137); and (ii) a claim *in rem*. The right to trace into a mixed fund was not restricted to cases where the defendant was the person who had mixed the moneys, or where the fiduciary relationship, necessary for a proprietary claim in equity, existed between the parties to the action.

The claim *in rem* only is discussed in this extract.

LORD GREENE MR: The first question which appears to us to fall for decision on this part of the present appeals may, we think, be thus formulated: Did the power of equity to treat Diplock "money" as recoverable from the charity, which undoubtedly existed down to the moment when the cheque was paid by the bank on which it was drawn, cease the moment that the "money" by the process of "mixture" came to be represented by an accretion to or an enlargement of the chose in action consisting of a debt already owing to the charity by its own bankers? Wynn-Parry J, in effect, decided that it did. His reason for taking this view, shortly stated, was as follows: The principle applicable was to be extracted from the decision in *Hallett's* case ((1880) 13 ChD 696) and that principle was in no way extended by the decision in *Sinclair v Brougham* ([1914] AC 398). The principle can operate only in cases where the mixing takes place in breach of a trust, actual or constructive, or in breach of some other fiduciary relationship and in proceedings against the trustee or fiduciary agent: here the mixing was not of this character, since it was effected by an innocent volunteer: there is no ground on which, according to principle, the conscience of such a volunteer can be held in equity to be precluded from setting up a title adverse to the claim: in every case, therefore, where a "mixture" has been carried out by the charity, the claim, whether it be against a mixed monetary fund or against investments made by means of such a mixed fund, must fail in limine.

Now we may say at once that this view of the inability of equity to deal with the case of the volunteer appears to us, with all respect to Wynn-Parry J, to be in conflict with the principles expounded, particularly by Lord Parker, in *Sinclair v Bougham*. If Lord Parker means what we think he meant, and if what he said is to be accepted as a correct statement of the law, Mr. Pennycuick, who argued this part of the case on behalf of the charities, admittedly felt great difficulty in supporting this part of the reasoning of the learned judge. We shall deal further with Lord Parker's observations on this topic when we come to them in our examination of *Sinclair v Brougham*. But here we may conveniently summarize what we consider to be the effect of them as follows: Where an innocent volunteer (as distinct from a purchaser for value without notice) mixes "money" of his own with "money" which in equity belongs to another person, or is found in possession of such a mixture, although that other person cannot claim a charge on the mass superior to the claim of the volunteer he is entitled, nevertheless, to a charge ranking pari passu with the claim of the volunteer. And Lord Parker's reasons for taking this view appear to have been on the following lines: Equity regards the rights of the equitable owner as being "in effect rights of property" though not recognized as such by the common law. Just as a volunteer is not allowed by equity in the case, e.g., of a conveyance of the legal estate in land, to set up his legal title adversely to the claim of a person having an equitable interest in the land, so in the case of a mixed fund of money the volunteer must give such recognition as equity considers him in conscience (as a volunteer) bound to give to the interest of the equitable owner of the money which has been mixed with the volunteer's own. But this burden on the conscience of the volunteer is not such as to compel him to treat the claim of the equitable owner as paramount. That would be to treat the volunteer as strictly as if he himself stood in a fiduciary relationship to the equitable owner which ex hypothesi he does not. The volunteer is under no greater duty of conscience to recognize the interest of the equitable owner than that which lies upon a person having an equitable interest in one of two trust funds of "money" which have become mixed towards the equitable owner of the other. Such a person is not in conscience bound to give precedence to the equitable owner of the other of the two funds.

We may enlarge upon the implications which appear to us to be contained in Lord Parker's reasoning. First of all, it appears to us to be wrong to treat the principle which underlies *Hallett's* case as coming into operation only where the person who does the mixing is not only in a fiduciary position but is also a *party to the tracing action*. If he is a party to the action he is, of course, precluded from setting up a case inconsistent with the obligations of his fiduciary position. But supposing that he is not a party? The result cannot surely depend on what equity would or would not have allowed him to say if he had been a party. Suppose that the sole trustee of (say) five separate trusts draws 100*l*. out of each of the trust banking accounts, pays the resulting 500*l*. into an account which he opens in his own name, draws a cheque for 500*l*. on that account and gives it as a present to his son. A claim by the five sets of beneficiaries to follow the money of their respective trusts would be a claim against the son. He would stand in no fiduciary relationship to any of them. We recoil from the conclusion that all five beneficiaries would be dismissed empty handed by a court of equity and the son left to enjoy what in equity was originally their money. Yet that is the conclusion to which the reasoning of the learned judge would lead us. Lord Parker's reasoning, on the other hand, seems to us to lead to the conclusion that each set of beneficiaries could set up its equitable interest which would prevail against the bare legal title of the son as a volunteer and that they would be entitled to share pari passu in so much of the fund or its proceeds as remained identifiable.

An even more striking example was admitted by Mr. Pennycuick to be the result of his argument, and he vigorously maintained that it followed inevitably from the principles of equity involved. If a fiduciary agent takes cash belonging to his principal and gives it to his son, who takes it innocently, then so long as the son keeps it unmixed with other cash in one trouser pocket, the principal can follow it and claim it back. Once, however, the son, being under no fiduciary duty to the principal, transfers it to his other trouser pocket in which there are reposing a coin or two of his own of the same denomination, the son, by a sort of process of accretion, acquires an indefeasible title to what the moment before the transfer he could not have claimed as his own. This result appears to us to stultify the beneficent powers of equity to protect and enforce what it recognizes as equitable rights of property which subsist until they are destroyed by the operation of a purchase for value without notice.

The error into which, we respectfully suggest, the learned judge has fallen is in thinking that what, in *Hallett's* case was only the method (there appropriate) of bringing a much wider-based principle of equity into operation—viz., the method by which a fiduciary agent, who has himself wrongfully mixed the funds, is prohibited from asserting a breach of his duty—is an element which must necessarily be present before equity can afford protection to the equitable rights which it has brought into existence. We are not prepared to see the arm of equity thus shortened.

It is now time to examine in some detail the case of *Sinclair v Brougham* ([1914] AC 398). Before us it was argued, on behalf of the respondents, that the principle on which it was decided was not that applied in *Hallett's* case ((1880) 13 ChD 696) but a different one altogether, invented with a view to solving a particular problem. We do not agree. The principle, in our view, was clearly the same; but in its application to new facts fresh light was thrown upon it, and it was shown to have a much wider scope than a narrow reading of *Hallett's* case itself would suggest.

We have examined with care not only the opinions themselves but the printed cases and the arguments of counsel as well as the judgments of the majority and of Fletcher Moulton LJ in the Court of Appeal. It is in the context of this material that the speeches must be interpreted.

The contest in *Sinclair v Brougham* was between shareholders and depositors in respect of a miscellaneous mass of assets distributable by the liquidator in the winding up of a building society. The deposits had been made, and the assets were used, in connexion with a banking business carried on in the name of the society but beyond its powers. Each of the two classes claimed priority over the other. Until the case reached the House of Lords the possibility that they might rank pari passu does not appear to have been considered. The majority of the Court of Appeal, affirming Neville J, gave the shareholders priority over the depositors. Fletcher Moulton LJ would have given the depositors priority over the shareholders. The House of Lords held that both views were wrong and that on the principle on which *Hallett's* case was founded, the two classes shared rateably. In one respect, no doubt, this application of the principle is an extension of it since, although the right of individuals to trace their own money (if they could) was preserved in the order of the House, the order provided for tracing the aggregate contributions of the two classes as classes. *Hallett's* case was, of course, based on the right of an individual to follow what he could in equity identify as his own money. The extension of the principle in *Sinclair v Brougham* was the obvious and, indeed, on the facts, the only practical method of securing a just distribution of the assets. The importance of the point must not, however, be overlooked in considering the arguments and the speeches.

Apparently it had not occurred to any of the judges in the lower courts or to any of the eminent counsel who signed the cases or argued in the House of Lords that *Hallett's* case ((1880) 13 ChD 696) had anything to do with such a case as *Sinclair v Brougham* ([1914] AC 398). There is not a mention of it in any of the judgments below or in either of the printed cases or in argument in the House of Lords until Lord Haldane LC ([1914] AC 398 at 404, 406, 407) suggested that the principle of *Hallett's* case might apply. The point thus offered was accepted by counsel, who proceeded to base arguments upon it. Mr. Cave and Mr. Tomlin (as they then were), submitted on behalf of the depositors that *Hallett's* case was really based, "not upon trusteeship in the narrow sense, but upon ownership" and argued that if the property of B is found in the hands of A, prima facie, A "is in a wide sense in a fiduciary relationship towards B because equity affects his conscience with regard to that particular property". This proposition, as stated, was not accepted by the House. From it counsel deduced the consequence that the depositors were entitled to priority in respect of the moneys which they had deposited. This argument was, of course, quite different from the other two arguments adduced on behalf of the depositors, viz., that based on money had and received and that based on the principles enunciated by Fletcher Moulton LJ in his dissenting judgment.

Mr. Upjohn and Mr. Younger (as he then was) for the shareholders agreed that (subject to a qualification not material on the facts) "money paid under an ultra vires contract does not become the property of the society but remains the property of the payer, and so long as he can identify it he may trace it through any number of changes and claim it on the footing that it is and always has been his property". But a claim based on property was, they said (and this relates to the point mentioned above) impossible in that case because no tracing order could be made without identification and the doctrine of tracing could not be applied to the collective claims of the depositors as a class. They also said that *Hallett's* case was confined to fiduciary relationship in a strict sense.

Now it is to be remembered that the arguments of counsel on either side were directed to claiming priority for their respective clients and much of the reasoning in the speeches is directed to negativing these claims to priority. The House held that although the equity underlying *Hallett's* case was applicable, the result of its proper application was that the conclusion sought by both arguments was wrong and that the fund was divisible rateably between the two classes of claimants. We may call attention in passing to the manner in which the House dealt with the argument of counsel for the shareholders that there could be no tracing save in favour of an individual who could follow and (in equity) identify his own property and that in consequence there could not be what would be in substance a tracing order in favour of a class. This argument does appear to raise a technical difficulty. But the House brushed it aside. Lord Sumner's speech contains the clearest exposition of the reasons for dealing with it in the manner approved by the House. He said ([1914] AC 398 at 459): "My Lords, I agree, without recapitulating reasons, that the principle on which *Hallett's* case is founded justifies an order allowing the appellants to follow the assets, not merely to the verge of actual identification, but even somewhat further in a case like the present, where after a process of exclusion only two classes or groups of persons, having equal claims, are left in and all superior claims have been eliminated. Tracing in a sense it is not, for we know that the money coming from A went into one security and that coming from B into another, and that the two securities did not probably depreciate exactly in the same percentage, and we know further that no one will ever know any more. Still I think this well within the 'tracing' equity, and that among persons making up these two groups the principle of rateable division of the assets is sound." This does at least show that in applying the equitable principle equity is entitled to adopt that method of application which in the circumstances of the case will lead to an equitable result.

We now proceed to consider some of the salient facts in *Sinclair v Brougham* ([1914] AC 398).

The case is complicated by the fact that the claims of the depositors came to be considered at a time when the society was in liquidation, with the result that the shareholders came into the picture as competing claimants against the assets. But a problem precisely similar in all essentials would, as it appears to us, have arisen if the depositors had claimed to trace their money while the society was still a going concern. In that case the shareholders would not have appeared as claimants at all; the competition would have been between the depositors and the society. In the actual case the shareholders were the claimants but all that they could claim was such money as the society itself could have claimed as between itself and the depositors. We shall not be thought disrespectful if we call attention, perhaps rather more emphatically than was sometimes thought necessary in the opinions as delivered, to certain distinctions which must be borne clearly in mind. The first is the distinction between the directors and the society which could not be bound in any way or for any purpose, directly or indirectly, by the ultra vires acts of the directors. The second is the distinction between the society and the shareholders who were only entitled to such equitable rights in the assets as the society itself could have claimed, for that was all that the liquidators had the right to give them.

The third distinction is of no less importance, that between the ultra vires business (which was not in law the society's business) and the assets requiring distribution which were in the society's name and of which the society was the legal owner. So far as we have been able to discover, all the assets in question stood, as we would have expected them to stand, in the name of the society—they were, as Lord Dunedin said, "in the society's strong box"—and it was thus that they came into the hands of the liquidator. None of them was in the name of the directors who were, therefore, not necessary parties to the proceedings. In view of the argument addressed to us and of the judgment of Wynn-Parry J on the point, this is important and for the following reason. The starting point of the claim of the depositors was the existence of a fiduciary relationship as between themselves and the directors: that relationship arose from the fact that the depositors had entrusted their money to the directors for the purpose of a business which could not lawfully be carried on, so that the directors must be treated as holding the money on behalf of the depositors. If the directors had paid the money of a depositor into their own banking account he would have had an action against them exactly similar to the action in *Hallett's* case and it would have been correctly said that the directors could not be heard to set up a title of their own to the money standing in the account adverse to the claim of the depositor. But nothing of the sort could be said if the directors paid the money into the account of the society at its bankers. Neither the conscience of the society nor of its liquidator (if it went into liquidation) could ever come into the picture on the basis of a fiduciary relationship since the only parties to that relationship were the directors and the depositors. The society could not have been a party to it, since it had no power to accept the depositor's money. If, therefore, in such a case, the depositor could claim a charge on the society's account with its bankers the claim must have been based on some wider principle.

What can that principle be? In our judgment it must be the principle clearly indicated by Lord Parker, that equity may operate on the conscience not merely of those who acquire a legal title in breach of some trust, express or constructive, or of some other fiduciary obligation, but of volunteers provided that as a result of what has gone before some equitable proprietary interest has been created and attaches to the property in the hands of the volunteer[15].

In *Re Tilley's Will Trusts* ([1967] Ch 1179, [1967] 2 All ER 303)[16] the testator, Henry Tilley, appointed his widow as an executrix and gave her a life interest in his estate with remainder to his children, Charles and Mabel. Mrs. Tilley, with the help of a bank overdraft, embarked on a highly successful career as a dealer in property. By 1952, having dealt with some properties, she had accumulated £2,237 trust capital, and over the years had thoroughly confused this trust money with her own private funds. She had overdraft facilities for over £22,000 in 1939, and by 1945

[15] See also *Re J. Leslie Engineering Co Ltd* [1976] 1 WLR 292, [1976] 2 All ER 85.

[16] (1968) CLJ 28 (G. H. Jones). See also *Scott v Scott* (1963) 109 CLR 649; Restatement of Restitution, § 142.

the overdraft was £23,536. She died in 1959, leaving an estate valued at some £94,000. The plaintiff, as executor of Mabel's estate, brought an action for an account of what was due to Mabel's estate.

The question was whether the property should be treated as Mrs. Tilley's, or whether all or part of it should be treated as belonging to the trusts of the testator's estate, and if so, in what proportions.

UNGOED-THOMAS J held that it was all her own free estate, on the ground that trust moneys had not been used for the property purchases. He said (at p. 1193): "The trust moneys were not invested in properties at all but merely went in reduction of Mrs. Tilley's overdraft which was in reality the source of the purchase-moneys."

If, however, trust moneys had been applied in the purchase of the properties, these properties would have been owned partly by Mrs. Tilley and partly by the trust, in proportions in which moneys from those sources had been used to make the purchases.

UNGOED-THOMAS J said at p. 1182: "The plaintiff claims that Mabel's estate should, in virtue of Mabel's half-interest in the estate, subject to Mrs. Tilley's life interest, have half of the proportion of the profits of the purchases made by Mrs. Tilley to the extent to which the defendants, as her legal personal representatives, cannot show that those properties were purchased out of Mrs. Tilley's personal moneys. The defendants, on the other hand, say that the plaintiff is entitled only to a charge on the defendants' bank account for half the trust moneys paid into that bank account with interest, i.e., half the sum of £2,237, which is shown to have been paid into that bank account, and the interest on that amount.

I come first to the law. The plaintiff relied on the statement of the law in Lewin on Trusts, 16th ed. (1964) at p. 223, and some of the cases cited in support of it. That statement reads:

> 'Wherever the trust property is placed, if a trustee amalgamates it with his own, his beneficiary will be entitled to every portion of the blended property which the trustee cannot prove to be his own.'...

So the proposition in Lewin on Trusts, which I have read, is limited to cases where the amalgam of mixed assets is such that they cannot be sufficiently distinguished and treated separately; it is based on the lack of evidence to do so being attributable to the trustee's fault.

The defendants relied on *Re Hallett's Estate* ((1880) 13 ChD 696), with a view to establishing that the trustee must be presumed to have drawn out his own moneys from the bank account of mixed moneys in priority to trust moneys, with the result that property bought by such prior drawings must be the trustee's exclusive personal property. In that case the claim was against a bank balance of mixed fiduciary and personal funds, and it is in the context of such a claim that it was held that the person in a fiduciary character drawing out money from the bank account must be taken to have drawn out his own money in preference to the trust money, so that the claim of the beneficiaries prevailed against the balance of the account. *Re Oatway* ([1903] 2 Ch 356) was the converse of the decision in *Re Hallett's Estate*. In that case the claim was not against the balance left in the bank of such mixed moneys, but against the proceeds of sale of shares which the trustee had purchased with moneys which, as in *Re*

Hallett's Estate, he had drawn from the bank account. But, unlike the situation in *Re Hallett's Estate*, his later drawings had exhausted the account, so that it was useless to proceed against the account. It was held that the beneficiary was entitled to the proceeds of sale of the shares, which were more than their purchase price but less than the trust moneys paid into the account. The law is reviewed and the principles stated by Joyce J who said ([1903] 2 Ch 356 at 359–361):

> 'Trust money may be followed into land or any other property in which it has been invested; and when a trustee has, in making any purchase or investment, applied trust money together with his own, the cestuis que trust are entitled to a charge on the property purchased for the amount of the trust money laid out in the purchase or investment. Similarly, if money held by any person in a fiduciary capacity be paid into his own banking account, it may be followed by the equitable owner, who, as against the trustee, will have a charge for what belongs to him upon the balance to the credit of the account. If, then, the trustee pays in further sums, and from time to time draws out money by cheques, but leaves a balance to the credit of the account, it is settled that he is not entitled to have the rule in *Clayton's* case ((1816) 1 Mer 572) applied so as to maintain that the sums which have been drawn out and paid away so as to be incapable of being recovered represented pro tanto the trust money, and that the balance remaining is not trust money, but represents only his own moneys paid into the account. *Brown v Adams* ((1869) 4 Ch App 764) to the contrary ought not to be followed since the decision in *Re Hallett's Estate*. It is, in my opinion, equally clear that when any of the money drawn out has been invested, and the investment remains in the name or under the control of the trustee, the rest of the balance having been afterwards dissipated by him, he cannot maintain that the investment which remains represents his own money alone, and that what has been spent and can no longer be traced and recovered was the money belonging to the trust. In other words, when the private money of the trustee and that which he held in a fiduciary capacity have been mixed in the same banking account, from which various payments have from time to time been made, then, in order to determine to whom any remaining balance or any investment that may have been paid for out of the account ought to be deemed to belong, the trustee must be debited with all the sums that have been withdrawn and applied to his own use so as to be no longer recoverable, and the trust money in like manner be debited with any sums taken out and duly invested in the names of the proper trustees. The order of priority in which the various withdrawals and investments may have been respectively made is wholly immaterial. I have been referring, of course, to cases where there is only one fiduciary owner or set of cestuis que trust claiming whatever may be left as against the trustee. In the present case there is no balance left. The only investment or property remaining which represents any part of the mixed moneys paid into the banking account is the Oceana shares purchased for £2,137. Upon these, therefore, the trust had a charge for the £3,000 trust money paid into the account. That is to say, those shares and the

proceeds thereof belong to the trust. It was objected that the investment in the Oceana shares was made at a time when Oatway's own share of the balance to the credit of the account (if the whole had been then justly distributed) would have exceeded £2,137, the price of the shares; that he was therefore entitled to withdraw that sum, and might rightly apply it for his own purposes; and that consequently the shares should be held to belong to his estate. To this I answer that he never was entitled to withdraw the £2,137 from the account, or, at all events, that he could not be entitled to take the sum from the account and hold it or the investment made therewith, freed from the charge in favour of the trust, unless or until the trust money paid into the account had been first restored, and the trust fund reinstated by due investment of the money in the joint names of the proper trustees, which never was done. The investment by Oatway, in his own name, of the £2,137 in Oceana shares no more got rid of the claim or charge of the trust upon the money so invested, than would have been the case if he had drawn a cheque for £2,137 and simply placed and retained the amount in a drawer without further disposing of the money in any way. The proceeds of the Oceana shares must be held to belong to the trust funds under the will of which Oatway and Maxwell Skipper were the trustees.'

So, contrary to the defendants' contention, it is not a presumption that a trustee's drawings from the mixed fund must necessarily be treated as drawings of the trustee's own money where the beneficiary's claim is against the property bought by such drawings. Further, *Re Oatway* ([1903] 2 Ch 356) did not raise the question whether a beneficiary is entitled to any profit made out of the purchase of property by a trustee out of a fund consisting of his personal moneys which he mixed with the trust moneys, and so the judgment was not directed to, and did not deal with, that question.

I return now to the judgments in *Re Hallett's Estate* ((1880) 13 ChD 696). . . .

[His Lordship quoted extensively from the parts of the judgment which are extracted at p. 636, ante, and continued:]

Sinclair v Brougham ([1914] AC 398) considered *Re Hallett's Estate*. Lord Parker said (at p. 442):

> 'The principle on which, and the extent to which, trust money can be followed in equity is discussed at length in *Re Hallett's Estate* by Sir George Jessel. He gives two instances. First, he supposes the case of property being purchased by means of the trust money alone. In such a case the beneficiary may either take the property itself or claim a lien on it for the amount of the money expended in the purchase. Secondly, he supposes the case of the purchase having been made partly with the trust money and partly with money of the trustee . . .'

The next sentence I shall come back to later.

> 'In such a case the beneficiary can only claim a charge on the property for the amount of the trust money expended in the purchase. The trustee is precluded by his own misconduct from asserting any interest in the property until such amount has been refunded. By the actual decision in the case, this principle was held applicable when the trust money had been paid into the trustee's banking account. I will add two further illustrations which have some bearing on the present case.

> Suppose the property is acquired by means of money, part of which belongs to one owner and part to another, the purchaser being in a fiduciary relationship to both. Clearly each owner has an equal equity. Each is entitled to a charge on the property for his own money, and neither can claim priority over the other. It follows that their charges must rank pari passu according to their respective amounts . . .'

—again, I emphasise this—

> 'Further, I think that as against the fiduciary agent they could by agreement claim to take the property itself, in which case they would become tenants in common in shares proportioned to amounts for which either could claim a charge.'

It seems to me that when Lord Parker says in the sentence, to which I first called particular attention ([1914] AC 398 at 442), that 'In such a case the beneficiary can only claim a charge on the property for the amount of the trust money expended in the purchase' he is merely contrasting the charge with the right to take the whole property which is the matter he had just been dealing with; Lord Parker is not, as I see it, addressing his mind to the question of whether the beneficiary could claim a proportion of the property corresponding to his own contribution to its purchase. This interpretation of the passage seems to me to be the only interpretation which in principle is consistent with Lord Parker's view expressed at the end of the passage which I quoted, and to which I drew particular attention, where the purchase is made by the trustee wholly out of moneys of two different beneficiaries. In that case he says that they are not limited to charges for their respective amounts, but are together entitled to the whole property. But if each of two beneficiaries can, in co-operation with the other, take the whole property which has resulted in profit from the trustee's action in buying it with their money, why can they not do so if the trustee himself has also paid some part of the purchase price? And if two beneficiaries can do so, why not one? Indeed, it was conceded in argument that the passage should be so interpreted as suggested.

In Snell's Principles of Equity, 26th Edn (1966), the law is thus stated at page 315:

> 'Where the trustee mixes trust money with his own, the equities are clearly unequal. Accordingly, the beneficiaries are entitled to a first charge on the mixed fund, or on any land, securities or other assets purchased with it. Thus if the trustee purchases shares with part of the mixed fund, leaving enough of it to repay the trust moneys, and then dissipates the balance, the beneficiaries' charge binds the shares; for although under the rule in *Re Hallett's Estate* ((1880) 13 ChD 696) the trustee is presumed to have bought the shares out of his own money, the charge attached to the entire fund, and could be discharged only by restoring the trust moneys. Where the property purchased has increased in value, the charge will be not merely for the amount of the trust moneys but for a proportionate part of the increased value. Thus if the trustee purchases land with £500 of his own money and £1,000 of trust moneys, and the land doubles in value, he would be profiting from his breach of trust if he were entitled to all except £1,000; the beneficiaries are accordingly entitled to a charge on the land for £2,000.'

For the defendants it has been rightly admitted that if a trustee wrongly uses trust money to pay the whole of the purchase price in respect of the purchase of an asset a beneficiary can elect either to treat the purchased asset as trust property or to treat the purchased asset as security for the recouping of the trust money. It was further conceded that this right of election by a beneficiary also applies where the asset is purchased by a trustee in part out of his own money and in part out of the trust moneys, so that he may, if he wishes, require the asset to be treated as trust property with regard to that proportion of it which the trust moneys contributed to its purchase.

Does this case fall within that principle? . . .

It seems to me that if, having regard to all the circumstances of the case objectively considered, it appears that the trustee has in fact, whatever his intention, laid out trust moneys in or towards a purchase, then the beneficiaries are entitled to the property purchased and any profits which it produces to the extent to which it has been paid for out of the trust moneys. But, even by this objective test, it appears to me that the trust moneys were not in this case so laid out. It seems to me, on a proper appraisal of all the facts of this particular case, that Mrs. Tilley's breach halted at the mixing of the funds in her bank account. Although properties bought out of those funds would, like the bank account itself, at any rate if the moneys in the bank account were inadequate, be charged with repayment of the trust moneys which then would stand in the same position as the bank account, yet the trust moneys were not invested in properties at all but merely went in reduction of Mrs. Tilley's overdraft which was in reality the source of the purchase-moneys.

The plaintiff's claim therefore fails and he is entitled to no more than repayment of the half of the £2,237 . . ."

---

iii. CRITIQUE

Goff and Jones: *The Law of Restitution*, pp. 54–56

"The rule in Clayton's Case[17]

If an active banking account contains a mixed fund, composed of the moneys of beneficiaries under two different trusts, any loss as between the two trusts is borne in accordance with the arbitrary rule in *Clayton's* case, namely, first in, first out, which was conceived to apply as between a banker and his customer[18]. Judge Learned Hand condemned this particular manifestation of the rule in the following words[19]:

> 'There is no reason in law or justice why his [the fiduciary's] depredations upon the funds should not be borne equally between them. To

[17] (1816) 1 Mer 572.

[18] *Re Hallett's Estate* (1880) 13 ChD 696 at 700, per FRY J (the point did not arise in the Court of Appeal); *Hancock v Smith* (1889) 41 ChD 456 at 461, per Lord HALSBURY LC; *Re Stenning* [1895] 2 Ch 433; *Mutton v Peat* [1899] 2 Ch 556; *Re Diplock* [1948] Ch 465 at 554. Cf. *Re British Red Cross Balkan Fund* [1914] 2 Ch 419, where *Clayton*'s case was not applied.

[19] *Re Walter J. Schmidt & Co* (1923) 298 Fed 314 at 316; precedent, nevertheless, compelled the judge to apply the rule to the facts; see also (1950) 36 Cornell LQ 176 (Z. Chafee).

throw all the loss upon one, through the mere chance of his being earlier in time, is irrational and arbitrary, and is equally a fiction as the rule in *Clayton's* case. When the law attempts a fiction, it is, or at least it should be, for some purpose of justice. To adopt it here is to apportion a common misfortune through a test which has no relation whatever to the justice of the case.'

This denunciation is, in our view, most convincing. The loss should be borne *pari passu*. Both groups of beneficiaries can show an equitable title to the mixed fund; accordingly they should share it rateably according to their contributions[20].

Loss of the right to trace

In *Re Diplock*[1] the Court of Appeal posited three exceptional cases where the right to trace would be lost because it would be inequitable to allow the next-of-kin to follow their money. These are where the money has disappeared; where an innocent volunteer has spent the money on improvements to land; and where he has used the money to pay off secured or unsecured debts.

The first case is clearly unexceptional. But the second and third cases call for examination. The Court of Appeal thought that, if money had been spent on improvements to land, the land might not necessarily increase in value; that the property to which the charge would attach would be uncertain; and that, since the charge could only be realised by sale of the property, equity could not give to the 'innocent volunteer that which he has contributed so as to place him in a position comparable with that of the owner of the trust fund'[2]. As regards debts, the effect of the payment of the debt was to extinguish it, 'so that in order to give effect to the equitable doctrine . . . it would be necessary to revive the debt in some way. We do not see how it can be said to be unconscientious on the part of the charity to object to this being done.'[3]

It seems correct in principle that a person, whose money is used to pay off creditors, who have no notice of his claim, should lose his right to trace, for, in such circumstances, the creditors are in the position of bona fide purchasers. The claimant should, however, be subrogated to the position of secured creditors paid off with his money[4]. It is more doubtful, however, whether the Court of Appeal was right to hold that a claimant can no longer follow his money if the defendant has expended it on improvements to land. In our view, the right to trace should only then be lost if the defendant can show that he has so changed his position by making the improvements that it would be inequitable to require him to repay the money expended on the improvements[5].

20 (1963) 79 LQR 388 at pp. 401–402 (D. A. McConville).
1 [1948] Ch 465, [1948] 2 All ER 318, p. 643, ante.
2 [1948] Ch 465 at 548.
3 [1948] Ch 465 at 549; for a fuller discussion, see (1959) 75 LQR 234 at pp. 248–249 (R. H. Maudsley).
4 The claimant should also have a personal claim against the debtor who has used the claimant's money for his own benefit by discharging his debts.
5 Western Australia Trustee Act 1962, s. 65 (8).

Tracing at Law and in Equity Contrasted

It is clear from the foregoing discussion that the rules of tracing at law and in equity are significantly different. At common law, the requirement of 'identifiability' means that the right to trace is lost if the plaintiff's money is mixed with another's[6]; in equity, identifiability is no obstacle because equity will be prepared to impose a charge on the mixed fund to the extent of the plaintiff's contribution. Moreover, the rights of the innocent volunteer are apparently dissimilar at law and in equity; at common law an innocent volunteer must restore the property to the owner, whereas in equity his claim ranks *pari passu* with that of the claimant. For these reasons it is difficult to agree with the conclusion of Denning J (as he then was) in *Nelson v Larholt*[7] that it is 'no longer appropriate . . . to draw a distinction between law and equity'. Such a degree of fusion, as Atkin LJ's judgment in *Banque Belge pour l'Etranger v Hambrouck*[8] suggests, is desirable, for the objects of both sets of tracing rules should be the same. In our view, the requirement of fiduciary relationship should be abandoned as a condition precedent to a proprietary claim in equity, so that both a legal and an equitable owner should be able, subject to bona fide purchase and change of position, to follow property into a mixed fund, and if our criticisms were to be accepted the tracing rules at common law and in equity would work harmoniously together. As yet, however, the observations of Lord Denning must be regarded as an expression of hope rather than a statement of reality."[9]

QUESTION

Now consider again the relationship between liability as a fiduciary, the tracing remedy and constructive trusts; and Restatement of Restitution, §§160, 202–215.

[6] But see *Banque Belge pour l'Etranger v Hambrouck* [1921] 1 KB 321 at 335–336, per Atkin LJ.

[7] [1948] 1 KB 339 at 343; see also (1949) 65 LQR 37 (A. T. Denning). But see *G. L. Baker Ltd v Medway Building and Supplies Ltd* [1958] 1 WLR 1216, [1958] 3 All ER 540.

[8] [1921] 1 KB 321 at 335–336; quoted at p. 636, ante.

[9] For views to the effect that an outright legal owner has the benefit of the equitable tracing remedy on the ground that he is also the owner in equity, see (1975) 28 CLP 64 (A. J. Oakley); (1976) 40 Conv (NS) 277 (R. A. Pearce). The view is not supported by the authorities.

Index